WOMEN IN AMERICAN THEATRE

12/18/89

Dear Carol,

You made me remember how important theater had been in my life and how wonderful it can be as you grow.

Love ya,
Karen

WOMEN IN AMERICAN THEATRE

REVISED & EXPANDED EDITION

EDITED BY

HELEN KRICH CHINOY
LINDA WALSH JENKINS

THEATRE COMMUNICATIONS GROUP

To Our Children
Claire Nicole, Michael, and Bobby

Women in American Theatre, revised and expanded edition, is published
by Theatre Communications Group, Inc., the national organization for the
nonprofit professional theatre, 355 Lexington Ave., New York, NY 10017.

Originally published in 1981 by Crown Publishers, Inc.

LIBRARY OF CONGRESS CATALOGING IN PUBLICATION DATA
Main entry under title.
Women in American Theatre.
Bibliography: p.
Includes index.
1. Women in theatre—United States.   I. Chinoy, Helen Krich.   II. Jenkins,
Linda Walsh.
PN2226.W6   1980   792'.088042   80-16786
ISBN 0-930452-66-6

Designed by Sarabande Press

Manufactured in the United States of America
First Printing · August 1987

CONTENTS

7.   NEW PROBLEMS, PRACTICES AND PERSPECTIVES
Helen Krich Chinoy

SOURCEBOOK

INDEX

PREFACE
THE TURNING POINT:
WHICH WAY FOR WOMEN IN THEATRE?

Report has it that on her deathbed Gertrude Stein murmured to her dear friend, Alice B. Toklas, "What is the answer?" Overcome with emotion Alice remained silent. Gertrude, never at a loss for words even under heavy sedation in these last moments of her life, transformed what might have been some summing-up clichés into a final Stein conundrum. "In that case," she whispered, "what is the question?"

We take our clue from this mother of us all and say: What can we most profitably ask about women in theatre—indeed, in all the arts—at the end of the 1980's? For years, even centuries, the challenge has always been: Where are the women playwrights? Where are the women composers? Why are there no "mistressworks" to hang beside the masterworks in our museums? During more than a decade now, however, scholars inspired by the women's movement have been providing often surprising answers to these kinds of questions. Redressing the neglect of centuries, we have been uncovering the unknown legacy of women creators in all the arts.

Animated by the new understanding of the relationship of gender and theatre, for example, we sought out for the original 1981 edition of *Women in American Theatre* new and previously hard-to-find scholarship to document an impressive record of accomplishment and vision long obscured by discrimination and repression. Influenced as well by the "new history" and studies of popular culture, our investigations led us past the chronicle of a few big names to an exploration of neglected figures and ignored movements. Since the enterprise of theatre has been mainly run by men, women in both the business and the art of theatre have usually been seen only in terms of male definitions of success. By shifting our focus to include the many different places where women's "success" could be found—the art theatres and little theatres of an earlier day; community theatres, educational theatres, feminist theatres and regional theatres, as well as Broadway—we gained new insights into the largely untold *her*story of American theatre.

We opened the first edition of our book by going behind formal theatre performed mainly for entertainment and profit to explore distinctive "Female Rites" performed primarily for community and family bonding. In looking at "The Actress," the quintessential female presence, we offered important but unfamiliar performers instead of a run-down of stars, whom we did not mean to slight, but whose story has been at least in part available in popular books. "Where Are the Women Playwrights?" ranged from an ancestress who wrote plays to rouse the patriots against the British to a million-dollar-hit playwright of the 1920's, from experimenters in subject matter and form to conventional craftswomen. Covering the careers of producers, directors, designers, casting specialists, and teachers, "If Not an Actress, What . . . ?" suggested the struggles and successes of women in those jobs where being a woman was a severe handicap that could sometimes be turned into a unique source of strength. The studies of "Images" alerted us to the projections of female stereotypes or originals in a wide variety of plays written by both men and women. With some important additions—pieces on Gertrude Stein, Lillian Hellman, Lorraine Hansberry, Hallie Flanagan, early women directors, and a few others—this essential and still mostly unknown compensatory history appears in the revised and expanded edition of *Women in American Theatre*.

The feminist catalyst that started our "revisioning" of the past also stirred women to use the potent art of theatre as an instrument to raise their collective consciousness. In 1981 our section on "Feminist Theatre" provided one of the first surveys of this most obvious and direct reflection in theatre of the striking changes that were taking place in women's lives. For this new edition we reorganized and enlarged the "Feminist Theatre" section both to give fuller treatment to this important movement that was just taking shape in 1981 and to allow for retrospective assessment by such leading practitioners as Martha Boesing, Roberta Sklar, and Megan Terry. Women in theatre today need to understand the accomplishments as well as the struggles of feminist companies. Their history, recent as it is, is our heritage to cherish and to change. It will help women confront the new political, economic, and aesthetic problems that are before us at the end of the 1980's, a decade that started out with so much hope for a new women's idea of theatre.

The 1980's brought conspicuous new triumphs for women in every area of theatre. Major new awards especially for women, such as the Susan Blackburn Prize, were created; major old awards like the Pulitzer Prize, rarely given to women, were awarded in 1981 to Beth Henley for *Crimes of the Heart* and in 1983 to Marsha Norman for *'night, Mother*. In 1982 Ellen Burstyn was installed as the first woman president of Actors' Equity in its sixty-year history and Colleen Dewhurst followed her in this important position in 1985. In the various other professional associations such as the Society of Stage Directors and Choreographers, the League of New York Theatres and Producers, and the Dramatists Guild, the presence of newly active women began to be felt. Newspapers and magazines paid increased attention to women directors, producers, and playwrights. A few anthologies of scripts and several historical and critical books were published. Although Broadway remained inhospitable, more work by women was seen not only in the women's theatres but also Off and Off-Off Broadway and in the regional centers. The '80's seemed, indeed, to be the decade of women in theatre.

As women today try to consolidate the advances in theatre, however, many questions have again come to the fore. The struggle to make a place for themselves has opened up a new Pandora's box of women's issues. It's not that women don't know what they want—to recall Freud's famous question—but that what they really want is not exactly what they find they are getting. In gaining greater access, women have discovered that they must come to terms with attitudes, work relationships, and artistic values often at odds with what they had in mind for themselves, their art, and their society. The art critic Lucy Lippard put the paradox of women in the arts very well: "The entrance of more art by women into the establishment is certainly good for the establishment. . . . [yet] one of the questions we have to answer is whether women do want the same things that men have wanted: whether 'greatness' in its present form is, in fact, desirable."

To chronicle this complex development and its implications is the purpose of "New Problems, Practices, and Perspectives," a section that has been added to our book. In the limited space available we have offered a sampling of voices speaking out on the concerns of women in theatre today. "The Female Actor," "Here Are the Women Playwrights," "Women Backstage and Out Front," "Doubly Marginalized: Women in the Avant-Garde," the various segments of "Matrix: New Intersections of Gender, Identity, and Politics," and the concluding view of Judith Malina, "About the Future," put us in touch with important accomplishments and troubling questions.

Women in American theatre seem to be at the turning point. New opportunities wrested from the traditional power structure by the women's movement have attracted some younger women to seek success in traditional male-identified venues and on male terms. These women tend to be "self-absorbed," as one critic put it, interested only in individual careers; to some, "women's issues" are "baggage" from the past that must be unloaded. Even some who think of themselves as feminists report that they resent being called upon as woman artists to "have a position," to make a statement with their art, to be obviously political as women in the early feminist theatres were. They claim to be tired of the pressure of being feminists or simply of being "women" and want only to be artists. They want to get on with the "work" and they want to be paid appropriately for it. It is surely hard to "starve for one's art" when, on one hand, there is diminishing public and private support for the constantly escalating costs of making theatre and, on the other, novice women professionals in business all seem to have starting salaries of at least $30,000.

Yet for all the new mobility of women in theatre, individually and as a group they have by no means escaped the realities of persistent, albeit somewhat muted, discrimination and of the sharply contracted market of the Broadway theatre that many want to enter. When a show is being developed in the commercial theatre, women directors and designers still report being openly rejected as unsuitable to work on new or classic scripts by men; while men, who regularly stage and design plays by women, are often preferred by women playwrights and producers as a way of making their "product" more commercial. Regional theatres offer more chances to work, but there, too, women have hardly made a big dent in networks and institutional structures. Seeking to work in these professional theatres rather than in the often unfamiliar (although very lively) alternative ones in New York and across the country, a number of women confess among themselves to serious disappointments and frustrations. They find it very difficult to make careers in theatres where pressures to be "nice" and to play the roles of "earthmother, peacemaker, or group nurturer" conflict with the strengths necessary in tough administrative or professional situations. How to use and to value "the total self" remains for many women in theatre a problematic goal.

These evident conflicts and tensions lead once again to central questions about women in theatre. Where do women fit in? Where can they make a living, have a career, and create authentic theatre art from women's lives? Is there a feminine sensibility in theatre creation? Is it the result of nature (some essential female quality) or of nurture (the socialization that makes us feminine or masculine)? Do women directors approach their tasks in markedly different ways from the practices of male directors? Do women view the sacrifices and spoils of conventional success as men do? Can they or should they try to break the "Broadway barrier"? Do women playwrights have something special to say as women, not just as individual artists? Do they create in a distinctive way, use unique forms, speak a long-silenced "mother tongue"? What is the relationship between individual talent and women's common problems? What does it mean to be a feminist in one's life and one's art in the late 1980's? Is the personal still viewed as the political? What happens when women, so long outsiders, objectified as the passive Other, move into male roles and institutions? Do women have some responsibility for the life and work of other women artists and for the art and institutions of theatre? And what of female sexuality? How are race, class, and region related to gender in women's work? How are all these variables encoded in the theatre of daily life and in the closely related life of theatre?

These are some of the many questions raised and explored with new intensity and new theoretical variety in the concluding section of our book. In some form or other they have animated this volume from its inception and will continue to guide our study. The research and data gathered here and in the other books and investigations done during this decade, however, do reenforce the hypothesis suggested in our original introduction, "Art Versus Business: The Role of Women in American Theatre," which follows this preface. It leads us to ask the overriding, positive question: what do women artists have in their unique experience that can help both men and women enrich and restructure theatre art and life itself? The answers are everywhere in these pages and in the letters, articles, plays, and performances of many additional generous women who could not be included. They have to do with why and how women make art.

Ingrid Bergman's words about why she—an awkward and timid adolescent—got started as an actress capture the contradictions and almost violent drive articulated by many women: "I was shy and scared, but also a showoff. . . . I had a lion roaring inside of me that wouldn't sit down and shut up." The creative urge has been so strong that women have found ways to harness and to communicate it despite the absence of cultural and institutional assistance. They have tended to make art an integral part of their total lives rather than something set apart for special occasions. A women's trio in the opening of a musical play, *The Death of Black and White* by the young Kentucky playwright Judyie Al-Bilali, projects this involvement: "We are caught in the middle/of so much life/and life's middle is everywhere."

Working most often outside of professional structures for training and advancement—in kitchen corners, in community or regional drama leagues, in local pageants or children's plays, in feminist collectives or political troupes—women have often used their art for social bonding and for social challenge. Ruby Lerner, who was director of ROOTS (Regional Organization of Theatres South), speaks of a "community-centered vision" that contrasts with the "myth of the alienated artists. . . . It's a different way of seeing oneself as an artist. . . . The focus is more on the interaction between the individual and the community." And within the theatre company, too, it is the relationships that women seem to value most. Tina Packer of Shakespeare & Company, for example, says she has rejected the "intellectual fascism" and search for fame expected in the male-identified field of directing. She opts instead for "collective relationships," which "always came last" in other professional theatres.

Making art part of their daily experience and part of a group endeavor, many women have helped to undermine the notion of the "great artist," with its romantic, elitist bias. They tend to redefine talent as the "capacity for experience," for "penetrating the environment," for "opening the way to intuitive knowledge"—a quality to be cultivated by everyone, as Viola Spolin urges in her seminal *Improvisation for the Theatre*. The "woman in the audience" becomes "the acting partner" of the woman on stage, is the way feminist director Roberta Sklar puts it. "The actor demonstrates transformation, and the audience woman considers transformation in her own life." Finding it necessary so often to be accommodating, flexible, and open in order to work at all, women have often been the true *amateurs*—the lovers of their art.

These are some of the values at the heart of the female tradition in the arts. They may not be much in evidence in show business today, but they are alive in many individuals and theatres across the country. They are also alive in the pages of this book, including the Sourcebook which completes the volume— with information about Awards, Organizations, Studies, Festivals, Conventions, Feminist Theatres, Books, Dissertations, and Resources, and most of all with a Playlist of thousands of plays by hundreds of women. We hope what we have brought together in these pages will not only provide information, stimulate investigation and challenge preconceptions, but will also help women decide which way to go in theatre today.

HELEN KRICH CHINOY
LINDA WALSH JENKINS

WOMEN IN AMERICAN THEATRE

INTRODUCTION

ART VERSUS BUSINESS: THE ROLE OF WOMEN IN AMERICAN THEATRE

In the decade or more since the women's movement began, a number of books on the female experience in literature, in art and architecture, in film, and in dance have been published, but no comparable attempts have been made to identify a women's tradition in the complex art of theatre. Some excellent volumes of plays by women and some about women, some interesting articles on individuals and on the new feminist theatres, a symposium or an interview here or there have appeared. With the exception of the reissue of Rosamond Gilder's classic *Enter the Actress*, however, no overall study has tried to see how women have used and have been used in theatre.

Yet questions about women's participation in all aspects of theatre have become more insistent. As women with new self-awareness and enthusiasm try to use theatre to explore what it means to be a woman, they also look back in the hope of locating themselves in some female tradition that will help them understand their problems in the present as well as plan for the future. Despite the public life of theatre, we know very little about the role that women have played. It has not been easy to see a female network in the composite art of theatre or to find a sense of "we-consciousness," as Simone de Beauvoir calls it, among actresses, playwrights, designers, directors, and producers.

In this anthology we have juxtaposed in a single volume some of the many different things we are only now beginning to learn about women in all aspects of theatre. When viewed together in this way, the studies in this collection, varied as they are and gathered as they were without any single preconception or ideological thrust, do highlight some continuities in women's experience in theatre. The recurrent patterns that appear in these pages and in the body of research out of which this volume grew suggest that women's role in theatre has been special. From female rites to Broadway shows to sisterhood sessions, women seem to have found the sharing, collective, creative, community aspects of theatre especially congenial. They have tended to commit their energies to the nurturing art rather than to the competitive business of theatre. A brief overview of women's role based on this insight, which only a formal history could fully document, is sketched

1

here. It is offered as an introduction to the selections that follow in the hope
that it will raise questions for discussion and stimulate much-needed further
research.

As a starting point there is the striking evidence of women's continued
and extensive participation in theatre. Acting, of course, has been the
obvious career for women. If you were pretty but poor, or wellborn but
hard-up, with no useful skills but your feminine attractions to offer, the
stage was always a possible way to earn a living. In *Aria da Capo* Edna St.
Vincent Millay neatly satirizes the easy link of women and acting. When
Columbine complains that she can't act, Pierrot answers: "Can't act? Can't
act? La, listen to the woman! . . . You're blond, are you not?—you have no
education, have you? can't act! you underrate yourself, my dear!" In addition to their obvious but crucial function as actresses, women—often starting as actresses—have been involved in greater numbers and in a greater
variety of jobs than are indicated in the theatre history books, which usually
mention only the big names who made it on Broadway.

Many of these unsung women were born into theatrical families where
they learned to do all that was necessary. Some added management to
acting on the death of their fathers or their husbands; others started their
own theatres, often the first in an outlying area, out of the need to earn a
living for themselves or their children or a desire to enrich the life of a
community. There were those who were the power behind the scene,
managing actress-daughters, or those who enriched or almost ghostwrote
the plays of their husbands. Various strong, independent women served
theatre on their own terms, whether that meant playing male roles to satisfy
their own sense of power and authority or alternatively exploiting their
female sexuality in defiance of the "flabby, sanctimoniousness" of good
women who, they chided, dwindled into "nonentities" on marriage.

Liberated by their work in the very public, often vulgar world of theatre,
they wrote plays for themselves or for others to star in, courted commercial
success or struggled for personal expression. They organized companies,
trained young performers in their troupes and later in notable studios and
schools. They experimented with chemical and physical laws to devise new
scenic effects and directed the plays they wrote to ensure that they were
staged properly. They have been casting and dramatic agents, producers,
financiers, and lawyers for theatre. Especially since the turn of the twentieth
century, women have made their way into all the specialized positions in
theatre, where they can be found if you have a mind to look for them and
some sense of where they are most likely to be located.

For although many women have made their mark in theatre, it hasn't been
easy for them to do so on Broadway or in the mainstream of theatre. Their
accomplishments are celebrated in this volume, but at the same time the
limitations and constraints they faced are also clearly indicated. In show
business as in other businesses and professions, women have not easily or
regularly come into positions of importance or power in the major institu-

tions. They have been restricted by the blatant prejudice against letting women have any say where big money and decision-making have been involved as well as by their socialization into a passive but emotional self-image.

To the usual limits on female career aspirations—marriage, family, appropriate submissive behavior and acceptable feminine appearance—theatre has imposed further restrictions by being socially and morally suspect in puritanical, middle-class America. In a country where theatre was thought of as Satan's haunt and actresses often equated with harlots whose "lascivious smiles, wanton glances, and indelicate attitudes" threatened the ideal of "womanhood," the women who worked in theatre had a difficult time. Defined in this way by society, they could exploit their erotic attractions before an often largely male audience and make a rather free and easy life for themselves outside the limits of correct society. Or anxious to get on, they could fit themselves to the stereotypes acceptable to the popular audience—the innocent ingenue, the noble wife, the fallen woman. From the beginning, however, some women challenged the debased image of theatre and of women in it. Attracted by the stage, they tried to reform it and to raise the moral and esthetic level of the profession. Although they were sometimes snobbish, prudish, even priggish, reflecting what was thought appropriate when a "lady" turned to theatre, these women through their efforts over the years and in response to changing values eventually transformed their defensive attitudes into a dynamic idea of theatre in America.

Uncomfortable in the commercial theatre or barred from full participation there, important creative women have insisted that their theatre must be more than "amusement . . . prostituted to the purpose of vice," to quote Mercy Otis Warren, our first woman dramatist, or "more than an amusement" to catch an echo in a Sunday *New York Times* headline about Zelda Fichandler's Arena Stage. In an earlier day women dramatists and actresses spoke of themselves as "reformers" who would grace the theatre with "their own pure and blameless lives" or with the "benign influence of a noble womanly spirit," to quote Anna Cora Mowatt, the lady who wrote *Fashion*.

Olive Logan, actress, writer, bluestocking, suggested that theatre could become "a worthy channel for gifted, intelligent, and virtuous young women to gain a livelihood through" if producers would only get rid of the "leg business" made popular in hits like Adah Isaacs Menken's "nude" *Mazeppa* or *The Black Crook*. In her fascinating series of essays, *Apropos of Women and Theatre*, written in 1869, Olive Logan argued that a career on the decent, serious stage was one of the few in which women could earn equally with men and was therefore worthy of an aspiring, independent woman. Julia Marlowe, we can suggest, was such a young woman who deliberately prepared herself by hard work and careful study of Shakespeare to be a "moral force" in acting his plays. She conceded that what impelled her as an actress was "the dramatic attraction of the woman who stays pure." Her contemporary, Mary Shaw, equally idealistic, was impelled by the possibility of using the stage for a feminist vision. "Women exert a tremendous and virtually irresistible influence over the stage," she insisted. "Aristocrat of the arts and child of religion," she told the International Congress of Women in London in 1899, the drama "is a field for women." With Jessie Bonstelle, actress, director-manager of important stock companies, Mary Shaw projected a Woman's National Theatre devoted to communicating "distinctive feminine feeling or opinions," one of several such theatres planned in the early years of the twentieth century.

By 1931, Eva Le Gallienne, actress-director of the Civic Repertory Theatre, could look back on this heritage of high-minded activism when analyzing "Women's Role in the Theatre" in the *Alumnae Quarterly* of Smith College, which had just given her an honorary degree. Her point of departure was an attack on women by Gordon Craig, who had written that "to achieve the reform of the theatre, to bring it into the condition necessary for it to become a fine art, women must have first left the boards." Miss Le Gallienne's defense began in an apologetic, familiar vein, noting the absence of women in ancient theatre and the use of only "lower types of women" in "orgies of licentiousness" during the "degenerate days of Rome and the Renaissance." The modern movement in theatre, however, disavowing sexism and show business, was created by both men and women. Indeed, Le Gallienne suggested, at first somewhat hesitantly and then in stronger terms by the end of her comments, the modern theatre was in many ways the accomplishment of women. Looking at the achievements of, among others, Miss Horniman in Manchester, Lady Gregory in Ireland, Irene and Alice Lewisohn, Mary Shaw, and Minnie Maddern Fiske in New York, she pointed out that, as she saw it, women were really the "doers" in the development of the modern art theatre.

Looking today for what seems especially to distinguish the contributions of notable women, for a female network or feminine consciousness in American theatre, we find ourselves reinforcing Miss LeGallienne's suggestion that, counter to Craig's perverse admonition, serving the art of theatre has in many ways been the special function of women. The women who have made major contributions to American theatre have tended to identify themselves—whether they were actresses, playwrights, directors, or producers—with an idea of theatre larger than that of Broadway. In the 1920's Edith Isaacs, editor of *Theatre Arts* magazine, the journal of the art theatre movement, dubbed this alternative theatre "the tributary theatre." In her important essay, she rejected commercial New York theatre as "not an artist's goal," and urged Americans to go to "the four corners of the country and begin again, training playwrights to create in their own idiom, in their own theatres." In declaring that theatre must have a "relation, human or aesthetic, to the life of the people," she sounded a call to which women have responded with unusual dedication.

The association of women with regional, institutional, little, art, and alternative theatres is striking. Think of Susan Glaspell, who became an innovative playwright after founding the Provincetown Players with her husband, George Cram Cook; of Theresa Helburn, executive director for many years of the famed Theatre Guild; of Edith Isaacs, for over twenty-five years reviewer, editor, and manager of *Theatre Arts* magazine; of Rosamond Gilder, her disciple and associate, critic, historian, activist in the National Theatre Conference, ANTA, and voice of America through the International Theatre Institute; of Cheryl Crawford, cofounder with Harold Clurman and Lee Strasberg of the Group Theatre, and later collaborator with Eva Le Gallienne and Margaret Webster in the American Repertory Theatre; of Hallie Flanagan Davis, creator of the Vassar Experimental Theatre and the Smith College Theatre Department and head of the great Federal Theatre Project; of Margo Jones, director-producer in Dallas, "high priestess" of the post-World War II regional theatre movement; of Nina Vance of the Houston Alley Theatre; of Zelda Fichandler of the Arena Stage; of Judith Malina, guru of the Living Theatre; of Ellen Stewart, La Mama of the whole Off-Off-Broadway theatre movement.

Most of these women turned their backs on making it on Broadway. They rejected what sociologists consider the male preoccupation with power and climbing the ladder in the "cash nexus world." Their concerns have tended to be with the values of what has been called the "status world" in which love, duty, tenderness, individuality, and expressiveness are central. Their activities belong to the tradition of female rites in which, as Linda Jenkins has pointed out, performance events are used primarily for family and social bonding rather than largely for entertainment and profit.

Eva Le Gallienne, to stick with her instructive experience, turned against what she felt was the "stultifying effect of a successful engagement" as a leading lady to try her hand at special matinees of "better" plays. Her determination to stage Ibsen, Hauptmann, and Chekhov led to the founding of the Civic Repertory Theatre where the satisfactions of ensemble playing, repertory scheduling, low prices, and free training for performers replaced the triumphs she could have easily had as a star. Other leading actresses also freed themselves from being "commodities" in the hands of producers to head their own companies or join institutional theatres or even just tour an individual production that would allow them to perform personally and culturally meaningful plays. Think of the great Minnie Maddern Fiske, who was called the "most civilizing force" of the stage of her day, of Katharine Cornell, of Lynn Fontanne, of Helen Hayes, of Julie Harris, and Irene Worth, among many others.

Many of these women tend to look on their companies as family units within a larger community group, sharing, supporting, learning, and teaching. They reject the "atmosphere of hysteria, crisis, fragmentation, one-shotness, and mammon-mindedness" of the Broadway system as inappropriate for the "collective and cumulative" art of theatre. They tend to turn away from the "nameless faces and the anonymity" of New York to places where they have a "feeling of roots." They tend to work for a theatre "which is part of everybody's life . . . where there is a theatre in every town providing entertainment and enlightenment for the audience and a decent livelihood along with high artistic goals for the theatre worker." This sampling of quotations, it should be noted, like most of the illustrations here, antedates the new feminist theatres where these nurturant, supportive, cooperative, community values have become the basis for a new kind of theatre that can even call itself, as one feminist troupe does, "It's All Right to Be Woman."

Perhaps because they were not locked into the show business esthetic, women won the major prizes offered early in this century with plays that aimed at being more than just hits. Josephine Preston Peabody, for example, won the competition for a play to inaugurate the new Shakespeare Memorial Theatre in 1910 with her poetic drama, *The Piper*, and Alice Brown won the $10,000 prize offered by Winthrop Ames for her *Children of Earth*, chosen over 1,700 other manuscripts. Although not a stage success, the play has been praised for the "note of repressed and insurgent desire for participation in life" its heroine expressed.

It was out of this kind of need to tell what Megan Terry was later to call "the psychic news" that women early on in the century began the experiment with dramatic form and staging techniques that now characterizes the *New Women's Theatre*, as Honor Moore calls it in her fine collection of plays. Rachel Crothers, in exploring the conflicts of the "New Woman" as artist and wife-mother, extended the range of the social-problem drama of the day. She thought women's evolution the most "important thing in modern life" and felt herself very avant-garde when among other innovations she made her heroines over thirty years old. "No more is it necessary to confine heroines to ingenues, stage age seventeen," she declared in the early years of this century.

While Crothers in her almost fifty years of acting, writing, and directing represents the older ladylike tradition of "ethical concern" brought to the theatre, the new bohemian artists, the Greenwich Village feminists, probed the psyche of their characters in new forms that seemed invented especially to express the troubled spirit of modern woman.

Alice Gerstenberg's *Overtones*, for example, produced by the Washington Square Players with a set by Lee Simonson, used the then novel Freudian concepts of ego and id to project the divided selves of her two characters. Each woman is shadowed by a veiled alter ego who speaks her innermost feelings in this one-acter that is thought to be the first American play "to depart from realism to show the unconscious."

In Susan Glaspell's *The Verge* (1921), done by her Provincetown Players, the struggles of the heroine to enlarge the boundaries of her life, to be "stabbed to awareness," are paralleled in some ways by the playwright's struggle to extend the boundaries of her dramatic form. She calls for striking expressionistic lighting and scenic effects, provided originally by Cleon Throckmorton, to image forth the search for "otherness" and "apartness" that makes her heroine reject home, husband, and child in a mad vision of passion and self-realization. In Glaspell's more realistic plays, the an-guished heroine often does not appear, but the discovery of her "suppressed desires" is the device for dramatic action and tension.

In Sophie Treadwell's *Machinal* (1928), designed by Robert Edmond Jones, the playwright uses stream-of-consciousness passages and expressionistic sounds, rhythms, and images to suggest the "mechanical, nerve-nagging" environment that drives her young woman to illicit love and to the murder of her husband, once her boss. When the young woman cries out "I won't submit" as she is led to the electric chair, Treadwell thrusts a powerful image of women's anguish and revolt at audiences.

An interest in the downtrodden, the unfulfilled, and the defeated is often found in women's plays. In addition to the few just mentioned, there are many in which the trials of Indians, workers, farmers, Blacks, lesbians, and antiwar activists are dramatized. Rachel France's important anthology, *A Century of Plays by American Women*, is the place to find some of these usually unavailable plays. Despite great difficulties Black women playwrights from Angelina Grimke to Lorraine Hansberry, Alice Childress, and Adrienne Kennedy have, along with actresses and directors like Rose McClendon, Ruby Dee, and Vinnette Carroll, raised their voices to document and celebrate the "life, experience, and humor" of Black people. Women have also pioneered in other neglected areas, providing children's creative dramatics, settlement-house culture, and prison entertainment.

Even some of the scholarly studies written by women have been devoted to ignored subjects. Long before the Black movement and women's liberation, Edith Isaacs's *The Negro in the American Theatre* showed the significance of Black art as one of our few native resources, and Rosamond Gilder's *Enter the Actress* told of women who were pioneers in theatre rather than queens of the stage. Even Marilyn Stasio's recent *Broadway's Beautiful Losers*, full of plays that have "failed as commercial products" despite the fact that they had "merit as theatre art," supports the view that, for all the varied reasons suggested here, women have generally been for art rather than business in American theatre.

This brief overview with its selective illustrations may seem an overstatement made to isolate a female tradition. Certainly when the history of women in theatre is written, it will detail with more than the few suggestions possible here those many talented women who made it in the man's world of theatre because, as Anita Loos once put it, "I was just a girl writer who liked money" in a field where girls, she felt, were mostly smarter than men. They were "doers," not just "dreamers," to recall Le Gallienne's observations. But in reviewing the wide range of activities represented in the pages of this collection and in related research, one learns again and again that much of what women did was dedicated to realizing a dream of a different kind of theatre. Perhaps this concluding sketch of the career of one woman will capture the essence of the special spirit that seems to have animated many of the women in American theatre.

During the "full, lean years" of the Depression, a tiny woman in a fedora hat cast a huge shadow which covered the whole land with the vision of a different kind of theatre. Hallie Flanagan Davis, during the few short years of the Federal Theatre Project, made the tributary the mainstream. The educational, regional, experimental art theatre became our national people's theatre. When she was appointed national director of the Federal Theatre Project in August 1935, the *New York Times* wrote that "the boys—the local gentry for whom the theatre does not exist outside Manhattan—did not quite know what to make of that." To them the appointment "represented 'art.' . . . There was headshaking. What this project needed, they said, was an old-line Broadway manager who knew the commercial theatre's devious ways."

There were many reasons why Harry L. Hopkins, with President Franklin Roosevelt and, we might add, Mrs. Eleanor Roosevelt supporting him, wanted someone outside the commercial theatre, but here we only want to ask what were some of the qualities that Hallie Flanagan Davis brought to the job.

Born in South Dakota and brought up in Grinnell, Iowa, she belonged to the vast reaches of America that Broadway thought of as a "dumping ground" for some of its products. Although she eventually became part of the Eastern scene, she always recalled, in often lyrical prose, the great quiet prairies and the "long summer days and long winter evenings" of a "serene childhood" and youth spent in the spacious West.

At Grinnell College she, like the rest of her group, was "imbued with the Grinnell conception of public service" and she developed a strong sense of the importance of being "part of an institution." She wrote of herself, "I can't imagine just being a floating rib someplace." She could not imagine theatre apart from the life of a group.

She started her first work experience like a latter-day Nora trying to earn money in secret for her ailing young husband by giving drama lessons, one of the few skills this young wife had. When her husband died, she thrust herself into teaching to earn money for herself and her two children. Her first notice came as a playwright when she won a prize offered by the Des Moines Little Theatre Society in a regional contest open only to Iowans. This success plus her effective productions at Grinnell College led her to Professor George Pierce Baker's Workshop 47 at Harvard, where she earned a master's degree. With her small son Frederick, this indomitable little woman went east to learn the art of theatre after suffering the death of both her husband and her seven-year-old son Jack. Professor Baker, she recalled, "believed that I should give up everything and write plays. But I couldn't—I had a family to support!" All her active life she was concerned to support herself and her family; her work was for her no fanciful creative outlet but a serious economic commitment. But the work was also more than just a job.

She went back to Grinnell, where she used all she had learned at Harvard. A production at her Grinnell Experimental Theatre of *Romeo and Juliet*, into which she confessed that she "secretly" poured her remembrances of her young husband, won the attention that led to the award of a Guggenheim Fellowship, one of the first given to a woman. It also won her a position at Vassar College, where President Henry MacCracken asked her to set up another experimental theatre.

With her Guggenheim Fellowship she traveled to Europe to see the *Shifting Scenes*, as she would call her book about the journey. Her exposure to the innovations of Craig, Reinhardt, Stanislavski, and especially Meyerhold sharpened her awareness of and commitment to theatre as a dynamic instrument to serve the people as they change the world around them.

In the next few years at Vassar she and her Experimental Theatre became the "dynamo," to use another word that would become a title of one of her books, that "releases youth's burning energy . . . into the power of creative change." She foreshadowed the later Living Newspapers in her Depression documentary and call to action, *Can You Hear Their Voices?*, and she found ways of transforming classic dramas into contemporary actions. Her innovations attracted the attention of educators, artists, and critics, as well as government officials, and led eventually to her appointment as the national director of the Federal Theatre Project.

When this "soft-spoken slave driver," as she was admiringly called, took on the Federal Theatre Project to employ out-of-work performers, she tried to realize for the nation the values of the kind of theatre in which she had worked. With her associates she tried to create a regional, popular, educational art theatre in which, as Harry Hopkins told her in urging her to take the appointment, "the profits won't be money profits."

Without arguing the success or failure of the Federal Theatre or the mistakes or limitations of Hallie Flanagan Davis, we can observe that she brought us closest to the realization for the nation of the dream widely shared by the other women discussed here. In her Federal Theatre, the profits were human. Papa, who might have been an actor, a playwright, a designer, or a technician, had a job even if the salary was only twenty-five dollars a week. The roots were regional. The theatre tried to "explore sources of native American life." The accomplishments were national. Theatre became for a new audience of millions an artistic medium "of free expression," an "access to the arts and tools of civilization," and a "bulwark of the democratic form of government."

From the female shaman with whom our volume opens to the Broadway star and on to the feminist activists with whom it closes, this large vision has shaped the role of women in American theatre. Liberated, mostly by circumstance and sometimes by desire, from male pressure to "make a mark in the world" and "develop the ego," women have served the art and the people.

HKC

1
FEMALE RITES

A section on female rites opens our collection on women in American theatre because these performance events, interesting and important in themselves, can also help us understand how women have functioned in our theatre. Indeed, exact definitions of "ritual" and "theatre" continue to elude theorists since these two activities share so many features. Often it is context, not content, that determines whether a performance event is one or the other. It is widely accepted now that no event is clearly one or the other. Rather, ritual and theatre belong to the same family of human behavior in which the major variables are whether or not an event is purely esthetic or is believed to be socially or spiritually efficacious.

If we look to the end of the ritual/theatre continuum where performance is solely for fun—and profit—emphasizing the here and now, making no attempt at social bonding, we find some women but few relative to the number of men there. If, however, we look at family and public performance events in which social and religious bondings are established, we find women. They are decorating and embellishing the parade floats, church interiors, schools, and homes; they are managing the feasting and preparations; they are singing in the choirs, if not on the stage; they are lighting candles and playing the organ; they are guarding order and dignity.

These roles in performance have been women's rights. It would help us greatly to understand why, for example, there have been few women directing on Broadway, if we look to the broader "theatre" of American life to see what society has not only allowed but expected. Traditionally women have not been encouraged to create anything "for fun," but rather to create for others, for community, for social and religious good, and for the maintenance of order. Often woman is herself a social decoration; even her self-adornment is done for the pleasure of others and might be understood as her way of being a visual artist within sex role demands.

When we look for women in the ritual and ceremonial aspects of American life, we see great diversity and contribution. Shakers, possessed by the spirit of Mother Ann, created events that combined pantomime,

10

singing, and clowning. Psychologist Rev. Audrey Bronson and her jazz-pianist sister lead her congregation through spiritual experiences in the Sanctuary Church of the Open Door in Philadelphia. Storyteller Laura Simms advertises herself as approaching her performances as a ritual theatre art. Sculptor Suzanne Benton uses masks to create performance happenings she calls rituals. Composer Pauline Oliveros combines meditative techniques and figurative theatrical elements in her *Crow Two, A Ceremonial Opera.*

As women in contemporary society challenge old ways, they can look to rites for reform and reconsideration. Jewish feminists, for example, are revising the traditional seder and Haggadah to give themselves a more active role and to make the language more inclusive of Jewish women past and present. Even the consciousness-raising groups that were such an important part of the women's liberation movement of the early 1970's became events with gestures, stories, interactions, and patterns that began to have the aura of ritual about them.

Material in this chapter is arranged to suggest what Richard Schechner has called the ritual/theatre continuum. The first essay surveys Native American women's sex role expectations and observes their place in the range of events in their tribes. In considering these events and women's participation, we may reflect on ways in which sex role expectations with regard to contemporary theatre may be a relic of other tribal pasts. We can see parallels between the ways in which Native women have been "overlooked" by field-workers and historians and the ways in which other American women have been overlooked.

In the events of the Woman's Crusade of 1873–74, Women's Trade Union League, and National Woman's Party we see women who performed according to role expectation—prayer, song, saving the home, friendship, bonding, decoration, parade, and pageantry—but took their performance into a context in which it made a political statement.

By contrast, and ironically, in American beauty pageants women perform in ways that have not been appropriate for modest homemakers and home-savers—showing off their bodies, calling attention to themselves by singing, dancing, acting. Yet they are seen as bolstering, not challenging, the given order. It might be noted that beauty pageants by minority groups, such as Miss Black America and Indian Princesses, have not existed merely to ape the Miss America pageant; they have challenged white America's ideal of beauty. Through public events like Miss America and homecoming parades American society judges the premarital (virgin?) female on the basis of her physical beauty, bearing, and other potential (talent) for embellishing her future family (primarily her husband?). But the postmarital female, Mrs. America, is then judged on her ability to bake pies and sew. Perhaps TV commercials form an ongoing Mrs. America pageant, as we see our contestants tested on dirty collars, coffee-making, and floor-waxing.

Starhawk's account of the ritual event grounding a "Take Back the Night" march reminds us of the unbroken, though always threatened, tradition of witchcraft and ancient goddess religions. Barbara Ann Teer's ritual work with the National Black Theatre and the ritual drama created by At the Foot of the Mountain might be said to straddle the ritual/theatre continuum. Teer looked to ritual sources as an alternative to Anglo-European theatre, while At the Foot of the Mountain created *The Story of a Mother* both to display a mother's life through imitation/enactment and to engage the audience in an actual ritualistic summoning of individual mothers.

Finally, Adrienne Kennedy has made female rites of passage part of the dramatic core of her plays. In her plays we encounter social rituals that form woman's identity with its resultant agony. As a playwright, Kennedy is at the other end of the continuum from the traditional female performance role, and yet in her work we connect with the female shaman introduced in the first essay. Kennedy, like a shaman, understands and reveals balance and imbalance in the rites that create a female.   LWJ

SEX ROLES AND SHAMANS

LINDA WALSH JENKINS

The first "theatre" on the North American continent was the performance activity of hundreds, perhaps even thousands, of Native cultures. Some of these performance traditions continue into the present day, and new events have been and continue to be created. When theatre texts select photos or drawings of Native events for chapters on "primitive ritual" and "beginnings of theatre," they tend to select exotic and romantic images such as George Catlin's paintings of Mandan buffalo dancers (male) or photos of ceremonies in which live snakes are handled by men. When thinking of Indian performances the most common images are probably those of a male Plains warrior dancing in full regalia, men sacrificing their flesh in the Sun Dance, or some of the Southwest Indian events that appear in magazines like *National Geographic*. Hollywood films and mythology of the Old West have helped place the Indian male activity at the forefront of the popular imagination. What of the roles and contributions of Native women in these performances, particularly in the time prior to the reservation experience at the end of the nineteenth century?

When historians or ethnographers describe performance events in Native American cultures, they rarely refer to the participation of Indian women, so even finding the women in the available evidence from past centuries is a job requiring a patient sifting of elements. The temptation for scholars, it seems, has been to assume that if women aren't mentioned, they aren't important and their activity is not a topic to be pursued. However, there is enough evidence to assume that women were involved in performance and that their story has not been fully recorded or told.

There are many problems in the very nature of fieldwork that keep knowledge of women's activities invisible to the outsider. Most researchers were and are people whose knowledge of theatre/performance is very slight and who saw/see Indian performance solely as a part of the culture's social/ religious complex, not as theatre. Even the most thorough and valuable recorders do not give us much evidence for rehearsal process, methods of teaching and transmitting performance techniques, or aspects of an event other than the actual performing. For example, recorders were not noting that even when only males are dancing they are wearing costumes, and in many instances those costumes were made by women, so the women have not only participated in the event, but the dance is an exhibition of their art, their visions in kinetic sculptures. Usually the informants to field-workers were male (Arctic surveyor Knud Rasmussen noted that men had greater periods of idleness, women always had work to do, so men had time to talk with field-workers).[1] As men and women in most tribes often had very separate activities such that they almost had two separate cultures (in some instances they even had separate languages, with the women understanding both languages but the men not understanding the women's), most male informants could not speak knowledgeably about women's deeds or thoughts. Within tribal traditions there may be biases that obscure women's work. For example, according to Black Elk, all of the seven sacred rites of the Oglala Sioux were the results of male visions, even the menstrual rites.[2] The author does not investigate for us if it was traditional for the Oglala to credit men with such contributions. In oral traditions it is tradition, not the "hard fact" of Western science, that determines how history is recorded.

Some of this lack of visibility is desired by the women themselves. Minnie Two Shoes, an activist with the American Indian Movement, explained in a meeting at the University of Minnesota in 1974 that it was to the Indian women's advantage to keep men like A.I.M. leaders Russell Means and Dennis Banks in the spotlight. That permitted the women to behave as a true underground, traveling freely under the noses of the F.B.I., teaching the children, carrying on the work. She criticized non-Indian women for failing to understand the strategy of anonymity, for believing every woman should strive to emulate male leaders and want their fame.

Taking her cue and looking for American Indian women in historical materials with an eye to finding them between the cracks, I find women present in (and significant in their contributions to) performance at almost every age, every stage of life, sometimes out in the thick of the dancing and singing, sometimes on the "fringes," making it all happen. Most Native American tribes recognize and celebrate through performance the para-doxical nature of life: life can be known and life cannot be known, life is explicable and mysterious at one and the same time. That which can be known—the ordered relationships among people, between people and the natural world, within the natural world, the stars and cycles of living, and so forth—is honored and symbolically expressed through performances. Performances also celebrate, dramatize that which cannot be known directly, that which is sacred and can only be dramatized symbolically. In each tribe the symbols used, the conventions followed, are particular to the collective consciousness and memory of that tribe. Although some of these performances follow patterns that were established long ago in tribal history, they may be altered as individuals bring new visions to them.[3]

In most cases, what the men and women did in traditional Native theatre was determined by sex role, based on division of labor in the tribe. Women's primary performance responsibilities, like larger tribal responsibilities, were to celebrate ordered relationships, decorate, provide for the group welfare (feasting), maintain the group's dignity. But there is evidence that sex role division is not always strict and that in some cases women perform in the same ways as men, often while retaining their gender identity as women.

The following information and descriptions should not be considered a composite portrait of the Native woman in performance, as tribal variances make any such composite impossible. But generally, when participating according to sex role, women were involved in performance as young girls (premenstrual, pure, not yet possessing women's "power"), in menstruation rites, as postmenstrual women of childbearing age, and as old women (past childbearing). As young girls they often participated in the performances of male societies—they were the virgins, carrying the major symbols of the tribe's purity and honor, even leading processions and dancing between the males and the rest of the tribe (this was particularly prevalent in Northern Plains cultures). John Neihardt recorded from the Oglala Sioux holy man, Black Elk, this description of the girls in his elk ceremony:

> The four virgins represented the life of the nation's hoop, which has four quarters. . . . The four virgins wore scarlet dresses, and each had a single eagle feather in her braided hair; for out of the woman the people grows, and the eagle feather again was for the people as in the bison ceremony. The faces of the virgins were painted yellow, the color of the south, the source of life. One had a daybreak star in red upon her forehead. One had a crescent moon in blue, for the power of the woman grows with the moon and comes and goes with it. One had the sun upon her forehead; and around the mouth and eyebrows of the fourth a big blue circle was painted to mean the nation's hoop. . . . One of the virgins also carried the flowering stick, another carried the pipe which gives peace, a third bore the herb of healing and the fourth held the sacred hoop; for all these powers together are women's power.[4]

The young girls also danced with young boys in children's events (as in certain Southwest dances today in which children perform as clouds). Their menstrual time was handled variously—for some tribes only the women and a male holy man had contact with the girl; in others there were (and are) elaborate private and public aspects to this rite of passage that took days and involved the whole tribe.[5]

Once a girl began menstruation she entered women's society in a new way. Women of childbearing age were charged with the domestic responsibilities of the people—theirs was the daily round of cooking, sewing, gathering, making the home and camp tidy and harmonious. In some tribes they fished or did some small-game hunting or farmed. It has been assumed by most scholars who have mentioned them that these women were not permitted to dance because their "bleeding" made them taboo or that the constant domestic chores kept them from having time to make dance preparations. Women who were menstruating probably were kept in isolation from the tribe, but otherwise these women performed and aided performance to a surprisingly great extent. There were songs, dances, and ceremonies to celebrate the birth of a child, and there were women's social dances of all sorts (basket dances, friendship dances, special dances traditional to or made up for the various women's social groups, performances of women's societies formed as a result of female shamans' visions). Women created parades and honoring dances (the Scalp Dance) for war leaders. In a great many tribes they danced, imitated, narrated, and sang together with the men, participating in bawdy sketches or enacting tribal legends.

Ample illustrations of almost every aspect of the range that women's performing and performance participation took may be found in one complex of events, the Winter Ceremonial of the Kwakiutl of what is now British Columbia. Franz Boas observed women beating skin drums (it is often thought Native women did not drum) and noted that in one society's dances one woman's duty was to sing all the sacred songs.[6] He recounts numerous instances in which women were involved in comic sketches, including a takeoff on white society which involved an old woman and Indians dressed as policemen and a judge. Four men dressed as policemen came into the lodge where everyone was gathered, wanting to know if all were there and determining that one person was missing. They went out and returned with an old woman, who was handcuffed. They then held a mock trial to punish her for her absence. The judge pored over his law book and fined her seventy dollars; she offered seventy blankets instead, claiming she was poor and had no money. The judge accepted the exchange. Then her friends protested, "That is always your way, policemen. As soon as you see anyone who has money, you arrest and fine him." The old woman was released and then seventy blankets were brought out by her relatives and distributed to the group, so the whole skit was a prelude to a giveaway. This sketch, which he witnessed in 1895, while obviously something made up after contact with white society, nevertheless suggests that for the Kwakiutl it was conven-

tional to create such satirical sketches and that they were quite at ease with
having women involved.

For a radical shift in tone and style, Boas gives a long description of a
woman who was chosen to "throw" the supernatural power into the people
because she had performed that role more than anyone else. A male leader
threw the power into the group of people and she was told to try to catch it
and do the same.

> When she caught the spirit, the sound of whistles which she had hidden
> in her mouth was heard. Four times she ran backward and forward, then
> she threw the supernatural power among the people, who stopped. . . .
> Then they began to laugh and to utter their cries.

And so she went through the various houses, singing the sacred song of the
power thrower.

Thus by looking at the Kwakiutl alone we can begin to see the mature
Native woman as a much livelier person and more complete participant than
popular conceptions by non-Indians suggest. Further reading into other
tribes of very different cultures than that of the Kwakiutl, such as the
Cherokee and the Cahuilla, confirms that the Kwakiutl women were not
alone in being active in this realm of performance activity separate from sex
role demands.

However, in keeping with the labor assigned to them as women, there
were performance roles that they carried out either alone or sometimes in
concert with the men. They and the old women bore much of the responsibility for the overall event arrangements. If men in their family were performing, women might help gather properties and other performers needed
and do some of the sewing. In tribes that used tipis the women (who usually
owned the tipis) took down the regular encampment, moved to the performance site, and pitched the tipis in whatever special manner was
appropriate for the event. They cooked the food, which sometimes had to
feed many visitors for many days. They were responsible for the overall
harmony and dignity of the occasion. The observance of proper order and
procedure in all these aspects of the tribe's life was part of keeping the whole
life of the people balanced.

In addition to helping with the feasting and arrangements, older women
sometimes guarded the periphery of a performance event, offering songs,
prayers, and ceremonies to keep evil influences out of the occasion. Similarly, they often made songs at times of death. An old woman might actually be
the major personage in an event—in the Blackfoot Sun Dance, for example,
Sun Dance Woman performs a pivotal role, beginning and ending the event
as well as providing focus for many observances within the event.

Allied to this presence of an old woman as Sun Dance Woman is the
frequent practice of having a female or feminine presence as the spirit that
bonds a performance. In the Pawnee Hako a series of events occur that are

male-performed, but the whole Hako complex is dedicated to and overseen by the mystery of Corn Mother. Sometimes the feminine presence (such as Mother Earth or Female Rain) is represented by a masked person (often, but not always, male), and at other times She is invoked through prayer (the Hako). Nevertheless, She is there as a spiritual presence and Her feminine nature pervades the male activity—again, a way of creating and celebrating balance.

To the non-Indian some of these various roles and responsibilities may seem trivial, and indeed have been treated as such in most scholarship. Although to the theatre specialist every aspect of stage and "house" management is considered significant, these elements in Native performance have been ignored. But there is nothing trivial to Native peoples about any gesture or contribution to those events that honor and express ordered relationships; they make life whole and keep it whole.

Performing as a shaman was not part of a woman's sex role expectation. In some tribes, it seems that role was expressly forbidden to women, or at least that is what field-workers were told.[7] The shaman, who lives to understand the sacred, performs variously depending on the culture. It is generally agreed that the shaman bridges and reveals the realms of paradox—what can be known and what cannot be known. First the shaman makes and keeps contact with mystery through dreams and visions, then performs an event either by taking the participants into the edges of the realm of mystery or by going into that realm as participants observe. In the latter case, the observers are at least touched by the presence of mystery. An individual is chosen for this task by virtue of the power of his or her visions, and the people's recognition of that power. The shaman has received a great deal of attention in Western psychoanalytic and theatre theory in the past decade or more as the "technician of the sacred" whose technique is "to cure by means of ecstasy."[8] Typically, the performance consists of the shaman's singing/dancing/drumming, with or without helpers, over a person who is ill, in the presence of family and other tribal members. The shaman experiences (or appears to experience) an ecstatic state and often takes the ill person and the others into the same state. Often the shaman sucks a stone or object out of the sick body or performs some other such astonishing and "impossible" feat—this aspect of the event has most fascinated Westerners, who seem more anxious to cry "fraud" than to pay attention to the shaman's imitation of paradox. The shaman "cures" through creating ecstasy or some other liminal experience, bridging the known and unknown, restoring the balance between the two for the person who is ill and the tribe. The "fraudulent" feat need not be believed any more than a contemporary audience believes Peter Pan actually flies; in the success of the illusion the shaman confirms the power to contact the world of mystery.

Some contemporary women are shamans, and while their visions, chanting, and performance may be somewhat influenced by contact with Christianity and non-Indian ways, we can see in them the tradition of female shamans. Flora Jones, a Wintu shaman, uses trance performances to heal. In these her spirit helpers arrive (trickster suckerfisher, black wolf, star, moon, mountain spirits) and speak through her voice, sometimes arguing or joking with one another, and with their presence she discovers a patient's ills. When a person is close to death, Flora may perform the Soul Dance, a ritual dance at midnight, performed to the beating of sticks.[9]

Mesoamerican (Mazatec) shaman María Sabina discovered her powers with the teo-nanácatl (psilocybin mushroom) when she was eight. She cured with herbs until she married and began having children, which she says left her no time for the teo-nanácatl. One of her night vigils, in which she chants and calls forth her visions, is recorded by R. G. Wasson and others.[10] Joan Halifax's abbreviation of that text leads us into the woman's performance, into the realm of her spirit. Following is a fragment of her vision chant:

> Woman who thunders am I, woman who sounds am I,
> Spider woman am I, hummingbird woman am I,
> Eagle woman am I, important eagle woman am I,
> Whirling woman of the whirlwind am I, woman of a sacred,
>   enchanted place am I,
> Woman of the shooting stars am I, yes Jesus Christ says,
> Clock woman am I, yes Jesus Christ says. . . .
>
> Jesus oh Mary, holy child, the arm and the hand of the lord
>   of the world.
> Dangerous things are being done, tragedies are being worked out.
> We are left only perplexed, we mamas.[11]

María Sabina's statement that her children left her no time for the teo-nanácatl is a clue to one of the reasons why there were far fewer female shamans than male—with the strict division of labor, a woman was usually restricted during her childbearing years. She found it difficult to maintain the sometimes several days' long vigils and concentration required of a shaman and at the same time fulfill her first role. However, there were often other women around to help. Perhaps in this hesitancy to permit women to be both female and shaman there is some fear that women would have too much power (more than males) if they can bear children, bleed, be the source of the people, and simultaneously have access to mystery as shamans.[12] To further discover the female shaman we will have to search carefully between the lines of tribes' performance histories; and as none of those have been written, she is even more elusive. But she and her sisters were essential to the first theatre in America and carry those ancient traditions into the present.

TRAMPLING OUT THE VINTAGE

SUSAN DYE LEE

There are many ways of understanding the Woman's Crusade of 1873–74. It can be seen as an evangelical temperance revival, as a female protest against the saloon, as the feminization of a male-dominated reform movement, and as a militant extension of home-centered values into the community. Without neglecting these themes, this article also considers the Crusade as a kind of pentecostal melodrama, a spectacular nineteenth-century version of street theatre in which pious, retiring housewives publicly presented themselves as victims of male drinking habits and collectively dramatized their demands for an end to the liquor traffic. As a result, thousands of wives, mothers, and sisters not only managed to bring their grievance to the attention of a nationwide audience, but learned to accept themselves in a new role—that of social reformer.

During the winter of 1873–74, anyone traveling through the towns of Ohio or of its neighboring states saw a novel sight indeed. Bands of praying women were on the march. Their destination? Any place in the community that sold intoxicating spirits. Their mission? With peace, prayer, and persuasion to convince rum-sellers that salvation lay in forsaking the traffic in liquor.

The Woman's Crusade, as it came to be called, was the most remarkable confluence of women, evangelism, and temperance witnessed in the nineteenth century. Whatever animated these crusaders—an addicted relative, abused wives, broken families, righteous indignation—their motives were translated into a female insurrection whose outlines were shaped by the necessities of evangelical piety. The Crusade resembled a gospel temperance revival, featuring prayer, exhortation, and soul-saving. Even militant tactics of direct confrontation and civil disobedience were rationalized by a belief in the moral superiority of women and their mission to act as God's instrument in restoring communities to sobriety. As a result, the movement combined the fervor of a revival with the dramatic spectacle of pious housewives invading male territory to plead for a redress of their grievances. A newspaper correspondent in Newark, Ohio, reported that he would never forget

> the touching and imposing spectacle that burst upon my view as I beheld walking calmly, solemnly, and deliberately, over two hundred ladies, representing our best society, enshrined with silence and beautified by tears. The streets were crowded by thousands as they moved, and many a head was uncovered as the ladies passed, as if they had a special power from God.[1]

Susan Dye Lee, whose Ph.D. dissertation at Northwestern University focussed on the WCTU, is completing a study on the links between temperance, suffrage, and religion.

The Crusade began on Christmas Eve of 1873 in the quiet town of Hillsboro, in southwestern Ohio. Prompted by a temperance lecture on "The Power of Woman's Prayer in Grog Shops," a group of seventy-five ladies dedicated themselves to a campaign against intemperance and began going to saloons to pray for the conversion of liquor dealers.[2] This revolutionary idea—of a prayer meeting "with the locale changed"—soon spread to hundreds of cities throughout Ohio, Indiana, Michigan, Illinois, western Pennsylvania, and upstate New York. From town to town, women "who had never even tried to speak or pray outside their own homes were moving rough men to tears with words of tender eloquence."[3]

The most common, definitive feature of the Crusade was saloon visitation. Because this tactic contained the dramatic element of contrast—of the physically weaker sex pleading with the stronger—of morally superior women appealing to spiritually inferior men—the Crusade commanded a widespread audience, from throngs of street spectators to newspaper readers as far away as Europe. No approach to the problem of intemperance had ever so effectively captured the imagination of press and public alike as did the saloon prayer meeting of the "woman's whiskey war." A reporter in Waynesville, Ohio, described a typical visitation:

> I dropped my pencil a moment to attend an afternoon meeting, held, by permission of Mr. Bowman, at his saloon. It was the most remarkable and impressive scene I have yet witnessed. . . . The ladies sang some beautiful hymns, then the leader called on a very nice-looking old lady to pray. . . . Men that had probably not heard half a dozen prayers in as many years were deeply touched; and as the ladies rose from their knees, there were tears on almost every face. Not a man seemed to have stirred during the prayer, but at its close the band sang with great force and beauty,
>
> *"Tell me the old, old story,"*
>
> and one by one, reverently and in silence, the men dropped from the room. The very genius of primitive Christianity seems to have descended upon some of these praying women. . . .[4]

The crusaders frequently alluded to Christ's atonement when they thought of "going into the low part of town and entering one of those vile dens which respectable people abhorred at a distance. . . ."[5] If Christ died to cleanse his children of their sins, he surely expected them to undertake soul-saving in a spirit of loving sacrifice. "We knew the blessedness of being reviled and persecuted for Christ's sake," said one woman, ". . . and we all felt it was sweet not only to work, but to suffer for His sake."[6] In this respect, the temperance protest became a means of experiencing Christ. "Never have we felt ourselves nearer heaven," said one crusader, "than when kneeling on the floor of a drinking house, praying for the keeper and for the success of the Woman's Crusade."[7] Many hymns the ladies sang during their visitations reflected this desire for redemption through suffering:

> *I am coming to the cross;*
> *I am poor and weak and blind;*
> *I am counting all things dross,*
> *I shall full salvation find.*[8]

Another popular hymn, which the women often sang when their entreaties met with failure, affirmed their identification with Christ:

> *Must Jesus bear the cross alone?*
> *No there's a cross for me.*[9]

Identification with suffering not only had its sources in the evangelical quest for holiness, but in the women's personal feelings of oppression as well. Woman as victim in need of rescue was often the message that praying bands conveyed in their visitations. In Springfield, Ohio, a teacher who brought her entire class of young ladies to a saloon to sing "Say, Mr. Barkeeper, has father been here?" asked in prayer:

How long! oh, Lord, how long! must we suffer on and on, while we have left the power to suffer? Oh, God, consider the tears of the oppressed, for on the side of the oppressor is power, which Thou alone can crush.[10]

Correspondents on the scene presented a similar image in their descriptions. An observer in Jeffersonville, Indiana, wrote:

In their solemn march, they have been compared to a funeral procession; and well they may, for there are mothers there who mourn their first-born slain, and there are mothers, wives, and sisters who are pleading for the lives of those dearer to them than life itself.[11]

Underlying this appearance of passivity, however, lay feelings of militant determination. The crusaders saw their visitations as contests with sin, and placed their experience in the tradition of familiar Biblical stories of good battling evil. In their accounts, they likened themselves to Hebrew children passing unscathed through the fiery furnace or to Daniel in the lion's den. In this sense, the Crusade was a sexual confrontation in which women, impelled by the moral urgencies of evangelicalism, attempted to impose their values on men. Crusade minutes were laced throughout with belligerent war imagery. The ladies "enlisted in the ranks," sought out the "fortress of the enemy," engaged in "hand-to-hand combat with the rum power," and demanded a saloon keeper's "unconditional surrender."[12]

Some saloon keepers were not won over by tearful professions of love from the praying ladies. At Savegaut's Saloon in Wheeling, West Virginia, a fist fight broke out and the "police rushed in and cleared the way with their clubs, and delivered the ladies." In New Vienna, Ohio, the proprietor of the

Dead Fall Saloon "baptised the crusaders with buckets of dirty water," and in another town a saloon keeper's angry wife drenched the band in beer. In a cock-fighting saloon in Cleveland, the group leader was set upon by dogs, and in Carthage, Missouri, the praying women were pelted with rotten eggs. Such abuse made stirring newspaper copy. On May 5, 1874, "Black Tuesday" in Bucyrus, Ohio:

> Women were thrown down, were dragged and wrenched by brute force from posts and rails to which they clung; were seized by ruffians who were intoxicated, and carried several rods from their companions.[12]

Opposition only spurred the crusaders' determination. When locked from a saloon, they moved their theatre of operation into the street. Since they conducted street work despite the severe weather conditions, the women presented a heartrending sight. At Ripley, Ohio, for example, the ladies were not permitted to hold a prayer meeting in Reinert's Saloon, and so:

> Down on their knees the ladies fell upon the pavement, in snow and sleet, with a most pitiless wind blowing. Men stood with uncovered heads, and the crowd wept. . . . Close against the pane a mother bowed in prayer, and a moment later the door was opened, and Mr. Reinert said, "Ladies, I will quit the business. . . ."[12]

Much as they suffered from the weather, the crusaders were delighted with the sympathy that such scenes roused. "I saw that instead of being a disaster," said Mother Eliza Stewart of Springfield, "it was often an advantage, as we had so many more auditors on the street than we could have in the saloon. It excited the sympathy of the throng for the women, and their indignation against the saloon-keeper. . . ."[13] "It was a sight calculated to melt the stoutest heart," admitted a reporter in Hillsboro, when the ladies were locked from Dunn's Drugstore and conducted their prayer meeting on the cold flagstones instead.[14]

Exhortation through prayer was not the only tactic used by the crusaders in their campaign to eliminate the liquor traffic. They soon devised other, quite ingenious means of applying social pressure to strip drinking of its respectability. Pledge-collecting, a favorite antebellum practice, resurfaced during the Crusade. In Delaware, Ohio, for example, the young ladies of Ohio Wesleyan University refused to associate with any young man who had not signed the pledge.[15] In Waynesville, Ohio, "books were kept in which the name of every man entering either saloon was registered; the result was a large falling off in the patronage."

Few temperance men questioned this novel reversal of leadership roles. Faith in the redemptive power of women was a shared assumption. "We men must take back seats and be ready to do whatever the women command," said a Cincinnati partisan.[16] The women agreed. They were in charge. "We deem it important," said one committee of crusaders, "to keep this work in the hands of the women of our city."[17]

Nowhere was the truth of this development more visible than at mass temperance meetings, where the full force of community opinion was brought to bear on nonconformists. At these public gatherings, the evangelical belief in the right of "the female brethren" to self-expression reached full flower. Crusaders, along with ministers, offered prayers for the deliverance of their communities. Moses T. Handy, a reporter for the *New-York Daily Tribune*, described the scene he found in Mount Vernon, Ohio:

> The meeting, to use a homey Western expression, run itself. Nobody presided. The meeting progressed with the greatest religious fervor till a young man made his appearance and crowded his way to the pulpit, where, facing the audience, with an excited gesture he called their attention. "Ladies," he said, "I have come to tell you that I can't hold out any longer; I, too, give in. I shall not sell any more liquor, and I want to sign the pledge."[18]

Like a protracted revival meeting, the confrontation gripped communities all over the Western states in a fever pitch of suspense.[19] Praying bands grew in number. Stories of whole towns gone dry were widely circulated in the press. "The world has seen nothing like this woman's temperance movement," said one of its zealous advocates. "It is sweeping over this country like a magnificent prairie fire."[20]

The surrender of a saloon keeper, particularly when he was the final holdout, prompted a mass celebration in communities where it occurred. In Xenia, Ohio, for example, the "siege" of an intransigent rum-seller ended on February 19, 1874:

> Mr. Steve Phillips, proprietor of the "Shades of Death," invited the ladies to enter, and announced that he would never sell anything intoxicating in Xenia again. Then the ladies, joined by the spectators, sang,
>
> "Praise God, from whom all blessings flow,"
>
> while the liquors were rolled into the street. A half-barrel of blackberry brandy, the same of highwines, a few kegs of beer, and some bottles of ale and whiskey, were soon emptied into the street, amid the shouts of an enthusiastic multitude. . . . On every side nothing was witnessed but smiles, laughter, tears, prayers, hand-shakings, and congratulations.[21]

At Hillsboro, the crusaders knocked bungs from barrels and cheered as their contents spilled into the gutter. "I didn't know I was so strong," said one woman, "but I lifted that axe like a woodman and brought it down with such force that the first blow stove in the head of a barrel and splashed the whiskey in every direction."[22] Millennial feelings of great joy permeated all these community celebrations. Typical was the one at South Charlestown,

Ohio, where the citizens formed a triumphal procession, marched to the saloon of the last man to surrender, and to the accompaniment of a brass band, serenaded the owner. Christ's kingdom on earth had arrived. Said one: "Who will blame us for feeling unspeakably happy? for we saw the light gleaming over the hill tops."[23]

The millennium was short-lived. By the end of summer, the Crusade had worn itself out. Gradually, bands of temperance agitators ceased their visitations and saloons opened for business as usual. Clearly, the Crusade had not succeeded in abolishing the traffic in liquor.

By other standards, however, the Crusade was not a failure. Intended as a mission to save the souls of liquor dealers, the Crusade instead became a transforming experience for the participants. It brought thousands of women out of their homes and into the community. It gave many their first opportunity to speak publicly, to lead groups, to formulate plans, and to execute goals. Uniting in a cause women could identify with gave the crusaders a chance to express shared feelings of sisterhood. And, having learned the power of association, they began to organize beyond the local level. In November of 1874, over one hundred delegates at a convention in Cleveland formed the National Woman's Christian Temperance Union, an organization that was to command the largest following of American women in the nineteenth century.[24] The Crusade not only broke down sectarian boundaries, but also showed women how to liberate themselves from second-class status in the temperance movement.

The crusaders had made an irreversible debut into public life, and they were aware of it. It "startled me into an active thinking life," said one. It gave me "broader views of woman's sphere and responsibility," said another.[25] For many participants, then, the Crusade was a watershed experience, one they celebrated whenever and wherever they gathered for the rest of their lives. By significantly altering their self-concept, the Crusade changed women's ideas about themselves and their relationship to the larger society. As Frances Willard asserted, "Going out on the street brought women face to face with the world's misery and sin," and for the crusaders home would never be quite the same again.[26]

FRIENDSHIP AND RITUAL IN THE WTUL

ELIZABETH PAYNE MOORE

Since the publication of Carroll Smith-Rosenberg's "The Female World of Love and Ritual: Relations Between Women in Nineteenth-Century America," scholars interested in women's history have become increasingly concerned with the nature of female ritualized behavior and with what has been labeled "woman-bonding."[1] Female rites such as visiting, gift-giving, and parties served to refresh ongoing relationships, to intensify women's identification with each other and to create a "female world." These women, of course, were from á fairly homogeneous background and were not "public" women involved in a career or reform activities.

One sees, however, some of the same phenomena among a group of women who associated together as the Women's Trade Union League (WTUL) more than fifty years later. Founded in 1903 during the annual convention of the American Federation of Labor, the League worked to organize unskilled, mostly immigrant, working women into trade unions and to educate the public on the needs of working women. Few organizations could claim a more sociologically diverse membership. Jewish seamstresses, Italian finishers, and Swedish bootworkers came together with middle-class "allies" to work for the improvement of conditions of women workers. Membership included Margaret Dreier Robins and her sister, Mary Dreier, former debutantes from Brooklyn Heights society, as well as Rose Schneiderman, a Polish immigrant seamstress, and Elizabeth Maloney, a Chicago waitress.

Members organized women into union locals and provided support for strikers during most of the nation's major labor upheavals of the period. It was they who conceived and then secured the passage of federal legislation providing for the nineteen-volume pioneering survey which paved the way for much of the legislation of the Progressive Era. These women were purposeful, serious about themselves, and passionately committed to changing the social and economic structure in important ways.

But this is the "official" side of their lives and their organization. Underlying their public endeavors, the fabric of their personal relationships and their social life together provided an encouraging context for accomplishing goals that they had set for themselves in the broader society. Female rites like birthday and anniversary parties, open houses, and choral groups as well as pageants, festivals, and celebrations of strike victories gave women immediate, face-to-face contact across class and ethnic barriers. Such communal experiences did not obliterate the personal hostilities nor mute the

Elizabeth Payne Moore, who teaches history at the Art Institute of Chicago, wrote a Ph.D. dissertation on Margaret Drier Robins and the Women's Trade Union League at the University of Illinois-Chicago Circle.

cultural differences that such a diverse membership inevitably brought to the organization, but they did give form to the women's quest for fellowship and "solidarity."

A close look at the organization reveals that both workers and allies expressed a yearning for what they called "a larger life" or as the Lawrence picket sign demanded, "Roses as well as bread."[2] David Dubinsky, president of the International Ladies Garment Workers' Union, readily acknowledged that a union "could not hold working women just by a dollar more in their pocket and a short work day. You had to give them something more. . . ."[3] Indeed, much of the ritualized social behavior observed in the League was later institutionalized in the Amalgamated Clothing Workers' Union and the International Ladies Garment Workers' Union, predominantly female organizations.[4]

That the women's voices and the particular content of their protest arose precisely when they did was no accident. Female garment workers at the time were America's lowest-paid industrial workers, but that does not in itself explain the intensity of the women's protest since women seamstresses had been among the poorest-paid workers throughout the nineteenth century. Several important segments of American industry had mechanized and subdivided work during the 1880's and 1890's, but the garment industry was the first large one which employed a majority of women to divide work intensively. The large Chicago manufacturer of men's clothing, Hart, Schaffner, and Marx, for example, moved "inside"—a term used to denote the assemblying of all work processes under one roof—the same year the League was organized, 1903. The speeding-up system typical of the highly competitive garment factories, especially of the newly emerging women's ready-to-wear industry, and the seasonal nature of the trade resulted in fourteen- to sixteen-hour days, six-day weeks, and three- to five-dollar weekly wages—a way of life which made one feel "so dead that one never sees anything," according to a young Russian-Jewish seamstress.[5] Constant tiredness and fatigue were the ultimate threats to natural growth and to the development of one's potentiality, not the least of which was one's potential motherhood, a fact always in the back of the women's minds. In essence, factory time was being substituted for human rhythm.

In addition to offering avenues for cultivating friendship and expressing sociability, then, the League's social gatherings provided space for experiencing what these women saw as a more natural rhythm. As such, their activities helped members confront discontinuities they faced in the broader society by providing emotional sustenance—what one sociologist calls emotional "nutrition"[6]—to women who often found their social environment enervating. Seen negatively, their choral singings, parties, and pageants presented a mere countervailing force to the monotony and fatigue of factory life.[7] Seen more positively, however, they were oriented to stimulate, to arouse and deliberately to play with the emotions in order to elicit creativity and hence evoke new self-perceptions. Although they did not necessarily do so, at times the female rites practiced by League women led to "an awakening"—the libidinally loaded euphemism they used to describe a young woman's budding interest in the labor movement. The Chicago WTUL, for example, sponsored Sunday afternoon poetry readings as one of its first activities, and through reading poetry, Margaret Dreier Robins felt, young women became alive to the fact that each had her own story and message to tell. "And so," she later recalled, "one of the first demands in the old days when we were simply reading poetry was for classes in public speaking."[8] Robins obviously felt that reading poetry together had inspired women to develop skills—mastering parliamentary law, English grammar, and public speaking, for example—which would enable them to enlarge their scope within the broader society. In 1915 at their biennial convention, for example, one member thought that the League had "grown in surety and strength of purpose to somewhat the proportions of a women's labor parliament," but in tone and atmosphere the convention seemed more like a "jolly family gathering."[9]

Their parties ranged from small, intimate occasions at a member's home to large banquets celebrating a significant event in the history of the League or perhaps a recent strike victory. Life-cycle events like birthdays and anniversaries were the focus of special attention. Often women composed songs or poems for the occasion, detailing events from the life of the one whose birthday was being celebrated. Historians of women working in documents of the Progressive period are frequently amused at the extent to which the female reform community celebrated September 6, Jane Addams's birthday. Yet birthday celebrations were common among all women's organizations, clubs, and friendship circles. Birthdays evoked a feeling of basic human *prima materia*—everybody had birthdays—at the same time they focused on the biography of a particular and "special" person.[10]

Not merely preliminary to "serious" work, neither were their social gatherings and celebrations peripheral to the League's identity as a group. In 1924 Samuel Gompers, with whom the women had had a constant tug-of-war, began a drive to assimilate the WTUL under the auspices of a Women's Department in the AFL. Most members energetically fought the move, rejecting male unionists' criticism that they had been ineffectual in their work. Agnes Nestor, a Chicago glove worker and the first woman to head an international union, wrote Robins that year describing a recent party sponsored by the League. She wished, she wrote, that Gompers and other proponents of the absorption plan could have attended "our Girls' dinner," since it was exactly the kind of activity that Illinois Federation of Labor President John Walker and other critics had warned against the League's sponsoring. "We had 111 at the dinner and fully one hundred were trade union women and most of the program was singing. . . . We had so much singing that it really was everybody's party. It was a great success. I tried to picture the men getting it up or arranging it."[11]

Drama especially appealed to League women. They read and acted out parts of plays, sometimes writing the plays or pageants themselves. "The festival of life" or "the pageant of life" were metaphors frequently used to describe the richness and diversity which they felt lay beyond the horizon of most working women but which could nevertheless be tapped and experienced via drama. Robins had a highly developed sense of the dramatic, had directed her younger siblings in plays as a child and enjoyed "the something which happens to each of us when for the moment we are caught up in a spirit of exaltation."[12] The League's plays and pageants frequently dealt with themes in the history of women or labor, but the purpose of their dramatic undertakings was less to inform than to encourage creativity. Through writing plays, staging pageants, and acting parts, it was hoped that women would discover their own hidden potentiality. Although sometimes didactic, their plays and pageants were essentially celebrations of the powers and capacities of womanhood, allowing women to experiment with roles or ways of being not otherwise encouraged.

League members enjoyed giving each other gifts. Although complex, the ritual of giving gifts seems to have functioned largely for these women as what sociologist Barry Schwartz calls a "generator of identity."[13] As in other rites observed in the League, gifts gave women a freedom to experiment and even to "play" with their self-perceptions. The gift of copies of Ibsen's plays to Rose Schneiderman from a group of women whom Schneiderman had just organized into a union local conveyed how those women saw her as well as what she had evoked in them.[14] The giving of gifts furthermore helped create a system of "gratitude imperatives" without which any group, especially one with women from such diverse backgrounds, could not have long sustained itself. Accepting gifts bonded the recipient to the giver and helped transcend incipient hostilities.

Historians have frequently interpreted the social and leisure-time activities of the League as deflecting time and energy away from the serious task of economic reform, and on occasion—but very rarely—some of the activities were criticized by working women as the charitable concerns of the middle-class allies.[15] One could, however, more appropriately invert this critique: for many of the League women there would have been little energy or vision to tackle economic reform without the intimate, ritualized social contact that the women had with each other. Clearly their social activities were not mere epiphenomena, but neither was there a straight line of evolution from, say, celebrating one's birthday or writing a poem to organizing a new union. The relationship between their social life together and their reform efforts was more subtle and circuitous than that. It was ultimately a matter of being energized and of taking courage—literally of being *encouraged*—or as Leonora O'Reilly had written in her diary, a matter of women saying to other women at crucial times, "go ahead . . . we believe in you."[16]

RITES AND RIGHTS

CYNTHIA PATTERSON AND BARI J. WATKINS

At first glance, the relationship between pageants and the modern women's movement reveals a curious historical irony. In September 1968 members of various radical women's organizations demonstrated against the Miss America Pageant in Atlantic City, New Jersey, for the oppressive image of women the competition perpetuated. The radical women's street-theatre tactics captivated the mass media and provided the American public with its first front-page exposure to the emerging women's liberation movement. Over fifty years earlier, however, the radical women of the National Woman's Party had staged rather than disrupted pageants to protest the same legal and cultural subordination of women in American society. In both instances, women activists acted from a recognition of the power of pageants to create a public image of women. The crucial difference between the radical women of the 1920's and the 1960's lies not in their objectives but in their tactical alternatives. In the 1920's, the Woman's Party organized pageants to depict women in the positive imagery of equality, while in the 1960's, beauty pageants presented an image of women against which women activists rebelled.

Since the early nineteenth century, pageants have held a special place in the development of "female rites." First used by women reformers, church groups, and by schoolteachers to present dramatically social ideals and female solidarity, the female rites of pageantry as an organizational style unique to women's groups and clubs developed naturally into a part of the organized women's movement. Since the Seneca Falls Convention of 1848, women's organizations have frequently utilized the theatrical *rite* of pageantry to promote and publicize their political commitment toward the attainment of various *rights* for women in American society. In this context, the Woman's Party's "Equal Rights Pageants" represent a significant and highly innovative expression of the idea of "female rites" in the history of women in American theatre.

In 1923, the Woman's Party proposed the first Equal Rights Amendment to the U.S. Constitution. By that time, the mass organization supporting the drive for suffrage had disbanded, leaving the Woman's Party as the sole representative of radical feminism in the United States. Viewed as outsiders, the Woman's Party faced a long and disappointing struggle to preserve the earlier spirit of the women's movement.

The Woman's Party's equal rights program aimed at replacing legal inequalities and cultural beliefs in women's innate inferiority and natural

Cynthia Patterson, Associate Athletic Director at Northwestern University, wrote about the National Women's Party and Feminism for her Ph.D. in history there. Bari Watkins, Dean of the College at Rollins College, Florida, was formerly director of the Program on Women at Northwestern.

domesticity with the ideals of equality, liberty, and justice. To secure these goals, the Woman's Party adopted a strategy of legal reform and education designed to eliminate the institutional and cultural barriers underlying the subjugation of women in American society. While the passage of the ERA formed the core of their legal program, the Woman's Party viewed the process of education as the essential prerequisite for transforming cultural attitudes toward women and employed a wide variety of techniques to diffuse their ideas throughout society. The most interesting and creative of their tactics, however, were the Equal Rights Pageants.

From 1923 through 1925, the Woman's Party sponsored three national pageants and a series of state and regional pageants. The basic theme in each pageant was the historical evolution of the women's rights movement. The first major pageant, held in Seneca Falls, N.Y., July 1923, marked the seventy-fifth anniversary of the Seneca Falls Convention of 1848 when the women's rights movement in the U.S. was officially initiated. As the prototype of the Woman's Party style of pageantry, the Seneca Falls celebration demands careful consideration. The event, worked out in sumptuous detail, involved an opening processional, musical productions, and a series of tableaux. At nightfall, a processional of one hundred women dressed in purple flowing gowns, singing the "March of the Woman," paraded from the local Episcopal church to the lake area where a bilevel platform stage stood. Following the processional, approximately five hundred banner girls arrived on barges from across the lake. The banner bearers, dressed in white and carrying the purple, white, and gold banners of the Woman's Party, were joined by women representing various professions, and together the ensemble encircled the stage and the audience. Then, after a brief silent interlude, Madame Vander Ver, a professional opera singer, performed Handel's *Largo* with lyrics written by Hazel Mackaye, the pageant's director.

When the entire processional had been completed, the lights revealed a higher platform upon which the entire delegation to the 1848 Seneca Falls Convention was represented, complete with hooped skirts and high beaver hats. The climax of the ensuing tableaux occurred when Lucretia Mott followed by Elizabeth Cady Stanton stepped forward and Stanton recited the "Declaration of Sentiments" adopted at the 1848 Convention. As Stanton read the list of principles, trumpets sounded and her words were flashed in light against the darkened sky. Lavinia Egan captured the spirit and format of the pageant in her description of this moment which appeared in the Woman's Party's weekly journal:

From the darkness below the stage came a solitary figure, frail, grey-clad, Quaker garbed, fearless Lucretia Mott. . . . The picture of the intrepid woman who seventy-five years ago dared to emerge from the darkness of ignorance and prejudice and age-old traditions and stand forth against the whole world for a principle was strikingly manifest. . . . Elizabeth Cady Stanton and Lucretia Mott clasped hands in the pact of comradeship and co-operation in the great work of freeing one-half of the human race. The symbolism of the thing was superb; the dramatic impact on the mind of the spectator was tremendous.[1]

The closing recessional preserved the idealistic and dramatic quality of the performance as the entire cast sang "Onward Christian Soldiers" and disappeared behind the stage.

The rhetorical flair and idealism conveyed in both the pageant and Ms. Egan's description of the event prevailed in all of the Woman's Party's pageants. The major pageants in Colorado (September 1923) and Westport, New York (August 1924), repeated the basic scheme of their predecessor. The Colorado pageant added the story of the Western pioneer women and their contributions to women's advancement and to the historical drama of the women's movement. At Westport, the historical scope of the pageant was extended even further as women's struggle for equality was re-created on the stage from ancient Greece through the contemporary equal rights campaign of the Woman's Party. In each case, the artistic imagination and ingenuity of the Woman's Party conveyed to thousands of Americans a vision of a better society in which women had finally triumphed in their battle against inequality and subjugation.

The Woman's Party's motives for staging pageants involved much more than a simple desire to entertain. As an instrument of education, the pageant was uniquely suited to overcome the obstacles the Woman's Party confronted among women and throughout the culture. The Woman's Party regarded women as the worst victims of the cultural indoctrination and perpetuation of Victorian notions of womanhood which remained as the major restrictions upon women throughout the 1920's. Blinded by blissful ignorance and false consciousness, content in her subjugation and traditional roles, the American woman of the 1920's stood out as the primary target for the Woman's Party's educational arsenal. Further, the political apathy, materialism, frivolity, and conspicuous consumption which seemed to dominate the cultural mainstream presented a related, added source of frustration to the Woman's Party in their educational endeavors. With the Equal Rights Pageants, the Woman's Party believed that it had created an educational medium powerful enough to convert men and especially women to their cause of equality and to transform cultural attitudes toward women.

In 1923, Hazel Mackaye, the Woman's Party's pageant director, explained the educational purpose and methodology underlying these colorful events. "The one consuming passion of the American people," she initially posited, "is to make money. . . . The next most absorbing passion is the search for an outlet for the sensuous emotions which have been repressed by the grind of the business world." According to Mackaye, these emotional needs were manifested in the popularity of recreational indulgences such as jazz, car racing, melodramatic sentimental movies, and bootlegging. Given this set of priorities, she continued, everything, whether merchandise, ideas, or even religion, must be "sold to the public." Thus, the Woman's Party believed it had to find some medium through which they could educate and inspire an anti-intellectual, apathetic, and self-deceiving public. The Woman's Party's solution appears as a variation of the "do as the Romans do" approach: "To get into the game . . . and 'sell' our program to the public." Since the Woman's Party could not bestow monetary profit or social prestige upon individuals, it must reach the public through its other main interest—having a good time.

The pageants, Mackaye pointed out, provided individuals with "a chance to take part in a 'big show,' done on a large scale, with color and beauty—a chance in short to have a good time." Once a public audience was attracted to the event, the success of the educational process was ensured as the nonbelievers were converted to the righteousness and urgency of the Woman's Party's program. With rhetorical flair and conviction, Mackaye described the impact of the pageants on both the cast and the audience:

> The realization came to them that these women today were going on with the noble traditions of the past; that they were forging ahead to win the goal so grandly and so uncompromisingly demanded by those intrepid women seventy-five long years ago. Not one of those women or girls who participated in the pageant could ever again feel indifference toward the cause of Equal Rights. And the same was true of the ten and twenty thousands in the audience. Their imaginations had been touched, illuminated. They were, for the moment, lifted to an unaccustomed but none the less pleasurably thrilling plane of idealism—where all the sordid, petty matters of the ordinary lives ceased to exist.

Once the flame of idealism, the desire for equality, liberty, and justice, had begun to burn in the hearts of men and women, the Women's Party felt assured that it could never be extinguished. "Through the pageant therefore," Mackaye concluded, "we found that friends were made for Equal Rights who could never have been gained by any other method, at once so winning and so disarming."[2]

Yet the meaning of female rites as rituals in relation to the Woman's Party goes even deeper than the party's commitment to theatrical rites as a medium for social expression by women. Like all cultural rituals, theatre possesses an internal structure of meanings revealing as much about the artist's perception of him/herself as about the relationship between certain artistic forms and corresponding social and cultural conditions.

In this context, the "Equal Rights Pageants"[3] were also an important symbolic manifestation of the Woman's Party's self-image as a vanguard of idealists whose thoughts and actions were carrying forward the historical struggle of women to achieve equality. The Woman's Party's conviction that their ideals were righteous, their sense of mission, and their belief that victory was inevitable emanated from their reflections regarding their own historical importance. For example, the Seneca Falls pageant of 1923, celebrating the seventy-fifth anniversary of the beginning of the women's rights movement, explicitly expressed their self-perception as "torchbearers." During the pageant the symbolic torch of women's emancipation was passed on from the pioneers, Lucretia Mott, Elizabeth Cady Stanton, and Susan B. Anthony, to the Woman's Party. The Woman's Party thus created their own past. By drawing a direct historical linkage from themselves back to the early feminist pioneers, the Woman's Party engaged in a search for a continuity of opposition and for historical antecedents to their ideological beliefs.

The Woman's Party's creation of a usable past signified a crucially important aspect of their collective identity and ideological system. Their ability to find themselves in their selective past allowed them to justify their contemporary position as an unsuccessful, criticized, and often ignored extremist group while simultaneously providing them with "proof" that they were the end point rather than the beginning in the evolution of a historical movement. Thus, the pageants were as important and meaningful as rituals for the Woman's Party as the Woman's Party hoped they would be for their audience.

Finally, we are left with yet another historical irony. The Woman's Party lost their battle in the 1920's to liberate women and create an egalitarian society. Perhaps, if their pageants had been the effective tool of cultural education the Woman's Party intended them to be, there might never have been an antipageant protest some fifty years later in Atlantic City.

CROWNING MISS CALIFORNIA, AGAIN

JAMES H. BIERMAN

The *San Francisco Chronicle* had already gone to press with its Sunday paper when Deanna Rae Fogarty was crowned Miss California on Saturday night, June 23, 1979, and the coronation was not considered of sufficient importance to bother holding a space for it. Monday's paper devoted half its front page to the eighth annual Gay Freedom Day Parade, but contained no coverage of the Miss California Pageant. Twenty years ago, the paper would not have missed the event. Ten years ago, the outraged protests of the

James H. Bierman, Professor of Theatre Arts at the University of California at Santa Cruz, has written extensively about popular entertainment for such journals as *The Yale Review, The Drama Review,* and the *SoHo News.*

women's movement brought it back to the limelight, but in 1979, the Miss California Pageant seemed harmless. It was not negligible, however, to the sponsors who paid $114,500 to broadcast the event live on seven West Coast network television stations or to the audience which filled the 2,000-seat Santa Cruz Civic Auditorium to capacity for three nights in a row at a cost of six dollars per seat for the two preliminary showings and twelve dollars for the final pageant. Despite the ups and downs of public opinion the Miss California Pageant has managed to hold its own over fifty-six years.

Being Miss California or possibly Miss America, with the crown and scepter which accompany the office, is the closest thing to obtaining royalty possible for young women in a democratic society, short of marrying a prince of Monaco, and the image of success which comes with it is still very much a piece of the American Dream. More than 100,000 women annually apply to compete in local pageants. Seventy thousand enter the competition and their numbers are reduced through local pageants, state pageants, and finally the Miss America Pageant to one queen. This program is supported by 250,000 volunteer workers who labor with astonishing civic zeal for the cause. Their cooperative efforts contribute to the mammoth structure of the Miss America Pageant, a nonprofit organization which franchises subsidiary state pageants, which in turn sell franchises to local pageants.

Being a nonprofit operation employing only one full-time staff member, the Miss California Pageant is unique in the field of popular entertainment in that it is entirely free of profit motive. This independence attracts a staff of volunteer workers whose dedication is not diluted by financial concerns. It also means that the pageant can exist unfettered by a need for the approval of popular or monied interests. Ironically, the events and the queens they produce continue to be a product the public purchases. A total of 2.8 million people watched Deanna Rae Fogarty receive her crown on 24 percent of California's televisions. The ratings from 8:00 to 9:00 P.M. on June 23 were the highest in the West. Had she been chosen as a finalist in the national pageant at Atlantic City, over 65 percent of the television viewing audience across the country would have watched her belt out "Mein Herr" and "Wilkommen."

The Miss America Pageant remains a cornbelt phenomenon which focuses on the amorphous middle of America. It demands community involvement and tends to establish itself best in those small communities where the involvement is highest. San Francisco sent no candidate to the 1979 Miss California Pageant, while such places as Morro Bay, Reedley, San Luis Obispo, Fresno County, and Lake County were represented. In general, the geographic distribution of the local pageants coincides with the political distribution of the population, with the more conservative areas producing the most contestants. Out of the thirty-three contestants participating in the Miss California Pageant, nine came from the Los Angeles—Orange County area.

Local pageants begin in July of the year previous to a given Miss California

Pageant and continue through April of the next year. Some, such as the San Joaquin County Pageant, involve thorough and rigorous screening processes. In 1978, 125 applicants were interviewed, and twenty-nine were selected to compete. Ten finalists selected from preliminary pageants were then given ten weeks of intense training in such required areas as walking, dress, hair styling, and developing their talent. Then on a final night of competition, Parlisha Sophia Watts, a nineteen-year-old student at San Joaquin Delta College, was selected. One of three Black candidates to make it to the state finals, she sang a rendition of "I've Got Love" that was spunky, brazen, and "Black." She eventually came in third in the state, winning the $1,000 scholarship award for second runner-up. To put on her local pageant, the people from the Miss San Joaquin County Pageant Association raised $19,000, of which $15,000 went to producing the event and $4,000 was divided up in scholarship prizes.

Irony was not lacking in the selection of Gil Stratton, a well-known Los Angeles television sports commentator, as a cohost for the final night of the Miss California Pageant. In fact, the pageant bears greater similarity to a sporting event than to any other recognizable genre of public entertainment. The highly specialized behavior demanded in a pageant requires a special training without which no woman stands a chance. There is no such thing as a "natural" in the pageant just as there is no such thing as a person who has a natural ability to pole-vault. Such behavior must be learned and can only be developed through training. Similarly, during pageant week, a Miss California candidate is required to perform activities and present herself in ways which are unlikely to be repeated in her life.

Despite this, one of the ideological themes of the pageants is individualism. At the outset, the general chairman of a pageant receives a memo from the pageant's executive secretary, Ruth McCandliss, headed *Re: Let the Contestants Be Themselves*, which encourages them to allow the candidates to nurture their individuality:

> We encourage the National Finalists to show their individuality, and this holds true where dress is concerned. We strongly advocate "good taste" in the selection of wardrobe, a hair style which is becoming to the contestant and comfortable for *her* to wear, and a reminder that what is worn under her dress or swimsuit is her own decision. . . . If a young woman can enhance her appearance (within the confines of good taste)—then the more power to her.
>
> So please do not permit anyone to question any addition(s) to wardrobe (swimsuit or dress) which the modern woman considers an aid in making her a more attractive person.
>
> You must, of course, operate within the framework of instructions from State Pageant Headquarters when selecting wardrobe. Certain requirements are made regarding type of swimsuit, dress for Judges Interview, rehearsal clothes, etc.

Allowing contestants to wear padding as they choose is hardly an expression of individuality. As it is, all the 1978 Miss America candidates came within an inch or two of the standard 36–24–36 or 35–23–35 measurements (the twelve-inch hourglass), and padding merely serves as an aid to conformity, rather than individuality. Nonetheless, the rhetoric of the pageant continues to stress the American ideal of individuality, and a late 1960's style belief that a person's success depends on the development of her own individual potential. Deanna Rae Fogarty expressed this ideal when asked about her role in the women's movement. "We all do it on our own successes. I'm not out to fight for them. Women will have to draw their own strength from within. This [indicating her body] is only an exterior."

Despite the rhetoric, serious pageant candidates have very little room for personal expression in dress, hair, makeup, or even self-presentation. To begin with, each must conform to the numerous conditions of a twenty-nine-page rule book, with five full pages on swimsuits alone, which they are given upon arriving at Santa Cruz. This book contains such a stupefying list of stipulations that a pageant week promises less freedom for the participants than basic training or state prison. During the stay in Santa Cruz, each contestant is attended by a close entourage of chaperones from their local pageant area and hostesses from Santa Cruz. The hostesses—"outstanding women of the community who are selected because of their abilities, graciousness, and joy in being with others"—act as constant companions to the contestants, picking them up at their motels, delivering them to the Santa Cruz Civic Auditorium, the site of the pageant, and returning them to their motel. They have full charge of all the contestant's activities, interviews, pictures, recordings, and any other appearances and must accompany her at all times unless she is in the company of her chaperone. The chaperone is described as a "companion and friend, buffer, champion, and watchdog." Her particular function is to be on constant surveillance for the possibility of "unacceptable and uncomfortable situations." Except on stage, no contestant has contact with the outside world except through the mediation of a chaperone or hostess. In particular they are protected from men—even fathers. As the rule book states:

> So many fathers are handsome and young looking, and could easily be taken for your "gentleman friend." Therefore, we limit them as to contact with you, as we do all other males.

This constant guard also assures adherence to a conduct code which prohibits attendance at unscheduled parties, meetings, or social events, smoking in public, imbibing alcoholic beverages or entering any establishment where alcoholic beverages are served, taking unprescribed drugs or tranquilizers, or being in the presence of judges or men.

The pageant has a history of being attacked by conservatives and liberals and it has become so defensive that it obsessively protects the contestants. If anything, it has erred on the conservative side of the issue, but this has been, in part, stimulated by a desire to distinguish itself from a host of imitations that have spun off from the Miss America Pageant over the years: Miss U.S.A., Miss Universe, Miss Rheingold, Miss Subways, Miss Chinese-America, Miss California Rodeo, and so on. Anyone on the staff of any Miss America Pageant would be quick to explain that these are merely "beauty" pageants whereas the Miss America Pageant (and its state and local counterparts) is a "scholarship" pageant. These women are selected on the basis of the "whole person," not just their bodies.

The swimsuit competition is the area where the Miss America Pageant is forced to be the most defensive. In the 1970's the contestants were finally allowed a choice which extended beyond the one-piece paneled swimsuit, but the regulations which still apply don't amount to much of a liberation. Above all, the regulations steer clear of any hint of sexiness in the suits with such guidelines as "the fit of the suit in the bust and crotch areas must be smooth and trim and not revealing. Pay particular attention to these areas when making the selection." It is this concern which probably resulted in relaxing the requirement of the "panel" suit and not the fact that it had been long outdated. In effect, the front panel served to call attention to the crotch rather than hide it.

A woman parading on a ramp through the Santa Cruz Civic Auditorium in front of 2,000 fully clothed spectators wearing an outdated single-piece swimsuit with matching four-inch spike-heeled shoes (in style again) while Jack Fisher and the Miss California Orchestra play cocktail-lounge music presents an absurd image. Although the pageant took place on the Santa Cruz beach until 1954 where swimwear was more appropriate, its history does little to justify its present form. The stated justification announced to the audience during the pageant is that "it enables our judges to determine health qualities, the attitudes our contestants portray while meeting this more difficult part of our program, and the self-discipline she possesses in caring for herself." The contestants are told that the swimsuit competition is the "health portion" of the competition permitting the judges to evaluate their "form, carriage, proportions, skin tone, etc.," while the judges' instructions direct their attention toward such abstract qualities as "beauty, figure, grace, poise, and posture."

Despite the confusion about the purpose of the swimsuit competition, there can be little doubt that the pageant would lose its appeal without it. Joseph Merkel, the press director of the 1979 Miss California Pageant, inadvertently revealed this attitude when he said jokingly of the swimsuit competition, "It's the name of the game." It is the element of the Miss America Pageant most often included in the imitation pageants. However, in their effort to distinguish themselves, the Miss America Pageant has not been able to abandon the swimsuit competition, realizing that it is essential to its popularity. As the judging goes, the swimsuit competition carries one-sixth of the weight. Each candidate has a personal interview which carries an equal weight, as does her appearance in evening gown competition. The talent competition is given an importance equal to the total of the other three parts, thus allowing it half the emphasis, but it is difficult to imagine any woman with a less than shapely body possessing enough talent, poise, or personality to be Miss America.

Five judges sit at an elevated table by the stage-left side of the ramp. Normally composed of three men and two women, the panel is drawn from "pageant family": producers, directors, chaperones, and fashion and grooming specialists involved in other state pageants. They are also experienced judges, having developed an expertise in recognizing the specialized behavior demanded. Because the judges are longtime products of the pageant system, they tend to pick winners who perpetuate the values previously encouraged. Their aim is toward conformity with other judges. Being housed in the same hotel, the Dream Inn, it is understandable that the judges spend time together and discuss candidates, influencing one another with comments about their favorites. Veteran judge Al Castagnola supports this behavior. "It's natural to talk about the job, and it's better to openly discuss the merits of each girl. That way the judges' decisions are more considered and more informed."

The most abstract judging comes in the evening gown section of the entertainment. Each contestant steps up to a microphone and is given fifteen seconds to introduce herself to the audience, present her background, ambitions, and philosophy of life.

> Good evening, I'm a twenty-one-year-old senior at Cal Poly-Pomona. My major's elementary education because I would like to have a part in molding the young children who'll be our citizens of tomorrow into integrated persons: physically awake, mentally alert, spiritually alive. I wish to further my education by obtaining my master's degree in music at U.S.C. Thank you.

She then steps onto the ramp and parades across, making two stops, one in front of the judges, one across from them, where she then executes slow-motion militarylike turns, stopping periodically with her feet poised at right angles to each other. As in the swimsuit competition, contestants move with a special motion like models; their shoulders drawn back a little farther than normal, their heads a little higher. There are specific technical qualities to these walks which the beauty experts among the judges (usually the two women) recognize and evaluate, and points can be gained or lost depending on the amount of scapula showing or skin tone, but usually the judges respond to instructions which tell them to evaluate poise, grace, and general appearance.

Since such qualities are difficult to quantify, it is hard to imagine the judges remaining totally objective. Judges develop their own way of looking for the required qualities. "I don't look at the gown," says Al Castagnola,

"I look for poise, presence, command of the stage, how a girl radiates. I look at what she's doing when she's not in the spotlight. Is she on stage? Is she smiling?" It is evident that a lot of outside behavior is counted in evening gown competition and the contestants are instructed never to appear during pageant week without makeup, proper dress, and a smile.

Another aspect of the contestant's performance that spills over is the personal interview. "The interview keeps coming back all the time in your mind," confirms Castagnola. The contestants appear before the panel of judges for a five-to-seven minute interview in which they are asked questions ranging from "Who is the Prime Minister of Canada?" to "What is your opinion of [California's] Proposition 13?" or "What are your feelings about marriage?" Interviews are scheduled over the two days of preliminary judging and, as they are videotaped, they have the added formality of TV lights and cameras, as well as the presence of the panel of judges set up like a press conference. Such conditions would normally be intimidating to candidates, except for the fact that, like all other parts of the competition, they have had thorough coaching from a trained and experienced team which probably included hours of practice interviews and briefings on current events. The judges are instructed to evaluate "personality, mental alertness, vocabulary, voice, general knowledge, personal appearance, sincerity and manners," but they also look for specifics. For instance, they will ask questions which the contestant cannot answer to see how forthrightly she will acknowledge her ignorance. They will also test the political inclinations of the candidates, and few will risk their chances by offering anything but guarded conservative responses.

The easiest part of the judging is also the weightiest, the talent competition. Often the talent displayed is one which is developed, with considerable coaching, for the occasion, and since it must be demonstrable through performance, singing and dancing are the most frequent choices. Out of thirty-three 1979 Miss California finalists, twenty-five sang or danced or did both for their two-minute, forty-second presentation. In past years, certain talents have been more likely to produce winners. Classical musicians have a higher probability of winning than the practitioners of such unusual talents as roller skating or baton twirling. Very unusual talent displays, such as the sign-language presentation of poetry, stand very little chance of winning. Those who sing tend to do songs popularized by well-known singers such as Garland and Streisand in the style of those singers, and looking at this portion of the pageant, one often sees the shadows of other more famous performers on stage. In effect, the competition inadvertently serves as a homage to the popular heritage of women.

What the judging aspires to in all its aspects is a Miss California who is talented, beautiful, and intelligent. There is a functional aspect to this, since the judges remember that they are selecting someone who will serve as unofficial state hostess for the coming year, presiding at numerous civic functions as well as other pageant functions and commercial engagements. Furthermore, the Miss America-Miss California pageants have identified themselves as "scholarship" pageants since 1945, serving the cause of women in their totality rather than that aspect which is represented by the bathing beauties of the original 1921 pageant.

Despite the fact that they attracted vociferous opposition from the women's movement in the late 1960's, the pageant represents the largest scholarship organization for women in the world. Since 1950 the Miss California Pageant has awarded over $144,650 in scholarships. Local and state pageants throughout the United States hand out approximately $2,000,000 annually, and the Miss America Pageant alone offers another $116,000 in scholarship prizes. As a result of the diligence of volunteer fund-raising efforts, these figures are rising. The local pageants of the Miss California Pageant increased their awards from $16,325 in 1970 to $48,000 in 1978. The Miss California Pageant prize monies increased from $8,000 to $13,500 in 1979 alone—these funds coming from the Campbell Soup Company, the Gillette Company, the Kellogg Company, Santa Cruz financial institutions, the Shoong Foundation, and others. Contestants are allowed to put their winnings toward any form of instruction they select, and the choice normally ranges from law school to voice lessons or beauticians' school. All are met with equal favor by the pageant organization. In addition to scholarship prizes, pageant winners collect thousands of dollars' worth of gifts such as cars, furs, wardrobes, free hair styling, free travel, free room and board, etc., and they are capable of earning a considerable amount from their modeling or appearance fees as a reigning queen. In all, the awards are sufficient to attract many contestants who would not otherwise be part of a beauty pageant. Feminists can find numerous reasons for objecting to the mode of selection of scholarship recipients and to the compromises involved in creating this public image of women, but they are still obliged to acknowledge the amount of financial support that can be gained.

The Miss California Pageant at the Santa Cruz Civic Auditorium is now structured for TV, a change that affects the contestants and the whole spirit of the "live" event at the same time that it extends the audience from 2,000 to 2.8 million. Despite nostalgia for the old days when the pageant was held on the beach, and evident problems arranging the current format, the "pageant family" remains committed to the event for the "civic involvement it generates," in Al Castagnola's words. It is now an institution so thoroughly established that it exists of and by itself.

TAKE BACK THE NIGHT

STARHAWK

Rallies, meetings, conferences, and demonstrations raise power—but rarely do organizers think about grounding it afterward. Grounding does not have to be elaborate—simply remembering to formally end each working session will help earth the power. Group members might simply take hands in a circle and sit quietly for a moment. Recently, there has been a growing tendency in the feminist movement to incorporate ritual into conferences and demonstrations, for the express purpose of grounding and channeling the power raised. The following is an account of a ritual several women and I created in November 1978, as part of a conference on violence and pornography, with the theme "Take Back the Night!" The climax of the weekend was a march through the North Beach section of San Francisco, the heart of the topless-bottomless and massage parlor scene. The ritual took place in Washington Square Park, at the end of the march.

The women pour in from the street. It takes so much longer than we expected. I had no conception of 3,000 women in a mass. . . .

Witches, at the front of the march, aspurge North Beach with salt water. They chant Laurel's couplet:

Wipe the slate clean,
Dream a new dream!

At Broadway and Columbus, the artists create a mini-ritual around their float. In the front, it is a giant, candle-lit Madonna; behind, slabs of dead meat and pornographic magazines. A strong symbol of images that squeeze women into narrow, hurtful roles. They bring out the float, chant, tear the pornography into confetti. Holly Near sings.

We wait at the park, too nervous to leave and risk not getting back in time. The Witches arrive at the entrance to the park, form a double line, a birth canal. They hold lighted candles and incense and sprinkle the women with salt water as they enter:

From a woman you were born into this world,
By women you are born into this circle.

We are onstage (the back of Anne's truck). Our backdrop is the lit facade of the church: an irony. Lennie Schwendinger of Lighten Up has created beautiful lighting for us—it is the first time I have done a ritual so theatrical, where the bright lights cut us off from the crowd, who become "audience." Our pool of light seems the only world—and I'm not sure I like it. Behind us, in the trees, a woman's acrobatic troupe, Fly By Night, perform a slow, aerial dance.

Starhawk, peace activist, feminist therapist, teacher, and witch, is the author of *Dreaming the Dark* and *The Spiral Dance, A Rebirth of the Ancient Religion of the Great Goddess*, 1979, from which this selection is taken, pp. 130–132. Published by permission of Harper & Row.

Nina leads the chant:

> *We're taking back the night,*
> *The night is ours!*

The women are not dancing, as we had hoped. The audience-performer image is too strong—they are watching us. I feel awkward, unsure of what to do. The chant dies away—still, crowds are flowing into the park. . . .

Toni Marcus begins to play her violin. The sound carries over the park, electric, magical. . . .

We can put off starting no longer. I take the microphone, and say that we should turn for a moment and look at each other, at how beautiful we are, how real we are. . . .

I say, "We have been taught that women's bodies are unclean, that our sexuality degrades us, that we must either be Virgins or whores. But we accept neither image! Instead we raise the banner of the naked Goddess, whose body is truth, who is within us, in the human spirit.

"We say that our bodies are sacred, because they bring forth life, because they are life, because they give *us* pleasure, because with them we make, build, think, laugh, create, and do. . . ."

Lee and I lead the responsive chant:

> *Our bodies are sacred,*
> *Our breasts are sacred,*
> *Our wombs are sacred,*
> *Our hands are sacred. . . .*

It builds and builds.

> *Our voices are sacred,*
> *Our voices carry power!*
> *The power to create!*
> *The power to change the world!*
> *Let go—let them become sound—*
> *Chant without words—let them be heard!*

The voices roar into the night. Not a cone—it is too strong, too amorphous—a tidal wave sweeping out of the park.

It stops. Quietly, I lead a soft, low chant. A humming—the buzz of two thousand bees, a deep throb. . . .

Over it, Hallie leads the meditation:

"Softly, softly now begin to feel the earth's energy beneath your feet as She dances with us. . . .

"Close your eyes . . . feel your strength sparkling through your body and women around you. This is the power generated by our marching, our chanting, our dancing, our destruction of the symbols of violence. . . . Know that each of us, and all of us together, have the power to change the world. Feel the effects of your action rippling out into the world . . . reflect on how your life will be different. . . .

"Open your eyes and look about you . . . see our strength in one another's face . . . know that we are strong. Know what the women of old knew . . . that the night must belong to us. Know that we are women who take back the night. Know that the night is ours!"

Cheers, laughter, screams, kisses. Some of us touch the earth. The women follow. The ritual is done.

RITUAL AND THE NATIONAL BLACK THEATRE

BARBARA ANN TEER

We didn't do our first piece until '71. But before that the standard of art was created. The standard was basically what I call the five cycles of evolution. We went through what I call the "nigger" cycle, the "negro" cycle, and militant, nationalistic, and revolutionary cycles. We analyzed each of those cycles from a social point of view, a religious point of view, a political point of view. We found out about the colors, the foods, the lifestyle of the family, the relationships of people within each of those cycles. Each performer was required to go through each cycle. Each person had to keep a notebook of pictures and experiences when they went into each cycle. They would have to dress their cycle; they would have to live around those people. It was a total educational process. Then when we got to the revolutionary cycle we found it was all the same. . . .

In the meantime, we were having symposiums on Sunday where we invited all of the major figures in the black world to come and address themselves to the community about whatever was going on. Rap Brown, Stokely Carmichael, James Foreman, my sister Fredrica Teer, and Congressman Charles Rangel all spent a Sunday afternoon with a hundred people or more. We would rap and talk and exchange and try to get in touch with what this overwhelming force was that was called blackness. It wasn't simply a skin color to me, it never was, but it was what made me unique. We decided to perform after these two-and-a-half years. We realized that we had a standard, but we didn't have a form to hold the standard, and that's when I started creating rituals. Ritual is the theatre. Our first production was *The Ritual* and it was done on Channel 13. It was so popular they got a thousand phone calls, and the show was aired three time consecutively back to back. That caused the show to go national. We then got a lot of different job offers, none of which I

Barbara Ann Teer, founder and director of the National Black Theatre, is quoted here from her interview in Karen Malpede, *Women in Theatre: Compassion and Hope*, New York: Drama Book Publishers, 1983, pp. 226–227. Printed by permission of Karen Malpede.

took because they were all too commercial, and I thought it would water-down this thing.

In those days people used to get possessed, just go right out, you know. The drums would take them out. They would talk in tongues, and they would tell stories, and they would share with me all kinds of things when they came back. They experienced a freedom I had never seen before. I was just loving every minute of it. I couldn't sleep at night I was so turned on. I began creating exercises and processes and techniques to handle the energy and I continued to go to my mentors, who were church people.

Ritual got us a semivisibility in the black world. We started touring college campuses and black studies programs performing *The Ritual to Regain Our Strength and Reclaim Our Power*. During the performances people would get so turned on they would spontaneously start running up and down the aisles just celebrating themselves—you never saw anything like it. By this time I had changed all the standard theatrical titles. I said we were not actors, we were liberators. Our theatre wasn't a theatre—it was a temple. Our techniques were in a form I called ritualistic revival—we were doing revival form, we weren't doing play form.

THE STORY OF A MOTHER, A RITUAL DRAMA

MARTHA BOESING, IN COLLABORATION WITH

THE WOMEN AT THE FOOT OF THE MOUNTAIN

The Story of a Mother is a kaleidoscope of images which explores the relationship between mothers and daughters. Scripted scenes about the myths, the key memories, the repressed feelings and, finally, the bonding of mothers and daughters are interspersed with structured audience-participation events in which all present are invited to see the world as their mothers did, and to speak both the spoken and the unspoken words which hang in the air between all daughters and their mothers. Music for the production was improvised on guitar, reed flutes, and percussion instruments (water glasses, clay pots, temple gongs, sticks). Traditional songs were also sung and three songs were set to music by Roberta Carlson. Following is an outline of the play with its five open-ended ritual segments that change shape from audience to audience. Included with the ritual segments is some actual "audience response" material that Ellen Anthony

---

Martha Boesing, for years artistic director of At the Foot of the Mountain in Minneapolis, is a director and playwright with a long list of credits. She was awarded the Bush Grant for play-wrights in 1984 and an NEA Fellowship for 1986–87. Members of the collective who created *The Story of a Mother* in 1977 and 1978 were Martha Boesing, Aurora Bingham, Cecilia Lee, Jan Magrane, Phyllis Jane Rose, and Robyn Samuels.

recorded and transcribed. The complete play text may be obtained by writing Martha Boesing, At the Foot of the Mountain, 3144 Tenth Avenue South, Minneapolis, MN 55407.

A. MOURNING

1: The Big Mother (the play begins and ends with a gigantic Mother figure created by one actress sitting on another's shoulders, the two of them covered by a long white dress with apron, the upper actress wearing a mobcap).

2. The actress wearing the cap takes it off, descends from the other's shoulders, and becomes a daughter who mourns her mother's death.

3. The other actresses, as chorus, catalog the means of her death (She died washing the dishes . . . hanging out the laundry . . . mashing the potatoes . . . flushing out the diapers, and so on to the end . . . reaching out for love).

4. Daughter speaks to the mother at graveside of what she would have done "if only you could have looked at me."

5. All sing "Sometimes I Feel Like a Motherless Child."

6. Images of Loving and Fighting: Scenes of familiar ritual interactions.

7. Performers chant and sing, calling forth Mother, which leads the audience into the first open ritual.

RITUAL 1: The Calling Forth of the Mothers

One of the actresses speaks to the audience improvisationally, using the following outline:

Be aware of your breathing, just breathe. Call for your mother, whatever name you would use, until she appears. See her in front of you. Notice age, standing or sitting, what she is wearing, how her hair is, hands, all physical characteristics, what she is doing. Approach her or let her approach you. Look at her, speak, touch. Ask her: Can I enter you? Slowly enter in whatever way is right for you. Turn around. Fit your feet, legs, thighs, genitals, pelvis, hips, stomach, spine, chest, breasts, shoulders, arms, wrists, hands, fingers, neck, head, chin, cheeks, mouth, nose, forehead, eyes, skull, into hers (one at a time). Be aware of yourself as her, what you are doing, where you live, how you feel, and so forth. When you are ready, open your eyes, see the world as she saw it.

(If it is a small group, the actress may call on each person in the group, but with a large group the audience is asked to speak voluntarily.) Actress, as Mother: There were certain things which I always said over and over again. Are there things that you always said that you would like to say again now?

The audience members, speaking as their mothers, call out "I always said" and finish it with a phrase appropriate to their own mothers. (Examples from production experience: I told you so; Now don't worry about money, money comes when you need it; If everyone else jumps off the bridge, are you going to, too?; You made your bed, now lie in it; Make your bed; But I'm not everybody else's mother; Wait till your father comes home; I hope you have three just like you; You'll never know how much I love you; This hurts me more than it hurts you; You know they're only after one thing.)

When everyone has spoken, the actress says: Close your eyes. Get in touch with that part of you which is not your mother. Leave her in the same way that you entered her. See yourself as separate from her. You might want to tell her what it felt like to be her. Say goodbye. When you are ready, open your eyes, see the world again as you see the world.

B. HIDING

1. Hide and Seek: Rituals of attention-getting.
2. The Mother's List of Things to Do: A mother sits rocking, listing all she has to do while a daughter begs for attention (take chair to upholsterer, put up storm windows, get driver's permit for Curtis, call furnace cleaner, In a minute!).
3. The Calls for Dinner (the familiar words, phrases, responses of family at dinner time [Everything's getting cold on your plates! I hate this vegetable crap—Daddy says crap!]).
4. Baby Feeding: A pantomime with chorus and song in monosyllables.
5. It Says in the Book: Conflict between a mother's instincts and what "the book" says (It says in the book not to pick her up when she's crying).
6. Closed Doors: The child overhearing mother's secret sounds, muffled anger, stifled sobs, sexual sighs; the mother finding and comforting the child.
7. Goodnight Rituals.

RITUAL 2:   The Healing (Redeeming of the Daughter)

Actress 1 brings a bowl of water and washcloth to Actress 2. 1 chants, "The mother says to the daughter . . ." as 2 says something truthful to daughter and washes her. Other actresses do this. 1 invites the audience to speak as mothers or become their mothers and say something to the daughter, beginning with the phrase, "I want you to know." Actress 2 washes another actress in response to each one who speaks from the audience.

Examples from production experience: I did the best I could; I didn't know how to love you; I didn't want to hurt you; I envy you; I need you; Dad and I are glad you're a girl; I like you the way you are; You're the most important woman in my life; Most of the time I felt afraid; You'll always have a home.

C. INITIATING

1. The Daddy Jig: To a square dance, the calls repeat familiar phrases about "Daddy" (Actress 1: Right-hand star if you don't mind the bother, Left-hand star   Actress 2: You're just like your father   Actress 1: Move to the center and give me a shout   All: Your father won't like it Actress 1: Now move on out).
2. The Rape Dream: Daughter recounts a dream of rape that follows the

formula other women who have rape dreams will recognize; the mother comforts.

3.   The Shampoo: Ritual scenes of Preparation (We'll make you all pretty for Daddy); Wetting (The water is not too hot); Soaping (No, I won't get soap in your eyes); Rinse (Daddy won't recognize you because you're so clean and sparkling; Boys, boys, boys, that's all you ever think about).

4.   Making Up: The little girl watches the mother get ready for going out (Can I watch? When you die can I have it? What's that blue stuff for? Are all mothers as pretty as you?).

5.   Your Father Is a Wonderful Man: The actress asking the little girl questions was also putting on makeup and at the end of "Making Up" she transforms into a mother who descends the stairs in anticipation of the father's being an audience for her entrance. He isn't there, he's late, so she has a monologue in which she tells her daughter all the wonderful things about her husband (You're a lucky girl to have your father for a father . . . I could fill a whole book with things you don't know about your father that I could tell you about him).

6.   Menses Image: The daughter throws bloody bandages to the mother, who catches them, crosses to the daughter and slaps her face.

7.   Menstruation Scene: Mother-daughter interaction on day daughter's period starts.

RITUAL 3:   The Words Never Said (Giving Voice to the Scream)
The audience is invited to speak as the mothers they are, or to become their mothers again, and say something that was never said, beginning with the phrase, "I never said."

Examples from production experience: Sometimes I hate you; I'm sorry you turned out to be a girl; I'm jealous of you; I need a mother, too; I believed in you; It would be easy; I was perfect.

D. SEPARATING

1.   The "Do You Like Yourself" Clichés: Familiar female self-deprecation.

2.   The Hysteria Transfer: The mother begins with self-hatred (I hate this chair, I hate the cleaning, I hate my husband, I hate my eyes); she is countered by the daughter (Your eyes are beautiful), but then the roles transform and the daughter takes on self-hatred while the mother consoles.

3.   The Chicken Monologue: A daughter at the dining room table recounts a fight between her mother and father, and as the father puts the mother down and the mother retreats from the fight, the daughter chokes on a chicken bone.

4.   One actress comes to the choking daughter like an animal mother, licks her all over, the daughter relaxes and is healed.

5.   The Big Mother (seen in the opening scene) reappears on a darkened

stage and lights six candles that have been set out as another actress sings "Mother" (M is for the million things she gave me, etc.).

RITUAL 4:   The Words Never Said (Adorning the Mother)

The Big Mother takes center stage and opens her arms as if to invite the audience into them. As the actresses and members of the audience say things they never said to their mothers that they always wanted to say, long colorful ribbons are placed on the Mother's arms and about her neck and hat. Audience members can come out of the audience to do the placing, or they can remain seated and the actresses will place the ribbons for them. Each person begins with the phrase, "I never said."

Examples from production experience: I want to grow up to be just like you; Thank you; I'm glad I'm your daughter; I realized you had a hard life; I don't want you to die; I respect your choices; You were right; You're the strongest woman I've ever known; I need you; I like you the way you are; There's a lot of you in me; I'm proud of you; I appreciate all you've done for me; I want to know who you are.

When the audience response is finished, the Big Mother says, "I lit the candles for you. And he always said . . ." An actress responds as "he": "What-cha lighting the candles for? What a dumb thing to do to light the candles." At that the actresses blow out the candles and Big Mother disappears.

E. BIRTHING

1.   Plate Scene: Angry mothers in chain of putting down plates, picking them up, arguing with children, driven to the point of frustration and hysteria (Do you think I'm a slave? Is that what you think? Hired help. I don't do this for pay, I do this for you . . . Nobody cares about me. Nobody cares what I feel. Who am I? I am nobody. That's who I am. Nobody likes me). For a moment there is a tableau of images of women killing themselves or their children with broken plate shards.

2.   Actress in monologue speaking as her own mother: One actress as daughter whispers repeats of the mother's refrains as the mother recites her own sense of life and how she's come to terms with it.

3.   Big Mother enters with teardrops on her face. She goes to center stage and slowly takes them off, dropping them to the floor.

4.   A child is born from under Big Mother's skirts.

5.   Big Mother sings lullabies to the child.

6.   Acknowledging the Woman Hating: Mothers and children, in conversation, review familiar comments and phrases (When my hair was black, they used to say I was a tease . . . but once I started getting these gray hairs, I was a useless old hag; Whenever I reached out to touch people, they said I was acting needy, or that I was an easy catch. Just like a woman. But if I kept my hands to myself, they said that I was cold, probably frigid). The mothers say that this was done to keep women apart, to keep mothers and daughters

apart. A mother says, "I'll tell you what, I'll give you my arms. They're damn strong. They've carried laundry and groceries and suitcases and dirty diapers and boxes of books and wastebaskets full of cat shit and all my sleeping children upstairs and down. And they're very soft. They've held all of the people I've loved, sometimes all night long." The daughters reply, "Just like a woman, she said."

RITUAL 5: Communion

The actresses carry bread to the audience and give some to each member of the audience, saying softly to each either "Nurture yourself with this food" or "Let the mother within feed the child within." They might give bread to one person at the end of a row and ask the audience to pass the bread along, offering bread to one another with these phrases. As they do this, one actress remains onstage and sings "The Song of the Mother."

THE SONG OF THE MOTHER

We will walk through the streets of this city which sleeps,
which sleeps, my daughter,
you and I.
You carry the bowl,
I'll bring the grain,
On this parade through the city.

We will walk through the streets of this city which sleeps,
which sleeps, my daughter,
you and I.
I'll take the ashes,
you bring the jonquils, daughter,
on this parade through the city.

We will walk through the streets of this city which sleeps,
which sleeps, my daughter,
you and I.
You carry my heart,
I'll carry you, my little daughter,
on this parade through the city.

THE BIG MOTHER'S FINAL SPEECH

One actress becomes a child curled up on the floor and then grows into the Big Mother (a reversal of the opening image): "How could anyone tell this story? It's too long. It's hundreds of thousands of years long. It's been writing itself since the world began—every day of every year and every minute of every day. I mean, history is so much simpler than this story of a mother. (Pause) We've survived. That's something to tell. Through the dirty dishes and the children sitting on our laps and the men leaning on our arms and the tyranny of their myths and their movies and their songs, we have survived. And who could say what it is like? In the end the only thing to say is that we go on living—with all of our beings we go on living. And the entire planet depends upon our ability and our willingness to do it."

THE INTRODUCTIONS: THE CONCLUSION

Each of the actresses introduces herself and her mother's name, inviting the audience to stand and do the same: I am Cecilia, daughter of Margaret; I am Phyllis, daughter of Mary Jane; I am Martha, daughter of Mary; I am Jennifer, daughter of Martha; I am Aurora, daughter of Lena; I am Jan, daughter of Marilyn; I am Robyn, daughter of Liela May.

"LESSON I BLEED": ADRIENNE KENNEDY'S BLOOD RITES

ROSEMARY K. CURB

"Lesson I bleed" is the opening line of Adrienne Kennedy's play *A Lesson in a Dead Language*.[1] The syntactically ambiguous line might well serve as a slogan for all of Kennedy's plays, since the female characters in other plays are obsessed with blood as well.

To become a woman means to bleed. The phases of progression from girlhood to womanhood all involve bleeding: menstruation, sexual initiation or deflowering, and childbirth. The three uniquely female rites of passage are naturally terrifying to a girl/woman experiencing them for the first time because all three involve internal pain never before experienced and the sight of blood coming out of her body. Since blood means life and loss of it means death, the uninitiated girl is frightened that something vital has torn loose inside of her and she is dying. Not only does her changing adolescent body seem an alien and uncomfortable garb forced on her against her will, but she has a sense of being transformed into her mother. Her mother and other older women may contribute to her sense of confusion about becoming a woman by calling menstruation "the curse" and indicating that menstrual bleeding is shameful—a dark female secret that must be hidden from men lest they ridicule and reject her simply for being female. Numerous patriarchal religions regard menstruating women and women who have given birth as unclean.[2]

In contemporary American culture, the adolescent girl discovers that the

Rosemary K. Curb, Associate Professor of English and Coordinator of Women's Studies, Rollins College, Florida, has published widely on feminist and black theatre in *Chrysalis*, *Modern Drama*, *Theatre Journal*, *Melus Journal*, *Women's Review of Books*. With Nancy Manahan she co-edited *Lesbian Nuns: Breaking Silence*.

rituals associated with menstruation, e.g., asking the male druggist for sanitary napkins, can be painfully embarrassing. Popular culture reinforces adolescent insecurity by advertising an array of products to hide the "curse" of menstruation. Where misogyny is the rule of patriarchy, a young woman quickly learns to hate her imperfect and uncontrollable female body. Menstrual blood is the sign—almost the antisacrament—of the inherited guilt of womanhood.

In *A Lesson in a Dead Language* Adrienne Kennedy uses the words *blood* or *bleed* thirty-four times in a play so short that it has only thirty lines of dialogue. The effect of the repetition is to load the word with symbolic significance. Blood is not only the sign of the guilt connected with being a woman, but in the play it is also symbolically associated with loss of innocence and even patriarchal assassination. The play is set in a brightly lighted classroom furnished with ordinary school desks, but there theatrical realism ends. The female teacher is costumed as a huge White Dog from the waist up. The dominating presence of highly colored life-size statues of Jesus, Joseph, Mary, two Wise Men, and a Shepherd encircling the room suggests that the play is set in a Catholic school. The extraordinary White Dog costume which makes the teacher's speech seem to come without mouth movements and makes her gestures large and stiff is perhaps a child's perception of the medieval nun's habit and the remote, partly female, creature within.

The White Dog and statues overpower the pupils by their actual bulk and by the weight of tradition and symbolism which they carry and with which they threaten the students to confess and conform. The seven girl pupils wear white organdy dresses, white socks, and black shoes. The virginal costumes are school uniforms more appropriate for church processions than classroom work. The number seven (often considered the perfect, magic number) suggests that the pupils represent all girls at the threshold of adolescence.

Apparently a Latin lesson on the assassination of Julius Caesar is in progress. The last line of the play, "Calpurnia dreamed a pinnacle was tumbling down," is one pupil's laborious translation from the lesson. Calpurnia's vision foretells not only the immediate assassination but perhaps the complete downfall of patriarchy in the public sphere symbolically acted out in private as the drooping impotent phallic pinnacle.

The White Dog's opening line "Lesson I bleed" is a dictation to which the pupils respond in unison: "I bleed." Perhaps punctuating the teacher's announcement "Lesson: I Bleed" would eliminate the ambiguity and clarify that what follows is a brief but bizarre excursion into female sex education. Perhaps the line is also a pun in Black dialect summarizing the whole theme of the play: "I better not grow up less'n I bleed an' get blamed for grown-up crimes an' on top a' that get accused a' tryin' to do 'way with my elders an' ancestors." Menstrual blood represents a double curse for adolescent girls.

To bleed is to be cursed with a messy inconvenience, but not to bleed indicates a major alienation from parental and societal approval: unwanted pregnancy, the proof of premarital sex. Therefore, the opening line can also be read as a moral command: "Lesson I (one): Bleed."

In the play, bleeding is associated with the death of the White Dog, Julius Caesar, and the figures represented by the statues. The White Dog, who is Mother as well as Teacher, instructs the pupils to write one hundred times on the blackboard, apparently as punishment for their misdeeds, "Who killed the white dog and why do I bleed? I killed the white dog and that is why I must bleed." Large circles of blood are visible on the backs of the pupils' white dresses when they stand at the blackboard. The blood is evidence of their guilt.

Collectively blaming the assassination of the White Dog on the pupils, even though only one of them is guilty, is similar to blaming all Jews for the death of Jesus, the whole Roman Senate for the death of Julius Caesar, or a whole class for a dirty picture of the teacher which only one student drew on the blackboard. Collective punishment for presumed collective guilt is a phenomenon familiar to children, slaves, and other oppressed groups. Although the slaughtered dog is described by one pupil as "a charming little white dog [that] ran beside me in the sun when I played a game with lemons on the green grass," the dog is not merely a child's pet whose death is the result of an unfortunate accident.

The White Dog in the play represents the whole world of elders and ancestors from Christianity and classical antiquity down to the two most powerful female authority figures in the adolescent girl's life: mother and teacher. The adult women who have long ago suffered through the adolescent rites of passage seem to derive sadistic satisfaction from the sufferings of those to be initiated into womanhood and thus issue warnings laden with their own fears and repressions: "My mother says it is because I am a woman that I bleed," say the pupils in unison. Furthermore, elders threaten to incarcerate the insubordinate. One pupil says, "Teacher, my mother is sending me to the Asylum if I don't stop talking about my white dog that died and my bleeding and Jesus and the game in the green grass. I asked her who made me bleed. The conspirators, she said. . . . And she said everything soon bleeds away and dies. Caesar, too."

Another of Kennedy's adolescent characters, Kay (Sister Rat) in *A Rat's Mass*, is sent to the State Hospital in Georgia by her mother when she fails to accept adolescent changes quietly. Growing up is generally portrayed in Kennedy's play as a dreadful irreversible passage from which death is the only escape, and mothers never console daughters or ease their passage through adolescence.

Set in the memory and imagination of Brother Rat, *A Rat's Mass* chronicles the fall from innocent bliss of Sister and Brother Rat (Kay and Blake). Brother Rat imagines them hiding from Nazi conspirators who leave in their wake dying baby rats and dying gray cats hanging from rafters with sunflowers in their mouths—a suggestion of castration.[3] Although bloody rats certainly present a more terrifying image than the white dog, animal imagery in all of Kennedy's plays is associated with frightening uncontrollable sexuality. Here the animals are not only dead but unsexed as well. However, as in nightmares, the dreadful beasts (adolescent sexual desire), refuse to stay dead but instead return bloody and mutilated to mock their murderer. That Kennedy would identify societal taboos against female adolescent sexuality with Nazis is curiously appropriate. Since the Nazi goal was to achieve a pure (in every way) homogeneous Aryan race, the Nazis condoned hunting down and slaughtering all aliens: Jews, homosexuals, the aged and infirm. For an adolescent Black girl to awaken sexually is to become acutely conscious of her alienation from society on many levels. She is warned by her mother to fear premarital sex and pregnancy out of wedlock as a fate worse than death, but the white male-dominated culture simultaneously tells her that she is a promiscuous bitch just because she is Black. She acknowledges her bloodiness and her sexual yearnings as proof of her hopeless bestiality. Naturally she expects to be hunted down and slaughtered by those in power.

The female authority figure in *A Rat's Mass* is neither mother nor teacher but a fellow classmate, a white girl named Rosemary, who has worms in her hair and who has so dazzled Blake (Brother Rat) with her Medusa charm that he will do whatever she says. The turning point in the adolescence of Brother and Sister Rat is their fatal act of incest. At some time in the past, Rosemary ordered Kay and Blake to have intercourse on the slide in the playground to prove their love for her. Later, the slide becomes an aisle of blood for Sister Rat, who confuses the slide, slippery and red with the blood of her defloweing, with the red carpet runner in church and the blood itself with the Communion wine.[4]

Sexual initiation is a rite of passage into the adult world for both Brother and Sister Rat, who now see sex everywhere. However guilty Brother Rat may feel, the chief victim of Rosemary's plot is Sister Rat, who not only bleeds, and consequently sees blood everywhere, but fears she is pregnant. No real baby ever comes, but Sister Rat is obsessed with the vision of dead baby rats. Furthermore, she tells Blake in her letters from the asylum that she hides under the house (like a rat) and gnaws (like a rat) sunflower petals—a symbolic acting-out of her deflowering and gnawing away of her own genitalia. To force her brother to share her agony, she sends him the gnawed petals in letters.

Before the play opens, Rosemary has gratified her voyeuristic curiosity by pandering to Brother Rat's desire for her approval and has played the panderer in their union. Rosemary appears in the play more like a phantom than a participant in present action. Of course, the only present action is Blake's reminiscence. Because Rosemary is aloof from the rat world (as white and Catholic), she remains untouched by the suffering, which she causes.

Before their fatal incest, Brother and Sister Rat were as innocent as the pupils in *A Lesson in a Dead Language* before the death of the White Dog. Sister Rat remembers: ". . . we lived in a Holy Chapel with parents and Jesus, Joseph, Mary, our Wise Men and our Shepherd. People said we were the holiest children." The same Christian Nativity figures which dominated the White Dog's classroom hover over the two chilren in *A Rat's Mass* and move on and off stage in procession, speaking in unison much like a Greek chorus, until they abandon the finally lost adolescents to their rat world.

Sexual sins make Kay and Blake more ratlike; both have rat tails. Blake has a rat head and a human body, and Kay has a human head and a rat belly. The partial metamorphoses are symbolically appropriate since Blake willed the sin which Rosemary counseled, and Kay exhibits it in her belly. After the Nativity figures desert them (loss of grace?), Kay and Blake act more ratlike and their voices sound more like gnawing.

In *A Beast's Story*, set in "the gloomy house of a minister in a drab section of a midwestern city," the beasts are members of a Black family obsessed with sensuality. Parental fears and conflicts make it impossible for the budding adolescent Beast Girl, costumed in a white organdy dress, ever to grow into healthy womanhood. Beast Woman, her mother, tries to thwart her daughter's passage into womanhood through sexual initiation. "I keep the ax to maintain her innocence," she says. Like the labyris of the Amazons, Beast Woman's ax is a weapon of defense against male invaders. The mother is obsessed with the blood of her own deflowering. Of her daughter's birth she says, "I went into labor at my dead sister's funeral. Twenty hours later she was born." If the daughter is a substitute for the dead sister, she can only prevent her daughter's death by preventing her going through the rites of passage which lead all women to death. Beast Man says to her, "You spoke of death at our wedding."

The conflict within the Beast family is brought to a crisis when a boy called Dead Human invades as Beast Girl's lover and husband. Although the girl desires sexual union with the boy, her parents' taboos and phobias freeze her budding sensuality, and she drops her bridal bouquet and runs to her mother. About her passage through the marriage rite, Beast Girl says, "It was morning when I awakened, a red sunrise morning, the first day of my marriage. At last I knew who I was . . . no shadow of myself, I was revealed . . . to myself." The imagery suggests that Beast Girl thought herself liberated from her parents' fears, but according to the boy she fled from the marriage bed the first night: "You said I had raped you like your father had raped your mother the night you were conceived. You fled from our bed." Furthermore, no fruitful union of boy and girl is possible since Beast Girl and Dead Human say her parents made her kill (abort?) her baby "with quinine and whiskey." In the end, with great force and fury, Beast Girl smothers her husband with a pillow and smashes her father's skull with the ax.

The Owl Answers reaches a similar but opposite conclusion: mother and daughter grow more and more bestial and deranged as their struggles with sensual desire and repulsion intensify until violent suicide is the only escape for both of them. The mother stabs herself with a butcher knife, which the daughter later uses on herself. Although *The Owl Answers* is longer and more complex than any of the three plays previously discussed, it focuses on the personality fragmentation of She who is Clara Passmore who is the Virgin Mary who is the Bastard who is the Owl rather than on adolescent rites of passage. Nevertheless the Bastard's Black Mother who is the Reverend's Wife who is Anne Boleyn is as reluctant to see her daughter through the sexual initiation and childbirth rituals as Beast Woman.

She says, "On my wedding day the Reverend's Wife came to me and said when I see Marys I cry for their deaths, when I see brides Clara, I cry for their deaths." In the play the death of Mary means the death of the Virgin Mary and every woman's deflowering. The Reverend's Wife carries a vial of blood, the sign of her own passage and perhaps a trophy of survival. Early in the play she holds up the vial and says, "These are the fruits of my maiden-head, owl blood Clara who is the Bastard Clara Passmore to whom we gave our name, see the owl blood, that is why I cry when I see Marys, cry for their deaths, Owl Mary Passmore." The name she gives her daughter carries the curse of her confusion: as owl she is doomed to be obsessed with sensuality and eventually fall prey to it, but as Mary is equally doomed to a sexual frigidity forced on her by her mother's fears. Later when the mother is becoming more like an owl, she screeches what has become a parrotlike incantation—the formula of a ritual spell: "The Reverend took my maiden-head and I am not a virgin anymore and that is why you must be Mary, always be Mary, Clara."

Cursed with such a heritage, the daughter cannot pass beyond her mother's fears. Her sexuality is frozen in frustration. Furthermore, she has incorporated her mother's fear of rape so thoroughly that she describes it as if it happened to her. She is conditioned to regard all men as rapists and any expression of her own sexuality as the signs of a fatal disease. Even more devastating to her development is her conviction of her own worthlessness caused by her mother's continual rejection and denial of affection.[5]

Lack of maternal affection also warps Sarah in *Funnyhouse of a Negro* into a rigid, fearful woman who has retreated from reality into a fantasy world populated with alter egos. Like Beast Girl and She who is Clara Passmore, Sarah the Negro is obsessed with the rape of her mother by her father at which she was conceived. All three young women regard their existence as the hated product of their mother's fall from innocence. It is understandable that the mothers express no warmth for the product of their violation and that they try to prevent their daughters from growing up. Sarah's mother goes insane. Her single line is a warning to her daughter: "Black man, black man, I never should have let a black man put his hands on me. The wild black beast raped me and now my skull is shining." Like Sister Rat, the mother is locked up in an asylum for failing to adjust quietly to female bondage to male violence.

Sarah experiences her mother's rape obsession in all of her multiple personalities. The prime fear is the return of the father from the jungle to rape her. Beast Girl and She also fear rape by the father. Sarah says she wants to bludgeon her father to death with his ebony African masks. Instead she hangs herself. Taking out anger against the male oppressor/rapist on oneself and blaming self for being a victim is a response familiar to women under patriarchy. Sarah's first appearance with a bloody face and a noose around her neck foretells her fate. Sarah's bloody face is reminiscent of the bloody circles on the pupils' dresses, exhibiting the guilt of passage to womanhood. The main symbol of impotence and death in *Funnyhouse of a Negro* is loss of hair. Sarah's alter egos carry their fallen hair in red bags, which suggest menstrual blood and the blood of deflowering.

Passage into womanhood need not be a death sentence. The naturally flowing blood of menstruation and childbirth need not be regarded as shameful or terrifying. However, in a culture which makes women alien objects to be used and abused by men, women learn to hate their bodies and their sexuality. In societies where women are bought as commodities and discarded as casually as paper cups, women realize that they have no value in themselves except insofar as they conform to their expected role as detachable and disposable vessels of male pleasure and caprice. Adrienne Kennedy's plays vividly dramatize the horrors attendant on female adolescent rites of passage under patriarchy.

2

THE ACTRESS

"Women have risen to greater heights of achievement as actresses than in any other art," writes Rosamond Gilder in her landmark study, *Enter the Actress*. Without doubt acting has been and remains a unique art and career for women, for in performance the very fact of being female is what is being featured. More is involved in performance, however, than the gender awareness of the actress. Since acting on stage is intimately tied to social role-playing and the ceremonies of our collective life, the many different parts played by actresses are reflections of the many different ways of being female.

Yet we don't really know very much about the complex dynamics of how the actress uses herself to become an important emblem of what each era means its women to be. Although discussions of acting have become more sophisticated explorations of psychic need and social ritual, the distinctive interplay of person and role in the experience of the actress has gotten little special attention. Most discussions of the actress still recall Victorian concern about the morality of women on the stage or raise the perennial question of female pulchritude and youthfulness as prerequisites for success. We don't seem to have gotten much beyond Noel Coward's "Don't Put Your Daughter on the Stage, Mrs. Worthington."

From the research and the resources of this volume a few observations are offered here to introduce the wide-ranging essays on actresses that follow. Putting these materials together will, we hope, stimulate much-needed research on the career and the public images projected by the actress.

From shopgirls to society ladies, the theatre has been a way out for women. In the theatre they have risen up the social ladder, earned equal pay, and developed independence. For those who came from theatrical families, entry to the field was usually taken for granted. One thinks of "Little Minnie Maddern"—later the great Mrs. Fiske—who played bits in Shakespearean productions when she was five or six years old, having earlier made her debut singing and dancing with the Maddern Family Concert Company. For women of working-class origins, the stage has always been a means of moving up socially and economically. In turn, "ladies" fallen on hard times, like the famed Anna Cora Mowatt, found the theatre, despite its taint of immorality, to be the only paying outlet for the good looks, genteel manners, musical skills, and elocution lessons that had been part of their social education. Lotta Crabtree's career offers a stunning example from the early days of what was possible. As she made her way from rough mining camps in California to become a national favorite, she amassed a fortune estimated to be over $4 million at the time of her death in 1924.

With the increased participation of women from all walks of life early in this century, they seemed to turn in greater numbers to the theatre. Anecdotes from the period suggest that daughters were doing what their mothers only dared to dream of—they were trying to go on the stage. By the late 1920's, it would seem that New York was almost overrun by women wanting to act.

There has been much to attract women over the years to the theatre beyond the economic advantages. With few options usually open to them—at least until very recently—most women have led lives marked by subordination and submission. On stage, however, they saw a chance to exercise a kind of control usually absent from their daily experience. Geraldine Page, for example, speaks of that "most wonderful sense of freedom" that comes when as an actress you feel "that you, and only you, are in control." Acting allows women to capitalize on those characteristics of emotionality and exhibitionism by which they are usually socially defined. Aware of the dichotomies in their lives and accustomed to playing many different roles off stage, they can find on stage an outlet for personality traits developed by the female experience.

Being on the stage, however, also encourages qualities usually associated with men's lives: initiative, self-reliance, ambition, and independence. Traveling on tours, hoisting your own luggage, living in hotels alone or with fellow troupers, competing for parts, bargaining for salaries, angling for career advantages—all these activities have given the actress an independence few women have had an opportunity to acquire. Although many have been concerned to be thought conventionally respectable in a profession said to be morally dangerous, especially for women, actresses have nevertheless been part of a unique subculture with its own standards. Long before most other women were able to do so, they could dress as they liked, smoke cigarettes, take lovers, have children outside marriage, and live a generally liberated life-style.

Ironically, however, these "free" women are the very ones who have embodied for their particular era the accepted image of women—the passive heroine, the fallen woman, the flapper, the gossip, etc. Although their profession permits them greater personal liberty off stage, their sexual attractiveness, their dominant histrionic power, and their vibrant personalities are used on stage to convey the social stereotypes fashioned for conventional patrons mostly, although not exclusively, by male dramatists. On stage, paradoxically, the actress has usually been a "commodity," as Jean Dalrymple once put it. She has been used, manipulated, exploited for her talents in a theatre that has allowed her little say about what she does. The structure of show business has provided the actress few opportunities to express her sense of self despite the control her magnetism can exercise over audiences. Mae West put it crudely but well when she said in looking back at the 1930's that actresses—and actors, too, for that matter—"were considered big hunks of meat to be bought, sold, and packaged."

"If the playwrights would just talk over matters with the actress," suggested Mary Shaw, they would not continue to produce those "man-made women caricatures" that most actresses are forced to play. She herself made choices of roles in accordance with her feminist beliefs, as the study of her in our collection reveals.

Actresses have sought to gain personal control over their performances in many different ways. Some by their extraordinary intuitive genius have cut through clichés to expose a unique inner life. One thinks especially of Pauline Lord and Laurette Taylor. Others, more conscious of what they might do, have started their own theatres or managed their own companies where they could determine what roles they would play. From the early days Minnie Maddern Fiske, Eva Le Gallienne, and Katharine Cornell come to mind. Others associated themselves for longer or shorter periods of time with important companies or studios whose esthetic or social views they shared or could help to shape: Lynn Fontanne and Helen Hayes at the Theatre Guild; Stella Adler, Frances Farmer, and others at the Group Theatre; Ruby Dee with the Harlem Players and various other Black theatres; Kim Stanley, Maureen Stapleton, Anne Bancroft, and Geraldine Page among many others at the Actors' Studio.

In recent decades as leading actresses have suffered from "lack of work, inferior plays, and short runs," they have sought a way out by playing in unique women's vehicles, some written by the actresses themselves. Julie Harris's *The Belle of Amherst*, Estelle Parsons's *Miss Margarida's Way*, Irene Worth's *Love Letters*, Gretchen Cryer's *I'm Getting My Act Together and Taking It on the Road*, and Ntozake Shange's *For Colored Girls Who Have Considered Suicide/When the Rainbow Is Enuf* are recent different responses of women performers. Across the country these and many other notable actresses are using their skills to project a fresh image of American women.   HKC

ANNE BRUNTON MERRY: FIRST STAR

GRESDNA DOTY

On December 5, 1796, Mrs. Anne Brunton Merry[1] made her American debut in her most celebrated characterization, Shakespeare's Juliet. That performance was a turning point for Philadelphia's Chestnut Street Theatre as well as for the professional theatre in the United States. Billed as "late the principal actress at Covent-Garden," Mrs. Merry's appearance gave Americans their first opportunity to witness a talent from the first rank of performers in the English-speaking world. No other actor previously appearing in the United States had ever held a position as a first-line performer at either of London's two patent theatres, Drury Lane and Covent Garden. The significance of the occasion was not lost on theatre-going Philadelphians. Two separate reviews in Philadelphia's *Gazette of the United States* supplied details of the performance. "Dramaticus" praised her for those qualities admired in the British Isles: "feminine sweetness," power to mark the passions, "melodious" voice, "natural, easy and appropriate action." Additional comments referred to her most powerful scenes: "In her speech, act IV, when she drinks the sleeping draught, she thrill'd every heart with horrid sympathy; and her dying scene was inimitably fine. In justice we must say, that this elegant and powerful actress is a most valuable acquisition to the American stage." In the same newspaper another critic signed "W" compared her to Mrs. Marshall and Mrs. Whitlock (Sarah Siddons's sister), both of whom had previously performed the role in Philadelphia. Apparently Mrs. Merry exerted force which Mrs. Marshall lacked, but not the "masculine coarseness" of Mrs. Whitlock. A decided artistic triumph, Anne could not "fail at once to establish her own fame, and to reflect honour on the American drama."[2] Moreover, the debut brought $1,200 into the company treasury and her portrait into many homes. On the day following her debut, *Claypoole's American Daily Advertiser* announced the availability of Mrs. Merry's portrait as Juliet: plain, fifty cents, and colored, one dollar.

For the twelve years between that first appearance until her death in 1808, Mrs. Merry, as "the sun of the theatrical solar system," established and maintained a new standard of excellence for actors. In addition, she served briefly as manageress of the Chestnut Street Theatre and became a respected social matron while carrying out the duties of a wife and mother. Accomplished by the age of thirty-nine, her achievements seem remarkable, but they are matched in their unusualness by her personal life and career, both more dramatic than any role she ever portrayed.

Gresdna Doty, Professor of Speech at Louisiana State University, is the author of *The Career of Mrs. Anne Brunton Merry in the American Theatre*, and of many articles on American and British theatre in *Theatre Survey*, the *Quarterly Journal of Speech*, and other journals.

Born in London in 1769, Anne spent her early years in the provinces where her actor father shared the boards with talents no less than those of Sarah Siddons at the Theatre Royal, Bath. When she was only sixteen, her father discovered her talent one day when, returning from rehearsal, he heard her reciting one of Calista's speeches. He learned that she knew the entire role, as well as those of Juliet, Belvidera, and Euphrasia. Soon after, Anne's recitations convinced manager John Palmer that he should arrange for her debut on the Bristol stage. Only eight months later, Thomas Harris, manager of Covent Garden, brought her to London hoping that a "youthful wonder" would counter the powerful attraction of Mrs. Siddons at the rival Drury Lane. William Dunlap, who later became manager of New York's Park Theatre and first historian of the American theatre, recorded his impressions of Anne's extraordinary debut, which he saw while visiting in London:

> The extraordinary self-possession of this young lady, not yet sixteen, when she appeared at Bristol the preceding year has been recorded by a witness, and it apparently did not desert her on this occasion. Her voice, never exceeded in sweetness and clearness, did not falter, her action was perfect, she was the Horatia of the poet, and London confirmed Mr. Palmer's opinion that she was "another Siddons."[3]

During the first season, Anne played ten new roles in forty-seven performances, an impressive schedule for a sixteen-year-old girl. She drew audiences described as brilliant and overflowing, but, in spite of her mercurial rise, she did not displace Sarah Siddons, reigning queen of the London stage. She did, however, launch a seven-year career at Covent Garden and learned the rigorous demands of touring when she traveled to visiting summer engagements in Norwich, Birmingham, Manchester, Liverpool, and as far away as Belfast and Cork. By the time she was a stage veteran of twenty-two, the course of her life changed dramatically when she fell in love with poet, playwright, and politician, Robert Merry.

Wealthy, handsome, and charming, and son of aristocratic parents, Merry had attended Harrow and Christ's College, Cambridge, but he soon abandoned his academic pursuits for a social life in London and on the Continent, overlaid with prominence as a poet and a rabid interest in the French Revolution.[4] Merry also attempted playwriting, which ultimately brought him in contact with Anne Brunton when his work was produced at Covent Garden. In August 1791 they married over the protest of his family, who objected to Anne's stage career. Merry told his sister, however, "She ought to be proud he had brought a woman of such virtue and talents into the family."[5]

Whatever domestic bliss the newlyweds enjoyed was soon clouded by Merry's literary and political interests which eventually proved disastrous to the young couple. Although Mrs. Merry terminated her Covent Garden engagement, before long financial worries persuaded the couple that Mrs.

Merry should resume her acting career. When Thomas Wignell offered Anne an engagement at his Chestnut Street Theatre in Philadelphia, Anne had little choice but to accept.

When Anne sailed for the United States in October to resume her acting career, she was twenty-seven years old, but no longer the fledgling actress. She was an experienced performer with seven years of successes and failures as a leading actress at Covent Garden earned by playing over 50 roles in more than 352 performances. Also, she was more sensitive to the emotional range of life, a knowledge acquired through the stress of a marriage troubled by financial and political anxiety.

Anne's success was immediate and continuous. She became the principal attraction and leading actress in Philadelphia, but she also dominated the wider theatrical scene wherever the company traveled: on one occasion to New York, in its annual fall and spring visits to Annapolis and Baltimore, and in its summer engagements at theatres in Alexandria, Georgetown, and eventually Washington. Her box-office draw was so clearly established that, when her husband died suddenly in 1798, William Dunlap, manager at the Park Theatre in New York, negotiated with her to accept a permanent position with his company. Anne bided her time, however, and corresponded with "connections" in London about her future. At the same time she maintained her place with the Chestnut Street Theatre. Anne's ultimate decision to renew her engagement with Wignell in the midst of some of the darkest financial months of the company's history confirms her basic respect for and trust in the manager, whom she married three and a half years later.

Anne's theatrical career took another dramatic turn when Dunlap renewed his attempts to bring her to New York in 1801 for "starring" performances at the Park during the summer. She agreed to a contract stipulating a salary of $100 per week plus a clear benefit, a sharp contrast to the $30 per week offered to other performers. Arranged in March, the appearances were scheduled for July. In June, however, Mrs. Merry requested a release from her commitment because of ill health. When Dunlap begged her to reconsider since he had borrowed money in the belief that her appearances would enable him to repay it, she agreed to make the effort. Soon after, Mrs. Merry journeyed to New York, where the actress "for the first time in America was brought forward as [what is now called] a star."[6] Also impressed by the occasion, a fellow actor, William Warren, noted in his daily journal that "Mrs. Merry is acting as a Star in New York."[7] Anne returned to Philadelphia with $750 from benefits in addition to her salary and having established herself as a "prodigious favorite in New York" and a decided advantage to the box office at the Park Theatre.[8]

Understandably, Dunlap arranged another New York engagement with Mrs. Merry in the following spring when her appearances created the cultural event of the season. Dunlap may have intended a third consecutive starring visit, but several events interfered. On January 1, 1803, the actress married Thomas Wignell, manager of the Philadelphia theatre. The marriage seems to have been the inevitable result of their mutual trust and close professional relationship and, possibly, a change in values for the actress. Evidence indicates differences between the personalities of Mrs. Merry's first and second husbands. From descriptions by those who worked under his management, Wignell emerges as an opposite of the dashing, fun-loving, and quixotic Merry. At age thirty-three and in her circumstances, the young widow may have admired and needed the steadfastness which Wignell possessed.

From testimonial and description, Wignell appears to have been a fitting partner for the actress, whose private conduct from her earliest professional years was such "as would grace a woman of superior rank."[9] With a similarity of values, character traits, and interests, the newly married couple had every reason to anticipate a happy marriage. But the happiness was short-lived, for only seven weeks after the wedding Wignell died following a brief illness.

On the day after the funeral, the newspaper carried a significant and melancholy announcement which marked the beginning of a new phase in the theatrical career of the now Mrs. Wignell. The advertisement stated that the theatre would continue to operate under the direction of Mrs. Wignell and Alexander Reinagle (Thomas Wignell's partner) with the assistance of actors William Warren and William Wood. Anne performed during the Baltimore spring season, but after its close withdrew to await the birth of her daughter, Elizabeth, in the fall.

The spring of 1803 must have been another difficult period for the actress. Once again she had the sole responsibility for maintaining herself. She also had the increased burden of the management of the theatre in addition to rearing her child. She faced several choices: returning to England, continuing with the Chestnut Street company as comanager and leading actress, or accepting an offer from Dunlap to join the Park Theatre company in New York. Her decision to remain in Philadelphia and assume the management of the company for a four-year period may have been influenced by an unfulfilled hope of securing the help of her brother, John, also an actor. Charles Durang commented that he "was sorry to see her harrass'd by some of the performers." He also, however, amusingly describes an instance when, as a youth, he beheld her exert her authority in matters of the wardrobe.

Cain was extremely careless in his dressing, and even at times manifested a want of cleanliness. His "tights" . . . looked like a loose garment thrown on his person hap-hazard. On one special occasion, he was playing Romeo to the Juliet of . . . Mrs. Wignell. . . . At the fall of the curtain, at the end of the play, . . . amidst the most thundering applause . . . Mrs. Wignell arose, as we thought, obviously excited, and hastened to the green-room.
. . . With the rude curiosity of a boy, we followed her to the green-room,

for we did love and honor our managerial queen above all others. With evident feeling, she directed the master tailor, McCubbins, to be called to her; she also desired the presence of Mr. Cain, before he disrobed himself of his Romeo habiliments. After the two persons thus summoned appeared before her, she descanted in very strong terms upon the dress of Mr. Cain, rebuking both the actor and the costumer, for their violation of everything like propriety and suitableness in "her Romeo's" dress. . . . She concluded by ordering the master of the robes to make an entire new dress for Mr. Cain, and to be very particular hereafter, when he had a principal part to play with her, to see him suitably equipped at all points.[10]

In her personal character Anne also influenced the managing of the theatre, for Durang testified that the greenroom "was a drawing room in every sense of the word; where the presence of Mrs. Merry, Mrs. Whitlock, Mrs. Melmoth, Mrs. Wood, and other ladies of cultivated intellect and polished manners, were examples to the younger members of the profession, who felt a restraint and respect before them."[11]

Duties as manager and mother, as well as leading actress, left Anne little time for social life; yet Durang remembered her as the "directress" and social matron, a position not always accorded to actresses. Durang also recalled Anne's impressive arrival at the theatre:

The coachman was a genteel white man, dressed in a kind of half livery—a gray surtout, buckskin breeches, and fair-top boots.[12]

One of Anne's chief contributions as manager was in setting and maintaining high standards of performance, but by April 1805 she turned over her share of the management to William Warren in order to devote herself to serving as the leading actress for the company and to rearing her daughter.

Her withdrawal from the management also permitted her to accept another starring engagement in New York during the summer. She made "an impression such as no other actress in this country could ever make." One New York critic wrote: "When we say we do not think we ever saw Mrs. Wignell play better, it may be readily believed it approached the perfection of histrionic art. Her powers are in full maturity and she gave us last night their best exertion. Who that once has seen her wondrous exhibitions, can afterwards receive any satisfaction from the attempts of any other actress in a similar line that the American theatre can boast of?"[13] At the conclusion of the successful engagement she retreated to Annapolis for the remaining summer, to await Warren's return from England with fresh recruits for the company. With two new actresses from London to share the acting roles in the fall of 1805, Anne reduced her schedule. In the following summer, she again went to Annapolis until late in August, when she married William Warren.

Durang has revealed that "there was some surprise expressed" over the Wignell-Warren marriage.[14] To some, Warren obviously did not appear as a likely husband for Anne Wignell. Such sentiments were expressed as late as 1811 by George Frederick Cooke, the visiting British star, who explained to Dunlap: "So . . . this is the widow's third choice. . . . Upon my word the good lady seems to descend with every husband: first Merry, then Wignell & then Warren!"[15]

Dunlap, however, remembered Warren "as a pleasant companion and an upright man," and Fennell identified him as "a man of honour and of trust . . . his name is fixed on a firm base of general integrity." Such descriptions suggest that Warren and Mrs. Wignell were suited to each other in temperament and values. Drawn together by long and close association, they had not only embarked on American theatrical careers at the same time but also had remained with the same company for ten years. During that time they had shared the successes and failures of the Chestnut Street company, as well as their own personal misfortunes and now each needed a parent for an orphaned child. Anne Wignell, at thirty-seven, undoubtedly was content to share the rest of her life in the United States with the man who had become one of her oldest and closest associates.

Her new domestic status did not alter her professional life; she continued to perform leading melodramatic, pathetic, and tragic roles. During the following February, she interrupted her regular performance schedule in order to return to New York to help revitalize a languishing season at the Park Theatre. Once again "very crowded" houses and "boundless solicitude for tickets of admission" were the pattern for her engagement.[16] In the autumn she accepted another starring engagement, this time in Boston. She returned home with $1,350 profit, concluding the last of her starring engagements on a triumphal note. The subsequent year was equally successful, but in June, at the age of thirty-nine, she died in Alexandria, Virginia, after giving birth to a stillborn son. A large cement vault marks her grave in Christ Church yard in Alexandria.

Although Anne is not well known in the American theatre and her career in the United States spanned only twelve years, she deserves to be remembered, for she probably exerted more influence than any other professional woman in America up until the time of her death. Arriving at the Chestnut Street Theatre at the age of twenty-seven, she won acclaim as the "most perfect actress America has seen." Serving as director for only two years, she set the high standards of her own art for the company as a whole. She was the first performer whose artistic superiority made her visiting engagements prestigious events which could command unprecedented financial remuneration. She dramatically demonstrated to fellow actors as well as managers the advantage and the potential of importing actors of great reputation. Thus her stardom was born, and in subsequent years the star system became widespread. She was admired as an artist, but she was equally respected for her own personal character. As her obituary testifies, her "spotless and unsullied Fame" did much to convince the early American public that "an unblemished reputation is by no means incompatible with theatrical life."

ENTER THE HARLOT

CLAUDIA D. JOHNSON

Few professional situations could be as paradoxical as that of the nineteenth-century woman who went on the stage for a livelihood: the vocational possibilities of a stage career were afforded women in few other segments of nineteenth-century life. The salary of an actress was comparatively good; she was able to compete with men on an equal basis of talent and public appeal; and she could, in the theatre, secure positions of management. To reap these benefits, however, the actress had, by virtue of her association with a profession blemished in the eyes of the public, to relinquish important valuables of Victorian womanhood—a special, even reverent esteem afforded the ideal mother-wife, as well as the sympathetic support of her nineteenth-century sisters. The lonely gulf which existed between the actress and society as a whole, especially its women, was created and perpetuated by a hostile church which dominated American society and commanded the adoration of its women in particular. Although the attitude of the religious public toward actresses was based on ignorance and gross distortions, it was, irrefutably, a strongly held and widely held view, subsequently, a reality to be dealt with. It is only with a recognition of this climate of hostility that one can appreciate the courage of the nineteenth-century actress and the irony of her situation in the theatre—at the same time the worst and the best of worlds.

Because the Protestant churches and its ministers in America were the principal and admitted opponents of the theatre, the position of the actress and her profession must be regarded in the light of the status of the church. Despite the country's earlier abandonment of a state religion and the clear constitutional separation of church and state, Protestant churches in particular grew to be uncommonly forceful in the century.[1]

Virtually every Protestant sect in America, with the sole exception of the Episcopal Church, officially and unequivocally declared the theatre to be the haunt of sinners.[2] The Reverend Robert Hatfield and the Reverend Dewitt Talmadge, for example, both believed that young men and women were better off dead than in the briefest association with actors. Hatfield puts his case in what he obviously regards as a rhetorical question: "Let me ask you, my young friend, justly proud of your sister, would you not rather follow her to her grave tonight than to know that tomorrow she shall stand at the altar and pledge her faith and trust her precious future to an actor?"[3] The

Claudia D. Johnson, Professor and Chair of the English Department, University of Alabama, has published six articles and three books on American theatre, including *Shakespearean Burlesques*, *Memoirs of the Nineteenth Century Theatre*, and *American Actress*, of which the above article became the first chapter.

Reverend Talmadge, who in the 1870's officiated over the largest church congregation in New York, declared that most people would rather see their children "five feet under the ground of Greenwood," than "in a month's association with actors."[4]

The exact extent to which the general public actually shared the view of the church about theatre would be difficult to determine, but it is clear that many theatrical people *believed* that the public held the same low opinion of them voiced by the clergy. In short, the actress and actor both worked in what they perceived to be a hostile climate. John Hodgkinson, an actor writing at the turn of the century, speaks of "strong and widely-held prejudices" against the profession.[5] Writing in 1827, Mrs. Trollope concluded that the general public in America did not approve of theatrical exhibitions.[6] Albert A. Palmer, one of the most successful theatrical owners and managers in the last half of the century, estimates that at least until mid-century seven-tenths of the population looked on stage attendance as "almost a sin." He observes some improvement in the attitude of the public toward the profession by the 1880's and 1890's.[7] Daniel Frohman, the "star maker," another outstanding producer of the period, corroborates Palmer's conclusion that as late as the 1860's antitheatrical bias was far-reaching.[8]

Actresses, of course, were not blind to these opinions of them. Anna Cora Mowatt, born into wealth and social standing, recognized "the prejudices of the world against the profession as a body." The actor, she wrote, "dwells on the outer side of a certain conventional pale of society, which he is allowed to enter only by courtesy, unless it is broken through by the majesty of transcendent talents."[9] Another actress, Clara Morris, reared at the opposite, lowest end of the social spectrum, reached the same conclusion—that members of her profession had labored under a cloud of disapproval throughout most of her career. "Even the people who did not think all actors drunkards and all actresses immoral did think they were a lot of flighty, silly buffoons, not to be taken seriously for a moment." Although the cloud of public suspicion was slowly lifting in the last decades of the century, Morris leaves no doubt about having felt its presence in the 1860's: "The actor had no social standing; he was no longer looked down upon, but he was an unknown quantity." By the 1880's and 1890's, Morris believes that some members of her profession had "won some social recognition."[10]

The conflict between the large religious public and the stage produced a rhetoric so powerful that it was bound to cause the stage and the actors suffering. Several successful managers, William Wood, Sol Smith, and Noah Ludlow, who harbored no little bitterness about the church's antipathy toward actors and thought the matter of sufficient importance to record in their memoirs, indicate its destructive effect on the profession.[11] Although the frontier, less tradition-bound, less religious, and often eager to attract entertainments and actresses, might be expected to be less biased against the theatre, it was far from free of harassment on the part of religious settlers. Noah Ludlow, writing of Ohio in 1828, Sol Smith, writing of Alabama in 1835, and a minor actor named Watkins, writing of Ohio and New Orleans in the 1840's, all attest to the clergy's stance and its significant impact on the professional and personal life of the actor.[12] As late as Lincoln's assassination, the general public was capable of extraordinary invective, and in 1870 the minister of an Episcopal church in New York City refused burial to an actor. Although the press and much of the public objected to the refusal, the case was certainly not an isolated one.

To work in an age when women were denounced for not remaining sequestered, pure, and religious undoubtedly made it difficult for the actress to maintain her self-esteem. There is certainly no denying, in a century that saw the phenomenal growth of the theatre, that good actresses received the plaudits of the playgoing public and that, occasionally, some of them, like Charlotte Cushman, even came into contact with genteel society. But actresses were also aware that such occasions were exceptional and that their professional success was quite another thing from social success or public respect. All the plaudits in the world did not alter the general public's view of the actress as a "low order of society . . . very properly debarred from respectable society."[13] Actresses on the American stage rarely, if ever, whined about social snubs, slander in the press and from the pulpit, or their inability to move comfortably in polite society. This certainly does not mean, however, that they were unaffected by the climate of opinion. Mary Ann Duff, along with some of her family, was compelled to break off all relationships with her former theatrical associates and conceal her identity as the foremost tragedienne of her day.[14] One reads of Fanny Kemble discovering with a shock that her American husband and his family would not allow her friends who were actors and actresses to set foot in the house where she lived.[15] Anna Cora Mowatt writes of being brainwashed against the theatre by her minister when she was a child, of feeling personally insulted when a theatre manager offered her an acting job, and later, being accused of betraying her class when she decided to become an actress. Clara Morris writes of her mother's being "stricken with horror" at the idea of her daughter turning to the theatre as the only likely means of helping shoulder the family's financial burden. Later, Clara, herself, came to feel that actresses were, in effect, barred from going to church. The "exclusive spirit" of churches, as she put it, kept many actresses away from the most significant comfort and meaning afforded most women in the century. In an age when the minister was the Idol of the Ideal Woman, he was the adversary of the actress.

Most of the expressed disapproval of the theater and actresses could be traced to nineteenth-century sexual mores and the commonly held belief that all or most actresses led immoral lives both on and off stage. With the sole exception of prostitution, to which it was often compared, no single profession was so loudly and frequently condemned. Olive Logan, herself a nineteenth-century actress and writer, declared that misconceptions about the actress had produced an unhappy result: "The name of a poor stock actress is a synonym for what is lax in the sex."[16]

The religious public rested its case against actresses not only on inappropriately applied historical evidence from Restoration England, but also on their assurances that no "lady" would do on stage what actresses did. In the first place, ministers believed that actresses' participation in "a deception" could not fail to infect their personalities. As the Reverend Robert Hatfield made plain, "men and women whose nightly business it is to act a lie . . . who are trained to assume the most contradictory passions and moral states, have no power to prevent this life of falsity and sham from reaching most disastrously upon themselves." Other objections to on-stage behavior can be divided into three categories: first, costumes that revealed too much flesh; second, scenes that required flirtation; and third, scenes that required physical contact with male actors. The few ministers who admitted to having been to the theatre believed that what they had seen there was sufficient evidence to call for the wholesale condemnation of all actresses: "lascivious smiles, wanton glances, dubious compliments, indelicate attitudes, kissing, with a variety of vain and sinful practices."[17] Even worse, women were "twirled and handled" on stage, and their clothing was, by ministerial standards, more often indecent than not.[18] Mention is also often made of such proofs of "immoral behavior" as "heaving bosoms, languishing glances, voluptuous attitudes" of actresses in the execution of their roles. Even worse was the immodest physical displays of falling "into the arms of men" on stage.[19]

The reputation of the actresses for immorality may have come as much from what was reputed to go on behind stage as what occurred on stage. The ubiquitous greenroom was, in the minds of many, a den of unspeakable iniquities: "The associations of the greenroom are blasting. It is a terrible ordeal through which but few can pass unsinged. The whole land ever and anon rings with some new outcry of shame or cruelty."[20] Even though American theatres had from the beginning banned everyone except actors from their greenrooms, the attitudes of outspoken enemies of the theatre were evidently formed from readings in the history of the Restoration stage when greenrooms were often used as "places of assignation." The same clergy who faulted actresses for "acting a lie" seemed unconvinced, at the same time, that what happened on stage was make-believe. Love scenes that began on stage were, it was suggested, continued backstage, an assumption which caused several actresses to insist that love scenes on stage were often played between men and women who hated each other and refused to speak to, much less touch, each other off stage.

The clergy believed that actresses deserved denunciation on the basis of their off-stage as well as their on-stage and backstage conduct. No woman could remain on the stage and keep the purity of a saintlike femininity:

The effect of the kind of life led by players is peculiarly pernicious to female character. It strips it of all its loftier attributes, its softer and more delicate charms. Sensibility, modesty, and refinement are gradually extinguished by the unfeminine and indelicate business of the stage, and nothing is left but the hackneyed and haggard form of injured humanity, covered and bedecked perhaps, by false and tawdry ornaments. A few female actors may have preserved their virtue, but, alas! how many have lost it forever by their connection with the stage. And if others have not been entirely ruined by this means, how greatly must their characters have suffered in purity and elevation, by the dark forms of evil with which they come into such close and continual contact.[21]

Not only did the clergy succeed in defaming the actress as immoral in an age which held its women to a virtue narrowly defined—on the same grounds, it drove a particularly cruel wedge between the actress and most "respectable" women of her day by discouraging theatre attendance. Frances Trollope observed in her travels throughout America that the clergy had little influence on the theatre-going habits of American men, but that its influence on women was enormous. Clerical disapproval was, she wrote, the principal reason why women avoided the theatre. Furthermore, it is only women, she writes, and not men who "deem it an offense against religion to witness the representation of a play."[22] Certainly there were many reasons quite aside from theological ones which discouraged wholehearted female attendance at the theatre—the third tier set aside for prostitutes, the rowdiness, and the violence—but the church's concepts of morality and female psychology also contributed to the widely held conviction that contact with the theatre and actresses was particularly detrimental to female character. Those human faculties, specifically the imagination, the senses, and the emotions, which the actress appealed to in her profession, were precisely the faculties that could be used to destroy womanly virtue.

The aim of any upright Christian, and especially the good Christian woman, was to keep emotion and imagination in quiet, unexcited moderation. The duties of home and church, the simple amusements of reading and attending occasional lectures were not dangerous. One could even read dramas without experiencing notable harm. The danger came in seeing plays on stage, for there the viewer would be excited by scenic effects, by direct and "overwhelming appeals to the senses."[23] The Reverend Samuel Winchester: "The tendency of theatrical amusements is to produce injurious excitement. The passions are inflamed, the sympathies are excited, and a multitude of various emotions crowd upon and often overwhelm the soul."[24]

These warnings were meant for all people, of course, but they had greater meaning for women than they did for men because of the century's view of the emotional constitution of the sexes. Men were perceived as not only stronger in body but in reason and resolution as well. As a consequence men had better defenses against the theatre's corruption. The character of woman, as distinct from that of man, is described by a physician of the day as being intuitive, imaginative, emotional, and affectionate. A column in the *Christian Spectator* warned ladies against attending the theatre because their imaginations so easily led them into depravity:

> A mother might fear the polluting comedy for her son but the more absorbing tragedy for her daughter . . . and it is not to be imagined that the delicate mind of a female, young and imaginative as she may be, can be agitated by scenes like these . . . and yet suffer no depravation.[25]

Woman was thus more liable to taint from the theatre than was man, and her reputation less likely to recover from stains of any nature. Plays that openly mocked religion and piety, portrayed evil, particularly adultery, in attractive or sympathetic ways, used obscene language or were performed by immodestly clad actresses were distasteful to any decent Christian. However, ladies, more than gentlemen, were blemished in viewing these unholy spectacles. Male critics of objectionable plays were invariably more horrified at the prospect of the language from stage reaching the ears of a wife or a daughter than their own ears.

The subsequent double standard meant that what was often publicly pronounced to be sauce for the gander as well as the goose in Christian society was in practice sauce only for the gander. A respectable male's visit to a tavern or his enjoyment of a cigar in public, while reprehensible, was largely expected and easily forgiven. The respectable female, on the contrary, was not expected to break the same rules without serious and lifelong ruin of her reputation.

The perils which women might fall into as a result of association with the theatre were believed to be much worse than those which awaited men. Theatre-going was actually feared as a kind of addiction very like the addiction to heroin; once having gotten a good dose of it, it was almost impossible to give up. Instances were cited of boys being led to the gallows in their search for money to attend the theatre, or men dying sad, premature deaths from dissipation brought on by association with the theatre. As drastic as these cases sounded, the extremes to which theatre addiction led the average man were not believed to be nearly so disastrous as that which awaited women. For the price of a theatre ticket, poor men pilfered and stole, but women were led to sell their bodies as well as their souls. This is the warning of the Reverend Griscom, frequently quoted in tracts and newspaper columns:

In the case of the feebler sex, the result is still worse; a relish for the amusements of the theatre, without the means of indulgence, becomes too often a motive for listening to the first seducer; and this prepares the unfortunate captive of sensuality for the haunts of infamy and a total destruction of all that is valuable in the mind and character of woman.[26]

As a result, actresses found few of their own sex, with the exception of prostitutes, in the audiences for which they performed, particularly in the first half of the century. In the first place, the portion of the theatre open to respectable women was very small. The third tier was restricted to prostitutes and their companions, and the pit was restricted by custom to men and boys. Women who were not prostitutes were limited largely to the boxes or portions of the lower tiers. The appearance of "ladies" in any part of the house in the first fifty years of the century was sufficiently infrequent to draw attention to the occasion and was always especially noted by observers. Actors in their memoirs eagerly mention the appearances of ladies in the audiences they played to. It seemed to be proof of the moral acceptability and stature of the company. For example, Tyrone Power, a nineteenth-century Irish actor, made special note of the uncustomary spectacle of "American ladies of the best class" in a New Orleans theatre,[27] and Charles Dickens in the 1840's commented on the very few women in the Boston Theatre, all of whom were sitting in the front of the boxes.[28] Certainly a few very fashionable, upper-class women frequented theatres like the Park and some working-class wives brought their whole families and picnic lunches to the Bowery, but for most of the century, respectable women did not support the theatre in any significant numbers even in the cities. Of the New York theatre in the 1840's, Meade Minnigerode writes, "Ladies in general seldom attended the theatre, except to see a Fanny Elssler, or an occasional opera, or some visiting dramatic star."[29] J. S. Buckingham, Frances Trollope, and James Boardman report the same situation in what were then frontier theatres. Although productions like Uncle Tom's Cabin and The Drunkard opened the theatre to a few more respectable women in the last half of the century, continual clerical attacks would never let the actress be assured of any widespread support from the rest of the female population.

There is considerable irony in the fact that, while the actress endured disparagement and ostracism by reason of attacks on her virtue, she appeared in reality to be no more and no less virtuous than other women, even by narrow nineteenth-century standards. Attacks on the virtue of actresses prompted numerous defenses from the men of the American stage. W. W. Clapp, for instance, claimed that there was "no class in the community more remarkable for constancy and devotion in their domestic relations,"[30] and a stage comedian called William Davidge supported actresses in The Drama Defended by writing that "there are now in the city of New York, who have retired from the duties of their profession, those whose chastity, truthfulness, and domestic accomplishments, as daughters, wives and mothers, are second to none, not even the most opulent in this vast metropolis."[31] When actresses and ballet girls do become immoral, he wrote, it is no more often than women in other fields and, furthermore, not the fault of their association with the theatre.

Nor, wrote Davidge, is there any validity in the argument that actresses are just naturally sinful because they work in close association with men. Do not men and women work together in factories and churches without being corrupted or maligned?

Theatrical women as well as men rose to defend the honor of their sister-actresses, including the lowly ballet girls who were so often the prey of stage-door johnnies or "mashers" as they were then called. Anna Cora Mowatt came to the defense of actresses after she had acquired some firsthand knowledge of the theatre, indicating how very wrong she had been in her self-righteous disdain for actors. In the theatre, she found to her surprise, "refined and accomplished ladies, exemplary wives." She also declared: "My views concerning the stage and my estimate of the members of dramatic companies, had undergone a total revolution. Many circumstances had proved to me how unfounded were the prejudices of the world against the profession as a body." She further found that women in the theatre led lives of "unimpeachable purity, industry, devotion to their kin," and she found them "fulfilling the hardest duties of life with a species of stoical heroism."[32]

The mother of Clara Morris had declared when Clara was a child that she would rather she and her daughter continue as lowly domestics for the rest of their lives than that Clara accept a job as a ballet girl in a theatrical company. But Clara's observations as an adult actress belied everything of which her mother had been so fearful. She claimed that in all her years in the theatre she had never seen but one instance of even a breath of scandal in the theatres where she had been employed.

The truth seems to be that American actresses were as willing to uphold Victorian morality as were other women of the day. Theatre critic William Winter, a staunch defender of conventional nineteenth-century morality, passed harsh judgment on several famous actresses like Laura Keene for what he considered to be irregular personal lives, but it was his observation in *Vagrant Memories* that sexual morality was no better and no worse in the theatre than it was in other segments of society. A modern historian's research has led her to the same conclusion about actresses: Elizabeth Dexter writes, "It appears probable that the majority of them were as correct in their conduct and had as much essential goodness as any other group of women."[33]

In an important way, of course, it does not really matter whether public opinion of actresses was justified; the simple fact of the matter is that they were frequently regarded as little better than harlots. Actresses had economic advantages; they had the applause of a special group of playgoers; and in a few exceptional instances they were welcomed into the homes of respectable people. None of these things, however, altered the persistent day-to-day reality of the ordinary actress—that for most of the century she labored under the unrelenting scowl of the religious mainstream in an intensely religious country. The courage and, one concludes, the usually silent suffering of the actress in the performance of her professional offices can only be valued properly in the light of this disagreeable historical reality.

WOMEN IN MALE ROLES: CHARLOTTE CUSHMAN AND OTHERS

YVONNE SHAFER

In the New York season of 1819–20 there was a performance described by George C. Odell in his *Annals of the New York Stage* as a "futile novelty":

> An early, but unfortunately, not the last female Hamlet in New York was shown on March 29; I cannot conjecture what led Mrs. Bartley to this attempt, on her benefit night. Perhaps Mr. Simpson should have played Ophelia.

Earlier in the century actresses had appeared as Young Norval, Romeo, and other characters created for men. Students of theatre history are familiar with the number of actresses celebrated for "breeches roles" and know that Bernhardt and Siddons performed Hamlet, but little attention has been given to the large number of American actresses throughout the nineteenth century performing male roles in regular commercial theatres with full supporting casts. Why did the actresses choose to impersonate men? Were they successful? What does the phenomenon reveal about the nineteenth-century theatre and women's role in it? By focusing on the foremost impersonator of males on the American stage, Charlotte Cushman, in the context of females in male roles, answers to these questions can be found.

There are several reasons actresses occasionally played male roles. The prime reason for Miss Cushman and others who did so repeatedly was a natural inclination toward masculine behavior and appearance. For example, Miss Lydia Kelly, a successful Romeo in the 1820's, was never at home in genteel, feminine roles. One critic said, "her Amazonian walk alone is sufficient to scatter and annihilate a whole drawing room full of dandies."

Yvonne Shafer, who teaches in the School of Theatre, Florida State University, has published many articles and several books, including *Approaches to Teaching Ibsen, Ibsen's A Doll House*, and *Henrik Ibsen: Life, Work, and Criticism*.

Miss Kelly was very popular, however, playing breeches roles and male roles. "Though not regularly handsome, though in fact somewhat masculine in appearance and manner, she radiated sunshine to the rear places of the largest theatres." Lydia Kelly's most successful female roles were those which were strong and dominating, such as her "hearty and buoyant, if somewhat masculine" Beatrice in *Much Ado About Nothing*.[1] For actresses whose appearance and manner did not conform to the nineteenth-century conception of femininity and beauty, playing the part of a male provided an opportunity to act in a way which seemed natural and which gave vent to the urge to dominate the action.

Another major reason for actresses to play male roles was the increased opportunity to show off their abilities. It is obvious that in a theatre dominated by Shakespeare, the great roles were those written for men. Compared with Macbeth, Lady Macbeth is a small role. Compared with Hamlet, Ophelia is a small role. Also for many of the major female roles in Shakespeare, dominating women such as Miss Cushman were simply not suitable. At one point in her career, Miss Cushman considered the novelty of playing Romeo one night and Juliet the next, saying, "If Fanny Kemble is not too old and fat to play Juliet, then I am not."[2] To her friends, however, the idea was simply laughable, and she continued to play Romeo.

The quest for novelty led many actresses to play male roles to draw a crowd. Odell indicates that it was a fairly standard business throughout the nineteenth century for women to play Hamlet, or other male roles, especially on a benefit night. An example is provided by a Mrs. Barnes, who often played male roles as a novelty, and who played Hamlet many times in the 1820's.

Natural inclination, a wish to display ability, and novelty all figure as reasons for actresses attempting male roles. Perhaps some of them, consciously or unconsciously, shared another motivation with Charlotte Cushman: the urge to take the lead and compete with men in a very direct way. Certainly in her attempt at Hamlet, Miss Cushman presented a direct challenge to Edwin Booth. Actresses playing Romeo, Oberon, Hamlet, and other leading male roles undoubtedly found pleasure in playing the central part while men played the roles of Tybalt, Lysander, and Laertes.

A final reason for the continued performances of men's roles by women is provided by the answer to the second question, "Were they successful?" The answer is clearly, and perhaps surprisingly, yes. The general public and the critics accepted the convention and the actresses drew large audiences and often received excellent reviews. One indication of success is the large number of actresses, many unknown today, who played men's roles: Mrs. Bartlett, Mrs. Hamblin, Mrs. Shaw, Mrs. Sefton, Miss Ellis, Mrs. Hunt, Mrs. Coleman Pope, Mrs. Brougham, Fanny Wallack, Mrs. Alsop, Miss Glyn, Melinda Jones, Madame Ponisi—to list only some of them. Another indication of success is the large number of male roles performed by women, often throughout their careers. Charlotte Cushman played sixteen male roles, many played by other actresses. These included numerous Shakespearean roles, leading parts in nineteenth-century tragedies such as *The Lady of Lyons,* and, of course, the popular role of Norval in *Douglas.* There were also the many character roles in an interesting play, *Ladies at Home, or Gentlemen, We Can Do Without You,* with an all-female cast.

Odell usually described such performances in an ironic or negative manner, using phrases such as "freakish exhibition." But Odell was writing from a later viewpoint, and the critics of the time simply accepted the idea, in general, as they accepted the idea of a fifty-year-old Juliet, or as later critics accepted a two-hundred-pound Carmen.

Audiences, too, responded positively to the ladies playing men. In 1820–21, Mrs. Barnes drew the biggest receipts of the season at the Anthony Street Theatre when she played Richard III. A Miss Clifton playing Count Belino in the 1831–32 season, played additional performances "in consequence of the applause bestowed by a brilliant and crowded audience."[3] When Miss Cushman played Romeo in 1860 many persons could not get seats, and some people in the theatre were forced to retire because of the crowds and the heat.[4]

There were of course occasional jeering reviews, even for some of the great Miss Cushman's performances. Some incidents in the theatre annoyed the actresses. When Miss Cushman played Romeo in Boston there was a loud raspberry from a man in the audience during a love scene. Miss Cushman led the Juliet from the stage, and returned to say, "Some man must put that person out, or I shall be obliged to do it myself." The crowd responded with cheers and threw the man out.[5]

In summary, one can say that the ladies who played the many male roles throughout the century received some negative criticism, but for the good actresses who acted not merely for the novelty, the reviews were serious and positive, and the audiences large. On the whole, the attempts were successful, as indicated by the fact that a number of actresses repeated the roles so many times and to such large houses. Fanny Wallack, for example, played Romeo and other male roles as a standard part of her repertoire for many years.

Fanny Wallack and other lesser actresses of the nineteenth century never had the stunning and continued success in male roles which Charlotte Cushman enjoyed. The critical and popular response to this actress seems incredible to a contemporary reader, especially one familiar with the portraits of her in Victorian dress, with a portly figure, a large bosom, and a rather grim mouth. She played these roles first when she was in her twenties and continued to play many of them when she was in her fifties. She began by playing Patrick in *The Poor Soldier* in New Orleans when another actor became ill. She moved to Albany in 1837 and played a number of male roles in a stock company. As her biographer Joseph Leach comments,

By the end of her Albany sojourn, upstate New York knew Charlotte Cushman as an able young actress especially adept in "breeches parts," so skilled in male impersonation that no one seriously objected to a woman's daring in Victorian America to change her skirts for the revealing costumes and aggressive demeanor of men.[6]

Her early success led her to play a great many male roles, including the following: Claude Melnotte in the *Lady of Lyons,* Cardinal Wolsey in *Henry VIII*, Aladdin, Hamlet, Oberon in *Midsummer Night's Dream*, Romeo, Orlando in *As You Like It,* and Richelieu.

Of all these roles, Romeo was her most popular one and received the most critical acclaim both in England and America. In 1845 she performed the role at the Haymarket in London, with her sister Susan as Juliet. There are many rave reviews in the Charlotte Cushman Scrapbook and in the biographies.[7]

Charlotte Cushman returned to America for the 1849–50 season, and as Odell says, "A real thrill must have pulsed through the season when, on May 13th, Charlotte Cushman came in as Romeo [the part in which she had been acclaimed in London, assisted by Fanny Wallack as Juliet]." The *New York Times* reviewer noted the immense size of the audience and the enthusiastic response. His review found in the Cushman Scrapbook was typical of the praise Charlotte Cushman received in America and indicates the style of the performance:

> Romeo is, perhaps, the most difficult character to represent in the whole range of drama, and we know no one who can play the part but Miss Cushman. . . . In Miss Cushman's picture of Romeo there is nothing sickly, or subtle, or morbid. It is the love of a young, glowing, unreflecting Italian, rich in passion and tenderness, and yet in its hottest glow chastened with a delicacy—a love not of mere sensuality, but of sensuality spiritualized by imagination, and revelling in the frankness of unhesitating trust. It is such a love as manifests itself where the imagination is ardent, the blood hot, and the soul refined.

Considering these reviews and the enormous audiences which came to see the performances, it is not surprising that Miss Cushman played the role of Romeo throughout most of her career with various Juliets, including her sister and Booth's wife, Mary Devlin. Naturally, not all critics liked her in the role—one wag remarked that her Romeo was so "ardently masculine" and Juliet so "tenderly feminine," that the least Miss Cushman could do, once the engagement was over, was to marry her sister.[8] Negative or amused criticism of this sort, however, was unusual, and although she is remembered today for Lady Macbeth and Meg Merrilies, in her lifetime she was as popular as Romeo as she was in these female roles.

Another popular male role in Miss Cushman's repertoire was that of Cardinal Wolsey in *Henry VIII*. She performed the role in full productions and as part of the readings she gave later in her life. A typical review noted her vocal quality—deep, rich tones which lent reality to her interpretation. Writing in 1870, when Miss Cushman was fifty-four, a Pittsburgh reviewer found in the Scrapbook commended her choice of Wolsey as an appropriate role, and said she "gave her greatest exhibition of genius":

> Notwithstanding her age, which is advanced, Miss Cushman yet retains her physical energy apparently unshaken, while her intellectual fire has certainly not paled in the progress of years. She is fitted, at this stage of her life, for the deepest and strongest emotions that a poet or prose writer has set upon paper. Looking at her upon the stage it would be more difficult to conceive that she could yet portray with any marked degree of appropriateness the tenderer passions. Passages from King Lear would be more to her taste than Juliet moonshine.

Neither critics nor audiences liked her in all the male roles she played—clearly, novelty was not enough to make a success. When Miss Cushman played Hamlet, she felt she was quite good, but almost no one else did. Some writers called her performance "bizarre," and certainly there must have been a good deal of merriment over the prospect of this sizable woman struggling into the tights she borrowed from the diminutive Booth when she played the role. Ironically, Booth seems to have loaned Charlotte his costume for Hamlet many times despite their rivalry. The Players Club library has several letters from her to Mary Devlin requesting the use of the costume.

In challenging Booth, of course, she was competing with the greatest Hamlet of the time. On one occasion she wrote to Mary Devlin:

> My engagement was cut short in New York, because as they told me Mr. Edwin *would* commence there or act otherwheres—I was to have acted *Hamlet there* but they prevented it because Edwin was going to do it.[9]

There is no doubt that Booth felt her urge to play Hamlet arose from a wish to show that she could play it better than he. She felt that his acting was "flimsy" and "pale," that he was a "mere willow" in *Macbeth*. Booth wrote a friend saying, "Cushman is doing so-so at the Boston. She is down on me as an actor; says I don't know anything at all about 'Hamlet,' so she is going to play it here in February."[10] Lawrence Barrett often acted with Miss Cushman and admired her work so much that he wrote several pieces about her after her death. Barrett's comments on her Hamlet, however, reveal a feeling that the challenge to Booth was a futile effort on her part.[11]

Perhaps not too much should be made of the reactions of rival actors, but their comments do reveal the professional courtesy which actors extended in lending costumes, supporting her in the lesser roles, and offering advice on stage business, as well as the competition which figured in Miss Cushman's assumption of male roles. Booth, at least, regarded her effort as a direct challenge to his interpretation.

A more important consideration than the attitude of other actors toward Miss Cushman's assumption of male roles is her own attitude. Her choice of these roles seems to relate very directly to her physical and psychological characteristics, and to her outlook on the role of women in society. Shortly after Cushman's death in 1876, a close friend, Emma Stebbins, wrote a book about her in which the author attempted to disguise the real reasons that she played Romeo and other male parts.

> Although Miss Cushman's early training as a "utility actress" at the Park Theatre had obliged her to make herself familiar with many male parts, it was not her choice to represent such, and notably in the case of this impersonation, Romeo. She was led to her choice of this play as the one in which to present her sister to an English audience by her strong desire to be enabled to support her fittingly herself. By acting Romeo, she would add to her sister's attraction, secure her success, and give her that support which it would be difficult otherwise to obtain.[12]

Stebbins's view is simply not correct. Writing in 1894, W. T. Price, in *A Life of Charlotte Cushman*, stated: "There is not only no apology needed for Charlotte Cushman's Romeo as her female biographers seem to imagine, but it was one of her most remarkable achievements." He then presented his viewpoint that off stage Miss Cushman was performing the dominating role normally played by a man in terms of supporting all her relatives, handling business affairs, traveling and working in different places, and establishing households of which she was the head. He concluded that it was natural for her to choose to play the dominating male role on the stage, since "she was playing the part of a man in these serious relationships of life."[13]

Her dominating personality and physical appearance led her naturally into such a position. She felt that she had a handicap in traditional roles normally played by beautiful women, and her acting in female roles was characterized by a restlessness and constant movement, because she felt that to play with repose one had to be beautiful. In male roles she was spared comments on her lack of conventional beauty, and was spared invidious comparisons between herself and beauties like Mrs. Siddons. Her size, too, made it difficult for her to play the role of a woman who was dominated by a man, and one critic wondered at the probability of Bill Sykes being able to kill her Meg Merrilies. She herself complained to William Winter, "The actors who come on for Macbeth are, usually, such *little* men; I have to look down at them."[14] Actors who performed with her were keenly aware of her size, too. Booth remarked that when as Lady Macbeth she urged him to kill Duncan, he felt an inclination to say, "Why don't *you* kill him, you're big enough."[15] When Forrest was in the audience and she said, "All the perfumes of Arabia will not sweeten this little hand," Forrest laughed aloud and said, "*Little* hand! Why it's as big as a codfish!"[16]

Obviously, then, it was her physical qualities, and her attitude toward them, that drew Miss Cushman to male roles. Playing Romeo and other male roles certainly did not embarrass her, nor was she embarrassed to dress and behave according to her inclinations off stage, despite the comments of friends and relatives. The writer Melville met her and found her a very masculine "strange creature" wearing a "man's collar, cravat and Wellington boots."[17] Elizabeth Barrett Browning was dismayed by what she described as a "female marriage" between Charlotte and the young actress Matilda Hays, who played heroines to Charlotte's heroes (in the *Lady of Lyons* and *Romeo and Juliet*, for example). In a letter to her family regarding a relationship with the sculptress Emma Stebbins, Charlotte said, "I love her very much, she is the finest nature I have ever been in contact with."[18] In 1858, Miss Cushman temporarily retired from the stage, moved to London, and lived with three other women as, in her words, "jolly female bachelors."[19] That this mode of life was known and accepted is indicated by a number of comments by writers at the time.

Charlotte Cushman's relationships were with women who had aspirations to raise the status of women through writing and art—as she felt she was doing. Price wrote, "Eliza Cook fell in love with her, and read her own poetry to her, some of the sonnets being on Charlotte—and they spent much time then, and in after years, in the company of each other."[20] Another writer Charlotte encouraged was Geraldine Jewsbury, who wrote a novel titled *The Half Sisters*. It was a defense of women's right to free love and the need to prove themselves capable of more than marriage and motherhood. The central character was modeled after Charlotte, and the author wrote to her, "We are touching on better days when women will have a genuine normal life of their own to lead, and no longer feel their destiny manqué if they remain single."[21] Miss Cushman supported and assisted Emma Stebbins, and tried to help her win a major commission for a piece of sculpture, saying, "In this way *women* will raise the statue."[22] Through playing leading roles, Miss Cushman was able to stand as a highly visible symbol of successful and independent womanhood, and in playing roles men usually played, and receiving more acclaim than any other Romeo at the time, she showed that women could compete with men. She must have taken a great deal of pleasure in playing Orlando in the all-female production of *As You Like It* performed by 150 members of the Professional Women's League.[23]

Charlotte Cushman's efforts to raise the status of women, her dissatisfaction with her lack of typical feminine beauty, and her natural instinct toward domination all led her to play male roles. With the exception of Hamlet, these were popular and critical successes. Her male rivals may not have liked what she did, but had to take her seriously, especially in view of her general success. She seems to have made a clear appraisal of herself and her circumstances, and to have played roles which brought her fame and earned her a great deal of money. This gave her the means to live as she chose and to assist other women in various ways and to encourage the artistic efforts of women with independent outlooks. The position she achieved brought her admiration, critical acclaim, a very active social life, and wealth.

There is nevertheless some evidence that however successfully she adapted to her circumstances, she could have wished them otherwise. Although she played men's roles, she would have preferred to play really fine roles written for women. She acted the part of Richelieu, but her real desire was expressed when she wrote to a playwright wishing to have a play with

> a woman of strong ambition, who is at the same time very wily and diplomatic, and who has an opportunity of a great outburst when her plans are successful—in short, a female Richelieu.[24]

Later actresses had the opportunity to play such roles as the American theatre changed. New playwrights and changing social views presented an increasing number of dominating women's roles in realistic dramas such as *Margaret Fleming, Mrs. Warren's Profession,* and *Ghosts.* With the increasing emphasis on realism in the theatre, the number of women playing men's roles decreased. In the twentieth century attempts at Hamlet by actresses such as Eva Le Gallienne and Judith Anderson have been regarded as notable oddities, and the former is certainly more likely to be remembered for her portrayal of Hedda Gabler and the latter for her Medea. As a phenomenon of the nineteenth century, the actresses playing male roles revealed a challenge to the male domination of the stage, a taste for novelty, and the willingness on the part of the critics and audiences to accept the process as one of the many conventions of the nineteenth-century theatre. For individual actresses, playing male roles offered the possibility of psychological satisfaction, star billing, public acclaim, and increased income—all major advantages for strong independent female performers.

ADAH ISAACS MENKEN IN *MAZEPPA*

LOIS ADLER

Adah Isaacs Menken "is the sensation of the New York stage," said one review. "Her rare beauty and the tantalizing audacity of her performance defy description. She must be seen to be believed; anyone who misses her at the Broadway Theatre will be denying himself the rarest exhilarating treats."[1] The penny press went all out for Menken, famous as the first lady to play the male lead in *Mazeppa* while strapped to the back of a real horse—and in the "nude" no less! The date was April 30, 1866. The former "Mrs. J. C. Heenan," ex-wife of the boxer "Benecia Boy," had come a long way from her days at the Bowery.

Lois Adler, Professor of Theatre, Manhattan Community College, is a former actress who coordinates a new theatre program. A longer version of this paper was read at the American Theatre Association, 1977.

The Oxford Companion to the Theatre attributes the first playing of Mazeppa by a woman to Charlotte Crampton in 1859; a listing in Odell's Annals of the New York Stage for such a performance on January 3, 1859, at the Bowery would seem to corroborate this, although other commentators do not mention it. Odell quotes from a handbill (presumably) which said that Crampton was "the first actress to attempt the part with her two beautifully trained horses, Alexander and Black Eagle; executing the most intrepid feats ever performed by a lady." However, she didn't do it in the nude, nor was she tied to the horse's back, which gives Menken the edge.

Menken first played the role on June 3, 1861, in Albany. The Oxford Companion to the Theatre errs in claiming San Francisco, 1863, as the place and date of the initial performance. It also gives Menken's real name as Dolores Adios Fuertes—an absolutely super name—but one of several "real" names that Menken made up along with conflicting tales of her birth and background.

In fact (faulty reportage and crumbling, nonpaginated newspapers aside), the material involving Menken is a mass of contradictory statements, historical inaccuracies, and heresay provided mainly by Menken herself. She used extensive PR and was also the source of the "facts" behind the publicity—all these having achieved legitimacy through continued repetition, unfortunately. When Adah Bertha Theodore—and that was her real name—married Alexander Isaacs Menken, so one story goes, she claimed she told his devoutly religious family that she was the daughter of a Portuguese rabbi. That this tale undercut the story of her conversion from Catholicism to Judaism seemed not to matter. The penchant for the "Spanish Style" and the related stories seem to have surfaced very conveniently in 1861, right after the death of Lola Montes (Marie Dolores Gilbert) whom Menken identified with and emulated. She began using the name Dolores with her intimate friends at that time and later announced this as her real name to the European press.[2] She was Swinburne's "Dolores."

The idea for Adah to do Mazeppa came from the actor James Murdoch, who had played in Macbeth with Adah in Nashville, according to biographer Paul Lewis. Supposedly, sometime in 1861, Adah was in a sketch at the Broadway called Ha Ha Horsie, in which a group of girls cavorted around wearing imitation horses' heads while one girl rode a horse. At one point the horse reared, and our Adah (one of the horsies) grabbed the reins, helped the girl to dismount, then leaped onto the horse's back while the audience applauded wildly. When Murdoch heard of the incident, he suggested that she do Milner's dramatization of Byron's Mazeppa or the Wild Horse of Tartary lashed to the back of a real horse. None of the male Mazeppas had ever done that scene on the horse; they had used dummies. Apparently, no one in New York wanted to chance a woman doing that stunt, although Murdoch had seen her ride (she was trained by her stepfather, supposedly) and he knew she could do it. The manager of a company playing at the Green Street

Theatre in Albany, Captain J. B. Smith, was interested, and so they went off to Albany. Once there Murdoch supervised the building of a spiral ramp; it was his idea that she should ride out through the audience on this runway so that everyone could see her. In his book, *The Stage,* he never mentions any of these things, though he gives a vivid account of what it was like to play Macbeth opposite her improvised Lady Macbeth.[3]

At this point, Adah came up with the second innovation—she would wear flesh-colored tights to simulate nudity while strapped to the back of the untamed horse. According to her account, she was "ordered" never to answer questions from the press or anyone else as to whether she wore tights or was really nude. The wardrobe mistress, Emma Hazeltine, was also sworn to secrecy.

Adah practiced at least an hour a day on the runway. But at the dress rehearsal in the afternoon before the opening, something frightened the horse, which bolted and toppled off the runway. Adah, according to Lewis, "having broken the bands of light paper which served as bindings, leapt out of the way of the horse, grabbed the reins and spoke quietly to the horse— then mounted her and insisted on trying it again and again until it was perfect." News of this spread and the house was sold out by evening. While this is an amusing story, that same Captain Smith, in an interview printed by Mr. H. P. Phelps in the *Albany Mirror* on October 25, 1879, reminisced about how he came up with the idea for Menken to do *Mazeppa*. He had seen her in another company in Albany and thought that it would be perfect for her and that it would be a great success. Certainly for an era bound up with spectacular scenes on the melodramatic stage, this was a good guess. His description of Menken's initial nervousness and what happened in rehearsal when the horse bolted, throwing her and injuring her, is in marked contrast to her account. He does say, however, that she was very plucky and tried until she got it right; he quoted her as saying, "No one ever saw me show the white feather."[4]

On the evening of June 3, 1861, Menken opened in *Mazeppa,* appearing in the "nude" in staid Albany. She followed the tradition of using a black horse popular since the late 1850's; the horse's name was Belle Beauty. Certainly a black horse was more fearsome and wild-looking for a naked lady—even if she was playing a man. There is a marvelous litho in the Townsend Walsh Scrapbook at the Lincoln Center Library of Adah dressed as a Tartar warrior, looking like Brunhilde-cum-Odile. She is on a black horse, wearing a black cape, black boots, carrying a black shield and with black, flowing hair.

The *Albany Express* said, "The house was crowded; we can safely say that it was the largest audience that has been seen for years within the walls of the Green Street Theatre. Miss Menken has proved herself to be a heroine in the fearless manner in which she succeeded to the top of the theatre on the back of the horse Belle Beauty. The place has been got up in fine style."[5] The run was brief, but Menken made a hit in Albany. A clipping in the Townsend

Walsh Scrapbook states that the straps used in the "binding scene" were still in view over a bar in Buffalo.

For the next two years, Menken toured with *Mazeppa*, visiting Hartford, Philadelphia, Pittsburgh, Wilmington, and Louisville (where she played Pip in a version of *Great Expectations*; she was an ardent admirer of Dickens, with whom she later became friendly), but the dates are difficult to verify. Paul Lewis says she was back in Albany for her return engagement in January 1862 and was earning a high salary playing to capacity audiences. We do know that she brought *Mazeppa* to Baltimore in November 1862, where after a few performances she was arrested as a Confederate spy. She was accused of being involved in some plot with a well-known Confederate sympathizer, who it seems gave her several gifts. This was the story of her most recent husband, Robert Henry Newell, writer and literary editor on the *Sunday Mercury*, who was summoned to Baltimore to bail her out (she had divorced J. C. Heenan, the famous boxer, several months earlier).[6] Her own story was that she was talking to some admirers after the performance and was overheard praising Jefferson Davis.[7] In any event, this scandal produced fabulous receipts at the box office; people flocked to see her despite the tense war atmosphere. It is difficult not to draw the obvious conclusion that Menken devised this whole thing as a publicity stunt—perhaps the initial box-office receipts were not good or she perceived some possible threat to her drawing power.

Offers came from California during the Baltimore run, and Adah knew when to move on, when to conquer new territory. In the summer of 1863, she left for California, where she entertained the miners and sporting men for about a year. She felt San Francisco was her town and the feeling appears to have been mutual; the show was a tremendous success and she was personally very popular. Her friends were the Western literati: Mark Twain, Bret Harte, Charles Warren Stoddard, and other writers on the well-known magazine, *The Californian*. It was Charles Henry Webb's review in *The Californian* that contained the famous quote: "The Menken is unrivalled in her particular line—but it isn't a clothesline."[8]

Menken was clever enough not to submit *Mazeppa* to overexposure in San Francisco; she interspersed it with performances of *The French Spy* and *Black-Eyed Susan*, playing the male leads. In addition, she toured other parts of California like Sacramento, and at one point took off for Virginia City, Nevada. By doing this, she warded off the possibility of using up her San Francisco audience. She was earning $500 a week in California and was reportedly offered $2,500 down payment for an engagement in Virginia City.[9] In March 1864, Adah agreed to the offer in spite of the fact there was no theatre. She found a substitute and flamboyantly (in the style of the Old West) put her production of *Mazeppa* in an old amphitheatre on the outskirts of Virginia City. As she told it, Lewis reports she had men coming up on stage handing her silver pieces while she dispensed kisses; this was her arrangement, after gently chiding them for throwing money at her—which was their customary way of showing appreciation. After her Nevada triumph, Menken returned to San Francisco that spring for the final run of *Mazeppa*. A new influx of people plus those natives who had not yet seen the notorious lady assured her of an audience and secured the financial success of the run. Adah benefited enormously from this Western tour, not only financially but in terms of star status and future bookings. It afforded a gold mine of exotic adventures for the publicity mill, particularly for the tour of Europe she took in 1864.

Menken returned to the United States and appeared in *Mazeppa* at the Broadway Theatre in New York on April 30, 1866. This is considered by some biographers to be the first performance of Menken's *Mazeppa* in New York, although there is considerable disagreement about where this performance fits into the history of the production. Whatever the case, Menken came to New York as a star, having acquired fame in Europe; and this was the best way to arrive, considering the theatrical fare she offered.

Paul Lewis's version of opening night—he dates it June 12, 1861—is based on a mixture of information supplied from books written by Menken's friend, Ed James, and her husband, Robert Newell, and her own diary.[10] She was billed as an "extraordinary artiste": an epithet that appears on an early handbill found in Lincoln Center (*Menken Portfolio*) advertising her appearance as a danseuse in a vaudeville sketch in Louisiana. Lewis says, "The suspense and thrills were built up by posters displaying a black stallion, teeth bared, rearing its front legs pawing the air. Lashed to the animal's back was a cleverly concealed figure of a woman who appeared to be nude, with black hair to the waist, bare arms and with a look of wild terror on her face."[11] There was real excitement and gossip about Menken appearing "nude"; and to add to it, Menken had cut her hair in a mannish bob a few days before opening night, according to Lewis. The first night was sold out. Boxes were ten dollars each. Booth and Whitman, her friends, were reported to be in the audience.

Just before curtain time, Adah pulled what can only be called a "kitsch" stunt. First the houselights were dimmed, then they rose again slowly, while ushers passed out copies of Adah's poem "Pro Patria" (poetry and writing in general were her lifelong passion and she got a great deal of it published). After a few minutes, the lights went out and the curtain went up.

Here is Lewis's description of the appearance of Cassimir, based on Ed James's account: "He [she] appeared in skin tight breeches, a deep plunging man's shirt and calf high boots . . . sitting on a pasteboard rock. 'Yonder sits the brooding Cassimir,' says another character." Adah's voice was "uncommonly husky" and her stage speech was something all her own: "a mixture of Southern, Spanish, and the rounded English of Edwin Booth." James thought she showed great agility and said her acting style appeared to be distinctly her own: ". . . she made up for her lack of polish by her emotional intensity. . . . She was a hot-blooded young woman, even if she wasn't exactly the character Cassimir." One gathers from all of this that Menken had presence and tremendous sex appeal on stage as well as off.

As for the big scene, Lewis says, "The horse reached the runway at the rear of the theatre, then cantered down towards the front stage again—Adah giving commands continually. When horse and rider reached the stage, the curtain closed swiftly and the spotlight was extinguished. Cheers rang out."

At her curtain call, Menken proved a real showman. She appeared completely covered from head to toe in a scarlet cape. Suddenly she was sobbing and there was Edwin Booth rushing to her side. Supposedly she took fourteen curtain calls.

While the *Herald* was not enthusiastic, the *Tribune* was positively virulent: ". . . the atmosphere reeked with vulgarity."[12] Horace Greeley himself in the *Tribune* was supposed to have attacked her with statements like, "An actress who uses her naked body to entice audiences into a theatre should be barred by legislation from the stage." Apparently this started a running battle between them, with Adah taking out ads to answer him. The publicity was fabulous and kept her constantly before the public. She called Greeley unfair; she admonished him for criticizing something he had not seen. She urged him to see the performance and when this didn't work, she dared him to show up: "See me in my notoriety!"[13] He finally did show up and ultimately, though he was never able to praise the show, became a friend.

George Wood, manager of the Broadway, answered the critics by saying, "To see Miss Adah in the natural beauty of her womanhood, costumed as she is costumed, is alone worth the price of admission."[14] The *Courier* declared, "the female *Mazeppa* is the sensation of New York. It should continue to draw crowds for months to come."[15] Another of the reviews said: "She is Aphrodite and Diana; a marble statue of exquisitely molded perfection."[16] The *Evening Daily News* said: "May a lady be naked? She lives, she breathes . . . we salute the naked lady of New York." The *Post* said: "She is so lovely she numbs the mind and the senses reel—although we must confess that the play is a dreary excuse for a theatrical entertainment; yet we would be willing to see it again just to see her." The *New York Clipper*, rather than giving an actual review, recapped Menken's European reviews and discussed her previous success in California.[17]

It was said that Menken was popular with the suffragettes. One can see why. Adah, ever the admirer of independent women (she thought Hester Prynne heroic—simply hated little Pearl), espoused the cause or might have *said* she did. Certainly Ms. Menken never hid the fact that she found domesticity distasteful nor did she conceal her dislike of "good" (obedient) women. She considered them bores. Once, after submitting her writing to *Harper's* magazine, she said, "As for Ladies magazines, I want no part of that flabby, sanctimonious collection of trash which good women read so avidly. If I had a favorite recipe, I would send it to them and they would pay me well for it. But I have never been an accomplished cook, thank the Lord. I will be rich enough to pay someone to cook for me—even breakfast."[18] Adah's most famous comment, made in a letter to her friend Robert ("Racy") Reese after his marriage in 1864, revealed definite insight. She said, "I believe good men should be married, but I don't believe in women being married; somehow they all sink into non-entities after this epoch of their existence. This is the fault of female education. They are taught from the cradle to look upon marriage as the one event in their lives. That accomplished, nothing remains."[19]

Immediately after the New York run of nearly a month, Menken left for Europe. There she repeated her past success, adding to her list of admirers and friends the names of Dumas Père, Gautier, and George Sand. She died in Paris in 1868, penniless, at the age of thirty-three, and was buried in the Jewish section of Père Lachaise Cemetery. Later the body was transferred to Montparnasse Cemetery.

From all of the above material, one thing seems abundantly clear—that Menken's projection of her physical attractiveness, not her histrionic ability, was the dominant theatrical attribute. Newspapers referred to her as "statuesque" and as "Aphrodite." Paul Lewis maintains that she was about five foot seven with a perfectly shaped figure; and with full lips that were painted crimson. He quotes Newell as saying that "Adah was a symbol of desire . . . all who saw her, wanted her immediately."[20]

It is obvious that Menken had a real talent for what might be called dramatic display. She had a sense of what her audience wanted whether in the theatre or out of it. In an age that lusted after spectacle and variety (a partial reason for the popularity of breeches roles), when advertising was everything, Menken knew how to advertise. She was her own best publicist. She was the prime female example of that special brand of showmanship which is usually associated with men, specifically those who were engaged in "popular entertainments" during the second half of the nineteenth century. Her production had less straight dramatic quality than any of the previous productions of *Mazeppa;* much dialogue was cut and greater emphasis was placed on her "postures" both on and off the horse. This touch of "burlesque" combined with her imaginative, melodramatic approach to publicity, created a product that was closer to a circus or a Wild West show. It was this total approach that made Menken's *Mazeppa* a great hit.

LYDIA THOMPSON AND
THE "BRITISH BLONDES"

MARLIE MOSES

References to Lydia Thompson and her so-called British Blondes are most frequently found in discussions of the "leg business" or "naked drama" of the last quarter of the nineteenth century. Thompson has been credited with, or blamed for, the establishment of "nudity," i.e., the display of female legs, clad in tights and topped by short skirts or trunks, as a box-office attraction in the United States.

The revealed female form had been introduced on the American stage by Adah Isaacs Menken and had reappeared with the *danseuses* of *The Black Crook* and *The White Fawn*, but the phenomenon of women in tights, kicking and dancing on stage, appears to have settled into U.S. theatre history with the long run of *Ixion, or the Man at the Wheel*, which opened at Wood's Museum in New York on September 28, 1868, with Lydia Thompson in the title role.

After a highly successful run to capacity crowds, the company moved to Niblo's Gardens, establishing a total long-run record of forty-five weeks. A tour of the Eastern United States followed, the success of the troupe proving so profitable that, with only minor exceptions, for the next six years the company toured as far as California and played to enthusiastic American audiences, returning occasionally to New York and making intermittent voyages to England to secure new scripts, recruit new actors, and order new scenery and costumes.

Most treatises on the subject of modern burlesque cite Thompson and the female members of her troupe (which included men as well) as the first "queens" of burlesque—or at least as its "progenitresses."[1] Certainly the several extant photographs of the Blondes appear ludicrously prurient in their intent. And it was true that burlesque was regarded as a substandard literary form. History, however, has been unkind to Thompson and her associates, seizing on the evidence of the photographs and, more significantly, on the scathing reportage of the contemporary American press, and ignoring the contradicting evidence—especially the evidence of Thompson's stature in the English theatre.

Remembering that the New York stage of the 1860's was working to overcome its reputation as a rowdy, undisciplined, and unclean institution, it is not difficult to imagine the outrage engendered by the appearance on stage of women in tights. The scantily-clad Parisian dancers of *The Black*

Marlie Moses, Professor of English, Rhode Island Junior College, read a version of this paper at the American Theatre Association, 1977, and had a paper published in *Dramatics*, 1983.

Crook had subsided from the stage, and now for the second time in a decade the theatre had been invaded by a *foreign* element,

> an army of burlesque women who took ship for America, and presently the New York stage presented one disgraceful spectacle of padded legs jiggling and wriggling in the insensate follies and indecencies of the hour. . . . They do not either act, dance, sing, or mime; but they habit themselves in a way which is attractive to an indelicate taste, and their inefficiency in other regards is overlooked.[2]

So ran the accusation of the well-known actress-turned-author, Olive Logan, whose lengthy diatribes in magazines and in her books, *Before the Footlights and Behind the Scenes* and *Apropos of Women and Theatre*, consistently attacked the Thompson actresses for their "bleached blonde hair" as well as their "padded limbs." What Logan feared above all else was that the "naked drama" was debasing both actresses and the acting profession.

Others who believed the stage was imperiled by the Thompson company included the editors of *The Spirit of the Times*, who claimed that the burlesque company had

> not only enticed to their exhibitions a new public element from the suburbs, but so drained the old theatrical audiences of a percentage of their followers, that in a little while, nearly all the dramatic houses were forced to recruit their companies with lascivious attraction.[3]

The Spirit of the Times was especially antagonistic toward Thompson's husband, Alexander Henderson, the manager of the company, calling him a "shovel-nosed shark of humanity" and accusing him of indecent conduct with his actresses. Henderson was actually engaged in a fistfight by the drama critic of the *Spirit* but was vindicated in the ensuing court case he brought against the newspaper.

The battle waged by *The Spirit of the Times* went on for months, but it was a tame contretemps compared to the case in Chicago, a few months later, of the *Chicago Times* versus Lydia Thompson and Alexander Henderson.

Wilbur Story, editor of the *Times*, had had some trouble securing a box at Crosby's Opera House, where Thompson's company was performing. Taking out his anger in print, he went beyond the boundaries of editorial privilege, calling the company actresses "bawds" and "ladies of the evening," in issue after issue of the *Times*.

Lydia Thompson, according to the newspaper accounts of the trial, had endured enough. She proceeded to Story's residence, along with Henderson, her press agent Archie Gordon, and her friend and fellow trouper, Pauline Markham. The culprit was identified and held fast while Thompson plied a leather horsewhip to his neck and shoulders, following which the entourage rode straight away in a carriage. Thompson was arrested, tried, and fined $100, which she later testified was well worth the satisfaction she achieved.

Despite continually swelling box-office receipts and consistently favorable audience reception, Lydia Thompson's burlesque company never enjoyed a prestigious reputation in America. Lavish testimonials and benefits tendered her on her various American tours, as well as occasional testimonials in the press by such respected personages as Shakespearean scholar Richard Grant White did not seem to offset the tarnished reputation which she suffered during her initial engagement.

A member of her original company, for example, married Brander Matthews, the distinguished critic and scholar. All during his life he tried to cover up the fact that his wife, Ada Harland, had come to this country as one of the Blondes. In his autobiography of some 460 pages, Matthews devotes only a single line to his marriage—to a "Miss Ada Smith of London."[4]

Theatre historians have unwittingly perpetuated this tarnished view of Thompson and her theatrical associates—a view based primarily on her American reception. When one studies Thompson from the British vantage point, an entirely different reputation emerges. It might, therefore, be useful to examine briefly the life and career of the London actress.

Born in London in 1836, the young Lydia Thompson made her debut at age sixteen as a ballet dancer and won London hearts both as a dancer and later as an actor in Christmas pantomimes. Before she was twenty she had established herself as an outstanding Principal Boy in burlesque, pantomime, and extravaganza. On the basis of her London success she toured the Continent, including Russia, to high public acclaim. In later years, after her American success, she would tour India and Australia.

She was married twice, the first time to a nontheatrical businessman, to whom she bore a daughter, Zeffie Tilbury, who was also to pursue an acting career, the latter part of which she spent in Hollywood, where she died in 1947.

Thompson married Liverpool theatre manager Alexander Henderson in 1867, following which he acted as the company's business manager, planning not only the American tour but all of Thompson's subsequent productions. A year after Henderson's death in 1886, Thompson had a hand at theatre management, leasing the Strand in London. Despite capacity sales and lavish critical appraisal, the two productions mounted under her management were financially unsuccessful and she was forced to surrender her lease.

She continued to play her Principal Boy parts for years; well into her fifties she was the subject of unabashed praise and amazement over the extreme youthfulness of her face and figure.

The press in England was as generous as it was calumnious in America. Newspaper and magazine articles contained tributes to her gentility, modesty, kindness, sweet disposition, good humor, and flawless good taste. A magazine reporter stated that he couldn't help feeling awed in the presence of "the quiet little lady to whom all the world has paid homage, who has probably been applauded more than any living person."[5] Reviews of her performances unfailingly praised her grace of movement, her singing, her captivating style of comedy. The Victorian press, in short, adored her.

There is no hint of disapproval of her scanty costumes or suggestive dialogue, simply because both of these phenomena were part and parcel of the burlesque/pantomime tradition. The Principal Boy was a beloved part of this tradition, and British audiences loved and revered their Principal Boys. On the question of tights, Thompson was quoted in the *New York Herald* in 1895: "Some ladies upon the stage object to put them on. Why? Shakespeare's most lovely heroines wear tights—Rosalind, Viola, Imogen don them, and Joan of Arc as well." And on legs: "Many aver it was I who brought legs into prominence both in England and America, which statement is ridiculous. Legs were very much in evidence long before I was born or crossed the ocean."[6]

Probably the most dramatic testimonial to Thompson's integrity and popularity in England was the farewell benefit accorded her by her peers in 1899 on the occasion of her formal retirement from the stage. The event was staged at the Lyceum Theatre under the directorship of Sir Henry Irving. The General Committee of 106 included not only such theatrical luminaries as Pinero, Jones, Tree, Daly, Boucicault, D'Oyly Carte, and Forbes-Robertson, but also a glittering roster of royal sponsors. The farewell address was especially written by William S. Gilbert; following Thompson's delivery of the lengthy poem, there was reportedly not a dry eye in the house.

It would be a mistake to omit Henderson from this discussion of Lydia Thompson's conflicting American and English reputations. He first comes to the historian's attention as the manager who took over the Prince of Wales Theatre in Liverpool and refurbished it with such exquisite taste and with such painstaking attention to detail that it is not surprising to learn that it was directly from this Liverpool theatre that the Bancrofts made their way to London to set up their own Prince of Wales so renowned for its bandbox decor. It was Henderson, moreover, who first produced the Tom Robertson dramas, *Society* and *Ours*, thereby launching Robertson even before the Bancrofts succeeded in immortalizing him in their theatre. In London Henderson was the successful manager of the Charing Cross, the Folly, the Comedy, the Avenue, and the Globe—all respectable and successful theatres.

Lydia Thompson continued acting in London and the provinces after her final American appearance in 1891, but following her formal retirement in 1899 she played only a few dowager roles. Neither England nor America recognizes her fully as the popular performer she was, unquestionably because of the fact that she so divided her enterprise between the two countries. But she led a full and active stage life that spanned fifty-three years, forty-seven of which were relatively uninterrupted. She was the first Englishwoman to import her own company to America, and the first star of either sex to play an entire unbroken season in New York. She popularized burlesque and extravaganza in the United States, although she always denied that she was the first to do so, and she created a sensation in the process.

One of her dubious contributions was to start a rage for blond hair on the stage, although in this respect it is interesting to note her comment in a newspaper interview written in 1895: "Why my company should have gained the appellation of the 'Blondes' I cannot imagine," she testified, "for they were nearly all dark."[7]

She also helped to introduce the word *burlesque* into the language as a term for entertainment which utilizes suggestive songs and scantily-clad female dancers. Despite her occasional detractors, she won the hearts of her audiences, and she received numerous tributes from a legion of fascinated admirers.

One of these admirers was the young and handsome Grand Duke Alexis of Russia, who became enamored of Lydia Thompson and pursued her vainly as she toured the American hinterlands. Word reached New Orleans in 1872 that Thompson was arriving soon, with Alexis in breathless pursuit. The Mardi Gras—a theretofore mild celebration—would coincide with the prince's visit, and the city fathers decided to foster a spectacle in keeping with the visiting royalty. The result was the first Mardi Gras of the present tradition, complete with King Rex, fancy balls, and magnificent parades, all in tribute to a romantic liaison that in fact never materialized. The only memento of Lydia Thompson's involvement in the event is the adoption of "If I Ever Cease to Love"—her musical trademark—as the official Mardi Gras song.

HENRIETTA VINTON DAVIS: SHAKESPEAREAN ACTRESS

ERROL HILL

The stage career of Henrietta Vinton Davis encompasses all of the promise and frustration experienced by Black actors of her generation. She was born in Baltimore, her father being a talented musician who died prematurely. At

---

Errol Hill, Professor of Drama at Dartmouth College, is a director, playwright, and scholar with numerous publications including *The Theatre of Black Americans* and *Shakespeare in Sable,* in which this piece appears.

fifteen she graduated from a Washington school and took a teaching job in Maryland, but was back in Washington in 1878 as secretary in the office of the Recorder of Deeds. She became a student of Miss Marguerite Saxton, an esteemed elocutionist, and made her professional debut as a public reciter at Marini's Hall in Washington, D.C., on April 25, 1883. On hand to introduce her was the man under whom she served in the recorder's office, the leading Black statesman in the country, the honorable Frederick Douglass. It could not have been a more auspicious start to a long and brilliant career on the concert platform and legitimate stage.

Miss Davis was advertised as "the first lady of her race to publicly essay a debut in Shakespearean and other legitimate characters." Her recital program included speeches of two of Shakespeare's heroines: Juliet (from *Romeo and Juliet*) and Portia (from *The Merchant of Venice*). Clearly elated with this new evidence of race progress and conscious that the artist was a local resident, the *Washington Bee* rhapsodized:

> She came forward and from the time she said her first line to the close of the last sentence, she wrapped the whole audience so close to her that she became a queen of the stage in their eyes. One moment all was serene and quiet, deep pathos,—the next, all was laughter. . . . She is our first American lady leader, she will in due season become our star on the stage of tragedy and the drama.[1]

Miss Davis opened in Boston on July 17, 1883, appearing at the Young Men's Christian Union Hall on Boylston Street. Supporting her on the program were two Boston artists, the soprano Adelaide G. Smith and Samuel W. Jamieson, a pianist. She acquired professional managers who announced a tour immediately following her Boston engagement that included a number of towns and cities in the Eastern states. The Boston correspondent of the *New York Globe,* writing of her performance, recognized Miss Davis's potential as an actress but was not much impressed with her impersonations. He thought she would make a stronger impression in scene work with other actors than in solo recitations. However, a few weeks later at the Bethel A.M.E. Church in New York Miss Davis scored a notable success, her commanding presence and deep sonorous voice reminding her reviewer of Charlotte Cushman, first lady of the American stage. As Juliet in the potion scene from *Romeo and Juliet* she was "so true to the concept of a truly great artist as well as to nature, that the audience, electrified by the beautiful acting and the finished elocution of Miss Davis, applauded her to the very echo."[2]

At the end of her first season of performances, Miss Davis showed a marked improvement in her readings. She had added speeches of Rosalind in *As You Like It* and Cleopatra in *Antony and Cleopatra* to her repertoire, and expressed her desire to appear in a regular stage production next season supported by a full company of actors. This ambition seemed close to fulfillment when the *New York Globe* announced on March 29, 1884, that Miss Davis had been engaged by Thomas T. Symmons, manager of the Bohemia Dramatic Club, to appear at Whitney's Opera House, Detroit, on April 14. The club had evidently acquired an enviable local reputation and Mr. Symmons, himself a baritone soloist who subsequently took over Miss Davis's management and became her husband, planned to put his company on the road in a new drama with her as leading lady. There is no evidence that this project ever materialized. Miss Davis continued to build her reputation in frequent appearances around the country. In the May 3, 1884, issue of the *New York Globe*, an article entitled "Our Dramatic Artists" commented on her development as an actress:

> Miss H. Vinton Davis has shown undoubted talent as a delineator of Shakespearian characters. Her concepts are rich and original, while her stage presence is graceful, easy and natural. In humorous delineations she shows to good advantage, but her strongest forte is in characters like Lady Macbeth and Juliet. This artist is yet in her youth and has plenty of room in which to rise to an honorable position.

On a visit to Cincinnati, Miss Davis had teamed up with Powhatan Beaty in scenes from Shakespeare. The collaboration had worked so well that Beaty was invited to participate in an ambitious production at Ford's Opera House in Washington, D.C., on May 7, 1884. The program consisted of three scenes from *Macbeth*, *Richard III*, "which was performed almost entirely," and a scene from *Ingomar*. Miss Davis played Lady Macbeth, Lady Anne, and Parthenia; Beaty was Macbeth, King Henry VI, and Ingomar. Completing the company which was assembled for the occasion were a number of local amateurs, among them W. R. Davis, who made his stage debut as Gloster after King Richard, W.H.H. Hart as Earl of Richmond, and selected students from Howard University. Citizens and soldiers were supplied by the Washington Cadet Corps. Directing the production was Miss Saxton, the elocution teacher who had coached Miss Davis. The Opera House seating more than 1,100 was filled to capacity with a mixed audience of both races, the honorable Frederick Douglass and family occupying a private box.

The long and ecstatic notice in the *New York Globe* of May 17, 1884, commenced by saying that the three principals covered themselves with glory. It went on to discuss the performances of the leading actors:

> As Lady Macbeth, Miss Davis displayed wonderful powers of conception. While we failed to discover in her acting the dull, heavy, declamatory style complained of by some critics, to me it was plainly apparent that Miss Davis has great reserve dramatic powers, which have not been drawn upon because of the influence that always somehow represses the spontaneous outflow of genius in beginners. . . . The perfect adaptation of Miss Davis to her chosen profession is undisputed. She has earned the plaudits of professional critics, and her success has opened the dramatic door to

many. Thus leap by leap the colored man and woman encroach upon the ground so long held sacred by their white brother and sister.

Referring to notices in the white press about the production, this reviewer felt that the actors should be highly flattered because they were not criticized as colored people nor as beginners. Instead, they should regard such criticism as a compliment since every paper discovered among a few faults great merit in the embryo actors and actresses.

The review in one of these white papers, the *Washington Post* of May 8, 1884, is illuminating for its description of the atmosphere in the Opera House during the production. More than sixty years had elapsed since the African Company in lower New York was harassed by white patrons and forced to give up playing Shakespeare. The reception accorded these colored Shakespeareans in Ford's Opera House showed how little had changed in the mental attitude of those whites who refused to accept Black performers in productions of serious plays. The *Post* critic reports:

> There were many white people in the house who seemed disposed to turn to comedy the tragic efforts of the actors. In this they were not wholly successful, for the earnestness and intelligence of several of the leading performers were such as to command the respect of those most disposed to find cause for laughter in everything that was said or done. . . .
> The scene from *Macbeth* went creditably, all things considered, Miss Davis and Mr. Beaty showing a knowledge of the requirements of the parts which they essayed which, it is safe to say, surprised those in the audience competent to judge. The most enjoyable thing of the evening was *Richard III*. Here the "guying" disposition of the audience found ample opportunity to vent itself. . . . The combat between Richard and Richmond waked the most derisive plaudits from the auditors, and "Time" was repeatedly called by particularly irreverent individuals.

Over the next ten years, Miss Davis continued to perform regularly in an ever-widening circuit of cities, touring the South and West in addition to Eastern states. Her press notices grew more and more effusive. Appearing before a mostly white audience in Evanston, Illinois, in 1888, she held them "spellbound by the intensity of dramatic truthfulness she displayed" and was called "the most talented artist on the American stage."[3] In North Carolina, the *Goldsboro Argus* hailed her as "the greatest living genius of her race. . . . Her prodigious memory, her graceful control of every thought, word and action, her powerful delineations and her compass and modulation of voice are truly wonderful."[4] There were renewed calls for her to be accepted into a regular company presenting Shakespeare and other dramatic classics. The *New York Freeman* of January 23, 1886, found it singular that none of the brilliant musical and elocutionary exponents of the race had so far obtained a footing on the legitimate stage and cited lack of money as the principal drawback. It urged some public-spirited individual of means to take an interest in Miss Davis's career. All that was necessary to the fullest development of her dramatic powers, wrote the Boston correspondent of the *New York Freeman*, was an opportunity to be heard by the great devotees of the drama through free access to the competitive arena.[5] T. Thomas Fortune, writing in the *New York Age* of September 19, 1891, included Miss Davis among a few colored women actors who could achieve fame and fortune on the regular stage if only she could find a sponsor.

All appeals were in vain. Henrietta Vinton Davis, despite her manifest excellence as an actress, was unable to gain admission into the ranks of legitimate theatre companies, then exclusively under white management, because of her color. This racial boycott not only denied her professional fulfillment but deprived the theatre itself of a superbly talented actress whose art might have enriched the lives of countless playgoers. One would like to think that Shakespeare himself might have benefited from her interpretation of his heroines in properly mounted productions. The irony of the color bar as it applied to this actress is that Miss Davis was herself light-complexioned and not noticeably different from dozens of other actresses on the professional stage with inferior ability but without the stigma of African ancestry. A description of Miss Davis's physical appearance occurs in the Buffalo *Sunday Truth:*

> Miss Davis is a singularly beautiful woman, little more than a brunette, certainly no darker than a Spanish or Italian lady in hue, with illustriously expressive eyes and a mouth moulded upon Adelaide Neilson's. . . . We could not help thinking what a magnificent Cleopatra she would make to a competent Antony. She has made the part a study, we have been informed since seeing her in Association Hall, and hope to view her in it some day. Her reading of *Mary, Queen of Scots* was also very fine and elicited much applause.[6]

Miss Davis appeared but once with the Astor Place Company in its rather cursory production of *Damon and Pythias* in 1884. The next year she was billed to play Desdemona to Beaty's Othello in Cincinnati but there is no mention of the production in the available records and one is left in doubt whether it ever occurred. Then in 1898, after fourteen years of concert recitals, she was at last seen in a full-scale production of a play that she helped to write. This was an original five-act drama of the South entitled *Our Old Kentucky Home,* written in conjunction with the colored journalist J. E. Bruce. In it Miss Davis had the role of a Creole slave, Clothilde, whose courageous attack on a fort helped to bring about the end of the Civil War and reunite her with her lover, one of the freed slaves who had enlisted in the Union Army. The show toured the Eastern cities with marked success. Two years later, the *Colored American* carried a terse and ominous announcement: Miss Davis had signed for *The Country Coon,* one of the best shows to be presented next season. The title of this show would place it solidly among

the minstrel-cum-vaudeville type of variety acts that Black performers produced regularly for touring in second-rate theatres across the country. It was
the last place one would look for an artist of the caliber of Miss Davis. She
had done everything that could possibly be expected of a dedicated actress
to maintain the integrity of her art, which was directed toward the interpretation of dramatic masterpieces; now in utter frustration she was reduced
to playing in the popular music hall. She had presented a range of Shakespearean characters: Juliet, LadyMacbeth, Cleopatra, Ophelia, Portia, Desdemona, Lady Anne, and Queen Elizabeth, as well as other tragic heroines
from the nineteenth-century drama: Calanthe, Mary Stuart, Parthenia,
Leah, not in their completeness—that privilege had been denied her—but in
dramatic monologues and selected scenes to universal commendation. Now
she would play what? It is small consolation that the details of her assignment in the coon show are not known. The experience must have been
soul-destroying for Miss Davis was back on the concert circuit in 1901,
extending her itinerary to the great Northwest and West Coast where she
stayed for some three years before returning to her adopted home city of
Washington. In 1903 she revived *Our Old Kentucky Home* in Denver and
again played Clothilde, recited at the Palm Garden in New York in 1908, and
one final appearance occurred at the Trinity Congregational Church in
Pittsburgh in 1909 when she doubled in the roles of Zingarella, a flower girl,
and Dominique, a comic character, in the production of another original
play entitled *Dessalines* written by W. Edgar Easton. She had been acting
continuously for a quarter of a century and more. The *Colored American* of
February 22, 1902, provides a fitting summation to the career of this distinguished artist:

> Miss Davis is a remarkable woman, and had she not been handicapped by
> unfavorable racial origin, she would today by virtue of her acknowledged
> talents take rank with dramatic artists of the Leslie Carter, Maude Adams,
> Julia Marlowe and Henrietta Crosman school. This thought strikes us,
> since Washington is so honeycombed with prejudice against the Negro to
> the point that in few theaters can we secure a decent seat and colored
> traveling companies cannot secure dates—why could not an enterprising
> manager organize here a stock company on the order of Lafayette Square
> and produce plays of current human interest, adapted to the refined tastes
> of our best people who now refrain from attending the existing theaters
> because of the unjust treatment they are compelled to endure? The natural
> head of such an organization would be Miss Davis. With such a versatile
> artiste, capable of assuming roles from tragedy to light comedy, and a few
> other actors as a nucleus, a stock company of undoubted drawing qual-
> ities could be built up in a season. An adequate theater could be con-
> structed or a suitable hall could be remodeled to serve the purpose at a
> moderate expense. Now why not a theater for our people as a solution of
> the embarrassments that now confront us?

MARY SHAW: A FIGHTING CHAMPION

ROBERT A. SCHANKE

The most marvelous thing in the twentieth century is woman's discovery of woman.[1]

To me [there is always] the sustaining thought—the equality of woman's value as compared with man's. . . . We [women] must develop ourselves and must not allow our habits of thought, our inheritance, to retard our best expression. We must search for things within ourselves, not in our environment, and we must not drug ourselves with formulas and compromises.[2]

These words, modern as they appear, embody the goal of a woman who spoke them nearly seventy years ago, actress Mary Shaw. She led protest marches, organized strikes, founded women's clubs, and addressed international audiences. Flouting both critics and public opinion, she used the theatre as a vehicle for her feminist ideas.

Even before she became a Broadway star, Mary Shaw was an ardent champion of women's rights. On December 6, 1892, she enrolled as a charter member of the Professional Women's League, an organization dedicated to bringing "together women engaged in dramatic, musical, and literary pursuits with the purpose of rendering them helpful to each other."[3] Housed in their own building at Sixty-eighth and Broadway, the League sponsored numerous benefits, symposiums, bazaars, and exhibits—all focused on promoting the advancing role of woman in society. At monthly meetings, members performed plays, read position papers, and generally sought means to improve the status of the professional woman. By 1902 the League boasted 500 members, including such leading ladies as Ada Rehan, Mrs. Fiske, Helena Modjeska, Blanche Bates, and Lillian Russell.

Shaw served the League faithfully. For over twenty years she sat on the board of directors. In 1893 she starred as Rosalind in the League's all-female cast of *As You Like It*. Mme. Janauschek played Jaques. Scheduled for a single matinee performance on November 21, 1893, it proved so popular that in late January 1894 the League revived the production for one week.

But her work for the League was not limited to acting. In the spring of 1894 she organized a conference and symposium in New York entitled "The Woman of the Next Century." Joining her in reading papers were Maude Banks and Mrs. James Herne, wife of the playwright. Shaw granted interviews and presented speeches. She spoke out particularly on behalf of women artists. She recognized that one of the handicaps facing actresses

Robert A. Schanke, Director of Theatre at Central College, Pella, Iowa, has completed a book on *Ibsen in America, A Century of Change*.

who want equality with men is "that so many of them are unable to eliminate their sex consciousness."[4] Women have been brainwashed into believing they are inferior, but they must change that image. "Women," she demanded, "exert a tremendous and virtually irresistible influence over the stage. Not only the plays, but also the actors must please the women or fail hopelessly. The women who support our stage may make it, or they may mar it."[5]

Shaw resolved to be a woman who "made it," who influenced the stage. For many years she lacked the necessary credentials. She had played minor roles with the Boston Museum Stock Company for two years, had joined Augustin Daly's New York company for one season, and had supported famous stars in national tours for nearly ten years. Not until 1899, after acting for twenty-one years and promoting the women's movement for ten, did she merge her two interests: theatre and the fight for women's rights. The playwright she first turned to, the one whose female characters symbolized the very apotheosis of the emancipated woman, was Henrik Ibsen.

Her choosing Ibsen aligned her name with the controversial, contemporary theatre. His dramas had polarized theatre-goers. Leading the conservative attack, puritanical William Winter of the *New York Tribune* called Ibsen a writer "of a number of insipid, and sometimes tainted compositions, purporting to be plays. . . . He is an offence to taste and a burden upon patience." But leading Ibsen's defense was Shaw's friend and feminist leader Annie Nathan Meyer. Detecting "his strong sympathetic belief in the future of woman," she saluted Ibsen as "a prophet of the new womanhood."[6]

Mary Shaw agreed. When she chose to star in Ibsen's *Ghosts*, she realized the significance:

> Most of our plays and books and laws are masks. They lull us to sleep, give us moral peace. Ibsen had the courage to lift one corner of the mask and look at the dreadful thing, and there was a chorus of shrieks. Then, when he tore the mask away, pandemonium. The grinning mask which Ibsen tears away in *Ghosts* is the duty of wifely sacrifice in woman.[7]

When she chose to star in *Ghosts*, Shaw believed she had embarked on a holy crusade. Armed with her personal convictions and directed by internationally famous Emmanuel Reicher, stage manager of the Deutsches Theatre and a friend of Ibsen's, Mary Shaw performed one of the outstanding roles of her career. Praising her "cosmic range, suggestive power, profundity and extreme telling simplicity," critic Arthur W. Row hailed her performance as one of the "great moments in great acting."[8] She seemed, thought a critic for the *New York Dramatic Mirror*, June 10, 1899, like "a real woman." The *New York Times*, May 30, 1899, pronounced that "this was Ibsenism's greatest night in New York thus far." Mary Shaw had "achieved a new triumph."

Soon after this professional triumph, Shaw received a personal reward.

She was elected to represent the American theatre at the International Congress of Women held in London, June 26–July 5, 1899. Among the other American delegates were Susan B. Anthony, Rev. Anna Howard Shaw, and Mrs. May Wright Sewall. The goal of the Congress had remained constant since its formation in 1888: to promote unity among working women of the world and to apply the Golden Rule to all of society. When Mary Shaw arrived in London she joined 3,000 other women representing the countries of the world.

On June 30, 1899, Mary Shaw addressed the professional section of the Congress on "Drama as a Field for Women." Before the overflowing crowd, she proclaimed "that the drama was the aristocrat among the fine arts, and was a child of religion." To aspiring actresses in the audience who feared persecution, she declared, "Women who felt the dramatic instinct within them might enter the profession with confidence and hope. In spite of persecution, the drama at the present day enjoys a popularity the equal of which is given to few other institutions."[9] Her listeners were so impressed that they hastened to honor her. Henry Irving entertained her in his theatre. Herbert Beerbohm Tree invited her to act with his company. The honors culminated when she received an invitation to lunch with Queen Victoria at Windsor Castle and to travel there from London in a special train bearing an enormous banner: *Her Majesty Queen Victoria's Guests*.

Ironically, once Shaw returned to New York City after the Congress, she encountered persecution and opposition. Friends and colleagues criticized her diversity of interests; a true actress, after all, should be devoted to theatre alone. Managers chastised her for going to London, arguing "that an actress must be an actress and nothing else, to the public." The moment an actress appears as a lecturer she forfeits "that fascination of mystery" which is important to her art.[10] Indeed, even the critics, wearying of her feminist pronouncements, endorsed William Winter's observation: "Miss Shaw has shown signs of taking a more serious view of herself than anybody else ever has taken or ever will take."[11]

But unwilling to compromise her principles, Shaw resumed her feminist crusade. After a long run in *Ben Hur*, she joined actor Frank Gillmore as codirector and leading lady for George Fawcett's new theatre in Baltimore. In addition to the stock company productions typical of the period, they planned an Ibsen series of *Ghosts, A Doll's House, The Wild Duck*, and *John Gabriel Borkman*. Following its Baltimore run, each play would tour major Southern cities. The series opened on November 11, 1902, with *Ghosts*, advertised as "one of the dramatic surprises of the season." And that it was, for the production closed after three performances. A *Baltimore American* critic hailed Shaw's "artistic touches," but he regretted that the large audience had been shown such a "morbid and gruesome drama." In answer to mounting protests, Fawcett announced that since it was "not a play for the majority of theatregoers," he would halt the Ibsen series and send *Ghosts* on the road.

In spite of the setback in her plans, Mary Shaw continued her defense of Ibsenism. As time approached for the five-month tour, she anticipated the public's growing awareness that Ibsen "exerted an influence for good."[12] The critics' reactions during the tour rivaled those she had received four years earlier. The *New York Times*, January 27, 1903, recorded that her "sterling performance" of Mrs. Alving seemed as tragic as Hamlet or Phaedra. Another New Yorker noted that Shaw challenged comparison with the great Eleonora Duse. In Chicago, W. L. Hubbard of the *Chicago Tribune*, May 8, 1903, praised the "spirit of naturalness" and the "harmony of ensemble." He singled out Mary Shaw as an "actress of distinctly agreeable simplicity and directness of method." The production proved so popular with Chicagoans that a special return engagement of three performances was held a few weeks later.

Once the Chicago run finally ended, Shaw began a venture unprecedented in American theatre history: a thirty-seven-week tour of Ibsen's *Ghosts*. In a series of one-night stands, the trailblazing company traveled to Wisconsin, Minnesota, North and South Dakota, Colorado, Wyoming, Nevada, Nebraska, Iowa, Kansas, Missouri, Tennessee, and Kentucky. They played to farmers, cowboys, cattle punchers, and wheat harvesters. In Genoa, Nebraska, they even appeared before a tribe of Indians! By the time Shaw returned to Chicago in March 1904, she had performed *Ghosts* 225 times in fifteen months and had traveled over 16,000 miles.[13]

Fortified by the tour's success, Shaw expanded her repertoire by again attempting an Ibsen series, premiering her ambitious project on March 2, 1904, with *Hedda Gabler*. The determined actress held definitive views about the title character:

Hedda Gabler is a distinct type of twentieth century woman. She is symbolic inasmuch as she typifies some of the gravest complexities to be met with in certain modern women. She is a skeptic. She has no ideals. She has the twentieth century lust for money and power. Being a woman, she knows that these can only be obtained through a man; she wishes to gain wealth and influence through man, but will give nothing in return.

In her performance of Hedda, Shaw intended to illustrate "the penalty women pay for tampering with social laws."[14]

Regardless of her noble aims, the Chicago reception was decidedly hostile. Critic W. L. Hubbard in the *Tribune* of March 3, 1904, had hailed Shaw's performance in *Ghosts*, but he now berated her for portraying the ignoble Hedda. The *Chicago Record Herald's* James O'Donnell Bennett in March 1904 denounced her incessant movements, flounces across the stage, constant fidgeting, and wringing of her hands. He thought she made Hedda "downright rude." Echoing the attacks of many critics, Amy Leslie of the *Chicago Daily News* on March 11, 1904, charged Shaw with presenting a "gospel of despair, of revolution, of dethroning tenets and creeds." The actress had contracted for an evening run at the large Steinway Hall, but once the theatre owner saw the notices, he persuaded the local fire commissioner to condemn his theatre as a fire hazard.[15] Refusing defeat, staunch Mary Shaw continued with matinee performances at a vaudeville house.

A less decisive woman might have yielded, might have returned to playing safe and popular scripts. But for Mary Shaw, opposition "only spurred her on" to more feminist advocacy.[16] She chose, therefore, to star in what became one of America's most sensational premieres, George Bernard Shaw's *Mrs. Warren's Profession*, a play focusing on a woman who avoids starvation and the bleak life of the factory by resorting to prostitution. Through the title character, the playwright had intended to "advocate moral reform."[17]

Nevertheless, even the intelligentsia opposed the play. Indeed, the editors of *The Theatre* magazine in December 1905 ran a two-page argument entitled "The People vs. George Bernard Shaw." Labeling him a literary anarchist, they insisted that the play was "wholly unfit for public representation." Such attacks created a sensational climate before the Broadway opening. While the play was in rehearsal, the secretary of the Society for the Suppression of Vice in New York, Anthony Comstock, warned producer Arnold Daly against bringing the show to Broadway, announcing that "whatever outrages public decency and is injurious to public morals is indictable."[18] William McAdoo, New York City Police Commissioner, echoed support: "If New York should adopt his [Shaw's] moral code I would resign my Police Commission in an hour." He personally censored many lines of the script and threatened to close the production if his orders went unheeded. Furthermore, all of the playwright's dramas were banned from the open shelves of the more than thirty libraries in the city.

By the time the company arrived in New York, the atmosphere was tense. On opening night, an estimated 10,000 people crowded around the theatre. Scalpers sold tickets for as high as thirty dollars apiece. Once the play began, all seats were sold, hundreds were standing in the aisles, and nearly 3,000 were turned away. Extra police were ordered to handle the curious mob. The following day, however, the press spared no venom:

> The lid was lifted by Mr. Arnold Daly and the limit of stage indecency reached last night. . . . It defends immorality. It glorifies debauchery.

> But "the lid" was lifted for only one night. The morning after the opening, the production was closed, and Arnold Daly and the cast were summoned to court to answer charges of appearing in an immoral play. Only after an eight month legal battle were they acquitted. The presiding judge noted that "if virtue does not receive its usual reward in this play, vice at least is presented in an odious light" and ruled that the play could be performed.[19]

Following the court decision, the play reopened on Broadway but created less excitement. Rennold Wolf of the *New York Telegraph* remarked that all seemed comparatively tame now that the play bore "the stamp of the court's approval." Even so, all seats were sold out, and scalpers again sold tickets on the sidewalks. As before, Mary Shaw's performance received commendation for being "a treat in itself." Wolf ranked her as "one of the truly distinguished actresses on our stage." But regardless of the acting, most critics still agreed that the play was definitely "unfit for the general theatre."

When the limited Broadway run closed, Mary Shaw embarked on another crusading, coast-to-coast tour, supplementing *Mrs. Warren's Profession* with *Ghosts* and *Candida*, another feminist play. Soon after the tour, she selected to star in another feminist play, this one dealing with a growing issue in American politics: women's suffrage. She held firm beliefs on the subject. In fact, she insisted that the very "principle of democracy [was] at stake." Votes for women, she argued, meant "one step further toward the goal of self-government."[20]

Little wonder that the play entitled *Votes for Women* attracted Shaw's attention. Written by Elizabeth Robins, an American actress living in London, the plot revolves around Vida Levering, a suffragette who accidentally meets her former lover and his fiancée. Many of Vida's lines provided Shaw with ammunition for the women's movement:

> Some girls think it hardship to have to earn their living. The horror is not to be allowed to.
> We have to learn [to] get over our touching faith that, because a man tells us something, it's true.

When the character addressed a suffragette rally in Trafalgar Square, she presented an impassioned plea for women:

> We must get the conditions of life made fairer. We women must organize. We must learn to work together. We have all worked so long and so exclusively for men, we hardly know how to work for one another. But we must learn.

Vida's thoughts sounded so much like Mary Shaw's that some theatre-goers must have wondered if she were really acting.

Actually, the opening on March 15, 1909, did appear more like a political rally than a theatrical premiere. Suffragettes representing the Interurban Council of Women Suffrage Clubs, the Union Club, and the Equality League of Self-Supporting Women crowded the theatre. Members of the American Suffragettes were conspicuous with yellow buttons pinned to their lapels. Banners flew from the balcony. Women from the Harlem Equal Rights League marched during intermission with placards reading "Women vote in 4 Western States. Why not in New York?" Frequent bursts of applause accompanied entrances and exits, the rise and fall of the curtain, and emotion-filled lines of dialogue added to the excitement.

Although the suffragettes endorsed the production, the critics did not. Charles Darnton chastised the cast for its lack of polish. A writer for the *New York Times*, March 16, 1909, complained that the play was too obviously a propagandist tract that avoided realistic confrontation of the issues. Another *Times* reviewer attacked the characterizations: "The people who are opposed to suffrage . . . are insistently represented as unsympathetic, if not ignorant types, while all the virtue is on the other side." Even Shaw's performance was damned with faint praise. Her acting "was so much better than the play," wrote one critic, of the *Dramatic Mirror*, that he "felt sorry for her. . . . *Votes for Women* would have throttled the artistry from a Heaven-sent genius." The *New York Times* complimented her attempt at saving the script but recognized she was limited by a "wildly improbable scenario." Perhaps most pointed was Charles Darnton. Shaw's decision to perform in the play bewildered him, for it seemed nothing more than an inferior *Mrs. Warren's Profession*.

Unheedful of Darnton's advice to choose better scripts, Shaw continued championing feminist dramas, regardless of their quality. Only a few months after *Votes for Women* closed, she starred in Paul Bourget's *Divorce*, a lengthy discussion of the problems women encounter in common-law marriages. Critics denounced the tedious dialogue, stilted translation, and confusing plot. In addition, they unanimously condemned Shaw's performance. For over a decade Mary Shaw had used the theatre as a vehicle for her feminist ideas. With evangelistic fervor, she had starred in *Ghosts*, *Hedda Gabler*, *Candida*, *Mrs. Warren's Profession*, *Votes for Women*, *Divorce*, and *New York*, thereby linking her name indelibly with propagandist theatre and with the image of the emancipated woman. Her last three Broadway performances were such critical failures that she did not appear in New York for four seasons. Instead, she toured and wrote articles about the theatre. With the exceptions of her own revivals of *Ghosts* and *Mrs. Warren's Profession*, she never again enjoyed star billing on Broadway. Her politics had marred her career.

As her professional popularity waned, Shaw devoted even more time to championing women's rights. Foremost in her interest was the founding of a new woman's organization, the Gamut Club. A number of professional clubs already existed: the Professional Women's League, which she helped found in 1892, the Twelfth Night Club, the Charlotte Cushman Club, and the Rehearsal Club. But Shaw found all of these lacking in proper focus. "Tea table tattle, bridge, and banalities" had become their chief interest, she argued. Undoubtedly, a major impulse for her beginning a new club was her defeat for the presidency of the Professional Women's League by what she called "Tammany tactics."

Instead of a club for "rich women with fat pocketbooks" Shaw wanted "an aristocracy of brains." She declared the time was right:

> I consider the Gamut Club offers a wonderful avenue of education in tolerance and kindness and Christian charity. These are things women need to learn—loyalty to their sex and patience with each other and appreciation of the individual struggle every woman is making in her particular line of endeavor.[21]

Shaw's goal, therefore, was to provide a meeting place for the busy professional woman, a kind of "halfway house for rest and rendezvous."[22]

With Mary Shaw as president and Lillian Russell as vice-president, the Gamut Club officially began on July 13, 1913. Reasons for the name were twofold: it articulated the goal to represent most of the arts and professions and it bestowed honor on a men's club of that name in Los Angeles that had given Shaw honorary membership a decade earlier. The board of directors drew up unique qualifications for membership. All women were warned that they "must amount to something." If they were not professional artists, teachers, or doctors, they had to prove they were "vitally interested" in one of those areas. The board further announced: "Positively no parasites permitted. The Idle Rich are severely debarred."[23] Perhaps aided by these elitist restrictions, applications for membership poured in quickly. By October 1914 the roll books listed 250 members.

As president, Shaw organized a variety of club activities—monthly dinners, dances, and skits. At least once each year she directed members in a play. Since many of the women were theatre artists, she sought "to encourage dramatic and theatric material in the club whether in decorations, acting itself, or in playwriting, and to present plays not practical in the commercial theater."[24] One of her most popular productions was of a play she wrote herself: *The Parrot's Cage*. In the biting satire, Shaw gave five women costumed like parrots the opportunity to perch and to talk of feminism. The feminist Free-Souled Parrot struggled to break the chain around her leg and chattered, "I want to be free! I want to be free!" A sneering Idealist Parrot sniffed in reply, "A parrot's highest mission is to amuse."[25] In her *Impressionistic Sketch of the Anti-Suffragists*, Shaw had the "antis" recite their daily pledge:

> I pledge myself to remember each day, at every hour, that there are only two great moments in a woman's life. The first, when she gives her first kiss to her lover; the second, when she kisses her own little baby.[26]

But the activities of the Gamut Club had a serious side as well. Shaw urged members to support the "dress strike" initiated by the Women's Political Union in 1912. Women backing the strike pledged to buy no new clothes until 1915 when the suffrage amendment was to reach the referendum stage.[27]

Calling attention to the injustice done to women by the wanton slaughter of their sons, Shaw rallied club members for a Peace Parade to protest against World War I. When the Peace Parade actually occurred on August 29, 1914, Shaw and the Gamut Club led over 15,000 women from Columbus Circle down Broadway to Union Square. Wearing black and carrying no flags or banners, they represented a silent "prayer for peace."

Protesting was not the club's only involvement with the war effort. Once the country became involved, members labored with war drives, sold Liberty Bonds, made surgical dressings, helped the Red Cross, and hosted open houses for soldiers every Sunday. The Gamut was the first woman's club in

New York to open its doors as a canteen. Drawing on the talents of the members, Shaw presented a number of original one-act plays for the servicemen. One of the plays, *Wrong Numbers*, by Essex Dane, they toured to almost every camp and hospital within a fifty-mile radius of New York City, performing 439 times.

Yet the years following 1914 were not totally devoid of professional theatre work for Mary Shaw. In 1916, she toured *The Melody of Youth*. She starred in New York revivals of *Ghosts* in 1917 and 1918 and of *Mrs. Warren's Profession* in 1917, 1918, and 1922. Much of her time was spent working with Jessie Bonstelle to found a Woman's National Theatre. Their scheme called for a parent company in New York with subsidiary companies in other cities. Not wanting to antagonize commercial managers, they decided to limit productions to American authors and American actors. Men could perform for the company, but they would not be connected with the management. As Shaw argued, male managers make it "impossible to 'get across' any real and distinctive feminine feeling or opinions."

> Although 75 per cent of the theatre-going public is composed of women and consequently the managers are lying awake nights trying to secure productions which will make a hit with them, they obstinately refuse to accept woman's judgment. No matter what an author says, the play is remodelled and whipped into shape by those men in charge, who cause the heroines to talk and act not as real women would but as men think that women ought to talk and act.[28]

The idea for this new theatre was certainly unique. It failed, however, since the goal of raising $1 million to begin the project never materialized.

Shaw's final venture in theatre occurred during the 1927–28 season when she starred in Eva Le Gallienne's twenty-three-week national tour of *The Cradle Song*. Shaw's performance of the Prioress was hailed at every stop. The tour, however, provided Mary Shaw with more than critical acclaim; it opened up more platforms for her to speak out on women's rights. As in past tours, she spoke at many women's clubs. Her theme now—women must save the theatre. "The legitimate stage is in a perilous state," she proclaimed. "And only through the efforts and interest of woman can it be saved."

For over thirty years, Mary Shaw had struggled for the women's movement, using her talents as an actress to reach the public. Her persistent crusading prompted the editors of *McClure's* magazine to claim that she, more than any other actress in the country, stood for what was "new and daring and experimental in dramatic art." At a memorial service at New York's Little Church Around the Corner following her death in 1929, Edwin Milton Royle dedicated America's first stained-glass window in honor of an actress and pronounced Mary Shaw "a fighting champion." He recognized her challenging mind and authoritative performing had created "a distinct influence on the stage of her time." She had devoted both her career and her life to the advancement of women's rights. This pioneering actress, he concluded, had left a "trace on the universe."[29]

AILEEN STANLEY, HER LIFE AND TIMES
GRAYCE SUSAN BURIAN

The life and times of Aileen Stanley are synonymous with the life and times of popular entertainment in America in the first half of the twentieth century. She was a single woman headliner in vaudeville, she starred in three Broadway musicals, and she was among the pioneer performers in recording, radio, and television.

She was born Maude Elsie Aileen Muggeridge in Chicago in 1893, during the time of the great depression. She was named Maude after Maude S., the winning trotting horse of the day, but she was called Aileen. Her father died seven months before she was born. He had contracted typhoid from another daughter who died of the disease just three weeks earlier. But Aileen had two older brothers, Robert and Stanley, and her mother was young and healthy and was soon able to move out of the tenements in which they lived into a house that she opened up for roomers.

It was while living in the rooming house, being catered to and petted by immigrant boarders, that Aileen learned to be a great mimic. She used to sing for the boarders and sometimes mimic their accents. Stanley, two years older than Aileen, showed some musical talent also.

Their mother, Maria, being an enterprising woman, saw in the children's talents a way to earn some money and so raise their living standard. She set about getting a little act together which played at the various organizations around Chicago—the Shriners, Eastern Star, Knights of Columbus, all of whom paid the glorious sum of five dollars per show. The act proved so successful that Maria decided to try for the vaudeville circuits.

She sent out flyers that she had made: "Stanley and Aileen, the Peerless English Juveniles" (the family had come over from England just a couple of years before Aileen's birth) and sometimes "Premier Versatile Entertainers."

The act was very rough to begin with, but Maria managed to get them booked on the Western circuit. At eighty-two years old, Aileen could recall a song she sang during that first booking. One of the verses went,

Grayce Susan Burian, Professor, Department of Humanities, Schenectady Community College, runs the Theatre Program. This paper, presented at the Popular Culture Association, 1978, is based in part on her acquaintance with Aileen Stanley, who provided a rich store of personal materials, also used in a 1986 article for *Theatre File*, London.

Oh Auntie, Auntie, although we live in a shanty,
Just be contented, dear, and someday you will see.
Oh, when I get bigger, money won't cut any figure,
Then I'll have plenty for you, Auntie.

She remembered:

That little song was done in the middle of our act. We opened with a very pretty little sophisticated number called "Ere I Wander in the Bright Moonlight," and then Stan came out and sang in his lovely tenor voice and then did a dance. At that time I changed to a farmer outfit—with a little gingham apron, white socks and shoes, and a little umbrella. I wore pigtails under a little farmer hat. I came out and started with the verses and chorus of "My Auntie," and I would stop the show cold. Then I'd look to the wings and I'd say, "Here comes my best beau." That was my brother Stan. He had changed to farmers' overalls and came out and sang "Maria—you set my heart on fire, the highest flyer of all the Marias in town." Then we did a little dance together and we closed with a chorus of "Maria."

In late 1903, Stanley and Aileen toured from Chicago through the Middle West, reaching the West Coast early in 1904. Then they toured up and down the coast on the Pantages Time for more than a year. Of that tour, Aileen could recall at eighty-two the "storefront shows" that became popular at the turn of the century:

The theatre was a vacant store and the manager, who was employed by the telephone company by day, put seats in the store and made a theatre out of it with a rolling curtain that pulled up and down in front of the stage, which was just a platform with a wood scene painted on a back canvas. The footlights were gas lights and the manager pulled the curtain up and down—he did everything. The orchestra was a pianist. We did two shows, one at 7:00 and a late show at about 9:00. We were home in bed by 10:30. We were the only act, and this, plus a one-reeler, was the show. The admission charge was twenty-five cents for the first show and ten cents for the late show, and if the house wasn't full for the second show, the manager would pass the hat.

And so the three traveled on for years on the circuits going westward and back to Chicago repeatedly. They traveled with a sewing machine (Maria made all their costumes as well as their clothes), a box of toys, and two dogs. Maria tried to make the little rooms they stayed in like home, preparing home-cooked meals, sometimes holding a frying pan over a gas jet on the wall.

On these circuits they didn't play only two-a-day. Some theatres had four, six, and eight shows a day. Continuous vaudeville was becoming popular. The salary—a mammoth $50 to $60 for each week they worked. Why shouldn't they continue? Maria gave them their education. They were avid readers. This helped them to get past the Gerry Society that had sprung up in each city to keep children off the stage unless they could prove that they were getting their schoolwork done and living a normal life. Aileen was always a big girl. At six she looked nine. That didn't help with train fares although it did with the Gerry Society. Aileen tells of those times:

> Maria put short pants on Stan and little baby dresses on me because she couldn't afford to pay those fares. . . . When we got on the train once, a conductor got hold of me and said, "Listen, how old are you really?" And I said, "Well, if you won't tell anyone, I'm nine years old really, but six on the train, but when I come up for the Gerry Society, I'm sixteen."

The traveling continued. Sometimes they'd change their act, but it would take at least two years to get each act perfected. They played in Box Houses, sometimes called Honky Tonks, as well as storefront theatres, and sometimes even real theatres. In some of the out-of-way places in the West, Aileen remembered that the audience, which usually consisted of miners, would throw nuggets sometimes containing specks of gold at them, so she always had a pocket in her costume.

They soon got tired of traveling and since Chicago now had about seventy-five Nickelodeons or Five and Ten Cent theatres, Maria decided it might be good to settle back in Chicago for a while and have the children work in those. In 1911, Stanley and Aileen played Nickelodeons; they performed about twenty shows a day and received $65 a week.

It wasn't long before they had worked practically every Nickelodeon in the area. Stan then decided to try the burlesque houses of Chicago. One burlesque house in particular said that would take the two, but along with their act, Stan would have to be a straight man for other acts and Aileen would have to dance in the chorus and do little solo singing and dancing numbers between the acts. The house was the U.S. Music Hall on Harrison and State streets. There were eight shows a day, seven days a week. When she wasn't on stage, Aileen was rehearsing down in the stone basement. She claims that working at that burlesque house was the busiest time she ever put in. But it wasn't long before Stan became restless and ran off with a chorus girl with whom he formed a new act.

That left Aileen on her own, with the name Aileen Muggeridge—one that would never do on a marquee when she became famous. So instead of Aileen of Stanley and Aileen, she decided she would be Aileen Stanley, a single-woman act in vaudeville. She had a sweet personality, nice soprano voice, and charm; it wasn't difficult for her to move on to some of the nicer dinner places and cafés in Chicago. However, she longed to make the big time in New York. She made a short trip there but could find work only as a song plugger. Another song plugger she met and worked with for a while was George Gershwin.

One of the cafés she had worked for in Chicago, the North American, asked her back and she went. There an agent from the Orpheum Circuit, Harry Weber, signed her up and sent her on a tour through Canada and the Middle West and West again. After 1919 she toured almost without break on the United and Orpheum Times, perfecting her single-woman act. Soon she even played the Palace in New York and received a page and a half bad review from Sime Silverman, but she would return later to rave reviews from everyone. Her style—a sweet young thing always, fresh and wide-eyed, albeit a little overweight. At the height of her career she stood five foot eight in her stocking feet and weighed 149 pounds.

That same year—and she was almost twenty-seven years old, while on the Orpheum Circuit—Weber had her audition for a show in New York, *Silks and Satins*, written and produced by William Rock. She got the role, which was nothing more than Aileen singing her own songs. No real book. But while she was in *Silks and Satins*, she decided to try the record companies—maybe she could make Victrola records. At that time the companies were just experimenting with electrical recordings and reproduction. The equipment was still rather crude. There were no microphones as yet—the singers had to sing into a huge horn. The first company she tried was Pathé. They could use her. The Victor company wanted her exclusively but she decided only to freelance for a while. So when *Silks and Satins* was closing and about to go on the road, Aileen tossed a coin to help decide whether she should stay in New York to make records or go on the road. New York and the records won.

But while making records in New York she was asked to tour for Keith and Albee. She had a special contract that enabled her to play in New York after being outside for a certain time so that she could make her records, and for many years afterward, all her touring was planned this way. Usually her recording sessions would coincide with her dates at the Palace or other theatres in New York City. In between shows she would get into a taxi with a sandwich and her sheet music, eat and study on the way to the studio, record almost cold or with a rehearsal or two, and get back to the theatre for the next show.

Between 1920 and 1936 she managed to record over 215 sides for Victor, His Master's Voice, English Brunswick, English Decca, and many other English and American companies. By 1923 Aileen was recording exclusively for Victor and did so until 1930, and then for His Master's Voice in England until 1936.

She always continued her performing either on the circuits or in England. The year 1922 was typical of most of those Aileen spent on the Orpheum and Keith-Albee Times. Here is a rundown of the places she played between January and December 1922. Each city represents at least one week of performances: Des Moines, Davenport, Cedar Rapids in Iowa, St. Paul, New York City—both the Palace and the Coliseum—Chicago, Milwaukee, Chicago, Milwaukee, Chicago, St. Louis, Memphis, New Orleans, New York

City, Brooklyn, Washington, D.C., Baltimore, Philadelphia, New York City, Baltimore, New York City, Richmond, Atlantic City, Columbus, Indianapolis, Baltimore, Montclair, N.J., Buffalo, Toronto, Montreal, New York City, Philadelphia, Buffalo, Hartford, Cleveland. She did take a couple of hours off on January 4 of this year, while she was playing Minneapolis, to marry her accompanist, Robert Buttenuth, but this was done in between shows. She didn't miss a performance. This kind of touring would continue for years. From January to June rarely did she have a week off, and during the summer months she'd play fairs and special smaller engagements.

She did take time out from the circuits to star with Phil Baker in three Broadway shows for J. J. Shubert: *Night in Spain, Pleasure Bound*, and *Artists and Models*. It was during *Pleasure Bound* in 1929 that the *New York Post* reported on May 18: "When Aileen Stanley sings a new song, that song goes echoing from one end of the country to the other and across more than one continent, for over 25,000,000 victrola records of her songs have been sold, a mark that even Caruso himself never touched."

Why was she so popular? Possibly because throughout her career Aileen mixed humorous numbers with those that were sentimental, nostalgic, wistful. They were always on the light side. There were never any dark or tragic overtones, and rarely is any pain or genuine heartache expressed; even in a song like "It's All Over Now," the dominant tone or feeling is one of charm rather than grief. The main effect is one of unaffected, unpretentious innocence if not indeed naïveté. Even in her novelty songs these same qualities are what stand out.

Aileen also got in on the ground floor of broadcasting. She appeared with Rudy Vallee on the "Fleischmann Hour" and on the Paul Whiteman show many times. She did thirteen weeks of the "Oldsmobile Hour" and starred in many of her own radio programs both in the U.S. and England between the years 1929 and 1937. Her records had become popular in England, where she performed five different years, from 1925 to 1937.

From August 1923 to April 1935, her husband, Bob, kept a diary of every theatre or club date that they played, and also made significant notations on certain engagements. The diary helps to explain what glorious days those must have been during the twenties and early thirties for American performers in London. Aileen played the intimate supper clubs frequented by the upper crust of society, was one of their favorite entertainers and so joined in their amusements.

Aileen had a repertoire of about a dozen songs and would vary the songs at each engagement. Sometimes, if she had time, she would taxi to the hotel for a change of gown, or she would wear one gown on top of the other and remove the top one for a change. At times she used this trick in her act if she needed a quick change.

Many times after a busy schedule, she would also be invited to parties that sometimes lasted all night. Typical was an entry Bob made in his diary on

December 18, 1927. After a full evening of performing at several different clubs, Bob wrote:

> Wednesday night Prince of Wales gave party at Lady Benson's house—sent car for Aileen—had marvelous time—Prince drove us home personally at 5:30 A.M.

Of course, Aileen always had to sing for her supper at those parties.

By 1931 vaudeville was supposed to be dying, but not for Aileen. In 1931 she was booked solid, playing the picture houses which boasted movies featuring such stars as William Powell, George Arliss, Mary Pickford, Laurel and Hardy—but still offered vaudeville in between the showings.

In February of 1934 Aileen was back in London sharing the bill at the Palladium with Ethel Barrymore who was doing a one-act play, *The Twelve Pound Look*. It may be of interest to hear part of *Variety*'s review of the opening:

> It is a question whether the Palladium management didn't make a mistake in giving Ethel Barrymore the headline honors in the billing for the week of February 5.
>
> Hindsight is always clearer, and it is more than likely had they billed Aileen Stanley more elaborately they might have gathered a larger audience for the opening night. Miss Stanley, it may be recalled, was a most emphatic success here some years ago and nightly packed the Kit-Kat Club.
>
> Miss Barrymore, in Barrie's "Twelve Pound Look," . . . appeared and departed without creating any profound impression for or against.
>
> Miss Stanley, on the other hand, is modernity personified, with her interpretations of Broadway melodies, in a simple white silk gown cut on classic lines.

Miss Barrymore called on Aileen and asked what she would do in the light of such reviews. Aileen said, "Quit." Barrymore did so and then sent Aileen a beaded evening bag as a gift.

Aileen was utterly devoted to her career. When she married Bob Buttenuth, there was no notice of it in the papers. She kept her marriage a secret to all but her closest friends. Her life was devoted to her work, to rehearsing and performing. She rarely partied. After performances she went back to the hotel for a good night's sleep. In the morning she'd do some form of exercise, swimming if at all possible. The partying that she did in London was unusual for her.

She was happier when working and would allow nothing to interfere with work—not even her marriage. Bob wanted to relax and play after performances but he had to do so alone. Eventually this led to divorce. But they were always friends, right up to his death.

Because most people did not know of her marriage, she was often linked with other men by the press. One of those men was the Prince of Wales. On June 2, 1935, the *Minneapolis Sunday Tribune* ran an article on the thirty-eight women in the prince's life—speculating as to which he would marry. Aileen was one of those named, along with Wallace Simpson. The prince, however, knew Aileen and Bob were married, and when he and Aileen partied, Bob was always along.

In 1937 Aileen made her last trip to England, for the first time without Bob Buttenuth, now her ex-husband, accompanying her. *Variety* wrote of one of her appearances at the Holborn Empire: "Beautiful and attractive Aileen Stanley pays a quick return and brings with her a budget of new numbers. Her syncopated song-singing with the introduction of a tuneful 'blues' song or two is very attractive entertainment. A delightful personality is the gift of Miss Stanley and also the ability to render songs with the correct expression."

It was on her return from this trip, however, that Aileen discovered that vaudeville was in trouble because of competition from radio and movies, and the threat of television. Performers were no longer being offered huge salaries. She refused to work for less than her normal fee, which was quite high. The time did seem right for her to do what she had been thinking of doing, namely, to train and manage young singers. She opened a coaching studio that Bob Buttenuth managed, and from 1937 until 1959 coached and managed young singers from her four-room suite in the Brill Building. Then Bob died. She closed the studio and moved to retirement in Hollywood, where she still lives in a little four-room house on Hammond Street.

Aileen Stanley is indeed the epitome of the American success story. A woman with no formal education, who started her career playing one-night stands in storefront theatres and honky-tonks could entertain and be entertained by England's nobility. Hers was a special kind of growth, of education. She was endowed with natural resources that she was able to tap and to build on as she moved from stage to stage of her career and her life. Few people, no matter what the profession, can look back on a life of so much fulfillment and so few regrets. The very fact that she never quite achieved the status of a superstar, that in her prime she received featured billing more often than top billing, makes her career seem all the more representative of mainstream popular entertainment—a revealing chronicle of its performers and its audience.

THE ART OF RUTH DRAPER

MURIEL MCKENNA

On her casket lay a collection of shawls, not flowers. It was at her own request. To the people who came to mourn her passing it was a fitting symbol of the many characters those shawls had evoked under her matchless performance.

Ruth Draper, the inimitable, had passed away in her sleep at the age of seventy-two, in December of 1956. She had just opened in New York that week for what was an almost annual appearance, and had planned to start on another transcontinental tour with her cast of characters.

Ruth Draper! The name is almost synonymous with solo theatre. And theatre it was, uniquely her own, even though the costume was no more than one of those shawls, the scenery a chair or table on the bare stage. No matter. Her artistry transformed them into whatever illusion she wished to create, the stage was peopled with other characters who were visible in the imagination of her audience as if right there on the stage.

What should one call her? Some have called her a diseuse, but that term, meaning literally "a speaker of songs," suggests Yvette Guilbert and others of that type of entertainment. Although she gave new meaning to the word *monologuist*, that term has connotations of the old-style elocutionists with all their affectations. She considered herself a "character actress." She was a consummate actress and always a solo performer. Probably the best term would be "one-woman theatre," for that is what her performances really were.

Miss Draper was born in New York City in 1884. Her grandfather was Charles Dana, the famous publisher. Even as a small child Ruth was a delightful mimic and entertained her family and friends with her little character sketches.

It was in 1916 that she first appeared as a professional actress. She had a small part in a play called *A Lady's Name* at the Maxine Eliot Theatre in New York. It lasted for one season. After that she never again appeared in anything but her own monologues.

Until this time she had merely entertained family and friends and performed at private parties. It was not until 1917 that she turned professional, under the management of James B. Pond, who continued as her agent until 1928. After that Helen Arthur of Actor-Managers Inc. took over the management of her career.

In an interview[1] Miss Draper stated that there were three influences in her life that prompted her career. First, she had seen and been very much impressed by the work of Beatrice Herford, a popular monologuist of the time. Second, she saw the Chinese play *Yellow Jacket*, which showed her what could be done with little setting or properties. Last of all, she had

---

Muriel McKenna, who was a theatre major at the University of Wisconsin, is studying solo theatre.

encouragement from her great friend, Jan Paderewski, who was most per-suasive in urging her to go on with her work and to develop her talent to the full.

Throughout her career Miss Draper wrote everything she did for the stage herself. The sketches were not really written down; she often changed a number from performance to performance until it met her rigorous stan-dards of perfection. Sometimes this went on for as long as fifteen years before it sounded just right to her ears. One critic, in appraising her perfor-mance, remarked that it was "as if Fritz Kreisler were to give recitals every evening playing only his own compositions."[2]

Henry James, a very admiring friend, was fascinated by her work and wrote what he felt would be a very good number for her, in 1913. It was the story of a very pushy American woman in London, determined to be presented at the Court of St. James's. But Miss Draper was never able to perform it or any other piece that she had not written herself, much as she hated to disappoint her good friend who had gone to so much trouble.

Later, when she once asked Henry James for advice on what she should do with her life—whether to try to become an actress, or to go on with her writing, or to continue with her monologues, James is said to have replied, "My dear child . . . you . . . have woven . . . your own . . . very beautiful . . . little Persian carpet. . . . Stand on it!"

During World War I she entertained the American and British soldiers. Later, in 1920, she went to England. It was here, on January 29, that she made her first appearance as a professional (she had often entertained there at parties and affairs before that, however). It was the first of many appear-ances in England over the years—she was a great favorite. She gave a command performance at Windsor Castle in 1926 and was presented at court in 1928.

In the fall of 1921 she induced Aurélien-Marie Lugné-Poë, the director of the Théâtre de l'Oeuvre in Paris, to let her perform at that theatre and to receive 60 percent of the receipts. It was very successful and she made many appearances there up to as late as May 1950, when she gave her last performance. She had a similar sponsorship from Max Reinhardt in Ger-many.

Her manager, in December of 1928, decided on a very risky venture. She rented the Comedy Theatre in New York—with the specification that it was to be on a percentage basis, in order to make the expected losses as small as possible. Tickets were sold at regular theatre prices, the same as for any good, full-length play.

To everyone's amazement, Miss Draper, alone on the stage, with only a shawl or hat for costume, a table or chair for scenery, gave eight perfor-mances a week for twenty-six weeks. Receipts were greater than for most plays with a full cast and several changes of scenery. The next year she had an eighteen-week season with equal success, and over the years she came back to New York, as elsewhere, many times, to the delight of her devotees.

She made many transcontinental tours of the United States and performed in almost every corner of the world in the course of her long, very successful career.

She received many honors—honorary degrees from such prestigious institutions as Smith College, Cambridge and Edinburgh universities, the Catholic Guild of Ireland, and was made an honorary member of the Order of the Garter of the British Empire, rank of Commander.

One of the main differences between Miss Draper's work and that of those who came before her in the field is that she developed what one might call the "monodrama"—that is, two or three sketches were put together to make a short playlet of two or three acts. (Cornelia Otis Skinner was to carry this still further by making a full dramatic production of it, with full staging and costume.) These two- or three-act plays were as complete as a full-length play, as if all the characters were on stage and the stage fully furnished with all the stage settings of a play, so great was Miss Draper's ability to evoke the invisible characters in the imagination of the audience.

That was the most astonishing part of her performance. Her consummate artistry gave her complete independence of the ordinary trappings of scenery and stage setting, or even of costume in the ordinary sense of the word. A table or chair, a shawl or a hat, was all she needed to create the scene and the character. Her figure seemed to change, her face almost appeared to grow old or young as the character she portrayed. And, above all, the other characters in the drama seemed equally visible, one was fully aware of their presence also.

It was said that sometimes even the usually bored stagehands in the wings forgot their crap games for a while to watch this lone woman make a large audience see and feel a whole group of people on the stage and a full stage setting. Surely this was almost the ultimate in compliments to her artistry!

She had no superiors and few equals in her chosen specialty, which was high comedy—and high-quality theatre. In the course of her career she created some thirty-nine sketches, which included some fifty parts in all, in six or more languages—and there were about two hundred invisible characters besides. As mentioned before, they had not been written down, but Charles Bowden and Richard Barr, her managers in 1948, finally induced her to record some of the best. Some of the titles of her numbers were: *Three Women and Mr. Clifford; In a Church in Italy; Three Generations of Jewish Women at a Court of Human Relations; Three Breakfasts; A Scottish Immigrant at Ellis Island; On a Porch in Maine; The Italian Lesson; At the Court of Philip IV; Doctors; Dalmatian Peasant Woman; Showing the Garden; The Children's Party; Opening the Bazaar; At an English Country House Party*—to name only a few of the better-known ones.

From the titles alone one can see the wide range of her ability. She had a "camera eye" for the minutest, faintest details of action and movement, and a "camera ear" for the slightest, barest nuances of sound, inflection, and rhythms in speech. She would sometimes speak in any of six languages;

at other times, as in the *Dalmatian Peasant Woman*, she would indicate the accent and rhythm of the language even though not able to speak it. In one sketch she is said to have spoken French with a Polish accent. Some of these numbers merit further description and discussion, with the opinions expressed by critics.

One of the best known of her monodramas is *In a Church in Italy*. As the scene opens we see an aristocratic Englishwoman who has come with a friend, apparently to copy a painting for which the church is noted. She is having difficulty, so they pack their materials and go off. Soon an old Italian woman enters and wanders among the tourists who have come to see the church and the painting. She is begging, so some give her money, others ignore her, and she goes off muttering to herself. Then a swarm of American tourists comes in, one of whom is equipped with a guidebook, determined that she and all the others will not miss anything they should see there. As they leave, a young Italian girl enters for a quick, clandestine tryst with her lover. Soon a small group of German tourists enters, stolidly viewing each thing as described from the guidebook. Finally, after they have gone, an old Italian woman, obviously troubled, comes to pray, drops to her knees, lifting her eyes in trust and peace as the curtain falls.

All this, of course, is accomplished by Miss Draper alone on the stage. One is as aware of the invisible characters as one is of the speaking parts. The change is accomplished with only a shawl or a funny hat. The variety of accents and language is enormous—from proper upper-class English to the soft, liquid Italian of the breathless girl.

Three Women and Mr. Clifford is a short monodrama in three acts. In Act I we are in Mr. Clifford's office, where we meet Miss Nichols, the perfect secretary. She manages Mr. Clifford's phone calls, soothes his worried aunt, takes orders from Mrs. Clifford, neatly arranges things when his wife and his mistress want to go to the same play on the same night, sees that he knows about his appointments, and then goes off to join her fiancé. About fourteen invisible characters enter the office or can be visualized at the other end of telephone calls in this act.

In Act II we meet Mrs. Clifford, waiting for their car after the theatre. She greets a few friends, works her way to the car, and once inside on the way home begins a long monologue of worries and complaints. We are aware of her husband sitting silently beside her, occasionally chuckling at her recital of the latest escapades of their sons. As they pass the museum, the wife grows sentimental, wishing that they could go there together again since he hasn't been there for ages. Mr. Clifford leaves her at the door and goes off for a walk.

In Act III we meet the lovely "friend," Mrs. Mallory. She is no "mistress," just a charming, cultivated woman of middle years. She is seated on the edge of a large armchair. Mr. Clifford, of course, is in that armchair. She chats happily about the busy, pleasant day she has had. She has been to the museum to see their favorite pictures. She laughs at the escapades of the boys, and so on. As to their "affair," well, it will just have to wait till the children need him less and can understand things better. She can wait.

The costume for these three acts consisted of the following: a smock for Miss Nichols, an evening wrap and small bag for Mrs. Clifford, and a lovely shawl for Mrs. Mallory. The scenery was equally sparse: two tables, a telephone, a pad and pencil for Act I; a small loveseat for the back seat of the limousine in Act II; and a large armchair in Act III. Yet the effect was that of a fully produced play with many characters and full scenery. One of the critics wrote of this monodrama: "It came very close to being one of the finest statements on the stage of the tragedy of many lives—of selfish wives, at least, with the man a weakling."[3]

Three Breakfasts is the story of another marriage, somewhat like the Broadway success, *The Four-Poster*. This one, unlike the Clifford story, ends happily as the couple discover the real values of life. In Act I we see the young bride as they are moving into their first house, an old-fashioned farmhouse. By Act II, fifteen years have passed. The couple is now wealthy, living in a palatial home in the city, but the eager, tender, loving wife is now a bored society matron. By Act III, many years have passed. The wife is now an old lady, somewhat feeble, but alert and happy, back again in their beloved farmhouse. Of Miss Draper's performance in this monodrama, one critic wrote: "Watch the way she stirs a phantom cup of coffee with a phantom spoon. It tells you things about the way human beings stir coffee which we never noticed before, and the discovery interests us and fascinates us."

Three Generations of Jewish Women at the Court of Human Relations is another monodrama in three acts. One is aware of the three women and also of the kindly judge who is trying to do his best to take all three people into consideration as he makes his decision.

First we see the grandmother, bent and worn, wearing a black shawl in peasant fashion. She is reaching eighty years of age and is very angry with her granddaughter who wants to leave them to go out west and marry a "no-good" who drinks and has no real job. She and her daughter are completely dependent on the granddaughter Rosie for their care.

In the second act, the shawl has dropped to Miss Draper's shoulders. The mother, forty-seven years old, is tired and discouraged from a life of continuous struggle. Rosie wants to put her crippled mother and aged grandmother in an old ladies' home so she can marry and go out west with the "no-good" young man who drinks and has no real job. Rosie is needed at home; she is their only support.

The shawl drops to the floor. We now see Rosie. The change is impossible to describe; it has happened so suddenly. Rosie is almost twenty years old. She has looked many places and has now found a very nice home for her mother and grandmother, in the country. Her fiancé has a job offer out west; she can't take both old women with her. There is nothing to do but locate them in a nice place where they will be cared for. Her fiancé is a good boy; she is not wild. The judge tells her to bring the boy to see him and also a letter from the uncle who is said to be offering him a job out west. The judge will decide on Wednesday at ten o'clock. Rosie goes off happily with mother and grandmother.

In performance Miss Draper's whole body and face seem to shrivel up and age as the grandmother, become a little younger as the mother—and, suddenly transformed, she is twenty. A masterpiece of conjury.

Miss Draper did not actually write down her monologues, as we noted earlier. She was finally induced to make recordings of some of her better-known works in a series of albums called *The Art of Ruth Draper*. Some of these were also printed in a book about her with the same title. But neither the printed page nor the recordings are completely satisfactory as a measure of her talent. The words, cold on the printed page, do not read particularly well. Gestures, facial expression, slight movements—all those intangibles that complete the performance—cannot be seen from the printed page or the recordings. She was a consummate actress; every movement made the picture more complete.[4] One had to hear and see to fully understand the unusual art by which she alone created many characters on the stage.

UTA HAGEN AND EVA LE GALLIENNE
SUSAN SPECTOR AND STEVEN URKOWITZ

In 1937, when she was seventeen, Uta Hagen wrote to Eva Le Gallienne asking for an audition to join Le Gallienne's acting company. Inspired by the state repertory theatres she had seen in Europe with her parents, Hagen wanted to break into the theatre doing "the classics." In America at the time only Le Gallienne was regularly producing major plays from the European repertory on the professional stage.

Le Gallienne, although she had already interviewed hundreds of young actresses for her Civic Repertory Theatre, sensed something special in Hagen's letter—"The handwriting alone was full of character and individuality. . . . The phrasing too was striking; it was forthright, honest and simple, and the choice of words was intelligent and original; one felt a personality there." She invited Hagen to read for her at her home in Westport, Connecticut.

The personality that showed through in Uta Hagen's letter had been

Susan Spector, Assistant Professor of Speech and Theatre at Baruch College, City University of New York, wrote a Ph.D. dissertation on Uta Hagen at New York University. Stephen Urkowitz, Associate Professor of English at Hofstra University, recently published a study of *King Lear*. Quotations by courtesy of Uta Hagen and from Eva Le Gallienne's *With a Quiet Heart: An Autobiography*, New York, 1953.

nurtured in an extraordinarily rich soil. Her father was a prolific writer, a noted art historian and composer who had been responsible for the revival of Handel's operas in Germany in the 1920's; her mother, an accomplished concert singer. Their home was a gathering place for professional musicians, artists, and the brightest lights of the university and political community in Madison, Wisconsin. As a girl she studied dance and music in Europe and America and performed in school and at home.

Late in April 1937 Hagen traveled to Westport. In the audition Le Gallienne recalls she read a speech from Shaw's *St. Joan* "quite badly . . . I was ruthlessly honest with her . . . talked to her about it, gave her a few pointers, and asked her to think it over for an hour. . . . The improvement was startling." In the abbreviated prose of her journal, Hagen recorded her own impression of the interview: "She started drilling me on [*St. Joan*], and finally made me say it right to her. She practically hypnotized me, and it got better. She doesn't like my voice when it goes up and gets breathy, and said I needed more diaphragm control (which she emphasized by whacking me there). Then she talked and yelled at me. Made me sight-read Ophelia and Nina from *Sea Gull*. She said maybe I could work in her company in the fall. I don't even know if I want to. Oh well."

Le Gallienne planned to play Hamlet in the summer production she would direct on Cape Cod. She would rehearse from the end of June until the end of August, when eight performances would be given in the Cape Playhouse, Dennis, Massachusetts. Most of the cast was drawn from the members of her defunct Civic Repertory Company, but she couldn't find a satisfactory Ophelia.

Early in June she wrote to Hagen, offering her a week's trial in the role—no guarantee, no pay, no expenses. On June 23, Hagen arrived to begin work.

Le Gallienne's plan was to have a month of small rehearsals, meeting with groups of actors as they were available to come to her home in Westport. Set and costume designs and the preliminary shape of roles were to be hammered out before the full company assembled late in July.

During her trial week, Hagen spent her mornings studying alone. Her journal for June 26: "Went canoeing, practicing lines and songs as I paddled. At about 11:30 I paddled for shore vigorously because of a wind, and suddenly tipped over and fell in the water. My watch didn't stop but my swell new copy of *Hamlet* and my hair got pretty wrecked. Came back dripping." Afternoons were spent rehearsing and watching Le Gallienne working with other performers. In her free time, Hagen wrote letters, practiced piano and recorder, and exercised in dance workouts. On Le Gallienne's suggestion she began reading extensively, beginning with Karl Mantzius's six-volume *History of Theatrical Art*.

Le Gallienne was *in loco parentis* for Hagen, who had just turned eighteen, coaching her in her role, of course, but also looking after her health and her diet, and even reproaching her after a wild night out. The girl was brought into conversations with the company designer and manager, the actors and production people. She was made to feel part of a fine enterprise with high aspirations.

At the end of the first week, after a long rehearsal Le Gallienne said, "By the way, Miss Hagen, I think you can tell your parents it's all right now. But you've got to work hard." Accepted, Hagen went outside and wept for a quarter of an hour.

To Le Gallienne's steady stream of concern and approval, Hagen's parents added a flood of supporting letters, cards, and packages from home. One box, for example, brought cake, marmalade, cream, a hairbrush, bubble bath, and candy. A long letter from her father has this glowing parenthesis: "(By the way, read an ad today at the grocer's; it was about olives. They were distinguished as large, ex-large, giant, jumbo, colossal, ex-colossal, super colossal. Now I wonder what your Ophelia will be like—*super*, or ex-super-colossal?)"

The full company began work in Westport on July 27, and then moved to Cape Cod on August 8. Fencing-master Giorgio Santelli arrived to choreograph the last act swordplay and to give fencing classes to all the actors. Hagen, who had woven some of the fabric for the production's costumes, began embroidering during her breaks in rehearsals. She eventually did the decorative work on her own costume and on Osric's. And once the move to the Cape was accomplished, Le Gallienne began giving her twenty dollars per week for expense money. For the first time she was being paid to work in the theatre. In her journal she wrote, "Ahem! Am I proud."

In addition to company rehearsals, Hagen spent time on the set alone— walking, practicing, studying. Le Gallienne took time to affirm her faith in Hagen's talent and to give her perspective on what lay ahead: "Before we started [rehearsing] Eva walked with me and was wonderful. She said she believed in me, that I had great talent, was very good in the part and born for the theatre. But that I shouldn't believe the things people told me because I still had a hell of a lot to learn and in 10 years I might be a great actress. I wasn't yet, and she and I knew it. We also had high standards and because I was intelligent she hoped I wouldn't believe praise and let it go to my head."

The work grew more strenuous, approaching the August 23 opening. Le Gallienne's attitudes and graciousness under pressure show up repeatedly in Hagen's journal. After the final dress rehearsal she records her own jitters and Le Gallienne's supportive ease: "I was stinking! Make-up bad, couldn't be heard, felt practically nothing & for the first time did everything in a daze. Also dried up once which has never happened before. Everything else was wrong too. Timing of music, trumpets, etc., very poor. God! It was frightful! Eva stayed sweet and pleasant throughout. How she does it, I don't know!!! I think more of her and admire her more as an artist and person than anyone in the world next to mom."

On opening night, Hagen received flowers and telegrams from her family and friends in Madison and Berlin. "I went to the theatre at 7:30 and was rather dazed till curtain time. . . . I got more and more excited. As a whole the production went well, with a few technical flaws. . . . The feeling and sweep as a whole was better than ever before, but now I can spend the week polishing off thousands of tiny things." (She made meticulous notes detailing changes or reminders for her next performances.)

Hagen's Ophelia was applauded and acclaimed, and, although the reviews were mixed for the production as a whole, audiences were enthusiastic throughout the run. Le Gallienne remembers: "The theatre was crowded every night. I was aware that many people came out of curiosity, expecting to see a freak performance, a ridiculous sort of stunt; quite a number, I suspect, came prepared to scoff. But when the curtain fell at the end of the play, the silence for several moments was electric, and then the storm of applause broke loose and the shouts and 'bravos' brought tears to my eyes. I have seldom been so happy, though I found the eight consecutive performances almost unbearably exhausting."

Critics particularly praised Hagen's work on Ophelia's mad scene. Four Boston writers called it "realistic," "appealing," "excellent," and "clever." The local Cape Cod papers said, "The strength and beauty with which she endows it ranks only second, in the production, to Miss Le Gallienne's last scene." And, "She took the stage to herself for several minutes and in a vague, distracted way that fitted the role perfectly, she won the audience's complete attention and respect. Her exit was the occasion for immediate applause, the only time the play was so interrupted." In her journal, Hagen's response to these reviews was circumspect: "My press notices were good, but I certainly didn't take them to heart considering the bosh they wrote about other things!"

Hagen's second performance was a real letdown after the success of her debut. Le Gallienne had warned her of the second-night dangers, but they were nevertheless a painful shock to Hagen. On later evenings Le Gallienne came to Hagen before the performance to talk about her makeup, to chat about her parents' expected arrival, or to go over a problematic detail. This attention calmed her and eased much of the jittery anxiety she felt.

On August 26 Hagen's family finally arrived, and she was reunited with the source of so much of her talent: "Shortly before twelve I was walking across the street when I heard shrieks and honkings, and there was the family. God, I nearly died of joy." That evening, while her brother Holger was shouting "Bravo's," she took her first "final curtain calls" with Le Gallienne and other leading players.

But the next day's matinee was, in Hagen's estimate, "stinking." The theatre overheated in the sun, and the performers were physically and emotionally drained. "Before the mad scene Eva said, 'You've got to speak up, my girl. The soliloquy was bad.' It threw me way down in the dumps. The whole performance was awful."

Hagen knew that her performances had been erratic, but she worked hard and felt a real sense of her own improvement as the week came to an end: "It was the last performance and [it] made me very sad, but I felt it was the best. Of course there were little things that still left me very unsatisfied, but on the whole it was the strongest. Eva had given me some hints in the afternoon and I took them to heart, regaining a lot of the truth and simplicity I was beginning to lose. Before the performance she said, 'Do your best now!' And I tried. Afterwards, when I meant to give the Ophelia ring back, she made me keep it, and I floated. . . ."

Hagen's parents and Le Gallienne spent a long afternoon together in Connecticut a few days after the company left Cape Cod. "I've never seen Eva before as she was this afternoon," Hagen wrote. "Never so alive, so brilliant and witty, and so deep in telling of the past and plans for the future. . . . And to hear daddy and Eva having deeply intellectual talks, and to have Eva beg mother to sing, etc., means more to me than I can put down in words. . . . Eva said to them, 'You can't know how wonderful it is to be near people who understand.'"

The repertory company Le Gallienne hoped to include Hagen in for the next season failed to materialize. Instead, Hagen went to New York in October and within two months began her Broadway career, starring with the Lunts in *The Seagull*. In *Respect for Acting* (1973), Hagen wrote, "I am grateful to Eva Le Gallienne for first believing in my talent, for putting me on the professional stage, for upholding a reverence for the theatre, for helping me to believe that the theatre should contribute to the spiritual life of a nation." More than any technique or style, in their work together on *Hamlet* it was the sense of the high calling of theatrical art that was passed from one generation to the next.

WOMEN MIMES IN AMERICA

BARI ROLFE

Women pantomime players came to America from France and England at the end of the 1700's. They played in dance companies such as those of Ravel and Alexander Placide, whose ballet-pantomimes were popular fare throughout the new United States. Ballet-pantomimes consisted of stories played in dance and mime, and were based on the innovative *ballets d'action* (mimed dances) of France's great ballet master Noverre. Themes were mainly those of myth and legend and, in the United States, equally mythical stories about American Indians and colonial life. Mime as an art form as we know it today, however, existed primarily in the clown turns of the circus

---

Bari Rolfe, who has taught mime at many institutions, is the author of *Mimes on Miming* and *Movement for Period Plays*.

and the comic sketches in music halls and vaudeville. Players were at first imported from Europe; then American pantomime began to emerge in the nineteenth century. It was out of this background that performers, men and women, developed their skills in the direction their artistic sensibility carried them.

The women discussed here, with the partial exception of Angna Enters, came to mime from dance while most male mimes came from vaudeville, circus, or music hall. The women have usually been their own choreographer-directors, and their presentations tend toward dance-mime. Since about 1950 mime as an art form and body of technique has been well enough established that performers can enter it directly.

The following brief biographies are those of some of the women in American mime who built careers and achieved some recognition. Yet to be heard from are the dozens of young women soloists, members of companies, and clown mimes, who are on their way toward achievement and recognition.

ANGNA ENTERS (b. 1907)

Although she studied and performed dance, Angna Enters came to mime through painting. Her portraits taught her that "human beings don't always talk . . . they act in certain ways for which no words are the equivalent." In order to find out how human beings acted, so as to better paint them, she began doing motion studies with herself as the character; soon she needed to show her portraits-in-motion to audiences. Even later, as a concert-mime, she prepared a new piece not by rehearsing it but by painting on canvas the images in her mind.

Her extraordinary career, beginning at age seventeen, started with thirteen New York performances in three years, of some thirty-nine sketches. The output continued nonstop: yearly concert tours throughout the United States and Europe; painting, sculpting, with exhibitions throughout the country; writing of several volumes of autobiography, plays, articles, film scripts; composing music, designing costumes and sets, directing plays, and teaching, until the mid-1960's.

Enters's unique presentations were hard to label; it wasn't traditional acting, said the drama critics, nor traditional dance, said the dance critics. She tried various terms: dance-forms, episodes, dance-mime; and finally chose "The Theatre of Angna Enters." She also learned that certain strictures obtained on the commercial stage at that time: "a woman comic was either a mimic, doing takeoffs on prominent people, or a grotesque, or a clown." It was uphill work for this artist who did not fall into any of these slots.

She delicately and wittily blended acting and movement, never patronizing, always inventive. Her unusual programs soon elicited enthusiastic response from critics in music, art and literature, as well as theatre and dance.

To Enters her stage pieces were social commentary in the tradition of Greek and Roman mimes, using a past period as a mirror to see/show one's own time. Her characters were women (an exception was "Boy Cardinal," a movement study of a child ecclesiastic) from many times, places, and circumstances, for her range was phenomenal. Art critic Louis Kalonyme commented (1925) that "while they are all based on feminine phases" they were all different. Using classical, popular, and jazz music (the first to do so) she drew her characters from ancient Greece, the Middle Ages, and the seventeenth century on; they were courtly ladies, prostitutes, a pianist, painter, flapper, cook; from France, Russia, the United States, Spain, and Asia; and dozens more women from every society, from every period.

Enters's programs were unforgettable, say many who have seen her, and not only for their novelty. Her talent, plus concepts based solidly on proven acting principles, resulted in presentations of intelligence, sensitivity, and imagination; they were "unique," "subtle," "amusing," "witty," "tragic," and "comic," to quote a few of the critics. In her writing she was simple, clear, poetic, and profound; the validity of her ideas concerning mime is confirmed by time—ideas as true today as when she formulated them.

TRUDI SCHOOP (b. 1904)

Dancer Trudi Schoop formed a comedy troupe in her native Zurich, and went to Berlin in 1929; her comic ballet became "the talk of Europe" as she built her early reputation in political cabaret. Critics compared her to Chaplin and to Grock, the famous Swiss clown-mime, because of her effective pantomime with expressive eyes, hands, and childish grin. At the 1932 International Dance Congress in Paris, the companies of Kurt Jooss and Trudi Schoop won the first and fourth prizes respectively. Thus, when she came to America, brought by Sol Hurok in December 1935, she was an established dance-mime of reputation.

She began her tour in New York, where most critics gave rave reviews to her "flawless ensemble"; the least complimentary lauded her comic abilities but considered her material to be more suited to musical comedy than the concert stage. Others found that same humor to be a universal language of simplicity and satire, worth a thousand words because her eloquent pantomime communicated to all nationalities. They called her brilliant, hilarious, original, inventive, magnificent, delightful; she was "a female Chaplin," "Europe's most riotous comedienne," "the comical mistress of pantomime," and "the funniest girl in the world." Schoop wrote and staged her own two/three-act comedies. Oskar Schlemmer, of Bauhaus fame, designed the costumes for one of her pieces. On her return to Europe after five tours in the U.S.A., World War II began. Schoop performed political cabaret in Zurich under the eyes of the Nazis, and later came back to the United States to tour with her company until 1947, when she settled in Los Angeles in order to set down roots. She painted, taught, and danced while a new impulse was germinating; it took the form of dance therapy, and she built another career in that field.

Themes of her performance pieces were varied. "Want Ads" was a series of short dramas based on newspaper ads. "Fridolin," in which she played the male lead character, showed the adventures of a dreamy, naïve youth, and represented her own conflicts with society. There was "Barbara," a dancing clown, and "Blond Marie," the story of a maidservant who became a stage star. Her pieces were humanistic, gently satirical, ironic, antisentimental, and never bitter, and she "stripped life, its funny and tragic situations, to simple, bare essentials."

From comedy to therapy may seem to be a big leap, but Schoop was uniquely qualified to bridge the two. For one, humor itself can be therapeutic. For another, she was fascinated with human expression, its variety and meaning, and with communication through movement—qualities which served her in both areas. She could well understand the schizophrenic who "played out in his own theatre fragments of comedy, slapstick, and tragedy." She found that "imitation was a determinative part" of working with patients—they copying her movements and she theirs; copying, or imitation, became a way to acknowledge them, to validate what they were doing. Patients also imitated the outward signs of a feeling or idea; perhaps they could not respond if asked to "feel angry," but could follow directions to stamp or grimace or punch a pillow. The same technique is used by other therapists: Charlotte Wolff (The Psychology of Gesture) imitated her patients' movements in order to learn something of their inner motivation. Actors, too, employ the same means of utilizing the outward gesture to get to an inner justification.

Schoop maintains a busy schedule of classes and lectures in the United States and Europe. Pioneer and practitioner, she synthesizes the two creative fields of art and science.

LOTTE GOSLAR (b. 1917)

Elfin-clown Lotte Goslar, who has loved elves since childhood, resumed in the United States in 1940 a career cut short in Hitler Germany. She had been especially fortunate in having as guides and colleagues some remarkable people who let her develop in her own, special way: Palucca, from Mary Wigman's school, a dancer highly appreciated by the Bauhaus people, and the two great comics of the Liberated Theatre in Prague, Jan Werich and George Voskovec, with whom she worked for a year. Then she came to the United States for extensive touring in revues, in cabarets and concerts, including ten years at Hollywood's Turnabout Theatre with Elsa Lanchester.

This dancer-clown-comic-mime has choreographed for operas, ballet companies, children's theatre, and film sequences. She organized her present company, Pantomime Circus, in 1954 and since then has toured the U.S.A. and Europe, including appearances at various mime festivals.

Critics emphasize Goslar's considerable comic gifts. The truly funny situations are often tinged with compassion and tenderness; a few pieces are tragedies. However, the traditional sad/glad clown is an image she rejects; for her, simply to be funny is itself a gesture of courage. Her serious side is sometimes, not often, offered to the public. Bertolt Brecht wrote a tragic clown scenario for her; she has another story about a soldier, and still another tragic piece about a child.

In some of her sketches the protagonist is a woman: grandma, fond nanny, would-be carny queen; others feature the androgynous clown: a flower, an insect, a mushroom. Goslar sees two kinds of clowns: the one with the personal act, like Grock, Rivels, or Dimitri, and the knockabout, rough-and-tumble clown, in which category women are not found. As the first kind, her personal clown originates in her own reaction to nature, people, animals, and trees.

Critical comments about Goslar are refreshing to read: "endearing, indomitable dumpling," "irresistible," "inspired madness," "tender poetry," she performs with "humor, grace and understated parody"; "with a face like a gallant, easily discouraged potato and a heart big as a frying pan," in that happy phrase of Clive Barnes.

Her themes are varied: a disgruntled flower at the mercy of sun, wind and rain; a shy, nasty child dance prodigy; a smug nanny ruffling the hair of her concert pianist protégé during his performance; a motherly flower pouring nectar for hungry bees; an aging carnival dancer vainly competing with younger girls.

Goslar also draws, designs costumes, and writes children's books. That her work appeals both to adults and children attests to its breadth, honesty, and humanity.

BARI ROLFE (b. 1916)

Like most women mimes, I began as a dancer in dance companies and as a soloist in cabarets and theatres, in the mid-1930's in and around Chicago. After an on-stage fall that slipped a disk, and after somewhat recovering, I involved myself in little theatre, some of it political, and gained some acting experience. When I resumed dance on a noncommercial basis, my dances tended to be little stories in movement; not knowing what to call them, they remained "dances."

In 1955 I saw Marcel Marceau on his first American tour. Unforgettable moment! I pointed shakily from my seat in the top balcony to the tiny white figure below: *"That's* what I want!" After some years of relentless scraping and saving, I arrived in Paris where Marceau had offered to supervise my training—although not in his company as planned but with his teacher, Étienne Decroux. But in a few months I knew that Decroux's style of mime was not for me, and I was fortunate enough to find, late in 1963, the school of Jacques Lecoq.

Lecoq's work gave me more than I'd hoped. My motivation had been to become a better performing mime, but there I found so many doors opening into a world of meaningful movement, of mask, clown, and physical theatre, that I wanted only to teach this great store of movement understanding and challenge. I managed to live very nicely, first by teaching modern dance, then as part of a three-person mime company at the Crazy Horse Saloon, plus mime classes in theatres and universities and as choreographer for a company of drum majorettes.

After three years of Lecoq's two-year course, where to go? Herbert Blau, over a Paris lunch, advised me to return to the States, for "a new wind was blowing through acting training there," and I could teach in university drama programs despite my lack of any academic degree. This turned out to be true; I worked in professional training programs at the University of California at Los Angeles and the University of Washington, the drama department at California State University at Northridge, and gave workshops at many other colleges, theatre companies, and dance studios. The time was right, for mime was beginning to be recognized in the United States both as an art form and as a useful skill for actors for its insight into meaningful movement and its ability to enhance the physical aspects of theatre. In the few years from 1972 to 1978, many American theatre departments introduced mime to their courses; the professional organization, International Mimes and Pantomimists, was formed; the *Mime Journal* began publishing, then *Mime, Mask, and Marionette,* and two major festivals took place: LaCrosse 1974 and Milwaukee 1978. I was fortunate enough to be a part of all these events, writing and teaching mime, and was the first American to participate in a European mime festival, with an invited paper, at Prague, 1971.

3

WHERE ARE THE
WOMEN PLAYWRIGHTS?

A wonderful anecdote in Dore Schary's autobiography, *Heyday*, tells a lot about the difficulties of women playwrights in the American theatre. A play written when Dore Schary was a young man was read by producer Walter Wanger who, misled by the unusual name, sent the following cable to Harry Cohn, head of Columbia Pictures in Hollywood. "Dore Schary should be signed up—she writes tough—like a man."

The ironic inversions in the punch line here make an important point. Playwriting has always been viewed as man's work, and the women who have tried to intrude have found the going rough. Major critics and big-time producers have said it straight out: women can't write first-rate plays. Even Lillian Hellman, without doubt the major American woman playwright, was faulted by George Jean Nathan for the "generic female inability" to master an "economy of emotion." The producer John Golden in a speech giving a "national achievement award" to Rachel Crothers in 1939 yet insisted that "there were few, if any great women dramatists—the reasons obvious: They were congenitally good, sweet, tender, loving, shy . . . so protected that they could never have seen the side of life . . . that one should know, see— perhaps, even live, to be a great dramatist."

There you have the characteristic answers influential men have offered to the perennial question: Where are the women playwrights? The women writers see things differently. They wonder what there is about the theatre as a medium that has kept women from full participation. Theatre as a highly public expression and a risky investment, they realize, has been outside of what has been defined as women's sphere. Playwriting is a skill that can only really be learned as part of a group working together in a highly technical physical plant, and they know that women have not usually had access to the camaraderie of the production process or the complex instrument of professional theatre.

Although some of these difficulties are shared with male writers who also find theatre a forbidding form, women face the put-down of male producers and directors, the ridicule of family and associates for even trying to make it,

129

and their own guilt and frustration at sacrificing personal needs of self and children for the niggardly rewards of theatre. They are sometimes in a double bind. Brought up to deny themselves and their strong emotions and sexual drives, they find it difficult to expose what they really feel. If they do manage to give form to their "suppressed desires," they are chastised or feared for subverting the accepted female image. If not feared, female subject matter is often rejected as the dull, uninteresting minutiae of domestic life unrelated to the big world of male activities.

Paradoxically, despite these potent obstacles, the number of women dramatists in the history of American theatre is surprisingly large. As always in uncovering women's past, we discover findings that belie what we have been taught. The play list in our Sourcebook contains more than six hundred women playwrights, and this is by no means a complete accounting. Although the names may not be known to the larger public, these playwrights have played an important and occasionally outstanding and original role in the development of American theatre. They have won Pulitzer Prizes, Drama Critics awards, and Obies. From their pens have come some of the all-time hits—from East Lynne to Abie's Irish Rose to Harvey.

One can trace women writing for the stage back to the very beginnings of American theatre to an occasional revolutionary bluestocking like Mercy Otis Warren. Some of the actress-playwrights of the mid-nineteenth century were close observers of the native scene, writing "original society plays" that treated American themes somewhat realistically at a time when most plays were romantic or melodramatic spectacles.

At the turn of the twentieth century, in the wake of the struggle for women's emancipation, women playwrights almost seemed to take over the processing of popular commercial productions for an increasingly female audience. Stories in newspapers and magazines featured the new phenomenon: "The Women Who Write Successful Plays." What many of these women wrote, like the men with whom they competed, were those serviceable melodramas, farces, mysteries, and comedies that made up the season during the teens and expansive twenties. Working as "pros," they tended to look on playwriting as a "business."

Important as these professionals were in making a place for women in the theatre, they did not challenge—except by their presence—the conventional views of women and the esthetic limitations of Broadway. Only a few were able to bring something of women's concerns to the mainstream—the ever-active Rachel Crothers, Zona Gale, and Zoe Akins, for example. It was, however, largely in the more congenial atmosphere of the little, art, and institutional theatres that the more venturesome women dramatists began to expose aspects of women's lives long hidden from view. They enriched the social dramas of an earlier day with penetrating psychological insights which they tried to project in effective dramatic action. One can find in the seminal experiments of Alice Gerstenberg, Susan Glaspell, Sophie Treadwell, Hallie Flanagan, Gertrude Stein, and others, some of the subjects and the structures now widely used by today's women playwrights.

The strong, individual voices of Lillian Hellman, Clare Boothe Luce, Mary Chase, and Lorraine Hansberry carried women playwrights into the mainstream during the years from the Depression to the 1950's despite the severe cutback in the number of Broadway shows. In the 1960's the experimental Off- and Off-Off-Broadway theatres, like the earlier little theatres, were responsive to women writers, and a whole new generation of exciting playwrights came from these creative nurseries—Megan Terry, Rochelle Owen, Rosalyn Drexler, Adrienne Kennedy, Myrna Lamb, and others. Some of these women banded together to produce their own plays in theatres that would, as they put it, be stripped of "sexism and violence."

In the 1970's women, finding theatre a powerful instrument for consciousness raising, began writing plays with great abandon and coming together in feminist theatres. As this book goes to press there is a strong sense that the time is ripe—not for the "great woman dramatist," a concept itself at odds with the antihierarchical women's movement, but for the rich dramatic vision of autonomous women and men created by the many women writing for the theatre today.   HKC

MERCY WARREN,
SATIRIST OF THE REVOLUTION

ALICE MCDONNELL ROBINSON

Although Harriet Beecher Stowe's role in rousing antislavery passions before the Civil War through her novel and the play based on it is well known, the part played by another New England woman, Mercy Warren, in an earlier war, is almost totally unknown. In the days before and during the Revolutionary War, Mercy Warren stirred up hatred for the Tories of Massachusetts and admiration for the American Revolutionaries through a series of plays.

Mercy Otis Warren was three years younger than her brother, James Otis, who was one of the most brilliant, and one of the most outspoken, of the early patriot leaders. Like her brother, she had always had a love of study. She had been allowed to go with her brother when as a boy he studied with the Reverend Jonathan Russell, their uncle by marriage. The Reverend Russell had been educated at Yale and was entrusted by Colonel Otis, their

Alice McDonnell Robinson, Associate Professor of Theatre, University of Maryland, Baltimore, has published in *Players Magazine* and *Educational Theatre Journal* and is co-editor with Milly Barranger and Vera Mowry Roberts of *Notable Women in the American Theatre*, 1987.

father, with the job of preparing his oldest son for Harvard. In the Reverend Russell's library were not only the Greek and Latin classics but also the works of Pope, Dryden, Milton, and Shakespeare. Mercy Otis received nearly the same education as her brother, but, of course, she was not allowed to go to college. After his graduation from Harvard, James spent two years at home studying for his master's degree. He seems to have shared much of his reading and his thoughts with his intelligent sister. In 1754, at the age of twenty-six, Mercy Otis married a former classmate of her brother, James Warren.

The home of James and Mercy Warren in Plymouth became a meeting place for the patriots. Through her brother and husband, Mercy met John Adams and his wife, Abigail. She knew Samuel Adams, John Hancock, and later Washington and Jefferson.

She might have remained a simple housewife rearing five sons and writing poems on nature and friendship in imitation of Pope and Dryden, had not her beloved brother become, as she was later to write, "the first martyr to American freedom."

James Otis and Samuel Adams led the Massachusetts House of Representatives in the struggle against the strict rule over the Colonies imposed under the rule of George III. In 1769, her brother James, in a rage against some customs officials who had printed scurrilities against him, published in the Boston Gazette a notice giving the names of certain men who had "treated the characters of all true North Americans in a manner that is not to be endured." The next evening, Otis walked, unarmed, into the British coffeehouse frequented by his enemies. He was instantly threatened, the lights were put out, and his enemies attacked and beat him with canes and swords. Otis never recovered mentally from this attack. He returned to the Assembly in 1771, but he was not himself. In December of that year he was carried off in a post chaise bound hand and foot. It was at this time that Mercy Warren, at the age of forty-four, took up her pen to fight the battle her brother had helped to begin.

In 1772 the propaganda battle by the patriots was at a low ebb. With her brother unable to lead the patriots in their opposition to the English rule, Mrs. Mercy Otis Warren now began to use her pen to keep before the people her brother's ideals. She allowed excerpts from her first propaganda play, The Adulateur, to be printed anonymously in the radical paper, The Massachusetts Spy, on March 26 and April 23, 1772. In 1773 she published anonymously in pamphlet form a revised five-act version of the play. This longer version was probably published to take advantage of the patriots' outrage over the Hutchinson-Oliver letters in which Hutchinson had written that he doubted that the colony three thousand miles away could enjoy all the same liberties as the parent state and that "there must be an Abridgment of what are called English Liberties." This statement seemed to confirm the patriots' worst thoughts about Thomas Hutchinson, then acting governor. Hutchinson was the arch-villain in Mrs. Warren's play.

Mrs. Warren had never seen a play, for Boston had not allowed the players to perform in their city. She read history and philosophy and, when she felt inspired, she put her thoughts into poems. Her favorite themes for her poems were nature, friendship, philosophy, and religion. Most of her poems were written in rhymed couplets imitative of the poetic models of the day, Alexander Pope and John Dryden. But now she used her pen to write in dramatic form, using blank verse. She was familiar with the plays of Shakespeare, Molière, and Joseph Addison. The model for *The Adulateur* was probably Addison's heroic tragedy, *Cato*, for she included a quotation from *Cato* on the title page of her pamphlet.

Mrs. Warren's purpose, as she later wrote, was to "strip the Vizard from the Crafty"; those politicians against whom she directed her satirical pen were the wealthy Tory oligarchs who represented the British king and opposed the elected Assembly of Massachusetts. Chief of these men was Thomas Hutchinson who, when the play was published, was governor of the colony. At the time of the Boston Massacre, when the play takes place, Hutchinson was the lieutenant governor, president of the Council, Chief Justice, and judge of Probate. As early as 1762, James Otis had spoken out against the same man's serving as both legislator and supreme judge. After Hutchinson became governor, his brother, Foster, became justice of the Common Pleas; his wife's brother-in-law, Peter Oliver, became Chief Justice; and his son, Thomas, became judge of Probate. This was the tight little group of oligarchs who were the target of Mercy Warren's satire.

The time depicted in *The Adulateur* is 1770, just before and during the Boston Massacre. *The Adulateur* follows quite closely the actual historical events. Of the aristocratic oligarchy of Massachusetts, Mrs. Warren uses among her characters:

Rapatio, Governor of Servia	(Thomas Hutchinson)
Limput, Married to Rapatio's Sister	(Andrew Oliver)
Hazelrod, L.C. Justice, Brother to Limput	(Peter Oliver)
Meagre, Brother to Rapatio	(Foster Hutchinson)

The characters were not, of course, identified in the pamphlet, but the close relationship of the characters made their originals easy to determine.

Opposing these four characters are four Boston patriots, each given an appropriately heroic Roman name:

Brutus, Chief of the Patriots	(James Otis)
Junius ⎤	(Samuel Adams)
Cassius ⎬ Patriots	(John Adams)
Porteus ⎦	(John Hancock)

Mrs. Warren's primary purpose in writing *The Adulateur* in 1772 was to arouse the patriots and unite them once again to oppose the "tyranny" of

Britain as they had done at the time of the Boston Massacre. She drew her characters in strong black and white. She was, however, surprisingly advanced in her thinking about the human dignity and equality of men. She ranks, along with Samuel Adams and Thomas Paine (who had not yet come to this country), as one of the most democratic of the Revolutionary War leaders. In this play she depicts the wealthy and powerful oligarchs as contemptuous of the common people. On the other hand, Brutus and his fellow patriots believe in the dignity of the common man. Mrs. Warren was well aware of the social revolution that was going on at this time.

In *The Adulateur*, the patriot leaders also stand for liberty and freedom. Through them Mrs. Warren describes some characteristics of a government which would assure greater freedom to the people. First, no one man should have too much power, as had Rapatio, surrounded by fawning relatives and parasites. Second, a good government should assure justice for all, and judges must be free from influence by the executive branch of the government. Third, the government should have no standing army.

Mrs. Warren seems already to have visualized an independent country, for she has Brutus wish for a "gen'rous, free and independent people." She calls her readers to immediate action, and she seems to encourage physical opposition. Her leaders are resolved that before they will be slaves they will "pour out" their "choicest blood" and with their daggers "force a way to freedom."

Through her depiction of the heroic leaders of the patriots, headed by her own brother, Mrs. Warren attempts to define for the first time in original American drama the "true" American. This idealized American is trustworthy, unselfish, freedom-loving. He scorns title, position, and money that are attained at the sacrifice of honor. He respects the common people and believes in a government based on the will of the people. He has a vision of greatness for America.

Mrs. Warren's play seems to have helped to discredit the two chief victims of her satirical pen, Thomas Hutchinson and Peter Oliver. The names of Rapatio and Hazelrod which she gave them stuck to the two men.

In 1773, Mrs. Warren published in the *Boston Gazette* some excerpts from a new propaganda play called *The Defeat*. This play was evidently never published in pamphlet form. In *The Defeat* Rapatio and Limput appear once again. The patriots with the names of Honestus, Cassius, Rusticus, Hortensius, and Lucius are members of the Massachusetts Assembly. In this play, the patriots are once again victorious. In the third act, which is merely summarized in the newspaper, a battle takes place in which "Rapatio, his Abettors and Creatures are totally defeated" and "freedom and happiness" are restored to the people. In the final scene of the play, Rapatio laments his lost peace of mind which he basely sold "for flattering titles and more sordid Gold."

In *The Defeat*, liberty is again set up as an ideal and is even triumphant. Several references are made to native rights or native freedom. This is an early mention of that "natural law" which the patriots were beginning to claim to be over and above mere governmental law. Mrs. Warren enumerates four rights which the government should protect. The government should protect the right of assembly, should assure the right of the legislatures to meet and make laws without intimidation, should allow freedom of the press, and should protect the people from a standing army. Most of all, Mrs. Warren, as she had done in *The Adulateur*, warned against a government in which one man has too much power. She also helped to destroy the effectiveness of Thomas Hutchinson as governor of the colony, and in 1774 he was recalled to England to report to the king in person.

Before Mrs. Warren's third play appeared, certain important events took place. In December 1773, the famous Boston Tea Party occurred. As a punishment for the dumping of the tea, the British ordered that Boston Harbor be closed. The very next day after the closing of the harbor, the news of Parliament's so-called Intolerable or Coercive Acts reached Boston. Among the Coercive Acts was one that stated that the governor should appoint his Council instead of its members being elected by the House.

The news that the king had signed the Coercive Acts arrived in August, along with the list of thirty-six men who had been appointed by the king to serve as councilors. These councilors at once became the object of the patriots' contempt. The mob "persuaded" all but sixteen of them to resign their appointments. The sixteen who refused to resign had to seek protection from the British soldiers who made of Boston almost an armed camp. General Thomas Gage had now replaced Thomas Hutchinson as governor.

Early in 1775, Mrs. Warren attacked with her pen these sixteen councilors who had refused to resign their appointments. This play, which became her most popular one, is called *The Group*. The first two scenes were printed in the *Boston Gazette* on January 23, 1775, and reprinted three days later in *The Massachusetts Spy*. On April 3 the *Boston Gazette* advertised that the play was for sale in pamphlet form. The pamphlet edition published in Boston included four scenes and an epilogue. A short time later, pamphlet editions were published in both New York and Philadelphia. These pamphlets included only the two scenes which had appeared in the newspapers and may have been copied directly from the newspapers. The last two scenes and the epilogue contained in the Boston edition seem to anticipate the fateful day, April 19, when the British troops marched out of Boston to seize military stores at Concord.

In her prologue to the play, Mrs. Warren set forth her purpose in writing it:

> *Hear this and tremble, ye who 'scape the laws;*
> *Yes, while I live, no rich or noble knave,*
> *Shall walk the world in credit to his grave;*
> *To virtue only, and her friends, a friend,*
> *The world beside may murmur, or commend.*

All of the characters in *The Group*, with the exception of Hazelrod (Peter Oliver, formerly the "adulateur") and Sylla (General Gage), are councilors appointed by the king. They are given names like Brigadier Hateall, Hum Humbug, Sir Sparrow Spendall, Beau Trumps, Simple Sapling, and Crusty Crowbar. Though *The Group* was published without identifying the characters, there are five extant copies of the play with a key written in. Few of these Tories are known by name today.

In *The Group* Mrs. Warren has no virtuous patriots to praise the ideal of freedom. Perhaps her cry for freedom and liberty sounds even louder by being voiced by the Loyalists. Most of Mrs. Warren's councilors realize that through their own weakness they have rejected the great ideal of liberty.

In the epilogue, Mrs. Warren voices, through "a Lady reclined in an alcove," her faith in the final victory of the Americans over the British troops. Many "painful scenes" will follow, the lady says—

> *Till British troops shall to Columbia yield*
> *And Freedom's sons are Masters of the field.*

Mrs. Warren, writing the final scenes of this play just a few weeks before Lexington and Concord, tried to give the untrained militia the confidence to face the British troops.

The success of *The Group* seems to have made Mercy Warren feel a little guilty about the picture she had drawn of the Tories. She began to wonder if such cutting satire was suitable for a lady to write. She wrote her friend John Adams to ask him what he thought. John Adams responded in a letter to her husband: "My most friendly regards to a certain Lady, tell her the God Almighty (I use a bold style) has entrusted her with Powers for the good of the World, which, in the Cause of his Providence, he bestows on few of the human race. That instead of being a fault to use them, it would be criminal to neglect them." Abigail Adams added her own comment to the letter. "I observe," she wrote, "my friend is laboring under apprehension, lest the severity with which a certain *Group* was drawn was incompatible with that benevolence which ought always to be predominant in a female character. . . . Yet when it is so happily blended with benevolence, and is awakened by the love of virtue and abhorrence of vice . . . it is so far from blamable that it is certainly meritorious."

Perhaps these words helped to reassure Mrs. Warren that her satire was necessary to the cause. However, *The Group* seems to have been the last of Mrs. Warren's dramatic satires. Some scholars have credited her with two more satirical plays, *The Blockheads; or, the Affrighted Officers,* and *The Motley Assembly,* but there seems to be no proof that she wrote either of them and their style is quite different from *The Adulateur, The Defeat,* and *The Group.*

In 1805, at the age of seventy-seven, Mrs. Warren published her three-volume *History of the American Revolution,* which she had begun in 1775.

In 1814, hearing that the copy of *The Group* in the Athenaeum in Boston had been attributed to one Samuel Barrett, Mrs. Warren asked her old friend

John Adams to vouch for her authorship. Adams, seventy-nine years of age at the time, traveled to Boston and wrote on the last leaf of the pamphlet: "August 17, 1814. The 'Group' to my certain knowledge was written by Mrs. Mercy Warren of Plymouth. So certifies John Adams."

About the same time, Mrs. Warren wrote at the end of her own copy of *The Adulateur*: "Though many years have elapsed since the above sketches were written and time has meliorated the resentment felt against those who strenuously endeavored to enslave the American colonies, they were in the busy period of the Revolution deemed a just portrait of the characters mentioned in the preceding pages; and all who are acquainted with the historic records of those times will compare historic and dramatic narration and accede to the justice and truth of the description." In October of that same year, 1814, Mercy Otis Warren died. Through her plays she had been an active participant in the struggle for a new nation.

LOOKING TO WOMEN: RACHEL CROTHERS AND THE FEMINIST HEROINE

LOIS GOTTLIEB

In 1931, Djuna Barnes interviewed Rachel Crothers for the *Theater Guild* magazine. She asked how, from such an early point in her career (around 1908), Crothers had been able to overcome masculine resistance and take charge of the production of her own plays. Crothers referred specifically to several women who had helped her and offered the following generalization: "For a woman, it is best to look to women for help; women are more daring, they are glad to take the most extraordinary chances. . . . I think I should have been longer about my destiny if I had to battle with men alone."[1] Coming as late as 1931, Crothers's affirmation of women's capabilities and her assertion that women play an important role in the destinies of other women contradict the generally held belief that by the second half of her career, beginning in the 1920's, Crothers's plays depict the failure of the American women's movement and repudiate the feminism so apparent in her earlier plays.

The term "feminism" in relation to Crothers's plays can certainly cover everything from fearless exposés of sex antagonism and injustices to women to a benign focus on women at the center of the dramas. The role of feminism in her plays clearly changes from a coherent and optimistic ideology to a rather shadowy and amorphous afterimage. Crothers's feminist

Lois C. Gottlieb, who teaches in the Department of English, University of Guelph, is the author of *Rachel Crothers*.

heroines change, too, from energetic and clear-sighted rebels to women who are confused, dissatisfied with the sense of emancipation surrounding them. These are developments in feminism, as Crothers saw it, however, not reversals or failures. And they can be understood best through the plays themselves, within which Crothers developed the theme of woman's evolution—her purposeful and inevitable progress. In these plays she created a particular kind of feminist heroine crucial to that evolution: the woman who looks to other women, to give help and to get help, in order to advance woman's development.

Between 1899 and 1906, Crothers's apprentice years as a playwright, her feminist heroines reflect society's views of their specialness. Such women stood out from most other women as a studied contrast in dress, behavior, and attitude, with greater intellectual capabilities and a usually recognizable professional or working role. Crothers further emphasizes the distinguishing external qualities of these women by contrasting them with the more traditional women characters, who tend to be unpleasant, difficult, weak, or malicious in these early plays.

The superiority of these incipient feminist heroines is partially a negative factor in their lives. They lose, or almost lose, the men they love, not, ostensibly, because the men devalue their superiority, but because they overvalue it. The superior women themselves often overvalue their strength and competence, and they seem to chasten this excessive pride by giving up the men they love to "needier" women, that is, women whose whole lives are love.

The superior sufferer is tacit evidence of woman's evolution, but she does not advance that evolution. When she looks to other women to help them, what she sees are traditional women and what she helps them to are women's traditional goals: marriage, respectability, protection. The social injustices which limit the superior women to lonely nobility are only indirectly commented on. Far from seeing herself in the mirror of other women's lives, the superior sufferer is defined by her unlikeness to the common run of femininity.

Rhy McChesney, in Crothers's first theatrical success, *The Three of Us* (1906),[2] is really a "transitional" heroine and reflects Crothers's difficulty in bringing her feminist out of the closet. She attempts to advance woman's evolution by defying the double moral standard, which insists on man as woman's protector, and she explicitly dissociates herself from the "fear" of a compromised reputation that is supposed to curtail the activity of "all good women." Crothers gives Rhy a forceful declaration of independence by which to demolish the age-old role of the masculine protector. As she says to both the villain and the hero: "My honor! Do you think it is in your hands? It's in my own, and I'll take care of it, and everyone who *belongs* to me. I don't need you—either of you." But Crothers also has Rhy pose as a helpless woman so that her brother, whose ego has been damaged by having a strong sister, can enhance his self-image by defending a woman's honor.

Between 1908 and 1914 Crothers wrote a series of social problem plays, American style, in which the feminist heroine is far more comfortable with her strength than earlier heroines, is consciously motivated by her desire to help other women break out of boundaries, and is explicit in her belief in women's evolution and its beneficial impact on society. Crothers's central women of this period are not "youngsters" and several of the most interesting characters are in their mid-thirties, expressing Crothers's conviction that modern dramatists no longer had to "confine heroines to ingenues, stage age seventeen."[3] These are, in fact, experienced women, successful in business and the arts. Bettina Marshall of *Myself Bettina* (1908) and Frank Ware of *A Man's World* (1909) have traveled and lived abroad; Victoria Claffenden in *Young Wisdom* (1914) is a college graduate; Ruth Creel and Ann Herford in *He and She* (1911) have developed themselves as journalist and sculptor, respectively, through discipline and long apprenticeship; and Beatrice Barrington in *Ourselves* (1913) steeps herself in a personal as well as theoretical knowledge of the causes and cures of the great social evil, prostitution.

Crothers endows these women with more freedom of experience and thought than her earlier characters, and the questions they debate and the battles they fight supply far more abundant evidence of woman's emancipation than one could glean from earlier plays. Bettina, for example, in the manuscript of *Myself Bettina*, refuses to define woman's honor exclusively by her reputation and condemns marriage as the means to restore a "fallen woman's" honor. Frank Ware, in *A Man's World*, writes social protest novels exposing the brutality of women's lives on the Lower East Side, where poverty and prostitution are inextricably linked to keep women in bondage and where both phenomena are traceable to the "man's world." Frank also tackles the problem of woman's sense of psychological inferiority to man and her dependence on masculine attention for status and self-respect. *He and She* questions the impediments placed by men before the artist woman and critically examines the charges of inherent inferiority, unnaturalness, selfishness, and injustice to husbands and children which were part and parcel of the emotional baggage the artist woman was forced to contend with. In the manuscript of *Ourselves* the premise is that prostitution is a "man's business"—and a big business at that—and that society has been sidetracked from resolving the problem by focusing on the women when the more effective approach would be to start "locking up the men."[4]

On almost every point, these central women are acutely and critically conscious of the status of women, but an equally conspicuous feature of their character is their attempt to impart this consciousness to other women, not only to teach them about their bondage, but also to see the freedom of their own lives reflected in the lives of more women. In two of these plays, *Myself Bettina* and *Young Wisdom*, Crothers perceives the helping within a family context, as an older, more experienced, and more emancipated sister attempts to encourage or hasten the advancement of her more domesticated or confined sister. In three of these plays, women turn their attention to a wider sphere of women, enlarging the notion of sisterhood from a familial to a societal relation. In *A Man's World*, for example, Frank sets up a girl's club on the Lower East Side to provide a center of learning and support in an environment hostile to woman's freedom. Frank's ideal of woman's self-sufficiency and strength does not endear her to all women—particularly to women of her own class who are alienated by it. Thus, when Frank tackles the problem of women who are psychologically, though not economically, dominated and diminished by the operation of the man's world, her helping meets with some resistance. Lione Brune, a temperamental and haughty opera singer, acknowledges that "All men are pigs," but resents what she considers Frank's "show" of independence from men and refuses to adopt it for herself, since she fears the reprisal of a manless existence. In another dimension, Clara Oakes, a timid, unsuccessful miniature painter, is fearful of Frank's disapproval because she is tired of being strong and self-sufficient and is, in fact, humiliated by her spinster status. Clara does gain a measure of self-respect, however, when she accepts Frank's offer of a job as a resident art teacher in the ghetto girls' club. In *He and She*, Ruth Creel, a successful young journalist with an entirely emancipated view of woman's nature, spends a good deal of time encouraging the artistic development of her friend, Ann Herford, a thirty-six-year-old wife and mother who has had a late start developing her considerable talent as a sculptor and is still uncertain of her abilities. As Ann cheerfully contends with patronizing solicitousness toward her work and family interruptions, Ruth argues that Ann has genius and ought to resist everything that threatens it, including her father and her husband. Eventually, Ann acknowledges the inhibitions these men have placed on her advancement, and although she has secretly created designs for her sculptor husband to enter in an important public competition, she follows Ruth's advice to enter them under her own name, and she beats her husband for first prize.

Crothers's portraits of rebels and reformers are more complex than this brief survey might suggest, or to put it another way, her plays are less programmatic than the "dramatic tracts" written by other feminists. Two plays of this period offer insights into some of the drawbacks of the reform movement. In *Ourselves*, for example, Beatrice Barrington is a type of privileged, wealthy, sheltered reformer whose desires to help women needier than herself exceed her ability to do so and blind her to the urgent need to understand the situation of women in her own class. She takes home a prostitute from a reformatory in order to work out theories of the benefits of a refining influence on the lives of fallen women, but Beatrice's housekeeper has far more impact on the young woman and has far more luck becoming her intimate than does the wealthy woman. And the young prostitute, rebelling against being treated as an "experiment" rather than a person, ultimately refuses further "refuge" from her patroness and returns to the slums, convinced that self-help, not patronage, is the best process for freeing women like herself.

In the manuscript of her final play of this series, *Young Wisdom*, Crothers depicts a naïve and breathless heroine who delights in reading aloud from her mentors, such as Mona Caird and Ellen Key—both well-known anti-Victorian critics. Victoria argues for the merits of free love and "trial marriage," and is swept away by an excess of enthusiasm for woman's evolution. As she breathlessly declares: "The future of the world depends on women. . . . Men don't evolute at all, you know." Through Victoria Crothers pursues the possibility that radical feminist thought may misguide woman's evolution, and this play, like the others, displays the moderate position Crothers took as a feminist on the subject of woman's evolution. While the four earlier plays reflect the middle-ground position, "that with the development of society is bound up henceforward the more complete and perfect evolution of women,"[5] this last play shows Crothers's rejection of "the attempt of a few extremists to exalt the wonder woman at the expense of the man."[6]

The heroines of this period bear witness to the increasing numbers of women affected by the women's movement. Their activity reflects what journalists called a growing "sex loyalty" or "sex solidarity" among women, which the women's movement had generated and which could be put to work to aid the evolution of all women. Crothers publicly praised the growing sex-loyalty for its success in closing two particularly divisive gaps: the moral chasm between "good women" and the "woman who has strayed from the path of conventional morality," and the personal division between "the home woman" and her "self-supporting sister,"[7] whom she resented. She also acknowledged that her own progress in the theatre had been aided by sex solidarity: she received important professional help when Maxine Elliott, the star to whom Crothers had sold *Myself Bettina*, allowed Crothers to stage and direct it. As Crothers noted, Elliott had "such an admiration for and faith in the work of woman, that she was delighted to find a woman who could shoulder the entire responsibility."[8] Sex loyalty, however, also placed Crothers on the defensive, when some feminists denounced *Young Wisdom* and Crothers took to the papers to defend herself and her play against charges of "hypocrisy" and pandering to the box office. Crothers argued that she had already proved herself a "natural woman's champion," the "most ardent of feminists" and saw no discrepancy between her belief "in women and their capacity to earn their daily bread in the same field and on the same footing with men," and her intent to satirize the "theories involved in the advanced women, to laugh *with* them, not at them," at the funny, chaotic results which would ensue if "the radical ideas" of "the most militant feminist" were at once adopted and acted upon.[9]

Between 1914 and 1919, Crothers wrote a group of six plays, which replaced social problems with sentiment and which were modeled on the popular "gladness" plays, of which *Pollyanna* is probably the best-known example. For the only time in her career, Crothers abandoned both the themes of woman's evolution and the feminist heroine, and their absence

makes a striking difference. Women characters in conventional mold, financially dependent on men, once seen in secondary roles in her earlier plays,
now took center stage.

With the 1920's, however, Crothers reintroduces a feminist perspective,
but the comic mode which she adopted and perfected in this decade compli-
cates her treatment of woman's evolution. As comic figures the central
women of the twenties lose their previously idealized characterizations as
well as their long hair. Where the rebellious reformers were almost entirely a
collection of superior women, the twenties heroines are either immature,
ordinary to a fault, or, in some cases, less than ordinary. Two of these
heroines, Teddy Gloucester, in *Nice People* (1921)[10] and the daughter, Mary,
in *Mary the Third* (1923),[11] are frenetic flappers, barely out of their teens.
Minnie Whitcomb is a pathetically mousy music teacher in *Expressing Willie*
(1925),[12] and Nancy Marshall, a figure in several one-acts published in 1926,[13]
is a "feminist opportunist," selfishly exploiting suffrage gains to further her
political career. The single superior woman, the androgynous female aviator
in *Venus* (1927)[14] is a figure of fantasy.

Another important feature of the comic characterization of these women
is that Crothers portrays them as products of their flawed society rather than
as superior to it. They show an excessive concern with self-fulfillment and
personal liberty, the watchwords of their day. When the twenties heroine
recognizes a social injustice to women, her solution is emphatically individual.

Along with the comic emphasis on "self," the plays reflect the weakening
of sex solidarity. Crothers's women of the 1920's will not look to other
women for help. For the flappers in *Nice People,* for example, women of the
critical older generations mirror a type of femininity distasteful to the younger women. As sex solidarity weakens, woman's role in helping other
women break out of boundaries is relegated to a secondary action or is
entirely ignored even while change for women remains at the center of the
plays. In two plays the evolution of women is expressed by magic, or
fantasy. The self-effacing Minnie of *Expressing Willie* finally achieves power
and confidence, but only through the satirized, pseudo-Freudian ritual of
digging deeply inside herself, freeing herself from "suppressions," and
releasing buried greatness. The female aviator in *Venus,* disgusted by sex
antagonism on earth, prepares to emigrate to Venus in order to live the
androgynous life.

In looking to the women of the 1920's, then, Crothers highlights their
flaws and foibles and plays down their positive qualities. The feminist
heroine is a comic character who struggles to maintain equilibrium and
identity in the intoxicating freedom of postwar society, and Crothers portrays this as an age which wedged itself between generations of women as
well as between women of the same generation, isolating them from the
mutual help which had proved so effective in advancing women's progress
in the preceding era.

The four plays of Crothers's last period, 1929–37, do not easily lend themselves to a uniform reading on the status of woman's evolution; what they reveal about the fate of the feminist heroine after the 1920's is certainly too complicated to be supported by general reference to the "demise of the New Woman."[15] The novelty of being an "evolved" woman has worn off; only vestiges remain of the external, man's world to be fought. Therefore, the announcements of dissatisfaction, loneliness, depression, and boredom issuing from the most visible exemplars of the "daughters" of the new women are cause for attention. Thirty-year-old Kitty Brown, in *Let Us Be Gay* (1929), and thirty-six-year-old Mary Howard, in *When Ladies Meet* (1932), are both glamorous, creative, well-traveled, financially successful, and sexually liberated women, but far from being "completed" by their freedom, these women find their lives lacking and are beset by confusion and anxiety. The thirties home-women, however, make the same complaints. The two middle-aged Iowa housewives in *As Husbands Go* (1931) dread a return to the lifelessness and anonymity of their domestic roles after a revitalizing trip to Europe; and Susan Trexler, in *Susan and God* (1937), confesses to her daughter that she has spent most of her domestic life trying to fill it up with things outside marriage and family.

The evolved woman inherited a "freedom" from gross, external injustices but not a guaranteed place in the sun, freed from internal anxieties and fears. As a consequence, Crothers records a sense of disillusionment with the women's movement, and a tendency to blame it for deficiencies in woman's emotional life. As seventy-six-year-old Mrs. Boucicault puts it, in *Let Us Be Gay:* "Women are getting everything they think they want now, but are they any happier than they were when they used to stay home and let men fool them?"

The new challenge, then, for the woman of the 1930's, is to find "happiness" rather than justice or advancement. In the face of the Depression, the rise of Fascism, and the onset of World War II, it is not surprising that Crothers emphasizes the difficulty of this task. Her heroines tackle it with all the energy Crothers normally endows her advanced women, but a sense of disillusionment pervades the plays.

Far from being entirely negative about woman's evolution, however, Crothers's last plays deal with the continued process of woman's growth and Crothers carefully identifies her latest challenges. The plays appeal to woman to take a more accurate measure of the dimensions of the human male and discard the idealized myth; they demonstrate the necessity for woman to reject a "man-centered" distortion of reality but, at the same time, to assess honestly man's place in her emotional life.

One play from this period, *When Ladies Meet,* supplies a full and consistent critique of man's place in the emotional life of the evolved woman. Crothers concentrates on two women who have a man-centered reality. They have, consequently, not only inflated and idealized man—as protector, savior, and source of transcendence—but they have also accepted a "second-hand image" of woman, as she is reflected through man's eyes, and this is an image that divides women from each other as well as from themselves.

The two central women of *When Ladies Meet*—the ladies of the title—are built from the stereotypical models of antagonistic women—since they are the mistress and wife of the same weak-willed publisher. Mischance brings them together, ignorant of each other's relationship to the man. Each woman meets her "rival," without preconceptions and certainly without a predisposing hostility. In fact, the women like each other a great deal. Because mutual affection and trust have built between the women in the absence of the man, Crothers can deliver a far different recognition scene when each finally discovers the other's identity. Claire, the wife, sees that Mary, "the other woman," is not a "vile brazen slut" though throughout the long years of marriage with a philandering husband, she has consoled herself with the image of the "other woman" as a cheap seducer. Similarly, Mary sees that Claire, the "wife," is not the dull, unsympathetic creature of her lover's complaints—an image soothing to Mary's conscience—but rather is a lively, humorous, attractive woman. In short, the man-centered reality does not survive.

By eliminating man as the lens through which to view woman, Claire and Mary have both outgrown an imprisoning myth; the consequence is that rather than fight each other for the man, each rejects him, Claire leaving her husband and Mary ending her affair. Both have taken a more accurate measure of the dimensions of the human male, and Mary is an interesting example of a Crothers woman for whom this reality is not too hard to bear.

In fact, this reality is a prelude to Mary's taking a more honest look at man's place in her life, and she does so with humor. She is the "strong" and "intelligent" woman who "at last persuades herself that a man is *the* thing in life she wants" and as a consequence, she accepts the label of "the biggest fool of all!"[16]

It is one measure of the distance traveled by the evolved woman that Mary can acknowledge man's place in her life, without self-loathing or self-pity. She is no longer bound to the stoical silence that marked earlier feminist heroines, suffering loneliness and isolation. But the spectacle of an evolved woman, aggressively announcing that career, money, and acclaim have not brought her personal happiness or assuaged her loneliness, was disconcerting to those who had judged Crothers a feminist. Eleanor Flexner was particularly distressed by Mary's complaint, at the beginning of *When Ladies Meet:* "I haven't found *anything*. Except to know that I haven't *got* anything that really *counts*. Nobody *belongs* to me—nobody whose very existence depends on me. I am completely and absolutely alone." Flexner saw this as a significant sign of the failure of feminism.[17] For Flexner, "the wheel has come full circle." The progress of woman's evolution had not simply been slowed, but reversed.

When Ladies Meet is not, however, a cry from woman to reverse woman's evolution. In fact, the structure of the play argues that Mary's critical examination and honest assessment of her independent status advances, rather than reverses woman's progress. Mary's declaration of loneliness is heard at the beginning of the play; the action that follows comically exposes Mary's attempt to assuage her loneliness through an idealized lover. Crothers does not mock the loneliness as an unworthy or degraded emotion, but she does make comedy out of Mary's attempt to combat loneliness, mocking Mary's distorted, "man-centered" view of things.

Mary is a new type of feminist heroine in the Crothers canon, and she brings new dimensions of humor and insight to the conflict between the evolved woman and love. In terms of Crothers's career, Mary represents the last stage in the development of the theme of woman's evolution, begun three decades before, but she is evidence that through this last phase of her career, Crothers reiterated the importance of supportive bonds between women in the continuous struggle for woman's progress.

APROPOS OF WOMEN AND THE FOLK PLAY

RACHEL FRANCE

The first use of the term *folk play* in the American theatre appears to have been the Carolina Playmakers' *Carolina Folk Plays* on the program for their initial production at Chapel Hill, March 14 and 15, 1919. Credited with this term was Professor Frederick Koch, who hoped that, by beginning with a specific locale, a writer would eventually find his or her way to the universal. If a writer could view "the lives about him with wonder, why may he not interpret that life in significant images for others?" Koch asked. "It has been so in all lasting art."[1] Hamlin Garland was prompted to say of such efforts that "locality makes the American drama."[2]

There were, however, earlier plays about rural life, many of them written by women for whom the important issue was not locale but, rather, defining exactly who in America could be described as its "folks." These plays, ignored by Koch and Garland, would not be included in the standard canons of Folk Art.

Ruth Suckow's essay, "The Folk Idea in American Life," does much to illuminate this earlier group of plays about rural life. She attacks the view that folk art—especially in America—should be tied to regional peculiarities. Her folk were "hard-working people of a fairly religious call, with a strong

Rachel France, editor of *A Century of Plays by American Women*, wrote this paper as part of her larger study, *The Drama of Sex: Apropos of Women and the American Theatre*.

belief in education, Protestant, and to that extent Puritan."[3] Rather than simple people living close to the land, Suckow's picture of "folks" can better be recognized as "the silent majority."

Her essay, written in 1930, reiterates, with the clarity of hindsight, the effort—most fervent after World War I—to define native American culture as something distinct from and independent of European culture. This effort began in earnest toward the end of the nineteenth century, inspired, in no small part, by the nearly 15 million foreigners who immigrated to the United States between 1896 and 1914. These newcomers gave rise to the fear that America's boast of a classless society might only be realized at the expense of the native born.

This nativist point of view warrants mentioning because it was also espoused by the most prominent members of the women's movement. Suffragists found it especially ironic that so large a group of "foreign" men could expect to be enfranchised before "American" women. But, more important, it provides an exact reflection of the spirit which informed so many of the folk plays written by women prior to 1920.

In these folk plays middle-class white women bear the cultural burdens of American civilization; they are preserving their small enclaves from the corruption of outside influence. Intellectual or social pressures are brought upon them by men. However, these folk plays reflect the isolation of women from wider social structures. Men who engage in the activities of the world are seen essentially as foreigners to the rural sense of community and are cast aside. The imaginative constructs of folk drama render them negligible. Folk drama becomes, therefore, the drama of the woman's world.

Zona Gale's vision in The Neighbors (1912) should be taken as a vision of the upper Midwest which may have existed for her as a young woman. It is also one which she would subsequently reject as hopelessly naïve in Miss Lulu Bett, written less than a decade later.

Central to Gale's idea of "folks" in The Neighbors is the notion that human beings are fundamentally good—or, at least, "folks" are. Their finest instincts might lie beneath a rough exterior, but they can be brought out when the latent sense of community of folks to which they belong is realized.

Implicit in Gale's concept, also, is the idea that the community is held together by women. Of the eight characters in the play, six are women. They are all instinctively aware of correct social behavior. By word and by deed they will educate Ezra Williams, a woodcutter, and Peter, who suffers from unrequited love.

Gale shows how the women's influence comes into play when "neighbors" are faced with a problem. One of them, Mis' Carry Ellsworth, plans to adopt her orphaned nephew. He is to arrive that evening, but Mis' Ellsworth lacks the means to care for him properly. Only Ezra fails to respond to the situation with instinctive goodness. "Well, ain't that just like a woman!" he exclaims. "Always gettin' herself come down by a lot o' distant relatives to support."[4]

The women, however, quickly find the appropriate way to assist their friend and neighbor. Mis' Ellsworth, they know, would not accept money, "even if anybody had any to offer." Instead, they hit upon the plan to give her clothing and other supplies that she will need. The values of the community emerge. Charity, to these self-sufficient people, is indeed "nasty." Of prime importance is to be "folks."

It is Peter who displays the deepest flaw, one that keeps him from the community. Although he is one of them, Peter has yet to learn how to behave properly. "Folks is folks, no matter how different or similar," says Grandma. "They can't fool us. Folks is folks." Peter, with his predilection for lofty discussion, seems to be denying that he, too, is "folks." The women are aware that Peter needs to conform, since it is actions and the shared remembrance of the local landscape and family events which bind the community together.

The women, as Ezra notes, "tend to the society end of this town." His business is seen as inconsequential men's work; however, he is considered a member of the community, if only because of "the few little things my wife just sent over."

At the end of Gale's play, the neighbors learn that another home has been found for Mis' Ellsworth's nephew. The women gather to share her loss. "We all know," Mis' Abel begins. "I ain't had but one, but I know." Mis' Trot agrees, "Yes. I've got seven an' sometimes I'm drove most to death with 'em—but I know." And, although Mis' Moran "never had none," she too knows. "Mine's dead—all dead," Grandma adds. "But I know." And so does Inez know. Their remarks form a chant of "womanhood," the common sensibility which is the foundation of the community.

Although there are two men in *The Neighbors*, their presence plays no part in the women's lives. Only Mis' Moran mentions her husband. Feeling slighted by Mis' Abel, she complains, "If that ain't just like Jake's treatment of me." Apparently, the most useful male contribution, which is not female-inspired, is the eight dollars a month that Mis' Ellsworth receives.

In addition to the stress upon "womanhood," *The Neighbors* touches upon the conflict between the sexes. It is this conflict that is explored quite fully in Alice Brown's *Children of the Earth* (1913), where it is an important secondary theme added to the basic folk drama theme of country versus city. This four-act play has had an impact beyond its stage success, or lack of stage success, because of its subject matter—with the ultimate triumph of woman over man, and of nature over materialism.

Children of the Earth goes well beyond Gale's relatively simple assertion in *The Neighbors* that the sense of community is a natural aspect of rural life. Instead, Brown depicts a rural civilization which is still to be fully formed, focusing on that point in time when the community is threatened both by the materialism of the industrial age and by the unrefined sensuality of frontier days. Her heroine, Mary Ellen Barstow, must integrate the natural aspects of rural life, the feeling of union with the earth, with a profound sense of duty, to morality and the work ethic, to realize a new level of civilization—for herself and for the "children of the earth" for whom it is her special province to care.

It is difficult to comprehend *Children of the Earth* in terms of realistic passion. The play reads like a reconstruction of archetypal themes in American literature—in terms of the unique place of "womanhood." Brown tells her story in terms of Mary Ellen's relationship with two men. One of them, Nate Buell, is a city man who is "always looking out for the main chance."[5] He has been denatured, so no compact with him is possible. Peter Hale, on the other hand, represents the natural man. He is married to Jane, a dark woman of mysterious origin. Mary Ellen could, if she wished, win Peter for herself. However, their union would merely be a sexual one, as Peter's marriage to Jane has undoubtedly been. Instead, Mary Ellen symbolically weds both Peter and Jane. Their combined sexual energies will, hereafter, be sublimated by the need to care for the land and all its people. Thus, Mary Ellen finally succeeds in civilizing the wilderness.

Children of the Earth was an evocation of American life which drew upon certain nativist literary traditions. Brown has attempted to alter existing stereotypes by creating a new formulation for the role which women played in the making of America. The play achieved immediate favorable recognition by Winthrop Ames, who was anxious to promote the work of American dramatists. He offered a $10,000 prize in 1913 for the best play submitted anonymously by an American author. Augustus Thomas, Adolph Klauber, and Ames himself selected *Children of the Earth* from nearly 17,000 manuscripts. In 1915 the play ran for a disappointing thirty-four performances at the Booth Theatre in New York.

A salient fact about Brown, and authors like Neith Boyce and Susan Glaspell who also wrote about rural life, is that these women had left the small communities of their birth in order to participate in the theatrical life of New York City. Brown, for example, worked extensively with the Washington Square Players, who performed most of her one-act plays. The reality which pervades their work is the reality of remembered life seen through the prism of the cosmopolitan milieu which they had chosen. Part of this milieu was the avant-garde of a triumphant feminist movement.

The women they knew had fled the countryside in order to gratify their desires and instincts. Yet their plays reveal the life of farm women with reverence. While Zona Gale presented women as the triumphant moral arbiters of rural communities, city feminists saw farm women as nobly struggling to gain their rightful ascendancy. For city dwellers, the country became sentimentalized. They felt that it had natural values which were lost in the artificiality and materialism of urban life. In a sense they saw their own freedom as artificial. In the country, women coped with primordial realities. *Children of the Earth* had as its primary objective to show how a woman might transcend these realities. Her heroine gains ascendancy because Brown has made spiritual awakening an adequate tool for coping with sexual and material appetites. But Brown is quite obviously describing the ideal, rather than portraying the realities of rural life. Yet, it is precisely the ideal of woman's having natural moral superiority that informs three "realistic" plays about rural life which were written shortly after *Children of the Earth*.

Brown's own one-act *Sugar House* (1916) which Margaret Mayorga called "one of the best one-act plays that have been written in America,"[6] appears to be a realistic study of a married man who tries to set up housekeeping in an abandoned sugar house with his lover, a young girl. A mob comes to tar-and-feather the girl. The man's wife intercepts the mob, and by the use of moral persuasion manages to save the girl. Brown makes it abundantly clear that the crude men in the mob have no business meddling in the affairs of women. The husband recognizes that his wife has shown him the path of righteousness from which he must not stray.

Neith Boyce's *Winter's Night* and Susan Glaspell's *Trifles*, both written in 1916, also depict the harsh realities of rural life. Boyce and Glaspell share Brown's optimistic view of women's superior nature. But, unlike Brown, they do not depict happy reconciliations between their women characters and the men who would be agents of their oppression. Both Boyce's heroine, Rachel Wescott, and Glaspell's, Minnie Wright, have, in effect, found personal freedom in their lives, but it is a freedom made possible only after the deaths of their husbands.

Rachel Wescott was married to her husband Daniel for twenty-eight years. During all this time the couple lived with Daniel's brother Jacob. Daniel has just died and Rachel confronts her brother-in-law with her plans for a new life.

I've spent enough of my life here, Jacob, I never meant to stay here forever . . . I've had my ambitions, Jacob, and for all that I'm forty-seven I can't feel that my life's over yet.[7]

Jacob has silently loved Rachel and, with his brother's passing, assumes that he and Rachel will marry. However, Rachel intends to abandon Jacob despite his pleas that she either remain with him or take him with her. She is unsympathetic to his need for her and considers his proposal to be crazy. The situation can only end badly. Once rejected, there is nothing left for Jacob but to blow his head off with a shotgun.

This episode in the play serves to reveal fully the dark atmosphere enveloping the life that Rachel is escaping. The play is notable for the amount of sympathy the author directs toward Rachel and the cavalier way in which she disposes of Jacob. The two men in Rachel's life, her husband and her would-be lover, have existed only to be overcome before she can have a fuller life.

Rachel is unable to articulate why her life has been so barren. Yet Boyce makes it plain that Jacob is fundamentally wrongheaded in thinking that Rachel longed for a man's love. Rachel herself has been aware intuitively of a more profound need denied by her drab existence with Daniel and Jacob. Boyce's thesis is that Rachel has been yearning for esthetic fulfillment—the fulfillment available to ordinary women if only they will grasp for it.

Similarly, Glaspell's *Trifles* is about the drab existence of rural wives. Her biographer[8] describes the play as "precise realism," but the term "precise realism" is applied to two characters who never appear on the stage—John Wright, who has been murdered, and his wife, who murdered him. These characters are seen solely through the eyes of two women who accompany the men investigating Wright's death. Glaspell undoubtedly wanted the views expressed by Mrs. Hale, the neighbor's wife, and Mrs. Peters, the sheriff's wife, to be accepted as truth.

While the action of the play is an investigation, Glaspell has skillfully introduced what are two investigations. The men are simply looking for clues to a murder. Glaspell, with a touch of irony, has Mr. Hale remark at the beginning of the play that "women are used to worrying over trifles."[9] Unbeknown to Hale, it is such "trifles" which furnish the substance of the women's investigation.

In fact, it is the men who are, in Glaspell's eyes, interested in "trifles," like the identity of Wright's murderer. The women, on the other hand, with a finer grasp of ideal justice, realize that, although the murder of Wright was indeed "an awful thing," and a crime in the eyes of the law, that act was not the worst crime committed in the Wright house. The keynote to this is the description of John Wright by one of the women as a man who "didn't drink, kept his word as well as most, I guess, and paid his debts. But he was a hard man. Just to pass the time of day with him [was] like a raw wind that gets to the bone."

The men are destined to hunt in vain for their clues; the women quickly find what the men have missed. This discovery is not an accident; it is the result of their peculiarly feminine sensibilities which enable them to recognize the importance of what they find, a bird with a broken neck. They guess that Wright killed it. "Wright wouldn't like the bird—a thing that sings. He killed that too." They realize that the bird's death might well have been Mrs. Wright's motive for murdering her husband. "If there'd been years and years of nothing, then a bird to sing to you, it would be awful—still, after the bird was. Still."

Glaspell introduces the idea that the truly "awful thing" was not the murder of John Wright but the life that his wife had been forced to endure, isolated in the Wright home. Because they have neglected Mrs. Wright, the women feel implicated in the greater crime. "Oh, I wish I'd come over here once in a while! That was a crime! . . . Who's going to punish that?"

In partial expiation, the women decide to hide the incriminating evidence. The men, as it happens, are on the right track in their investigation. "It's all perfectly clear except for a reason for doing it. But you know juries when it comes to women. If there was some definite thing . . . a thing that would connect up this strange way of doing things." Their concern with the details of the most readily apparent crime is, in Glaspell's eyes, proof of the superficial masculine view of criminal justice. They casually assume that the women feel as they do. "I guess they're not very dangerous things the ladies have picked up . . . Mrs. Peters doesn't need supervising. For that matter, a sheriff's wife is married to the law. Ever think of it that way, Mrs. Peters?" Truthfully Mrs. Peters replies, "Not—just that way."

In *Trifles* Glaspell has clearly pointed to the dichotomy between men and women in rural life. Men are basically insensitive to the nature of women's lives. More important than that, their proclivity for the letter of the law bars them from a humane understanding of justice. The two women, with their sense of higher purpose, band together to protect another woman from what is clearly the injustice of man's law when applied to women. Glaspell in effect condemns John Wright to death for being insensitive to his wife's esthetic yearnings.

For critics like Arthur Hobson Quinn, folk drama had a different meaning. It comprised "a significant movement in this country which has to interpret the life of those natives of America who have retained the primitive culture of their ancestors, and whose emotions have remained in that inarticulate and unsophisticated state which allow them free expression and make them therefore well suited for the drama."[10]

Quinn's choice of a play to represent folk drama was Lula Vollmer's *Sun-Up.* This play not only presents primitive folk life located here in the mountains of North Carolina, but places the characters within the larger context of American civilization. Vollmer's heroine, Widow Cagle, reveals that most "primitive" women instinctively discover their essential bond with all other women. Both Widow Cagle and her son, Rufe, thrown by circumstances of World War I into contact with a larger civilization, instinctively formulate the then currently popular rationale for fighting the war.

Sun-Up is a notable departure from the other folk plays mentioned here, in that it places its characters within the framework of current events. Although first produced at the Provincetown Playhouse in 1923, the play was most probably written in 1918. Vollmer had come to New York that same year, at the height of America's war activity. The play was her response to the war while it was still going on. Burns Mantle reports that Vollmer's friends from the South brought her many stories of the reactions of Carolina mountain folk to the draft. "It took two weeks to get the play on paper but she spent the next five years in search of a producer."[11]

Lula Vollmer's primitive North Carolinians eventually see the war as a means of preserving American ideals. In fact, the war is responsible for Widow Cagle's recognition that she has a common bond with all other mothers. "As long as thar air hate—there will be feuds. As long as thar air women thar will be—sons. I ain't no more to you than other mothers' sons air to them."[12] This theme, readily apparent to less primitive minds, is revealed to the Widow Cagle through her dead son's spiritual message. Her truly womanly nature is awakened. "I heared you, Rufe. I never knowed nothin' but about lovin' anything but ye—till ye showed me hit's lovin' them all that counts."

Widow Cagle, as an example of primitive life, begins by opposing any intrusion by the government into her life. When the sheriff comes to investigate the failure of two mountain youths, one of them Rufe, to register for the draft, Widow Cagle voices her negative feelings about the government. Rufe, however, has had some schooling. "That little bit o' larnin' taught me to respect something a little higher than my own way of wantin' to do things." It has equipped him to understand the need for going to war, even at the cost of his own life.

Rufe's unarticulated feeling of patriotism combines with the only other knowledge he possesses, also unarticulated, of the world beyond his home—religion. Armed with his knowledge of God and country, Rufe can face his mother when she tells him, "It seems a little queer to me that ye air goin' off to fight the Yankees with Zeb Turner, the man who killed yo Pap, still alive."

The point Vollmer is making is that, even though her characters are innocent to the point of simplicity, their intuitive reactions and instinctive wisdom in time of national crisis draw them to the stated purposes of the national government—a government whose very existence is mythical to them, "somethin' a little higher than my own way of wantin' to do things." The government is identical with the "somethin' different outen the Bible."

Before her turn to patriotism, the Widow Cagle makes a very shrewd political analysis of her own. "Thar ain't no reason fer war, unless us poor folks fight the rich uns for the way they air bleedin' us to death with prices for meat and bread." But the newly patriotic Widow Cagle discards these Marxist ideas. Patriotism, Vollmer suggests, brings out womanly sentiment.

Lula Vollmer was the American playwright whose work was most often produced throughout the little theatre network, with *Sun-Up* her most popular play. *Sun-Up* brought folk drama into the larger context of American life. If the characters are unsophisticated, Vollmer's concept was not. It held that everything profoundly true must be simple enough to be understood by even the most primitive among us.

Theatre-goers could identify with Vollmer's characters in the sense that they represented American life in its purest form. Undoubtedly they served as an imaginative release from reality. Archetypes of the native American— simple, basically good, independent, and free—they carry over to this day in popular literature, in cartoons, and on television.

ANNE NICHOLS: $1,000,000.00 PLAYWRIGHT

DORIS ABRAMSON AND LAURILYN HARRIS

If a young woman with an Irish surname marries a young man from a Jewish family, someone is bound to refer to her as "Abie's Irish Rose." Explanations are seldom necessary. The expression has become a cliché, firmly embedded in our language.

It found its way into our traditional speech by way of a play that opened on Broadway, May 23, 1922, and closed—over five years later—on October 22, 1927. Eventually, *Abie's Irish Rose* became something of a national institution. It set a record for consecutive performances (2,327) and held that record for fourteen years. After that comedy had been running three years, Lorenz Hart wrote lyrics for Richard Rodgers's song "Manhattan" that included the line: "Our future babies we'll take to *Abie's Irish Rose*. I hope they'll live to see it close—someday." When it reached its 2,000th performance, the *New York Telegraph* noted that a group of Jewish and Irish children in attendance were not even born when the play started its New York run. Milton Wallace, one of the actors in the company, had cards printed listing *Abie's Irish Rose* as his permanent address.

Who wrote this extraordinary popular hit? The multitudes who have heard of the play usually do not remember (or, more likely, never knew) that its author was a woman—a rather remarkable woman named Anne Nichols. It is estimated that from this single play she earned a million dollars in royalties as author and millions more as producer.[1] The movie rights alone brought in two million. In addition, she wrote over twenty other plays, numerous vaudeville sketches, and was an active producing-manager. Indeed, hers is perhaps one of the greatest commercial success stories in the history of the American theatre. "There were weeks when I made $180,000 net profit," she once told Arthur Gelb. "I bought stocks and bonds and most of Flushing."[2]

Strangely enough, Ms. Nichols's theatrical achievements have for the most part been either belittled or pointedly ignored. She is seldom mentioned in current theatre history textbooks. She rates no separate listing in standard reference works such as *The Oxford Companion to the Theatre* or *The Reader's Encyclopedia of World Drama*. You won't find much attention devoted to her in the latest edition of the *Encyclopedia Britannica*, and the *Encyclopedia Americana* lists her name once (under the heading "Abie's Irish Rose"), while

Doris Abramson, Professor of Theatre at the University of Massachusetts, Amherst, is the author of *Negro Playwrights in the American Theatre, 1925–1959* as well as studies of early black women playwrights. Laurilyn Harris, who is Associate Professor in the Theatre Arts Program, Washington State University, has published articles in *Theatre Research International*, *Theatre Annual*, *Nineteenth Century Theatre Research*, and *Theatre History Studies*. Reprinted from *Players Magazine*, April-May 1976 by permission of the authors.

several paragraphs are devoted to the accomplishments of golfer Jack Nicklaus.[3]

This neglect may be the result of a deeply ingrained attitude shared by a number of male theatre critics and historians, an attitude perhaps best summed up by George Jean Nathan: "Even the best of our women playwrights falls considerably short of the mark of our best masculine . . . women, when it comes to the confection of drama, are most often inferior to their boy-friends."[4] Thus all American women playwrights, from Anna Cora Mowatt to Lillian Hellman, are casually dismissed as somehow "inferior" to their male counterparts, and one casualty of this bias is undoubtedly Anne Nichols. One has to search out old newspaper articles for any detailed information about her life and works. In most instances, she remains simply the name below the title of Abie's Irish Rose.

Anne Nichols was born in 1891 in Dale's Mill, Georgia, and reared in Philadelphia. Despite a rigid Baptist upbringing, her childhood ambition was to become an actress, and, at sixteen, she ran away from home with thirty-six dollars in her purse to pursue her ambition. Down to her last five dollars, she eventually landed a job as a dancer in a touring Biblical extravaganza called The Shepherd King. Then came several years of stock and vaudeville engagements, and marriage to a young actor, Henry Duffy. She decided to try writing when she realized that she and Henry were too impoverished to buy vaudeville sketches in which to perform. Her first effort, a melodramatic tear jerker, accidentally turned out to be funny, and the audience laughed hysterically. The embarrassed author fled to her dressing room, only to be met by the delighted theatre manager, who offered Anne her first important contract. That contract marked the beginning of Anne Nichols's career as a professional playwright.[5]

She wrote her first full-length play, Heart's Desire, in 1916, in collaboration with Adelaide Matthews. For various touring companies she wrote The Man from Wicklow (1917), The Happy Cavalier (1918), A Little Bit Old-Fashioned (1918), and Springtime in Mayo (1919). She also wrote the books for several musicals in 1919, among them Linger Longer Letty, which was constantly revived by its star, Charlotte Greenwood, throughout the twenties and thirties. (Eventually, under the title I Want a Sailor, it became Bob Hope's first starring vehicle.) For Fiske O'Hara, with whose company she had toured as far back as 1915, she wrote Down Limerick Way (1920) and Marry in Haste (1921). She again collaborated with Adelaide Matthews to write Just Married, which opened in New York in April 26, 1921, broke all stock company records in New York, Chicago, and London, and was apparently made into a movie three times.[6] In one of her infrequent interviews, Ms. Nichols wryly observed that although both Linger Longer Letty and Just Married were running on Broadway when Abie's Irish Rose opened there in 1922, people persisted in congratulating her on Abie's success by saying "Weren't you lucky to have your first play turn out to be such a hit!"[7]

But *Abie's Irish Rose*, while certainly not her first play, nor even her first successful play, was to overshadow all her other work. For it was the kind of popular hit that attracted a great deal of attention and engendered considerable critical response. So, to her surprise and dismay, the author found that she could never again be anyone but "that woman who wrote *Abie's Irish Rose*."[8]

She got the initial idea for the play from Fiske O'Hara, who told her about a young Jewish friend who had pretended his Irish Catholic fiancée was Jewish in order to win his Orthodox father's approval of their marriage. After the wedding, however, the father discovered the truth and rushed in horror from his son's house. Anne Nichols recalled later that the story made a strong impression on her: "I couldn't stop thinking about that mixed alliance, and all the prejudices which it brought in its wake." Ten minutes after the O'Haras left, she sat down to work on the play that was to become *Abie's Irish Rose*. She wrote steadily for three days and most of three nights. Her intention, she said, was "to write a play which might serve to overcome religious bigotry."[9] *Abie*, like all her best work, would be a comedy, but underlying the humor would be a serious message—a plea for religious tolerance.

At first glance, *Abie's Irish Rose* seemed unlikely to cause much of a stir in the theatrical world. The plot was amusing but unpretentious, revolving around the difficulties encountered by Rose Mary Murphy and Abraham Levy in their quest for some semblance of a normal wedding and a happy married life. The complications, including two belligerent fathers-in-law (each of whom makes Archie Bunker look like a model of tolerance), two well-meant deceptions (Abie introduces Rose to his father as Rosie Murpheski; Rose tells her father that she is marrying one Michael Magee), and three frenetic wedding ceremonies (one Methodist, one Jewish, one Catholic) are finally resolved when Rose and Abie manage to produce twins, an event which turns their hostile fathers into doting grandfathers, willing to take the first tentative steps toward tolerance and understanding.

Abie could hardly be characterized as an overnight success. The author spent three years just trying to get her play on stage, but it was rejected by every producer from New York to Hollywood. Finally, Oliver Morosco agreed to try it out on the West Coast. Nevertheless, despite its success there, Morosco was reluctant to attempt a New York production.[10] Ms. Nichols then took matters into her own hands. She mortgaged her home and used the money to produce the play herself at the Fulton Theatre.[11] The initial New York reaction to *Abie's Irish Rose* was lukewarm. Reviews were mixed, though not all were hostile (for example, William B. Chase, reviewer for the *New York Times*, liked the play and hoped for a long run.)[12] But the stinging adverse remarks of other well-known critics such as Percy Hammond, Robert Benchley, and Heywood Broun did affect the early reception of the play, and box-office receipts suffered.[13] However, Ms. Nichols sank every cent she had into the production, the actors took a salary cut, ticket prices were reduced, and *Abie* managed to keep going for two shaky months until it suddenly caught on with the theatre-going public.[14] The play that Benchley disparaged as the worst in town was on its way to becoming, in the words of George Jean Nathan, "the fourth biggest industry in the United States."[15]

Not that the critics gave up—in fact, some relentlessly hounded the play for the entire five years of its run. Most memorable were the barbs of Robert Benchley. Faced with the task of writing an original description of the play every week for *Life* magazine, the formidable Benchley produced minicritiques such as, "We understand that a performance of this play in Modern dress is now under way."[16]

Other critics were less clever but equally cutting. Some were disturbed and mystified by the success of such an "undistinguished" play, and wrote lengthy essays in which they solemnly tried to analyze the "secret" of *Abie's* popularity. To George Jean Nathan, the source of the play's success lay in its indebtedness to burlesque sketches such as the popular *Krausmeyer's Alley*.[17] To Robert Littell, it seemed significant that *Abie* "is nice to everybody. . . . There is no villain. Everybody on the stage is likeable"; yet, puzzled, he concluded "there must be a deeper reason than all these, a more human, a more subtle one."[18] The author herself put it more simply: "It has the love element, the comedy, and it tells facts, but tells them with a smile."

Anne Nichols had created a well-constructed blend of broad humor, sentiment, and gentle caricature, and audiences loved it. In addition to the Broadway production, there were performances of *Abie's Irish Rose* all over the United States and Canada. One company was in London; another in Sydney, Australia. The play was performed in Europe in French, German, Spanish, Portuguese, Swedish, and Russian. It was seen in China with an all-Chinese cast. It played eight months to packed houses in Berlin (Hitler didn't like it).[19] There were two New York revivals (1937 and 1954), two film versions (1928 and 1946), and a weekly radio show in the early 1940's. Touring companies continued to stage *Abie* for decades. As Ms. Nichols once said, "It has never stopped playing somewhere."[20]

But ironically, *Abie's* success was to prove a very mixed blessing for Anne Nichols. After an interview with her, Arthur Gelb wrote: "It brought its author spectacular fame and fortune—earning her more money than any single play has ever earned for a writer. But it also put a permanent crimp in her literary career, [and] hounded her personal life for four decades. . . ."[21] She went on to write, direct, and produce other plays after *Abie's Irish Rose*, but she gradually found herself forced to devote more and more time to the comedy she and others called her "million dollar hit."[22] One problem was that she genuinely loved and believed in her play, and felt compelled to keep an eye on it. "No matter what else I was trying to work on, I had a compulsion to check up on the various companies," she said. "And invariably I'd find that the minute my back was turned, the actors would start distorting the play by ad-libbing lines for laughs. I had to travel back and forth across the country constantly to keep them in check. I hardly found time to write any more."[23]

Then there were numerous legal battles, starting with Oliver Morosco's attempt to get an injunction to stop the play's opening in New York.[24] He failed, but later there was trouble with contracts, with booking agents, with managers trying to cheat her. She became involved in lawsuits to collect the money due her. In 1929 she sued the Universal Pictures Corporation for $3 million, charging that they had used her play as the basis for their film, *The Cohens and the Kellys*. She lost the case when that eminently perverse critic George Jean Nathan testified that the theme of young lovers thwarted by their parents went all the way back to *Romeo and Juliet*. The court then ruled that the idea had been used so often it was in the public domain.[25]

In 1962 she told Arthur Gelb, "I've always been haunted by the ghost of *Abie's Irish Rose*." She was trying to live quietly (she had divorced Duffy in 1924 and her son was living in California), but people still kept trying to meet her, to interview her, "wanting to know what makes me tick." In order to work in peace on her autobiography, *Such Is Fame*, she had finally withdrawn to the seclusion of Harwich, Massachusetts. Fearing further interruptions, she asked Gelb not to reveal where she was, stating that she needed about another three months of peace and quiet to complete the book.[26] One wonders if she ever got them. When she died four years later, her once-huge fortune substantially reduced by the Depression and medical bills, the autobiography was apparently still unfinished.

SOPHIE TREADWELL: AGENT FOR CHANGE

LOUISE HECK-RABI

As agent for change in American drama, Sophie Treadwell never ceased to be challenged by ways of arriving at something different and something new. As a dramatist, she did not identify the type of play she could do best and then refine that form until it was adjusted to that equipoise of playwright's intention and audience acceptance a commercially successful play required. She was never to find the best type of play for her to write to achieve commercial success, as did Maxwell Anderson and Rachel Crothers, for example. Nor could she identify what was best in her work and utilize that aspect of her talent to author hit plays.

There is an endearing lack of deliberation and calculation in Treadwell's

Louise Heck-Rabi, librarian, teacher, and playwright, published *Women Filmmakers: A Critical Reception* in 1984 and is now working on volume two in this series. Her Ph.D. dissertation at Wayne State University, 1976, was on Sophie Treadwell. Quotations from Treadwell's manuscripts and letters are used by permission of the Special Collections, University of Arizona Library, Tucson.

addressing herself to what was different and new in the writing of drama. She seems to have been temperamentally bound to an honesty that hurt. She kept up a frenzied work pace as she turned her dramatic impulses into a stage script which she would then refine, adjust, revise up to the opening night or the first rejection from an agent or producer. She would continue to make changes as she marketed her plays. Even over a period of years she would work on a script because she believed in her plays. Once done, however, she would not return to a type of dramatic composition she had already attempted. Indeed, the longhand first draft of a play was always something different, something new.

Her role as agent for change stems from these ongoing new attempts. From the laboratory of her temperament and talent, she would switch from one kind of play to another. These creative shifts were a counterpart to the many moves and changes of address in her personal life. The restlessness impelling her dramatic experiments and the rootlessness of her life experiences combined to cast her in the role of transformer of dramatic writing for the stage.

For Saxaphone [sic] is the most innovative of Treadwell's works. She was intrigued by the prospect of hitting upon a novel amalgamation of music, film, and dialogue which audiences would like. She sang and had written for films. The combination of her knowledge of music, film, and stage plus her proclivity for innovation resulted in the composition of *For Saxaphone*.

After *Machinal* Treadwell probably wanted to move on to a film-writing career where she could try out the new talking picture medium and also bring home good salary checks. In Box 27 of her papers in the Special Collection of the University of Arizona Library at Tucson, there are six film scenarios and two filmscripts. These are labeled "Work for United Artists"; one is titled *New York Nights*. She obviously thought that with the growing popularity of radio and talking pictures in the early 1930's, musical plays would become more successful than straight plays. A musical play rather than a musical comedy is what *For Saxaphone* is. Its use of constantly changing musical sound, frequent lighting and staging shifts, and unusual visual and verbal presences, suggest that the play may be more suited to the cinema than to the stage. The technical challenge of the play is, in itself, complex and forbidding. *For Saxaphone*, which was copyrighted June 4, 1934, is a musical mutation of *Machinal*. It centers on a protagonist who is given a core character, Lilly, and her three satellite selves. The play follows a progression of her life experiences.

Treadwell's preface to an early version of *For Saxaphone* best explains her artistic intentions for the play:

> The script is written to be played with an almost unbroken musical accompaniment. It is really words for music. I did this because I think our audiences' nerves, tuned to pictures and radio, now almost demand it of

any entertainment. The music is for the most part typical of music to-day,—where a saxophone is much heard, but there are also parts of a Brahms Symphony, some Viennese waltzes, Hungarian gypsy innovations, etc.

Also much use is made of voices (of people not seen)—bits of conversation here and there—incomplete—suggestive. I thought this gave a certain way to develop the story as well as giving the whole thing the living effect of something overheard. Anyway, our audiences are now trained to it through radio and have come, I think, to like it. The dialogue is written in a short repetitious rhythm, where I tried to create the empty, blatant blah effect of most of our talk today.

The play is done in fourteen scenes, all of which go one into the other through lights, voices, and music, as [sic] that the effect is of something seen, moving-by, and something overheard,—from all of which, a bit here and a bit there, inconsequential and seemingly unrelated, the audience discovers—writes the play.

All the scenes are planned to be done in different light spots—pools of light on a dark stage—no scenery—a door or a window, when necessary, set up as a separate piece—very little furniture—very few props. It must all create a sense of luxury and taste and the clothes, especially Lilly's, must be exquisite. In fact, her role is a sort of kaleidoscope of a beautiful girl in beautiful clothes.

To stand any chance at all the play must have an exceptional young actress to play Lilly. She must be young and she must be able to create a special mood around herself—a special aura (as some children—doomed to die in childhood—seem to do).

The four characters who comprise the central figure dominate the play, but in all versions Lilly remains the protagonist, while Minnie, Billie, Gilly dart into and out of the action. Chronicling Lilly's reaction to the events of her life as they swirl past her, the play deals chronologically with these happenings, as in *Machinal.* Treadwell's experiments focus on dividing these activities into scenes. From the fourteen scenes in the earlier versions, Treadwell pared the phases of Lilly's life to eight to be performed in two acts of four scenes each. In Version Eight there is Act I: Engagement, Wedding, Honeymoon, Moon, and Act II: Married, Knife, Flight, Flight's End.

In each version, Lilly's death is prefigured when a knife appears in the hands of a male exhibition dancer who is an accomplished knife-thrower. In all versions of the play Lilly is knifed by this dancer at the final curtain. In Version Five, dated December 1941, Lilly is not slain; she dances with a young man after her dancer-lover has departed.

As the characters sit at cabaret tables before and after the exhibition dancing, they converse about personalities in the newspapers, particularly current film favorites: Clark Gable, Ronald Colman, George Raft, and Rudy Vallee. Events of the day also emerge in the chitchat, lending a topicality to the play which may now cause it to seem dated. Treadwell lists in her cast of unnamed characters those seen and heard, those heard and not seen (voices), and characters seen, but not heard (visual presences).

Given the experimental factors in the play, the intricacies and difficulties to be anticipated in the sound plot and light plot, plus the difficulties of casting a first-rank Lilly, as well as finding a knife-throwing dancer and other carnival performers, *For Saxaphone* was obviously not a commercially viable product. Treadwell knew this, but, nonetheless, she tried to sell it as a stage or motion picture property. She failed, but the comments of those who rejected it afford a critical look at its strengths and weaknesses.

Treadwell first approached Arthur Hopkins with *For Saxaphone*; he relayed the script to William James Fadiman, a reader for Sam Goldwyn, Inc. in New York. Fadiman wrote the following letter to Hopkins on December 12, 1935:

> This play by Sophie Treadwell is most unusual and might even be called eccentric. The novelty and marked freshness of the background, setting, accompaniment and fusion of these elements with the story are factors that remain exciting in themselves but occasionally hamper the fluid narration of the story. . . .
>
> Since the fundamental *raison d'être* of this play is the unique rhythmic synchronization of dialogue with sets and characters, it seems difficult to imagine an important actress subordinating herself to these theatrical requirements. . . . I am afraid its presentation on the screen, depending as it does upon sheer story-line, would lose much of the bizarre construction that Miss Treadwell presents in the stage version. . . .

On April 20, 1937, Treadwell's agent Richard J. Madden in New York wrote this letter to Treadwell in Los Gatos, California, about the fate of *For Saxaphone.*

> . . . I wonder if you ever heard from Bobby Jones [Robert Edmond Jones], who was almost frothy at the mouth here before he left for abroad over your *For Saxaphone.* He declared to me that he absolutely "must produce" that play in autumn but at the moment he could not tell where in the world he would get the money except that it must be gotten. Of course, I think it would be swell if Bobby could follow up his promise and enthusiasm with performance. He is expected back here in a few weeks and I know, one of the first things he will devote himself to will be the promotion of *Saxaphone.*
>
> We had, through our coast office, some very exciting correspondence concerning a coast production by one of the Federal Theatre groups out there but I discouraged it, in view of Mr. Jones' attitude. . . .

Temporarily defeated, Treadwell replied to Madden from Old Trees Ranch, Stockton, California, on August 28, 1937:

Dear Dick, I got your letter today, and I'm really grateful that you are not tired of me and mine, but my decision about the script has not changed. I know that you have had them read by all the men that count and that's that,—they did not catch. I want them back now. . . . In the meantime, *Saxophone* is really not available. Just four days ago—unforeseen—out of the blue—I had a wire from a friend—in the theatre but not a producer—asking for a short option,—which I gave,—gladly. Mr. Hopkins gave him the play to read two years ago, but nothing came of it—until this wire.—So that is that.

It seems to be a law with me in everything that I never get anything—not even a chance at anything—until I completely give it up. . . .

The identity of this friend cannot be gleaned from the papers, but late correspondence testifies to the fact that Robert Edmond Jones remained enthusiastic about *For Saxophone*, and for a period of three years tried to stage it, but it was in vain.

On April 26, 1940, Jones wrote in longhand to Treadwell from Villa Riposa, Santa Barbara, California, a letter which describes their working relationship and mutual concern over the play.

. . . I think the thing for you to do is to forget about mechanical devices and let *me* worry about the inner and outer along the lines you outline. Don't put down any directions for scenery at all. Let the drama secrete its own form as a nautilus secretes its shell. Something entirely new might happen, never seen in the theatre before.— . . . I have always maintained that its only fault (silly word!) from a box office point of view is that it seems a depressed play—not tragic, but depressed. There is nothing wrong with this except that I don't think people would try to see it, and yet there is no adequate experimental theatre where such things could be put on. I dreamed of it for Central City once, but the backers there can't see anything that isn't in the festival spirit. However, *Saxophone* is perhaps beside the point,—I am leaving for New York—address 1 East 53d St. Keep in touch with me. All best in haste Bobby.

Treadwell replied to him May 8.

The new version of *Saxophone* is on its way to you. . . . (The depression of which you spoke to me—and so justly—is surely not in it any more—because the depression is not in me any more.)

You will, of course, see that the form of the thing had come to me from the motion picture and the radio. I think all plays will soon be played to music—whether they are written to be or not. Surely music plays a mighty role in the patience and absorption of a motion picture audience.—Consider sitting before some of that tripe in quietness' [sic] submitting to silence. . . .

I have tried to use these things—that have proven their mass entertainment value—to make a real SHOW. If you would like it and do it,—it could be an amazingly beautiful show,—perhaps a great show.

Some five years later, Treadwell tried again. She wrote a brief note, quoted in its entirety here, to Richard Rodgers. Dated March 4, 1942, it does not mention a play title, but does deal with a play with music.

Dear Mr. Rodgers, I am sending you today the first act of a play I am working on. I am thinking of it as being played to continual music. Would you look through it and let me know what you think of it? Something you said—casually—at Terry's [Theresa Helburn] last Sunday gave me the courage to send this along to you. I hope you do not find it any kind of an intrusion upon your time. I hope you may like i [sic] Cordial regards to you and Mrs. Rodgers, Sincerely,

We do not know if this play was a new venture or *For Saxaphone*. There is no letter of reply from Rodgers in the Papers.

In 1947, Treadwell was still relentlessly seeking a producer. Henry Souvaine thought well of *Saxaphone* and his letter comments astutely upon the form of the play:

I was very happy that I was given the opportunity to read your play *For Saxaphone*. Certainly this is beautifully written and an extremely professional job of creating believable theatrical illusion.

Technically, your form of projecting the plot development was, to me, continuously interesting. In fact, I wonder if the producers of "Allegro" didn't have a little thought communion with your writing studio in Newtown. It is a little unfortunate that "Allegro" appeared on Broadway before your play, although the similarities in technical treatment are nothing more than a coincidence. . . .

Did Treadwell anticipate the Broadway musical play in *For Saxaphone*? Probably not. But her good judgment of the necessary properties for a novel form for the stage or screen has been proved by the multimedia and total theatre shows of the '60's, and she accurately predicted the ubiquitous popularity of music in all stage and cinematic works.

THE COMIC MUSE OF MARY CHASE

ALBERT WERTHEIM

When Mary Coyle Chase won the Pulitzer Prize in Drama in 1945 for her comedy *Harvey*, she was only the fourth woman to win that prize since its founding in 1918. Zona Gale had received the prize in 1921 for the dramatization of her novel *Miss Lulu Bett*; Susan Glaspell for *Alison's House*, a play based on the life of Emily Dickinson, in 1931; and Zoe Akins for *The Old Maid* in 1935. What sets Mary Chase immediately apart from these other women dramatists is that she does not in her three major plays—*Harvey* (1944), *Mrs. McThing* (1952), and *Bernardine* (1952)—deal with the plight of women in society, and she is, moreover, a writer of highly imaginative comedy. A longtime resident of Denver, Colorado, and environs, Mary Chase does not write about New York or other East Coast cities, but sets her plays in what might be any medium-sized mid-American city, though Denver is probably her model. By freeing herself from specific social or political issues and by casting off the restraints of geography, she is able deftly and sometimes brilliantly to use her comic art to present man's eternal conflict between his imaginative world and the constricting world of social forms and social realities. Although at first glance a seemingly lighthearted dramatic gewgaw, a play like *Harvey* shares a common theme with such overtly serious works as Eugene O'Neill's *The Iceman Cometh*, Philip Barry's *Hotel Universe*, or Tennessee Williams's *Glass Menagerie*. Mary Chase's comedies, particularly *Harvey*, deserve the serious treatment they have not yet received from critics and even from their more enthusiastic reviewers.

One is tempted to say, and perhaps with some justification, that, written and produced during wartime, *Harvey* must surely have had immediate appeal to audiences wearied by the grim realities of global war and, consequently, eager to find escape in the fantasy world that Mary Chase offered.[1] Elwood P. Dowd, who takes leave of the worldly society represented by his sister Veta, his niece Myrtle Mae and their friends to share a life with a pooka, an invisible six-foot rabbit, is doing no more, one might argue, than the audiences of 1944 and 1945, who took leave of Germany, Japan, and Italy to spend a few enjoyable hours with Elwood and his invisible friend Harvey. Though these judgments may well be true, the fact that *Harvey* has survived beyond the World War II era, that it is still being successfully performed and enjoyed today, seems proof that the play has more than mere escapism to recommend it.

A usual procedure of comedy is to laugh at the illusions of comedy's

---

Albert Wertheim, Professor of English at Indiana University, has published widely on Shakespeare, Renaissance, and Restoration theatre as well as on modern British and American theatre.

central characters and, finally, to restore them to the level-headed, norma-
tive thinking of society. In Molière, for example, the Orgons, Argans, and
M. Jourdains must surrender their illusions and self-delusions to the worldly right reason of the Cléantes and Cléontes. In Mary Chase's *Harvey*, the
usual procedure is reversed, and we find ourselves identifying positively
with the benign fantasy world of Elwood P. Dowd and his pooka, and
rejecting the everyday world of social forms and social norms. And it is
precisely that everyday, normal world that is the object of Mrs. Chase's
satire and the butt of her comedy.[2]

The method of Mary Chase's comic art is one that step by step exposes the
ridiculous stiltedness, meanness, and sterility of what one might call "normal" or "expected" social behavior. To foster her increasingly negative
picture of normalcy, she makes her audience laugh at the comic posturing,
insensitivity and stupidity of "good society" and of the arbiters of normalcy,
the psychiatrist and his staff. At the same time, she builds up, both in the
audience and in her stage characters, an increasing affection for the eccentric
Elwood and his invisible friend. It is Mary Chase's triumph that before her
play is over, Harvey has become as real to Elwood's sister Veta Louise, to Dr.
Chumley, the psychiatrist, and to the theatre audience as he is to Elwood
himself. The transference of allegiance through comedy from the world of
reason to Elwood's eccentric world of imagination and fantasy is Mary
Chase's triumph and marks her sense that the imaginative, visionary world
is finally more estimable than the often hollow world of manners.

Appropriately, *Harvey* begins as a comedy of manners but one in which
the audience is not made to laugh, as is the usual manners comedy rule, at
the outsider but at polished society itself. The curtain rises on a comic picture
of the *beau monde* as it exists in Middle America. Veta Louise Simmons and
her daughter Myrtle Mae are giving a ladies tea complete with a laughably
off-key soprano singing "I'm Called Little Buttercup." She is accompanied
by an equally untalented pianist. With the sour notes of the songstress in the
background, Veta Louise, full of self-importance, is describing her fete to the
society editor of the local newspaper. Both the scene and the dialogue deftly
satirize the world of society ladies and the clichés of society column rhetoric:

> . . . a tea and reception for the members of the Wednesday Forum. You
> might say—program tea. My mother, you know—the late Marcella Pin-
> ney Dowd, pioneer cultural leader—she came here by ox-team as a child
> and she founded the Wednesday Forum. . . . Miss Myrtle Mae Simmons
> looked charmingly in a modish Rancho Rose toned crepe, picked up at the
> girdle with a touch of magenta on emerald. . . . The parlors and halls are
> festooned with smilax. (4,5)[3]

Into this caricatured depiction of a high society occasion and into a room
dominated by the severe portait of the late Marcella Pinney Dowd, "pioneer
cultural leader," saunters the dreamy, light-footed, socially uncaring

Elwood P. Dowd. His gait, his manner, and his unfashionable attire immediately single him out as an outsider in the world of social teas and Wednesday Forums. To Veta Louise's stilted telephone conversation with the society column editor is immediately juxtaposed Elwood's delightful and delightfully unpretentious telephone conversation with Miss Elsie Greenawalt, a woman unknown to Dowd who is selling magazine offers to his invisible companion presumably sitting alongside him on the couch. He promptly invites the strange telephone saleswoman to his sister's party as well. The mental delight conjured up at the thought of Elsie Greenawalt's making an appearance at Veta's socially pretentious tea helps pit Elwood's unaffected, affable world against the pretentiousness and off-key singing of Veta's.

Although Miss Greenawalt never materializes, Elwood himself comically crashes his sister's festivities. His encounter with Mrs. Chauvenet, society matron and society leader "dressed with the casual sumptuousness of a wealthy Western society woman—in silvery gold and plush, and mink scarf even though it is a spring day" (8), is deliciously comic. Having run through the social forms of inquiring after Elwood's health and inviting him to dinner, Mrs. Chauvenet is rendered speechless as Elwood proceeds to introduce her to his six-foot, invisible pooka. While Mrs. Chauvenet darts from the room aghast, Elwood and Harvey proceed to the parlor, where the invisible giant rabbit will duly be introduced to the remainder of Veta's socially prominent, shocked guests. The comic confrontation between polished society's decorum and Elwood's fancies is brilliantly made at the close of the play's first scene, in which Elwood reaches for a bottle of liquor hidden behind a handsomely bound book in the library. The volume that has served as a screen for Elwood's pint bottle of spirits is, of all things, a deluxe, limited edition of Jane Austen. In a wonderful comic stroke, Mary Chase lets Jane Austen, the novelist most clearly associated with the world of polite society, stand in for the whole world of decorous behavior and become the comic foil to Elwood and his alcohol-inspired but nonetheless charming, invisible companion.

During the first scene of *Harvey*, Mary Chase wittily satirizes normal social behavior and *society* in the limited sense of that term used in newspaper columns to describe the aristocratic world. Moving from Veta Louise Simmons's drawing room in scene one to a mental hospital, Chumley's Rest, in scene two, the satire begins to encompass a new and enlarged target. In her comic treatment of the sanitarium to which Veta hopes to commit her idiosyncratic, socially unacceptable brother, Mrs. Chase calls into question the ability of psychiatrists to define what is meant by normal behavior within *society*, in the more general application of that word, and to ask as well whether what the psychiatrists imply is normalcy is truly a desirable state.

A farcical misdiagnosis by the admitting psychiatrist at Chumley's Rest, Dr. Sanderson, results in a scene laden with comic irony as Sanderson assumes that Veta is in need of admission to Chumley's Rest and that Elwood, her charmingly "normal" brother, is quite understandably committing her. That Veta is forcibly carried off, stripped, and put through the rigors of hydro-tubs is her comic punishment for seeking to expose Elwood to these things. More important, however, the action satirizes and exposes the psychiatric establishment that would excise all idiosyncratic behavior, reducing humanity to some preconceived idea of uniform, monolithic normalcy. The psychological jargon so freely employed at Chumley's Rest is an analogous, but insidious version of the jargon found in society columns. The psychiatrists, as arbiters of what is proper in society, are the sinister first cousins of society columnists.

The ability of Elwood and Harvey to best the psychiatric staff at Chumley's Rest is a clear comic victory, as the humiliated Dr. Chumley screams at his blundering assistant:

> Doctor—the function of a psychiatrist is to tell the difference between those who are reasonable, and those who merely talk and act reasonably. Do you realize what you have done to me? You don't answer. I'll tell you. You have permitted a psychopathic case to walk off these grounds and roam around with an over-grown white rabbit. You have subjected me—a psychiatrist—to the humiliation of having to call—of all things—a lawyer to find out who came out here to be committed—and who came out here to commit! (41)

But of course Dr. Sanderson's error in judgment is not altogether an error, for Elwood Dowd has far more human feeling, social grace, and love of life than his sister or than the psychiatric staff, the arbiters of normalcy, themselves. And as the first scene of *Harvey* ends with the triumph of Elwood and Harvey over the world of good society as represented by Jane Austen, so at the conclusion of the second scene Elwood and Harvey triumph once more. In accord with the widened satiric focus of the second scene, the Jane Austen volume of the first scene is replaced with the published record of civilization itself, the encyclopedia.

Once again Mary Chase supplies a *coup de théâtre* as the first act curtain comes down on Wilson, the mental hospital orderly, looking up *pooka* in the encyclopedia:

> P-o-o-k-a. "Pooka. From old Celtic mythology. A fairy spirit in animal form. Always very large. The pooka appears here and there, now and then, to this one and that one at his own caprice. A wise but mischievous creature. Very fond of rum-pots, crack-pots, and how are you, Mr. Wilson?" How are you, Mr. Wilson? Who in the encyclopedia wants to know? Oh—the hell with it! (42)

The invisible presence of Harvey usurps the pages of the encyclopedia, the product of the Age of Reason, asserting himself and his world of imagination, myth, rum-pots, and crack-pots.

In large part, *Harvey* abounds in comic irony as Elwood P. Dowd and his long-eared pooka seem increasingly amiable and rational amid the rest of the characters of the play who are lost in the insane chaos produced by Mary Chase's excellent farce.[4] Elwood's innocent and accepting attitude, furthermore, increasingly wins audience affection, so that audience laughter is directed against the supposedly sane world and audience applause toward Elwood and his imaginary rabbit. In short, Harvey becomes more real than the dramatic caricatures on stage, and the audience, therefore, comes not only to approve of Elwood's fantasy but to share it. Harvey's triumph is made manifest when the portrait of the giant rabbit is hung over the mantelpiece replacing the severe portrait of the "lantern-jawed" Marcella Pinney Dowd, doyenne of Midwestern cultured society.

Beneath the comedy, however, is a serious questioning of the validity of the imagination. What makes Mary Chase so remarkable a playwright is that she uses the medium of comedy to present an issue that has most often elsewhere been treated tragically or with high seriousness. In Eugene O'Neill's *The Iceman Cometh*, for example, the playwright's central concern is the question of whether facing reality is better than living in the fantasy of one's pipe dreams. The would-be truth-teller in that tragedy, Hickey, attempts to strip the inmates of Harry Hope's bar of their dreams, forcing them to face reality. Hickey's initial success renders his friends moribund. They are once more revitalized when they reaffirm the validity of their pipe dreams. With medical metaphors, Hickey tells his friends:

> Oh, I know from my own experience it's bitter medicine, facing yourself in the mirror with the old false whiskers off. But you forget that, once you're cured.

Hickey's medicine, however, works no cures and, O'Neill's audience realizes, his is a medicine that can well be lethal to the imagination and the human spirit. The stern truth of *The Iceman Cometh* is likewise the stern truth of Ibsen's *The Wild Duck* and of other serious modern plays. In Mary Chase's hands, it is transformed into sparkling comedy. She, too, has a doctor and patient, but O'Neill's Hickey and his clients become the raw material for laughter in *Harvey*:

> *Dr. Sanderson* If you'll begin by taking a cooperative attitude—that's half the battle. We all have to face reality, Dowd—sooner or later.
>
> *Elwood* Doctor, I wrestled with reality for forty years, and I'm happy to state that I finally won out over it. (64)

Like Hickey, too, Dr. Sanderson and his mentor, Dr. Chumley, have a medicine, formula 977, which will drive away Elwood's rabbits and let him instead see his responsibilities and duties. And like Hickey's cure, it de-humanizes as the wise cabdriver's speech makes patently clear:

> Listen, lady. I've been drivin' this route fifteen years. I've brought 'em out here to get that stuff and drove 'em back after they had it. It changes 'em. . . . On the way out here they sit back and enjoy the ride. They talk to me. Sometimes we stop and watch the sunsets and look at the birds flyin'. Sometimes we stop and watch the birds when there ain't no birds and look at the sunsets when it's rainin'. We have a swell time and I always get a big tip. But afterward—oh—oh . . . They crab, crab, crab. They yell at me to watch the lights, watch the brakes, watch the intersections. They scream at me to hurry. They got no faith—in me or my buggy—yet it's the same cab—the same driver—and we're goin' back over the very same road. It's no fun—and no tips— . . . Lady, after this, he'll be a perfectly normal human being and you know what bastards they are! (88–89)

The cabdriver becomes the spokesman for Mary Chase's comic indictment of "normal" behavior. As Elwood avoids Dr. Chumley's cure and leaves with his fantasy world intact, with his invisible rabbit still very much there, the audience applauds with delight affirming thereby the necessity of dreams and the vitality of the life of the imagination.

In *Harvey*, Mary Chase makes her mark as a distinguished playwright, not a female playwright with a particularly feminine or feminist point of view, but a playwright willing to tackle an important and serious human problem and to do so through the medium of comedy. She continues to do this in her subsequent plays, although none matches the success and comic genius of *Harvey*. In *Mrs. McThing*,[5] produced eight years after *Harvey*, Chase attempts to recapture her earlier achievement. Again the world of good society, championed by Mrs. Howard V. Larue III of Larue Towers, is pitted against the mythic world of Mrs. McThing, the witch of the Blue, Blue Mountains. Mrs. Larue's world is one of social formalities and her desire is to keep her son Howay isolated within a circumscribed society that is at once beset by social snobbery and devoid of imagination. Her comic punishment is to have Howay replaced by a changeling, an attired stick that embodies the ultimate desires of Mrs. Larue's comically and often farcically sterile world. The real Howay has broken free from the mannered, constricted world of Larue Towers to join a mob of ridiculous gangsters at the Shantyland Pool Hall in the sleaziest part of town. When Mrs. McThing also translates Mrs. Larue into a kitchen helper at the pool hall, the sterile snobbery of Mrs. Larue slowly gives way to a spirit of acceptance and a new vitality as she is humanized by her stay among the fantastic mobsters.

Mrs. McThing was a Broadway success largely because Helen Hayes as Mrs. Larue, together with the precocious Brandon de Wilde as her son Howay, carried the play. This comedy, however, falls short of *Harvey* because it fails to go beyond a criticism of a very limited segment of society.

Beginning in the confines of Veta's home and satirizing her Wednesday Forum, *Harvey* proceeds in subsequent action to move to the Chumley sanitarium and satirize normalization of behavior in general. *Mrs. McThing* never goes beyond a satiric criticism of the insulated, overrefined, vapid life of Mrs. Larue and her society friends. After a pre-Broadway run of *Harvey* in Boston, where Harvey was portrayed by an actor in rabbit costume, Mary Chase wisely eliminated the visibility of Elwood's pooka. In *Mrs. McThing,* the fantastic world, the world of Poison Eddie and his gangsters at the Shantyland Pool Hall, is all too graphically represented. Likewise, perhaps distrustful of the audience's powers of imagination, Mrs. Chase, in the final moments of the play, has the powerful but hitherto-invisible Mrs. McThing make a double appearance, first as a frightening witch and then as a beautiful fairy godmother decked in rhinestones. The theme of *Mrs. McThing* remains the same as that of *Harvey:* the importance of imagination and fantasy to make human beings more than the stick figures of convention. Yet by giving a local habitation and a name, actualizing the fantasy world, *Mrs. McThing,* although a comedy of merit, falls far short of Harvey's triumph.

Mary Chase's third well-known comedy, *Bernardine,* first staged the same year as *Mrs. McThing,* explores new comic ground. It is a nostalgic, wistful remembrance by a young man, Arthur Beaumont, of the humor and mystique of the years when he was "Beau," the acknowledged leader reigning over the special preadult world of teenage boys. Entering in the prologue to *Bernardine* and dressed in his Air Force uniform, a mature Beau recounts his dramatic anecdote of earlier days when he reigned supreme as leader of the Kings. His monologue recognizes—and forces the audience to recognize—the universality and inherent comedy of that special time in the lives of the young just before they enter the adult world of responsibility. It is at once a time rich in pubescent fantasy and a universal *rite de passage,* that, when viewed with hindsight as it is in *Bernardine,* makes one aware of the comic nature of teenage posturing. As Beau explains to the audience in his prologue:

> There are quite a few of us retired Kings flying these days. But often in the service clubs and around we get together and talk about our lost kingdoms; high-school days in the old home town—a Hallowe'en world that is—with its own set of rulers, values, dreams, and a cockeyed edge to laughter.
> Here no adult can enter fully—ever. (1)[6]

And it is that "cockeyed edge to laughter" that Mary Chase seeks to recover in *Bernardine.*

There is much wistful comedy in *Bernardine* derived from the intersection of a straightforward adult world with the "cockeyed," exclusive world of teenage fantasy. There is as well some broad comedy derived from the scenes in which one of the teenagers, who is less sophisticated than he thinks he is, comes close to seducing an unusually attractive older woman. But *Bernardine* is a comedy that has higher sights than *Time Out for Ginger* or any number of Henry Aldrich comedies, for it suggests that the special world of the Kings with its concomitant special ideal vision of womanhood and sexuality, Bernardine Crud of Sneaky Falls, is a necessary part of growing up, a desirable prerequisite for adulthood. In both *Harvey* and *Mrs. McThing*, Mary Chase suggests an alternate fantasy world for the rigidity and limitation of diurnal existence. Her position in *Bernardine* shifts somewhat, for she suggests that the special imaginative world shared by adolescents can inform their adult lives in such a way that the memory of it will serve to humanize the rigors of adult life and prevent their becoming the stick figures of *Mrs. McThing*. Even the adults like Mrs. Weldy, who urge the young men to act responsibly, seem to understand this, for Mrs. Weldy ultimately advises her son and his friends to make the most of their adolescent years in the Shamrock, "You stay here—all of you—as long as you can" (109).

Mary Chase creates successful comedy from the time spent by teenagers in their idiosyncratic, closed fantasy world. At the same time, she emerges curiously close to a serious poet like Wordsworth, who also, in poems like "Lines Composed a Few Miles Above Tintern Abbey," emphasizes the special scenes of youth, which when remembered in tranquillity have the power to humanize the workaday world. One has the sense in *Bernardine* that those humorous, awkward, but halcyon days spent at the Shamrock visualizing Bernardine of Sneaky Falls will, in later life, bring Wordsworthian "tranquil restoration" and will lighten the "burthen" of a troubled and sometimes "unintelligible" adult world for Beau and his teenage comrades.

Where *Bernardine* falls short is in its ability truly to recapture the adolescent world. Mary Chase is a competent comic playwright, but she is, finally, no match for Wordsworth and his ability to recapture for adult readers the mystique of youth. *Harvey* continues to stand out as Mary Chase's major work, even perhaps her masterpiece, and it is *Harvey*, plus *Mrs. McThing* and *Bernardine*, that secures for Mary Chase an important place among those American writers who have championed the necessity of dreams, the life of the human imagination.

GERTRUDE STEIN: FORM AND CONTENT

BETSY ALAYNE RYAN

Gertrude Stein's disruption of the alternate reality—or fiction—of the traditional theatre is the unifying principle of all her plays, regardless of period. Insofar as she was able to accomplish this disruption, she rooted the experience of the spectator in the theatrical present, avoiding what she termed "syncopation," and established an immediate relationship between the spectator and the physical world of the stage. This relationship involved no identification with a fiction on stage, but a detachment from it and a focus upon the surface of the theatre experience.

If this description seems to bear some resemblance to the intent of Brecht, it is best to take the analogy no further, for Brecht rendered social and political realities for overtly utilitarian ends. Stein's concerns, on the other hand, lay solely in the realm of epistemology. Interested less in political and social questions than in everyday reality, she sought to transmit her knowledge simply and directly to another mind. This is not to say that her position was not political. As Marcuse has said, "The political potential of art lies only in its own aesthetic dimension. . . ."

Stein's plays are first and foremost attempts to call attention to the theatre experience. Forty-one of them refer often enough to themselves and to Stein's writing process to be considered metaplays, or plays about plays. Her inclusion of process as an integral part of her plays makes most of them self-referential at some point. . . .

The fictional aspect of the theatre is undermined by this self-reference. Once a play refers to itself as a play, the spectator acknowledges his presence in a theatre, and disengages from the fictional character of the proceedings. Contrary to traditional practice since the Renaissance, which posited the unreal (a flat painted in perspective) as the real (a town square), Stein posits the actual presence of actors and spectator as real.

Stein's plays are not pure attempts at metaplay, however. All of them have subject matter, however sketchy or disrupted. . . .

Stein's plays can be said to reflect nine broad categories of subject matter: identity, mystery, domestic life, conversation, war, movement, nature, sex and love, and religion. Most of the plays, save the ones concerned with identity, should be considered less explorations of topics than distillations of her life concerns.

Gertrude Stein is hailed today not only as an American innovator, iconoclast, and celebrity, but also as "a woman writer who knew women profoundly and expressed that knowledge." Both the form and the content of her plays are influencing women in theatre. Betsy Ryan taught theatre at the University of Illinois and the University of Iowa and is presently managing editor of a professional journal at UCLA and an independent scholar in theatre. This excerpt from *Gertrude Stein's Theatre of the Absolute*, p. 67 and pp. 115–129, copyright © 1984, 1980 by Betsy Alayne Ryan, is reprinted courtesy of the author and UMI Research Press, Ann Arbor, Michigan.

Domestic life of some kind comprises the subject matter of forty-three plays from *White Wines* in 1913 to *The Mother of Us All* in 1946. Stein's overriding concern in these plays, most of which reflect her own household, was in capturing the essence of day-to-day living. . . .

References, usually veiled, to love and sexuality are made in fourteen plays from *Old and Old* (1913) to *Yes Is for a Very Young Man* (1944–1946). These generally take the form of descriptions of Stein's own relationship with Alice Toklas, and become quite explicit once it is understood that her euphemism for orgasm was "cow," and that Alice's nickname for her was "baby." . . .

Nature provides the subject matter for forty plays and ranges from oblique references to birds, animals, and landscapes to plays based entirely on nature imagery. . . . Nature was obviously a source of delight and comfort to Stein, and forms the basis of what she termed her landscape plays, many of which are set in an actual nature landscape. . . .

Stein's preoccupation with movement within a landscape finds expression in the subject matter of thirty-two plays. . . .

Twenty-two plays, most of them occurring between 1915 and 1919, reflect Stein's preoccupation with conversation to such a degree that they can be considered metaplays. The number and variety of subjects combined with an overriding dialogue perspective makes these plays intensely conversational in tone. . . .

War is the subject matter of ten plays. . . . *Yes Is for a Very Young Man* (1944–1946) is the most complete depiction of life in wartime, the domestic situation . . . , the love affair . . . , and the war itself sketched with a thoroughness not approached in her other plays. The play deals specifically with the activities of the French Resistance . . . and Marshal Petain's "toy" army. . . .

Religion is the subject matter for four plays: *Lend a Hand or Four Religions* (1922), which presents four religions (first through fourth) as personages in a nature landscape, and *Four Saints in Three Acts* (1927), *Saints and Singing* (1922), and *A Saint in Seven* (1922), all of which sketch the saintly life. Stein was interested in saints primarily because of their self-contained existence, their ability to simply be. . . . The use of saints emphasized her static art since she could render them most completely, she felt, by not showing them doing anything. . . .

Seven of her plays are mysteries. . . . The mystery play is a prototype for all of Stein's plays, since she avoids presenting connections between events in all her plays in the few instances that events occur. Anyone who faces the plays and attempts an explanation spends much time reflecting upon what she so deliberately makes ambiguous and equivocal for the sake of her static art. The danger lies in positing meanings and connections for plays that depend on non-connections and non-significance for their very existence.

The subject matter explored most intensively in the plays is identity vs. entity, the overriding concern of her life and art. Does the essence of a person or thing depend upon its connections with extraneous things or upon a quality that issues from within? If the latter is the case how does one establish it? How does one really know who one is? *Identity a Play* (1935) is the first play to approach the question with any thoroughness. Written just three years after her first move into narrative (1932), it addresses directly the question of identity, and indirectly, perhaps, the question of her own integrity during this phase of her career. *Identity a Play* explores the ramifications of the deceptively simple Mother Goose rhyme "I am I because my little dog knows me. . . ."

Doctor Faustus Lights the Lights considers the subject in a different way. Doctor Faustus has sold his soul for the knowledge of electric light, and doubts the wisdom of that move from the beginning of the play. . . . In fact, he desires complete darkness after all the light he has seen. . . .

The parallels between the situation Faust finds himself in and Stein's own in the "identity" segment of her career—the time in which she exchanged the complete solitude of some twenty years of writing for recognition by an audience—are imperative to note. After writing her widely disseminated *Autobiography of Alice B. Toklas*, and *Everybody's Autobiography* in the early thirties, she wrote often about the consequences of fame for a writer, wondering openly in plays and theoretical writings whether it was possible to retain any sense of self in the glare of publicity and with the ever-present awareness of audience expectation. . . .

After the notoriety brought by her identity writing of the 1930's, Stein never wrote so clearly again. To write well, as she stated from the beginning of her career, a writer must have as little sense of her audience as possible. In her later plays . . . , Stein sought to combine writing as it is written with writing according to someone else's point of view. She withdrew from her audience to a large extent to accomplish this, and regained, at least in part, a solitude from which she could write.

There is subject matter in every one of Stein's plays, no matter how skeletal or veiled. As she said of painting, "The minute painting gets abstract it gets pornographic. That is a fact." Her plays always emerge from first-hand contact with things or persons. Still, the subject matter seems to be simple indeed, except for the few plays which explore in detail philosophical questions relating to identity and war. In fact, it is so very simple and multifaceted (99 percent of the plays reflect combinations of subject matter) that it can hardly be said to distract to any great degree from the surface of the theatre experience. Fictional though the plays are, they present only fleeting fictions, brief evocations of topics for the spectator to take in as he moves on.

Stein's innovation lies in her disruption of the alternate reality of the stage through manipulations of form and subject matter, both of which she expresses in essence, moment by moment, and forces to relate spatially within the landscape of the theatre. Through techniques of juxtaposition, repetition, modification, rhyme, simple language, and monotonous sentence structure she is able to keep the focus of the spectator on the present moment of perception. Through her use of hermeticism, non-logical expression, multiple perspective, and multiple stories, she achieves movement within her plays and confines the attention of the spectator to his experience in the theatre. Only four of her plays . . . even risk transporting that attention to fictional stage reality, and those plays need to be considered departures from her general technique and aesthetic.

LILLIAN HELLMAN TALKS ABOUT WOMEN

In *Pentimento*, published in 1973, Lillian Hellman wrote that she could not develop the plot Dashiell Hammett had suggested to her for the play that became *Toys in the Attic*. "I can write about men, but I can't write a play that centers on a man. I've got to tear it up, make it about the women around him, his sisters, his bride, her mother. . . ." In the last decade of Hellman's life, which was also the decade of the women's movement, interviewers drew from her some intriguing observations about her sense of herself as a woman artist and about women's issues. The following collage is a sampling of what she said on these topics.

1973—INTERVIEW WITH NORA EPHRON

Q.   Ever since *The Children's Hour* opened, you've been called a woman playwright and a woman writer. How do you feel about that?

A.   Irritated.

Q.   What do you think of the women's movement?

A.   Of course I believe in women's liberation, but it seems to make very little sense in the way it's going. Until women can earn their own living, there's no point in talking about brassieres and lesbianism. While I agree with women's liberation and ecology and all the other good liberal causes, I think at this minute they're diversionary; they keep your eye off the problems implicit in our capitalist society. As a matter of fact, they're implicit in socialist society, too, I guess. It's very hard for women, hard to get along, to support themselves, to live with some self-respect. And in fairness, women have often made it hard for other women. I think some men give more than women give.

1974—INTERVIEW WITH BILL MOYERS

M.   Why do you suppose there aren't more women writing plays or writing for the theatre today?

Nora Ephron, "Lillian Hellman Walking, Cooking, Writing, Talking," *The New York Times Book Review*, September 23, 1973, 2, 51. Reprinted by permission of International Creative Management, © 1973 by Nora Ephron.

The interviews on which we have drawn appear in full in *Conversations with Lillian Hellman*, edited by Jackson R. Bryer, Jackson: University Press of Mississippi, 1986.

H.   Well, of course, there always should have been. God knows why there weren't early. I think there are a lot more women writing now, not only for the theatre; there are a lot more women writing now than when I began or certainly fifty years before me when there were very few women writing anything. There're more women poets, there're more women novelists, aren't there?

M.   You once said I think that women's liberation is a matter of economics. Would you elaborate on that?

H.   Yes. I was misunderstood when I said it in a forum. I don't have to tell you how deeply I believe in women's liberation. I think some of its cries are rather empty cries because I think it all comes down to whether or not you can support yourself as well as a man can support himself and whether there's enough money to make certain decisions for yourself rather than dependence. In that particular discussion that was quoted one of the ladies brought up the point of she was not willing to do the cooking and lift the garbage cans. It seems to me it's not a question of who lifts the garbage cans but whether you have enough money to get somebody to lift them for you or enough money to say to your husband look I've worked as hard as you've worked today, please lift the garbage cans for me; or please do the cooking, I've worked perhaps even harder than you've worked today. I doubt if there'll be any true women's liberation until women are capable of even being paid for bringing up children which I think should carry a salary with it. . . .

M.   You said you were dependent and yet you strike me as always being a fugitive from commitment. I know you lived with Dashiell Hammett for thirty years off and on.

H.   Yes.

M.   And I guess one could say that's a commitment, and yet in your writings and in your life there seems to be a hanging back from commitment.

H.   I don't think from commitment; I think you mean from marriage.

M.   I didn't mean it, but I'll accept that amendment . . . from both. Why from marriage? Then I'll move on.

H.   I've been, as a matter of fact, I think a little too committed. I don't know. I don't know. It isn't even that I had a very bad first marriage. I had a very pleasant first marriage to a very pleasant man called Arthur Kober. It wasn't at all a mean marriage, and we still see each other and are very fond of each other. I suppose I decided that it wasn't right for me. I don't mean that so many people urged me into it, but I thought I was better with no formalities. I was better if . . . I would stay longer if I felt free to go any day. I suppose that was it. . . .

M.   Did he [Dashiell Hammett] help you with your writing?

H.   Oh yes, enormously, enormously. I can't ever pay him enough grati-

Bill Moyers, "Lillian Hellman: The Great Playwright Candidly Reflects on a Long, Rich Life," transcript of an interview on National Educational Television, April 1974. Used by permission of Bill Moyers, Public Affairs Television, Inc.

tude for what he did beyond the obvious things that writers can help with. He was so enormously patient. And more than patient, he was honest, sometimes rather sharply and brutally honest. Without that I don't think I would have done very much.

M. Did he tell you this is no damn good?

H. Oh yes, indeed. In stronger words than that. In very strong words.

M. Did you take it from him?

H. Oh yes, I took it. Once in a while I would get terribly pained and miserable about it. Yes certainly I took it because I recognized that it had . . . I think you can always take what people say if you know there's no malice in it or no self-seeking in it. Then whether they're right or wrong, they've shown that amount of love to take the chance on your hating them which has always impressed me in people.

1975—INTERVIEW WITH STEPHANIE DE PUE

Q. You were recently named Ladies Home Journal Woman of the Year, in the Creative Arts, and cited for "embodying woman's potential as an artist since the production of your first play."

So many women seem to have the conflict, "Shall I be like Mommy, and be safe, or be like Daddy and do something?" I recently read an article which notes that women of noticeably great achievement have often been raised by, or particularly close to, their fathers . . .

A. Well, I suppose so, but then most girls are closer to their fathers.

Q. It's an awful, sociological phrase to use, but do you feel you've made a valuable contribution to younger women by being a role model, a woman of accomplishment?

A. Oh, I wouldn't answer that question for anything in the world.

Q. You wouldn't?

A. No. Certainly I don't think I've been—how can you look at yourself that way, looking in the mirror to say, "I've been something." I don't do that, I don't look at myself that way. If it's happened, I'm delighted, and if it hasn't happened, it doesn't worry me. I don't see myself in such terms, they're too high for me.

Q. Well, you have now lived through two women's emancipation movements. Do you think the second will stick better than the first?

A. My youth couldn't have been called a women's emancipation movement.

Q. There were a great number of women who became doctors, lawyers, etc., and in the '40's–early '60's they got lost . . .

A. Yes, but I don't think it was a movement, in the sense of women's liberation. There were a great many women for the first time, not even for the

Stephanie de Pue, "Lillian Hellman: She Never Turns Down an Adventure," *Cleveland Plain Dealer*, December 28, 1975, sec. 5, 2, 8.

first time, it began in the '20's, beginning to work, beginning to sleep around, beginning to live with people they weren't married to.

But I don't think there was any real movement, just a pocket of people in certain cities. Most of the people I went to college with, for example, I don't think went to work.

Q.   Well, it's a common aphorism, that one of the greatest temptations for women is to think they can simply be rather than do. Have you found that so yourself?

A.   I think women almost have to be more sort of interested in a personal life than men have to be. I don't mean because men don't want one, any more than women do, because I think they do.

But I think women, no matter how liberated they are, feel more pressed to look for a personal life, whether it's a husband or a lover or a house or children or whatever it is, than men feel pressed to.

1976—INTERVIEW WITH CHRISTINE DOUDNA

A. . . . I was lucky. I was successful, early, I was twenty-seven years old. Women *have* been put down, there's no question of that. For centuries and centuries.

Q.   In a speech you said of the women's movement: "Some of its cries are empty cries." You talked about someone who was complaining about carrying out the garbage.

A.   I don't think it's of any great moment who carries out the garbage. I think it is important that people be economically equal. So that if somebody feels like walking out, there's a way for her to earn a living rather than suffering through a whole lifetime because she can't. Most people of decent manners, living together, automatically divide the jobs anyway, whatever they are. My own nature would have forbidden anybody depriving *me* of what I thought were my rights. I would have walked out.

Q.   Isn't that an extreme way of resolving a problem? Suppose you don't want to walk out over who carries out the garbage?

A.   I would think in a decent relationship you don't have to keep a daily score of who does what. It doesn't matter who washed the dishes. It seems to me a thoroughly middle-class argument and I have no interest in it.

Are you going to legislate this? Is every mother in the world going to bring up a son who says, I won't put my wife down? And is every mother going to bring up a daughter who says, I don't dislike men and won't make them pay? A great many women put men down very badly. Particularly upper-class ladies.

Christine Doudna, "A Still Unfinished Woman: A Conversation with Lillian Hellman." From *Rolling Stone*, no. 233 (24 February 1977), 52–57. Reprinted by permission of Straight Arrow Publishers, Inc. © 1977.

Q.   Do you think some women use the women's movement as an excuse for letting out hostilities which are really a lot more complicated?

A.   I guess many do. But I don't know any. Most women want everything. They want "leadership," they want to be darlings, they want to be Marilyn Monroe and they want to be Madame de Maintenon. At the same time they want to be president. There is no oneness about any movement.

Q.   Does the fact that young women have an easier time of it today than fifty years ago make you unsympathetic to their concerns?

A.   I'm not sure young women do have it easier. Yes, there are more jobs available, but for whom? I'm not sure Negro women have it any easier than they did when I was growing up. I'm not sure poor women have it any easier.

Q.   As a writer and a woman, how do you feel about the alterations in language that many feminists advocate?

A.   I hate "Ms." There really isn't anything like making small battles in order to lose big ones. That's what the whole women's movement has been about to me. The big battle is equal rights, whether one likes to face it or not. Even that may never solve it, but the small battles just won't do. These are diversionary movements.

Nobody can argue any longer about the rights of women. It's like arguing about earthquakes.

Q.   Do you think there's such a thing as feminine sensibility in literature?

A.   Sure. I think sometimes it's extraordinarily good and sometimes it's awful. The present crop of feminine porno writers is below contempt. Masculine stuff is very seldom porno in quite as nasty a fashion.

Q.   Erica Jong, for example, is somebody who . . .

A.   I'm not going to discuss people by name. Whoever thought sexual liberation had anything to do with liberation?

Q.   Anaïs Nin talked about how a lot of her creativity had been taken up by personal relationships. Have you ever experienced that as a conflict?

A.   Oh Christ, what a silly thing to say. That's like saying a lot of your creativity has been taken up by drinking or going swimming. It's your choice. Silly, self-pitying remark. You chose it, you wanted it.

1979—INTERVIEW WITH MARILYN BERGER

MB.   One of the things that I think women forget is that there is a price to be paid for the extraordinary freedom that a woman like you has. Do you feel you've paid a price?

LH.   Yes. Yes, I've paid a price.

MB.   What price?

LH.   Well, I think I said it earlier, that there would have been safer,

Marilyn Berger, "Profile of Lillian Hellman," transcript of five-part interview broadcast originally in 1981. Copyright © 1979, KERA Public Communication Foundation for North Texas. Used by permission of KERA-TV, Dallas/Fort Worth/Denton, Producer.

pleasanter ways to go. And as you get older, of course, perhaps you think . . . I don't think much about them really. Things turned out the way they did. Some prices, but I have no regrets for that price. Prices are to be paid for everything. There's no way to live without paying the price, and the price is. . . . It would be very hard for me to regret my life. It's turned out . . . I was very lucky.

MB.   I think people who do well and work hard often say they're lucky, but it's a little more than luck.

LH.   Oh yes, it's a great deal more than luck. I don't mean to underplay it. I worked very hard. I don't mean to say it's lucky in the sense of throwing dice.

MB.   Was not having children a price you paid?

LH.   Yes, it was certainly one of them. I myself should have said it. I hesitate always to say it because it sounds, I don't know. I back away from saying it. Yes, of course it was a price I paid. However, I could have had the children. Hammett wanted them, as indeed you know I was married once, and my husband wanted them. It was my choice.

MB.   I didn't know that Hammett wanted them.

LH.   Yes, he wanted them too.

MB.   That must have been very difficult not to at a time . . .

LH.   Well he wanted to because I was pregnant. I'm very fond of children and I would have had a nice time with children. That I certainly regret. But now they'd probably be grown up and unpleasant. . . .

MB.   Do you think in retrospect that your life as a dramatist would have been any easier had you been a man, not a woman?

LH.   No.

MB.   Was it easier because you were a woman?

LH.   No.

MB.   Neither.

LH.   No, I don't think so. It might've had certain minutes where it would have been easier to have been a man and where I wouldn't have had to . . . so the personal things didn't become quite so personal, if you know what I'm awkwardly trying to say. There might have been that if I'd been a man, but I don't think it would've made much difference.

MB.   Another question that's been raised is whether your books, coming out at a time of great movement for women's liberation, have been lucky in their timing.

LH.   I think they have been.

MB.   And have you found yourself being considered as a standard-bearer for causes that you really have nothing to do with at all because you happen to be a woman and . . .?

LH.   Yes. Yes, I have found that and been amazed by it. But then I have to say that in a sense, I understand it because I'm sure that I also had such people when I was young. I don't remember who they were, but I'm sure I also had such people too who I admired because they had done certain things that I was about to do or wanted to do. Sometimes my admiration was misplaced. Sometimes it wasn't. I am all for women's liberation. I am not, as I said before, not for the offshoots of women's liberation. I mean, I believe it must begin with economic liberation. There must be equal pay for equal work. . . .

MB.   You describe without any fuss an abortion you had done in your twenties. What do you make of the anti-abortion movement today, the right-to-lifers in this country?

LH.   Well, legal abortion, of course, in my mind is a very necessary and very properly advanced movement for people who either cannot, which is, I think usually the case, or even if they do not want, which is almost the same case since the child would not be loved or cherished if it's not wanted or taken proper care of, as one sees by child abuse . . . constant child abuse, certainly from people who had never wanted the child. It's a very necessary, civilized, proper act. The other is very irreligious to me. I have just the opposite theory. The anti-abortion law is a very irreligious law to me. It's forcing on people that which they cannot properly cherish and understand.

1981—INTERVIEW WITH SYLVIE DRAKE

"It hasn't gotten down to the basic issue," she said about the women's movement. "I said once that I don't give a damn who carries out the garbage. It's not the point of proof. The question should be addressed totally in economic terms: equal pay for equal work. Unless it does that, it's never going to attract any but unhappy middle-class women. It is a working-class woman's problem.

"It's almost come down to being a dislike of men, rather than an acceptance of the pleasure of men. Men have brutalized women, certainly, but the issues have been strange issues, often meager, minor complaints. And the enmity is strange.

"Child-bearing and -rearing is a very important function of women and always will be, please God. Yet it's absolutely absent from the discussion—perhaps because it is in the hands of women with very little interest in bearing or rearing children. I think—I hope—that when it's in the hands of simpler women, if ever, it will straighten itself out."

LORRAINE HANSBERRY: ARTIST, ACTIVIST, FEMINIST

MARGARET WILKERSON

Lorraine Hansberry wrote *A Raisin in the Sun*, the first play by a black writer to win, in 1959, the New York Drama Critics Circle Award. She was also the first woman and youngest playwright to win that award. Born in 1930, she lived a brief, intense, socially committed life, dying in 1965 at the age of thirty-four. Her short span of years yielded five published plays (one of which was completed by her former husband and literary executor, Robert Nemiroff), and more than sixty magazine and newspaper articles, poems and speeches. Among her unpublished works are several playscripts, filmscripts and adaptations, including a treatment and preliminary notes for a play on Mary Wollstonecraft, the 19th-century feminist, and a stunning opening scene for a play on the great Haitian liberator, Toussaint L'Ouverture. She wrote the text for *The Movement*, a photographic essay on the Civil Rights Movement. *To Be Young, Gifted and Black*, a dramatic compilation of her writings prepared by Nemiroff, toured the country after her death, playing to thousands on campuses and in communities, and adding a new and vital phrase to the American idiom. An activist artist, she spoke at Civil Rights rallies, writers' conferences and confronted Attorney General Robert Kennedy in a controversial meeting with black leaders about the role of the FBI in the Deep South.

Hansberry was a fiercely independent thinker who trusted the intellect instinctively. The roots of her philosophical views lie in Chicago, the place of her birth. Her childhood there held curious contradictions. On the one hand, she grew up in an upper middle-class family; her father was a powerful realtor who built his fortune on the sale and rental of kitchenettes to relieve the crowded housing conditions of blacks. He won a Supreme Court case against housing discrimination. Her mother, at one point a ward committeewoman, helped to manage the buildings and tenants, but had plenty of time for the leisure-time activities typical of the bourgeoisie. The parents taught their four children pride in themselves and in the race, and nurtured in them the belief that their possibilities were (or should be in a fair society) limitless. On the other hand, she lived in Chicago, a city of racial/ethnic barriers and boundaries. The burgeoning population of blacks, increased periodically by waves of immigrants from the South, was literally confined by restrictive covenants to a fifty- to sixty-block-long area with a few small neighborhoods nearby into which blacks had moved. Despite her family's financial resources, they could not purchase any home they could afford, nor could they eat in certain restaurants, nor even try on shoes in some of the city's major department stores. Wealth may have freed her mind and spirit, but it could not free her colored body. . . .

Her abhorrence of narrowness and parochialism later led her to an awareness of the hidden alliance between racism and sexism long before it was popular to do so, and to shape a vision cognizant of the many dimensions of colonialism and oppression. Anticipating the Women's Movement of the 1970's, Hansberry was aware of the peculiar oppression under which women

Margaret Wilkerson, Associate Professor in the Department of Afro-American Studies, University of California, edited the anthology *9 Plays by Black Women*, 1986. Excerpted from Special Issue (1986) Women in Theatre, *Theatre Annual*. Published by permission of Margaret Wilkerson.

lived and the particular devastation visited upon women of color. Recognizing its devious forms, she argued forcefully that anti-homosexual attitudes were linked to the oppression of women and man's predilection to gain mastery over other men. . . .

For Hansberry, nothing was "more universal in the world than man's oppression of man." This issue is what "most great dramas have been about, no matter what the device of telling it is . . . ."[1] Blacks, women, homosexuals and any others whose oppression is profitable will be victimized. Within her highly political and humanistic world-view, all art was social—whether intentionally so or not. And it was her role as artist to expose the myths and illusions of her time and culture so that the human race could achieve its true stature. . . . She believed that "man is unique in the universe, the only creature who has the power to transform the universe . . . . [to] impose the reason for life on life . . . ."[2] Like a sculptor molding clay she could create characters, structure a world in which the beauties and absurdities of human action could be exposed or treasured, as the case might be.

In the early 1950's, Hansberry worked as a journalist and associate editor for *Freedom*, a black, progressive newspaper in New York City founded by Paul Robeson. During this time, undercurrents of social protest were quietly growing, despite the Red Scare, McCarthyism and hearings by the House Un-American Activities Committee. Numerous violations of human rights, brutality of the Deep Southern variety, and labor protests filled the pages of *Freedom* as Hansberry gained an education in politics, culture and economics unparalleled in any university curriculum. While she treasured this work, she found journalism ultimately too restrictive—for one had to stick with facts, even if they obscured deeper truths. . . .

In *A Raisin in the Sun* (1959) we see her first successful attempt to transform the experience of her early years in Chicago into a drama which captured the deferred dreams of a race of people, while exposing the materialistic dangers of the society which evokes, then frustrates those dreams. . . .

A Raisin in the Sun dramatizes the seductiveness of American materialistic values by depicting the aspirations of a black family, the Youngers, who live in Southside Chicago of the 1950's. The title and theme are taken from a Langston Hughes poem, "Harlem," which asks: "What happens to a dream deferred?" Three generations of Youngers live in a cramped kitchenette apartment. When $10,000 insurance money is payed to Lena Younger (Mama), the elder of the household, she places a down payment on a house (in a white neighborhood) to the dismay and anger of her son, Walter, who dreams of capitalizing the windfall by investing in a liquor store. Moved by Walter's frustration, Mama gives him a portion of the money—which he promptly loses in a dubious business deal. The financial crisis which he precipitates becomes a critical test of Walter's personal values. . . . "There ain't no causes," says Walter, "there ain't nothing but taking in this world and he who takes most is smartest—and it don't make a damn bit of difference how."

It is indeed a moment of truth for a black man who seeks enough material resources to improve his family's economic situation and to provide his son with a future. Those aims seem acceptable enough. However, Walter's dream is dangerously flawed: he also seeks the kind of material wealth which comes at the price of deceit and oppression. . . .

House, secretaries, cars are all emblems of the success he seeks. But the dreams of Mama and Walter differ dramatically. Mama wants the family to advance materially without becoming materialistic, while Walter embraces materialism and power—of the kind which has already limited his opportunities. He seeks merely a transfer of power, not a change in the systems of power. . . .

Hansberry had seen the dangers of such confusion in her own brothers, who upon their father's death inherited his business, but little of his philanthropic vision, social commitment and business acumen. Eventually, through a series of mishaps (some of which were not of their own making), they lost their property in Chicago and moved west. Despite Hansberry's comfortable life, she rejected the fruits of capitalism and the conspicuous consumption of the bourgeoisie, dressing simply even as a high school student, and ignoring her mother's urgings to buy expensive clothes so that she would be in style. Here, in a 1961 interview, Hansberry explains the difference between material need and materialism.

> . . . there are thousands, millions of people in the United States who don't have too much of anything. They don't have enough and there's a fine and important distinction between that kind of material base of life which simply provides what people need to live a decent life and the middle-class preoccupation with acquisition, with affluence, with these things that they can demonstrate to their neighbors to show that they are keeping up with the fashions . . . .[3]

Hansberry, however, was not satisfied simply portraying the economic disparity between the poor and the wealthy. She proceeded to attack materialism even when it appeared in the midst of poverty. . . .

The Sign in Sidney Brustein's Window (1964), the second and the last of her plays to be produced during her lifetime, offers even more striking examples of Hansberry's objectivity towards her material. The play, which shocked some critics because it was not about black people specifically, focused on Sidney Brustein, a Greenwich Village intellectual, who, through his new and struggling newspaper, supports a local politician's campaign for office. The play charts Sidney's personal odyssey towards self-realization and affirmation of his responsibility to engage and act in this world. Some early notes on this play indicate that Hansberry originally intended the title to be *The Sign in Jenny Reed's Window* with a female character as the central figure. However, over a period of time she decided that it would not suit her purposes. While speculation continues as to why she made this change, her choice demonstrated her ability to write authentic, convincing male characters, if she had not already proven that talent in *A Raisin in the Sun*. One suspects that the final structure of the play with its male protagonist served her social statement as well if not better than a Jenny Reed would have. For while Sidney is the central figure, he is educated to his own chauvinism, intolerance and self-indulgence by three sisters who collectively present a tapestry of women victimized by this society.

The primary woman in Sidney's life is Iris, his wife, who tolerates the "Pygmalion-like" relationship which initially attracted and continues to hold her husband. Despite his progressive outlook on society, Sidney's views on women are nearly Neanderthal. He demeans Iris's attempts at intellectual discourse and reinforces a girl-child image, complete with flowing hair and idyllic ignorance. When Iris begins to rebel against this image (she eventually cuts off her beautiful hair) Sidney is shocked. . . .

Mavis, his sister-in-law, is portrayed as a bourgeois matron—the stereotype of the uptight gentile whose racial prejudice and provincialism come through in the simplest of conversations. Sidney and his friends enjoy many laughs at her expense. Yet it is Mavis who teaches him about courage—she who has lived with the secret that her straight-laced husband has supported a young mistress and illegitimate son for years, and who has made peace with that knowledge. Noting Sidney's shock, Mavis comments on his naivete.

> Sometimes I think you kids down here [Greenwich Village] believe your own notions of what the rest of the human race is like. There are no squares, Sidney. Believe me when I tell you, everybody is his own hipster.[4]

Sidney can only salute this woman whose humanity and intellect he had ridiculed.

Finally, Gloria deals the death-blow to his smugness. Gloria, the high-priced prostitute who had the fantasy that she could leave her mink-lined, sordid profession with its dope addiction and violent repercussions, by marrying Alton, a young black man. Sidney's last illusions are shattered when Alton breaks the engagement and Gloria commits suicide, while Sidney lay in a drunken stupor, wrapped in his own disappointments. Gloria is the most tragic victim, symbolizing the ultimate, perhaps, in the oppression of women. Mavis has reconciled her disappointment and made a life, such as it is, with her husband. And by the end of the play, Iris has asserted herself and forced Sidney to view her and himself in a different way. The possibilities for their relationship begin at the end of the play. But for Gloria there is no new beginning—at least not in this life. She had become trapped in a role which her world made attractive, a role which she continued to accept and to which she became addicted. Her end is inevitable self-destruction. Hansberry places in the hands of this "Greek Chorus," the Parodus sisters, the true "education" of Sidney and reveals the varied permutations of women's victimization.

Her handling of the only homosexual character in the play exemplifies her ability to use material without regard to her personal experience or preference but to expose ignorance and pretentiousness wherever she found it. By the time this play was written, Hansberry had already written some plays, short stories and essays exploring the theme of homosexuality and denouncing homophobia. By this time she had also become comfortable with her own lesbianism and was involved with a circle of intimate women friends. Yet David, a playwright in *The Sign in Sidney Brustein's Window* who is a homosexual, embodies many of the characteristics personally detested by Hansberry. He is a whining, self-indulgent character who wears his sexual preference like a chip on his shoulder, daring anyone to knock it off . . . . Even so, Hansberry later grants David his humanity and complexity by exposing his painful sojourn through his life as a homosexual.

Again, here is Hansberry the intellect, controlling her characters (and her own emotions) and insisting on distance between herself and her subject matter while utilizing the knowledge and memory of passionate encounters. Only in this way can she command her universe to yield the truths which she seeks for her audience.

This imposition of will suggests a "dark" side to Hansberry which is as much aware of the brutal, selfish, irrational side of humankind as she is of its transcendent potential. *A Raisin in the Sun*, in fact, whose upbeat ending sometimes obscures the danger into which the family is moving, had a different ending in an earlier version. This earlier ending showed the family seated in the darkened living room of their new home, shades drawn, family armed, awaiting the inevitable attack by their hostile white neighbors. Probably no other line dramatized this idea more effectively than Sidney's speech near the end of *The Sign in Sidney Brustein's Window*. Now having faced the abyss of human corruption and suffering, he acknowledges his pain—but pushes through it to action. The line is written as one sentence with practically no punctuation so that the words tumble out of Sidney in an emotional outpouring. But even as he is swept up in this passionate response, he imposes his own will and intellect on that rush of words—directing them towards action when they could just as easily lead him to withdrawal from the world.

[I am] a fool who believes that death is waste and love is sweet and that the earth turns and men change every day and that rivers run and that people wanna be better than they are and that flowers smell good and that I hurt terribly today, and that hurt is desperation and desperation is—energy and energy can *move* things. . . .[5]

WOMAN ALONE, WOMEN TOGETHER

HONOR MOORE

Until women go to war, scale Mount Everest, or have major moral concerns—in short, until their experience becomes less domestic and more dramatic—they will not write great plays. Such were the clichés about women playwrights when I went to college. The women's movement has changed that. It provided the sociological environment for many new female playwrights to emerge and brought about changes in consciousness that enabled women dramatists to bring so-called nondramatic feminine experience to vibrant theatrical life. The catalyst was the consciousness-raising group. Whether or not a woman joined such a group, she inevitably during the last ten years began to experience her femaleness in a new way. If she was a writer, her own experience and perceptions, instead of seeming inappropriate for the theatre, became a rich source for her writing, became also something to celebrate. This change of attitude is, I think, itself responsible for the kinds of plays, both in form and content, that American women are now writing.

Since the plays women are writing do not employ, strictly speaking, new forms, and since the dramatic technique seems to come so urgently out of the need to bring specific material to dramatic life, I will speak of strategies rather than forms. Approaching women's experience through the strategy of telling the story of an individual woman's struggle for autonomy results in what I call "the autonomous woman play," while choosing the strategy of dramatizing a situation which involves a group of women (or women and men) results in "the choral play."

When autonomy became an issue for many women, women's individual struggles became material for drama. The autonomous woman plays have one female protagonist, a fragment of whose journey toward autonomy we share. Some, like Alice Childress's *Wedding Band* (1973) concern a woman's survival of the death of someone she has been close to. Childress's Julia, a Black woman in 1918 in South Carolina, discovers herself in the process of her white lover Herman's death. Others place the struggle in the context of an argument between male and female; in Ruth Wolff's *The Abdication* (1969), a seventeenth-century Swedish queen abdicates her throne and in the course of confessing her sins to a cardinal with whom she has fallen in love, gains spiritual independence. Still other plays like Ursule Molinaro's *Breakfast Past Noon* (1968) and Gail Kriegel Mallin's *Holy Places* (1979)[1] take on the struggle of mother and daughter. Molinaro's is a play of manners in which mother's and daughter's values clash in the context of such issues as smoking and whether the mother approves of the daughter's lover; Mallin's is a

Honor Moore, playwright and critic, published the anthology *The New Women's Theatre* in 1977 and a collection of poems in 1987. She is writing a biography of her grandmother, Margaret Sargent.

poetic play in which the daughter resists her mother's love in order to resist the ordinariness of her adored father's death.

In these plays we are given heroines with a variety of lives and situations, but it is the way these women's inner lives are drawn that gives the plays their power. The feminist movement affirmed for women the truth of their inner lives and gave them a sense of the validity of their perceptions. It is this validation that gives the playwrights a context in which to bring female emotional reality into the theatre. The plays almost never adhere to traditional fourth wall convention. In Corinne Jacker's *Bits and Pieces* (1975), for instance, the heroine, a widow, is visited by her dead husband whom the other characters don't see. He is not a ghost as he might be in a more traditional play, rather a "piece" of Iris's previous life which has continued into the present to lure her to the past, back to a less autonomous self.

Francine Stone puts her heroine Anna (*Dead Sure*, 1977)[2] in a crisis situation: the husband whom she has left holds their children hostage and threatens to kill them if Anna doesn't return. Anna is a feeling rather than a thinking or reflective woman. Stone breaks into the "action" with tiny flashbacks and imaginings, Anna imagining what would happen if she did go back—almost a hallucination. For example, lights come up on Anna alone on the stage:

> *She is standing at the table, but the shaft of light extends no more than an arm's length around her. As she talks, she pulls a comb through her hair, paying no attention to her grooming. She encounters a bad knot and fights it mechanically. All the while she is thinking:*
>
> ANNA
>
> I'm . . . back. Is that what you want?
>   *(Starts again)*
> Should I see them? Are they all right?
>   *(Starts again)*

and

> Don't say anything. There's nothing to say.
>   *(Starts again)*
> No I'm not staying.
>   *(Starts again)*
> If only you'd said something. . . .

Because of the extreme stress of Anna's conflict these solitary moments heighten the drama. Stone's strategy is effective in dramatizing the sense of being in two places at once, of suppressing an inner reality to deal with an outer one, a way of experiencing many women share.

In other autonomous woman plays, the protagonist is divided into several selves, each of whom expresses different versions of the woman in question.

Usually the conflict is between a self acceptable to (male) society and a savage self who cannot conform.

A young girl in white sings, "I'm Lise, little Lise from Nuremburg . . . " to a delicate music-box melody. This is Myrna Lamb's heroine's memory of her perfect child-self, the self that was pleasing to her Marlene Dietrich-like mother. For the purposes of her opera *Apple Pie* (1975)[3] Lamb divides Lise in two, one an idealized child-self, the other the present woman-self who is too sexual, too ambitious, too much.

In Marsha Norman's *Getting Out* (1978),[4] a violent Arlie batters around her prison cell while Arlene, Arlie rehabilitated and eight years older, lives her first day out of prison. Arlie's youthful female life force is expressible only through violence, her actions screaming her refusal to buckle under to society's expectations of demure womanhood. As if a memory or a present specter, Arlie bounces, invisible, through rehabilitated Arlene's present apartment: the two actresses do not acknowledge each other directly, but there is a sense of forces resisting each other. When the guard who has driven Arlene home to Louisville after eight years of prison moans, trying to embrace her, "Arlie, Arlie girl, I'm sorry . . . " Arlene bats back, a mirror of her past, as Arlie seethes in her prison cell across the stage: "I'm not Arlie. Arlie would have killed you. . . . " Again we as women identify with her sense of being two people, one who would break all the rules, the other who keeps that rule breaker in line.

In other plays like Susan Miller's *Nasty Rumors and Final Remarks* (1979) and my own *Mourning Pictures* (1974) the protagonist engages in two dramas, one with herself witnessed by the audience, another inside the play. Miller's Raleigh, dying in intensive care off stage, appears vibrant and alive to replay moments with her mourners or to correct their perceptions of their common past. In *Mourning Pictures*, Margaret continually shares with the audience what events in her mother's dying mean to her growing sense of herself as an adult, a woman rather than a daughter.

If the autonomous woman plays say "This is what we have in common" by showing an individual woman, the choral plays say "There are many different kinds of women, each unique, but with much in common," by showing us the drama of a group of women. The autonomous woman plays give us women in isolation, women taken apart. The choral plays show us women together, women seeking integration by attempting community, much as women did in consciousness-raising groups. Though plays about individual women are still being written, most of the autonomous woman plays were written in the early seventies, while the choral plays are more recent—as if experience of women's groups had been their impulse.

Some of these plays are actual choral pieces rather than plays. Ntozake Shange's *For Colored Girls Who Have Considered Suicide / When the Rainbow Is Enuf* (1975),[5] which the author calls a "choreopoem, " and Susan Griffin's *Voices*,[6] also written in poetry, are two examples. Neither piece has a plot;

rather they are communal tellings of several women's lives, rituals in which the women move from isolated, oppressed, and painful pasts into a strengthening and newly communal future. At the end of *For Colored Girls* its characters, six women, come together in pain and slowly emerge to embrace each other and sing "I found God in myself and I loved her fiercely. . . ." *Voices* ends with a young woman's turning away from suicide:

ERIN
What held me like a magnet was the possibility of death, but I am curious . . .

In other plays, we witness groups of women in actual situations. Some, like Wendy Wasserstein's *Uncommon Women and Others* (1977)[7] and Leigh Curran's *The Lunch Girls* (1977)[8] are realistic; others, like Aishah Rahman's *Unfinished Women Cry in No Man's Land While a Bird Dies in a Gilded Cage* (1977),[9] are more poetic and abstract. Rahman's takes place one day in 1955, alternating between a home for unwed mothers where six women—Black, Hispanic, and white, all pregnant by Black men—have twenty-four hours to decide whether to keep their illegitimate unborn children, and an elegant Manhattan apartment where Charlie Parker, the Black jazz saxophonist, is dying in his rich white mistress's "gilded cage." Parker is meant by the playwright to "represent all the reasons why the women's men aren't there." The counterpoint between the world of women (six identically dressed pregnant women on a stage is quite a spectacle) and the death throes of a Black male artist who has been exploited and destroyed by white society gives the play a perspective that adds to its power.

In Wasserstein's *Uncommon Women*, a comedy about seven classmates at Mount Holyoke, men are present only as the male voice which, over a loudspeaker, periodically intones ideals of womanhood in the form of selections from the college catalog. These exhortations—that the students be "uncommonly" fine, that they dress properly, etc.—provide the play's comic tension. *Uncommon Women* begins at a reunion lunch years after graduation and flashes back to a year in the late sixties when most of Wasserstein's heroines were seniors. It is a play about a female community which, because it is insulated from the real world, can afford to scoff at the male values which emanate from the loudspeaker, even though falling short of those standards causes the young women considerable pain. Wasserstein has compassion for characters and events (women growing up, rejection by boyfriends, female eccentricity) that would usually, in the theatre or on television, be subject to ridicule or satire: we laugh *with* rather than *at* her uncommon women. In one hilarious scene, three women examine a first diaphragm as if it is some unfortunate variety of jellyfish; in another, all seven women dance joyously to a bouncy calypso beat—the choice of dance music makes the scene poignantly ironic: "If you want to be happy for the rest of your life/Never make a pretty woman your wife . . . " In spite of its truthful view of woman's situation, *Uncommon Women* is a comedy in the classic sense. All is resolved: the young women, however "uncommonly," have survived their college years; their communal act of memory has acknowledged and soothed, shared pain has receded, and the past is suffused in golden light.

Curran's *The Lunch Girls* is a darker play. Its characters are women of less privilege than Wasserstein's Mount Holyoke students. They have grown up—some are mothers—and there is little money or glamour in what they do. The play sees them through a day of work—they wait the lunch shift at a seedy Manhattan key club dressed in net stockings, spike heels, and skimpy chorus girl outfits. The locker room where we see them transform themselves from ordinary women into spike-heeled, net-stockinged, skimpily dressed kewpie dolls is no utopia. The lunch girls have become hard women and their dreams are charged with desperation: they yearn toward mere survival; a man who, if he couldn't care, would at least pay the way; a chance to play Ophelia; a way out of an unwanted pregnancy. The community these women would form is vulnerable to their own need for what the men—customer, pimp, husband, boss—can give them and what they must betray to win it. This vulnerability is pungently demonstrated when one of them notices the glint of an eye in one of the knotholes in the locker-room wall: she retaliates with hair spray and the peeping Tom howls with pain, a temporary victory. Curran offers no easy healing, and when Vicky, who wants to leave the club and get her kids into commercials, speaks of unity, she is tentative: "I just heard what ya said the other day about gettin' along and how nice it'd be if we all, ya know . . . really made an effort . . . I wanta help ya. . . . "

Most of these plays derive at least some of their dramatic impact from the fact that they look at pre-women's movement times from a post-women's movement point of view: this is the way it was, it has not been clearly seen before. There is not yet a body of playwrighting work that deals with the new communal future or that concerns women characters with feminist values and aspirations, if you will, the Mount Everests that women have begun in the last ten years to climb.[10] What are the dramas in a woman's life when her life is a life she has freely chosen? Tina Howe's *The Art of Dining* (1979)[11] is the first such play I know. In form an autonomous woman play, it treats an evening in the life of Ellen, in her mid-thirties the "co-owner and chef extraordinaire of The Golden Carousel."

It is a November night and Ellen and Cal, her husband and maitre d', prepare for the evening clientele. "These are the various works in progress," the stage direction says, hinting at Howe's metaphoric intention: that a woman chef be taken for a woman artist whose works range from "Pears in Cointreau with Frozen Cream" to "The sauces, Hollandaise and Velouté." *The Art of Dining* is a comic symphony to the creative process as experienced by women. It is the rare woman artist who would not identify with Ellen when, after raging at her husband's unconscious interference with her art (he compulsively eats her key ingredients), she says:

ELLEN

I can't do it all by myself, I just can't . . . it's too hard . . . so much to do. . . . I get lost sometimes, afraid I've done something wrong. . . . You're not helping me . . . tell me it's fine . . . tell me it's fine.

But Ellen perseveres with her creation. "Just let me cook," she snaps, and impulsively crowns the evening with crepe suzettes, a second dessert for everyone. "I don't believe this!" one diner says. "It's extraordinary!" says another. The play ends with what is literally a communion in Ellen's culinary art, a communal ingesting of the flaming triumph of one woman artist. Says a stage direction:

. . . The fury of the November wind increases outside and the light from Ellen's bonfire burns brighter and brighter as the diners gather close to its warmth. Ellen stands above them with a fierce radiance. Purified of their collective civilization and private grief, they lift the fiery crepe to their mouths and start to eat as the curtain slowly falls.

The women playwrights who have most successfully developed original theatrical voices are those whose work has continued to be put on by one theatre or producer: Joseph Papp has produced more than one play by Howe, Shange, Lamb, and Miller; the Actor's Theatre of Louisville has done the same for Marsha Norman; the Phoenix, after producing *Uncommon Women*, commissioned another play from Wasserstein; and the American Place Theatre has begun the Women's Project to develop women playwrights and directors. Because a play requires production to be a completed work of art, it is this kind of support, as much as the support of the community of theatre women, that will enable what is probably the strongest surge of women playwrights in history to continue to invent forms to suit their content, characters to express their perceptions, aspirations and visions.

4

IF NOT AN ACTRESS, WHAT . . . ?

"If not an actress, what . . . ?" is the big question for many women who want to do something in theatre. While accepted, even encouraged as performers and occasionally as playwrights, women have largely been excluded from most other aspects of show business. The creative and technical side of the production process and the manipulations of money and public relations have been more or less off limits to them. "Not strong enough," "no technical understanding," "lack authority," "too emotional," "no head for economics," are the sorts of responses made until recently to women who have wanted to work at the various trades and arts of production.

A closer look at what women have actually done in those areas usually labeled "for men only" suggests that it is not the tasks to be done that pose the problems for women but the hierarchical power structure of theatre. If the job is lowly, the organization experimental or community-oriented, or the artistic skill new, women are likely to be found doing the work. Once the job becomes an executive or top administrative one or the organization successful or nationally important, or the skill formalized into a profession, women's role seems to diminish and their original pioneer work often ignored or forgotten. This process is not peculiar to theatre, but is endemic to women's participation in American life, as Gerda Lerner has pointed out in *The Majority Finds Its Past*. For women's careers in theatre it has resulted in both lack of opportunity and a neglected history of accomplishments.

In the nineteenth century when theatrical production was not highly specialized, women, starting as actresses usually, could become involved in every aspect of production. There was Laura Keene, for example, acting, directing others, making costumes, designing and painting scenery, organizing publicity, and writing or adapting plays; or Mrs. John Drew, progenitor of theatre's royal family, brilliantly managing the Arch Street Theatre in Philadelphia; or the early founders of Augusta's theatre described in the following pages.

Greater division of labor occurred in theatre at the end of the last century

192

just about the time the energetic "new woman" made her appearance. Although being male remained an important determinant of success in such new careers as that of director, designer, and technician, a surprising number of women turn up in these positions. Obviously they were not among the "men who direct the destinies of the stage," as the new directors of Broadway were hailed, but they were directing in Hull-House, in the Toy Theatre of Boston, in the Neighborhood Playhouse, in the Washington Square Players, and the Provincetown Players. Few recall, for example, that some of Eugene O'Neill's earliest plays were directed by women: Nina Moise, whom he greatly admired, and Ida Rauh, whose direction could be innovative or "punk," as he put it. Rachel Crothers directed all her own plays, feeling as "passionate" about production as about the script, and many other women playwrights as well as actresses have directed and produced their own work and that of others.

From the 1920's on there was almost an "old girls' network" of directors, producers, and even designers. The short-lived Woman's Theatre, initiated in 1926, took as its objective "to promote woman's work in the theatre and to render aid and give counsel to all who may apply. Whether she has a voice to be heard—a play to be read—a desire to act—or to paint scenery—whenever a woman asks our advice or seeks our aid in securing an audition, we assist her without charge." There are many examples of women turning to women to break the domination of men in various careers. A notable example of women working together was the American Repertory Theatre of the 1940's created by Cheryl Crawford, Eva Le Gallienne, and Margaret Webster. The major productions of Shakespeare done by Webster made her the best-known woman director in America.

Despite the impressive record of achievement that still waits to be fully explored and written up, young women continue to be discouraged by their teachers and their socialization from preparing themselves to be directors and producers. Although there are now over one hundred women members of the Society of Stage Directors and Choreographers and many more outside of its membership, they are rarely employed by producing organizations that repeatedly claim to be unable to find competent women directors. Our studies and Sourcebook belie these discriminatory statements. They will, we hope, facilitate and speed up the change which a new, forceful generation of women directors and producers is trying to make.

Women as designers and technicians still find themselves in an overwhelmingly male field. Here the long hours, the physical labor, and the need to supervise male stagehands have been used as excuses to keep women out. But from Aline Bernstein, set and costume designer of the Neighborhood Playhouse and the Theatre Guild, who was the first woman admitted to the Scenic Artists Union, to Peggy Clark Kelley, distinguished especially as lighting designer, who was the first woman to be president of this union, women have shown that their talents and skills can overcome barriers erected by the male domination of the production process.

In lighting, the newest artistic dimension of theatre, women have been the innovators—from the experiments of Loïe Fuller to the accomplishments of Jean Rosenthal and Tharon Musser. So, too, as costuming a show became a professional task rather than an adjunct of the actor's stock-in-trade, women like Lucy Barton, Willa Kim, and Pat Zipprodt came to dominate what would seem a natural field given women's upbringing.

There is no career in theatre untouched by women, although one must repeat that they are most active and successful where new roles are being defined and where salaries are low but human rewards high. They have been great teachers. They have cast our shows and movies and nurtured talent as play and actor agents. They have set standards and transmitted values as critics, and guarded rights as theatrical lawyers. More needs to be done to show that women have been there in theatre all the time. More needs to be done to break the hold of stereotypes that continue to keep women out of jobs that history tells us they have done with distinction.

HKC

WOMEN OPEN AUGUSTA'S FIRST THEATRE

MARY JULIA CURTIS

In 1790 two women opened a theatre in Augusta, Georgia, on the marshy banks of the Savannah River. Pioneers of the Georgia backcountry, they staged *George Barnwell*, *The Beaux Stratagem*, and other cut-down versions of eighteenth-century dramatic fare. Their theatre was a converted school-room, their producers were a debating society, and their newspaper critic a clever Englishman writing under the name of "Zoilus." The two women, Mrs. Ann Robinson and Miss Susannah Wall, professional actresses who had begun their American careers in the civilized city of Baltimore, must have asked themselves time and again during the 1790–91 season in Augusta, "How did we ever end up here?"

Their first performance, which we know about from a review in the *Augusta Chronicle*, was held on June 17, 1790. The women had put together a kind of variety show with sketches and songs, designed to amuse their audience of legislators, jurors, litigants, and judges who had assembled in Augusta, the state's temporary capital. Among Mrs. Robinson's selections was a parody of a legal dispute between Farmer A and Farmer B. Farmer A had a bull; Farmer B had a boat. *Bullum versus Boatum* had appeared in the *Charleston* [S.C.] *Morning Post* on July 14, 1786. The narrative, interspersed with great dollops of "true law Latin," concluded with the farmers being

---

Mary Julia Curtis, Professor of Dramatic Art, University of Nebraska at Omaha, read a longer version of this paper at the American Theatre Association, 1977.

"non-suited" with the judgment. So the bench permitted Farmer A and Farmer B "to begin again—*de nova.*" Whereupon, Mrs. Robinson caught her breath, gave a yank to her corset, and began again. She "kept the house in a continual laughter." Miss Wall, the beautiful ingenue, enchanted the Augustans with airs like "Sandy o'er the Lea," sure to please homesick Scots in the house. The reviewer of their opening performance trusted that "those ladies and gentlemen who did not attend will not deny themselves the pleasure of being there on next Wednesday night."

Who was Mrs. Robinson? G. O. Seilhamer in his *History of the American Theatre* wistfully speculated that she was the lady-love of George III and that having lost his attentions she eventually sailed to America. Unfortunately that was another Mrs. Robinson. Our Mrs. Robinson first appears in American theatre annals as Mrs. Dennis Ryan. She and her husband were performing in Baltimore with a company managed by Thomas Wall, the father of Susannah. In 1783 Ryan assumed the management of the Baltimore company and in June of that year took it to New York to entertain Tory and British audiences—a risky partisan business. When the British withdrew, Ryan petitioned the magistrates in Philadelphia for permission to perform but was turned down. Within two years the Ryans sailed for Charleston, South Carolina, which had always been a lucrative stop for earlier touring companies. The Ryans' season proceeded smoothly for three months until smallpox broke out and the company fled back to Baltimore.[1] Ryan died in the following January, leaving his widow with an infant and in charge of the company. She was married again to a Mr. Robinson whose identity remains a blank. Mrs. Robinson, as the "late Mrs. Ryan," returned to Charleston in the spring of 1789 with at least two charges: Charlotte Wall, daughter of Thomas, and her son, Dennis Ryan. The trio struggled to perform in the city which by now had turned its back against theatre people. Thanks to unruly conduct at Harmony Hall, South Carolina passed legislation against theatre in 1787.[2] So Mrs. Robinson and Charlotte Wall labeled their performances "olios," "rehearsals," and "concerts," and offered the legal dodge of the "Lecture on Hearts." In 1790 Mrs. Robinson doggedly moved her "family" on to Augusta. Charlotte, however, had dropped out of the group, and her place was taken by Susannah.

Susannah Wall, if one believes the *Augusta Chronicle,* June 26, July 3, and October 9, 1790, must have been a beguiling creature. There were odes composed to her beauty. Fulsome praise for her singing enlivened the pages; and an acrostic with her name was printed up to amuse her. She may have had some acting experience before her arrival in Augusta and like her sister have been led onto the stage at a tender age.[3] Whether experienced or not, the *Chronicle,* June 19, 1790, noted that she sang "with exquisite taste, judgment and precision."

Mrs. Robinson and Miss Wall elicited support from the newly formed Dramatic Society, which consisted of "gentlemen" who fitted up the theatre, supplied musical accompaniments, and assumed the male roles in the plays.

According to the *Chronicle* of July 31, 1790, the society was the third of its kind in Augusta's early days. Before its appearance, there had been the Academic Society and the Library Society.[4] With the arrival of Mesdames Robinson and Wall, the Library Society was temporarily displaced, however, by the Dramatic Society, which met regularly on Saturday nights. The gentlemen's success as theatrical enterpreneurs can be measured by the ferocity with which they were attacked. One Augustan wrote to the *Chronicle* of September 4, 1790, complaining that "gentlemen have taken up the business of players." That the correspondent spared Mrs. Robinson and Miss Wall may attest to his Old World manners with the ladies. But he contemptuously deplored "the constant buzzing of the theatre, which salutes our ears in every quarter of this little town."

Unlike Charleston, which had outlawed theatre, Augusta opened its doors to Mrs. Robinson and Miss Wall. The "establishment," in fact, provided the facility in which they performed. When Mrs. Robinson and Miss Wall opened their theatre season on June 17, 1790, it was in a building that also housed the General Assembly and the Superior and Inferior County Courts. Five days later, at a meeting of the board of trustees of the Richmond Academy which ran Augusta, the members resolved to enlarge the downstairs room by knocking out an interior wall. On June 23, the evening following their propitious board meeting, Mrs. Robinson and Miss Wall made their second appearance in the "theatre." With the backing of the board of trustees of the Richmond Academy, which included other influential Georgians besides the governor, the actresses enjoyed a legal security and political privilege rare in the new Republic.

Aside from the surprising historical fact that two women started Augusta's theatre and did a wide range of theatrical productions, there is another remarkable feature of the 1790–91 season: the quality of the theatrical reviews submitted by "Zoilus" to the *Chronicle*. Here was an arresting critic whose standards had been set in the English playhouse and whose observations revealed a depth and maturity in his reading of plays. He did not even spare Mrs. Robinson: "It were to be wished that Mrs. Robinson would, in future, pay more attention in committing her parts to memory: In *Deborah* she was very deficient in this point."

Stung by this remark, Mrs. Robinson somehow got word to "Zoilus." In his next review in the *Chronicle* of October 2, 1790, and his last, he added a paragraph which should have placated her:

> Mrs. Robinson, at present, stands in a more delicate predicament than is perhaps generally known: It is not left to her choice to take a favorite Character, or one to which she can render most justice. The play is struck out by the Society; her part is consigned to her without being even consulted; and whether it is acceptable to her or not, she feels herself under an obligation of performing it, by her agreement with the Society.

Throughout the winter of 1790–91, while Miss Wall was worshiped as a muse and the "Sweetest Syren of the Augustan Stage," Mrs. Robinson was trying to maneuver the Dramatic Society to work out a more favorable arrangement. Even though the society met regularly at the Theatre on Saturday night,[5] Mrs. Robinson was either not welcomed or not listened to. On December 4, 1790, she addressed the society by means of an announcement in the *Chronicle:*

> Mrs. Robinson earnestly requests the Gentlemen of the Dramatic Society to convene this evening, in order to determine on some measures relative to their engagements with her.

A performance of *Douglas* and *Thomas and Sally* followed in February 1791, but it was the last recorded production of Mrs. Robinson and Miss Wall working in consort with the gentlemen. Something in their arrangements had soured.

On May 1, Miss Wall married a local Army officer and settled down to domestic obscurity, no longer to adorn the stage.[6] Her decision left Mrs. Robinson professionally stranded in the last outpost of the English speaking world. To add to her distress, her ten-year-old son, Dennis, who was subject to fits, had disappeared.[7] Sometime during that month Thomas Wall, Susannah's father, arrived in town with Lawrence Ryan, who was Mrs. Robinson's son and Dennis's brother. Three of them—Thomas Wall, Mrs. Robinson, and Lawrence Ryan—gave the concluding performance in the theatre on May 21.

A Mental Evening's Amusement

> Mr. Wall (of Amherst County, Virginia, and formerly an actor in the Richmond Theatre) will exhibit a . . . Lecture on *Heads* . . . [and] a critical dissertation on NOSES . . . Mrs. Robinson will also join . . . in a scene taken from Shakespeare's CATHERINE AND PETRUCHIO. . . . An epilogue addressed to every body, not aimed at any body, will be spoken by Lawrence Ryan, in the character of NOBODY.[8]

Their final performance coincided with George Washington's presidential progress to Augusta. Three days before, in their theatre, he had been served a banquet and honored with toasts. Visitors from every possum corner had been attracted to Augusta to see Washington and, of course, the actors took advantage of the crowds.[9]

By May 21, the closing night of their season, Mrs. Robinson had decided to make Augusta her home and was advertising the opening of a school for young ladies. Three years later the Richmond Academy offered her the use of a Lot 79, which usually included the tenement on it, "for seven years, free of rent."[10] During the winters of 1797 and 1798–99, Mrs. Robinson traveled to Charleston to perform with the Placides at the Charleston Theatre. At the time of her benefit in 1799, she made a plaintive appeal to the Charlestonians:

> Whoever recollects her former exertions, and first-rate theatrical abilities, in the gay day of youth and spirits [when Mrs. Ryan] with her continued attention to please, will contribute their mite to render the evening of days easy.[11]

She returned to Augusta that summer and attempted at least one performance in July and another in October in her old "theatre," also known as the "Court-House." After she reopened her school in November 1800, she too faded into the Augusta community like Susannah. The only possible trace of her existence appears in the City Council Minutes of 1806 in which she received $10.00: "Paid to the Poor of the City."[12]

Two troupers of courage and tenacity, Mrs. Ann Robinson and Miss Susannah Wall sought employment where theatre was not only legal but encouraged by the city fathers. Their stage, fitted up in a large room, continued to be used by the Charleston Theatre company until 1823. Their productions aroused "Zoilus" to print four signed critical pieces of a level "Charleston knew intermittently, and Savannah, not at all."[13] And their audiences, mostly immigrants from the British Isles, devoured their theatrical fare like manna from the Old Country. The two of them made a unique and enterprising team, unparalleled in American theatre history.

ART THEATRE IN HULL-HOUSE

J. DENNIS RICH

In September of 1889, two young women, Jane Addams and Ellen Gates Starr, moved into a deteriorating old mansion in the middle of an immigrant neighborhood on Chicago's Halsted Street. In this tenement setting, they established Hull-House, one of the first settlement houses in America. The young women hoped to be neighbors to the poor, to share in their life experiences, and to work with them to improve their lot. The cofounders of Hull-House, especially Jane Addams, soon were recognized as pioneers of the modern social movement in the United States. According to Addams, the settlement "was an experimental effort in the solution of social and industrial problems which are engendered by the modern conditions of life in a great city."[1] The visual arts, music, and drama were integral in the effort "to provide a center for a higher civic and social life." "The universal desire for the portrayal of life lying quite outside personal experience" was encouraged through programs in the arts.

J. Dennis Rich taught in the Department of Communications and Theatre, University of Illinois at Chicago Circle, and managed the Circle Theatre.

It is significant that their effort to "socialize democracy" began theatrically. Among the first recorded activities at the settlement house was a dramatic reading from Hawthorne by Mrs. Sedgewick, the first resident at Hull-House. In the early years, young people were drawn to the settlement by the opportunity both to observe and to participate in dialogues, cantatas, charades, parlor magic, and festivals. Though such theatrical experiences offered a release from the day-to-day circumstances of the slum-dweller, the actual production of plays at Hull-House had to be deferred. Both the people living in the neighborhood and the first residents regarded the theatre with some suspicion. The population attended the theatre, but they did not encourage participation in it. Indeed, they feared the stage even if they were fascinated by it.[2]

Jane Addams wisely turned her attention away from the theatre and toward the development of the other arts. "Picture exhibits, lectures, concerts, classes in handicraft, and choral clubs were in part established for the purpose of providing an alternative to the commanding and nearly always insidious appeal of melodrama and vaudeville."[3]

But the "insidious appeal of melodrama and vaudeville" was the source of Addams's conviction that an exposure to the theatre was important in the education of young people. She was aware of "the persistency with which the entire population" attended the theatre. And, she interpreted such attendance as fulfilling a need for imaginative expression. It was the way in which this need was fulfilled that gave her cause for concern.

The young men told us of their ambitions in the phrases of stage heroes, and the girls, so far as their dreams could be shyly put into words, possessed no others but those soiled by long use in the melodrama.

The neighborhood theatre, "such as it was, appeared to be the one agency which freed the boys and girls of that destructive isolation of those who drag themselves up to maturity by themselves, and it gave them a glimpse of that order and beauty into which even the poorest drama endeavors to restore the bewildering facts of life."[4] Addams reasoned that if the theatre had so powerful an impact upon the lives of the urban poor, then Hull-House had to offer an alternative to the popular melodrama. She believed that a theatre which depicted life more truthfully would attract the young people of the neighborhood and would encourage understanding in place of escape. Her belief led to the creation of one of the first art theatres in America.

When the visual arts and music became established at Hull-House, the idea of a theatre at the settlement became possible. A cautious initial effort to incorporate the drama was made with the establishment of the Shakespeare Club in the early 1890's. The purpose of the club was to encourage good reading and to attend professional performances of Shakespeare's plays. In addition, professors and graduate students from the University of Chicago often were invited to lecture about the play club members were reading. The literary approach and the importance of the playwright assured respect for this early venture into the drama. Gradually, the readings brought about the realization that "a very widespread desire existed among the children and young people to act, and that satisfaction of this desire under educational auspices and high standards leads away from instead of toward the professional stage."[5]

Seven years after Hull-House opened, the theatre which Jane Addams hoped could be established materialized. A theatre in which young people might better "understand life through its dramatic portrayal" was created at Hull-House in January of 1896 with the performance of William Dean Howells's play, The Sleeping Car.[6] The event marked the birth of the first settlement theatre in America. In the February 1896 Hull-House Bulletin, Addams reported, "There seems to be a general awakening on the matter of plays. . . . We hope this enthusiasm will be utilized to produce plays of good standard. A simple, healthful play, with real characters is most delightful, and beneficial to both the actors and the audience."[7] During the remainder of 1896, five additional dramatic performances were presented on the stage in the Hull-House gymnasium. Both the productions and the process of rehearsal were praised. And in the following year, Addams suggested the establishment of an agency within Hull-House whose sole purpose was theatrical production.

In April 1897, Shakespeare's As You Like It was produced at Hull-House, under the direction of a Chicago advertising executive, Walter Pietsch. The play was so well received that Addams appointed Pietsch director of drama at the settlement. In October of the same year, Pietsch formed the Hull-House Dramatic Association. He immediately set goals for the new organization. First, he declared that the object of the Hull-House Dramatic Association was "to raise the standard of all plays at Hull-House"; second, he sought to recruit the most talented young people at Hull-House to act under his direction; finally, he began working toward the construction of a theatre facility.[8] By October 1898, Addams was able to announce that "Plans are being drawn for a new building."[9] The new theatre was completed one year later, in October 1899.

The completion of the new theatre extended the influence of the drama at Hull-House further into the immigrant community around Halsted Street. Among the events which inaugurated the new stage was a production undertaken by "a large colony of Greeks near Hull-House."[10] The Return of Odysseus, a dramatic adaptation of Homer's Odyssey, was performed in Greek. Addams reported that it was "a unique experiment to have genuine Greeks portray Homer."[11] This particular production was important to the developing theatre at Hull-House for a variety of reasons. First, the production encouraged other ethnic groups in the neighborhood to stage dramas in their own languages. Similar projects were soon sponsored by Lithuanians, Poles, Russians, and Italians living in the immigrant community. Second, the play was the first Hull-House production to attract attention outside of the immediate neighborhood. Finally, the production represented the Hull-House commitment to establishing a drama which "gives beautiful and significant expression to local loyalties and traditions,"[12] in other words, to a drama which had a rightful place in the community.

The construction of the new theatre established the drama on an equal footing with the other arts at the settlement. Under the supervision of Jane Addams, the theatre began to serve as "a vehicle of self-expression for the teeming young life" in the neighborhood. But Addams was not content simply to see the facility in use. She wanted the drama to go beyond the goals of "recreation and education." She believed that the Hull-House theatre would be able to provide an alternative to the popular melodrama because it was unfettered by commercial considerations. In lieu of the pursuit of profits, Addams argued for the pursuit of truth, for a theatre in which it was possible to "attempt to expose the shams and pretenses of contemporary life and to penetrate into some of its perplexing social and domestic situations." She hoped that the stage would become "a reconstructing and reorganizing agent of accepted moral truths" in which ideas could be tested.[13]

Addams's strong belief that the theatre at Hull-House ought to encourage new standards for the drama attracted the attention of others. As early as 1899, one of the leading writers and thinkers in American realist literature, William Dean Howells, wrote that the Hull-House stage

> seems to me a real Théâtre Libre, and for us an opportunity for a conscientious drama which is quite unequalled in America, so far as I know. You are not only going to bring a harmless joy into the lives of those poor neighbors of yours, but you are going to give a chance for honest and faithful work to those intending playwrights who are now locked out of the temples of the theatrical trust. Who knows but you are indirectly founding an American drama. . . .[14]

Howells's dream of founding an American drama never materialized at Hull-House. But by the turn of the century, the first American settlement theatre was on its way to becoming an important art theatre. Eventually, the vision which guided Jane Addams in the creation of a theatre at Hull-House also provided the impulse which led to the formation of important American experimental theatre companies such as the Provincetown Players and the Theatre Guild.

Jane Addams's revolt against the values of the monopolized commercial theatre entered a new phase at the turn of the century. Walter Pietsch resigned his position as director of drama at Hull-House. In 1900, Addams appointed Laura Dainty Pelham, a theatre professional, to replace Pietsch.[15]

Pelham became a Hull-House resident and assumed various responsibilities at the settlement. Despite her professional background, the retired actress expressed no interest in transforming the amateur group at Hull-House into a professional company. She realized from the beginning of her association with the theatre that its primary function was to provide an outlet for the young people in the neighborhood. At the same time, Pelham did not compromise her professional standards. It would appear that Laura Pelham was prepared for her role as director of drama by Jane Addams. Pelham's commitment was similar to that of Addams; that is, the promotion of artistic integrity over commercial considerations. Under Pelham's guidance the settlement was able to produce plays which, though performed by amateurs, came to be regarded as "professional" by Chicago audiences and newspaper reviewers. In this remarkable woman, Jane Addams found a leader capable of bringing her idea of a theatre to complete fruition.

Pelham assumed leadership of the Hull-House Dramatic Association under difficult circumstances. Apparently, Walter Pietsch resigned his directorship because he had, in some way, displeased Jane Addams.[16] Whether or not this assessment is correct, Pelham stepped into her directorship during a period in which plays were not being produced at the settlement, and in which the enthusiasm that productions such as *As You Like It* had generated was dwindling. The new director's first goal was to unify a disintegrating company of young actors. If she was going to create serious theatre at Hull-House, she first had to establish herself as a competent artist.

To achieve this end, Pelham utilized the dramatic form which Addams had so often criticized—the melodrama. Pelham's first production, presented in December 1900, was *A Mountain Pink*, by Morgan Bates and Elwyn Barron. Addams, writing in the *Hull-House Bulletin* of Autumn 1900, strained to find justification for the play. She observed that it "mixed the more usual dramatic ingredients of love and a lost heiress" but that it was of interest to residents and the neighborhood because Mrs. Pelham had acted in the play professionally and would "play her original part" at the settlement.[17] Pelham, in her defense, was pragmatic. She argued that she had chosen the melodrama for practical reasons:

> The company was most familiar with that type of play; my own experience was largely along such lines of work; and the neighborhood from which we expected to draw our audience still loved the old-fashioned drama with virtue triumphing over vice suitably downed in the last act.

Pelham's judgment appears to have been correct. *A Mountain Pink* played to an audience of over a thousand people in three nights, and it created the sense of unity which the director perceived as necessary if she was to build a cohesive company of young actors at Hull-House.

In October 1900, even as she was rehearsing the melodrama, Laura Pelham was working to create an atmosphere in which a different kind of drama could flourish. In support of her cause, she invited the famous actor Joseph Jefferson III to speak to the Hull-House Dramatic Association about theatre as a serious art form. "His advice and encouragement," Pelham reported, "were a great inspiration to us, and the work of our first years was largely based on the plan he outlined."[18] The Hull-House Dramatic Association did not immediately abandon the production of light entertainments in favor of more serious work. Rather, Pelham limited membership in her company and worked to raise the standards of performance.

Beginning in the winter of 1904, literary merit became a criterion for production. Safe entertainments were, for the most part, discontinued. "The first mile-stone" in the new approach to production at Hull-House was the very successful American premiere of Ben Jonson's pastoral drama *The Sad Shepherd.*

The decision to give a new direction to theatrical activity at the settlement coincided with a change in the Halsted Street neighborhood, as the Irish and English-speaking French "neighbors were being crowded out by Italians, who did not care for performances in English."[19] The immigrant community continued to be served by the Hull-House clubs and by productions, but Pelham was more easily able to undertake the production of a different kind of drama. Jane Addams's desire for socially significant theatre could now be satisfied.

Jane Addams's vision and Laura Pelham's professionalism, when combined, resulted in the creation of a true art theatre in Chicago. Plays by Shaw, Pinero, Galsworthy, and Ibsen came to dominate the Hull-House stage.

Eventually what was now called the Hull-House Players achieved recognition both in America and abroad as "the first and most important settlement theatre in the United States" and as an "example of Little Theatre with sociological aspects."[20] Maurice Browne, often called the founder of the art theatre movement in America, acknowledged a debt to Hull-House. He wrote, "The Hull-House Players gave plays of distinction with skill, sincerity and understanding. Mrs. Pelham, not I, was the true founder of 'the American Little Theatre Movement.'"[21]

WOMEN DIRECTORS—THE EARLY YEARS

SHIRLEE HENNIGAN

The first women to direct on the American stage were actresses. They directed or "staged" the plays in which they acted, sometimes working with another person who was not in the cast—frequently this was the producer, theatre manager, or author of the play and might additionally have been the

Shirlee Hennigan, Professor and Chair, Drama/Speech Department, Lewis Clark State College, Idaho, wrote her Ph.D. dissertation on Women Directors, at Washington State University.

actress's husband. (Directing the plays they acted in was common practice for male actors as well.)

The actresses in the early part of this century who staged the vehicles in which they starred include Minnie Maddern Fiske, who usually worked with her husband, the producer Harrison Grey Fiske; Olga Nethersole, who ran her own repertory company and was produced by her husband, Louis Nethersole; Margaret Anglin, who was famous for her Shakespearean roles; Marie Dressler, who did primarily farce and revues; Mary Shaw, noted for her Ibsen and Strindberg heroines; Josephine Hull, best known in later years as James Stewart's sister in both the stage and film versions of *Harvey*; and Jane Cowl, Henrietta Crosman, Elsie Janis, Grace George, and Margaret Wycherly. Some of these actresses not only staged the shows in which they performed but also produced them, joining the ranks of a number of other women who produced shows, including playwrights Dorothy Donnelly and Rachel Crothers.

It should be noted here that in the first quarter of the century there were a great many plays written by women produced for the commercial Broadway theatre. In the 1925–26 season, a random year chosen for examination, there were fifty-four women playwrights produced in the New York professional theatre. Some were co-authors with male playwrights, and some, like Rachel Crothers, Catherine Chisholm Cushing and Dorothy Donnelly, had two or three plays of theirs on the boards that year, in which better than one in eight authors of Broadway plays were women.[1]

Female and male stars continued to stage their own vehicles through the 1930's. Some of the new women who did this double duty were Blanche Yurka, Auriol Lee (who became a director of importance, staging most of the plays of John Van Druten until her death, when he assumed the direction of his plays), Alla Nazimova, and Estelle Winwood. One actress who stands out as a consistent and persistent director is Eva Le Gallienne. At her Civic Repertory Theatre, established in 1926, she directed herself in some twenty plays. She also directed plays in which she did *not* act at her theatre on Fourteenth Street, where her prolific group was critically acclaimed. After the Civic Repertory Theatre closed in 1932, Le Gallienne staged plays on Broadway at the Shubert and Broadhurst Theatres. In her productions she appears to have consistently used women designers such as Aline Bernstein and Irene Sharaff. In the 1940's she joined forces with Cheryl Crawford and Margaret Webster to found the American Repertory Theatre, where she shared directing chores with Webster. By the later forties the phenomenon of performers— of either sex—directing themselves seemed to die out.

Just as acting seems to provide a natural access into directing, so playwriting offers a similar ingress. Since the beginning of the century there have been women playwrights who have also directed. Rachel Crothers is an early and prolific example. Her first Broadway success was *Myself-Bettina* in 1908; it was produced by Maxine Elliot, who also starred. Two years later her next show, *A Man's World*, was produced by the Shubert Brothers and ran for seventy-one performances. Between 1913 and 1940 she directed nineteen of her own plays and several written by others; some of her plays, such as *As Husbands Go* and *When Ladies Meet*, were long-run hits. This record makes Rachel Crothers one of the most prolific American playwright-directors.

From the opening of the century until the 1980's the list of women writers who directed their own work is a long one, including among many others Margaret Mayo, Anita Loos, Sophie Treadwell, Anne Nichols, Rose Franken, Lillian Hellman, June Havoc, Megan Terry, Elaine May, Julie Bovasso, Amy Saltz, Maxine Klein, Maria Irene Fornes, Elizabeth Swados, Julianne Boyd, and Lucia Victor.[2]

The emergence of women who were primarily directors committed to staging plays rather than either acting in them or writing them followed the early actress- and playwright-directors. Such a woman was Agnes Morgan. Although her important career spanned close to a half century, she is almost totally unknown today, something this brief review hopes to rectify.[3]

Agnes Morgan seems to have been interested in theatre all her life. At Radcliffe she acted in plays and upon completing her Master of Arts degree became a protegé of the famous Harvard professor George Pierce Baker. He sent four women abroad to study the continental theatre for a year; Agnes Morgan was the only one to stay the full year and complete the assignment. When she returned she became a member of Baker's seminal 47 Workshop.

After leaving Cambridge, Agnes Morgan met Helen Arthur, who was working in New York at the Henry Street Settlement. She encouraged Morgan to join in the theatre activities started there by the philanthropic sisters Alice and Irene Lewisohn. When their theatre became the Neighborhood Playhouse on Grand Street in 1915, Agnes Morgan's career as a director began in earnest. From that date until 1927 she directed a long list of plays by such distinguished authors as George Bernard Shaw and Harley Granville-Barker that gave the theatre a reputation for artistic achievement. Morgan also wrote the book and lyrics and directed five "editions" of *The Grand Street Follies*, which brought commercial success and popular interest to the Neighborhood Playhouse.[4]

When the Lewisohn sisters, who were also directors, closed the Neighborhood Playhouse in 1927 believing it had completed its period of experimentation, Agnes Morgan and Helen Arthur founded their own company. Originally calling it the Grand Street Follies Company and later incorporated as the Actor-Managers, it existed until 1939. Operating on Broadway and using many of the actors and designers they had been working with, the new company functioned as a cooperative and was among those mentioned in a 1927 newspaper article as part of the "feminist movement in drama."[5]

In 1928 Agnes Morgan directed for the Shuberts a production of *Maya* by Simon Gantillon that caused a uproar. This sympathetic portrait of a French prostitute in Marseilles was closed by the police on charges of corrupting the morals of youth. Protests were made to Mayor Jimmy Walker by leaders of

New York society and theatre, and although Lee Shubert deemed the show "beautiful, very, very beautiful," he did not fight to reopen it.[6]

In the next decade Agnes Morgan remained very active, doing new editions of *The Grand Street Follies*, directing on Broadway, in summer theatres, and for the Popular Price Theatre of the Federal Theatre Project in New York. Her company also worked at the Casino Theatre in Newport, Rhode Island, where she staged, among others, a play Laurette Taylor wrote for herself to star in. Program credits for their Newport enterprise reveal a unusually large number of women in charge of the operations of the theatre.[7]

From 1934 until the end of her career in the 1960's (she probably died around 1970 in obscurity), she was associated with Frank Carrington at the Paper Mill Playhouse in Milburn, New Jersey. In 1982 the general manager who had worked with her there paid tribute to this forgotten, pioneer woman director. "She was a beautiful person and a real theatre person. She came to rehearsal completely prepared. She knew exactly what every person from the lead to the lowliest chorus person should do, and exactly where they should be. . . . She had a great feel for the theatre . . . remarkable . . . a fantastic person."[8]

HALLIE FLANAGAN: PRACTICAL VISIONARY

PAULINE HAHN

In an address entitled "The Search for New Standards in the Theatre," Francis Fergusson names four key American theatrical figures: Robert Edmond Jones, Harold Clurman, Thornton Wilder, and Hallie Flanagan. Jones, the poet, he calls frustrated by the parameters of a designer's role. Clurman, ardent proselytizer, and his Group Theatre never fulfilled their bright promise. Wilder, metaphysician for the common man, was co-opted by Broadway and his work grew facile. But Flanagan he calls a "Statesman": a leader and a thinker who "in a crucial experiment demonstrated the potential theatre life of this country." Her ability to sustain more than one large concept at a time (rather than settling for a least common denominator of things) resulted, Fergusson says, in the winning of a new audience which grew to trust the theatre and found itself transformed in the very magic way of which Jones dreamed.[1]

Hallie Flanagan was a visionary, most eloquent and expansive when communicating with her great good friends, T.S. Eliot and Gordon Craig; but whether with lumberjack or senator, she was unyielding in her use of the broad historical perspective, judging herself and all around her by the highest and best in theatrical history. It is only fitting that our reevaluation of her be conducted within these same dimensions.

Pauline Hahn, an actress of stage, screen and television, is Visiting Professor of Theatre at Vassar College and is writing a dissertation on Hallie Flanagan at Columbia University.

"Half a century from now," Hallie Flanagan once pondered in a speech, what will "historians speaking of this period . . . have to say. . . ." She imagined what we would know of the Federal Theatre Project, of which she was the national director. She described, in this and in other writing, the vast tapping of artistic energies, the public works, the inspired rejuvenation of artists roused from abject humiliation and despair, pride restored to them, and the patriotic sense of responsibility which comes with national service. She spoke of the revolutionary movement away from precious, glittering, irrelevant theatre, the switch from "the 400 to 4 million," as she put it, to the theatre which, "by a stroke of fortune unprecedented in dramatic history, can fulfill its necessity . . . to help reshape America." She said that historians of the future would point not only to the natural wealth rescued from oblivion, but also to the formation of a national (and by that she means to include every single type of American, from farmer to coal miner) trust and faith and passion for the theatre because of its immediacy, its relevance, and its accessibility.[2]

That was a great deal for her to have expected from us, the historians of today, but she depended upon it, no doubt all the more so after her beautiful theatre had been abolished. Little could she have guessed that the Federal Theatre Project would be relegated to a one-line mention in history books, and she to a bored, obligatory, four-word phrase, set off by commas.

How did it happen? How could we as a nation have sustained such an attack of amnesia? How could we have developed such indifference? The major critics of the time—theatre critics and thinkers from all over the world—hailed the Federal Theatre Project and Mrs. Flanagan as of monumental significance, not only to America but to the larger history of world theatre. The best playwrights here and abroad—Eliot, Shaw, O'Neill, Auden, Toller—rushed to have their works performed, for scarcely any remuneration, by the most important theatre of its day. Some of our greatest talents had their start with the Federal Theatre Project, and many of them arguably did their best work there. National theatres of Europe sent representatives to study the workings of a true theatre. Theatre became a daily subject of discussion and a true avenue for dialogue. Everyone who was anyone was sure that this was the making of an American national theatre, with Flanagan as its head. She was recognized to be not only the conceptualizer of a unique, indigenous, American national theatre, but was undoubtedly, for American theatre, the major unifying, international force of her day.

For almost fifty years, however, Hallie Flanagan and her Federal Theatre Project have been ignored, forgotten. How does one get written out of history? This is a complex question, the more so because it is one which must be explored not merely as a unique issue but in relation as well to many other women who have made important contributions to the theatre and to other fields and who have likewise been forgotten.

Tentative answers concerning Hallie Flanagan's disappearance fall into two areas of discussion: the political and the conceptual. The political may be easily disposed of, although the details are full of charges and countercharges. It consists of hostility towards liberals; fear of leftism and accusations of leftism, particularly during what Stefan Kanfer calls "The Plague Years"; and the complex mechanisms involved in culturally institutionalized sexual bigotry. The conceptual requires a deeper kind of analysis which I would like to suggest.

Let us begin by examining what Hallie Flanagan meant by theatre and what sort of theatre she attempted to create. Here is how she envisioned a national theatre:

> *The theatre has never been greater than its audience.* When audiences have been big, varied, and exciting, plays have been big, varied, and exciting. When the Greek plays were given in those exposed arcs cut from stone, the audience assembled from all Greece. They came to a festival to see plays chosen by the government and paid for by government money, and they expected the plays to be good. They were good, good enough to last three thousand years. In the Middle Ages the crowds jostling through the streets stopped to heckle and applaud the street players, investing the plays with their own vitality. So too, in Elizabethan England it was a noisy crowd and a big crowd that jostled into the pit to see a play by Will Shakespeare. The plays had to be tremendous, and they were.[3]

She then traced the process by which the theatre became small and precious and finally—in America—both geographically and financially inaccessible, until there were only two choices: the worker's theatre or mass media.

> It was logical and it was inevitable that the stage, having become the property of a few, became so special that the masses of people had to turn to the cinema and radio for their theatre. Thus the 12,000 [unemployed] people in our rolls are not there entirely, or perhaps even primarily, because of the general economic situation [the Depression].[4]

In an address she said:

> No doubt every one of us had thought at some time of some form of state or national theatre like institutions in European countries. We had thought, perhaps, of careful planning by wise committees, of the greatest actors, writers, designers, plays, all housed in appropriately magnificent surroundings, of an academy of dramatic training for gifted youth.
>
> If the loss of that dream still seems great, balance against its dignity its danger, the danger from which the American stage has always suffered— imitativeness. The pattern for our Federal Theatre has to be different, a pattern dictated by necessity, demanded for immediate use, utilitarian and functional.[5]

Now she described her audience:

There is no yawning in the Florida Wheel, where our actors play the Turpentine Circuit, audiences coming in barefoot with lanterns to see. Forty million people: lumberjacks in Oregon, sharecroppers in the South. Nothing is too good for this audience. It is their theatre. Only a theatre which springs from or penetrates into city, town, village, and farm can be called an American Theatre.[6]

That is enough to give us a good notion of where she stood on audience. Now, let us turn to subject matter.

Tremendous things are happening in the world of politics, in the field of light, in the realm of science; and if the theatre cannot capture some of the quality of this excitement in the plays it does and the way it does them it will die of yawning, with or without government subsidy!

We must see the relationship between the men at work on Boulder Dam and the Greek chorus.

Giving apoplexy to people who consider it radical for a government-sponsored theatre to produce plays on subjects vitally concerning the governed is one function of the theatre.

The relation between art and necessity lies at the root of the Federal Theatre.

Theatre: not the frosting on the cake but the yeast which makes the bread rise.[7]

This last should not be taken lightly. In one of Flanagan's articles she described theatre in an ideal society as explaining economics to the farmer who feeds starving economist and actor alike. Compare this to her comments on her own theatre, where "our actors are themselves the protagonists . . . a vital force . . . not a decoration."[8]

The precondition for Francis Fergusson's correctly placing Hallie Flanagan in theatre history was his having already, in *The Idea of a Theatre*, placed theatre itself correctly into history:

Hamlet's charge to the players expresses the perennial need for a direct and significant imitation of human life and action which can be played as music is played. But though we may assent to Hamlet's definition, if we read it attentively, we shrug it off the next moment.

If he could ask the players to hold the mirror up to nature, it was because the Elizabethan theatre was itself a mirror which had been formed at the center of the culture of its time, and at the center of the life and awareness of the community. We know now that such a mirror is rarely formed.[9]

What Hallie Flanagan was proposing—and what she in fact created for four years—was exactly this sort of a theatre, a real theatre, the kind we know nothing of, but the kind which every great theatre in history has been.

As Fergusson puts it, it isn't easy to even focus upon the *idea* of a theatre. We tend to assent without thinking, and if we do think we confuse it with "lyric poetry or pure music, on one side, or with editorializing and gossip, on the other"; and if we do not confuse it, we "shrug it off the next moment."

In our theatre of marketplace, of "alternating crusading and racketeering" (in Fergusson's words), it is easy to forget and for things to change shape. The regional theatres, which were the legitimate offspring of the Federal Theatre Project, have become as bland and homogenized as the Broadway theatre of the '30's. The people's theatres of which Flanagan spoke—radio, film and now television—have only speeded up the dulling process. Then, of course, the unexpected and inexplicable occurred. The heart of the Federal Theatre Project records disappeared for thirty-five years. The Dies Committee—HUAC— became fat and ferocious, savaging decades with fear and silence. And, strangest of all, the very generation of historians which should have passed on an understanding of her concepts and her theatre instead rarely mentioned her.

An explanation is required of us. Perhaps Flanagan is ignored because we cannot understand her theatre, while her theatre is ignored because we cannot understand—or categorize—her.

Envied for her fabulous (if fictitious) White House connections, she was the very emblem of *la nouvelle femme arrivée*. Undoubtedly the most powerful theatre producer of her day and, in very truth, a pivotal figure in theatre history then and now, Hallie Flanagan is, in fact, the double object of ironic ill fortune. In the political climate of the '30's, the grotesque fate of a moderate like Hallie Flanagan was to be classified simultaneously as "red" and "red-baiter" (Joseph Losey's characterization of her in a letter to the author), so that it was judicious simply to pass over her.[10] In the equally grotesque sexual-political climate of our (endlessly) transitional period, the status of a woman alters radically as she steps out of earshot, on the implicit principle that, although we all certainly know that some women are superior, any woman whom we have not personally seen to be superior is not one of them. Thus "cultural slippage" allows a key figure in American theatre to fall silently into oblivion.

Yet we must remember that as she looked ahead to the future, she placed her trust in us to see her contributions clearly. In 1986, the fiftieth anniversary year of the founding of the Federal Theatre Project, we are beginning to recover her heritage. The archives of the Federal Theatre, rescued from oblivion by Dr. Lorraine Brown and Dr. John Connor, have been restored and made available at George Mason University. Here the Institute on the Federal Theatre Project and New Deal Culture has become the center for oral history, performances, displays, publications, and discussion. Perhaps now historians will be able to fulfill properly the injunction Hallie Flanagan gave us a half century ago.

ALVINA KRAUSE: A GREAT TEACHER

BILLIE McCANTS AND DAVID DOWNS

Alvina Krause is generally considered to be one of America's great teachers of acting, yet she has not acquired the fame, public recognition, or financial reward of Lee Strasberg, Stella Adler, or the very few others who have also earned distinction for teaching an art some believe can't be taught. She developed her own unique approach to the teaching of aspiring actors during her long and remarkable tenure in the School of Speech at Northwestern University, 1930–63. She is sometimes called a "maker of stars" for having taught now-prominent performers such as Patricia Neal and Charlton Heston, but she never considered herself in that light. The program of acting study she created at Northwestern was designed to train an actor to bring life and humanity into a theatre in which the play not the actor is the star.

For twenty years she and her friend Lucy McCammon produced her kind of theatre during the summers at the Playhouse in Eagles Mere, Pennsylvania, while continuing to build the acting program at Northwestern. After her retirement in 1963, at age seventy, she spent nine years traveling the country lecturing and conducting theatre workshops often booked back to back in a schedule that would have staggered someone half her age. The Bloomsburg Theatre Ensemble in Pennsylvania, formed by her students in 1977, produced plays emanating from Alvina Krause's extended vision of humanity.

BILLIE McCANTS: ALVINA KRAUSE ON WOMEN IN THEATRE

Born in 1893 in New Lisbon, Wisconsin, a little town which then saw few of its young men and none of its women go to college, Alvina Krause knew from an early age that she would go. "I think I wanted always to be a teacher. . . . I was drawn to theatre because I was always interested in why people are what they are. . . . I would sit back and watch grown-ups, and people would say, 'She's shy. She doesn't talk much.' One summer day, I think I was a junior in high school, I didn't have anything else to read, and I picked up a volume of Ibsen, *A Doll's House*. Great heavens! What happened to me? I can't describe it. I didn't understand *A Doll's House*, but there was something there dealing with women and their society, and I read all of Ibsen."

There is a pause. "That smile was over the first marriage proposal I had. On Senior Day. We were out gathering stuff to decorate the high school. Here was this young man proposing to me, and I laughed. It was so ridiculous. I said, 'Why I'm going to have a career. I'm going to do things. I'm not going to get married.'"

But, she is asked, doesn't she believe women can have a career and a

---

Billie McCants, a freelance writer from Michigan, interviewed Alvina Krause in Bloomsburg, Pennsylvania, in 1978 for her article "Eternal Astonishment," from which this segment is excerpted. David Downs, Associate Professor in the Theatre Department of Northwestern University, studied with Alvina Krause in Bloomsburg in 1972.

marriage and babies? The eyes reveal the extent to which Alvina Krause has pondered this difficult question. "Yes, I do. They'd still better know what's important to them. It would take a pretty big woman. It would take clear insight. But it *is* possible. As women, we will have to come to an understanding of that."

Is it true, as rumor has it, that Krause is particularly demanding of women students? One recalls the much-repeated story of the night that Patricia Neal was a catastrophe in *Twelfth Night*. Afterward in the dressing room, the beginning actress told her teacher, "I shall never act again. Never." To which Krause replied, "Never again? You dare call what you did tonight *acting*? See you tomorrow at nine." Krause admits, "I don't take women unless I am convinced that they can take it, from me and from what will come after. The theatre has always been primarily men, and it's getting worse." When women today ask if she was handicapped by being a woman, she answers, "Well, it all depends on what you mean by handicapped. I had to work quietly, slowly." When she joined Northwestern there were only two other women on the speech faculty. One was Winifred Ward, distinguished founder of the children's theatre movement; the other was a costumer. "Oh, yes, a woman could teach costuming. There were the three of us. That was it. Women were not wanted." Krause was the first woman to direct a major university production there. Now she comes forth with her remarkable laugh, "But I did get to do what I believe in."

DAVID DOWNS: A TEACHER OF LIFE

If Alvina Krause were a violinist, I would probably be a teacher of the violin. When she entered and altered my life, I was searching, however unknowingly, for a human being whose comprehension of life's truths went beyond the obvious. Krause had discovered those truths for herself through theatre. "Theatre," she says, "is life given form, given meaning." And to teach theatre, she had to teach human life. I am not the only student who came "to life" with her guidance. She saw me, she searched me, and she set about the task of helping me. It is her way.

We started with Chekhov for, as she says, you can't fake Chekhov. "You *must* come to a total understanding of, and a full creation of, the human beings who live behind those spoken words." During a rehearsal of a scene from *Uncle Vanya*, Krause was helping a student understand Sonia's concern for a drunk Astrov as he plans to ride off into the storm. But Krause was teaching more than acting. She stood behind me, held her arms around my chest, put her head next to mine. "Why do you drink, David?" I froze. Her arms held tight, her voice gently, directly, profoundly continued. "It hurts me deeply to see you doing this to yourself. Talent like yours is rare. It must not be wasted." Before I could move, she released me and said, "That's what is troubling Sonia. Continue." And we instantly went on with the scene. I stopped drinking.

Krause teaches with the belief that the artist cannot be motivated by personal neuroses. In her vision of theatre, the actor must be as passionately motivated as is the playwright by concern for humanity. How does one teach concern? You keep at it, she says. Goals formed; my life took direction. Her constant association of every character, every drama, with parallels in contemporary life so connected theatre with the guiding forces of human life that private preoccupations simply disappeared. "Work to reach true understanding of others. And not with your intellect alone," she warned. "That's not enough. You must understand with your muscles, your senses, your total self." For Krause theatre is not simply a craft to be taught, a profession to be learned. For her, theatre is an art and a way of life.

When the opportunity came for me to teach at Northwestern, Krause urged me to pursue it. "Take the job. I will always be at your side." And so she was. The daily acting journal that had formed the mainstay of my training with her in Bloomsburg became a daily teaching journal in Evanston. She returned my weekly installments with extensive notes, suggestions, comments, questions. And behind all of her help was the insistence that I develop my own approach to teaching. "Exercises are nothing," she wrote. "My exercises worked for me. Find your own exercises. So long as the principles you illustrate are true, the goals you exemplify are right, you will find your own way." As the years go on, I am not surprised to discover that she was right. Alvina Krause profoundly exemplifies life in and through theatre. I will ever be thankful it was not the violin that so stirred and compelled her life.

PEGGY CLARK KELLEY: REMINISCENCES OF A "DESIGNING" WOMAN

I always wanted to be an actress. Although both my parents were scientists—my father was Professor of Anatomy at the University of Pennsylvania and other universities and he and my mother did research on blood circulation and published articles together—they were both active in theatre. Wherever they lived they started little theatres so that I grew up

Among the credits of this distinguished lighting designer are the Broadway productions of *Brigadoon, Gentlemen Prefer Blondes, Wonderful Town, No Time for Sergeants, Auntie Mame, Mary, Mary, Bye, Bye, Birdie,* and *Flower Drum Song.* In 1968 she was elected the first woman president of the United Scenic Artists. In 1977 her alma mater, Smith College, awarded her a medal, citing her "pioneering achievement in a predominately male profession." These "Reminiscences" were edited by Helen Krich Chinoy from an interview conducted by Jacqueline Van Voris for *Mosaic,* a study of Smith College alumnae on the occasion of the college's one hundredth anniversary in 1975. Published by permission of Jacqueline Van Voris and Peggy Clark Kelley.

with this love of theatre as well as with exposure to the sciences and to the liberal arts. What got in my way as a budding actress was my height. I just kept growing and growing. I'm five eight and three-quarters. At Smith College I always had to play the men's parts in our all female productions. I begged Samuel Eliot, our professor, "Can't I be something other than a spear-carrying servant. I really want to act." "Well, Peggy," he replied, "I can't see you as a woman, and you couldn't be a noble, so you'll have to be a slave." This was a rather devastating thing to say to somebody who was just seventeen and having her problems growing up. I said to myself: "If this is going to be the way casting directors look at me, my career as a great actress in the American theatre is over before it's begun. In the big world out there, they won't cast me for men's parts; the men can do it better." I decided to concentrate on my other love, which was painting and design. I *had to* be part of the theatre. I took all the art, costume, lighting, scene design and architecture and drafting courses I could. Smith College gave me all the things I wanted, I thought the theatre in our old Students Building was *mine* and I did everything for the shows we put on. At Smith we had no feeling that if we were in design or production we were being women in a man's field. It was our field; it was our theatre. You were as good as anybody else, and that is a marvelous thing to learn somewhere in your life.

At Yale the situation was rather different. I got into Yale without any problems because Donald Oenslager, who was head of the scenic design program, had studied at Harvard with Oliver (Pete) Larkin who was my professor at Smith. When they found that I had had architectural drafting, they put me to work drafting the first major production of the year. They assigned me to various crews, and everybody was pleased. I thought, "Well, this is fine. I'm going to get to do exactly what I want." It seemed a marvelous extension of the major I had created for myself at Smith. The courses I took on my own, drafting at Smith and extra lighting at Yale, provided the skills that I've earned my living by far more than the courses that were prescribed for me.

When I came back for the second year, however, I had to prove myself all over again. Their whole attitude at Yale at that time seemed to be, "Let's not waste time on the women because they're going to get married and are not going on professionally. We'll use the women on crews if they do well, but we won't give them the extra plums in design because it's the men we're interested in." The women at Yale were mainly in acting or in costume design. There were very few who went into scenic or lighting design.

By the time I got to the third year in the design program, there were only two boys and I getting our degree in design. It was the hardest year for the three of us. We had to do sketches to compete for the right to design the major productions, of which there were four each year on the main stage. The first show was about Carlotta and Maximilian. I liked my designs best, but they gave the assignment to one of the men. I was very upset. At that point, I got a note from the vocational office at Smith that there was an opening in Florida in an interior decorating shop for twenty-five dollars a week. It was during the Depression, remember. So I wrote home and I said, "I have been a burden to you all long enough. I'm going to take this job and quit; obviously they're not interested in me. I'm a woman and I'm never going to get anywhere in this man's world." My father was teaching anatomy but he got somebody else to take his classes. He and my mother drove up to New Haven for the weekend and took me out to dinner at Savin Rock. We sat and looked at the ocean, and he said: "Now look here, Peggy; you have talent, you've gone this far, you're doing well, we've talked to the faculty, they're intrigued with what you can do, they think you have promise. Finish and get your degree. You don't have to worry about being a burden, because Granddaddy is paying for it." They said, "Look, there must be some girl who desperately needs that job, and you don't need it. Anybody can sell antiques or interior decorating things but not everybody can design scenery and so, if you'll finish the year out we'll give you the next year, if you want to travel—look at the theatre—even go to Russia [which in 1938 was quite a thought] or go to New York, or whatever you want, since we're not paying for this year at all. And it will mean so much to Granddaddy." My grandfather got the first Ph.D. they ever gave at Yale in Zoology. My father got his A.B. at Yale. They felt I should have that Yale degree. After all, none of us knew any way to go in the theatre except the academic way; we didn't have family connections with theatre or anyone to turn to to say: "Here's somebody, can she be an apprentice or something?" That's why I was doing it the academic way, and I knew that once I got through Yale I would need a year of internship, working with a designer, to find out what happened professionally before I could try my wings at designing, even though I was convinced from when I finished high school that I could design better than anyone. What can I tell you? If you don't have that kind of feeling about yourself, do something else, because it's a hard row to hoe.

Anyway, I finished the year out; I got to design the next production, which was most interesting, and I got to light it too; nobody'd ever done the sets and lighting before, at Yale. Then I was mad because I couldn't do the costumes, because I didn't like what the costume designer did, but that's another thing. While I was at Yale I took the exam for the Theatrical Designers' Union and passed it. Young people do that quite a lot now but they don't always pass it. So that, when I graduated, I was also a member of the United Scenic Artists, which meant that I could work on Broadway. I was qualified. I stamped my thesis, which was *Sadko*, the opera by Rimski-Korsakov, with the union stamp. Oenslager was so funny, he said, "Well, we all take an oath never to harm a brother member—I had to pass you."

John Koenig, who was a third-year design student at Yale my first year and took the exam the same time I did, had done some designing professionally, so I said, "Look, next year you're going to get a lot of shows to do and I would like to be your assistant." He said, "Fine, if you pass the exam let me know." We exchanged addresses. When I went up to Green Mansions to design for the summer, I let him know. In midsummer, just when they were going to repeat the things they'd already done, I got a wire from him to hurry on down to New York. I went to work as his assistant. The only thing my family had to help with, and did, that year they had promised me, was to pay the union initiation fee. I went right to work in New York as Johnny's assistant. Also, then, I got some little costume designing things to do. I was very busy. I wouldn't let John pay me as much as he should have, according to the union, because I didn't think I was worth it. That was a nice bargain for him, too.

I learned a lot about where everything was, but I didn't learn enough. I had to find out about the whole union situation with stagehands and how that works, on my own, because nobody at Yale knew anything about it. I learned how important your crew is in professional theatre and how helpful and how wise a good carpenter, electrician, property man can be. For years people came from Yale and got shows to design and only did one. They might've been good but their shows never worked, because they came with arrogance and with this feeling that union crews were a necessary evil. It's terribly easy for the professionals to destroy a young person just entering on the scene. Working with Johnny, I learned these things. I was just his assistant, but I did all his drawing and found his props. I laid out lighting and saw that through because nobody did much about lighting at that point. I learned all about the shops from the good to the bad. I had an important experience working with Johnny on *Here Come the Clowns* with Eddie Dowling. Johnny had an interesting set, but he wouldn't leave me places to get lights in as I had asked him to. I couldn't do anything about it; I was just his assistant. I came in one day and the house electrician warned me that something was going on. They all liked me because I never tried to put on airs. I came with humility and good manners because I figured they'd been paid to do this job for a long time; they must know something, which was not the attitude of the recent Yale graduate at that time. Well, here was Abe Feder relighting the show. You see I hadn't any contract; I was just Johnny Koenig's assistant. I don't know what Abe expected me to do, but I looked it over and I stayed and I watched, but I never liked him very much for it. Also he was cutting holes in the scenery where I'd asked Johnny, "Couldn't we make space for things?" Being brought in specially, Abe could do that a lot. But then I figured, "Gee whiz, there's more to this than anybody's told me, I'd better find out a little more about the whole situation; who does what to whom and so forth." I worked with Stewart Chaney on some shows, but I waited before doing any lighting on my own until I really found out how it's structured and about production electricians, etc. Nobody told me these things before.

Then, of course, there was always the resentment against a woman. These older men, for the most part, did not want to work with young people, and they certainly didn't want to work with a woman. There were some that were so arrogant, so arbitrary, and so impossible that even though you'd worry through and you'd work it out, you didn't work with them again if they couldn't adjust to you. They also would try each crew—they are like children—to see how far they can go. If they're focusing lights for you and they're up on the ladder and you know where you want the light aimed and you know you want it shaped a certain way, well, they'd swing it, they'd do all sorts of things to see how much you'd put up with. But I had more patience; I had to learn it because I knew that if I were up on that ladder I could do it so fast, but I'm not allowed there, I don't belong to the stagehands' local. They don't have very many women. Once, during the war, in Texas, the wife of a business agent, when he went to war, got taken into the stagehands' local, but I've never heard of any other women. They've had to take some Blacks in here and there, so possibly there's hope for us other second-class citizens.

But the stagehands made a lady out of me, I've never appeared in slacks in the theatre. It's much more practical to wear pants when you're lighting a show, but they resent that. Now people don't so much, it's changed; but they did in 1938 when I was starting out. Women who would work in the theatre and would come in practical work clothes—slacks or trousers of one sort or another—all of the men would say, "Ahaa, a lesbian; she's trying to look like a man, trying to do a man's work." So I always wore, as neat as I could, a suit, but a skirt. It would be much easier to go around with pants but that whole image wouldn't work. I never wanted to have anybody think I was trying to pretend to be anything I'm not; I'm me. Well, I was doing everything. I was painting on the paint frame, you know, assisting designers, designing sets when they came my way, but they weren't hits so they didn't count, and designing costumes. Lighting just finally fell on me and happened.

There are a lot of things that make lighting a very good field for a woman because you have to be patient with these technical people who have to do the manual labor for you. It's no good going up and punching them in the nose; you've got to get it accomplished with a certain amount of cajolery and flattery, but also knowing what you want, and that it can be done. That was another thing in our famous talk, when my family convinced me to stay on at Yale, was that my parents said that I was saying that there was no hope for me, "I'm a woman and obviously they are putting barricades up here." "Well," my father said, "you're a woman, and of course it's harder because there's resentment against that. First of all, however, you've got to know your job better than any man and do it better. Don't have a chip on your shoulder that it's because you're a woman that you're discriminated against. But once, if you've made it and done something right, then it should be easier, because you *are* different."

They were right. They have always encouraged me in whatever I wanted to do and stood by, and that's wonderful. I think not everybody has that kind of family.

But being a lighting designer was hard. Each time a woman comes into the lighting field it's easier for them and eases up for everybody else. Jean Rosenthal had been lighting shows for WPA; she wasn't in the union yet, but she was about four years ahead of me at Yale. She'd also been lighting Martha Graham ballets and she worked with the Mercury Theatre. She had a harder time because she was the first woman to do lighting exclusively. After me, Tharon Musser was the next one to do lighting.

There are many women in the theatre now working in all fields. It was difficult that first year or two when I was doing everything, and we were working out of the Depression getting fewer shows each year. The union had a stewards' list where you signed up to work, and then when you got to the top of the list, they'd have a call for men to work in the paint studios. So, say there were three or four jobs that day, they'd call the three or four top people on the list and you'd draw which studio you went to. The first studio I drew I had to trade, change with another member, because they had no facilities for women. They had no extra toilet or anything there, so that limited the number of shops I could work in. I had to go where there was a separate toilet; that's the state law. Now they have to put them in for everybody, but then you couldn't send a woman where there wasn't at least a place for her to change her clothes and go to the bathroom. But once I got to the studio; no problem at all. They knew I could draw things up so I'd draw out the drops to scale, measuring them up from the designers' sketches. And then, on the paint frame, Joey Deluca was little and I was tall so we'd work along there; he'd paint in the middle and I'd go up high, and then I'd go down, sit below and paint that. But it was all very, very good experience.

Once people find that you know your job and that you're not really making a big issue and can control yourself not to cry at the wrong time or any of those ridiculous things, then they don't worry about your being a woman, at least I don't think they do. I don't worry about it, it was difficult at first; it's difficult for any young and different person to break into a new field. You can look at Ibsen's *Master Builder* and see the resentment of the old for the young; it goes on just as much as the sex problem. There are not as many women hired to design sets as there are women who *could* design beautiful sets. I think there's a prejudice in the minds of the producers or backers. Unless you're very young, you don't necessarily go around showing people your portfolio, but there have been women who designed scenery off and on all through the years. You've had combinations of people like Jean and Bill Eckart who did it as a husband-wife thing, and Helen Pond and Herbert Senn, I don't think they are married, but they've collaborated together. And of course, Aline Bernstein, she was still designing, not only costumes, but sets when I first came into theatre. Irene Sharaff did that lovely production in the thirties of *Alice in Wonderland* for Eva Le Gallienne's Repertory; mostly she's noted as a marvelous costume designer. Of course, there people accept women. In terms of hiring designers; if they had the choice they'd rather, all things being equal—equal experience, equal background—most producers would take a man ahead of a woman just because they think they are probably less trouble. I think that you have to learn, when you get into a situation, when you really want to fight with somebody because they're doing it wrong, not to do it because men can say all kinds of things to each other or they can hit each other or something and get something settled, but if a woman starts to yell or scream at somebody she sounds like a shrew, and right away you're handicapped there. I never knew, in certain situations when people would yell at me, just whether I was going to burst into tears or yell back at them and tell them in four-letter words what I really thought of them. Mostly I'd just simply sit and analyze, and then it turned out all right. It freezes you up when somebody yells, if the stage manager gets upset or something. But I wasn't brought up to be a fighter in terms of the words and the yelling, screaming kind of thing; I'm not good at that, I hate it. I hate to have to yell, but I will not give up my idea. I'm a fighter in terms of the bulldog—of holding on—and I do have confidence in myself.

MATRIARCHS OF THE REGIONAL THEATRE
DOROTHY B. MAGNUS

More than a quarter of a century ago, three intrepid women director-producers, Margo Jones, Nina Vance, and Zelda Fichandler, led a significant revolution in the American theatre. It was a revolt against commercialism, centralization, the joblessness of theatre artists, and the failure to experiment with the classics or new plays. They were disenchanted with the Broadway theatre for perpetuating these ills. They waged a battle for the survival of good live drama in new regional theatres that sprang up from local impulses and the determination of these strong individuals.

"Neither the building, nor the organization, nor the finest plays and actors in the whole world will help you create a fine theatre if you have no consistent approach of your own, a true philosophy of the theatre."[1] So said Margo Jones, first of the distinguished matriarchs of the regional theatre. On June 3, 1947, modern American regional theatre was born with the opening

Dorothy B. Magnus is Emeritus Head of the Speech Department and Theatre Director, Winona State University, Minnesota. A longer version of this paper was delivered at the American Theatre Association Bicentennial Convention, August 1975, in Washington, D.C.

of Margo Jones's Theatre '47 in Dallas. According to historian Joseph Zeigler, throughout her theatre's history until her death in 1955 she "served as
high priestess of the movement and a measure for all others." Margo Jones
achieved her eminent position not only through her life and her work,
which were the same, but also through her book, *Theatre-in-the-Round*,
which has been called "the nearest thing to a bible in the regional theatre
world—an extraordinary self-testament which makes awesome reading because it is prophetic and above all pure."[2]

She tells her story in part this way:[3] "My interest in theatre started very
early. . . . At eleven I knew I wanted to do plays, and up went a sheet in the
barn where my sister and my brothers joined me in my first producing-
directing venture. . . . Until I was fourteen, I did not have a chance to see a
professional production of a play. New vistas opened to me in Fort Worth
when I watched Walter Hampden as Cyrano. . . . I went to a girls' college
[Texas State College for Women] where the drama courses were crowded
with aspiring actresses, and I was the only student interested in directing. . . .
I did a certain amount of acting in college plays, but always with the clear
understanding that I was doing it to acquaint myself with the actor's viewpoint and problems." She speaks of being an avid reader of the classics and
later of new scripts.

At the time, no graduate program in drama was available from her alma
mater; she took her master's degree in psychology but held to her interests
by doing the thesis on "The Abnormal Ways Out of Emotional Conflict as
Reflected in the Dramas of Henrik Ibsen," case studies of the behavior of
three of Ibsen's female characters: Hedda Gabler (suicide), Ellida (hysteria)
in *The Lady from the Sea*, and Irene (insanity) in *When We Dead Awaken*. She
had the opportunity to direct one of these plays, *Hedda Gabler*, on her first
directing job a year later, after a summer of study at the Pasadena Playhouse. The next step in her education was a trip around the world. She went
to theatres in Japan, China, India, England, France before she had seen New
York.

While she was abroad, the Federal Theatre was started. Upon her return
home, she became assistant director of the Houston Federal Theatre. Following the collapse of that project in Houston, she went abroad again, this
time to see the Moscow Art Theatre Festival, which she covered in a series of
articles for the *Houston Chronicle*. On this trip, she also saw Berlin and
Warsaw and revisited London and Paris.

When she returned this time, she knew she wanted to have a theatre of
her own. The Houston Recreation Department offered her a job teaching
playground directors to do plays with children in the various parks of the
city. The department had a small building with a stage which was used for
square dances three days a week. Since she believed her place was primarily
in the little theatre movement, she asked to use that small building free of
charge to produce plays provided she kept up her other duties in recreation.

The moment she received permission to use the theatre, she announced in a press release that the Houston Community Players had been formed and that *The Importance of Being Earnest* was to be the first production. The play was done, ran two nights, and she managed to get one review in the newspaper. Since the theatre was not available for the second production, Elmer Rice's *Judgment Day*, the cast performed in a courtroom, which now seems mildly prophetic of what was to come.

The Houston Community Players also presented the classics—Shakespeare, Molière, and others. While gathering material for his book, *Advance from Broadway*, Norris Houghton visited Margo's theatre and wrote that one of her most provocative statements was: "My most successful box-office productions have been the classics. I always have to sell standing room for Shakespeare, Ibsen, or Chekhov."

In the spring of 1939 she was introduced to theatre-in-the-round at a theatre conference in Washington, D.C. She saw a production in a hotel ballroom that impressed her so much she felt she could do something similar in Houston. "I remember that on the train back to Houston, I shocked a girl sitting next to me by springing up from my seat all of a sudden and exclaiming, 'Why not!'" Her theatre in Houston was too hot for summer productions; theatre-in-the-round seemed to be the answer. "All I had to do," she said, "was to persuade one of the hotels to give me an air-conditioned room on the mezzanine. I succeeded in this, and we produced six plays during the summer. It was my first direct experience with theatre-in-the-round."[4]

During World War II, she moved to university theatre as a faculty member of the Drama Department of the University of Texas. There she directed three new plays and worked on several theatre-in-the-round productions, including one of new scripts. At the end of 1943 she decided that her way in the theatre pointed to the formation of a permanent resident professional theatre with a repertory system, producing new plays and classics. In the summer of 1944 she received a grant from the Rockefeller Foundation to develop her plan and do research on the few professional theatres of that time. Besides her theatre in Dallas, she envisioned the creation of similar theatres throughout the country; she was for the principle of decentralization.

Before she had time to get well into the research project, she answered a call from New York to codirect Tennessee Williams's *The Glass Menagerie*. It meant adding the training of the Broadway stage to her experience. Besides, she said, "I believed in Williams and I loved the play."

While the search for a suitable building for her theatre in Dallas was in progress, Margo took two leaves of absence to direct plays on Broadway, one of which was Maxwell Anderson's *Joan of Lorraine*. She returned home with the determination that the job in Dallas could be delayed no longer. An attractive, modern building of stucco and glass brick was finally located on the Fair Park Grounds. It was air-conditioned and adaptable to theatre-in-the-round. In the spring of 1947 all papers were signed with the approval of the State Fair Association and the City Park Department. On June 3, Theatre '47 opened with William Inge's *Farther Off from Heaven*, which, when he became famous, he revised and retitled *Dark at the Top of the Stairs*. Margo considered the search for new plays a great adventure. Williams's *Summer and Smoke* was brought to Broadway directly from its debut in Dallas. Likewise, Jerome Lawrence and Robert E. Lee's *Inherit the Wind* moved directly from her theatre to Broadway in 1955. The two authors now offer an award each year to the person or theatre in America demonstrating the most initiative in finding and producing important new scripts.

Theatre '47 completed its season with enough funds to start Theatre '48 with a twenty-week plan; Theatre '49 ran for thirty weeks and Theatre '50 followed the same plan. As to the name, she says: "Suggested by a theatre in Prague, it is changed every year on New Year's Eve in order to remain contemporary at all times. The audience that night is asked to attend the performance a little later than usual and to join the actors, after the play, in greeting the new year and the new name of the theatre."[5]

It was Margo Jones's conviction that "a theatre person is good in proportion to the inspiration, amusement, beauty, and education he can give to others. I want for other people what I want for myself; to live life to its fullest, to see good plays, to read good books, to see great paintings, to hear fine music. . . ." Until her premature death, this distinguished pioneer made her theatre a place for these passionate beliefs.

Following in the footsteps of trailblazer Margo Jones was a handful of disciples who created the theatres that were to form the backbone of the regional theatre revolution. First of the disciples to make history was Nina Vance, who had worked with Margo Jones and the Community Players in Houston. Reared in the tiny community of Yoakum, Texas, she comes from a background boasting a pioneer spirit typical of the rigorous Depression life in the rural Southwest. She received her B.A. degree from Texas Christian and did postgraduate work at the University of South Carolina, Columbia, and the American Academy of Dramatic Art. The same year Margo started her theatre in Dallas in 1947, Nina began the Alley Theatre in Houston, in a friend's dance studio, with the support of more than a hundred interested Houstonians. The inaugural production, Harry Brown's *A Sound of Hunting*, opened late in November 1947 and ran for ten nights. In 1948 the Alley, then an admittedly amateur group, presented five more plays. They were respectable audience-pleasers, among them Lillian Hellman's *Another Part of the Forest*, Clifford Odets's *Clash by Night*, Somerset Maugham's *Caroline*. By 1949 their playhouse was condemned and the Alley found new larger quarters in an abandoned fan factory. Soon Vance decided that star performers were needed to save the Alley from financial crises. They became an Equity company when Albert Dekker came to play in *Death of a Salesman*.

Actors and directors like Signe Hasso, Chester Morris, Alan Schneider, and William Ball worked on the Alley's "postage stamp stage."

The Alley was selected by the Ford Foundation as one of the first regional theatres to receive major financial help in 1960. The theatre received a three-year grant of $156,000 to enable it to attract known actors away from Broadway with the promise of $200-a-week salaries over forty or more weeks each season. Of the total money needed, the foundation's grant provided half (the first $100 per week per actor), and the theatre was required to supply the other half. The Alley was on its way to full permanence, with some national recognition, but still it was limited by its much too small fan factory theatre.

In 1962, the theatre received the largest of a series of Ford matching grants to regional theatres for the construction and running of a new theatre. Nina Vance chose New York architect Ulrich Franzen, and together they set out to design and build a mammoth theatre that looms above the Civic Center in downtown Houston on land donated by the Houston Endowment.

The theatre opened its new $3.5 million two-theatre playhouse in October 1968 with Brecht's *Galileo*. Concurrent with the move into the new theatre came other major changes; from a half-dozen actors in the late 1950's to more than three times that number now and from 225 seats in the fan factory to nearly 1,100 in the new building, which includes a replica of the fan factory stage.

Zeigler has said of these leaders of regional theatres that they "started their theatres in order to create places for themselves to direct plays. . . . It is significant that today most of these people direct plays rarely if at all. Early in the life of their theatres they discovered that no one else wanted to do the 'dirty work' of management, without which the theatre would collapse. . . . Soon, however, the dirty work began to get not only cleaner but also very interesting and far more dynamic than the interplay of actors."[6] Nina Vance exemplifies this pattern of moving from director to producer.

Margo Jones once wrote: "The production of classics is healthy, but . . . the seed of progress in the theatre lies in new plays," and Nina Vance shared this belief. The first new play presented by the Alley Theatre, Ronald Alexander's *Season with Ginger*, was produced in 1950. Later retitled *Time Out for Ginger*, the play became a Broadway success starring Melvyn Douglas. Another Alley premiere, in 1955, was James Lee's *Career*, which the Alley dedicated to the memory of Margo Jones. That play later went on to Off-Broadway success and was made into a film starring Dean Martin and Shirley MacLaine. The Alley had its first playwright-in-residence, Frank Gagliano, in 1960. His play, *The Library Raid*, was produced in Houston. Later the work went to Off Broadway as *Night of the Dunce*. Another Alley playwright-in-residence was Paul Zindel, then an unknown writer of novels and plays. His play, *The Effect of Gamma Rays on Man-in-the-Moon Marigolds* was premiered by the Alley in 1965. The play then disappeared, except for a showing on educational television, until it was mounted at the Cleveland Playhouse in 1969 and went on from there to Off-Broadway success and the Pulitzer Prize.

Nina Vance's prestigious theatre of the Southwest has been called the most regional of the regional theatres. Full credit goes to the financially astute and successful director-producer who started her penny-postcard recruitment of theatre supporters with two now famous words, "Why not?" Miss Vance died in the winter of 1980.

Zelda Fichandler shares billing with the other two matriarchs of the regional theatre revolution. Indeed she is one of its most persuasive advocates. Looking back twenty years she says, "Some of us looked about and saw that something was amiss. What was essentially a collective and cumulative art form was represented in the United States by the hit-or-miss, make-a-pudding, smash-a-pudding system of Broadway production. What required by its nature continuity and groupness, not to mention a certain quietude of spirit and the fifth freedom, the freedom to fail, was taking place in an atmosphere of hysteria, crisis, fragmentation, one-shotness, and mammon-mindness within ten blocks of Broadway."[7] Zelda Fichandler's Arena Stage was, in its inception, like the Alley's, modest in scope but high in ideals. Fichandler named Jones as the person who influenced her most: "She showed me the road. And in 1949 she took the time to talk to a frightened young girl to encourage her objectives and stiffen her right arm." In 1950 the Arena Stage began at a time when Washington's only roadshow theatre, the National, had closed its doors rather than integrate. Its first home was in a dilapidated neighborhood in northwest Washington in the old Hippodrome movie theatre with 247 seats.

Boston-born Zelda, who received her B.A. from Cornell, was finishing her M.A. at George Washington University when her mentor there, Edward Mangum, impressed by her ability included her in his planning for a theatre. She was the one who had the time and the energy to work night and day on the idea. She found the old movie house, cleverly skirted antiquated Washington regulations requiring a fire curtain (an impossibility in an arena theatre) and obtained a special allowance for the new theatre (which prohibited the use of the word "theatre" in its name).

The Arena Stage differed from the Alley in that from the start it was professionally staffed and had an Equity company. Early members included George Grizzard, and Alan Schneider was the resident director. The inaugural production was *She Stoops to Conquer*, followed by *The Glass Menagerie, The Hasty Heart,* and *The Importance of Being Earnest*. The theatre rediscovered and found success with plays which had been commercial failures on Broadway, notably *Summer of the Seventeenth Doll, Epitaph for George Dillon,* and *The Disenchanted.*

For five years Zelda forged ahead with Arena Stage despite great financial odds and difficulties, not the least of which was audience support. A narrow segment of the population, upper middle income, highly educated, professional, seemed to form the audience core for regional theatre; the common man, it was found, is fairly uncommon among those who attend live professional performances. Recognizing the need to broaden the base of audience support, Zelda said, "If we wish to attract . . . the 'new working class'— engineers, technicians, researchers, and teachers—who are not economically depressed or sensorially dead, then we must attract them with the directness of our work, its abrasion, its physical energy, its source within life. . . ."[8] By the mid-fifties, the theatre had gross receipts of $121,000 and had outgrown its first musty home. Halfway through a successful run of Agatha Christie's *The Mousetrap* in its American premiere, the theatre closed and the search began for a new location. An abandoned brewery to which still clung the stale aroma of long-since-emptied beer kegs became the second home in 1956. The opening play in the "Old Vat" was an expanded version of Arthur Miller's *A View from the Bridge*, directed by Alan Schneider.

In 1961 a new 796-seat Arena Stage Theatre was built, becoming the largest new theatre constructed for a permanent professional company, and the first professional theatre in America built specifically in arena style. It grew out of Zelda's decade of experience with the arena form and solidified her commitment to it. What had started from simple economic and structural necessity had evolved into a positive philosophy of theatre for Zelda who extolled the circular form. The new theatre opened in 1961 with the first American professional production of Brecht's *The Caucasian Chalk Circle*.

Like the Alley Theatre, the Arena Stage was an early favorite of the Ford Foundation. When the time came to build the new theatre, however, there was an acute need for funds. The only way to obtain gifts was to be nonprofit. Arena Stage was therefore reconstituted into a nonprofit parent organization, the Washington Drama Society. A stream of funding proposals has emanated from Zelda, who is considered the best writer of grant proposals in the regional theatre and an acknowledged genius of theatrical subsidy on the East Coast. Her Arena Stage has become *the* major nonprofit theatre institution in the East outside New York.

In January 1971 Zelda opened the $1.5 million Kreeger Theatre as an addition to her Arena Stage, "christening it with the American premiere of the British comedy, *The Ruling Class*, by Peter Barnes."[9] For the new addition to her building, Zelda programmed an "Old Vat" Room, in honor of former days, a place for the company and the audience to gather, and wonder, together. During the 1950's Zelda Fichandler's interest in new plays was steady. In the early years of her theatre she presented the premiere production of Robert Anderson's *All Summer Long*, which went to Broadway, Robinson Jeffers's *The Cretan Woman*, and Josh Greenfeld's *Clandestine on the Morning Line* (financed by a Ford Foundation Grant).

A stunning leap forward in the growing interest in new plays came with the premiere of *The Great White Hope* at Arena Stage in Washington in 1967.

This one premiere was a major turning point of the regional theatre revolution because it proved the national power of new plays. As director Edwin Sherin later pointed out, "It all happened because of the whimsical and radical genius of Zelda Fichandler . . . she has the vision of a seer. She believed in it!"[10] Howard Sackler's *The Great White Hope* was a gargantuan undertaking for Arena Stage. Despite a grant of $25,000 from the National Endowment for the Arts, Arena Stage lost $50,000 on the two-month premiere; but the theatre gained something that could not be measured in dollars. It gained for itself a place in the forefront of the modern American theatre, as representatives of the nation's media flocked to a regional theatre to report on the latest rage.

In the fall of 1968, the play opened on Broadway (after having been sold to the movies for nearly $1 million) with Arena director, Edwin Sherin, and Arena star James Earl Jones, plus a large portion of the Arena company riding with the play onto Broadway. The show received immediate laudatory reviews and went on to win many theatre awards, including the Pulitzer Prize.

Now Zelda began to concentrate more and more on mounting premieres. The season after *Great White Hope* she premiered Arthur Kopit's *Indians*. In the next three seasons, Arena Stage offered premieres of Arthur Giron's *Edith Stein* (directed by Zelda); Stanley Greenberg's *Pueblo* (subsequently seen by millions with Hal Holbrook starring in the Emmy award-winning televised version); Jay Broad's *A Conflict of Interest*; and Michael Weller's *Moonchildren*. For her efforts in new plays, Zelda was given the Margo Jones Award in 1972, by then long overdue. The record of the recent seasons is testimony to her continuing dedication with six premieres of which *The Ascent of Fuji*, directed by Zelda during the 1974–75 season, was only the second play by a Soviet writer to be shown in the West in nearly a decade.

Thanks to the three intrepid women pioneer director-producers who led the revolution against Broadway, theatre in America has penetrated the so-called hinterlands. The shackles of Broadway have been broken, and the winds of change have blown over theatre U.S.A. in large part because these three woman have said, "Why not?"

THE LADY IS A CRITIC

CAROLINE J. DODGE LATTA

The lady is a . . . critic? An American female theatrical critic to be exact! Preposterous? At the most a rare species? Yet over seventy women[1] in the United States currently practice this profession full- or part-time although

Caroline J. Dodge Latta, who teaches at Columbia College, Chicago, and is artistic director of the Studio Theatre, has written entries for *Notable Women in American Theatre*, and is on the Joseph Jefferson Committee in Chicago.

their identities usually are known only to those who live in their circulation area. A few may gain prominence outside of their own particular sphere of influence but national recognition is elusive. There is no woman today who holds a position of national theatrical influence, who has the stature of a Walter Kerr or the household familiarity of a Clive Barnes.

One apparent reason for their anonymity is that female theatrical critics exist almost universally outside the mainstream. If they work in New York (and approximately 41 percent do, the heaviest concentration of female critics anywhere in the country), either they are to be found as assistants to the regular drama editors or as "second stringers" on the city's major newspapers and magazines. They may also be found as primary reviewers on the many secondary specialized newspapers New York and its environs support. The majority of female critics are, however, far removed from the theatrical center. They are scattered nationwide—in Nashville, Houston, Chicago, Los Angeles.

Yet women do comprise 23 percent of the practicing theatrical critics in America today. To understand the range of criticism in our time and to explore the possible uniqueness of female criticism, we need to know who these female critics are, how they entered the field, where and how they work, and what special perspective, if any, they bring to their criticism.

It is interesting to note that women's responses to theatre were among the earliest to appear in print in Colonial America. Despite the social opprobrium frequently attached to women attending theatre, women managed to get some of their views about performances circulated. One of the earliest was one "Arabella Sly" who wrote the *Virginia Gazette* in 1756 asking about the "propriety of laughing at a scene without shielding her face with her fan"[2] at a performance of *The Beaux Strategem*. "Arabella" was generally "highly delighted" with the performance she attended, but another woman writing a few years later earned the distinction of registering in print the first unfavorable artistic critique written in America. In the May 6, 1760, *Maryland Gazette* "Clarinda" chastised "the bad manners of an actor who showed obvious resentment toward the audience when he was hissed, and who stopped the action of the play to instruct them not to applaud." She was also horrified "by the practice of the low comics who, being unsure of their lines, improvised vulgarity. These improvisations were even more offensive because they occurred in *Hamlet.*"

Even the artistic battle lines between the sexes were firmly drawn in these early days before dramatic criticism or theatrical reviewing as a profession existed in the Colonies. (Criticism emerged as a separate form of writing in the 1790's.) An exchange of letters in the New York press in 1761 between "Philodemus" and "Armanda" placed "Armanda" in the undignified position of defending her disputed right to view a theatrical piece and express her opinion of it. She found it necessary to mount a personal attack on her male opponent, "characterizing him as an old man whose early life was debauched and who now sees evil in everything."

Despite these lively beginnings, women theatrical critics fell curiously silent during most of the nineteenth century. Not until the 1890's do two names dislodge themselves from the anonymous group of women who attended the theatre and who surely discussed in detail its personalities, scandals, shortcomings, and artistic merits. Mildred Aldrich contributed pieces on theatre to *Arena* (1892, 1893), the *Boston Journal* (1894), and the *Boston Herald* (1895).[3] Amy Leslie, former light-opera singer and comedienne, wrote a review of a "touring company's [1890] production of *Castles in the Air*, sold it to the *Chicago Daily News*, and was hired as drama critic,"[4] a title she was to hold for the next four decades. In 1936 Ishbel Ross in *Ladies of the Press* briefly mentions four other women drama critics—Ada Patterson (*Theatre* magazine), Wilella Waldorf (*New York Post*), Carol Frink (*Chicago Herald Examiner*), and Leone Cass Baer (Mrs. H. W. Hicks) (*Oregonian*, Portland, Oregon). Ms. Ross laments that "there have been few good women drama critics . . . with the sustained reputation of a Percy Hammond or a Burns Mantle. . . ."[5]

Interestingly enough, Ms. Ross's list does not include either Edith Isaacs, Helen Deutsch, or Eleanor Flexner, yet these women expanded the opportunities open to drama critics in general, and to women in particular, further than any of their contemporaries. Mrs. Isaacs, who began her career as a theatre critic, became editor of *Theatre Arts* magazine in 1926 and made it the most influential theatre periodical of its day. Her editorial faculties were acute, her business acumen highly developed, and her critical eye keen, assuring the public of the finest coverage of the performing arts. Nine years later Helen Deutsch, a press agent, not a critic, singlehandedly coerced the New York drama critics into forming a "Circle." Its "mission" was to award a critical prize "for the best new play by an American playwright produced in New York during the theatre season."[6] Unfortunately, however, no women drama critics were charter members of the new society. In 1938 Eleanor Flexner, former contributor to *New Theatre* magazine, an outspoken proponent of social criticism and one of the few effective radical drama critics, published *American Playwrights 1918–38*. Her book was a scathing, often penetrating indictment of the failure of America's foremost dramatists to respond creatively to the economic conditions of the depression.

It seems appropriate that Rosamond Gilder, critic for Isaacs's *Theatre Arts* magazine (1937–48), first woman member of Deutsch's New York Drama Critics Circle, and advocate of Ms. Flexner's sentiments that the critic's "gift places him under a social obligation, to be a teacher and a guide,"[7] should head the list of the ten best and most representative women in the critical profession today. This list was developed during consultations with Joseph Shipley, Secretary of the Drama Critics Circle, and with various women critics. The women critics *emeriti* with Gilder are Ethel Colby (*Journal of Commerce*, 1940–70), and Claudia Cassidy (*Chicago Tribune*, 1942–65). Clara Hieronymus (*Nashville Tennessean*, 1956-present), Ann Holmes (*Houston*

Chronicle, 1948-present), Glenna Syse (*Chicago Sun Times*, 1958-present), and Edith Oliver (*The New Yorker* magazine, 1968-present) comprise a group of "old timers" who have served twenty years or more. Marilyn Stasio (*Cue* magazine, 1968–78, *New York Post*, 1978-present), Linda Winer (*Chicago Tribune*, 1979-present), and Sylvie Drake (*Los Angeles Times*, 1969-present) have been at their jobs for a decade or more. Through interviews and analyses of their writings I have sought to suggest how these important women critics see themselves and their work.

America's female theatrical critics feel that their job places upon their shoulders what Sylvie Drake calls an "extraordinary responsibility."[8] They point to roughly five traditional areas of that responsibility. The first is, as Glenna Syse points out, to one's publisher, and/or editor. The way to fulfill that responsibility is to be both readable and read. The prescribed method of achieving daily readership varies from individual to individual. Claudia Cassidy admonishes "never be dull."[9] Glenna Syse offers the precise formula "to tell what I saw and liked and why." Marilyn Stasio tries to "communicate a feeling of the reviewer's experience," to so capture the essentials with words that in reading her review, one sees the performance flash before one's eyes.

Editors often see the critic as a consumer guide for the audience, the second area of responsibility. Linda Winer deplores this conception of the critic, yet includes an answer to the consumer query somewhere in her review. Ideally she would like to believe everybody would and should go to anything and everything, but practically she realizes that people do not. Part of her hostility to wearing the consumer guide hat is that her relationship with the audience is more complicated than that. She is a member of that audience and her critique is written from that perspective. She wishes her review to bridge the gulf between audience and critic, to be a continuing conversation that she and the reader might have shared, had they stopped for coffee after the show. She is, she believes, as well informed a member of the audience as she can be.

Ms. Winer does not, however, write to instruct actors or directors, the third area of responsibility. Feeling she is not one of them, she does not presume to tell them their job. If the review helps them, all to the good, but her primary concern is directed to continuing her dialogue with her compatriot-in-arms, the audience. Ann Holmes weights this third area of responsibility—what is owed to director and cast—more heavily. Exhaustive self-study convinced her that she lacked sufficient knowledge to serve as a critic who could make informed judgments of use to performers. She actively pursued funding agencies and received three major grants to enable her to "fill in the gaps." She traveled throughout Europe and America observing theatre and the cultural scene. In 1969 she ventured into territory usually off limits to critics to watch prominent American theatre directors rehearse and mount their productions. Gaining a behind-the-scene's viewpoint made her, she feels, a more astute commentator and opened her eyes to the enormous benefits that could be achieved if cooperation between critic and director was standard.

Feminine critics widen responsibility from concern with a specific production to a fourth area: responsibility to the artistic community as a whole. Such a responsibility carries with it the inherent danger that artistic groups will confuse responsibility and loyalty. They will demand respect and praise where none is due, simply because of their existence. Nothing angers Glenna Syse more than being placed in the untenable position of being criticized by the artistic community for doing her job. Clara Hieronymus echoes her complaint. Theatre criticism in Nashville, up to the time she began writing in 1956, had been primarily social back-slapping, a product of a pleasantly patronizing tradition which passed out nearly unanimous accolades to most artistic endeavors. Ms. Hieronymus fulfilled her obligation to the theatre groups in her community by refusing to measure all dramatic activities by anything less than professional standards.

Objectively recording outstanding performances is, to Rosamond Gilder, the fifth and highest level of a critic's traditional set of responsibilities: a responsibility to posterity. As she eloquently states:

> The clearest insight that can be attained into the mysteries of this art [of acting] which dies with its creator—dies indeed with the moment of creation—is through the eyes of the observer who has recorded his impressions for our benefit.[10]

In her monthly dramatic reviews and in her book *John Gielgud's Hamlet*, a play-by-play description of the action that occurred on stage, including every facet of vocal and physical interpretation, Ms. Gilder reported clearly, allowing herself to serve as a medium by means of which great actors' performances could be faithfully and accurately transcribed.[11] The recorded echoes of these great performances reverberate throughout future productions. Such memories, Edith Oliver adds, actually enrich performances she is currently watching.[12] They are beacons which light up the past and illumine the future.

In addition to these five responsibilities, female critics cite the following: (1) a responsibility to new performers. Edith Oliver feels it her primary duty to welcome and encourage beginners, for theatre is reborn only with an unending flow of talent. (2) Ms. Oliver extends this responsibility to include encouragement of the fledgling playwright. She served as a dramaturge at the O'Neill Theatre Center new plays program. Lehman Engel in *The Critics* compliments Marilyn Stasio's ability in this crucial area. Ms. Stasio, he feels, presents the new playwright's best qualities and points out what, in her opinion, are his weaker areas, managing throughout the whole discussion not to sound discouraging. Felt responsibility is not confined to novice performers and playwrights. Each of these critics follows the careers of their protégés, hoping to be able to report substantial progress but capable of being brutally honest with both herself and her favorites. Edith Oliver's nine-year vigil over the charismatic but unfocused talent of James Earl Jones finally bore fruit in his rendition of Boesman in Athol Fugard's *Boesman and Lena*. Tennessee Williams's *Glass Menagerie* was championed by Cassidy in Chicago en route to New York as "honest, tender . . . brilliant."[13] What is not so well known is her 1961 critique acknowledging Williams's failure in *Night of the Iguana*, calling it "a bankrupt play."[14]

There is also (3) an unstated responsibility to the theatre at large. Edith Oliver worries in her October 25, 1969, *New Yorker* piece that "a theatre in which the artists—writers and actors—are subservient to the director seems . . . not revivifying but decadent." Ann Holmes laments in "The Musical Show" the lack of public and private support for this unique American contribution to the theatrical world.[15] One has only to read between the lines to realize that both statements are evidence of these women's concerns about the health of the theatre in general.

Harold Clurman has written, "Critics are parts of communities, each with its own particular history and need."[16] (4) Female critics apparently take this statement to heart, for they express movingly and convincingly the fulfillment they experience when they feel they have met this responsibility. Clara Hieronymus speaks of the necessity of knowing her community, of a twenty-five-year commitment to one place, of her unique niche, of valuing what happens here and of being valued in return, of the reward of watching her comments result in raised expectations and ultimately better theatre. Lehman Engel notes Claudia Cassidy's "courage . . . in behalf of her charge: Chicago."[17]

Rosamond Gilder carries responsibility to one's community a step further. (5) She reminds the theatre of its (and by extension her) responsibility to society. Such a responsibility often requires a critic to serve as a scourge compelling all concerned—be they artists or no—to "try to understand more clearly the satanic workings of the world around . . . [them] and attempt, at least, to use . . . [their] gifts to elucidate its meaning and thereby contribute to a better future."[18]

During World War II Rosamond Gilder focused her criticism on an analysis of the effects—adverse and advantageous—of the war upon the theatre and conversely the effect of the theatre on the war and its wearied participants. She reminded her readers that "this war will not stay out of the theatre as others have." Yet as "comedy followed comedy," she did not accept the apparently inescapable conclusion that the theatre influenced the war only by providing "momentary escape from fear and care." She contended that the theatre was capable of affecting the war in much more positive ways, as a powerful propaganda weapon.

In the end, however, she tempered her enthusiasm for propaganda. Rather, the critic should encourage the theatre to be filled with action designed to affirm the dignity and nobility of man. (6) This statement translates into a sixth level of responsibility: a responsibility to take, whenever possible, the optimistic viewpoint, not in the spirit of naïveté with head buried in the sand but honestly to find, delineate, and affirm the good. Sylvie Drake's definition of the art of criticism as an act of construction, of discrimination, not of enmity, and Marilyn Stasio's fine essay on the theatre's "vital resources,"[19] are examples of positive, courageous, deeply thought and deeply felt expressions of affirmation.

In his book *Creativity in the Theatre* Dr. Philip Weissman speaks of the critic as lacking nurturing qualities. He points out that many renowned critics have been biologically childless and suggests that this barrenness may "extend from his personal to his artistic self."[20] Yet the articulated concerns of these women critics—the necessity to watch over the charge, to follow its progress, encourage its growth, remind it of its duty to others, and provide it with the best of all possible worlds—seem to be variations of nurturing behavior. Have learned feminine behavior patterns unconsciously influenced the viewpoint and writings of female critics? Ann Holmes, longstanding drama critic of the *Houston Chronicle*, would contend that women bring no special perspective to their work and that the job of reviewer demands sensitivity, not gender. We are certainly not yet ready to answer any of these questions about female or male critics; indeed we are just beginning to try to formulate ways of looking at critics and criticism.

The women's movement of the last decade has brought about a new consciousness and understanding of the problems feminine acculturation has created for female critics. For instance, part and parcel of the need to affirm is the need to affirm the self. As Linda Winer states, "I was raised to make people like me, to not make trouble, to please people, to make them more comfortable." Such admonitions are, of course, directly counter to the job of a critic. "It is irrelevant," she continues, "if they like you, yet it was a hard lesson for me to learn that my job was not a popularity contest and that professionally I must do all the things I was taught not to do in polite society." The affirmation of the self is made more difficult because men, not women, are the accepted authority figures; there is an ingrained trust in men's opinions that has given them the credibility edge. These realizations have made female critics, like all minorities, harder on themselves than on others. Women critics have often in fact so steeled themselves to a man's world that hearing another woman's voice in the theatre is a revelation. Linda Winer cites the Chicago production (not the television version) of Wendy Wasserstein's *An Uncommon Woman and Others:* "Listening to a woman's concerns as a woman really touched me."

Interestingly enough, most female critics, with the vocal exception of Linda Winer and Glenna Syse, do not acknowledge experiencing any difficulties in being a woman in the critical profession. Sylvie Drake feels women have always been more readily accepted in the arts. Ann Holmes points to her grants as evidence of the lack of discrimination she has experienced. Clara Hieronymus attributes any resentment toward her as due to a "southernism" (resistance to professional standards), not to her femininity. Rosamond Gilder states that she arrived on the scene after the vote had been won and as such never experienced male prejudice. And Claudia Cassidy suggests that being a woman had given her certain advantages.

Still one wonders whether women critics pay a higher price than men. Linda Winer suggests that pressures on a female critic's personal life are enormous. "We have the crazy schedule of a doctor always on call but not the excuse we are saving lives." In a traditional marriage the male critic's nightly absences are covered by the understanding wife and mother, but in a dual career marriage the strains of two competing careers, especially when the woman's demands so much time, can lead to collapse.

Although the price may be great, it is evidently not great enough to deter these women. They find their profession fascinating. "I am," says Sylvie Drake, "finding myself lately more and more interested in expressing what the critical process is to me." Claudia Cassidy points to the challenge of searching for the right chemical combination that would make a production perfect.[21] At the best of times Ann Holmes considers herself a creative artist when she succeeds in abstracting the performance into another form that will make almost as great an imprint as the production itself. Marilyn Stasio speaks of the fun of it all,[22] and Linda Winer of the continual excitement of knowing there is always so much more to learn, the factor that after all is what makes any job worthwhile. As she describes it: "We are performers with the typewriter, not parasites of the arts, but rather part of the process, part of the circle of performance." And what is more, she adds, "We are beginning to be admitted to the critical fraternity." The year 1979, for instance, saw two breakthroughs into this fraternity. Glenna Syse became the first woman critic (and the first critic outside the New York area except for Eliot Norton in Boston) to be on the nominating committee for the Tony Awards (five people who see everything on Broadway) during its thirty-three-year history. And Linda Winer was the first woman to be asked to participate for an entire week as a master critic at the National Critics Institute, Eugene O'Neill Theatre Center, Waterford, Connecticut.

Although women have traditionally found equality and advancement easier in the arts, this has primarily been as actresses who would seem to professionalize the emotionalism usually identified as female. Women critics, along with women playwrights and directors, have had to combat the stereotypes in order to practice the "masculine" intellectual skill of judging. Those women who have had the courage to open up the critical "fraternity" need to be studied and celebrated. This paper offers a start on that task.

"CASTING BY JULIET TAYLOR"

INTERVIEW BY HELEN KRICH CHINOY

As the credits flash by at the end of films like *Julia*, *The Turning Point*, *Close Encounters of the Third Kind*, *Interiors*, *An Unmarried Woman*, you may not notice the name of Juliet Taylor, but "Casting by Juliet Taylor" has become the hallmark of some of the best films made. Paul Mazursky praises her "off-beat ideas." Woody Allen says, "She towers over other casting directors. She is not just a packager or someone who moves bodies through; she is someone who is sensitive to the performers."

The job of casting director is one of those little-known tasks that is essential to making movies today. As an independent casting director, Juliet Taylor brings together actors, directors, screenwriters, and producers, often providing a link between those who work on stage and those in films. This histrionic matchmaking requires very special personal qualities and skills, ones Juliet Taylor has in abundance. In the following interview, she talks about her background, her work, and her own sense of herself as a woman in a special job.

I suppose that somewhere in me at the start there must have been the desire to be a performer because I get such vicarious pleasure out of working with actors in casting. At Smith College, however, I was interested in all aspects of theatre which I was given a chance to study. That's how Smith contributed to what I am doing now since there's no specific training or preparation for casting directors. I gained a sense of theatre and performance; my critical faculties were developed as well as my ability to read a script and interpret it appropriately, which is very important.

After graduating from Smith, I took a six-week secretarial course, and came to New York. I got my first job, as a receptionist for David Merrick, through someone who had gone to Smith. It makes a big difference, getting that first job. After all those years in school, I thought it was fine being in the world, earning ninety dollars a week, working six days a week. I felt I was fortunate to get a paying job in the theatre where it wasn't easy to find work. After six months a former Merrick casting director whom I had gotten to know asked me if I wanted to become a kind of secretary-apprentice in the office of Marion Dougherty to which she was moving. Marion Dougherty, who had been the biggest casting director for live television for a long time, was now so busy doing film casting that she was setting up her own company. She was interested in someone who wanted to learn about casting but would do the secretarial work as well. I took that job, and never left—I

Juliet Taylor was interviewed by Helen Krich Chinoy, December 1979. It was especially gratifying for Professor Chinoy to explore the career of casting director with her former Smith College student.

234

stayed longer than anyone else. I ended up inheriting Marion Dougherty's business just by hanging in for five years.

Marion Dougherty was a wonderful person to work for. Interestingly enough, at first I found her more exacting than a man would have been. In a way, I was quite intimidated at first. But as time went on, that changed.

She's one of those people who once she knows and trusts you is very generous. She would share with me what she was thinking and how she felt about different parts and different actors and directors. She would include me in the process and let me sit in on things. It was a small office. She was also very generous with credit. She would tell a director that a certain actor had been my idea. That's very rare. Most people don't do that. When she left New York, she essentially left me her business through an agreement we made. It was very nice.

I've thought a lot about whether being a casting director is a career that is particularly congenial for women. Marion used to say women did it because men couldn't make enough money in it. Women would accept the pathetic salaries that men would not. That is partially true, but not entirely because men are doing other jobs in theatre that aren't that lucrative. I think that some of the personality ingredients that are needed by casting directors tend to be associated with feminine qualities. To enjoy casting and to be good at it, you have to be interested in people. You spend an awful lot of time getting to know other people. They never get to know you really. It involves a lot of curiosity and patience. I think women tend to have more of these qualities than men.

I couldn't put my finger on just what attracted me to the work except that it was a way of becoming very emotionally involved in a project. You're not always talking about concrete things; you're talking about people and feelings about them. In casting you are working on this instinct about someone, a feeling about whether they are going to project a certain quality. You develop a close relationship with directors and actors. You give them a sense of bringing something to life. Casting requires other capabilities as well. We do a lot of negotiating. There are a couple of casting directors who won't do negotiating. The ones I can think of are women. Maybe they don't feel comfortable. But I enjoy that aspect. I don't really understand what it is to be a casting director unless you have to cast within a specific budget. Anyone can cast anything if you have enough money. You have to have a sense of what the finances are. I find that interesting and challenging.

Marion taught me that you can create an environment that makes everyone comfortable. Her office was in a cozy brownstone. It wasn't at all officey. This would make the director feel relaxed. Most important was what went on in the reception area. I think that everyone who is a casting director has usually started out as a secretary. It's the way you learn to be kind and friendly to the actors who are usually very nervous. You learn not to overbook the day so that people don't have to wait a long time.

What Marion did which was really innovative in casting was that she eliminated the "grocery list" style of casting using huge numbers of people. Everything became very personal. Only people who were specifically right came in. By not having that cattle-call feeling, you eliminate a lot of the tension. You explain the scene to the actor so well that he or she feels comfortable with it. You give them the most information they can possibly have before they go in so that they don't feel like pawns in a game. They don't feel so vulnerable and at a loss. They feel like it's a one-to-one situation. That's really important. I think it's the whole key.

Casting women—I don't know if I have cast enough women's pictures to speak about the problem, although I did cast *Julia, An Unmarried Woman,* and *The Turning Point.* I do enjoy casting good women's roles, but I don't get much opportunity to do that. You really don't, even now. Even when the women's roles are leads, so many of the supporting roles are not. It seems as if all the background characters are always men. You don't get that many opportunities to cast an interesting group of women. I'd enjoy doing that. What goes into the choice, I guess, is my own instinct about what certain kinds of women are. To a certain degree I feel that there are only certain kinds of images of women that are acceptable to American audiences. As their leading ladies or their men's love interest, they seem to prefer women who are kind of vulnerable. That is the difference between the women who star in films in Europe and those who star in films here. There is much less variety and much less strength in the women in films here. There is an image problem. I've several times come up against directors who say that some woman is too strong. That's the reality we work with. I don't know if that's something to criticize. I think our vision is somewhat limited.

A woman to be cast has to be very lovely looking and between the ages of twenty and thirty-five. A few who have proven themselves go on working but most just stop working by the time they get to be forty. Whereas the men over forty, if they are talented at all, are starring in every television series in America. That is when they become most valuable and get paid fortunes. For women there's no counterpart to that experience.

A picture I thought really captured the female experience was Claudia Weill's *Girlfriends.* It was a very low-budget film. I helped her sort of off the record. That's a film that never could have been made by a man. I've also worked for another woman director, Joan Silver. Each director—male or female—has a very different style. I think, however, that the women do have different ideas of sexuality. I think that they are a little bit more courageous in both the casting of men and of women, in terms of who they think is attractive. They are far less predictable in their choices.

Although most of my work is for films, I am a theatre person. I really enjoy theatre. I'm interested in new playwrights. I spend most of my time looking for actors in the theatre. All the new people are in the theatre. Once people get into films, they have already made it. Most successful film actors are stage-trained. You have to be because after you get by on whatever your personal charisma is that makes you magical and interesting on film, you have to have something to draw on. You have to have resources. Unless you're really an actor, you run out and the work becomes very thin. The only place you can learn is on the stage. The only film actor I can think of who didn't have any real stage background is Jack Nicholson. Not all actors who are talented on the stage have a big impact on film, but most do at some point in their careers. Very few good actors aren't personable on screen. But there are a few who aren't.

To young women who find casting an intriguing job, I'd say that it's a wide-open field. In New York now, there's more work than there are casting directors to do the job. The difficulty is getting training. There are very few casting directors to work for. Most of them can't afford to have more than one or two people working for them. Some people start as agents and switch to casting. Some start out at advertising agencies, casting commercials or soap operas. I'm glad I didn't have to do that. I think it warps your point of view.

For myself, I find working with so many different people and different points of view very interesting, really lots of fun. I like working independently . . . I have a two and a half-year-old son and a twelve-year-old stepchild. I try to balance my personal life and my business life. I close my office door after six P.M. My husband, Jim Walsh, who's a theatrical producer, and I share the household responsibilities and we have an old-fashioned Scottish nanny to help out. I'm glad my job doesn't require me to travel these days. In the future there might be other possibilities—production, etc., but right now my life is full and busy. I'm enjoying what I'm doing.

5

IMAGES

Theatre is an imagining of human life and relationships. A theatre event displays apparent experience in such a way that those who witness the event may have their beliefs about actual experience confirmed or challenged, or both. Theatre studies have only begun to explore the nature of image-making in performance, the relationship of theatre images to social reality, the difference between the stage image and the image embedded in literary text. But there is wide consensus that gender display in theatre, as in other arts and media, has a very powerful effect on the hearts and minds of a society. In *Gender Advertisements*, Erving Goffman "shares with contemporary feminists the felt conviction that beneath the surface of ordinary social behavior innumerable small murders of the mind and spirit take place daily," notes Vivian Gornick in her Introduction. Goffman demonstrates how images that forces dominating society have determined to be socially useful can stifle members of both sexes.

Indignation has been expressed more and more insistently in the past decade or so over what have been perceived as restrictive and inaccurate images of women, minorities, and other peoples who experience themselves as oppressed and second-class in American society. This perception is not new, but recently a great upswelling of voiced concern has brought the issue into light for research. Most theatre research efforts have been directed at identifying negative portraits, usually static concepts, in dramatic literature (woman as whore, woman as shrew, woman as passive). But this is only a beginning—the real research is ahead of us.

There is a preponderance of theatre that displays women as either whore or madonna, foils to male heroes or Beatrice to Dante, sex objects and confections (as in a pseudo-burlesque show even titled *Sugar Babies*), frivolous and not to be taken seriously. Even those women with strong characters must conform to patriarchal rule—Shakespeare's heroines, the Duchess of Malfi, Hedda, or even poor Nora who walks out with no place to go and must surely in actual life be destined for the paternalism of welfare. But those who would study the image of women in theatre should not be satisfied with this cataloguing or this single gender approach. We must look at male roles and various gender relationships to perceive the full implications of gender images for the society as a whole. For example, in pursuing gender study, not just looking for women, we can see that in much of American drama, especially the drama around the time of the Depression and the world wars, the males are themselves weak or absent (consider *Awake and Sing*). What are the social implications of this image to both sexes?

As we have only begun to ask the necessary questions in our pursuit of the meaning and implication of stage images, we cannot expect to find a vast body of research and analysis of the subject. Even an approach that should be a useful tool, such as semiotics, will take time because interpretation itself is influenced by the interpreter's own personal system for reading gender behavior. But clearly a rigorous approach to the study of gender and theatre is needed and has much of value to yield to us. We need research that considers the visual image/icon on stage as it is shaped by director/performer/designer: What gender values are being reinforced or created by the "stage picture" alone? We need more study of audience response to the apparent experience of the theatre event: How closely will they allow it to approximate their perception of actual experience and how much challenge will they allow? Is there a gender differentiation with respect to who really censors stage images that challenge socially institutionalized images?

These and other such questions arise as we give credence to this area of theatre study and as we begin to recognize the relationship of gender display to sex role socialization on the part of both men and women. Practitioners of the art of the theatre should be students of this topic because virtually every choice made in theatrical production is informed by and influences socially held notions about gender behavior. This chapter surveys some of the work done to date. It suggests some approaches that see the female character in action, in drama, rather than in a still image; it delineates aspects of the Black female in drama, shares Susan Glaspell's clever feminist twist on the male detective image, and explores the use of (and problems with) creative drama to wrestle with sex role stereotypes. In this chapter, then, we show some first efforts in this research direction, hoping others will be encouraged to pioneer.

LWJ

THE SECOND FACE OF THE IDOL:
WOMEN IN MELODRAMA

ROSEMARIE K. BANK

To a measure, scholarship in each generation sees within the phenomena it studies the image of itself. Thus, to the nineteenth- and early twentieth-century reader or critic, American melodrama presented female characters who epitomized the ideal woman of that period—chaste, virtuous, nurturer of home and family, charitable servant and defender of the weak and downtrodden, loving wife, sister, sweetheart, and mother, loyal friend, and the cornerstone of a stable, productive, and decent society. This image of women supported cherished preferences for certain kinds of female behavior, behavior which was rewarded by idolizing women as kinder-hearted and morally superior to men, albeit thereby more naïve and dependent, less rational and self-motivated, and unfit for the world of making and doing. This view of the women in nineteenth- and early twentieth-century stage melodrama can still be found in contemporary scholarship.

There are female characters in melodrama who confirm this interpretation, but scholars today, given the general social-intellectual climate, need not automatically dismiss the idea that the image of women in American melodrama has more than this one aspect to it, just as theatrical scholarship in the past two decades has revised the general notion that melodrama and popular theatre did not merit scholarly attention.[1] Though as yet little contemporary cultural history of nineteenth- and early twentieth-century drama has emerged, a gradual shift in the depiction of women in American melodrama in the decades after the Civil War has been identified, a shift toward action. Much of the earlier, more passive, portrait of female characters has been delineated by David Grimsted in *Melodrama Unveiled*[2] (although that work is not primarily concerned with the image of women in the American plays from 1800 to 1850 which it examines). From his analysis, however, a shift appears to exist in the later melodramas of the century and those of the early twentieth century. Twenty-one of these comprise the sample for this discussion.[3] Although the selection is partial and does not isolate all variables, it is suggestive and illuminates the thesis at issue, namely that the image of woman in American melodrama from the Civil War to World War I has two aspects or faces.

The traditional view of the melodramatic heroine, and the one shared by those who do not know the form well, is of a kind, charitable, virtuous woman in trouble, usually of the villain's devising. Accordingly, the heroine

Rosemarie K. Bank, Associate Professor of Theatre at Kent State University, Ohio, has published articles and reviews in *Theatre Journal*, *Nineteenth-Century Theatre Research*, *Theatre History Studies*, and many others.

is most frequently pictured wringing her hands in helpless frustration and anxiety, throwing herself desperately and impotently at the feet of a cold and indifferent villain, or tied to railroad tracks or a sawmill—the ultimate victim—to be rescued in the nick of time by a man. These pictures—virtually a poster concept of melodrama—are remembered because they are striking (precisely the reason why managers used them in their publicity in the first place), but the vision they present of women in American melodrama is, at best, a partial one.

The female characters in late nineteenth- and early twentieth-century American melodrama often play an active role. They determine their fates in three major ways: they work at jobs outside the home, they play an active role in solving the problems that beset them, and they define the moral climate within which the action takes place. For example, in the sample, almost half of the heroines work outside the home. Their employment ranges from working as maids and domestics,[4] telegraphers, entertainers, and teachers,[5] to those who own their own businesses.[6] In addition to heroines, many other female characters are employed, largely in menial capacities such as cooks, washerwomen, maids, and the like. The criterion is simple: those who need to work do so.

No concept of long-term careers for women exists in the melodramas of this period, to my knowledge, nor any sense of work for wages as pleasurable and desirable in and of itself. On the one hand, this view is socially realistic, since many of the labors performed by the female characters in melodrama who must work are neither pleasant nor fulfilling, while on the other hand, the goal for women in these plays is to be good wives and mothers, not to have careers. Accordingly, any employment which prepares women for or which does not conflict with these roles is an acceptable preliminary or stopgap activity. In short, when the female characters in these plays have no other means of support or cannot live on what their men provide, they are expected to support themselves and to do their jobs well—and they do. A number of women in American melodrama can say with their British sister May in *The Ticket-of-Leave Man* (1863), "I pay my way."[7]

In addition to employment, the majority of heroines in late nineteenth- and early twentieth-century melodrama play an active role in solving the problems that beset them, for this is an area which vitally concerns even those female characters who need not work. In the twenty-one sample plays, for example, the central plots of one quarter (six plays) are resolved partly or fully through the actions of the heroine or another female character. This proportion is significant because the action of almost half of the sample (nine plays) is resolved by secondary characters or without the help of any agent (for example, by the death of the villain from accident or natural causes). The hero resolves the central action partly or fully in the remaining six plays. When plots are resolved through the action of secondary agents in melodrama, those agents are frequently women, and when a central plot is resolved by *one* major agent acting alone, that agent is as likely to be the heroine as the hero. It is not uncharacteristic of these plays that it is the heroine Laura in Augustin Daly's *Under the Gaslight* (1867) who breaks out of a tool shed to untie a man from the railroad tracks seconds before the train rushes by (in response to which he remarks, incidentally, "And these are the women who ain't to have a vote!").[8]

The specific things the female characters in melodramas do to solve the problems that beset them give the lie to the traditional view of a submissive, unenterprising, or defenseless creature. Deeds range from the exposure of corruption, to bringing the police, to tying up the villain or untying the hero, and so on, for examples of female courage and inventiveness abound in these plays, even though the characters are in most respects conventional women of their times. Indeed, the picture of a heroine slapping the villain smartly across the cheek or telling him off in public is a salutary antidote to the posters of heroines as victims.

The female characters in late nineteenth- and early twentieth-century American melodrama define the moral climate within which the action of the play takes place. Ethically, the heroine has the same moral status in these plays as the hero. She is considered not only capable of making moral choices, she is expected to act upon those choices and to defend her right. Socially, women are viewed as predominantly domestic beings, yet within the context of their own times melodramas give great importance and status to female characters as full partners not only in the domestic arena, but also in the vital business of securing virtue and exposing vice in society as a whole.

Poetic justice, that is, the rewarding of virtue and the punishment of vice, or the statement that this ought to be the case, is the cardinal ethical tenet of melodrama. Punishment for villainy may include death or imprisonment, but in many cases the villain is simply exposed and sent away. The reward for virtue for both men and women in melodrama is not great fortune; it is the establishment of happy family life. This is the goal for which all virtuous characters strive and it is the most frequent reward for their labors at the end of a melodrama. That reward is a heavy weight upon women, however, for the didactic devices of melodrama stress over and over again that if the family fails society falls, and women are the family. It is no accident that so few of the heroines of melodrama have mothers, for life was perilous indeed, as the hero of Bartley Campbell's *My Partner* (1879) says, for the "poor gal 'as had no mother to guide her."[9]

If the image of women in late nineteenth- and early twentieth-century American melodrama is highly proscribed and conventional in domestic matters, there is, as I have suggested, yet a "second face" to the idol. The moral force of women as people in these plays is considerable, for the female characters more than any other define what is right and wrong in life. They are actively concerned with human values in the broad sense: they help the poor, aged, sick, and helpless, often at great personal expense and risk; they are tolerant of frailty (even of their "fallen" sisters) and assist those who wish to reform; they are kind, loving, and hardworking when they or others are in need. What is more, the female characters in the melodrama of this period tell men what they ought to think and do morally, and the male characters—unless totally depraved—follow their advice. Such advice is easily overlooked in these plays because it tends to be expressed in the form of maxims, such as "Stick to your resolution to do right, and this funny old world that trampled you underfoot yesterday will receive you with open arms today."[10]

One may argue that such moral exertions—and they abound in all nineteenth-century melodrama—do not alter the course of the world, but these plays are, for the most part, concerned with a fairly intimate sphere, a world in which not even the male characters are involved with the "big issues." Within this sphere, personal moral questions *are the* questions, and it is significantly the female characters who give them utterance and definition. This image of women as moral forces in the world is, it would seem, a more positive picture than that shown by countless contemporary cinematic and televised melodramas in which female characters urge their male counterparts to do the wrong thing because it is safer, or in other ways give testimony to, seemingly, an innate inability to tell right from wrong much less to act when a moral imperative presents itself.

Thus far, I have suggested that the women in late nineteenth- and early twentieth-century American melodrama determine their fates by working for wages, by playing an active role in solving the problems that beset them, and by defining the moral climate within which the action of the play takes place. My objective in doing so has been to challenge the view of these characters as uniformly passive, helpless, naïve, irrational, and uninventive. Ethically and socially this case needs to be made so that we may gain a more accurate view of the depiction of women in literature and so discharge our obligations as social historians in our own times. Accordingly, there are many unasked questions to claim the attention of cultural historians in the coming years, such as, for example, the relationship of working heroines to employment patterns in American society, whether there really is a shift away from passivity in heroines' behaviors in melodrama after the Civil War, and, if so, is there a similar shift in the novel and popular fiction, and the tensions produced by the seemingly contradictory assertion that women are to be moral arbiters and yet may not participate in law or politics. The benefits of reading a play as a social document, as has been argued elsewhere,[11] are particularly evident for understanding the image of women which these plays project, and in relationship of that image to the sociocultural historical context out of which it grew.

There are also esthetic questions which must claim the major attention of theatre scholars because to conceive of the female characters of nineteenth-

and early twentieth-century melodrama, particularly of the heroine, as active affects our understanding of the structure of melodrama. The commonly accepted view of the action of melodrama envisions the hero and the villain in a tug-of-war for possession of the heroine or the heroine as a buffer between the hero and the villain. The tug-of-war concept is not supported by the facts. In this sample alone, for example, the villain has no designs upon the heroine's person or fortune in over half the plays. Further, there are a number of plays in which there is no readily identifiable villain, either because the villain and the hero are the same character or because the villain is something nonhuman, such as external circumstances or hard liquor. Though the triad appears in most melodramas of the period, then, it is not a structural necessity, since there are a number of melodramas both without villains, per se, and without a tug-of-war over the heroine.[12]

The concept of heroine as buffer[13] reflects an overemphasis upon the hero, which the action of many melodramas of the late nineteenth and early twentieth centuries does not appear to justify, for it is at least as frequently the case, if not more frequently, that action is centered on the heroine—what she does, what happens because of her, how she responds to actions initiated by others, and so forth. It is not, of course, wrong to see the hero as the central figure in the action when that is the case, but we ought not automatically assume that he is central. The male emphasis inherent in the concepts of tug-of-war and heroine as buffer slants the action of melodrama in the direction of sexual rivalry, whereas the central conflict actually appears to be ideological.

I have said here and elsewhere that poetic justice is the cardinal ethical tenet of melodrama, indeed that poetic justice is a structural necessity in melodrama (that is, that melodrama does not exist as a form without it). Since poetic justice is a statement about the world as it ought to be, the action of melodrama may actually reward virtue and punish vice, or simply establish the premise that this is the way things ought to be in the world. Given that the central conflict of melodrama is ideological, meaning, in this case, concerned with ethical matters, and given that this conflict is structural as well as ethical, then it follows that the character who is most involved with poetic justice is the character most central to the action of melodrama. I have stated that when an agent resolves the central conflict, that agent is as likely to be the heroine as the hero, and that the heroine is more likely than the hero to define the moral climate of the play. Given the close relationship between the ethical and the esthetic in nineteenth-century melodrama, then, the *active* heroine would be the character most likely to determine the structure of the play and to exemplify and express its cardinal ethical tenet. This is an orientation toward melodrama which defies the conventional picture of heroines and female characters as consistently submissive prizes in a male-oriented sex conflict, but it is an orientation which the data appear to justify.

Melodrama is a very cohesive form. Its dramatic and theatrical aspects are closely bound to ethical and social considerations. Nowhere is this clearer than in respect to the image of women in nineteenth- and early twentieth-century American melodrama, where structural interests lead to ethical considerations, the ethical to the social, and so forth. That we have seen only one face of the idol thus far is likely due to the general neglect of melodrama by scholars through most of this century, and to some critics it still seems a bizarre idea that anyone would devote the same analytical seriousness to the characters and action of a melodrama as to those of a comedy or a tragedy. Fortunately, this attitude has begun to change in the past fifteen years, and a more equitable and complete portrait of melodrama is emerging.

Less explicable is the constant neglect of melodrama as a data source by cultural historians who have freely turned to other popular American literary sources from the nineteenth century. Perhaps that attitude will also change as contemporary theatrical scholarship in the area increases and becomes available to other disciplines. Certainly, active intellectual cross-fertilization seems particularly appropriate in the areas of popular culture and the historical depiction of women. A significant piece of that picture, it seems to me, is the "second face" of the idol, a face which will define itself through studies more extensive than this summary essay, and which the present volume does so much to encourage.

WOMEN IN PULITZER PRIZE PLAYS, 1918-1949

JUDITH LOUISE STEPHENS

The rapid and continuous change which characterizes the twentieth century is reflected in the life of the American woman. Female characters in the literature of the century in turn reflect these many changes. Many books, articles, and scholarly studies have focused on the portrayal of women in American fiction. By comparison, few studies deal with women characters in American drama. Although there has been some critical examination of the women in the plays of a few of our leading playwrights, Eugene O'Neill, Tennessee Williams, Lillian Hellman, Rachel Crothers, and S. N. Behrman, a broader and more thorough analysis of women characters in a selected body of twentieth-century American drama is needed.

I selected the Pulitzer Prize plays for study because they offer a wide range of female characters in a variety of situations, and because they occupy a fascinating position in American dramatic history. The Pulitzer Prize plays

Judith Louise Stephens, Associate Professor of Theatre and Speech, Pennsylvania State University, Schuylkill Campus, wrote her Ph.D. dissertation on female characters in Pulitzer Prize plays, 1918-1975, at Kent State, and has published articles in *Theatre Journal* and *Theatre Annual*.

have been praised and maligned but seldom ignored.[1] Although controversy has surrounded the prizes, they have become a firmly entrenched
tradition.

This study covers the years of 1918 to 1949, from the first Pulitzer Prize for
drama awarded to Jesse Lynch Williams in 1918 for *Why Marry?* to the award
given to Arthur Miller for *Death of a Salesman* in 1949.

It seems appropriate that the first Pulitzer Prize for drama was awarded in
1918. This year begins the postwar era which is frequently chosen by
historians (as well as social and literary critics) to denote America's entry
into the modern period.[2] According to John Gassner, "it is one of the
commonplaces of contemporary American criticism that we have been in
possession of the best drama in the world since 1918."[3] Thus, the awarding
of the first Pulitzer Prize signals a new tradition in an American theatre
determined to break with the old. There are several reasons for terminating
this study after the decade of the forties: a span of those decades with
twenty-seven prize plays is sufficient in scope for one investigation; John
Hohenberg notes that after Columbia University President Nicholas Murray
Butler's retirement in 1946 "no succeeding president of Columbia University
sought to exercise the power that Nicholas Murray Butler has applied to the
granting of the Pulitzer Prizes"[4]; and the prize plays of the forties do include
the fresh new talent of playwrights such as Tennessee Williams, Thornton
Wilder, and Arthur Miller, whose works reflect some of the societal changes
brought about by World War II. In some of the chosen plays the female
character is the protagonist of the play; in others she is a central figure or she
is one whose action and presence figure most predominantly. This study
does not aim to compare the position of American women as seen in the
plays with the existing social conditions of each decade: it is not a sociological but a literary analysis. Each character was analyzed according to selected
dramatic criteria and critical reviews of the plays were examined with
particular emphasis given to commentary concerning the female characters.

The two specific aims of my study were: (1) to determine whether some of
the criticisms pertaining to the women characters found in American fiction
were valid when applied to female dramatic characters; and (2) to analyze
the central female characters in the Pulitzer Prize plays from 1918 to 1949
according to traditional dramatic criteria, noting what traits or characteristics were shared by those characters and what, if any, changes occurred over
each decade.

I identified four major characteristics of female fictional characters which
form a partial compendium of traits regularly assigned to women characters
based on conclusions reached by authors of books, articles, and dissertations who have explored modern literary female characters in some depth.
These characteristics are as follows:

1. *A preoccupation with love.* Most of the writers found that female fictional
characters are predominantly or exclusively concerned with love. Joanna

Russ, in an article entitled "What Can a Heroine Do?," found that women protagonists have been restricted to the confines of the "love story," which can have a number of variations such as falling in love, courtship, marriage, or the failure of courtship and marriage. Sample plots are:

How She Got Married. How She Did Not Get Married (always tragic). How She Fell in Love and Committed Adultery. How She Saved Her Marriage But Just Barely. How She Loved a Vile Seducer and Eloped. How She Loved a Vile Seducer, Eloped and Died in Childbirth. As far as literature is concerned, heroines are still restricted to one vice, one virtue and one occupation.[5]

After analyzing the women characters in five major Western authors, Simone de Beauvoir concluded that the woman is "required in every case to forget self and to love."[6] It seems that a woman character can be the protagonist of a love story but little else.

2. *Irrationality and emotionality.* June B. West studied the women characters appearing in the literature written between the two world wars and found that they were portrayed "as being slaves to their emotional natures."[7] Similarly, Katherine Rogers found, in all but the early novels of Sinclair Lewis, "the assumption that it is absurd for women to compete with men professionally, since they lack the necessary mental equipment—judgment, common sense, rationality."[8]

3. *Selfishness or selflessness.* The Eve-Mary Syndrome, or the prostitute-Madonna complex, is a phrase used to describe a certain dichotomy found in female literary characters. It refers to the tendency of writers to portray women as being one of two extremes: either extremely selfish (Eve) or extremely selfless (Mary), either a demon or an angel. Leslie Fiedler notes that the women in American novels are traditionally "bifurcated into Fair Virgin and Dark Lady, the glorious phantom at the mouth of the cave, and the hideous Moor who lurks within."[9] Judith Montgomery documents the favorable presentation of the dependent, selfless heroine in the works of Nathaniel Hawthorne, Henry James, and Edith Wharton. Montgomery places the demise of such heroines between 1900 and 1920, which marks the emergence of the bitter, destructive heroines of more modern times.[10]

4. *Passivity.* Mary Anne Ferguson documents the persistence of the submissive wife as a literary type. She cites examples ranging from Griselde in Chaucer's *Canterbury Tales* to the women characters of such modern writers as D. H. Lawrence, Dorothy Parker, and Sherwood Anderson.[11] Carolyn Heilbrun asserts that especially after the thirties, women characters tended to become only an event in the life of a man. She quotes a contemporary novelist as saying, "What do you do with women characters, except have the men characters make love to them? Then either they marry them or they don't."[12] It appears that women characters are commonly presented in the form of "being" rather than "doing."

I integrated these four characteristics with four traditional dramatic criteria for character analysis. These criteria are a character's basic motivation, the deliberation the character engages in, the decision that a character makes (or fails to make), and the action that the character performs.[13] A character's *motivation* is her basic goal or desire. It is what she wants above all else. It is the driving force, the underlying reason for decisions and actions. A character's *deliberation* is a mental process which involves a weighing of alternatives—a considering of different courses of action and their possible consequences. A character's *decision*, then, is the choice she makes. A character's *action* is the actual deed she performs as a result of her decision. Through performing this act she may or may not reach her initial goal. These aspects of character analysis were applied to each character by asking the following questions:

Motivation: What is it that the character most strongly desires? Does her goal or desire remain consistent throughout the play?

Deliberation: Is the character shown in the process of deliberation? If not, are periods of deliberation on her part referred to in the text? Is her deliberation exclusively of an ethical nature (based on moral values) or an expedient nature (based on practical considerations and individual desires)?

Decision: What is the nature of the character's decision? Are her decisions predominantly ethical or expedient? Is the character portrayed as extremely selfish or selfless through her decisions?

Action: Does the character carry her decision into action? What is the nature of that action? Is the action physical or verbal?

These four criteria of motivation, deliberation, decision, and action are related to each of the four major characteristics of fictional characters. In examining the *motivation* of each character, I can discover if she is predominantly concerned with romantic love. Irrationality-Emotionality can be related to *deliberation*. If a character is shown in the process of deliberation, she is not portrayed as a totally irrational being; even if her deliberation is only referred to in the dialogue, there is still some indication of a thoughtful, mental process. The Eve-Mary Syndrome, or a character's tendency toward either extreme selfishness or selflessness, can be related to the dramatic characters through an examination of their *deliberation and resulting decisions*. If a character engages in expedient deliberation, she is considering a way or a means of obtaining her goal. If she engages in ethical deliberation, she is considering her actions in the light of moral or ethical standards, and thus is not considered selfish. I examine women characters to see if they engage exclusively in ethical or expedient deliberation and if their resulting decisions indicate a consistent selfish disregard for others or an attitude of self-abnegation. Finally, passivity can be related to *action*. If a character's decision results in her taking an action of some sort, she cannot be thought of as a "passive" agent; if her action results from her own decision, which in turn was reached through her deliberation, the character will most likely be seen as one with power and force. This approach provides a basis from which the traits of female dramatic characters can be compared with those found in fictional characters.

This analysis is applied to twenty-eight female dramatic characters in the Pulitzer plays. From the first decade (1918–29), the characters are: Helen in Jesse Lynch Williams's *Why Marry?*, Ruth Atkins in Eugene O'Neill's *Beyond the Horizon*, Lulu in *Miss Lulu Bett*, Anna in Eugene O'Neill's *Anna Christie*, Jane Crosby in Owen Davis's *Icebound*, Jude Lowry in Hatcher Hughes's *Hell-Bent fer Heaven*, Amy in Sidney Howard's *They Knew What They Wanted*, Harriet Craig in George Kelly's *Craig's Wife*, Goldie McAllister in Paul Green's *In Abraham's· Bosom*, Nina Leeds in O'Neill's *Strange Interlude* and Rose Maurrant in Elmer Rice's *Street Scene*.

From the second decade (1930–39): Elsa Stanhope in Susan Glaspell's *Alison's House*, Mary Turner Wintergreen in Kaufman and Ryskind's *Of Thee I Sing*, Bus Nielson in Maxwell Anderson's *Both Your Houses*, Laura Hudson in Sidney Kingsley's *Men in White*, Charlotte Lovell in Zoe Akins's *The Old Maid*, Irene in Robert E. Sherwood's *Idiot's Delight*, Alice Sycamore in Hart and Kaufman's *You Can't Take It with You*, Emily Webb in Thornton Wilder's *Our Town*, Mary Todd Lincoln in Robert E. Sherwood's *Abe Lincoln in Illinois*.

From the third decade (1940–49): Kitty Duval in William Saroyan's *The Time of Your Life*, Miranda Valkonen in Robert E. Sherwood's *There Shall Be No Night*, Mrs. Antrobus and Sabina in Thornton Wilder's *The Skin of Our Teeth*, Veta Louise in Mary Coyle Chase's *Harvey*, Mary Matthews in Howard Lindsay and Russel Crouse's *State of the Union*, Blanche Dubois in Tennessee Williams's *A Streetcar Named Desire*, and Linda Loman in Arthur Miller's *Death of a Salesman*.

First, I compared the female dramatic characters with the four general traits of female literary characters and concluded that a *preoccupation with love* is the most common characteristic among the characters. Of the twenty-eight analyzed, all except Bus, a secondary character in *Both Your Houses*, were involved, to some extent, in a love story. Of the remaining twenty-seven, fourteen were primarily motivated by love. That is, they were making decisions and acting primarily on the basis of love. Out of these fourteen, eight were primarily motivated by romantic love. These eight are: Helen in *Why Marry?*, Ruth in *Beyond the Horizon*, Jane in *Icebound*, Jude in *Hell-Bent fer Heaven*, Goldie in *In Abraham's Bosom*, Laura in *Men in White*, Mary Wintergreen in *Of Thee I Sing*, and Alice in *You Can't Take It with You*. The remaining six of these fourteen characters were primarily motivated by love of their husband and/or family. These six are Charlotte in *The Old Maid*, Mrs. Antrobus in *The Skin of Our Teeth*, Miranda in *There Shall Be No Night*, Veta Louise in *Harvey*, Mary Matthews in *State of the Union*, and Linda in *Death of a Salesman*.

Although not fundamentally motivated by love, four of the remaining thirteen characters find their ultimate goal or are "saved" through love and marriage. These four are Anna in *Anna Christie*, Lulu in *Miss Lulu Bett*, Amy in *They Knew What They Wanted* and Kitty in *The Time of Your Life*. Also, two characters actively seek their goal in life through love or marriage. These two women are Harriet Craig in *Craig's Wife* and Nina Leeds in *Strange Interlude*. Neither woman is successful in her search but neither ever considers the possibility of pursuing any other course.

The seven remaining characters are not primarily involved in a love story; however, each of these seven women is in some way involved with love during the course of the play. These seven are Rose in *Street Scene*, Elsa in *Alison's House*, Irene in *Idiot's Delight*, Emily in *Our Town*, Mary Todd Lincoln in *Abe Lincoln in Illinois*, Sabina in *The Skin of Our Teeth*, and Blanche in *A Streetcar Named Desire*. For these seven women love is shown as a part of their life but does not play as predominant a role as it does with the women mentioned earlier.

All but one of the female characters in this study, irrespective of status or role, were involved, to some extent, in a love story. For most of these characters, the story focused on their success or failure in love or marriage. Thus, the contention that female literary characters are preoccupied with love is also true for most of the female dramatic characters in the Pulitzer Prize plays, 1918 to 1949.

Although most of the women in this study could not be called totally *irrational and emotional beings*, certain conclusions can be drawn from the analysis. Fourteen of the twenty-eight characters are significantly developed on the level of deliberation, or are clearly shown engaging in deliberation. But by itself, deliberation is *not* an accurate measurement of a character's irrationality or emotionality. Even though some characters are shown in scenes of thoughtful deliberation, three of them—Blanche, Sabina, and Mary Todd Lincoln—are portrayed primarily as highly emotional characters. All three engage in deliberation, and Sabina is a very emotional character; Mary Todd Lincoln and Blanche are both studies of mental decay.

Sixteen of the twenty-eight characters engage in highly emotional scenes. That is, they are shown crying hysterically, sobbing incoherently, or in some respect losing control of their emotions. Thus, the conclusion that women tend to be portrayed as emotional rather than rational beings holds true for the majority of the female dramatic characters in the Pulitzer Prize plays from 1918 to 1949.

Of the twenty-eight characters, only nine were found to suffer from the Eve-Mary Syndrome. Harriet in Kelly's *Craig's Wife*, Laura in Kingsley's *Men in White*, Sabina in Wilder's *The Skin of Our Teeth*, and Blanche in Williams's *A Streetcar Named Desire* were essentially selfish characters while Goldie in Green's *In Abraham's Bosom*, Charlotte in Akins's *The Old Maid*, Kitty in Saroyan's *The Time of Your Life*, Mrs. Antrobus in Wilder's *The Skin of Our Teeth*, and Linda in Miller's *Death of a Salesman* can be seen as selfless. However, we should note that Charlotte, Mrs. Antrobus, and Linda exhibit a brand of selflessness on which they seem to thrive; they lose self-identity but at the same time seem to take on an awesome and pervading power which becomes both a nurturing and destructive force. Nineteen were more complex than the terms "selfish" or "selfless" would indicate. Therefore, the contention that female characters are usually portrayed as either extremely selfish or selfless beings does not hold true for the majority of characters analyzed in this study.

Most of the characters in this study are physically passive. Out of the twenty-eight only two women—Rose of *Street Scene* and Veta of *Harvey*—complete a physical action which is a result of their own decision and which is not supportive of a male protagonist's more crucial action. The rest of the characters either perform their major action only verbally, or begin an action which is left uncompleted or unfulfilled, or perform an action which is in an auxiliary position to the male's. Thus, the female dramatic characters can be seen as passive when qualified in this respect.

In considering the four literary traits, then, the female dramatic characters conform to one on an unqualified basis: most tend to be preoccupied with love. The characters conform to two of the traits on a qualified basis: most tend to be emotional but not necessarily irrational, and most are, in certain respects, passive. Although there are some examples of the Eve-Mary Syndrome, the female dramatic characters do not tend to conform to this one trait. So, in these ways the female dramatic characters generally conform to three of the four traits which impose limitations on female literary characters.

In comparing the women characters in one decade to the others, it appears that the women in the plays of the first decade (1918–29) possess a stability, independence, and strength not generally found in the later decades. Out of the eleven plays studied for the first decade, all but three have a female protagonist. In contrast to this, the Pulitzer Prize-winning plays of the 1930's include one drama in which no female characters play a significant part. Out of the nine plays analyzed for that decade, only three characters can possibly be considered protagonists. During the 1940's a female protagonist is even more rare: among the seven Pulitzer plays, only one character, Blanche in *A Streetcar Named Desire*, can be considered the protagonist.

The most popular occupation of the women characters is that of wife or mother or both. In the decade of the forties a female character was more likely to be portrayed as a wife or mother than in the other decades. One character in each decade was portrayed in the role of a prostitute or mistress: they are Anna Christie in O'Neill's *Anna Christie* (the twenties), Irene in Sherwood's *Idiot's Delight* (the thirties), and Kitty Duval in Saroyan's *The Time of Your Life* (the forties).

Of the twenty-eight characters, ten are portrayed as having an occupation outside that of wife or mother. Only two of these ten work in a profession: Helen, a laboratory assistant in *Why Marry?* (1918) and Blanche, who had been a high-school English teacher, in *A Streetcar Named Desire* (1948). Three of the ten women are domestic workers or maids: Jane in Davis's *Icebound*,

Lulu in Gale's *Miss Lulu Bett* (the twenties), and Sabina in Wilder's *The Skin of Our Teeth* (the forties). Alice in Hart and Kaufman's *You Can't Take It with You*, Bus in Anderson's *Both Your Houses*, and Mary in Kaufman and Rys- kind's *Of Thee I Sing*, all of the thirties, are secretaries. Rose in Rice's *Street Scene* works in a real-estate office and Charlotte in Akins's *The Old Maid* of the thirties runs a day nursery for indigent children. Amy in Howard's *They Knew What They Wanted* of the twenties had worked as a waitress. In tabulat- ing the number of women working at an occupation other than that of wife, mother, or prostitute, we find that five out of eleven characters did so in the twenties and four out of nine characters did so in the thirties. In contrast, only two out of the eight characters analyzed from the forties would fit into this category: Sabina, the maid, and Blanche, who was a failure as a teacher.

Another change over the decades is that the characters of the thirties and the forties show less deliberation than those of the twenties. This decrease in deliberation might be related to the fact that fewer were protagonists of the plays. In any event, there was a marked decrease in the scenes of and references to deliberation for the female characters of the thirties and forties.

Probably the most obvious characteristic shared by all the female charac- ters is that except for Helen of the first decade and Blanche of the final decade, none of them was a professional person.

In overview, then, it seems that love for boyfriend, spouse, or family member is the most common motivation for the dramatic characters in the plays surveyed. The tendency to portray women as being primarily moti- vated by romantic love was most prevalent in the first decade. The tendency to portray the women as being primarily motivated by love of husband or family increased over the three decades. None of the characters analyzed from the forties is primarily motivated by romantic love but five out of eight of them are primarily motivated by a love for their husband or family.

The tendency to portray a female character working at an occupation other than that of wife, mother, or prostitute remained steady over the twenties and thirties but decreased during the forties. The tendency to portray a female character *successfully* working at a profession remained practically nonexistent for all three decades. The one exception is Helen, a laboratory assistant in the prize-winning play of 1918.

The majority of women are portrayed as emotional rather than rational beings. The female characters are most fully developed on the level of deliberation in the plays of the first decade. Scenes portraying women in the process of deliberation decreased in frequency during the thirties and for- ties.

The majority of women do not conform to the Eve-Mary Syndrome: that is, most are not primarily selfish or selfless individuals. However, there are nine characters who do conform to the syndrome. Since five of those nine were from the decade of the forties, it seems that the tendency to charac- terize women as being either selfish or selfless increased during this decade.

The majority of women are, in certain respects, passive on the level of physical action. Chances of the female character's having the status of protagonist tended to decrease after the first decade (1918–29). This suggests that the central female characters in the Pulitzer Prize plays, 1918–49, have generally received limited development, which accords with assumptions that women are primarily interested in love, are emotional, and are passive. I do not suggest that the playwrights have presented an inaccurate or false picture of women but only the repetition of a partial or limited picture. I do not suggest here that the use of love, as a character's main motivation, necessarily implies a repudiation of the playwright's creativity. But from this study I conclude that playwrights need to discover ways to express what women think and feel *other than* those thoughts and feelings centered on love, home, and family. They have long been accepted as part of a woman's life but they are not necessarily her whole life. I also conclude that the criteria of motivation, deliberation, decision, and action provide a workable basis for dramatic character analysis from both the traditional and feminist viewpoint.

THE WOMEN'S WORLD OF GLASPELL'S *TRIFLES*

KAREN F. STEIN

Susan Glaspell's murder mystery, *Trifles*,[1] explores sympathetically the lives of middle-aged, married, rural women, characters who would usually be minor figures in a play. In this way, *Trifles* (published in 1920) is a uniquely female and, indeed, feminist document.

Two New England farm women gather some personal belongings for Minnie Wright, jailed on suspicion of her husband John's murder. Observing the details of daily life in the bleak Wright household, Mrs. Peters and Mrs. Hale deduce the events which led Mrs. Wright to hang her tyrannical husband. The lack of a telephone, the shabby furniture, the much-mended clothing, and a canary with a broken neck bear mute but telling witness to the harsh meanness and cruelty of John Wright. Considering Minnie her husband's victim (like her symbolic analogue, the strangled songbird), the women conspire to hide the evidence they discover.

Trifles is an anomaly in the murder mystery genre, which is predominantly a masculine tour de force. We are used to seeing the detective as an active hero, proving his skill and ruthlessness in a brilliant intellectual game. In the classic sleuth story, the detective is hired by a desperate victim, frequently a woman, to solve a problem through his expertise. The hero may incur risks in his investigation, but his willingness to do so is further proof of his courage and power. In solving the mystery, the detective demonstrates his shrewdness and acuity. His successful investigation is the piecing together of a difficult puzzle; his reward for success is a handsome fee, the admiration

Karen Stein, Associate Professor of English at the University of Rhode Island, has published in *Modern Drama, Black American Literature,* and elsewhere.

of all who have observed him, and frequently, the love of the woman who hired him. But he remains intriguingly aloof, uncommitted.

The scenario of *Trifles*, however, is quite different. Here, the detectives are the very women that the powerful police, sheriffs, and detectives see as trivial, even ludicrous. Two middle-aged married women, lacking all glamour, they unravel the mystery from positions of weakness, not strength. Furthermore, as we will see, they utilize their intrinsic "femaleness," their triviality in the eyes of men, their concern with the minutiae of women's lives, to solve the mystery. What is most unusual, however, is that they do not remain objective observers; they become personally involved, and, through their successful investigations they gain human sympathy and valuable insights into their own lives. This growth, rather than the sleuthing process, is the play's focal point.

The women themselves are "trifles" to the busy, efficient men who leave them behind to tidy up while they (the men) investigate the murder of John Wright, searching upstairs in the bedroom for clues to the motive. The county attorney, intent on finding physical evidence, fails to pursue two references to Wright's meanness. But, as the women attend to the trifling details of packing clothes and cleaning up the kitchen, they observe carefully and come to understand the mystery of the missing motive. The clues are a strangled canary and the irregular stitching, indicative of tension, in a piece of patchwork Mrs. Wright was sewing. Thus, while the men search for—and fail to find—external signs such as forced entry into the house, their wives interpret the emotional significance of small details, learning of the narrowness of Minnie's life, her frustration, and her anger.

Interpreted similarly in its social and psychological contexts, the patchwork process becomes an objective correlative for the lives of these New England matrons. The patchwork quilt, composed of remnant fabric scraps and salvaged bits of old garments, is a uniquely American solution to the dilemma of keeping warm in an economy of scarcity before the introduction of central heating. Patchwork is a task demanding patient and painstaking attention to repetitive, minute details: a quilt may contain as many as 30,000 pieces, each one-half inch by three-quarters of an inch in size.[2] To women, in their homemaking role, went the task of hoarding the fabric scraps and stitching them into quilts. Girls were set to sewing samplers and quilt squares as soon as they were old enough to hold needles; they were expected to busy themselves with needlework whenever they had no more urgent chores. Through this apprenticeship, girls were trained in the docility and discipline which society values in its women. At the same time, the apprenticeship in quilting and other household tasks in a society with sharp gender-role differentiation bound women of a household together. Networks of female friendship and mutual assistance were central in the lives of eighteenth- and nineteenth-century women.[3]

Quilts were made primarily for their utility, but they also offered an outlet for creativity that often had no other available channel of expression. For the many women who had no knowledge of reading and writing, and who could not have spent their time in such nonproductive activities, patchwork became a means of artistic self-expression. In the quilt patterns and the names for them that their makers devised, women told the stories of their lives. Such names as "Baby's Blocks," "Log Cabin," "Corn and Beans," "Covered Wagon Trail," "Underground Railroad," and "Union Star" give us an insight into the daily routines and political sentiment of their creators.

The patchwork squares are pieced together in solitude, often in between and after the completion of the round of chores which was women's lot. The quilting itself, however, the joining of the patterned patchwork upper layer to the lining and the backing, was done in a communal setting, the quilting bee. Groups of women, friends and skilled seamstresses, would gather around the quilting frame to cooperate in the tedious task of quilting. The quilting bee was one of the main social events for women whose daily lives kept them isolated from each other. For many years, we have thought of the quilting bee as an occasion for idle gossip. But, we are gradually learning to understand and appreciate the importance of these parties as vehicles for sharing knowledge and camaraderie, for developing and strengthening social support groups, and for accomplishing a difficult job effectively.

Quiltmaking brought neighbors and friends together in a holiday spirit to cooperate in the production of useful and beautiful artifacts. In *Trifles*, as Mrs. Wright's neighbors view the separate fragments of the incomplete quilt, the mood is not festive but funereal. They have come not to join in the warm and social act of creation, but to clean up the debris of destruction. Through the sympathetic eyes of her neighbors, we are made to see the frustration of all Mrs. Wright's hopes for beauty, order, and happiness.

Observing the bits of evidence, a strangled bird which John Wright must have killed, the tight stitching which was the woman's reined-in response to this act of wanton cruelty, the women become poignantly aware of the emotional poverty of their neighbor's life. We feel with them her thwarted needs for song and companionship. Mrs. Hale reflects, "Wright wouldn't like the bird–a thing that sang. She used to sing. He killed that, too." Through the women's identification with her, we understand Minnie's desperate loneliness which drove her to do away with her brutal husband.

> MRS. HALE
> If there'd been years and years of nothing, then a bird to sing to you, it would be awful—still, after the bird was. Still.
> MRS. PETERS
> I know what stillness is. When we homesteaded in Dakota, and my first baby died—after he was two years old, and me with no other then—

Out of their sympathy for Mrs. Wright as a woman they perceive to be more sinned against than sinning, the neighbors conceal their discovery of the motive from the male investigators. After ripping out the uneven stitches and removing the strangled canary, they respond with terse irony to the county attorney's patronizing question about Mrs. Wright's quilting, "We call it—knot it, Mr. Henderson."

In their decision to conceal the evidence, the women in *Trifles* affirm their ties of loyalty and affection to other women. Mrs. Hale laments her guilt in letting this communality lapse: "Oh, I *wish* I'd come here once in a while! That was a crime! That was a crime! Who's going to punish that?" The need for cooperation is manifested throughout the play, in the references to shared tasks such as quiltmaking, and in their remarks about their own needs for companionship. In fact, the discovery and interpretation of the clues and the suppression of the findings is a shared process, diametrically opposite to the solo virtuosity usually displayed by male detectives. Further emphasis on the mutual understanding and aid women offer each other was inherent in Glaspell's title for the short story from which she derived this play, "A Jury of Her Peers." The women here realize, through their involvement in the murder investigation, that only by joining together can they, isolated and insignificant in their society, obtain for themselves and extend to others the support and sympathy that will help them endure the loneliness and unceasing labor required of them. For these women, solving the murder is not a disinterested act, but a cooperative endeavor which leads them to a knowledge essential for their survival as females in a hostile or indifferent world.

BLACK WOMEN IN PLAYS BY BLACK PLAYWRIGHTS

JEANNE-MARIE A. MILLER

In 1933, in an essay entitled "Negro Character as Seen by White Authors," the brilliant scholar-critic Sterling A. Brown wrote that Blacks had met with as great injustice in the literature of America as they had in the life of their country. In American literature, then, including the drama, Blacks have been depicted most often as negative stereotypes: the contented slave, the wretched freeman, the comic Negro, the brute Negro, the tragic mulatto, the local color Negro, and exotic primitive.[1] Black female characters have been scarce in only one of these categories—the brute Negro. They have been most plentiful as the faithful servant. In American drama, where, seemingly, many more roles have been written for men than women, Black or white, it is the Black female character who has faced double discrimination—that of sex and race.

Jeanne-Marie A. Miller, Professor of Theatre at Howard University, published "Images of Black Women in Plays by Black Playwrights," *College Language Association Journal*, vol. 20 (June 1977), 494–597, from which this excerpt is reprinted by permission of the *Journal*.

As early as the nineteenth century Black women were written about by playwrights of their own race. Melinda, in William Wells Brown's *The Escape*, for example, is a mulatto who is not tragic,[2] and Rachel, in Angelina Grimke's early twentieth-century play of the same name, is a young, educated middle-class Black woman who protests against the indignities suffered by her race.[3] Though there were many plays written by Blacks after the dawn of the twentieth century, the Civil Rights movement of the 1950's and the Black consciousness movement of the 1960's produced many new Black playwrights who brought to the stage their intimate inside visions of Black life and the roles that Black women play in it.

Alice Childress, a veteran actress, director, and playwright, in several published plays, has placed a Black woman at the center. Childress noted early that Black women had been absent as an important subject in popular American drama except as an "empty and decharacterized faithful servant."[4]

Childress's *Florence*, a short one-act play, is set in a railroad station waiting room in a very small town in the South.[5] The time of the play is the recent past. Emphasized is the misunderstanding by whites of Blacks, brought on by prejudice and laws that keep the two races apart. The rail separating the two races in the station is symbolic.

In the station a Black woman of little means, with a cardboard suitcase and her lunch in a shoebox, has a chance meeting with a white woman also bound for New York. In the conversation that takes place between them, the prejudices of the whites and their myths about Blacks are exposed, such as that of the tragic mulatto. Revealed also is the determination to keep Blacks in the places set aside for them by whites. Marge, the Black woman's daughter living at home, has accepted her place; Florence, the daughter seeking an acting career in New York, has not. Because of the revelations of the white woman, Florence's mother, en route originally to bring her daughter home and end her fumbling New York career, changes her mind and instead mails the travel money to Florence so that she can remain where she is. Thus, a docile-appearing Black woman, who stays in her place in the South, acts to help her child transcend the barriers placed there by those trying to circumscribe her existence.

Childress's two-act comedy *Trouble in Mind*, while concentrating on discrimination in the American theatre, also brings into focus the troublesome racial conditions in the United States of the 1950's.[6] The framework of *Trouble in Mind* is the rehearsal of the play "Chaos in Bellesville," a melodrama with an antilynching theme, in reality a white writer's distorted view of Blacks. The principal character, Wiletta Mayer, a middle-aged Black actress, a veteran of "colored" musicals, appears at first to have found a way to survive in the prejudiced world of the theatre. Coerced by the white director, however, she explodes and reveals her long pent-up frustrations. Specifically, Wiletta disagrees with the action of the character she is playing—a Black mother who sends her son out to be lynched by a mob seething with hatred because the Black man had tried to vote. Wiletta, alone among the play's interracial cast, demands script changes that will portray Black life realistically. Though she loses her job in the attempt, she in no way seems to regret the stand she has taken after a lifetime of acceptance.

In *Wine in the Wilderness*, Tommy Marie, a young Black woman from the ghetto, teaches real pride to her newly acquired middle-class acquaintances.[7] This play is set during the Black revolutionary period of the 1960's. It is one of those Harlem summers popularly described as long and hot. A riot is taking place outside the apartment of Bill, a Black artist currently engaged in painting a triptych entitled "Wine in the Wilderness"—three images of Black womanhood. Two canvases have been completed: one depicting innocent Black girlhood and the other, perfect Black womanhood, an African queen, this artist's statement on what a Black woman should be. The third canvas is empty because Bill has not found a suitable model for the lost Black woman, the leavings of society. Unknown to Tommy, she has been picked out by two of Bill's friends to serve as the model for that hopeless creature. At first sight Tommy is unpolished and untutored but is essentially a warm, likable human being. Once a live-in domestic and now a factory worker, at the present time she has been burned out and then locked out of her apartment as a result of the riot.

Later, dressed in an African throw cloth and with her cheap wig removed, Tommy undergoes a transformation as she overhears Bill, to whom she is attracted, describe his painting of the African queen. Believing that he is referring to her, she assumes the qualities he praises: "Regal . . . grand . . . magnificent, fantastic. . . ." For the first time she feels loved and admired. While Bill is trying to get into the mood to paint her, she recites the history of the Black Elks and the A.M.E. Zion Church, all part of her background. With her new look and the new knowledge he has gained about her, Bill cannot now paint Tommy as he had intended, for she no longer fits the image he sought.

The next day Oldtimer, a hanger-on, unthinkingly tells Tommy about the three-part painting and the unflattering role she was to play in it. She, in anger, teaches Bill and his middle-class friends about themselves—the hatred they have for "flesh and blood Blacks"—the masses, as if they, the others, have no problems. To the white racist, they are all "niggers" she tells them. But she has learned—she is "Wine in the Wilderness," "a woman that's a real one and a good one," not one on canvas that cannot talk back. The real thing is inside, she states.

Bill changes the thrust of his painting. Oldtimer—"the guy who was here before there were scholarships and grants and stuff like that, the guy they kept outta the schools, the man the factories wouldn't hire, the union wouldn't let him join . . ."—becomes one part of the painting; Bill's two friends—"Young Man and Woman workin' together to do our thing"—

become another. Tommy, the model for the center canvas, is "Wine in the Wilderness," who has come "through the biggest riot of all, . . . 'Slavery,'" and is still moving on against obstacles placed there by both whites and her own people. Bill's painting takes on flesh. Tommy has been the catalyst for change.

Unlike Childress's other plays, *Wedding Band* is set in an earlier period— South Carolina in 1918.[8] The central character, Julia Augustine, the Black woman around whom the story revolves, is an attractive woman in her thirties. A talented seamstress, she has only an eighth-grade education. The play opens on the tenth anniversary of her ill-fated love affair with Herman, a white baker who has a small shop. This illegal love affair is the theme of the play. In direct violation of South Carolina's laws against miscegenation, the pair has been meeting and loving clandestinely for years. On this day, in celebration of their anniversary, Herman gives Julia a wedding band on a thin chain to be worn around her neck. This day, too, is the first that Julia has spent in this impoverished neighborhood. She has moved often because her forbidden love affair has caused her to be ostracized by both Blacks and whites.

A series of encounters clearly delineates the kind of woman Julia really is. Though she is lonely between Herman's visits and sometimes allows wine to fill in the void, she is a woman of strength. She endures the criticism of her affair. She is unselfish, warm, and forgiving. With compassion she reads a letter to a new neighbor who cannot read. Unknown to her lover's mother, Julia sews and shops for her. When confronted by this woman who hates her and whose rigid racism drives her to exclaim that she would rather be dead than disgraced, Julia rises to her full strength and spews out the hatred that momentarily engulfs her. And even in her sorrow she is able to give a Black soldier a fitting send-off to the war and the promise that the world will be better for all Blacks after the war's termination. In the end, Julia forgives her weak, timid lover who is dying from influenza. He could never leave South Carolina for a region more suitable for their love and marriage, he explains, because he has to repay his mother the money she gave him for the bakery. In reality, history stands between Julia and Herman. South Carolina belongs to both of them, but together they could never openly share the state. The promised escape to the North and marriage never materialize. Julia stands at the end of a long line of Childress's strong Black women characters. In this backyard community setting of *Wedding Band* are other images of Black womanhood—the self-appointed representative of her race, the mother protecting her son from the dangers awaiting him in the white South, and the woman abused by a previous husband, waiting loyally for the return of her thoughtful and kind merchant marine lover.

The promising talent of the late Lorraine Hansberry was perhaps best displayed in the well-known *A Raisin in the Sun*, which portrays an interesting variety of female characters, none more so than Lena Younger, who has grandeur, strength, patience, courage, and heroic faith.[9] She is strong in the belief of her God who has sustained her throughout life. She mightily loves her family to whom she teaches self-respect, pride, and human dignity, protects them, sometimes meddles in their affairs, and does not always understand their needs and desires. Above all else, she wants a home for her family, a physical structure large enough to house them all comfortably. Acquiring this home would mean the realization of a long-deferred dream. She wants, too, to help Beneatha, her daughter, fulfill her dream of being a medical doctor. But the attitudes of the younger generation Lena sometimes does not fathom—Beneatha's toward religion and Walter's toward money which to him symbolizes success. The wise, sensitive woman that she is, Lena Younger realizes before it is too late that her son, in desperation, is reaching out to manhood at the age of thirty-five, and she helps him by making him the head of the household over which she has presided since the death of her husband. Theirs is a household of working-class people struggling to survive with dignity.

Beneatha, young, spoiled, spirited, and sensitive, has social pride. Her ideas about women's liberation and her interest in her African heritage were to burst in full force in the decade that followed the production of *A Raisin in the Sun*.

Ruth, Lena's daughter-in-law, a gentle woman, weary with life, loves her husband, who at first falsely blames her for his lack of materialistic success. She wants him to have that chance to be a man. In this household Ruth acts as a peacemaker between the generations.

A Raisin in the Sun is a drama of affirmation. Man's possibilities are manifold, and in this work this family, with the help of the women, changes its world, if only a little.

Like Childress, Hansberry turned to the past for materials for one of her plays. In *The Drinking Gourd*, a drama about slavery, written for television, one of the principal characters is Rissa, a cook who is also one of the more privileged slaves on Hiram Sweet's plantation.[10] On the surface, she is like the cherished, fictionalized image of the Black mammy who philosophically accepts her status, showers love and devotion on her white master and his family, forgives her white family of all wrongdoing, and hums or sings away all personal pain and sorrow. But unlike that unrealistic mammy, Rissa is concerned about her own family. To make life easier for her son Hannibal, she obtains a place for him in the Big House, only to have him refuse the favor. Slavery to him in any form is repulsive. After Hannibal is brutally blinded at the order of the plantation owner's son—for daring to learn to read—Rissa seeks vengeance for the crime. Though the fate is unknown of one son, Isaiah, who ran away from slavery, she assists blind Hannibal, his sweetheart Sarah, and Isaiah's son, Joshuah, in escaping from slavery to freedom. Moreover, for protection, she gives them a gun that she has stolen from Hiram Sweet's cabinet. Thus Rissa reverses the myth of the faithful, contented slave—faithful to her master and contented in her servitude. Unlike Carson McCullers's Berenice in *The Member of the Wedding*, who continues to care for her white charge while a mob seeks to murder one of her own family, Rissa rivets her attention on her son, while her white master, calling to her for help, dies outside her cabin. . . .

Unlike the majority of Black American playwrights, who use realism in dramatizing their ideas, Adrienne Kennedy, an avant-gardist, experiments with expressionism and surrealism. A poet of the theatre, she uses impressions and images rather than treat plot and character in a traditional manner. Despite the mode of treatment Kennedy draws her material from the Black experience. Her female character Sarah, in *Funnyhouse of a Negro*, is a young, tortured Black woman who has nightmarish agonies about being Black.[11] The action takes place on the last day of her life—before she commits suicide. The fantasy characters, all well-known historical figures—Queen Victoria, the Duchess of Hapsburg, Patrice Lumumba, and Jesus—represent the various selves of Sarah. In a monologue she reveals pertinent information about herself. The daughter of a light-skinned mother and a dark-skinned father, she spends some of her time writing poetry. She also spends time with a Jewish poet interested in Blacks. Because of guilt feelings about her treatment of her father, whose black skin she abhors, she imagines that she has killed him with an ebony mask and believes, at other times, that he committed suicide when Lumumba was murdered. After her own suicide, it is revealed by her Jewish lover that, in reality, Sarah's father is married to a white whore. The material possessions he has are those which Sarah herself craved—European antiques, photographs of Roman ruins, walls of books, Oriental carpets, and a white glass table on which he eats his meals. The pressures of being Black in America are the subject of this work. These pressures, in turn, have produced madness in this sensitive Black woman who has an identity problem as well as a problem with love, God, and parents.

In a second play by Kennedy, *The Owl Answers*, the racial identity problem is repeated.[12] The scenes, a New York subway, the Tower of London, a Harlem hotel room, and St. Peter's, are fantasies in the mind of the principal character, a Black woman named She Who Is. Her mother, a cook, was impregnated by a white man of English ancestry, who declared the child a bastard. But the child, now a woman, dreams about her white father's world. The English ancestors, whom she claims—Shakespeare, William the Conqueror, Chaucer, and Anne Boleyn—in rejecting her, jeer her. She cannot find her place in either the Black or white world.

Thus Black women in plays of many Black playwrights receive varied treatment, and their images, for the most part, are positive. The women often have great moral strength. In contrast to many of the white-authored dramas in which Black women have appeared, usually as servants dedicated to the families for whom they work, in the plays of Black writers, these women's concerns are for what interests them, mainly their own families. In many of these plays it is their lives that are on stage. In Black-authored dramas depicting ghetto lifestyles, Black women hold on to life, however harsh it may be, and sometimes work for a better future. In the dramas written by women, except in the plays of Kennedy, Black women often look to the future with optimism. Even Childress's Julia Augustine's plans for a move to the North with her lover terminate only with his death. In the plays written by Black males, Black women's happiness or "completeness" in life depends upon strong Black men. Thus Black playwrights bring to their works their vision, however different, of what Black women are or what they should be. Missing, however, is a wealth of dramas with positive images of Black middle-class women, Black middle-class women who work to improve the quality of life for themselves, their families, their race—the Mary McLeod Bethunes, the Mary Church Terrells, and the unsung Black women who help to improve the world, if only a little.

WHO PUT THE "TRAGIC" IN THE TRAGIC MULATTO?

WINONA L. FLETCHER

CROSS

My old man's a white old man
And my old mother's black.
If I ever cursed my white old man
I take my curses back.

If I ever cursed my black old mother
And wished she were in hell,
I'm sorry for that evil wish
And now I wish her well.

My old man died in a fine big house,
My ma died in a shack.
I wonder where I'm gonna die,
Being neither white nor black.
                    —Langston Hughes[1]

Nowhere is the spirit and tragedy of the mulatto captured with more poignancy than in this impassioned creation by Langston Hughes. The main

Winona L. Fletcher, Professor of Theatre/Drama and of Afro-American Studies at Indiana University since 1979, was in the prior twenty-five years Professor and Coordinator of Speech/Theatre at Kentucky State University, Frankfurt. She is currently researching the Negro wing of the Federal Theatre Project.

character of his poem, however, should by no means be misconstrued as "a figure of a poet's imagination." With or without public sanction or recognition, there exists in America a product of racial admixture known as the mulatto—in the flesh. This is no recent phenomenon since there is considerable evidence that "miscegenation doubtless took place from the first."[2] After the emancipation of slaves, the rate of increase among mulattoes accelerated more rapidly than among the darker members of the race, and the 1910 census revealed over 2 million persons who admitted belonging to this group.

It is generally known, however, that no census can reveal an accurate count of mulattoes, since the process of tracking down racial admixture is about as nebulous as the genetic phenomenon that permits one drop of Black blood to make a person "colored." It is difficult, if not impossible, to determine where Black leaves off and white begins or vice versa; yet we have become so obsessed with our attempts to make this distinction that long ago the question of color was catapulted into a national problem. This fact is the basic tragedy that underlies and permeates all the other "tragic" elements of the tragic mulatto. The myriad associations of "white" with right, might, and superiority and "Black" with backwardness and inferiority set the stage for the entrance of the tragic mulatto. Playwrights, both white and Black, have grappled with the theme of miscegenation for over a century and a half. This theme is directly responsible for establishing myths, stereotypes, and traditions both on and off stage—all of which have at one time or another been used, abused, refused, and manipulated by anybody who chose to do so.

Somewhere along the way there sprang upon the stage a convention that declared that the treatment of the mulatto must be sentimental, given to evocation of pity (and sometimes real fear); that the character must possess virtue and nobility; that the figure must be resigned to alienation from society and acceptance of a fate that results in shame for the possession of one drop of Black blood. Melodrama, the favorite of nineteenth-century playgoers, dictated the creation of this virtuous, noble, sentimental agent. The perfect real-life model for this dramatic character was the female mulatto slave. Already a victim of the white master, whose whims dictated her existence, her presence as his concubine aroused jealousy in the white woman, envy and hate in her darker sister, and despair in her own soul when she was prohibited by society from passing for white. She offered limitless dramatic possibilities. It was, therefore, generally agreed that the thus created "tragic mulatto" should be female although there are notable exceptions to this last mandate.

Harriet Beecher Stowe is credited with establishing the tragic mulatto prototype in her creation of Eliza (*Uncle Tom's Cabin*, 1852). The image of the fair-skinned mother clutching her young child as she frantically jumped the ice floes to freedom is one of the few pieces of "Black history" recognizable by most Americans. But Stowe is not wholly responsible for putting the "tragic" in the tragic mulatto—as researching and soul-searching reveal. While Stowe's infamous Black Uncle Tom overshadowed all other prototypes in the dramatization of her novel by George Aiken, the mulatto archetype remained popular throughout the Civil War and Reconstruction periods. Dion Boucicault discovered the figure and granted her a seat of dramatic prominence in his popular nineteenth-century drama, *The Octoroon* (1859). *The Octoroon* is a melodramatic treatment of a much beloved female whose discovery of her Black blood foils her plans to marry the white man she loves, and in one version of the play, leads her to sacrificially take her own life.

Other nineteenth-century white playwrights were captivated by the tragic mulatto (octoroon, quadroon) also: John T. Trowbridge, *Neighbor Jackwood* (1857); Charles Barton Hill, *Magnolia* (1862); Bartley Campbell, *The White Slave* (1882); Margaret Smith, *Captain Herne, U.S.A.* (1893). Nearly all romanticized the physically beautiful, near-white girl and her struggle for equality and understanding. In *Neighbor Jackwood*, for instance, the beautiful Camille, runaway slave, so white that her New England neighbors are unaware of her Black past, remembers:

CAMILLE:
To be a thing, a chattel, a slave—then to feel for the first time that I can call myself a woman, and in such an hour to find . . . Oh this is the beginning of life.

As late as the first decade of the twentieth century, Edward Shelton was keeping the tradition alive with *The Nigger* (or *The Governor*, 1909). The hero of this drama possesses a drop of Black blood that is so infinitesimal that he fooled even himself and would have spent his entire life "passing" had not his Black genealogy been revealed for political reasons. This unfortunate revelation instantly reverses his life and sets him on the new tragic course of the mulatto.

Despite society's attempts to check miscegenation by statute, playwrights continued to deal with the theme—more frequently with the process (miscegenation) than with the product (the mulatto). Plots more believable than the action of *The Nigger* were attempted by such major playwrights as Eugene O'Neill, *All God's Chillun Got Wings* (1924), in the twenties and on through the next decades to the sixties when Howard Sackler permitted Black Jack Johnson to flaunt his sexual habits with his white woman on stage and screen in *The Great White Hope* (1968).

Black playwrights have not been silent on this theme either. Editors James Hatch and Ted Shine seem to think that "miscegenation is the one theme on which both Black and white playwrights have always agreed: 'mixing is bad.' "[3] The point of view differs, but the product usually remains tragic, and the participants in the process are forced to accept the poetic justice meted out in the form of punishment or reward for the "sin."

William Wells Brown, Black contemporary of Mrs. Stowe, led his mulatto heroine through melodramatic, if not tragic, ordeals of resisting her white master before permitting her to escape to Canada with her Black husband. Melinda is permitted to preserve her virtue, at least, since as a tragic mulatto she could not preserve her racial purity:

MELINDA
Sir, I am your slave; you can do as you please with the avails of my labor, but you shall never tempt me to swerve from the paths of virtue.
—*The Escape: or A Leap For Freedom* (1858) Scene 5

Brown also permits his white antagonist to chuckle over his guest's mistaking of a servant child as the master's and replies, "If you did call him my son, you didn't miss it much. Ha, ha, ha!" (Scene 3).

Events in society and in the theatre conspired to keep the Black playwright's pen inactive during the sixty-odd years following Brown, and the real-life female mulatto joined the song and dance routines and found fame as a "high yeller" chorus girl helping to paint the picture of the "exotic Negro." Then, in the twenties, some Black writers rejected the exotic image and chose to use the stage for race propaganda. The mulatto shed another tragic tear.

In 1926, Black playwright Myrtle Smith Livingston used a Black man and a white woman as chief figures in *For Unborn Children*. Her treatment of character and point of view were different from O'Neill's 1924 approach, but there would be no difference in the resultant product. In Livingston's drama the Black hero rejects all family pleas:

GRANDMA CARLSON
Before we can gain that perfect freedom to which we have every right, we've got to prove that we're better than they! And we can't do it when our men place white women above their own!

MARION (sister)
Stay with your own race if it's color you want—we have women who are as white as any white person could be—My God! What is to become of us when our own men throw us down?
—*For Unborn Children*[4]

Leroy defies all customs and laws in his determination to marry his white beloved one, but oddly enough, makes the supreme sacrifice to give her up when he is told that he is himself a tragic mulatto. As he walks out into the threatening screams of the lynch mob, he consoles his grandmother with the words:

LEROY
Don't grieve so; just think of it as a sacrifice for UNBORN CHILDREN.

Livingston felt it was tragic for a Black man to marry outside his race, especially while he was still trying to prove his equality. The paradoxical nature of all of this compounds the tragedy which pervades the mulatto (Black, in general) attraction-rejection syndrome.

Writing three-quarters of a century after the appearance of *The Octoroon*, Langston Hughes, as did his predecessor Boucicault, left no doubt about the thesis of his play when he named his compelling drama *Mulatto*. Drawing upon society's early affirmation that an admixture of white blood tended to improve the Black breed,[5] Hughes created several mulatto characters to dramatize this belief. While the female mulatto appears briefly in Hughes's drama, the playwright chooses as his protagonist the tragic male figure Bert. Perhaps Hughes felt that this explosive assertion of manhood better suited the era of sociopolitical writing that characterized the thirties and, thus, he relegated the female to a place of subordination. It is both ironic and tragic that this early assertion of manhood was not a statement of *Black* manhood in the sense of the dramatic assertion of Black manhood of the 1960's.[6]

Nevertheless, Hughes raises his drama above the level of a mere problem play when he presents a strong-willed, rebellious, proud mulatto son of a white plantation owner and his Negro mistress. Convinced that his near-whiteness makes him superior to other Blacks, he defies his white father, loses control and kills him during a fight; he is then forced by the lynch mob to take his own life. The playwright's underscoring irony that Bert is too much like his white father to live brings real pathos to Bert's final recognition of the totality of his tragic situation. One is moved to ask—is there no other way? Or to pick up the lament "we have learned forever how well they die—cannot we learn now how to let them live?"

But there is yet another ironic twist. The female mulatto, Sallie (Bert's sister), is permitted to live, to suppress her outrage and revolt and to outwit her white father by preparing herself, at his expense, to "educate her way out of his control." But Hughes knew that her story had less dramatic value—at least to the audiences of the thirties. Failure to legitimize miscegenation, to permit the products of the act to live normal lives without circumvention only added fuel to their futile efforts to survive in a supercilious society—both on and off stage

The docile, saintly, noble, forgiving mulatto of Boucicault's day is certainly not present in the twentieth-century treatment of the character—but then neither are the same motivations for manipulation of the traditional stereotype. The Black revolutionist of the '60's is a good example of this change. Convinced that integration was never intended to be a two-way street and that many whites feared that it meant "mongrelization of the benefactors' race," the revolutionists began screaming "Black Is Beautiful" and rejecting everything white. In the midst of this movement of Black identity, the product of miscegenation became tragic for reasons totally different from Boucicault's octoroon who admonished herself for "the shameful single drop of Black blood which poisoned all the flood."

This new tragic mulatto is developed with horrifying intensity in the plays of Adrienne Kennedy. Ms. Kennedy turns from realism to a surrealistic world that can display the tortures and nightmares of her female character—a tragic mulatto searching for an identity that is trapped in conventions and torn by the paradoxes of living in a no man's (nor woman's) land. Symbols of these paradoxes are hurled out in rapid-fire order: smooth lily-white skin, black kinky hair, laughing white figures, pale yellow skin, ebony masks, etc. Sarah in *Funnyhouse of a Negro* and Clara in *The Owl Answers* are trapped in Blackness, desperately struggling to resolve their love/hate for Black/white, caught in the never-ending attraction/rejection syndrome.

> SARAH
> . . . he haunted my conception, diseased my birth . . .
> —*Funnyhouse of a Negro*

All of Ms. Kennedy's plays should be required reading for anyone seeking insight into what it means to be a tragic mulatto.[7]

As was the Little Red Hen in the well-known fable of that name, we are finally forced to face the issue: Who put the "tragic" in the tragic mulatto? Society, if forced to reply, would probably be as noncommittal and evasive as the Red Hen's followers. Their answers might go something like this:

"NOT I," said the Blackface Minstrel as he covered his face with burnt cork—denying white audiences a chance to see *real* Black folks in all their living colors on stage.

"NOT I," said the Abolitionist as she created one more "idealized abstraction" and penned one more sentimental phrase for the mulatto—evoking pity from white America who sighed, "There, but for the Grace of God . . .'"

"NOT I," said the Lawmaker as he wrote another law against racial intermarriage.

"NOT I," said the Theatre Audience, clinging to its safe and satisfying old stereotypes.

"NOT I," said the Klansman as he spewed out racial superiority and cut another length of rope.

"NOT I," said the Maker of Beauty Standards as she made millions selling skin whiteners and hair straighteners.

"NOT I," said the Black Revolutionist as he rejected the "polluted mainstream" and started his own brand of "racial purity."

And the beat goes on . . . ! Conventions have a way of hanging on, especially when they are deeply rooted in traditional thought patterns. As long as the mulatto is viewed as a social problem rather than a human being, as long as Blacks are caught up in the benevolence/malevolence, identification-with-the-aggressor-phenomenon, as long as "white" is elevated above "Black,"[8] there will be tragedy in miscegenation, and the resulting mulatto only an extension of this tragedy.

The tragic mulatto is a living product of society's conscious/unconscious attitudes and values and is willfully or unknowingly created by all of us. No matter how many laws we make—or break—until we escape first from our own conventional traps, we cannot effectively free her from the myths and conventions which engulf her; therefore, playwrights (and anyone else who chooses) will continue to manipulate her at will.

CREATIVE DRAMA: SEX ROLE STEREOTYPING?

LIN WRIGHT

Creative drama is improvisation with children. It is a group process. The leader helps the children perceive their world and then express themselves through the dramatic medium. The content of the drama can be based on curriculum materials or it may be developed around the personal interests and concerns of the children. Once the topic is chosen, the children under the guidance of the leader create the plot, characters, and settings. As they perform the improvisation, they create the action and dialogue. Participant evaluation of the improvisation is also an important aspect of the process. If creative drama is sensitively handled and the content carefully chosen, it should be fun for the children and an excellent means for their intellectual, esthetic, emotional, and social growth. Empirical research should verify these claims.

Relatively little research, however, has been conducted to verify the effect of creative drama with children, and the results in the few existing studies are generally less positive than anticipated. In all of the studies that include sex of student as a variable, boys have received scores different from those of girls on social, creative, and communication instruments after sessions in creative drama.[1] This sexism in the creative drama process was unexpected since the practitioners in the field claim to work with the individual child within the group for the maximum growth of each child. There is a need to discover the cause of these results and to develop means to assure nonsexist sessions for the children.

Dr. E. C. Irwin (1963) taught fifteen sessions of creative drama to 149 third-grade children to test growth in personal development from the drama process. The experimental boys made significant gains in social adjustment on

Lin Wright, Professor of Children's Theatre and Creative Dramatics at Arizona State University, has written widely on her specialty.

the California Test of Personality. The girls made significant gains on personal, social, and total adjustment.[2] Elissa Goforth (1974) discovered that fifty kindergarten boys and girls scored significantly higher on the Wallach and Kogan Creativity Series after sixteen creative drama sessions. She also found that boys in the classes with the least structure scored significantly higher (.001 level of confidence) than the children in the other drama classes.[3]

Dr. Lin Wright (1972) found thirty sixth-grade boys showing more growth in perception (a greater awareness of and a better interpretation of another's acts within a situation) than an equal number of girls after fifteen drama sessions. Feffer's Role Taking Task was the measure used.[4]

Mary E. Lunz (1974) found, after ten creative drama sessions, seventh-grade boys and girls showed significant improvement in communication effectiveness. When the data was analyzed for the effect of sex of the communicator, a trend appeared implying that "males responded more positively to the creative dramatics activities than the females."[5]

Dr. Irwin concluded that "a program of creative dramatics may possibly have a greater applicability to girls than to boys" in the third grade.[6] Lunz made a much stronger statement:

> The social and cultural implications are incredible. . . . The trend opens questions of preferential treatment for males by leaders, or the tendency of males to dominate the group activity. Experimentation with lesson structure in regard to how this factor is manipulated during activity is necessary to gain insight into the question.[7]

In the creative drama session the leader most often uses literature, history, current issues, other curricular materials, or the ideas of the students to motivate the improvisations. The literature used is often folk or fairy tales and characters from these stories are hopelessly stereotyped. Many children's books are also sexist. Leaders attempt to overcome this bias by having the girls play some of the stronger men's roles. This is not a real solution for the children know that the girls could not perform the tasks in "real life." Leaders can search for the few stories with strong roles for both boys and girls. New "nonsexist" stories are being published but care must be exercised with these materials because they often lack exciting characters and dramatic tension and will not play well. Text writers of history and social studies often suggest class activities involving role playing. History texts usually record the events of the brave men and supportive women from our past. The social studies problems are based on current social norms—which are usually sexist. Improvisations based on the children's ideas often reinforce sex roles. The ideas the children bring to the drama session are based on the current TV fare and whatever else they experience, see, and read. Most of this material is replete with stereotypes. The leader is a product of our sexist society and may have as much difficulty as the children envisioning nonstereotyped roles.

Solutions to stereotyped material are not easy. No one may really know what constitutes a nonsexist role, a role that respects the differences between the sexes but one that does not limit the activities either sex can perform. The leader can search for playable "nonsexist" material. *Pippi Longstocking, Charlotte's Web, The Courage of Sarah Noble, Pushcart War, A Wrinkle in Time* are a few stories with strong roles for males and females.[8] There are historical female figures of dramatic stature, such as Harriet Tubman, Sojourner Truth, Clara Barton, Susan B. Anthony, Helen Keller, who moved beyond the stereotypes of their era. If the leader can ask appropriate leading questions and conduct a discussion with tact and insight, it is possible to help children create their own stories in which the characters are not limited by sex.

Since both the participants and the leader of the creative drama session are products of our sexist society, often the process of planning, playing, and evaluating the improvisations reinforces sexist behavior. Anne Thurman, at a convention session examining sex role stereotyping in children's drama, raised four questions related to this issue:

1.   Do we give equal opportunity to boys and girls when we discuss, play, and evaluate our scenes, or do we let the boys dominate and the girls acquiesce?

2.   Do we call attention to sex distinction and role by allowing too many all-boy or all-girl scenes? Do we allow, acquiesce, or foster a large amount of small group planning in single sex groups?

3.   Do we discipline the boys more harshly than girls? Do we praise boys more than girls? Do we expect the boys to be more aggressive and noisy than girls?

4.   Are we conscious of sexist remarks or slurs as we have become of racist remarks? "Just like a girl, women drivers, dumb blonde, jock, my father says women are the weaker sex."

Trying to keep these questions in mind, David Saar[9] and I set out to team-teach boys to move beyond the typical roles they usually play and to see what techniques and materials might be of value in this process. We were concerned with the material we used, the roles we played in the entire drama context, the attitudes and expectancies we had for the children, the general group ambiance. The process of planning and evaluating with the children was every bit as important as the actual playing of the drama in dealing with sex role stereotyping.

Sixteen children were selected by their teachers from four fifth-sixth grade combination classes. The teachers selected the students who they felt would benefit most from the creative drama project. The students were told that the leaders were making a video film of the process of creative drama, a film that would be used to help train teachers and college students and show them "how much upper elementary students are capable of doing." The group met in the media center three times a week for four weeks. Each session lasted one hour.

The goal of the sessions, as stated to the students, was to develop an "improv troupe." Such a troupe is composed of individuals who are willing to share their ideas and also are willing to support the ideas of other group members. Each is willing to act out any ideas presented and to work to play off of any other member within an improvisation. The individual is always initiator and supporter in all three stages of improvisation, the planning, playing, and evaluating. This was an "adult" challenge and the students responded well to the approach.

All class activities—warm-ups, theatre games, pantomimes, story dramatizations, and original improvisations—were selected to help the students develop the dual roles of initiator and supporter. Means were devised to help as many students as possible develop their own ideas and present them to the group. The corollary of this was to help all students listen to their classmates, respect their ideas and be willing to support ideas from everyone.

The sessions started with small group pantomimes. We then created improvisations based on the idea of "what if" there were a series of unrecorded adventures of some of the sailors who became separated from Odysseus. This left us without the male leader and we hoped to "readapt" the story so the format could allow some nonsexist roles. Finally the children created a modern Odyssey: they chose to create a space journey.

Prior to the sessions we met with the children to explore their drama backgrounds and attitudes toward one another and apparent willingness to lead or follow. An outline of content and procedure for the twelve sessions was developed.

During the first two sessions the children were allowed to work in groups of their own choosing. The boys played with boys and the girls with girls. For the next session the children worked with those from their "pod." This placed them in groups of four, two boys and two girls each. While playing out the "unwritten" incidents from the Odyssey, the entire group worked together. Both boys and girls played sailors and monsters.

As we approached the creation of the children's space odyssey we evolved a scheme that put the children in boy/girl pairs. Each child had to develop an idea for the play, then combine her/his idea with that of the opposite-sex partner. These ideas were written and then presented to the entire group. Small groups volunteered to prepare these scenes under the direction of the initial pair of creators. These scenes were presented to the entire group and best segments were selected to incorporate into the final improvisation. One day was spent working on the final version which was filmed during the final class session.

The classroom teachers using informal observation felt that the drama experience had been very positive for the students and that there was carryover into the classroom. They noticed an improvement in the students' listening abilities. The students were more willing to listen attentively to others and then develop their ideas in relation to what had been said. Some of the students conversed more easily with adults and one boy with a learning disability had found his experience with drama a heady and unusual success. They reported discovering new abilities to perform and socialize in their students. In relation to leadership roles, they perceived greater changes in the boys, feeling that they had grown most in their ability to both lead and follow. They perceived a difference in leadership roles assumed by the girls.

The creative drama leaders noted that during the initial sessions two "natural" male leaders dominated the group. One girl acted as a leader with a small group of girls. By the end of the twelve sessions this had changed. Of the eight boys, there were the original two strong leaders and one newly emerged strong leader; two boys had assumed minimal leadership roles; three were followers. Of the eight girls, three strong leaders emerged; four assumed minimal leadership roles; one was a follower. Leadership qualities for the girls emerged most definitely in the final, original improvisation. All but one girl developed usable ideas and helped the group work to dramatize their ideas.

The girls had little difficulty supporting others' ideas throughout the sessions. The original female leader usually sought support for her ideas but if it was not forthcoming would willingly help develop the ideas of others. Of the boys, the three followers supported anyone's ideas; three boys tended to automatically support the ideas of their male peers but would support female peers only if the support of the whole group seemed strong. The newly emerged male leader was very group-oriented and very instrumental in bringing out everyone's ideas. The two original male leaders had difficulty supporting the ideas of other children. One tried, but retreated to "aloofness" when it became difficult. The other male leader would support others' ideas only if he could develop a means of gaining attention for himself in the process.

Three of the most successful male/female pairs were composed of a girl with leadership ability and a passive boy. In the fourth productive pair both the boy and girl were leaders but neither was acknowledged as a leader outside the drama group. The other pairs suffered in varying degrees from the boys' allegiance to each other rather than to the group.

The roles that the students were willing to play indicated some shifts in attitude. Initially the children tended to choose "male football player, female cheerleader" type roles. At one point one of the males commented that girls would have to stay in the boat because "girls don't fight." In the final story, the girls fought, played major roles, and were supported in these roles by most of the boys.

In conclusion, it is possible to effect positive change in the roles that boys and girls will assume in the drama process and playing, but this new flexibility will not carry over into the classroom unless the teachers create an atmosphere that will encourage these new roles. It is difficult to take basically sexist material (i.e., the Odyssey) and "turn it around" by an enlightened presentation. Original material, developed by the group under the leaders' guidance, can more easily be nonsexist. Presently, it appears that creative drama is as sexist as our society and is a means for continuing sex role stereotyping. From the work started in the Mesa schools it seems possible to begin to reverse that condition.

FEMALE PROTAGONISTS IN THE PLAYS OF SUZAN ZEDER

SUSAN PEARSON-DAVIS

Before the 1960's, most scripts in the field of theatre for young audiences were adaptations of traditional folk and fairy tales or popular children's fiction. Most fit neatly into the category of the well-made play; were realistic in style; had very familiar titles, few contemporary topics, and no controversial issues. Characters were usually less than three-dimensional since social and educational attitudes put narrow limits on what was considered suitable for children, and depth of characterization was thought to be confusing to them. But when television began bringing regular coverage of war and social unrest into most living rooms, society's view of children and what was suitable for them began to change. As it did, innovative scripts for young audiences began to appear.

Prominent among this new wave of innovative writers is Suzan Zeder, the author of eight plays for young audiences. Zeder, a Fulbright Scholar who teaches playwriting at Southern Methodist University, has won numerous awards for her scripts, including the Children's Theatre Association of America's Charlotte Chorpenning Cup for Best Playwright of the Year in 1978 and the same organization's Distinguished Play Award for *The Play Called Noah's Flood* in 1985 and for *Doors* in 1986. Although her scripts are innovative in many ways, perhaps her greatest contribution to contemporary theatre is her creation of child protagonists, particularly young female characters, who are recognizably contemporary and fully three-dimensional. Unlike the doll-like, passive, or sweet and sentimentalized girls in the traditional repertoire of plays for young audiences, Zeder's young female protagonists elude sex role stereotypes, struggle with difficult and contradictory thoughts and feelings which often lead to rebellious behavior, and grapple actively with the problems that confront them. In addition, these young protagonists are written in such a way that both children and adults can identify with them on their own level.

Probably the best known of these young female protagonists is ten-year-old Ellie Murphy in *Step on a Crack* (1976). Ellie has been raised by her single father, Max, for six years since the death of her mother. Max's remarriage to an attractive woman named Lucille fills Ellie with jealousy, brings out all her insecurities, and makes her behavior far from that of the "perfectly good little girl" she used to be. Ellie copes with her angry feelings and attempts to prop up her dwindling self-esteem by retreating to her own room where, with the help of two imaginary friends, Lana and Frisbie, who enter her room through

---

Susan Pearson-Davis, Associate Professor of Theatre Arts, University of New Mexico, Albuquerque, wrote this essay for her critical anthology of the works of Suzan Zeder, to be published by Anchorage Press.

her toy box, she creates and enacts fantasies of being rich, famous, and far
superior to Lucille. A third imaginary character, Voice, who represents Ellie's
own dark side, lives in Ellie's mirror. It is Voice that starts all the fantasies by
reminding Ellie that she is not as pretty, talented, or smart as Lucille.

Zeder's externalizing of Ellie's fantasies is highly theatrical and holds the
attention of even very young children by turning Ellie's thoughts into visible
action. But the psychological complexity inherent in the fantasies, such as the
use of Voice to represent Ellie's over-active self-criticism, also makes Ellie easy
to identify with on an adult level, in spite of her young age.

Zeder's adaptation of L. Frank Baum's *Ozma of Oz* (1981) gives another good
example of the complexity of her young female characters. Baum's original
Dorothy is brave, strong, and positive, but thoroughly one-dimensional. Even
when she is adrift on a raft in the middle of a stormy ocean, the reader never
sees Baum's Dorothy struggle with fear or any other attitudinal obstacle. By
contrast, Zeder has updated her play to the present and made Dorothy a
teenager with weaknesses and negative attitudes that get in her way. She is
accompanying her aging Uncle Henry because she has to, not because she
wants to. She is bored to tears by his ramblings about Australian history and
terrified when the storm strikes. Once they have been washed ashore in Oz,
and her uncle taken captive, Dorothy has to do things she never dreamt she
could do in order to rescue him. In the process, she learns that she has the
ability to think her way through a problem and that she has courage she can
act on in spite of feeling afraid. With the help of Ozma—who also differs from
the original in having the power to make people see "behind the mind and into
the heart"—Dorothy discovers that there is more to Uncle Henry than the
helpless old man she thought he was.

Not all Zeder's major, three-dimensional characters are children. Two of her
most fascinating and well-developed female characters, one of whom is over
forty, appear in her 1985 script, *Mother Hicks*. The play is set in a small town in
Southern Illinois during the Great Depression. Girl is a thirteen-year-old
foundling who has been passed from family to family all her life, alienating
most of them with her headstrong willfulness and refusal to follow rules. At
the beginning of the play she has just been left behind by yet another foster
father and forced to move in with the town mortician and his wife, whom she
does not like.

Mother Hicks is a mysterious woman in her forties who lives alone outside
this small town. She was a midwife in the town until a time ten years earlier
when the townspeople, in fear and ignorance, blamed her for the death of
several babies and ostracized her as an accused witch. In the atmosphere of
fear and loss brought on by the Depression, tales of her witchcraft spread; the
townspeople, including Girl, look on her with dread. But the two are destined
to meet when Girl is severely injured and brought by a young deaf man
named Tuc to be nursed back to health by Mother Hicks.

Both of these characters have to deal with the most difficult kinds of losses.

Girl, who had begun to hope that Mother Hicks was really her long-lost mother, discovers that although Mother Hicks can help her in some ways to heal the wounds of her repeated abandonment, she must "find her own name" and create her own identity before she can feel comfortable being defined as part of a particular family. Mother Hicks's own infant daughter died in the same epidemic that killed the babies she is accused of having witched. Her mysterious midnight visits to the graveyard every week, which have been used by the townspeople as evidence that she is a witch, are eventually revealed to be visits to the unmarked grave of her dead child.

Zeder's plays run the gamut from comedy to serious drama, from fantasy to realism, and from ancient to modern historical periods. Her young male protagonists, especially Jeff in *Doors* and *Other Doors*, are written with as much depth as the female characters. Zeder is primarily concerned with ordinary people coping with problems of everyday life, but these problems are ultimately universal in their scope: communication breaking down when one person withholds information from another "for the other's own good"; people searching for a sense of identity and meaning in life; and people struggling to have a voice in the decisions that are made about their lives.

Zeder maintains that she writes about rather than for children, and does so not for any particular social or educational purpose, but because she finds children fascinating and dynamic dramatically. She feels that it is extremely important for adults to "respect the child as having both magnitude and significant emotions" and refrain from condescending to children or trivializing their emotional difficulties, even in the well-meaning attempt to protect them. She carries this belief into her writing and validates the child's mind, world, and perceptions, emphasizing the universal presence of the child within the adult.

6

FEMINIST THEATRE

Although there is evidence of some feminist theatre activity during the beginnings of the women's suffrage movement and in Greenwich Village early in the twentieth century, it is only since the late 1960's that we have witnessed and documented a continuing feminist theatre. Approximately 150 feminist groups have produced theatre events in the U.S. since the '60's, and in the mid-'80's more than 30 were still active, with new groups forming as older ones closed. For example, Lilith Women's Theatre Collective, founded in San Francisco in 1974, served feminist energies in the Bay Area through perform-ances, readings and workshops until its closing in 1986. Undaunted, Terry Baum, one of the originators of Lilith, continues to pursue her writing and directing; and a new company, Mouth of the Wolf, emerged phoenix-like from Lilith's ashes, brought to life by Michele Linfante and others of the original group.

Why this need for feminist theatre? Certainly women have acted, managed companies, chosen scripts, and written for the professional Western theatre at least since the days of the *commedia dell'arte* troupes, but any feminist con-sciousness in their work was rarely acknowledged or encouraged. Although there are feminist notions in plays by women before the twentieth century, writers were not able to assume responsive women or sympathetic men as their primary audience. Even today, feminist drama created for the commer-cial theatre has to please men in power aesthetically and politically to achieve recognition and status. Feminist dramatists who work outside feminist groups still have to struggle with social suppression of their speech and sexuality. *The Search for Signs of Intelligent Life in the Universe*, written and directed by Jane Wagner, performed by Lily Tomlin, produced by the two of them in Broadway's Plymouth Theatre in 1986, seems an anomaly—an award-winning feminist piece in the heart of the traditional commercial theatre district. The achievement is explained, perhaps, as much by its nonconfronta-tional style as by the talents of its creators.

More often, feminist theatres provide an alternative to the establishment. From the beginning, feminist theatre has been compensatory by necessity. There is much to compensate for: oppression in almost every arena of society (including both radical politics and the avant-garde theatre movement); the invisibility of women's history and culture; an absence of active roles for women; little access to, and/or equality in, the professional theatre; the continued omission of women's life and language in men's theatre; a lack of visibility and validity for lesbian experience; and the repression of ancient feminist ceremonial traditions.

While seeking to compensate for these frustrations, lacks, and repressions, feminist theatres have fostered consciousness raising and used theatre to build sisterhood among women and bonds with feminist men. Though there is no universally accepted definition of "feminism," there is general agreement on the necessity of valuing and asserting female experience for personal and political change. A feminist theatre provides an environment in which a female artist can define herself in her own terms. Many women need to create in an atmosphere where the language of female experience prevails. Even if a woman intends to work in the male-dominated world, her own authenticity and possibilities for survival will be better nurtured by experience in a feminist situation—a fact that university theatre programs might well note for the future of their women students.

In the 1980's, several feminist theatre festivals have spread "the psychic news" (Megan Terry's term). The Feminist Amerikan Theatre coproduced the 1980 and 1981 Boston Womyn's Theatre Festivals. In 1985 the Boston Women in Theatre Festival assumed the task. The National Festival of Women in Theatre gathered feminists in California annually in Santa Cruz, 1981–85. Women's One World Festival, produced in 1980 and 1981 in New York City, was the genesis for the East Village's Cafe WOW. These festivals have also drawn feminist theatres from other countries. This national and international networking is not widely known. Even *MS.* magazine does not report on feminist theatres, claiming them to be an elite New York phenomenon, an assumption contradicted by our playlist and feminist theatres list.

Many feminist theatres and writers in the '80's began asking questions and attempting projects that grew out of the groundbreaking work in women's studies—exploring engendered use of space, gesture, and imagery, for example. Some addressed political issues of concern to both men and women with approaches informed by female experience, such as Minneapolis-based At the Foot of the Mountain's *Ashes Ashes We All Fall Down*, which put nuclear issues into the context of a woman's life while emphasizing a positive approach to the future. The "Matrix" section of this book addresses some of these newer developments.

There have been controversies and splits within the feminist theatres, some of which are suggested in this chapter. Many of the conflicts are just as common in nonfeminist companies, particularly the alternative theatres that began forming in the '60's: Is the art of the theatre more important than or separate from political goals or social ends? Should the group be organized communally, or with specialization of labor, or along more traditional hierarchical lines? How much effort should be expended in fund-raising and marketing? Should the group be open to anyone willing to work or should it be selective? Other disagreements arose over questions particular to feminist groups: Should men be allowed to perform or attend? How should one deal with sexuality within the company, the audience, the material selected for production?

Some feminist theatres are composed solely of women who perform exclusively for other women; there are others in which women-only companies perform for audiences of both sexes (sometimes holding women-only events); and in some companies men and women perform for mixed audiences. There is considerable variation in the type of performance space used, in the process by which decisions are made, and in the style and tone of the work done. But despite those differences, feminist theatres invite everyone to remove sex-role limitations and stereotypes from habits of thought—conscious and unconscious. It is the possibility of this new understanding that suffuses and motivates the work of feminist theatres.

LWJ

FEMINIST THEATRE:
A RHETORICAL PHENOMENON

PATTI P. GILLESPIE

Since the formation of the first feminist theatre groups in 1969, increasing numbers of people, mostly female, have joined together for the purpose of doing theatre—by, for, or about women.[1] Although the companies vary markedly in size, organization, repertory, working methods, and artistic excellence, all advocate or promote equality of opportunity *for* women, and all call themselves feminist theatres. Their nationwide and apparently spontaneous formation from coast to coast—without encouragement, leadership, or direction from a national organization—makes them an example of a grassroots movement seldom witnessed in the American theatre.

Although constituting a populist activity of considerable strength and vitality, feminist theatres have been largely ignored by established reviewers, critics, and scholars. Local media occasionally review individual productions and generate stories on indigenous groups, but newspapers and magazines with national circulations have, for the most part, neglected the phenomenon. For example, of the more than fifteen feminist theatres active in New York City between 1969 and 1977, the productions of only the Women's Interart Theatre

Patti P. Gillespie, Chair of the Department of Communication Arts and Theatre, University of Maryland, is the author, with Kenneth Cameron, of *Enjoyment of Theatre, Revolution and Revival*, and *Western Theatre*. An earlier version of her essay appeared in the *Quarterly Journal of Speech*, vol. 64 (1978), 284–94. Used by permission.

were regularly reviewed by *The New York Times* and *The Village Voice*. Five articles exhausted the attempts of established periodicals to deal with the theatres nationwide before 1977. Even underground newspapers and radical feminist publications treat the theatres and their works only occasionally rather than regularly; none attempt an analysis of the national phenomenon. Such inattention has predictably resulted in a public largely uninformed, or misinformed, about the nature of those theatres calling themselves feminist.

Reasons for the inattention are several. The most important can be briefly suggested. Feminist theatres, considered collectively, lack the unity and cohesion necessary for identification as a movement; their very diversity in size, repertory, format, and budget makes analysis and subsequent generalization difficult. Furthermore, the newness of the phenomenon, the inconstancy of the groups, and the decidedly experimental thrust of several have impeded inquiry by obscuring sources of information. Moreover, the artistic quality of the productions is often quite mediocre when judged by traditional criteria; established reviewers and media may consider coverage a waste of their time and space. Finally, the term *feminist theatre* appears now to engender controversy: some rather traditional producing organizations are beginning to embrace the term while other theatres, obviously devoted to the goals of feminism, are beginning to reject it outright.

But neither the inattention of the media nor the difficulty of the research excuses a casual dismissal of these theatres. The works of such feminist playwrights as Adrienne Kennedy, Myrna Lamb, and Megan Terry are now known, anthologized, and produced in nonfeminist theatres. Obies have been earned by plays and performers first seen in feminist productions.[2] But beyond such individual contributions, the national phenomenon itself has an importance not yet recognized and acknowledged by scholars. The formation and rapid development of feminist theatres nationwide is a rare example of an unpremeditated and vigorous people's theatre, a theatre apparently formed in response to strongly felt and shared needs. Whether by encouraging an adversary relationship with contemporary society or by promoting new images and possibilities for women, feminist theatres are credited with radically changing the perceptions of some viewers and the very lives of others. The most tantalizing questions, then, relate not to individual practitioners and theatres but to the national phenomenon. Why did these theatres form in such numbers and with such suddenness? Why did the theatres assume such diverse, and often quite nontraditional, characteristics?

Feminist theatres and feminism. Discovering answers to these and related questions requires recognition that all feminist theatres are rhetorical enterprises; their primary aim is action, not art. Each company is using theatre to promote the identities of women, to increase awareness of the issues of feminism, or to advocate corrective change.

The groups, if agreeing on little else, appear to share two convictions: that women in this society have been subjected to unfair discrimination based on their gender, and that theatre can provide at least a partial solution to certain problems arising from such discrimination. Did the groups not agree on the former, their public statements would be far different from those expressed. Did they not agree on the latter, they would have chosen strategies other than theatre for the exploration and promotion of their beliefs.

Certainly the suffragettes had their Bloomer plays,[3] and the 1920's and '30's were replete with agitprop dramas. But in neither instance were the *theatrical* (as opposed to the *dramatic*) practices so removed from those of the mainstream. Feminist theatres, on the other hand, sprang suddenly, spontaneously, and in relatively large numbers from no tradition and no political organization in particular. Such activity, at first, seems inexplicable. Analysis, however, suggests that the emergence is due to a peculiar confluence of historic circumstance and rhetorical need.

Formation of the theatres. Although theatre's potential as an instrument for education and change has been well known for centuries, the range of its possibilities was rediscovered and widely popularized during the 1960's. Experimental theatres arose to contradict long-held views of what drama and theatre could be. Attention centered on new kinds of plays, new sorts of organizations, new spaces for producing, new methods of training actors, and new audiences for performances. Asserting the political ends of art, the New Left developed street theatres and guerrilla events; probing the boundaries of life and art, the avant-garde focused on theatre as discovery, as process. The delayed appearance of the women's movement made possible its appropriation of certain theatrical practices popularized by the New Left and the antiwar demonstrators: performing in unusual places, presenting pithy and provocative skits, confronting audiences, proselytizing. During the 1960's, too, groups such as the Open Theatre, the Performance Group, and La Mama focused on self-exploration, group improvisation, collective organization, nonverbal communication, and physicalization; these techniques, too, became available to the feminists.[4]

Significantly, many women active in feminist theatres had prior experience in the avant-garde or the New Left. For example, women figured prominently in the Open Theatre. Of the fifteen women identified by Joseph Chaikin as particularly significant members of his group, ten are now, or have been at some time, involved in feminist theatre.[5] More telling, however, is that many women active in feminist theatre lacked prior training or experience in theatre but had been active in the New Left and antiwar coalitions which used theatrical tactics for the promotion of their causes.[6] In sum, by 1970, not only were new techniques of theatre available, but also by then many women had experienced the techniques firsthand.

But history alone is insufficient to explain women's ready adoption of theatre. The peculiar nature of the rhetorical problems facing advocates of women's equality also contributed to the grassroots movement. Recent studies have demonstrated several ways by which the rhetoric of women's liberation differs from other kinds of persuasive efforts.[7] First, the gender roles assigned to women at birth are not congruent with those deemed necessary for a successful rhetor. In fact, according to Campbell, "Insofar as the role of rhetor entails qualities of self-reliance, self-confidence, and independence, *its very assumption is a violation of the female role.*" Second, elimination of sex-role stereotyping requires both individual and social change. Thus, "All of the issues of women's liberation are simultaneously personal and political"; therefore, its rhetoric must be at once personal, dealing with the particular experience of individual women, and political, treating the organizations and structures affecting all citizens.[8] Third, as McMahan has shown, the rhetorical situation generated by liberationists is a paradox: even while proclaiming their equality, women are asking society to grant it to them. The responses to a rhetorical paradox are severely limited and may restrict communication through ordinary channels. It will be argued that theatre provides a mechanism by which women advocating radical change can overcome this particular combination of rhetorical problems. The question, why did feminist theatres arise in such numbers, is answered by considering them as tactical responses to problems faced by women advocates of equality.

Women chose theatre, in part, for the reasons that others proposing radical change have found it helpful. In conflicts where competing groups have vastly unequal power, the weak group often finds traditional forms of argument and public discourse inadequate. Low-power groups, therefore, often resort to techniques of violent confrontation and/or symbolic protest.[9] Women, a low-power group, tend to reject violent confrontation as a means of persuasion because they believe it to be based on male-dominated values, values which they question and strive to change. When violent confrontation is eliminated as an option, symbolic protest assumes a central position in planning.

Theatre is itself a kind of symbol. Like other art, theatre is a hypothetical construct to be appreciated and judged by its adherence to internal principles rather than by its fidelity to external "reality." Since theatre is performed for groups of people, its social component is stronger than that of most other verbal arts. Moreover, since living actors speak and act in front of a live audience, the sense of immediacy and urgency is greater than that of music, painting, lyric poetry, or the novel. In fact, the power of theatre to teach and convert has been recognized by figures as disparate as Plato and the Panthers, Bishop Ethelwold and Adolf Hitler.

But theatre remains a symbol, and thus deals in a world of hypothesis, not "reality." It therefore permits revelation of events, characters, and ideas without actually threatening either participants or viewers. A logical construct, theatre encourages reflection and empathy but does not require an immediate defense of, or attack upon, the world of the play. In a word, theatre is not debated. It does not demand (although it does permit) an agile exchange of ideas in the "real" world.

As a symbol, theatre says more than its literal meaning and means more than a single thing. Public address and debate are more nearly confined to the presentation of systematic arguments. Theatre has no such obligation: it can present a version of "reality" in all its complexity and contradiction. Thus theatre is particularly suited for promoting radical causes, causes which call for a restructuring of relationships and transactions, causes which lack specific, well-defined goals—in short, causes such as the liberation of women.[10]

Morever, theatre is, by its nature, especially well able to cope with an unusual demand of feminist rhetoric. Campbell argues effectively that an intimate interaction proceeds between the experience of a single woman and the public issues of all women. In fact she concludes that this inevitable relationship between the individual and social, the personal and the public, is a cornerstone of liberation rhetoric.[11]

Theorists as remote as Aristotle and as recent as Langer have observed that theatre is at once particular and universal, historic and philosophic. History deals with the real actions of real people; philosophy treats ideas and ideals; but drama constructs hypothetical, individual characters acting in invented situations. That is, within the play *Oedipus Rex*, Oedipus is a particular man-in-action; but *Oedipus Rex* is an artistic hypothesis, and so Oedipus, a logical universal. Because theatre, at its essence, displays both the particular and the universal, the individual and the totality, it is a strategy well selected to capture the intimate connections between the experience of a single woman and the political issues of all women. Whereas public speaking and debate can only assert such connections, drama can embody them, presenting them in all their intricacies and incongruities.

Finally, theatre permits a woman to function as a persuader without violating either her own past conditioning toward passivity or society's expectations regarding her appropriate behavior. The role of actress, unlike that of rhetor, does not violate gender-based expectations of conduct. Women have performed in the theatre at least since the sixth century B.C. and regularly in most countries since the late seventeenth century. True, actresses have been viewed by some as living on the fringes of respectability; but no one now is shocked by the presence of a woman on stage and few view the role as inappropriate.

Moreover, in the hypothetical world of the play, a female character can, with society's acquiescence, expose a social problem, defeat a male adversary, and experience economic and political success. Thus, an actress can, with a minimum of threat to either herself or members of her audience, embody traits, participate in situations, and articulate conclusions which in real life would be deemed unsuitable or threatening. While nineteenth-century audiences, for example, condemned the character Nora in Ibsen's *A Doll's House*, few attacked the actress for assuming the role. As a fictional character, then, a woman is free to decide, to take action, and even to attack contemporary practices with little reason to fear the renunciation or retribution of the audience upon her personally. Able to present a "view of reality" with no need personally to explain it logically or defend it rationally, even a timid woman may become bold enough to function actively as a persuader.

The formation of feminist theatres nationwide, then, can be appropriately viewed as response both to the historic possibilities of the 1970's and to the peculiar problems associated with liberation rhetoric.

Characteristics of the theatres. The confusing tangle of expressed goals, diverse structures, and varied methods of working likewise unsnarls when feminist theatres are viewed as particular responses to perceived problems. The traits of the theatres vary consistently with the answers to three questions: (1) What problem does the theatre target for solution? (2) What role is the theatre to play in its resolution? (3) What is the degree of social upheaval required for its correction?

Although the specific features of individual feminist theatres are, to some degree, unique, two major kinds of groups can be identified: those which are intent upon promoting women artists in particular, and those committed to assisting women in general. While the groups may overlap, theatres representing the two extremes can be cited and their practices compared.

Although less numerous, theatres which concentrate on the problems of women artists are often among the oldest and best known.[12] Such groups as Women's Interart, in New York City, observe that women artists have inadequate opportunities to show their work. There are too few women playwrights, for example. Of the several hundred plays produced in New York between 1969 and 1975, only 7 percent were written by women.[13] Women writers complain publicly that they are made to feel guilty about writing, that they are encouraged to consider their own efforts as mere "self-indulgent folly."[14] There are too few, and too inconsequential, roles for actresses. An analysis of Broadway and Off-Broadway plays produced between 1953 and 1972 reveals that only one-third of the available roles in the some 350 plays were for women.[15] There are too few positions open to women directors, women producers, women designers, and women technicians as well.[16] Feminist theatre, for groups such as Women's Interart, becomes a showcase for the works of talented women and a place of employment for female artists. Except for their preference for women artists and for plays which present women in nonstereotyped ways, these sorts of feminist theatres are largely undistinguishable from other professional, commercial, or community theatres. They tend to organize themselves into traditional producing units, with directors, designers, writers, and the like. Since their goal is to display art and artists in a favorable light, excellence becomes a major goal of each production. Generally these feminist theatres receive the most favorable notice from the established media and are most likely to be financially solvent, with permanent homes and organizations.[17]

But feminist theatre applies as well to the more numerous and amorphous performing units around the country whose aims coincide roughly with those of women's liberationists. These groups are often transitory and, to an outsider, may appear unorganized, haphazard, formless. These groups are apt to reject the traditional theatrical organization—a director atop a hierarchy of artistic specialists—in favor of loose aggregates of equal persons working collectively. Some aggregates include even the audience as part of the collective experience. A representative of such groups, It's All Right to Be Woman Theatre, considers that feature a central one: "Whereas theatre has been, to date, a combining of specialists, the essence of our theatre is to convey the collective experience . . . a theatre without separation of roles . . . a theatre without a stage to separate audience and players.[18] By and large the groups practice what they preach, and some go to considerable lengths to assure democracy within their theatre. Womansong Theatre, for example, omits the names of individual performers and switches parts among the performers at different productions.[19] Both the Cutting Edge and Women of the Burning City develop their scripts collectively.[20]

These groups often select plays and tactics designed to command attention, to shock, to alienate. Common confrontative techniques include attacks both on the norms of femininity and on basic gender-role expectations. *The Saga of How I Lost My Hairy Legs* assures a reaction by its treatment of a subject previously considered tasteless and unfeminine.[21] Myrna Lamb's play *But What Have You Done for Me Lately?*, depicting a desperate pregnant man in search of an abortion, forces a recognition of the issue of personal freedom by transposing gender roles.[22] Short guerrilla events performed in elevators of office buildings and department stores shock by their verbal assaults on familiar persons and institutions.[23] The New Feminist Repertory was praised by one feminist for giving "validity to ideas that have been expurgated from the range of attitudes permissible to 'healthy' people in the past few decades" and for understanding that "it is society that needs 'adjusting,' not the individual."[24] With such strategies, feminist theatres are merely using techniques already established as successful by the street and guerrilla theatres of the past decade.

In certain other respects, however, the feminist theatres are quite unlike their agitprop predecessors. The performance materials in feminist theatres, for example, are unusually personal. Such material serves to highlight the groups' informal, even vulnerable, style of production. It's All Right to Be Woman summarizes its practice:

> We make theatre out of our lives, our dreams, our feelings, our fantasies. We make theatre by letting out the different parts of us that we have pushed inside all our lives. . . . We make our music out of the tunes we hum to ourselves and the beats we tap out on a table top. Making theatre out of these private parts of ourselves is one way we are trying every day to take our own experiences seriously, to accept our feelings as valid and real. . . . To believe that what happens to us or what we feel or dream is important enough to share with each other and other women, that it is, in fact, the most important thing we have to share.[25]

Whether building scripts from interviews with the performers' mothers[26] or from dreams related by members of the audience,[27] the groups seem determined to make the theatrical event intimate, and from this intimacy to build a sense of common experience and, therefore, political commitment. A critic at a performance reports: "The personal voices of real women become the expression of feelings known in all of us. . . . Watching we were drawn into a sense of closeness with performers' lives, not just with their work."[28]

Women's movement and feminist theatres. Interestingly, the two kinds of feminist theatres parallel an observable division within the women's movement at large. Organizations such as the League of Women Voters and WEAL promote specific economic and social reforms. They are characterized by their moderate stance, their traditional methods, and their commitment to work through established channels of change. Similarly, moderate feminist theatres such as Interart, Los Angeles Feminist Theatre, and Washington Area Feminist Theatre aim to lessen the economic deprivation of women artists. The problems they address are the definable and practical problems of employment and salary. Their solutions are straightforward: to give women work, to show their art to the general public, to present that art in the most polished and acceptable way possible. Since the problem is to provide opportunities for theatre artists, the existence of the theatre is itself a partial solution. Moderate theatres, therefore, adopt traits which promote the continuance of the theatre. Since a high quality of artistry is important for the accomplishment of their primary goals, such groups contribute to the world of theatre as well as to the world of women—accounting for most of the significant new plays and playwrights, and serving most successfully as a conduit for introducing new female talents into the mainstream of the American theatre. Inasmuch as the social changes they advocate are not very profound, the existence and practice of these groups represent no threat, are readily acceptable to the media and to other theatres, and can exist in comfortable parallel with the theatrical mainstream.

On the other hand, in the women's movement at large, groups such as SCUM, WITCH, and Weatherwomen strive to change the whole fabric of society by attacking its attitudes and institutions. The approach is radical, the rhetoric combative, the aims revolutionary. Similarly, radical feminist theatres such as It's All Right adopt traits designed to cast doubt on accepted conventions of both content and form.[29] The radical theatres tend to reject traditional (scripted) plays, normal patterns of organization, accepted critical standards, polite language. The specific characteristics chosen as replacements depend, of course, on whether the theatre strives to promote lesbianism, explore the black experience, raise consciousness,[30] or name the enemy.[31] But in every instance, radical theatres select strategies which cultivate solidarity among adherents while encouraging antagonism, or at least apathy, toward previously accepted social norms. They do not practice persuasion of the many by the few; instead they organize themselves into leaderless groups which strive to break down traditional distinctions between the leader and the led, the actor and the audience. They do not strive to adjust their presentation to the expectations of an audience; rather they jolt the audience into new perceptions, new ways of looking at the world.[32] They do not promote a single program of change nor answer the question, "What do women want?" They present instead the different experiences of many women without attempting to resolve the consequent contradictions. In fact, theatres such as It's All Right incorporate all of the features which Campbell argues are unique to the rhetoric of women's liberation.[33] Consciousness raising, the "paradigm that highlights the distinctive stylistic features of women's liberation" rhetoric, can also serve as a model for understanding the radical feminist theatres. Both use affective as well as logical proof, rely on leaderless persuasion, resort to "violating the reality structure," and effect a transaction between the personal and the political. To such a posture established media and theatres predictably respond in kind: they attack, or ignore, the radical groups.

Summary. The phenomenon of feminist theatre grew out of a unique blend of historic circumstance and rhetorical problems. Politically powerless, many women chose to air grievances, explore possibilities, advocate change through the medium of theatre. They did so for some of the reasons that low-power groups of the past have exploited its persuasive capabilities. But the additional rhetorical problems confronting women (the conflict between the role *rhetor* and the role *woman*; the paradox inherent in the demand/request of equality; the peculiar interaction between the private and the public issues of liberation rhetoric) made theatre an unusually attractive option.

CARAVAN THEATRE

BOBBI AUSUBEL

Unlike most feminist theatres, Caravan was not founded as a result of the women's movement by a group of assertive women ready to do theatre. The fact that we were already in existence as part of the '60's experimental theatre movement, with a consciously political direction and with both men and women, colored the work we did. Caravan (1965–78) probably was the first feminist theatre to produce.

We were called Caravan because Stan Edelson and I, as co-founders and co-directors, organized it as a touring summer project of the American Friends Service Committee. We got a school bus, and we'd go perform for food and twenty-five dollars. The first summer we hit on what was to become the Caravan style, alternating between known published scripts and company-created original works, all of which raised questions about personal relationships to social and political happenings of the times. That first summer, in an elaborate environmental setting, we produced Max Frisch's comment on the

Bobbi Ausubel, Chair of the Theatre Division of Boston Conservatory of Arts, teaches acting, directs, and writes plays.

stockpiling of bombs amidst an indifferent public. That was followed by a company-created script, *We Shall Overcome???*, our multiracial ensemble piece that described the difficulties blacks and whites had coming together.

In the beginning the nature of our work was small. I didn't know it could be big. I come from a non-achieving working-class family, and it was just wonderful to perform in little coffeehouses. One day we got a review in the *Boston Globe* that said, "*The Maids* [Genet] is near genius." It seemed to me people were just rushing in. We had no chairs. I turned around and suddenly we had a business manager who spent my pennies on a roll of printed tickets. I was furious! What right had we to spend good money on tickets when you could give people pieces of cut-up colored paper instead? I had to learn to get paid for the work I do. Sometimes I wish I could go back to the old way when the stakes were lower.

The play that transformed me, and the theatre, and influenced Boston the most, was *How to Make a Woman*. At a Caravan planning meeting in my living room in January 1967—before the women's movement was dreamed of—I said, "I want to do a play about what it's like to be a woman in this culture, and how it is different from being a man." The men were supportive and the women cool, not wanting to be classified as "women," but as "people." We went into rehearsal. My role was to design improvisations and direct. Stan wrote the script from the improvs and from his wonderful imagination.

When we opened it at Club 47 in Cambridge, June 1967, the audiences came, clapped and left. This is in strong contrast to what happened one year later. The world outside the theatre was beginning to quake while we were re-rehearsing and changing the script before reopening it for our first full season at what became our permanent home, the Harvard Epworth Church in Harvard Square. Joe Volpe, an actor in the company, told me a friend had come back from the SDS (Students for a Democratic Society) meeting in Chicago and she had participated in a female liberation group that had formed there. We were stunned. Gradually what I had been saying in the play became clear to me, as it did to the rest of the group. We learned and understood, and relearned with the audiences, and rewrote for the next three years of the run.

How to Make a Woman was an "Ah ha!" experience for many. People began to stay for discussions, compelled to reexamine their lives. Both women's and men's groups were formed right there in the theatre. Then the women from these groups would come back and lead discussions for audiences at subsequent performances. The play made Caravan into a center of feminist energy in Boston. People would come back and squeeze into a space that held 200 people and sit on uncomfortable wooden benches, even during the anti-war riots when streetlamps were broken outside our windows and tear gas went off. What a way to do theatre! Alive! We were feeding and being fed.

How to Make a Woman tells the story of two women who find themselves in a dress shop (symbolizing the world) run by men. The men seduce the women into certain garments (gender roles) they have designed. The humorous hanky-panky of the designers' offerings begins to work on Mary, but is cut off when Aili prevents her companion from taking the "boob" baby girl's dress and instead forces her to make a dreamlike descent into the beginnings of time, from her birth through her girlhood, sexuality, marriage, and even old age. Then Aili too is forced to make a descent. Her fantasy recreates the terrifying role of Big Mama and the pseudo-liberated marriage. The women flee the shop at the end. The dreamlike sequences were expressed in physical movement-based acting, which was popular in the experimental theatres of the time and which often served as the basis for Caravan's acting style.

Looking back over the years I notice that I have always chosen to create plays about what has been most hateful or painful to me. The theatre process is one of exorcism, of transforming pain. I often start from confusion I have no distance from. For example, *Focus on Me* is about the part of us that hates women. It is an all-women's play; it had to be. For me it was about learning to accept my mother (and all seemingly "weak" women), to accept being a mother, loving my child self, my children. In the play a woman filmmaker is trying to make a film with another woman. She keeps putting her partner down. Like the society, she does not value nurturing and motherhood. So *Focus on Me* was about the process of loving another woman. It ran for eight months.

Caravan's successes were many. (I couldn't have said this years ago when the theatre closed and I felt like a failure.) We created new scripts centering on women, on male/female roles, for at least ten years. We recreated known dramatic literature (Brecht, Beckett, Euripides) in feminist terms. *Tell Me a Riddle* (an adaptation from Tillie Olsen's novella) and *Family* each won praise in Boston as one of the ten best plays of their respective years. Often, we got both mainstream and counterculture press coverage, which brought in a wide variety of audiences. We regularly got NEA and Massachusetts Council of the Arts grants. We influenced, among other theatre people, Megan Terry and Martha Boesing, who came to see *How to Make a Woman* at early stages in its run; Earth Onion, a women's theatre group, formed because we traveled to Washington, D.C., in one of our tours. Caravan took feminist ideas to Poland, where we toured for a month as part of the International Polish Experimental Theatre Festival. We nourished many actors and directors; we changed from a hierarchy to a collective.

Caravan transformed men and women together, understanding through painful and exhilarating group process that we were all socialized and forced into polar experiences. We, together, gave an artistic voice to the best of feminist politics: the uniting of the personal and the political.

OMAHA MAGIC THEATRE

Jo Ann Schmidman founded Omaha Magic Theatre in her native city in 1968, determined to create innovative theatre by and for the people of the Midwest. In the early 1970's she was a performing member/collaborator with the Open Theatre, while keeping the theatre going in Nebraska. In 1970 she played the title role in *Approaching Simone*, which won Obie awards for director Maxine Klein and writer Megan Terry. Schmidman's association with Terry has continued since, with Terry first writing for Omaha Magic Theatre, then joining full-time in 1974 as a playwright, literary advisor, and sometime designer. Schmidman writes and performs in addition to providing artistic direction and fiscal management.

Besides many skilled performers, a large group of Midwest painters and sculptors work with them, and they have four composers in residence. They have converted three storefronts to total theatre environments, produced more than seventy new plays and musicals, and televised many of these shows. The company produces a newsletter, *Magic Dust*, and tours the country, including schools, prisons and Indian reservations. Omaha Magic Theatre has never had a deficit, and in 1981 was named "One of America's Best Regional Theatres" by *Better Homes and Gardens*.

The theatre serves as a catalyst for the community while working closely with it. Megan Terry describes this relationship: "The audience tells us what they want to deal with. We do one piece a year which we think of as lending our skills to give voice to community concerns. The other seven plays we produce are for our own and our audience's artistic growth." *American King's English for Queens* (1978) voiced concern for sexism in language by examining it in family dynamics. Audience discussions after the performances acknowledged domestic verbal violence, and led to *Goona Goona* (1979), an examination of physical violence in the home. Terry designed *Goona Goona*, creating a soft-sculpture "house as a gigantic quilt." Terry describes her costume design "as a combination of puppets and football uniforms with padding so the actors wouldn't get hurt. They hit each other with baseball bats while depicting family violence."

Kegger, a portrayal of alcohol use and misuse among young people, was performed as a "model program" at the 1983 "Secretarial Conference for Youth on Drinking and Driving" in Washington, D.C., and televised by Omaha's NBC affiliate during prime time. To prepare the production, the company met with neurosurgeons, neuropsychologists, biologists, and drug counselors as they researched alcoholism. *Kegger* then toured through the Midwest

---

Compiled by Linda Jenkins from information supplied by the Omaha Magic Theatre, and from published interviews with Megan Terry conducted by Dinah L. Leavitt (in the first edition of this book), and by Kathleen Betsko and Rachel Koenig (in their *Interviews with Contemporary Women Playwrights*).

290 WOMEN IN AMERICAN THEATRE

and played to over 45,000 people. "Everyone is working now to find ways to have chemical-free fun. They've formed positive peer pressure groups within the schools to let kids know it's okay not to drink," Terry asserts. Schmidman adds, "The play is really about the ability of young people to make decisions: When do we become mature enough to know right from wrong—is there a magical age? Respect for the young and myth promoted by media are also dramatically set straight."

Omaha Magic's productions cover many performance styles and topics. For example, *100,001 Horror Stories of the Plains*, produced for the U.S. Bicentennial, collected stories from across the plains via a contest, then performed them in a family dinner-style setting for which people could either pay money or bring food to share. *Running Gag*, an exploration of the American fascination with running and jogging, was commissioned by and performed at the 1980 Winter Olympics in Lake Placid, N.Y., before touring the country. *Sleazing toward Athens*, a transformation play dealing with earning versus learning among today's college students, had sold-out runs in Omaha and toured the Midwest.

Not all of the theatre's work is overtly political or social critique. *Objective Love* is a musical performance event about love and the games lovers play; *Family Talk* is a play with music showing positive ways to create effective communication within the family; and *Astro*Bride* is a "McCluhanesque" sci-fi performance musical for one woman, three robots and a synthesizer. Terry emphasizes that for herself, Schmidman, and the Omaha Magic Theatre, "Art is about taking action. I believe in taking creative action. Theatre reminds you that you can transcend this discrete unit, the body, by combining imaginatively with your community in reacting with, for, and to the presentation on the stage that is meaningful to the community."

THE WASHINGTON AREA FEMINIST THEATRE

MARY CATHERINE WILKINS AND CATHLEEN SCHURR

The Washington Area Feminist Theatre was formed in 1972 to provide theatrical opportunities in an atmosphere that would not limit women, to train women in theatre skills, to produce plays designed to broaden the perception of women's capabilities on and off stage, and to promote an understanding of women's experience in society from a woman's point of view. WAFT produced three full seasons of plays—all written by women, a number of them world or

Mary Catherine Wilkins and Cathleen Schurr were both founding board members of WAFT. Wilkins, also a founding member of Back Alley Theatre, works in the Arts and Humanities Programming Department of the Public Broadcasting Service. Schurr, a founding member of what is now called Three for the Show, which Wilkins directs, is an actress and author, most recently of *Sexual Assault: Confronting Rape in America* with Nancy Gager.

Washington premieres, others revivals of shows that are part of the heritage of women in theatre. In 1976 WAFT's major production activity ceased because of both the termination of its relationship with a local college and an internal organizational breakdown.

As a feminist theatre, WAFT always aimed at a high level of artistic accomplishment while exploring the complexity and diversity of women's lives. All production work was performed by women; WAFT's primary commitment to women did not exclude men from audiences or casts, but they rarely functioned on production crews.

Successful production of two short plays for the Washington, D.C., chapter of the National Organization for Women as a part of the anniversary of women's suffrage during the week of August 26, 1972, encouraged some of the women who worked on the shows to discuss the formation of a feminist-oriented theatre. The only other women's theatre group in the Washington area at that time was Earth Onion. This women's collective, closed to new members, toured with an improvisationally based piece. The organizers of WAFT planned a different kind of theatre—one which would produce scripted plays and involve as many women as possible.

The six women who met initially included some who were attracted by the theatrical potential and some by the political potential. This mixture remained fairly consistent throughout WAFT's history. The initial group consisted of middle-class, college-educated, heterosexual, white women. The social class and education level of the group never changed substantially. However, by 1974 there were a number of lesbians working with the theatre. This change was disturbing to some of the heterosexual women, whose feelings were discussed at meetings of the WAFT board. There were continuing disagreements between those who wanted WAFT to be more politically radical—mostly lesbian—and those who wanted WAFT to remain moderate—mostly heterosexual.

By 1976, there were some black women working with WAFT and attending productions. Most of the founding board members were in their twenties, but one was in her forties, and two in their mid-fifties. Most of the women who took part in productions, especially as crew members, tended to be in their twenties or early thirties. The interchange between age groups proved to be valuable to the board and to the productions. New members were recruited at public meetings and workshops.

The outcome of one early workshop is illustrative of some of WAFT's basic principles in action. The workshop on "Technical Theatre" evolved into an "introduction to scene design" because of the interests and talents of two of the participants—an artist and an interior designer—who continued to work together, designing and constructing sets for the next three major WAFT productions. It was central to WAFT's definition of itself as an experimental theatre that women were supported in their ventures into new areas.

One of WAFT's problems was locating scripts by women playwrights. Finding the names of women writers and the titles of their plays involved extensive searching—of catalogs, anthologies, theatre histories, and library stacks. Then, finding the plays themselves was an additional problem. Contacts made by WAFT's script director, playwright Elizabeth Wilson Hughes, eventually brought in numerous original works.

These are some of the criteria that were applied to scripts: Is it written by a woman? What is its artistic merit? Are there more roles for women than men? Has it been produced frequently by other theatre groups? How does it fit with the other possibilities for the season? WAFT never produced a play written by a man, or one with more and/or better parts for men than women, or one of the commonly produced plays by women playwrights. Judgments about artistic merit and political content were most difficult because both are subjective. Frequently there were as many opinions as there were women in the room, but eventually, through compromise, a consensus was reached.

Although WAFT did not differ radically from traditional theatres in its production structure and process, it did differ in spirit. Feelings of self-confidence, self-reliance, mutual trust, and community were generated among the women who worked on productions because they were in an atmosphere in which women were in authority and where competence and achievement were the norms. This was sometimes difficult for some of the male actors; others, however, seemed to learn and grow from the experience. Conflicts also arose because some of the women resented the presence in a feminist theatre of even the few men who acted in productions. Although this issue was discussed frequently, WAFT continued to include men in the cast and in the audience.

During "Sound-Off" sessions after performances, the audience, including critics from metropolitan dailies and community newspapers, had a chance to exchange comments and questions with WAFT team members. Among the many disparate views, two comments were repeatedly voiced—that the play was too radical and militantly feminist, and that the play was not militant and radical enough. Men in the audience as well as in the cast were openly "astonished" that women were able to design and construct sets, hang light plots and manage an intricate theatre schedule while carrying on other jobs. Some critics consistently focused on WAFT's name and politics rather than on the artistic merit of the productions. Nevertheless, WAFT maintained generally good media relations, received the same coverage as other D.C. experimental theatres, and had its fair share of good and bad reviews. The theatre enjoyed the support of local feminist groups and publications, and by the time it stopped producing, it had achieved a reasonable degree of recognition throughout the Washington area.

In addition to its regular theatre schedule, WAFT also sponsored special events with the goal of encouraging women artists. These included a play contest, a Clearinghouse Bulletin for unpublished plays, and a program for women students from Antioch College. A grant from D.C.'s Commission on the Arts and Humanities, as well as organizational specialists brought in by the board of directors, helped the organization expand and work through problems.

WAFT began with no initial capital, but was able to raise money from box-office receipts, donations, small grants, workshop fees, contractual arrangements, and special fund-raising activities. The financial arrangement with Mount Vernon College, a women's college, was a great boon from 1974 to 1976: WAFT received free office, workshop and rehearsal space, and was paid between 10 and 15 percent of box-office revenues for productions and special events.

That arrangement was not renewed in 1976 when new administrators were not receptive to a feminist theatre on campus. At the same time, WAFT's board experienced an internal breakdown. These two factors forced a cessation of WAFT's major production activity. During the 1976–77 season WAFT produced a series of short productions, discussions and workshops designed to explore the impact of combining theatre with feminist politics.

A focal point of dissension during the period when the board of directors was trying to reorganize was WAFT's production of Lillian Mortimer's Victorian melodrama *No Mother to Guide Her*. During its run it was attacked by members of the board as "sexist" and "racist," and was said to lack redeeming artistic or political content. In an atmosphere of great confusion and many recriminations, the board decided that it could no longer function effectively as a group.

Since 1976, there have been a number of different small transition groups working to revitalize the organization, but the phoenix has not yet risen from its ashes. Whatever lies in WAFT's future, it can be proud of its concrete accomplishments. It has passed on a legacy which is alive in the groups that it inspired and in the women who worked with WAFT over the years.

WOMEN'S INTERART THEATRE

The Women's Interart Theatre functions as part of an extraordinary complex known as Women's Interart Center in New York City. The Center began around 1969 "with a group of women from several art forms meeting in lofts and in a Lower East Side firehouse," as Margot Lewitin, its long-time artistic director, recalls. "Each of us was supposed to present or perform some piece of work: a painting, a poem, a piece of music." Lewitin was asked in 1970 to help

---

Written and compiled by Helen Krich Chinoy from information supplied by the staff of Women's Interart Theatre and an interview with Margot Lewitin by Arthur Sainer, "Interart Walks a Tightrope," *The Village Voice*, August 7, 1984.

write a grant for a permanent home. When the group received some funding from New York State Council on the Arts, it moved into an then-abandoned city-owned building.

The participants used their $5,000 grant to renovate four floors of an industrial building on West 52nd Street, creating a theatre along with an art gallery and work facilities for artists. The Center dedicated itself to supporting independent women artists from different disciplines and to integrating the visual arts, music, dance, and theatre. Its participants believe that all the arts are interrelated and that to create them or present them in isolation is to limit their appreciation and growth. In addition to encouraging artists to work together, the Center supports efforts on the part of its participants, who include men as well as women, to learn new skills and experiment with new media and offers innovative training programs for both professional and beginning artists.

The Interart Theatre evolved within the context of the Center, coming into being more than two years after the Center itself had been formed. Lewitin recalls its informal beginnings:

> I'd been working at La Mama, stage-managing for a number of productions. After La Mama, I worked for Mobilization for Youth, but one day my job disappeared. I began spending a lot of time at the Center. Indeed I had nothing else going that particularly interested me. It was a good place to be. . . . Not until the 1972–73 season did we do our first theatre piece. I directed a play by Jane Chambers called *Random Violence*. . . . Whether I would ever have moved from stage-managing without Women's Interart I don't know. But being here somehow gave me the courage to begin directing plays.

The women's work nurtured and presented in the Interart Theatre is notable. As one of the oldest theatres in New York emphasizing the work of women playwrights and directors, Interart has staged over fifty productions, more than half premieres, almost all written or directed by women, whose creative growth remains the theatre's primary concern. Novices like Wendy Kesselman, who went on to win the Susan Blackburn award for *My Sister in This House*, wrote her first play, *Becca*, on a commission from Interart. The actress Estelle Parsons made her major directorial debut there in 1979, directing a large-scale *Antony and Cleopatra*. Other playwrights and directors who have worked at the Interart include Joyce Aaron, JoAnne Akalaitis, Kay Carney, Beverley Eamonds, Corinne Jacker, Salome Jens, Adrienne Kennedy, Françoise Kourilsky, Myrna Lamb, Lee Nagrin, Meredith Monk, Elinor Renfield, Amy Saltz, Nancy Rhodes, and Susan Yankowitz.

Interart Theatre's dedication to women has brought them important awards: in 1984, both a special Obie grant and a Drama Desk Award. In 1985, the Women's Committee of the Dramatists Guild gave its annual award to Margot Lewitin for her contribution to the development of women playwrights and women in theatre.

In addition to the recognition and the awards, this dedication to fostering women theatre artists has also brought the Interart Theatre a lot of headaches. "We walk a tightrope," Margot Lewitin told Arthur Sainer in a *Village Voice* interview in 1984:

> Some believe that the organization, with its many women artists, is inherently too feminist. Others think the Center isn't feminist enough. Some women's organizations feel that Women's Interart, by virtue of its existence as a women's cooperative, ought to be fashioning a very particular feminist ideology. It's true that we don't necessarily explore feminist issues. . . . In fact, the feminist community as a whole isn't that interested in art. . . . The truth is we don't have an anti or pro ideology. If we have a bias, it's simply in favor of supporting women artists rather than men.

The Interart's relationship to the projects of the Women's Experimental Theater, which Roberta Sklar and Sondra Segal co-direct, exemplifies their approach. Lewitin explains, "They develop, we house." But Sklar says that "they don't just leave us alone, they leave us alone with love and support." Yet Lewitin insists that Interart is "more than a collection of doting parental figures and discipline-free offspring." Over the years "we had to find a balance between being supportive and being stupid. At some point you have to make a judgment, you have to take responsibility for what you're putting up."

As a result of its open, supportive, responsible approach, Interart has offered productions that vary greatly in content and style. Its biggest "hit," ironically, was a play by a man, Franz Xaver Kroetz's *Through the Leaves*. But it was staged by a woman, JoAnne Akalaitis, and featured Ruth Maleczech and Frederick Neumann; all the artists involved won Obie Awards in 1984. Another notable project was transforming *Tongues* by Sam Shepard and Joe Chaikin for television.

Because women's work tends to be less well received by audiences and critics, there has been some concern that Interart may be playing down its women's aspect. Lewitin has said that "there are foundation people who genuinely feel that any organization that has the word 'women' in its title can't be serious about art." Without being dogmatically feminist, Interart fights this accusation by their continued dedication to providing a place for women artists.

Their major energies are now devoted to preventing the demolition of their building as part of the attempted gentrification of the Clinton Hill area, where the Interart Center's presence had brought other arts organizations like Ensemble Studio Theatre to the building and to the neighborhood. Having won the first stage of a battle with the city government to remain in their building in April 1986, Women's Interart is trying to implement an alternative community development plan, purchase the building, and continue to operate their multi-discipline center with its primary dedication to women in the arts.

NEW YORK FEMINIST THEATER TROUPE

CLAUDETTE CHARBONNEAU AND LUCY WINER

We two founded a radical, all-women's theatre company, the New York Feminist Theater Troupe, which began in December 1973 and gave what turned out to be its last performance in the spring of 1976. We and the other six original members of the troupe had, on a moment's notice, submerged ourselves in a whirlwind of planning sessions, rehearsals, and performances. In the first months a script was written, troupe members found, and performances staged at women's centers, churches, and colleges in New York and New England. This period culminated in a summer tour of western Canada, only six months after our first meeting. Though we went on to do a great deal more—we made a film, *Jeriann*, and staged a second theatrical production, *In Transit*—we were never again to match the energy, enthusiasm, and sheer productivity of those first six months.

It is hard to reconcile our knowledge that the troupe no longer exists with the feeling that it could still all be possible. And nothing—no amount of analysis, nor hours spent rehashing the probable causes of the troupe's dissolution—can mitigate the overriding sense of loss. If not for ourselves, then for those who come after us, there may be value in uncovering the problems.

Alternative groups, inevitably, confront a great many problems in our society. Much of what we faced would be shared by any troupe attempting to do political theatre. Yet certain problems were more acute because we were a group of women. Imbued with a sense of feminism, we wanted our troupe to be an arena into which any woman could step, even if only for a short while. Thus for one New York City production we encouraged a Frenchwoman briefly visiting the United States to join our cast. Knowing no English, she sat on a high stool in white face, playing an organ grinder, welcoming the audience to our show.

This flexibility was invigorating, even though the "polish" of the show might suffer. In fact, it was this kind of spontaneity and openness that the troupe sought. But it was much harder to attain in our permanent membership. We had hoped to create a troupe that would not only portray on stage but embody in its membership the various phases and modes of women's lives. Originally, our group had some range, particularly in terms of age. Some members were lesbians; others were heterosexual. But we never achieved the fully representative group we had envisioned.

Despite the fact that we were all involved in the women's movement, we had

Claudette Charbonneau and Lucy Winer were founding members of the New York Feminist Theater. Charbonneau has taught women's studies at SUNY Stony Brook and Brooklyn College, and is currently visiting professor at University of Tampere, Finland. Winer has completed three prize-winning films, including the most recent, a documentary of male attitudes, *Rate It X*, with Paula de Koenigsberg, co-produced by Charbonneau.

not fully and concretely grasped the actual constraints under which most women live. Child care, housework, husbands, unrewarding jobs—all would conspire to make it exceedingly difficult for most women to join an itinerant theatre. But we never did give up: a woman on welfare, mother of twins, joined us to work on the film and the second production. By then we had learned how difficult and consuming it is to sustain a theatre troupe, and how rare it would be for any but a very young woman to be free enough to jump in. The severe limits placed on most women's lives came sharply into focus when the troupe suddenly decided to embark on our tour of Canada. Who could dream of such a journey? Only women who were unmarried, women who had no set careers, women who weren't working to support others—only they could pack up and leave for two months.

Aside from the physical constraints, what of the emotional risks? All the original members had shown a dare-devil courage simply in joining. The prospect of an extended tour in a different country seemed a wonderful opportunity and we all knew it; and yet hours upon hours had to be spent in "emotional meetings," not discussing the very real practical issues like money and transportation, but unraveling vague and unidentifiable fears. In fact, whenever the troupe asked us to venture into new territory, to consider a new possibility, most of us experienced a ridiculously disproportionate amount of anxiety—a measure of just how strong and tenacious societal lessons of conformity and nonassertiveness can be. Joining the troupe meant overcoming more hurdles, both physical and psychical, than we had at first anticipated.

Lack of funding presented us with other, obvious kinds of difficulties. If nothing else, money provides a buffer. It can make the daily life of a troupe less harrowing, solving some of the constant, nagging problems—how to pay for adequate rehearsal space, how to transport props or the players themselves to out-of-town engagements, etc. Not to seek funding had been an early and a conscious decision. The troupe had arranged the first performance with no outside help or guidance and that sense of independence gave us tremendous energy. For a group of women to eschew the ordinary, established paths of support in itself made a political point. Clearly, our financial goals had to be modest. The fees we earned were small and the money made from one show had to be put toward the next. But we proved that an audience of women did exist and could be relied on to sustain radical feminist theatre. Our sense of independence was, of course, at the cost of other, important ideals. With money we might have been able to hire some of those women who could not join otherwise and thereby have given the troupe the broader representation we wanted. Nevertheless, if we were starting out again today, we might yet abide by our original decision.

The material the troupe performed centered on issues—the harmful and sometimes lethal side effects of available birth-control devices, the lack of equal work and educational opportunities, the sterilization of Third World women, the fear of lesbians, the medical treatment of women, etc. We used statistics and cited names. Our tone was not self-righteous; frequently, in fact, it was humorous. But there was no way the audience could avoid confronting in specific terms what it means for women to live in a male-dominated world.

Our first show, Lucy Winer's *But, Something Was Wrong with the Princess*, opened as a circus, a device offering many possibilities for exaggeration, slapstick, and improvisation. The scene culminated in a sideshow of freaks: Abortion Annie; Birth Control Bonnie; 'Lectric Lizzie, the survivor of many electric shock treatments; and Wonder Woman, the perfect housewife. The play also included original music, poetry, and scenes such as "The Socialization of Mary," "A Psychiatric Consultation," and "Dear John," a song describing a married woman's emotions as she decides to leave her husband. In contrast to the color and flair of the opening, the play closed in darkness: from all sides of the performance space we whispered and shouted the proverbial statements that have shaped women's sense of themselves—excerpts of anti-women passages from the Bible, fragments from the marriage ceremony, lines from television commercials, refrains from folksongs, and finally a mounting barrage of catcalls and sexual comments from men on the street.

None of the problems we faced had easy or obvious solutions. Those who were more committed found themselves pushing those who were not—a situation that drained and hurt everyone. The problem in our case was exacerbated, ironically, by elements which were assets: the substantial range in age and the dynamic qualities of several members. Because the most forceful were also the oldest, the sense of disparity was magnified. The troupe had trouble handling the different levels of energy and commitment in a way compatible with feminist ideology. "Emotional meetings" were helpful at times, but their effect was not lasting. There are limits to what consciousness-raising can do in the short run and the troupe lived very much in a short run crowded with the demands of rehearsal and performance schedules. Our failure to achieve a more equal and spontaneous involvement from all the members was a major cause of the troupe's decline. Those who felt "hammered away at" pulled back emotionally. Those who envisioned something more than a brief experiment began to lose heart at the prospect of constantly urging others on.

The disparities in involvement might not have been so debilitating if other divisions had not emerged. As a feminist theatre troupe we had a dual commitment—to politics and to theatre. How to maintain a proper balance became more and more problematic. The divisions arose subtly, as a question of emphasis and not of clear-cut choice. (Not even those who came to see acting as a lifelong pursuit wanted to be part of traditional theatre.) As the troupe got over the initial exhilaration simply at having put on a show, some began to have different expectations. Everyone wanted to put on a good production; but slowly the definition and conception of "a good production" began to change. The shift in expectations led to a shift in values. Spontaneity, flexibility, open membership had to be rejected if the "polish" of the performance were to come first.

The division between a grassroots political orientation and increasingly professional artistic hopes posed our most serious problem. Can the two be reconciled? A sensible balance might have been struck—if the troupe had had a more holistic sense of theatre and a clearer recognition of what the members really wanted and if, while we were trying to develop our range and depth as performers, we had also put more energy into being just as creative politically.

To dwell on difficulties, however, may obscure the most important point of all—that a group of women without experience or help created a feminist theatre troupe that lasted three-and-a-half years. We played every place and any place: in cafeterias, bars, prisons, day-care centers, classrooms, gymnasiums, ballrooms, and even a laundromat. The very real sadness we feel because the troupe no longer exists must not be allowed to cloud that reality. In this country and Canada, we reached thousands of women. Certainly we had wanted to build a more lasting structure. But it is perhaps a mistaken value to stress permanence, particularly if it detracts from the recognition that in existing at all we achieved something very hard and very wonderful.

THE LAVENDER CELLAR THEATRE

DINAH L. LEAVITT

The Lavender Cellar Theatre was founded in Minneapolis in 1973 by eight lesbian women; its final performance was given less than two years later. During that time the theatre collective performed six original productions for about two thousand people. The members had few theatre skills, little experience, no money, no scripts, no theatre building, and no clear idea of what a lesbian theatre was.

The founders originally intended their theatre to be a vehicle for telling the story of lesbian oppression and lifestyles. Complications arose immediately. Some of the women, fearing reprisals, refused to perform publicly outside the gay community; others, involved with gay rights, were unable to commit sufficient time to produce a play; and no one knew of a lesbian play to produce. Floundering, the core members decided to join the Alive and Trucking Company, a local socialist agitprop theatre. However, this plan was abandoned because the Alive and Trucking could not devote enough time to lesbian issues.

Dinah L. Leavitt, Associate Professor and Coordinator of the Theatre Program at Fort Lewis College, Colorado, published *Feminist Theatre Groups* in 1980, © by Dinah L. Leavitt, from which this segment is adapted by permission of McFarland & Company, Jefferson, North Carolina. The former members of Lavender Cellar Theatre gathered one day in summer, 1977, and allowed the author to glimpse what their theatre had been like.

In September 1973 the group, led by Marie Kent, gathered at the Lesbian Resource Center to reorganize. This time the women decided to use the theatre to explore and present the lesbian experience for lesbians. Member Nythar Sheehy says:

It started because lesbians needed something tangible to validate their experience; they needed something to get people to work together and as an alternative social function to bars. It also developed creativity and raised our own and our audience's consciousnesses.

One crucial element in the development of a cohesive lesbian community in Minneapolis was the Lesbian Resource Center, which in turn played an important role in the establishment of the Lavender Cellar. It provided rehearsal and performance space, acted as a financial backer for productions, and gave emotional support to group members; its own collective structure became a model for the theatre's organization.

Members adopted the collective structure because they wanted to overcome the usual management politics, competition, and hierarchy of established theatres. Besides collective responsibility for all work and decisions, the group used the concept to share both the group's and individual members' problems. Collective administration usually worked well because the group was small and stable in membership; its business-management needs were minimal; and its major production style—the revue—was well suited to group direction. However, members stated that the cooperative process was often overly time-consuming and that arriving at a consensus was often chaotic.

The company rehearsed an average of twice weekly with five rehearsals a week before each opening. Any member could submit a script for consideration or offer ideas for a collaborative piece. Following auditions, shows were cast and staff assigned by collective approval. Direction was cooperative:

People explored parts as they interpreted them and the director was more of a coordinator. When a total interpretation was necessary, a discussion was held with the entire cast.

The company employed a variety of acting and directing styles and techniques "as a means of getting in touch with the feelings the characters were expressing which had also been our own feelings." This developmental process, begun with *Prisons*, was expanded and refined through subsequent productions.

The first play, *Prisons*, a one-act by member Pat Suncircle, depicted the roles in which people are willingly and unwillingly cast and the consequences of defining one's role. Presented first at the Lesbian Resource Center in spring 1973, before the group's reorganization, the portable production was kept in repertoire and toured to conferences and meetings.

In December 1973 the group performed an occasional piece, *Scene at the Center*, a musical parody reflecting interaction and activity at the Lesbian

Resource Center. This piece, intentionally limited in its appeal, was performed only at the Center.

In February 1974 the company performed, again at the Center, a modern dance revue, *Isadora Is Arisen*, coordinated by Nythar Sheehy, and in May it presented *Women's Struggle Throughout History*, a reader's theatre production based on the writings of such women as Sojourner Truth, Gertrude Stein, and Susan B. Anthony. In fall 1974 the group put together a musical revue of eight short acts titled *Cabaret '74*. Like *Scene at the Center*, it was a celebration of the lesbian experience, designed to entertain and provide a social basis of unity for the lesbian community.

Cory, by Suncircle, presented in May 1975, was about a sixteen-year-old girl's struggle with family, friends, society, and self in dealing with her lesbianism. The realistic two-act drama employs a cast of ten, including two male roles, Cory's father and her friend, Douglass. The Lavender Cellar cast women in the male roles, costuming them as men. The audiences accepted the role/actress sex reversal as a convention of the theatre. The presence of nonlesbians would have created a group dynamic that the theatre believed would have been counterproductive.

Cory was enthusiastically received by audiences at the Center; and they remained after performances to discuss the play, the production, and lesbians' and women's issues. *Cory* fulfilled the group's objective of accurately presenting the lesbian experience. It also was successful as a meaningful exploration and experience for cast members. After *Cory* closed, the Lavender Cellar Theatre became inactive and remains so to date. Marie Kent explains, "After working on *Cory* for five months, we were exhausted, and no one came forward to relieve us."

The influence of the group was small by some measures, but if one considers the special, unique, and difficult goal it attempted to accomplish without role models, society's approval, or financial support, its limited appeal is both understandable and valuable. Lavender Cellar Theatre reaffirmed lesbian values and goals, contributed significantly to the Lesbian Resource Center's activity, engendered a sense of community through its performances and discussions, became a rallying point for women, fostered sisterhood and gay solidarity, and entertained, but the most important thing it did was simply to exist. For two years it performed lesbian drama, and that alone is a unique accomplishment.

AT THE FOOT OF THE MOUNTAIN

When Martha and Paul Boesing, Jan Magrane, and three others formed a theatre ensemble in 1974, they consulted the *I Ching*. The hexagram for "the springs at the foot of the mountain" gave them both a name and an image of sustenance. Although the composition and the direction of the theatre have shifted over the years, its evolution has been guided by that central idea of a theatre as necessary as water.

Organized in Atlanta, the group moved to Minneapolis to begin their politically committed work with a production of Martha Boesing's first two plays, *Pimp* and *The Gelding*. By the fall of 1975, all but Martha and Jan had left. Phyllis Jane Rose (then Wagner) saw their production of Boesing's *River Journal* that fall, returned to her job chairing a university directing program to direct the play there, but then quit her job and moved to Minneapolis to forge a collective with Martha and Jan. For Phyllis, Martha Boesing's play "crystallized the lesson of experience: that women and men relate hierarchically."

During the second half of the 1970's, At the Foot of the Mountain explored, and helped create for the rest of the country, the concept of a feminist theatre. Phyllis Jane Rose explains:

> Through the performance of Martha's plays (and "songs"), through the performance of scripts by other women, and through community events and rituals, we work *collectively* asking such questions as: How can we connect theatre with life? What is the correlation between the choices we make as performers and the choices we make as persons? How can theatre work as a spiritual and healing force in our community? How can theatre best serve radical political change? How can we stop giving in to a system in which power over others is the common standard for success? How does a women's theatre differ from the theatre of our heritage (theatre written and produced by men)?

The initial trio remained as the core of the theatre while many others passed through; by 1980 they needed to rest and gain perspective from the exhausting challenge of collective administration. Phyllis Jane Rose continued as managing director, and Martha Boesing returned as artistic director after taking a leave of absence. Jan Magrane resigned but a year later became producing director. The entire theatre reorganized using a board-of-directors structure similar to that of other not-for-profit groups so they could better compete for grants and other patronage. A full-time administrative staff allowed the artists not only to focus on such new plays as *Junkie!*, *Ashes Ashes*

Written and compiled by Linda Jenkins from personal knowledge of the company; discussions with Martha Boesing and Phyllis Jane Rose; an unpublished essay by Jeanyne Bezoier Slettom; At the Foot of the Mountain newsletters; and the introduction to *Martha Boesing: Journeys along the Matrix*, Minneapolis, Vanilla Press, 1978.

We All Fall Down, and *Haunted by the Holy Ghost*, but also to expand the programming to include such new projects as the Summer Workshop Program (culminating in the production of Martha Boesing's *Antigone Too*), the *Junkie!* film, the Broadcloth program (staged readings of new plays by women), and Jan's Coming of Age project (plays with adolescents and senior women). Nevertheless, Martha and Jan finally needed to move in other directions. Jan left in 1985.

In 1984, a decade after the founding of the theatre, Martha Boesing received a $20,000 Bush Foundation fellowship that allowed her an eighteen-month break from the company. She continued to work in association with ATFM, however, playing Fefu in Maria Irene Fornes's *Fefu and Her Friends* (directed by Fornes in 1986), and developing a new multiracial production of her *The Story of a Mother*; but she began reshaping her life as an artist. A National Endowment for the Arts grant in 1987 allowed her to develop further as a playwright.

Phyllis Jane Rose has taken the theatre in a new direction, creating a multiracial, multigenerational, and multicultural theatre company. The 1985–87 seasons included plays by Fornes, Adrienne Kennedy, and Marilyn Seven, a series of staged readings of historical scripts by African-American women playwrights, staged readings of new plays, performances by feminist comedian Janice Perry (aka "GAL"), a Mother's Day pageant created by performance artist Suzanne Lacey and co-directed with Phyllis featuring over 600 older women, a residency by Spiderwoman, and a touring repertoire of reprises of *Raped* and *The Story of a Mother* (scripted by Martha Boesing with the company's collaboration). In this way, the theatre continues to be a source of sustenance for the feminist political community—"the springs at the foot of the mountain."

SPIDERWOMAN

Muriel and Gloria Miguel and Lisa Mayo, the core members of Spiderwoman, are three Cuna-Rappahannock Indian sisters, born on the floor of their grandmother's house in an Italian neighborhood in Brooklyn. Central to their creations are their multicultural and female experiences, their political ideas, and the concept of "weaving" they take from their Native American heritage. The sisters describe the source of their name and the inspiration for their work as follows:

> Spiderwoman or Spider Grandmother Woman is one of the familiar household gods of the Hopi. Her divine powers, her unlimited wisdom and all-encompassing knowledge have made her a culture heroine of Hopi tradi-

---

Written and compiled by Linda Jenkins from articles by her and Diane Cartwright in *Alternative Theatre*, vol. I, no. 3, January/February 1975, p. 5; At the Foot of the Mountain's newsletter, Fall 1985, p. 3; and descriptions of the group in the Boston Women in Theatre Festival programs.

tion. She has prophetic access to the future and is familiar with all the languages of the world. Being a common spider she is ever present and ever ready to intervene, assist, counsel, guide and save.

We take our name from Spiderwoman, goddess of creation, the first to create designs and teach her people to weave. She always wove a flaw into her designs to allow her spirit to find a way out and be free.

We call on her inspiration in the development of our working technique "storyweaving," creating designs and weaving stories with words and movement. We work onstage as an ensemble, basing our productions on life experiences. We translate our personal stories, dreams and images into movement, and refine them into the essential threads of human experience. In seeking out, exploring, and weaving our own patterns, we reflect the human tapestry, the web of our common humanity. Finding, loving and transcending our own flaws, as in the flaw in the goddess's tapestry, provide the means for our spirits to find their way out, to be free.

Challenging the "one size fits all" view of feminism, [we] . . . use our diverse experiences . . . to defy such generalizations as "blondes have more fun" and "all women's theatre is the same." Our stories can be told or thought of at any time—on the street, over meals, in the tub. Then we rehearse, improvise and brainstorm to investigate various aspects of our stories, dreams and images. We usually begin with a theme, someone tells a story, another repeats it, and we work together to transform it into movement or reduce it to its essence.

Muriel Miguel, as director, makes the final decision as to what works and what doesn't with an eye to the creation of an entire production, but everyone in the group has a voice and doesn't hesitate to use it to express herself. This technique insures that a Spiderwoman production will be lively, entertaining and exciting. It also makes for a moving experience within each individual in the audience, as the personal chords sung, whispered, screamed or muttered by the performers strike up resonant reactions with the audience, who become a part of our web, as we become a part of theirs.

The idea for Spiderwoman began with a workshop of Indian and non-Indian women organized by Muriel Miguel at Washington Square Methodist Church in New York in early 1975, to explore this concept of storyweaving. They taught the audience Indian handgames, then one actress became Spiderwoman as she was fingerweaving and began to create a story. Others started weaving in their stories, dreams, and dances, as The New Wilderness Band (men and women) played gongs, bowls, rocks, a saw, flutes, and handmade instruments.

This experiment grew into Spiderwoman, as Muriel involved her sisters and others. They produced *Women in Violence* in June 1975, at New York's American Indian Community House. "I wanted to work with anger, with feelings about being boxed in, feelings about the Indian situation, the Indian Movement today, my own violence as a woman and as an Indian," Muriel has explained.

Their productions have been consistently original, unconventional, transformational events that weave together music, poetry, performance art, fantastic characters, dreams, and environmental art. For *Women in Violence* they used a prologue of Indian songs against a backdrop of quilts received in Sun Dance giveaways and large fabric "webs" sculpted by Donna Hennis. Diane Cartwright described their clown personae:

> Pamela Verge's militant-nun clown sprouted a grammar school nativity-play halo. A scrub brush for cleaning up the world protruded from a bandolier of bullets. Lisa Mayo . . . was garbed in clinging black—essential equipment outlined with white paint, long blonde locks topped by an oversize glitter bow. As the circus's strong woman, Gloria Miguel kept a flashlight hidden between the shiny metal-like strips of her skirt so that she might search for herself beneath the reflected image.

Other productions have included their semi-autobiographical *Sun, Moon and Feather* (three Native American sisters in Brooklyn plot to cross the bridge to Manhattan); *Grandma* (a Kiowa grandmother plans a giveaway, written by Hanay Geiogamah); *The Pause That Refreshes* (a risqué song-and-dance act about menopause); *Neurotic Erotic Exotics* (seven women of color explore experiences of oppression, developed in collaboration with At the Foot of the Mountain); *The Lysistrata Numbah!* (performed on European tour); *I'll Be Right Back* (an exploration of global survival, using folk tales, music, dance, animal sounds, and performance art chants); and *Three Up, Three Down* (a portrayal of tragic relationships, combining a contemporary love triangle among three women with a song about a withered plant and intermittent scenes from *Wuthering Heights* and *Jane Eyre*).

THE WOMEN'S EXPERIMENTAL THEATER

SONDRA SEGAL AND ROBERTA SKLAR

We founded the Women's Experimental Theater in 1976, together with Clare Coss, out of an insurmountable desire to discover our own voice and express it in a theatre where women spoke to women about what was important to them. It was started in a rush of seeking survival as we, alongside of thousands of other women, set out to tell our story.

For more than a decade we dedicated our time, energies, creative and

Sondra Segal, actor and teacher, is co-artistic director of Women's Experimental Theater and a creator of video documentaries. Roberta Sklar, director and teacher, was co-director of the Open Theatre with Joseph Chaikin; she is co-artistic director of Women's Experimental Theater and Director of Public Affairs in the New York City Department of Cultural Affairs. A full discussion of their work is in Cornelia Brunner's interview with Sklar in *TDR*, vol. 24, 2, June 1980.

economic resources to WET, where we reached out to an ever-widening audience of women who needed our work. The urgency and the desire flowed between theatre-maker and audience member in a charged, palpable, and powerful relationship. The subject of our work, though not topical, was always political. We addressed the subversive impulse in women's minds, an impulse to change, to seek expansion of being and a place in the world. We sought to delineate the interaction between the psychological and social worlds. Along with other feminist theatres, theoreticians, artists, and activists, we thought— and at WET, we made thought into theatre. Never before had we used ourselves so fully; never had we even imagined such use.

The three of us collaborated, working together and separately through several stages to create our first series of plays, *The Daughters Cycle Trilogy*. We started with research culled from hundreds of women who participated in workshops and interviews. After an inventory of what we had gathered, we wrote separately, exchanging ideas and material to develop a rough draft. More workshops and rehearsals were followed by more writing, as we also took on more specific roles.

In the research period, we were all actors, putting forth our ideas through improvised images. Sondra and Roberta each directed and acted, inventing exercises to create and generate material. Clare Coss, too, actively entered the actor research as well as writing dialogue and poetry that often extended beyond the parameters of the plays. All three of us wrote material and collaborated in decision-making.

Once the play was in rough-draft form, we would move into a more recognizable phase: the rehearsal of a new play. Roberta concentrated on directing; Sondra focused on performance, looking at the work from within; Clare revised the script. Up to this point we had been doing what we called "inspired writing," but now we would see specific problems in the text. Clare, who was brilliant at rewriting, would go home and fix it.

In performance you'd see Sondra on stage together with Mary Lum and Mary Lyon, the two other actors who worked with us throughout the trilogy (other actors performed in only one or two of the plays); you would see Roberta and Clare in the audience taking notes. We three assessed the work from our unique perspectives. Our roles as performer, writer, and director became more delineated but we continued to collaborate very closely, even as we learned to name what we did individually, to claim our work.

Over more than a decade we created two series of plays through this process: *The Daughters Cycle* and *Woman's Body and Other Natural Resources*. Throughout the work our use of humor was a frequent and deliberate choice to ameliorate the pain of seeing the experience of women in patriarchy. Our intention was to disturb, to challenge ourselves and other women, and to create good times—not to forget, but to remember through humor. We also sought to develop a feminist actor, one who gives testimony to the ability of women to change. Performer and audience member became partners in a process that moved towards change on both sides of the performing line.

The early years of work were devoted to mining our history of daughter-hood. All women are daughters—what could this simple universal truth mean? We were not alone in our passionate research. The mother-daughter relationship, and within it the commonality of daughterhood, gripped femi-nist thinkers in every field during this second wave of twentieth-century feminism.

The result of our labor was *The Daughters Cycle Trilogy: Daughters, Sister/ Sister*, and *Electra Speaks*. *Daughters* is a ritual that moves through themes of birth, the ambivalent and interchangeable nature of mother/daughter roles, the commonality of all women as daughters, and a reclaiming of all our matrilineage: "I'm Sondra,/ daughter of Lille, /Daughter of a woman from Austria." *Sister/Sister* is a search into the relations between sisters and how their childhood realities impact on their adult sisterhood. The third play, *Electra Speaks*, is an explosive work cutting across history and theatrical forms. Its transformational characters, Clytemnestra (the archetypal mother), and Electra and Iphigenia (archetypal daughters and sisters), confront domestic violence and its links to violence on a larger scale. Our Electra, however, does not collude in the murder of her mother. In a Chaplinesque gesture she attempts to sever her ties with the House of Atreus by flinging herself through the Greek archway of Home: "Electra steps out the door/she had never done this before." Separation leads to survival for Electra, the daughter born under a feminist sun.

In 1980 we turned our theatrical attention to another arena. Clare Coss left WET to continue her practice as a psychotherapist and to pursue her writing, while Sondra and Roberta began new theatrical research on the theme of woman's body and "obsession" as a state of mind. *Woman's Body and Other Natural Resources* is a humorous, compassionate, sometimes musical, series of plays about woman's profound relationship to food. Woman's body is food; she provides food; she binges and starves; she struggles to feed herself. *Food* focuses on the daily, unrelenting Family Dinner. After each performance, we were surrounded by audience members urgently reporting to us on their relationship to food. *Foodtalk* combines scripted "Testimony" by an actor with opportunities for the audience to join the actors on stage in naming the daily, unique, but universal concern with food. *Feast or Famine*, the culminating play, portrays woman's relationship to scarcity and plenty on a global scale. It was written and performed by Sondra and directed by Roberta; visual artists and musicians collaborated also, so that this work overlapped the field of perform-ance art.

When *Feast or Famine* was performed in 1985 for an extended run at Women's Interart Center, our home base, we found ourselves reassessing the demand for, need of and response to feminist theatre in the increasingly conservative 1980's that seek to put women back "where they belong," a period that the *New York Times* was calling the "age of post-feminism." Although thinking se-riously about women's lives is as important as it was a decade ago, it no longer seems to be a conscious, pressing part of a mass movement. The Women's

Experimental Theater is not currently active. The decline of economic and audience support tells us this is not the time. We have decided, however, not to formally close up shop. We want to remain open to the rumblings of a distant thunder—that of an old, or new, feminist need.

REBECCAH: REHEARSAL NOTES

KAREN MALPEDE

Rebeccah is a tale whose theme is the birth of the feminist imagination. It is a history of this century from 1905 to 1932, told through the life of one woman, Rebeccah, who becomes a bag lady. As Rebeccah sees how a new community can be built out of the garbage of this civilization, the tale changes tone from grief to joy.

The people who perform this play are workers. They carry all they need into the space with them. And all that they need has been found amidst the garbage on the streets of New York City. They tell a simple story directly. *Rebeccah* is meant to be performed in a circle, the audience surrounding the performers. The story is composed of narrative, song, chant, and moments of mutual turning—when characters exchange thoughts and feelings so deep their ways of being alter.

Rebeccah's tale begins in Kishniff, Russia, 1905. In a pogrom Rebeccah sacrifices her infant son, to save the rest of her family. The tale continues on the Lower East Side of New York City, March 25, 1911. Rebeccah's daughter, Sarah, is caught in the Triangle Shirtwaist Factory fire. Rebeccah becomes a bag lady; she dresses herself in the charred clothing of the victims of the fire. November 1931, Depression winter, Rebeccah founds a shantytown for homeless women and dies.

The *Rebeccah* company in April 1976 consisted of Tina Shepard (director), Karen Malpede (playwright), Linda Gutierrez (associate), and performers Sybille Hayn, Ellen Maddow, Gloria Mojica, Lois Weaver, and Pam Verge. After these rehearsal notes were made, Marcie Begleiter (designer) and performers Jan Cohen and Ann McGinnis joined the company.

April 4. We meet at the Chelsea Theater. (Burl Hash, then a producer at Chelsea, had lent us rehearsal space.)

Rebeccah's beginning: the suffering. Tina is correct to say that the temptation of the company is to rush through to the Depression where the play flowers,

---

Karen Malpede, co-founder with Burl Hash of the New Cycle Theatre in 1977, has been a passionate spokesperson for feminist theatre and the peace movement. She has challenged the avant-garde theatre to emulate feminist theatre's commitment to community and regeneration, inspiring collective projects and providing leadership through her books and plays: *Three Works by the Open Theatre, People's Theatre in Amerika*, and *Women in Theater: Compassion and Hope*, all volumes edited by her, and *A Monster Has Stolen the Sun and Other Plays*, a collection of her plays published in 1987 by The Marlboro Press.

but that we won't be able to fill that part out until we go deeply into the beginning and middle sections where Rebeccah feels the sorrows that lead to her transformation.

The actors take apart the first narration, reading it a dozen different ways. Sybille beats out a steady rhythm, reading over it. Tina and Ellen try to sing it different ways. They try to *daven* (the Jewish prayer rhythm). They try story-telling where each person adds a sentence when they feel the need, that is, when they are motivated by their own remembrance of the "event."

April 7. After the warm-up we hide on stage. First in the dark and then in the light and then we stand in a circle for a long time and speak about the experience. From the hiding two contrary emotions emerge that will resonate throughout the play—a sense of responsibility for everyone else and a wish to dissociate one's self from the others' fates. And another that some people speak of: waiting to see at what moment what you do will make a difference, hoping always for the chance to act. Then the reverse of this (which I feel!) of having hidden and then not wanting to look—of hoping not to be seen because I have stopped seeing.

April 8. The play as a series of concentric circles converging at a center point, the most subjective, the turnings—which, however, would not be possible without the sense of historical and social reality. A cycle in this way, too, beginning with the songs: the most direct connection between actors and audience and material; then the narratives, the survivors speak; the chants are the victims undergoing the psychic changes necessary to end their victimization. The true subjective center is when the victim renames herself or himself survivor.

April 12. Today the warm-up is a Balkan sound, or several. Tina says she feels like she's coming home to sounds she used to make but stopped because they were not music. The Balkan sounds are a folk tradition carried on by women—men's voices, I'm told, cannot do the thing. It is a sound made far forward in the face and not supported by the breath. A strong, somewhat harsh, nasal sound which combines in quite wonderful harmonies. This kind of singing is part of many cultures—Gloria says it sounds Indian, and it also sounds somewhat Appalachian.

Now I can see the large cycle in the play: the pogrom is the recognition, the Triangle fire is the renunciation, and the Depression is the rebirth. Or, like the ancient seasonal rites from which the theatre once derived, and in which women played a major part, first the battle, then the lamentation, then the regeneration, the rebirth. Within this large cycle there are many smaller ones. So the play is a series of circles in this way, too.

April 27. Ellen has composed a beginning pogrom song. I am delighted with it. In Balkan mode it is vibrant and angry and in it I suddenly feel the seeds of all the play becomes—as though in this first song of defeat and despair there is also all the energy for the later struggles and for Rebeccah's triumph.

As Gloria sings a Balkan song her voice trembles and slips from flat to sharp on the note and I see before me the courage of the person seeking to create— that blind faith that the shape will be attained if persistent effort is made. And when she's done, Tina utters my thought, "There was a nice edge about it, as though you were almost falling off, but didn't." Yes, the danger was very present and rang through all of us.

April 28. Art is about the coexistence of opposites: good and evil, pain and joy, temporal and eternal time. The opposites coexist in a balance. Our work is to shift the balance from evil toward good, from misery toward joy, from prose toward poetry. To weigh good in the balance before the mind, the eye and all the aspirations of the heart.

So I see more and more the different balance in the parts of *Rebeccah*. Today, the factory chant becomes a work song. It reminds us of the unused creativity inside these young women workers; each of them takes a turn supplying a line to this song and from the catalog of their ills they have crafted together an ironic and bitter, but consciously created song—they have put themselves into the world this way, beyond the harsh limits of their deadening work, they speak.

I think, too, that the Depression chant is—and is in actual fact since its first verse was literally chanted into my ear by a homeless man as I crossed the Lower East Side one day—another expression of this creativity which lives inside of the oppressed, and another manifestation of the force of conscious shape.

I remember what Rebeccah says to the women while she dies.

> *Now you've found the edge of brave emotion,*
> *stay there,*
> *surging up with each new wave of feeling,*
> *working away at the shape of the world—*
> *though the refashioning takes forever—*
> *no more considering stopping*
> *than a wave in the middle of the ocean*
> *considers not reaching shore.*

SPLIT BRITCHES

Lois Weaver, Peggy Shaw, and Deborah Margolin are the ongoing members of the Split Britches company, which began in 1980 with a production by that name, now considered a masterpiece of feminist theatre. They have created

Written and compiled by Linda Jenkins from information on the company in the Boston Women in Theatre Festival program, an unpublished essay by Sue-Ellen Case, and several unpublished interviews: Beverley Pevitts, 1982, Kentucky, with all three company members; Rhonda Blair, 1986, Massachusetts, with Lois Weaver and Peggy Shaw; and Alisa Solomon, 1986, New York, with Shaw.

remarkable, witty, and provocative women-centered work since then from their home in the East Village and the WOW (Women's One World) Cafe. Their collective vision has been described as being "at the overlapping point of Sapphic poetry, *Mad* magazine, and the Talmud."

Lois Weaver's entry into feminist work was with Spiderwoman; she began with the original storyweaving project and remained with the group for over seven years, directing, acting, and touring Europe and the U.S. Peggy Shaw met Lois and Spiderwoman in Europe (their second tour) while traveling with the gay cabaret Hot Peaches. The only woman in that group, Peggy built sets and costumes and performed. Spiderwoman invited her to help them with a cabaret they were creating, *An Evening of Disgusting Songs and Pukey Images.* Peggy recalls:

> I wasn't used to doing all that emotional kind of stuff. We spent our time [in Hot Peaches] writing new material, sewing on sequins, working with a piano player, changing all the he's to she's and she's to he's in all the songs. In Hot Peaches if you were mad at someone you could yell about it onstage and that was part of the show, but you weren't supposed to do that in Spiderwoman. Me and Spiderwoman kinda went like this [crashing noise] for the two years I was in it. But we all learned a lot and we're all still doing theatre.

Meanwhile, Lois Weaver had begun to conceive of the Split Britches project. Based on stories about her family—especially about three of her aunts—in the Blue Ridge Mountains, what finally emerged was a three-actress tour de force organized by the device of tableaux resembling family photos, with Lois narrating. The stories and gestural performances demonstrated the company's trademark—the split subject. The sisters struggle with their dependencies and their need for independence as they give the audience a funny, thoughtful, touching, sensuous theatre experience.

The original work on this project was done within Spiderwoman in 1980; they brought in Deborah Margolin to script the piece in 1981, and she eventually took over one of the roles when an actress left. With Lois directing, the three actresses told stories in character, told personal stories, sang, and worked transformationally, with "gesture leading from one world to another world."

Work on *Split Britches* inevitably caused a break from Spiderwoman in 1981 because it was hard to have two directors in one company (Lois Weaver and Muriel Miguel), and because the two groups were growing in different directions. Later Lois joined the show as an actress. In 1982 her family saw the piece and were so excited they corrected and embellished certain details. After each show, her father could be found in the lobby with the family album, telling stories to the audience.

Each of the three women in Split Britches brings complementary skills to the company. Peggy Shaw contributes a visual eye and design artistry. Moreover, "She's our political thermometer, our radical," Lois explains. "Peggy can cut through a lot of bullshit and say, 'Get real.'" Deborah Margolin brings a wild sense of humor and strong writing skills. Lois Weaver is the director and acting teacher, combining her college Stanislavski training with sound and movement impulse work growing out of her participation in experimental theatre in the early 1970's. To Lois these approaches are the same system: "I felt they were different words, but they were talking about the same things. So I tried to make some connections in order to use sound and movement as a solid base for teaching acting in a traditional setting." In rehearsals and in the workshops the group offers, Lois teaches what she calls "multiple-choice acting":

> You stand in the center of a wheel in the moment of performance, and at that center you have many things you can choose from. That moment of choice creates a live moment-to-moment performance. When you pre-choose, that is, when you take on a character which is very structured, you lose that moment-to-moment breathing.

Since 1982 the company has created several shows, taught workshops, and worked with the Cafe WOW to establish a genuine community theatre. *The Tennessee Waltz* involved eleven WOW women who developed original scenes, monologues, and music using Tennessee Williams's characters (they were unable to get rights for actual texts).

Other productions include *St. Joan of Avenue C* (based on Brecht's *St. Joan of the Stockyards*, developed with dramaturg Alisa Solomon), *Patience and Sarah*, *Cinderella*, and *Upwardly Mobile Home*. The latter features three women living in a van near the Brooklyn Bridge while a friend tries to win them a new mobile home in a camping-out contest. The three women are rehearsing a revenge play, "The Shanghai Gesture," which they hope will be their big break. *Upwardly Mobile Home* explores what it takes to survive in America; in one memorable image the three of them are in one skirt, singing "I Like to Be in America" in Yiddish. Playing femme and butch respectively, Lois Weaver and Peggy Shaw have also created roles that parody conventional gender representation, which they play on the street and in performance-art and cabaret venues as well as in their theatre productions. Theorist Sue-Ellen Case describes the strategy and the effect:

> On a given day, the butch may be wearing a man's blue suit from the 1950's, complete with shirt and tie. She may also imitate the walk and gestures of the kind of man who would have worn that suit. She disrupts the image with earrings, pant legs that are too short and a flamboyant, Elvis-style haircut. The femme might be wearing turquoise high heels, a turquoise cocktail dress (also from the 1950's) and a turquoise feather boa. Her colors complement the colors of her partner's suit. She, too, may imitate the walk and gestures of the woman who might have worn such a dress. She disrupts the image by relating to her lesbian escort and by wearing the dress in wrinkled, dirty condition, with no nylons and dirty shoes.

They transport these same costumes onto the stage, replete with gestures and characterization, as part of one of their performances. Their local audiences are familiar with their roles both on the street and on the stage, connecting the public persona with character, or drawing connections between stage and street, public self and theatrical character. Onstage, these costumes and gestures last only a short while, as part of a series of images the actors assume and then shed. Or, in some of their plays, these costumes remain on the actor, overlaid with other costumes, until the audience perceives layers and layers of differing gender-wear, differing period pieces, differing ages and differing class and ethnic accoutrements.

During their production of *Beauty and the Beast*, some of the roles played by the femme include a Salvation Army officer, the character of Beauty, Katherine Hepburn, and Lady Macbeth. Some of the butch roles are an old woman sometimes allied with the Salvation Army, the Beast, Perry Como, and James Dean. The Jewish actress takes on the characters of a rabbi, a Jewish stand-up comedian, a ballerina representing Beauty, and Beauty's father. At one point, the butch is wearing the dress of the old lady, the cape of the Beast, and Perry Como's sweater, while the Jewish actress is wearing the clothes of the rabbi, a tutu, and at one point, a dress hanging around her neck on a hanger. . . .

What is the difference between an actor, a celebrity, a social role, or a self-conscious system of gestures? Which character is the owner of the play, the protagonist, the "lead," the subject of the drama? If there is something like a subject position in this kind of performance, it is that of a collective subject.

Here's how the members of Split Britches describe their work:

L.W.   We just tried to tell our stories the best way we could and we wanted to be funny and loud and raucous and crazy. And we wanted to reclaim a lot of roles that had been denied us—to be fat if we wanted to be fat, and to be a country western singer even if we couldn't sing, and to be Juliet if we were sixty. We consciously talked about those things. And we talked about our own experiences most all the time. We rarely ever talked about technique or theory or certainly politics. Our lives are political. In fact, sometimes we were intimidated by the feminist community. After the show we'd be putting on makeup and the women in back were going "Oh, no!" We were closet women. We were the women they'd been talking about all this time. We were questioned about our "dialectical thesis" and we didn't know what they were talking about, because we were just trying to create theatre from our experience as women.

P.S.   This woman in Lexington was going to report in the *Times* and *Newsweek* about the work we do, and we said, "No way, honey, if that's your intention, forget it." Because that's the end of us as we know ourselves. It would be all over.

L.W.   We choose to love the characters we play: In *Beauty and the Beast*, a Salvation Army uptight sergeant who thinks everybody should be Christian, and an Hassidic rabbi who hates women and thinks she's a man and doesn't want to be with us in the first place. We have an eighty-six-year-old lesbian vaudevillian who thinks everything is a show and she's James Dean and she's senile.

D.M.   Everybody has a scene where they break loose. Lois is a Las Vegas-type singer in San Jose giving a reading from *Macbeth*, building up to "unsex me here." Peggy does Perry Como, lipsynching to "It's Impossible"—she misses the chair and the sound shuts off. The rabbi does a standup comic routine. You see the desperate wishes they have for themselves.

L.W.   The criticism we get from men is, "Nothing happened, there's no climax, there's no plot."

P.S.   This guy came and he hated the show. He said, "Even Shakespeare didn't have the nerve to have three women alone onstage without men for over an hour."

D.M.   A lot of our strength comes from not looking around to see, "What do people think?"

L.W.   We are really lucky. We are able to do our own work. The thing that we're most worried about is being true to ourselves. We're not worried about getting cast, about someone deciding to produce our play. It's personal. It's like what I always thought it meant to be an artist.

FEFU AND HER FRIENDS

BEVERLEY BYERS PEVITTS

Maria Irene Fornes explores basic feminist issues in her play *Fefu and Her Friends*. Although set in 1935, the play explores lives of contemporary women. The sensibility, the subject matter, the "universal" female characters, and the very structure of the play are clearly feminist. The women's lives viewed in *Fefu* are seen, especially in the second part of the play, as being repetitive and capable of being viewed in any random sequence; yet even as women we do not respond negatively to this suggestion. In the very repetition of the four scenes that are played simultaneously we view intimately women's need for women. Although the title character says women need men because we cannot feel safe with each other, the other characters prove her wrong as they interact.

Beverley Byers Pevitts, Professor and Chair of Theatre, University of Nevada, Las Vegas, is President of the Association for Theatre in Higher Education. She edited the Special Issue (1986) "Women in Theatre" of *Theatre Annual*.

In *Fefu and Her Friends* Fornes defines what can happen when women recognize their own worth, and each other: "And if they shall recognize each other, the world will be blown apart." The play is fluid, structured like music, a "fugue," says the playwright. The play takes place in an affluent New England home. Eight female characters are introduced: they discuss woman's loathsomeness, settle relationships among themselves, rehearse speeches, and recount visions. Fornes's characters speak as selves, not in the stereotypical roles of mother, daughter, bitch, witch, or virgin. She breathes into her characters humor and intelligence. The loving of one's self and the despising of one's self are both examined, as well as woman's inclination *not* to trust other women.

As they are moved from room to room of Fefu's house during Part Two, the audience is brought into the play. The cyclical four scenes reveal the characters tenderly interacting, bound up in each other's lives. By moving to the characters' spaces, the audience comes to know the reason(s) all eight of these women are getting together. One discovers intimately with the performers "how woman feels about being a woman."

Fefu is cinematic, in both structure and acting style. Part One and Part Three, both set in Fefu's living room, contain all of the characters. The four scenes that nest between the two framework parts each contain only two or three characters. These "substance scenes" present not plot but character development and relationships. The play incorporates stop action, jump cuts, and replay as the audience moves from room to room to see the four scenes in Part Two. As each scene is repeated four times, the rooms have simultaneous life. The scenes and the parts of the play are interrelated by accretion. The through line of action, the passage of time, is merely the sequence of events. The women arrive, they greet each other in Part One. They separate, they read, they share, they rest, they discuss, they play croquet in the second part. Part One is morning, Part Two is afternoon, Part Three is early evening, and contains the climactic event scene.

There are five different environments. Moving from room to room, kinesthetically experiencing the play, becomes more important than following a story. The movement is special because the audience is enclosed with the performers within the four walls. It is, as Fornes expressed it, rather like being a witness. The audience is experientially involved in the play, not following a linear story.

Scenes are intricately interwoven. Cindy and Christina are in the study through which Sue passes on her way with the soup to the bedroom where Julia lies in bed hallucinating. Paula and Cecilia revive and resolve an old relationship in the kitchen while Fefu and Emma play croquet on the lawn. The linkage of the four scenes is both linear and vertical. A rhythm of involvement and disengagement works through all six scenes of the play. Fefu, like Sue, weaves through two other of the four playing areas during the simultaneous scenes, linking the scenes together. Fefu moves through the study/living room to the kitchen for lemonade and back out to the lawn. The fourth (last) time she takes other characters with her while Paula moves to the study/living room to play the piano, and the audience comes together for the third part of the play.

Fornes says that with plot we are concerned with the mechanics of how we manage in the world; a play without plot deals with the mechanics of the mind, some kind of spiritual survival, a process of thought. The temporal awareness of the characters is related to the segmentation of the play's structure.

The central scene of the play is Julia's hallucinating scene in bed in Part Two. It is a moving scene in which the character speaks clearly thoughts many women know:

> The human being is of the masculine gender. The human being is a boy as a child and grown up he is a man. Everything on earth is for the human being, which is man. . . . Woman is not a human being. She is: 1—A mystery. 2—Another species. 3—As yet undefined. 4—Unpredictable; therefore wicked and gentle and evil and good which is evil. —If a man commits an evil act, he must be pitied. The evil comes from outside him, through him and into the act. Woman generates the evil herself. —God gave man no other mate but woman. . . . —Man is not spiritually sexual, he therefore can enjoy sexuality. His sexuality is physical which means his spirit is pure. Women's spirit is sexual. . . . Their sexual feelings remain with them till they die. And they take those feelings with them to the afterlife where they corrupt the heavens, and they are sent to hell where through suffering they may shed those feelings and return to earth as man.

Julia's thesis in *Fefu* is "the mind like the body is made to suffer to such a degree as to become crippled."

In the opening scene of *Fefu*, the title character points out that "women are loathsome." She gives the proof by reasoning the rational male way, by comparing woman to a rock that on the exterior "is smooth and hard and dry and clean" and is on the internal, interior, underneath side "slimy, filled with fungus and crawling with worms." This represents, she says, "another life that is parallel to the one we manifest." She continues, "If you don't recognize it . . . it eats you." This exterior appearance of woman can be readily compared to the image woman has been made into—the commercial view of the world (provided by men) into which women re-create images already created for them. The two sides of the rock represent how women feel about the image. If women do not realize it and recognize it, the underneath side does rot with the fungus and worms found there. If we do recognize this image, as Fefu later tells us, if we recognize ourselves as women, "the world will be blown apart." When this does happen, the reflection that was made by others will be destroyed and we will be able to rebuild ourselves in our own image, created by woman. The character Julia, trapped and oppressed, who at one point of her life was "afraid of nothing," and about whom the others wondered how one so young could know so much, is the one who is symbolically killed in the end of the play so that the new image of herself can emerge.

For many women becoming a feminist has caused a personal transformation. *Fefu*, like other contemporary plays by women, expresses this transformation, the transformation of the personal into mythos.

A RAINBOW OF VOICES

PHYLLIS MAEL

In 1975 three plays by women were produced which display striking similarities in form and theme: *Voices* by Susan Griffin, *Out of Our Fathers' House* by Eve Merriam in collaboration with Paula Wagner and Jack Hofsiss, and *For Colored Girls Who Have Considered Suicide/When the Rainbow Is Enuf* by Ntozake Shange. All three utilize the format of the consciousness-raising group to present a feminist variation of the archetypal journey in search of the self.

This journey has been depicted in myth, and in contemporary psychology it has become a paradigm for self-realization. Carl G. Jung has termed the goal of the journey "individuation," which he defined as the process of "becoming one's self."[1] Jolande Jacobi describes individuation as "a way to self-knowledge . . . to find meaning in life."[2] Through individuation the individual comes to know herself for what she really is and finds the god within.

In myth this journey was usually that of a single male hero guided or aided by females (or female symbols). If a female was the hero, she was usually aided by males (or male symbols) or often by negative female images such as jealous sisters or jealous goddesses. ("Amor and Psyche" in *The Golden Ass* of Apuleius is an example of the female journey in mythology.)

In these three contemporary plays, however, men are present only insofar as the women speak of them (the casts consisting solely of women), and the men are viewed generally as having blocked the self-realization of the women. In contrast, the women in these plays function as positive images (either as role models, comforters, or spurs to complete the journey to the self). There are no single heroes, nor is there a differentiation between traveler and guide, each woman being both.

This nonhierarchical, mutually supportive structure is typical of consciousness-raising groups. The basic purpose of such a group is to help each woman to break through her conditioning by enabling her to understand how society has prepared her to play certain roles. The group also breaks down her feeling of isolation by helping her to "recognize that what she had thought of as her

Phyllis Mael, Associate Professor of English, Pasadena City College, California, has published articles on contemporary drama by women in *Chrysalis, Frontiers, Kansas Quarterly*, and *Dictionary of Literary Biography*.

unique experiences are . . . shared and understood by other women. . . . Her sense of frustration, . . . futility and helplessness [thus diminishes and she can] begin to work positively toward altering and improving her own life."[3]

These goals are accomplished by "getting women to speak—only when they name their experiences can they begin to grow."[4] In these plays, the voicing of experience is achieved through what I call a rainbow of voices: as a rainbow presents a unity (light) and a diversity (the varied colors into which the light is separated), so do the voices in these plays. We hear individual women's voices moving from hope to disillusionment to despair to awareness. At times the individual voices merge to speak of the collective journey of women, and previously separate voices transform the isolated experience of a single voice into the mutually supportive and collective experience of Woman. The distinct voices thus interact with and respond to each other, either directly or obliquely, to create "a common language [which has the power] to create connections."[5]

This rainbow effect is most apparent in Griffin's play:

Five women of different generations and circumstances seem to be conducting five monologues. . . . Each at first perceives herself as uniquely trapped. . . . Never do they actually engage each other in dialogue. Yet they are, in a deep sense, *conversant* with each other; at times their actual words echo each other, and at other times they speak words in unison . . . no longer spiritually isolated.[6]

The first to speak is Maya, thirty-five, divorced, with two children, working on her dissertation on "The Death of the American Family." She opens the initial fugue of voices with a question: "What am I going to do?" During the play, she moves from hope through anger, despair, and awareness that her situation is not unique, to an informed acceptance of her situation. For Maya, who had fantasized the American Dream by marrying a young man who represented "Middle American Decency" and had played out all the fantasies of women—"sex queen, nymph, matron, lady in waiting," the voicing of her situation enables her to arrive at a qualified serenity, from which she states: "There is a kind of/stunning beauty/to the irrefutable truth/of . . . the/actualities of life,/uncovered from/veils of/myth and prejudice." The fantasies perpetuated by society can cause pain. Unmasking them is the first step to confronting the truth of the self and helps to mitigate that pain.

Kate, in her late sixties or early seventies, echoes Maya's "What am I going to do?" with "What is one?" Although living very different lives and belonging to different generations, both Maya and Kate arrive at similar truths about themselves as women. Both move from solitude to a sense of a shared experience with other women (Maya through a link with her grandmother, mother, and daughter; Kate through an unforeseen connection with her mother). This bond with other women seems to provide them with the courage to persevere, for despite approaching old age, Kate considers "death

... irrelevant./One goes on/with courage/and when/one loses courage . . . one goes on/anyway."

Whereas Maya represented "The Death of the American Family," Grace represents "The Death in Life of the American Family." For although still married, she can barely remember who she was before she became a wife and mother. The marriage has survived, but Grace's sense of self is in jeopardy. Through voicing her memories (of a strong, daring, active young woman), she acquires the strength to let the remembered self out of the metaphorical closet to which it has been relegated. And as she opens the door to that remembered self, she hears voices: "Strange women/speak to me./Women I have/never/met. Women who/I would never/know even/if they lived/next door to me. And I hear my own voice singing back."

Although in the staging the women do not hear or see each other, their shared experience is demonstrated theatrically in three ways. First, the individual voices interlock so that what one voice says is picked up or echoed by another voice. A second way of sharing and hearing voices is the repetition of a statement by each voice. At one point, each says separately "I was frightened" and then all say together "I was alone." But they are no longer alone, for the voicing erases their common loneliness. A third method of sharing is through voicing the collective experience of the American woman (expressing the outrage of women in slavery, dying as early settlers, suffering as pioneers in the West, or humiliated as adolescent sex objects in a sexist society). By voicing their common experiences and their shared history, each woman can listen to her inner voice and find her previously hidden self.

Like Griffin, Merriam presents the voices of specific individuals "whose life stories alternate and intertwine. . . . We hear women's voices testifying to struggles for maturity, independence, and relationships much like our own, reassuring us that the journey 'out of our fathers' houses' is worth taking."[7]

Unlike Griffin, however, Merriam takes her voices directly from diaries, journals, and letters of the historical characters portrayed. The six women, from the nineteenth and twentieth centuries in the United States, range from a little-known schoolgirl to Elizabeth Cady Stanton, founder of the National Women's Suffrage Association.

In the introduction to her book *Growing Up Female in America*, from which the play was adapted, Merriam explains that she selected these particular women in order to "restore our sense of the past . . . to give our lives today a continuity that has been lacking."[8] She wishes her audience to listen to "the striking contemporaneity" of the voices. She thus creates a "hypothetical conversation" or "consciousness-raising group among women who probably never met one another."[9]

Merriam describes the setting of the play as "the secret place where one would run off to think and be alone" and, at the end of the play, the need to "make the voyage of life alone" is voiced by all the women. But the play presents a "timeless interaction in which these women act out for both themselves and each other the stories of their lives." Thus, as in Griffin's play, the individual voices blend to create a collective experience without in any way obliterating the unique qualities of each individual experience. "Both together and alone they make the journey into a world of self-sufficiency and the 'solitude of self.'"

The play opens with a song depicting the house of the fathers as a "brick house . . . a high stone wall . . . a gate with a lock" from which the women must escape. Each rebels in her own way, for each has a different prison from which to escape. Whether radical (as that of Mother Jones and Dr. Anna Shaw) or hesitant (as that of Elizabeth Stern), the journey out of the house of the fathers to the self has been completed by the end of the play, and the voices join to speak of the loneliness of the journey. Merriam is not being ironic when she joins the voices to speak of solitude. For although the voices say "Nature never repeats herself," and they speak of "the solitude of individual life . . . and the need to cherish that individuality," the journey is shared in that it is a journey all must take in order to be fully human. The knowledge of the shared experience (just as the hearing of other voices) eases the journey for the individual.

In contrast with *Voices* and *Out of Our Fathers' House*, in *For Colored Girls* we no longer hear individual voices but individual poems which produce a cumulative effect: "The words of a young black girl's growing up, her triumphs & errors, our struggle to become all that is forbidden by our environment, all that is forfeited by our gender, all that we have forgotten."[10] Although Shange speaks in her Introduction of a "black girl" and although originally the play had Latins, Asians, blacks, but no whites,[11] Shange later acknowledged that the play "is a flash of humanity about women of all kinds at different times in their lives."[12]

Through the poems, seven women, wearing different colors of the rainbow, sing the songs, voice the lyrics, and bring into being the self that has been denied. The poems cover rite of passage, the search for identity, and various aspects of love relationships. As the poems move from youth to adolescence through adulthood, the journey moves individually and collectively from searching to finding.

The denial of the self occurred because "ever since i realized there waz someone calt/a colored girl. . . ./i been trying not to be that." By attempting to avoid a stereotype that the woman has been raised to consider repugnant, she fails to become herself. Only when the women refuse to debase themselves and are able to share the pride of being women, colored, and in love, can they continue their journey to individuation. Each can then recognize the self behind the stereotype and voice the price and conviction that affirm that self: "This is mine/that aint yr stuff . . . this is a woman's trip & i need my stuff . . . you cant have me less i give me away . . . wat i got to do/i gotta have my stuff to do it to."

That "stuff" is the essence of the self. And in asserting her right to her "stuff," the woman arrives at the end of her journey with a positive affirmation of self. "I waz missin somethin/somethin so important/laying me open to myself . . . i found god in myself/ . . . & i loved her fiercely."

In an essay on *For Colored Girls*, Toni Bambara has pointed out that "sister-sharing" (or sisterhood) enables one "to master pain and betrayal."[13] It also enables one to arrive at the god within which is the inner voice that is not controlled by society but emerges from within the individual. That sharing may occur through singing and dancing the individual and collective experience of the American woman as in *Voices*. It may occur through voicing the anxiety of oneself and of others as in *Out of Our Fathers' House*.

In all three plays, both separately and together, as the colors of a rainbow, the women help each other to articulate their own thoughts and feelings in order to move "out of their fathers' house" "to the ends of their own rainbow" to find the treasure worth the struggle—the self. Through the techniques and structures of consciousness raising, the plays transform the archetypal journey in search of the self into an experience that speaks by, of, and for women in the final quarter of the twentieth century.

PROCESS AND PROBLEMS

MARTHA BOESING

During its first decade of life (1974–84), At the Foot of the Mountain developed a process of working which sprang out of the feminist banner of the times: "the personal is political." But the roots of the work were to be found in the radical theatre of the sixties.

I worked at the Firehouse Theater in Minneapolis during that time. Like the Living Theater, Open Theatre and The Performance Group, we were involved in everything the sixties offered us, from politics to drugs, from burning draft cards to running around nude on the stage. The political was personal, the belief in change as an end in itself our private war-cry. We were aggressive and brave and willing to experiment with our own hearts and psyches to create our art. Resistance amounted to cowardice and we faced each other with an unspoken challenge to make each act more outrageous than the last. It was exciting. It was frightening. Some of us went crazy. The central aesthetic which emerged was that of transformational theatre. One actor often played many roles; characters transformed mid-scene into alter egos, animals, even

---

Adapted from a talk at Smith College, April 18, 1986, given as part of the festivities in honor of the retirement of Helen Krich Chinoy. See p. 44 for Boesing biographical note. At the Foot of the Mountain is a professional women's theatre based in Minneapolis.

trees. We questioned the notion of a single or static personality as we began to notice that each of us is really made up of many different images, feelings, attitudes and styles that are constantly changing depending on who we are with and what is expected of us. And we tried to create theatre that reflected this multitude of personalities within. We moved away from linear plays to ones built like mosaics or patterns on a quilt.

This transformational theatre became the aesthetic format of many women's theatres in the seventies. Plays were often layered, imagistic, nonsequential. Companies of five or six actors were called upon to play twenty to thirty roles in an evening. We gathered across the nation in consciousness-raising groups to tell our stories and talk about the many facets, the many roles we had been asked to play—wife, daughter, mother, lover, colleague, nymph, crone. We were "getting our feelings out"—some of us for the first time. And we were finding friends, sisters, who shared these feelings—anger, grief, and a common sense of having been silenced.

So, in our theatres, instead of asking each other to "leave your garbage at the rehearsal hall door," we invited ourselves to bring it all in—our personal problems, our headaches, our memories, our feelings toward each other. We were creating plays out of our own lives, our own issues, and there was no way that we could create characters and situations which had a true life unless we were willing to share the emotional fabric of our own lives with each other.

At the Foot of the Mountain started a practice which continues to this day. Before every rehearsal and every business meeting, we would sit in a circle and say what we were feeling. A simple practice; but not so simple. We discovered that we often didn't even know what we were feeling, although there aren't many different basic emotions. I had a friend who called it the "six-pack": glad, sad, mad, scared, loving, and we added ashamed, because as women we have learned to feel ashamed of almost every move we make. Sometimes we'd get into the thick of a complicated network of emotions about the work or about each other and "feeling circles" would go on for three hours. It seemed important to all of us to stay with each other through the difficulties in order to get to the truth of the work. Sometimes we'd identify the feeling, then reach out to establish the whole condition around it, the memories, thoughts, muscular tensions which arose from that feeling—and from that would emerge the day's character and scene work. Often we would work nonverbally, creating images of sound or movement out of the feelings shared in the circle. The social and political issues we were creating our plays about (rape, prostitution, madness, addiction, war) were always rooted in our own feelings and our own stories. "The personal is political." We took the banner literally and we explored it as deeply as we were able.

The process showed itself in the work in different ways. In an early production of my play *River Journal*, for example, we experimented with improvising the emotional line of the subtext of the play from night to night. We learned the lines and blocked the play, but allowed the actors complete freedom to improvise the feelings of the characters, responding to their own real feelings in the moment. A scene which was filled with rage one night might be played sweetly and deliciously, or etched in fear, on the next. It was invigorating, filled with surprise. Some of the actors loved the challenge, others felt the ground too loose beneath their feet.

When we worked on *Raped: A Woman's Look at Bertolt Brecht's The Exception and the Rule*, a production exploring the economic base of permissible violence to women, we began by sharing our own stories. "Well," we each began, "I'm one of the lucky ones—I've never been raped." But by the time we opened the show each of us had shared one or more rape stories. Some of us were victims of emotional rape; some were incest victims; some had lovers who refused to take "No, not tonight" as an answer; some had experienced mind rapes. For example, in college a creative writing teacher whom I adored said to me: "You're bright. You ought to do something you can do well. But you'll never be a writer. It's a genetic problem. Women's minds are filled with trivia. They can never be great artists." I didn't write again for ten years. That's a rape story.

Through the years we worked on plays about prostitution (*The Life*), addiction (*Junkie!*), nuclear war (*Ashes, Ashes We All Fall Down*), invasion (*Las Gringas*), always beginning with the premise that the personal is political, always using our own denials, our own fears, our own stories as the starting point for the larger social issues we were exploring. It sometimes meant horrendous encounters—with each other and with our own personal demons. For instance, I went through a profound depression while preparing the piece about nuclear war—several months of hiding under my bedcovers, desperate to avoid confronting the despair and helplessness I felt in the face of global death. It was never an easy choice, this plummeting.

And we didn't make it much easier for our audiences. We called these pieces "ritual drama" because in each work there were places where the audience was invited to enter in and take an active part in the event. There were litanies, written stories read aloud, testimonies. This work, again rooted in the aggressive audience encounters of the sixties, began for us with *Raped*, a popular piece which had a long run. One night when performing for an audience of friends in the women's community who had seen the play before, we invited anyone in the audience to stand up at any time and freeze the action by saying "Stop"—which we did—and share a rape story of her own. And they did. Many did. The play took on a different energy. The room was electrified by suspense. Both the wonder and the fear that the person sitting beside you might suddenly give witness, perhaps for the first time in her life, to her own oppression, brought a tension and a presence to the production which gave one the sense not that we were watching a play about change, but that real change was happening right here and now in this very room.

In *The Story of a Mother*, a play about the mother-daughter relationship in our society, we developed a practice in which we went into a trance state and entered into the bodies and minds of our own mothers in order to see and relate to the world as our mothers did. We then would improvise and rehearse whole sections of the play as our mothers. Then—as if we hadn't tortured ourselves enough—we worked with a therapist, a friend of the theatre, with all of us attending six or eight therapy sessions in which we were inside the bodies/minds of our mothers. It was frightening, revealing, and profound work. Most of us went into the play having conflicts with our mothers. We came out in a place of understanding of what their lives had been like, a place of forgiveness and love.

The secret of audience participation is to find a way to invite them in without coercion. It is never easy. I think it's important to admit from the start, by the way in which entry is offered, that the actors know more than the audience does, and that we are inviting them to take part because we have found the experience to be very rich and want to share this part of the journey. In *The Story of a Mother*, we led them through the meditation in which they would enter into the inner lives of their own mothers and then share in certain litanies such as "I always said . . ." and later "I never said. . . ." Within five minutes the audience had doubled—everyone was there with their mothers. At the end of the play we would say our names and our mothers' names ("I am Martha, daughter of Mary") and the audience would voluntarily join in until the room was ringing with women's names as the matriarchal lineage tumbled out into the space. I think that was our most successful personal work with an audience—direct, radical, and healing. It was beautiful to experience the power of the theatre to change people's lives.

One problem that emerges when working so closely and so intensely together is that a family system develops. We were committed to the work, but commitment to become a family had not been part of the contract. We met with resistance and fear. Some of us felt invaded, longed for more privacy, needed separation from the group. Others felt betrayed. We didn't always have the tools to deal with these problems as they arose. Today, I would urge a group working collaboratively to establish clearer boundaries between openness and privacy, to clarify expectations from the start, and to limit the shared personal life to that which is usable in the work, taking the rest, if need be, to a therapist. I would also encourage all company members to maintain a strong alternative life, a place to go for friendship and activities outside the theatre. Without it, we grow inwards as a group, elitist, incestuous, and often surprisingly lonely.

Our work was in the theatre and our goal was to become the finest theatre artists possible. To approach the material through the personal is not to negate the hours of labor involved in honing our skills—acting, moving, writing, singing, training new company members and pushing the old beyond their limits. It is important to mention this dedication to the craft because I think those of us involved in political theatre, or with any revolutionary art form, tend to become a little lazy. We say, "Well, the important thing is that we're women and we're getting our stories out. If the acting is a little sloppy, it doesn't matter." But it does matter. People's hearts and minds are opened because they are engaged and inspired by the images, the language, the artistry of the event they are watching. At the Foot of the Mountain tried to be diligent, though I often saw the mistakes and failures of the work. Then we were on to the next play before I had the opportunity to rewrite. When I left the theatre in 1984, I looked back over all my scripts, over twenty-five of them, and I said, "My God, I have created an entire body of work which consists of first drafts!"

So we need time. And a great deal of patience. The older I get, the tougher I get on myself. As women we must get tougher, we must put ourselves in situations where we are challenged by artists who have more highly developed skills than our own. At the beginning we needed the support and the love from each other that would give us a standing ovation simply in honor of our survival against overwhelming odds. But women's theatre is almost twenty years old now. We must sharpen our critical faculties and be willing to plunge in deeper. I still believe that women working together collaboratively have something to bring to the art—some real questions about both the form and the content which seem to limit much of our mainstream theatre. There is a kind of work that emerges from this intense, collective longing to communicate which is never attained in the plays by a single writer, mounted as a single production in a season. It has to do with community, with Jung's ideas about a collective unconscious perhaps, and it is a healing voice which is sorely needed on our planet right now. There are stories residing in the deepest parts of our souls which continue to be wrapped in silence. Our tale is not yet finished.

REFLECTIONS

ROBERTA SKLAR

When I was an undergraduate student at Hunter College in 1959, free speech, civil rights, and "Peace Now" were not yet household words. Off-Off Broadway had not yet begun. Feminism was unheard of. The sixties had not yet occurred. This was the world I entered as a young adult. My goal was to be an exceptional woman, for only in that way did I think I would get to do something!

In more than two decades of creating, writing and directing theatre I've had the privilege of living and working during three extraordinary phases of the

---

These observations are drawn from remarks made at a panel of women in academic and professional theatre in honor of the retirement of Helen Krich Chinoy from Smith College, April 1986, as well as from a brief talk at the Women in Theatre conference, New Haven, March 1982, and recent reflections.

American theatre. In the founding years of the Off-Off Broadway movement I directed new plays at the young Caffe Cino and Cafe La Mama. (As a novice I naively sought a career as a theatre director in a field virtually closed to women.) In the sixties as co-artistic director at the Open Theatre where we collectively created *The Serpent*, *Terminal* and the *Mutation Show*, I shared the vision of an alternative theatre for an alternative society. I've always experienced theatre, and myself within it, in a collaborative way—as a collective effort, a relationship, deeply interactive with its members, its audience and its time. For me theatre is most itself when it is integral to social change.

After working with the Open Theatre for several years in the development of a collective approach in American theatre, it slowly dawned on me that while I was speaking collectively, I neither understood my own voice, nor had something specific to say. The women's movement, through individuals and groups such as the It's All Right to Be Woman Theatre, suggested to me not only that I had a voice, but that I had a history of experience and a future that warranted articulating. There was reason to speak. It was in the context of feminist theatre, and especially within the Women's Experimental Theater, speaking solo and in unison with other women, that I found my voice.

Sondra Segal and I began working together in 1973 at the Womanrite Theater, and in 1976, together with Clare Coss, founded the Women's Experimental Theater. To work in a woman-identified way, a self-identified way, was the task. It took a lot of pain and it took rigor. We had been acculturated to a male world. We spoke in tongues. The language we had was not fully our own. We tackled the trivialization of our lives, resurrecting domains made small by sexism—the domestic sphere, the kitchen, childbirth, women's relationships, the female psyche, our bodies, our sustenance, our place in the world.

Women's theatre is a theatre of conversion. It's populated by women like myself who've converted through some sort of emotional or psychological "Ah ha"—a sense of revelation. We've been converted to ourselves. The "deity," if you will, that I attend is the woman within me. What I seek is a woman-identified theatre, one that serves me.

Like several other feminist theatre teams, Sondra Segal and I have worked together since the early seventies in a flow of artistic roles, attempting to create a women's theatre that would be a viable alternative to the aesthetic and economic structures of a male-dominated commercial and avant-garde theatre. Some say we should have first sought the money and power that would have given our institutions an enduring foundation. There may be wisdom here, but I think that the very process of consolidating power and wealth would have preempted the women's culture we sought to create.

Now in an age of conservatism equal to the 1950's, supported by the new economics and the movement of history, we are living again in an era unfriendly to the advancement and equality of women, an era at best dubbed "post-feminism." Once again women are disappearing from the horizon.

"Exceptional women" with "exceptional careers" are reappearing, and concurrently, feminist theatres are no longer surviving. Many of the women's theatres of the seventies and eighties have folded. So have the alternative health centers, day-care centers, consciousness-raising groups, women's presses, and women's production companies. Theatre does not exist in a vacuum. We are not unique, nor must we blame ourselves. I believe we are in a still period in the theatre, and as theatre so often does, it reflects the condition of the larger society. At this moment the path to creating feminist theatre may not be clear, but we must ask "Why?" and determine some of the tasks before us. What is the mission? What do we want to say? What do we want to change?

Although this wave of women's theatre has had a healthy life span, we are left with an incomplete legacy: a small number of groups creating and performing new works; a cache of largely unpublished plays; forays into feminist acting techniques, research methods and new forms that might better express our unspoken experience. We are sorely missing an articulated theory of feminist dramatic criticism to carry into the future. As a theatre movement we suffered dearly because such a criticism did not develop while we were more actively producing plays. We lack a substantial codification of our methods, of how we gathered material and information. The process in many of the women's theatres cut across race, class, and position and brought housewife and worker, lesbian and straight, secretary and executive, into the same workshop, the same consciousness-raising group, the same audience, each seeking self-knowledge and female universality. How these women came together and the process of research that informed us and created women's theatre are extraordinary parts of an untold history.

I hope that women, in every field, will not allow our work to fade from history; that we will record, not simply what we did, but what we intended. Feminism and women's culture have had a utopian aspect to them, and that's good. Our theatre is transformational; it changes something. When we create theatre, we must consciously ask: What is it we seek to change?

To focus attention rigorously on the questions that arise out of womanhood—that's the hardest thing. The temptation to join the male tradition is even greater than it used to be because more women have been allowed in. But the themes and the forms to be explored by women from a woman-identified perspective have barely been let in. Women require new forms to bring forth that which has so long been silenced. If we create only in existing forms, we can say only what has been said before. The theatrical articulation of more than half of the world's population cannot possibly be carried out in a decade by a handful of under-funded women.

For many years I worked exclusively at creating theatre with women, dedicated to women. I hope that in this work I did not only redress the past or ferret out silenced truths. I hope that I dreamed aloud a vision of a woman-loving future that would transform our theatre and our lives.

MAKING A LIFE IN ART: MEGAN TERRY INTERVIEWS

B/K. Megan, what message would you most like to send round the world?
MT. It's worth it to make a life in art. I want to tell everybody it's *possible* and it's worth it. I've lived long enough now to see what happens to people who don't follow their hearts.

DL. Do you identify yourself as a feminist?
MT. I am a feminist, but I'm many things. I'm a humorist and a humanist. I've been in the theatre since I was fourteen; I'm really a theatre person.
DL. What do you think a feminist theatre is?
MT. Everyone is an individual and each theatre company projects a different image. People want to try to determine that there's some kind of party line in feminism and there isn't. The most marvelous thing about the feminist movement is that there are no leaders. The leaders that the media has tried to make they've soon killed off, but it hasn't stopped the feminist movement at all. I think the reason for this is the lack of leaders. Each woman is her own leader. That's why it has such tremendous energy.

I was raised by women. I've always been interested in writing about women. I'm crazy about acting. I was brought up with very fine actors and many of them were women. There were no roles for them to play. I saw their pain and their struggle when they couldn't get jobs, not because they had no talent, but because there were no parts for them.
The women's movement enabled me to leave New York and give up that whole careerism business—the man's world of career stuff. I was always acting as the woman behind a man anyway. I was giving my energies to male careers. The movement also made me see really clearly that there's a necessity to write about very strong women so women can know that there have been strong women in the past. I'd been wanting to write about Simone Weil for fifteen years, but the women's movement gave me the courage to do it. Plus I'd built my technique to a point where I felt I could attack such a vast project.

If feminism is going to really move ahead, it's got to explore the possibilities of what a woman could be. We don't know what a woman could be like because we've had so many outlines and definitions forced on us. That's the most exciting thing to me. That's the true frontier. Women have got to take over

Megan Terry's more than fifty plays have broadened the American idea of theatre. A founding member of the Open Theatre and since 1974 Playwright in Residence at the Omaha Magic Theatre, in 1983 she received the Dramatists Guild's Committee for Women Annual Award in recognition of her "work as a writer of conscience and controversy and [her] many lasting contributions to the theatre." Her comments in this section were compiled by Linda Jenkins from two interviews with Terry: Dinah L. Leavitt (DL), published in the first edition of this book; and Kathleen Betsko and Rachel Koenig (B/K), published in their *Interviews with Contemporary Women Playwrights*.

the education of other women, because for too long we've been fitted into something that men want and the definitions that men have made. My own father refused to send me to college because I refused to join a sorority and reflect his values.

With the playwriting techniques we discovered or rediscovered in the sixties you can explore interior states. You can dramatize the interior state of being. Once inside one's head, body or soul, it's vast. Dramatizing that or showing all the possibilities, the ways to go, can really be done in the theatre and acted out in front of people. That's what's important for them to see. It can start a chain reaction. More and more people will come and say, "Ah, I can build on that."

DL.   I'm not sure what we are considering to be feminist drama.

MT.   Anything that gives women confidence, shows themselves to themselves, helps them to begin to analyze whether it's a positive or negative image, is nourishing.

DL.   How do you feel about the idea that if feminist drama is going to say anything new it has to say it in new forms?

MT.   It doesn't matter what the form is as long as you're telling the truth. The form is the least important thing. Telling the truth is the main thing. People get hung up on form because they've been to school too much.

I'm always fighting against critics because so many are biased whether they are feminist critics or male critics. They always want you to conform to whatever party line they're putting out. They want to use artists. It's the duty of the artist to criticize everybody including herself and her attitudes. The feminist movement really needs some criticism from artists so that we don't get so hidebound and serious. I refuse to be used.

DL.   Is there male and female art or is art just art?

MT.   It's art if *I* say it is. Art has always been whatever the establishment says it is. When I finally figured that out, I started proclaiming who I felt were artists, and I began praising and propagandizing all the work I liked. That is what women should do and stop worrying about rules.

B/K.   You teach playwriting. Are you spreading the word about women dramatists?

MT.   Constantly. Recently, I taught Emily Mann's *Still Life* at a university in Minnesota. My students were *outraged* that they'd never heard of this play, nor the work of Maria Irene Fornes, nor Roz Drexler, Rochelle Owens, Adrienne Kennedy, Sybille Pearson, Caryl Churchill, Pam Gems, Ntozake Shange, Julie Bovasso, Jo Ann Schmidman, Tina Howe. They knew none of these people, and they were getting their master's degrees! They were really angry by the time I finished with them.

B/K.   Do you believe that there's a female aesthetic in playwriting?

MT.   A female aesthetic could only happen if the next generation of women were raised all together on a desert island.

B/K.   So you don't think the innovations of women are in any way organic?

MT.   I really don't. How would you measure it?

B/K.   We don't know. That's why we're asking women playwrights this question. What we do know, after reading tons of women's plays and hundreds of their reviews, is that there are certain elements common to all: many of their plays are woman-centered, with a much higher percentage of female roles than plays by men.

MT.   This will probably continue until the balance is redressed. But after there's a balance, and we have the female characters living up there on the stage that we haven't had for a long time, that may all change again.

B/K.   There are some people who feel that there is a renewed but more covert war going on between men and women now . . . a deeper malaise setting in, separating us.

MT.   I think that men are negative because women are positive and on the rise! It's driving men crazy! Martha Boesing was telling me that in the thousand plays she receives each year, most have hopeful endings! Women are feeling positive and forward-looking. Plays men are writing often end with everybody dead, dying or neurotic to the point of no return.

B/K.   What can we do to heal this polarization?

MT.   Live your life as if the revolution had been a success!

B/K.   What advice do you have for young women in high school and college who are thinking about becoming a playwright?

MT.   Do it. See all kinds of performance, from polka dances to basketball games. Do you know what I miss in the world? Singing. There's a lot of noise, but there isn't enough singing lately.

DL.   What do you see as your future work?

MT.   I'll be in theatre. I'll be as surprised as you. I plan to keep Omaha as a base because the cost of living is reasonable here, and there's the chance to really understand how a whole community of this size [500,000] operates. I'm fascinated. It's not so big that you can't understand how it works. Also I got out of touch with America by going on so many world tours. I'm a great lover of our country in spite of what the critics or the CIA or FBI may think, so it's thrilling for me to be in the Midwest. Too many people go to New York and get caught up in the hierarchy of moving ahead, the male syndrome of success, and they forget their roots and write themselves out of what they came there with and then they start repeating themselves. They write the same play with different names. Once they get success they get isolated from people.

People in the East are always saying, "What are you doing in Omaha?" I answer, "I'm living a real life."

7

NEW PROBLEMS, PRACTICES AND PERSPECTIVES

This section provides a summary survey of experiences, opinions, and data to suggest some of the concerns of women in theatre today. Despite evident interest in women and their contributions in the 1980's, there is still much we don't know about individuals, groups, and institutions. The following eclectic gathering of voices is intended both to suggest the diversity among women and also to alert us to their recurrent problems and aspirations. Although each segment deals with a different aspect of the current theatre scene, they are all closely linked by common challenges and questions that in themselves grow out of the previous "Feminist Theatre" section. Cross-references to people, ideas, and techniques mentioned earlier, while not actually indicated, will be readily apparent to the reader. Indeed this final section that leads us to the cutting edge of theatre today grows out of the whole structure of this volume. Read together the parts comprise the overall view of women in American theatre this book has tried to provide.

HKC

THE FEMALE ACTOR

HELEN KRICH CHINOY

What's in a name is the question we might ask about the transformation of women performers today as they are moving from calling themselves "actresses" to sharing the generic term "actor" with men. By implication the new name confirms what we all know—that both men and women are players who can incarnate and project many roles, ones that cut across gender stereotypes as well as those of class, race, age, and routine psychological and physical encasements. The "actress" of the past was someone most often confined within the socially sanctioned assumptions about female looks, behavior, and potential, functioning to a large extent as the "object of the male

331

gaze." Her "self" was rarely invoked for her art, remaining locked away as her "secret." The change to "actor" or performer highlights the complex but central issue of how gender—a social construct—and the "secret self" are related to performance.

What follows is a sampler of experiences, questions, strategies, disappointments and triumphs related to the actor's use of herself to make a life in the theatre and to find the individuality, authenticity, and truth necessary for the art she wants to create there. The comments are drawn from a selection of living performers who range widely in age, artistic approach, career objectives, politics and lifestyle—from current feminists Roberta Sklar and Sondra Segal to Helen Hayes, who was already an actress at five when the century was the same age. Linking them here is not meant in any way to obliterate their diversity. Their observations, however, reveal certain common female experiences—the struggle to use oneself fully, to find meaningful roles, to have a career and a family, to make theatre that is significant socially and aesthetically as well as personally. The consciousness raising that led in the 1970's to the feminist theatre movement also emboldened other performers—some of them stars—to confront women's issues openly. In their individual ways these different female actors have been transforming their craft, their theatre, and their lives.

In the 1970's Roberta Sklar was exploring an Open Theatre exercise called "The Unnoticed Action" in which those "impulses that don't fit into social reality" were called upon. She realized that "for women, the internal reality is filled with the social suppression of womanhood. There are layers and layers of it. The first layers are rage and such, but then there is layer after layer of suppressed self-knowledge. That reality is the content of women's theatre. . . ."[1]

The "internal reality," the "secret life," and the "roar within" are images used again and again by various artists to identify what the new women's theatre is all about. Sklar, for example, began to explore "the distinct acting problems women have," and asked the basic question: "How do you act as a performer and a person when you have been taught not to *act*, not to do, not to take action? The performer is taking an action. The study of acting is an analysis of human behavior and a projection of that analysis." Instead of breaking down defenses as in traditional approaches to acting, feminists "located, supported, and built up strengths; literal strength and psychic strength. We worked with feelings. We knew that women unlike men have little trouble knowing what they feel or *that* they feel. Women are too often flooded with feelings. We had to learn to shape, control and consciously project our feeling."

Sondra Segal, with whom Sklar collaborates and whom she has called "an advanced feminist actor, perhaps the first," works "through her feminist consciousness" to create "a theatrical persona which allows for changeability, the constant switching of roles that is woman's experience. She works directly from the self." Sondra Segal herself says: "What I am doing is I'm telling what I know. I'm trying to speak personally and comment on it simultaneously. I think it is a skill that women have. I play a role, and it is something that I am taking on. It's not inherent and it's not unconscious. It feels very deliberate—a presentation to an audience of the choices I'm making. A demonstration. I have other choices; I know what they are. I am showing artifacts of our culture at the same time that I'm in it, subject to it, and I know it. The enormous pleasure in performing these works has been feeling understood for the first time."[2]

"The task for us is clear," Roberta Sklar has concluded. "Women have to learn to hear their own voice, bodies, impulses, to take them and use them, rather than assume that someone else always knows better. . . . I was learning to hear the intelligence of the woman actor." Her words recall those of Viola Spolin, one of the seminal but often forgotten inspirations of both sixties experimentation and feminist plays and players. It was Spolin's improvisational theatre games that not only introduced "transformation" exercises, but also offered a fresh understanding of "Creative Experience." "Everyone can act. Everyone can improvise. Anyone who wishes to can play in the theatre and learn to become 'stageworthy,'" Spolin wrote in the preface to her collection of over two hundred theatre games, *Improvisation for the Theatre*. She redefined talent as the "capacity for experiencing" at an intuitive and spontaneous level which releases "the untold potentiality of a personality." Her anti-authoritarian techniques suggested how "physicalizing" communication could liberate the spirit of "personal freedom" not only for the performers but for each member of the audience.[3] Her investigations helped to open up acting practice to women's newly articulated aspirations.

An unusual performance that exploded many conventional notions about gender, race, and physical qualifications was that of Linda Hunt in the film *The Year of Living Dangerously*. Her performance of the male Eurasian photographer, Billy Kwan, won an Academy Award, the first ever given to an actor for playing a person of the opposite sex. In addition, stage interpretations by this 4'9" tall, 80-pound artist of such major roles as Mother Courage, Saint Joan, and Aunt Dan, which Wallace Shawn wrote for her in *Aunt Dan and Lemon*, remind us forcefully of what real acting is all about.

Hunt says that it was seeing Mary Martin transform herself into Peter Pan that made her want to be on the stage. The challenge was to find a creative solution for someone of her size to become a performer. Studying with a "fabulous" acting teacher she had at the age of twelve "released" her "into really being able to use myself." With the support of her parents, she determined to be an actor.[4]

It was many years, however, before her talent was to find fulfillment. She studied directing at the Goodman School in Chicago, believing her size would limit her as an actor. But her time there and later in New York was one of frustration until the summer of 1970, when she began to study acting in her hometown of Westport, Connecticut, with Robert Lewis, whose interest and training turned her life around. Six years of playing at the Long Wharf theatre under the direction of Arvin Brown gave her professional credits in a variety of plays and led her to work again in New York, where she now felt better able to deal with the obstacles she faced.

"There are signs that people's notions of how certain roles should be cast, should be played, are breaking down," Hunt feels. She'd like to continue to see her size as "a mere technical problem." "I find you can change yourself without makeup. There's a certain physical attitude that begins to happen, bodily and facially, that is much stronger, much more profound, I think, than what you can do with makeup." Hunt learned from her experience playing Billy Kwan that "there are more important things in acting than size and gender. If you can create a character of great spirit, anything else about you can be fitted into the framework." She has "an almost political feeling" about her size. "We tend to judge people so much from what they appear to be physically. To open people's eyes about how circumscribed we are, in terms of our physical perceptions of things, is a political action."[5]

Robbie McCauley, actor, teacher, director, performance artist, who has appeared on and off Broadway in such works as Ntozake Shange's *For Colored Girls . . .*, Adrienne Kennedy's *Solo Voyages*, and Joseph Chaikin's *Tourists and Refugees No. 2*, found that much that was going on inside of her as a black woman performer "was not able to be spoken through some writer's words. Writing is something I've always done as an artist—journal-keeping, and writing down images. I always wanted to speak what was inside of me and I used to think I could do it through plays. I eventually found what I in fact wrote and began to speak by myself on the stage worked. I used the acting craft as a vehicle to say some of the things I need to say. That's essentially how I came to this performance mode."[6]

She has described her performance piece, *My Father and the Wars*, as "a series of stories that sometimes turn into songs . . . about this very forceful part of my life, which was my relationship with my father. It's almost like I'm speaking for him. He was in some ways just an ordinary guy. One of the things my father always did was rail about what was going on in the world. I lived through a time when one couldn't live without being part of the change. When I was young I lived down South. I lived under apartheid. In the South, it was black and white—Colored and White labels on the doors. Then I lived through a time when the labels were gone but the essence was still there. About racism, I think we are living through a time where apartheid is being confronted openly, and who knows what the resolutions will be politically. I think my father's voice is part of my voice. The contradictions of all the revolutions of our time—sexual, political—I find myself able to address in my work. How well I don't know, but the fact that I am able to address political issues through my voice is the thing that keeps me going."

In addition to Paul Robeson, Robbie McCauley counts Gloria Foster as an important early influence. Gloria Foster was the "actress who first spoke to me from the stage. I saw her perform *In White America*, a play about racism in America and integration. She did this monologue about a black girl going to a white school for the first time. The way Foster did it was incredible. I also knew with every breath I heard that I could do that—not in any arrogant or challenging way, but just I wanted to do that too. Over the years Gloria Foster has become a great actor in American theatre, although unfortunately her kind of art and range are not as well known as they should be. Her powerful voice spoke to me. I feel some sort of connection. As a force she's been influential and therefore the voice is passed on."

Robbie McCauley says she never felt she would have to make a choice between being an artist and having a full personal life. Although that was the message sent her, she didn't hear it. "I always wanted both." Now that she is a wife (married to Ed Montgomery, a musician with whose group "Sedition Ensemble" she performs) and the mother of a four-year-old daughter, she is finding out how hard it is to do both, in terms of being "tired and having too much to do." Of being a mother, she says, "There's nothing like it. I was surprised I hadn't heard more about it from friends who have children. I always heard how hard it is to raise a child, but the wonder of being a vehicle for another human being is unspeakable. These stories I'm telling in my performance are for my child even though she doesn't understand it. In a way, she's my audience."

Women as a "political issue" is not something separate for Robbie McCauley; rather it is part of her "international concept of freedom." "I make my words important, in creating text. It is my presence as a woman that is very influential in our work." She feels that black women's voices are getting stronger, helped by the writing of authors like Alice Walker. "I hope by telling the story to stir things up and to resolve some of the issues between generations, sexes, classes, and races—the things everybody thinks about." She believes the "action of the actor doubles for social action." Although she confesses it's a bit burdensome, "during the times I've lived, I can't see art as other than confronting the wrongs of society and trying to change them."

Colleen Dewhurst has been dubbed the "Mother Courage" of American theatre for her role as one of its most vigorous spokespersons. This dynamic veteran of almost forty years in the theatre was elected in 1985 to lead the profession as president of Actors' Equity. She has said that "something happened" to her when the Helen Hayes and Morosco theatres were torn down. The intimate Morosco was where she had her important successes in Albee's *Who's Afraid of Virginia Woolf?* and O'Neill's *A Moon for the Misbegotten*. "I understood that if a lot of people did not stand up for something, then they would knock down theatres, drop bombs, take away people's rights and do whatever they wanted. There comes a time to do something about things I care about or no one will."[7]

Dewhurst says that she has changed and grown in many ways during the last few years. The second woman to be president of Actors' Equity, following Ellen Burstyn, she says of herself: "Being the most disorganized woman in town, I couldn't believe I was selected, but I made it clear at the beginning that I did not intend to be a figurehead."[8] She turns up for all the causes—pro-choice, ERA, nuclear freeze. In the summer of 1986 she took a day from rehearsal of an upcoming show to go to Washington to highlight the disadvantages of the new tax proposals for actors, who would not be allowed essential deductions to stretch their poverty-level incomes. She has fought to preserve the beautiful historic theatres, and encouraged efforts at nontraditional casting.

Among the many issues, women in the theatre has been one of her passionate concerns. Again and again, she comes back to the absence of meaningful roles for women. "That's really the reason I haven't been on the Broadway stage in four years," she said in 1982. "I must have read a hundred scripts since 1978. I wanted something where I could be a multidimensional woman. There are no characters like that being written. It's a shame. The theatre needs plays about women. I also read many scripts with the same types of characters I've always played. I don't want a career that keeps repeating itself." In 1986 she said: "They say you're lucky if you made it before fifty, because after that, roles register down. Women are there, like the chairs and tables, but there's no life force. They do not determine what occurs. They are only reactors. There is no power within them, no desire left, no needs that are beyond reach. They are passive. I'm not interested in such characters."[9]

"I like ladies who are survivors," she has said. Her mother was a great exemplar for her. Her parents were divorced when Colleen was twelve; from then on it was "my mother and I alone. . . . She was a woman who was way before her time . . . a woman of great humor, incredible intellect." Although Dewhurst was "never raised to get married," she did marry three times, twice to George C. Scott, who is the father of her two sons. In various interviews she has talked about her attitude toward men, which seems to have put her at odds with some feminists, who have turned to her because of her "earth-mother" image. Although she is sympathetic to feminist concerns, she says, "I won't do anything antimale. . . . It's one of the more natural states to be with a man, but we're going to destroy everything in them that we want from them."[10]

Although she has done a good deal of acting on television, which she considers a very powerful medium that reaches all kinds of people; and would go to Hollywood, which she thinks of as a "cocktail party," if offered a good part—"something unafraid, with some depth"—she still loves working on the stage best of all. Even though making a living in the theatre is hard, she believes it is the only place where there are roles in which one can make a profound impact as she did in her greatest success, *Moon for the Misbegotten*. Josie is a role that has "all the facets of a real woman," one of those characters "who acknowledge their vulnerability, whose agony is laid bare." In the 1987 season she played O'Neill's wife, Carlotta Monterey, in *Dear Gene*, a one-woman show by biographer Barbara Gelb. Dewhurst has said that all of her roles were "parts of me that I sent to the front, and buried the rest."[11]

In the theatre today Dewhurst claims everyone is looking for the "great new play." She herself wants "to do something no actress had ever done before, speak words no one has spoken before, flesh out a character never seen before. . . . There are good writers out there: Marsha Norman, who wrote 'night, Mother, is an example. . . . As to women in theatre; we're doing better, but I think probably the most important thing right now is to find women writers who are writing with intelligence and compassion about both women and men. There are still two sexes."

Asked what she'd like to see in a new play by a woman playwright, Dewhurst has said: "A pause—while the woman who has 'done everything,' been successful, raised her children, looks backward and evaluates where she has been and where she is. We know our angers; now let's see what we have lost and gained by them." She has even offered to collaborate with a playwright willing to develop her thoughts.[12]

Joanne Woodward, actor, director, teacher, has especially in the last decade brought images of women usually ignored or forgotten to television, the screen, and the stage. From her films *Rachel, Rachel* and *The Effect of Gamma Rays on Man-in-the-Moon Marigolds* to her television plays *See How She Runs* and *Do You Remember Love?* and the stage interpretations of *Candida* and *The Glass Menagerie*, she has endowed "complex, sometimes downtrodden women" with her own sensitivity, intelligence, and power. Collette Dowling, author of *The Cinderella Complex*, pays tribute to Woodward's ability to "reflect the shifting, evocative aspects of Woman as she has emerged in the culture in recent years."[13]

Perhaps Joanne Woodward is able to use her beauty and talent in this way because she herself has gone through all the changes that have marked women's lives. Brought up to be a southern belle, married for almost thirty years to America's reluctant male sex symbol, Paul Newman, she seemed to have been torn in the early days between her upbringing that told her she should have "babies and be supported" and her desire for a career. She speaks of herself as something of a rebel when she came to New York to study acting at the Neighborhood Playhouse and struggled for acting jobs—"my idea of not conforming was to look a mess." Despite her stunning, Oscar-winning performance in *The Three Faces of Eve* early in her career, Hollywood had her playing the usual succession of "glamorous, or sexy and voluptuous types."[14] She faced the dangers of being turned into a "commodity" by the industry.

Woodward says of herself, however, that "I never really had the personality to be a superstar. I was having babies, staying home, studying philosophy at Sarah Lawrence, feeding the pets." She rejects the notion that she was taking a back seat to her husband's career. It was he who "literally shoved me out of the house to work. He directed *Rachel, Rachel* to revive my career when I was a total has-been."[15]

As she and her husband turned their backs on the Hollywood scene, however, her career took a different direction. "I've tapered off, but not by choice, I assure you," she quipped some time ago. "There are not many roles that come along that are right for me—unless you're willing to play a mechanical monster or be relegated to playing somebody's mother or in my case now, somebody's grandmother."[16] Instead Woodward gradually began the exploration of neglected women for which she has gained acclaim.

Joanne Woodward confessed some years ago that "I've come very late to a great many issues—probably in my thirties. And as far as the whole women's issue was concerned, probably not even until my forties. . . ." "I used to be happy to answer the telephone and say, 'This is Mrs. Paul Newman.' Now I say with neurotic intensity, 'This is Joanne Woodward'. . . . We are confused now, especially women my age. We were raised with certain attitudes and mores that just don't function anymore."[17]

Without abandoning the traditional roles of wife and mother of a large family, she has "come into her own" in her personal life and in her career. Although she is not one to talk much about her work or accomplishments, she has made opportunities for herself and others instead of waiting for things to happen. In addition to her many award-winning performances, she is directing for both stage and screen, teaching acting with her own company of young performers, narrating and hosting major cultural programs on television, and serving the many artistic, social and political causes she believes in from ballet companies to planned parenthood and nuclear arms control. Of the antiwar movement, she says that women's involvement is essential. "Women are the ones who raise the children, who give birth to the children. It's our children who will be destroyed along with us. And it seems to me, without being chauvinistic, that women have, perhaps, a greater sensitivity to what's happening and maybe a little more sensibility."[18] A 1986 project directing Shirley Knight in a short antiwar play, *The Depot* by Eve Ensler, for the Women's Project of the American Place Theatre not only brought together many of the vital current interests of this dedicated artist but also became the occasion for discussions with audiences about nuclear threat during a run at Interart Theatre.

Although Estelle Parsons is probably best known to the general public for her Oscar-winning role in the film *Bonnie and Clyde*, Hollywood has not been the place for her either. She did several films after her big success, which, she has said, "put my kids through private school and college," but there were not many scripts offered her that she felt were worth doing. She had been asked "to do horror movie parts with Bette Davis, Piper Laurie, Shelley Winters and others, but I've refused them. The characters are *not* real—I have to have a really grounded character, one that is psychologically sound and logical. Otherwise, I wouldn't know how to play it."[19]

It has been on and off Broadway that Parsons has made her mark in many different kinds of roles from the spinster-nursemaid Ruth in Joseph Papp's production of *The Pirates of Penzance* and Queen Elizabeth in the opera *Eliz-*

abeth and Essex to the tyrannical Miss Margarida in her very successful one-woman show *Miss Margarida's Way* and the many different repressed women in her one-woman feminist show *Orgasmo Adulto Escapes from the Zoo*, based on the script of Dario Fo and Franca Rame.

The variety of her roles onstage has been equalled by those offstage. Daughter of a New England attorney, she studied law for a year, and worked for a number of years as a writer, feature producer, and commentator on NBC's *Today* show when it first started. She left television work after her twin daughters were born, although initially she tried to keep going just as men do. "It was not possible to be married, have kids and stay in television," was her explanation. "I went on stage so I could work nights."[20] She turned to her long-time interest in singing and the stage, where she has continued to work ever since.

In her experience she has found that "most roles for women are stupid, stereotypical, male-written and male-directed." It was because *Orgasmo Adulto Escapes from the Zoo* offered "sharply delineated, full-bodied characters" that she was especially attracted to it. She did a translation for herself and consulted fully with Fo and Rame in Italy, devoting over a year to the preparations for the production, which she directed and produced. For the "marathon" role she worked intensely by herself in a loft with a devotion that she says was something of a "religious experience." "I would love it if I could be as alive in life as I am in the theatre. Life just doesn't have the intensity."[21]

Parsons was both attacked and praised for the message in *Orgasmo*—"the condition of women" and how "we're all prisoners of the male organ"—which she explains to the audience in the prologue. Her own interest, however, was not so much in the message. "I was more interested in their theatricality. I thought these pieces were wonderfully crazy and funny. They don't say the men are bad and the women are good—the women are as crazy as the men. One reason these plays are particularly important to me is because they're saying things that, as a woman, I don't say publicly, that I don't dare express in real life."[22]

It was not too surprising to discover that Estelle Parsons began turning to directing especially after *Miss Margarida's Way*. "As an actor you can't make decisions. *Miss Margarida's Way* was a transitional leap. It wasn't just acting. It was acting plus directing." Her first directorial undertaking was Susan Griffin's *Voices*, which, she felt, was good for an actor turned director since the five voices in the play are "different emotional aspects of one woman." Of the performers she worked with, Parsons has said, "I tried to get them to trust me, then themselves, to develop the courage to really work. We're working with organic American acting—what's called method acting. . . . [Parsons is a member of the Actors Studio.] We try to work right out of the inner life into the external form."[23]

The next year, in 1979, with the encouragement of Margot Lewitin of Women's Interart Theatre, she undertook a multiracial production of *Antony and Cleopatra.* "I wanted the production to represent, subliminally, much more the kind of life we lead, with the actors physically representing the world as it is now, particularly the world in New York. I wanted it to be multiracial and multilingual. . . ."[24] A subsequent happy development of Estelle Parsons' directorial approach to Shakespeare was the creation of her multiracial company, which has toured the boroughs of New York and performed on Broadway, playing Shakespeare for young audiences under the sponsorship of Joseph Papp.

In 1983 Estelle Parsons was the keynote speaker at the New York Conference of the Women's Program of the American Theatre Association. The topic of her talk, "Being Your Own Woman in Theatre," captures what has been her own objective as well as that of most of the women discussed here. In the Broadway theatre, "principally run by men," she found the difficulties greatest for designers and directors. She observed that she had only worked once for a woman director—Joanne Woodward in a television show. "That was an extraordinary experience. I wish there were more women directors." The problem she saw for all women in theatre was "maintaining your integrity, succeeding in the theatre according to your own vision."[25]

This brief survey concludes with some observations by Helen Hayes, who, as she herself humorously confesses, has become a "monument" in the American theatre. It is fascinating to see that for over eighty years she has had to deal in one way or another with some of the questions women are talking about more freely today—relationship to her stagestruck mother, use of her self in her art, finding more rewarding roles, and balancing career and family.

Looking back in 1958 shortly after a Broadway theatre was dedicated in her name, Helen Hayes recalled the time when "my youth, temperament, my own personal gifts were all that were necessary."[26] Early failures, however, led her to acquire not only some technique, "to learn the simplest, natural, truthful *means* of communicating through this instrument that is myself," but also to learn about "*what* to communicate." She developed what she called "her subway method" of studying her fellow riders so intently that her mother used to recall her to good manners by hissing "Stop staring."

"But I gazed outward to the world not inward upon myself," Helen Hayes recalls. "Someone I knew or observed was to become my bridge to a character I would portray. I've been too shy to use my own person. Maybe I don't have the courage to face myself. Maybe I don't want to seek inside myself too much. It embarrasses me to see a person picking away at himself like a monkey picking fleas. I do it, in my mind, to others all the time, but I just can't bear doing it to myself. . . . I learned there was never going to be any chance for me to use my real self or a remembered experience of my own or any of the things that help some actors." Even in parts "custom-tailored" for the charming young Helen Hayes, she felt she had "a hot potato in my hands because I literally didn't know how to be me on the stage. There I was face to face with myself, and there was nothing." She felt that she was always "falling back on the cozy little tricks that had stood me in such good stead for so long."

It wasn't until 1940, during her second try at Shaw's *Caesar and Cleopatra*, that she reports something "happened inside of me, that made it possible to communicate by using every part of me." In her long career playing everything from Queen Victoria to Mrs. Antrobus, she worked through problems of self, social expectations, and roles. For the character of Nora in O'Neill's *A Touch of the Poet*, one of her major late accomplishments, she felt that "all that has passed is prelude." She says she drew on her own life with her late husband, the playwright Charles MacArthur. It was the "absolute love" that he gave her that, she believed, helped her to understand and create Nora. "This was my great divestiture."

On her eightieth birthday, she spoke of having lost some of her enthusiasm for the theatre after the death from polio of her young daughter Mary in 1947 and of her husband seven years later. Her grief, she confessed, was that "I hadn't spent more time with Charles and Mary, that I'd gone off on road tours, that I'd gotten into the habit of serving the theatre."[27]

Despite Helen Hayes's great desire for privacy, the clash of public role and private life sometimes took place amidst great publicity. The famous "Act of God" episode, for example, was one that was retold very often in the early thirties. The story concerned the conflict with producer Jed Harris when Helen Hayes's tour in *Coquette* was interrupted by her pregnancy. Helen and her husband kept the pregnancy secret in hopes of gaining a bit of privacy for themselves, but it became a *cause célèbre* when she collapsed and had to take to her bed just before the last week of a two-year run. (She had to remain in bed for two months to protect the birth of her daughter Mary.) Harris refused to pay the cast for their final week, claiming that pregnancy fell into the category in the Equity contract of "fire, accident, strikes, Act of God." The actors sued for their wages. Equity eventually ruled against the producer, but not before all the papers were full of the story, which MacArthur kept from the resting mother-to-be. "Act of God" as the euphemism for pregnancies that interrupted runs was insiders' lingo in show business for many years.[28]

HERE ARE THE WOMEN PLAYWRIGHTS

HELEN KRICH CHINOY

"Where Are the Women Playwrights?" was the big question that headlined the May 20, 1973, Sunday Theatre Section of *The New York Times*. The question had been raised many times in the past by male critics and historians who regularly proclaimed women lacking "by nature" in those qualities needed for success as playwrights on Broadway. This feature story, however, coming in the early days of the women's movement, offered one of the few public forums for several women playwrights from on and off Broadway to voice their understanding of the special obstacles that confronted them individually and as a group in the always difficult struggle of women—and men—to survive creatively and economically in theatre.

Lillian Hellman, the most famous of the writers to respond, said she left the theatre when the "raw-money stuff" began to determine what plays were staged on Broadway. The ever-popular Jean Kerr quipped, "My mother keeps wanting to know why I don't write a play every year the way Neil Simon does. I have explained to her that (a) I don't have Neil Simon's talent, and (b) I don't have Neil's wife. . . . It may be that the new liberated woman has noticed that there are easier ways to make a name and/or a buck in almost any other line of work—creative or otherwise."

Gretchen Cryer, one of those younger liberated women, speculated: "Who knows how many potential playwrights there may be out there fixing bag lunches for their children who would be attempting to write their plays and get them on, were it not for the fact that they would guiltily consider their efforts self-indulgent folly." Renee Taylor, an actress turned playwright, laid the absence of women playwrights to the way women are "structured"— "pretty," "quiet" and "nice," "never allowed to be themselves," to have their "anger" or their "innate sexuality." Adrienne Kennedy, one of the most original voices in the black theatre, found women "lacking" in that "long dedication to art"; they were conditioned always to be listening "to the voices and needs of others." Rochelle Owens, who claimed women innovators were writing but not being produced, nevertheless also found that women "deplete their creative force and inspiration in the aeons-old traditional habit of overnurturing and pampering their 'genius' husbands." Clare Boothe Luce, a female voice from the heart of the commercial theatre, blamed the Broadway power structure, "dominated by male playwrights, directors and producers." In her opinion, "The question of why there aren't more women playwrights seems meaningless, unless women are now expected to save the theatre." Rosalyn Drexler, an avant-garde writer, seemed to suggest that women might indeed "save the theatre" in her comic vision of women artists "deployed about the city waiting to make their move. . . . At a signal which may be the clapping of one hand, all women playwrights will shoot the vapids and proceed to a secret rendezvous where a hidden store of explosive topics is waiting to be used. With proper handling, each sentence will find its mark."

In the next decade and a half many women did make the move Drexler prophesied. Their numerous plays can be found in the updated play list in our Sourcebook. A number of these women emerged from feminist collectives as well as from ethnic, community, and political theatres, where alternative values and structures encouraged a redefinition of the dramatist and her work. The new consciousness that led some dramatists to reject the traditional, commercial theatre completely also made those who looked to Broadway and the regional theatres more vocal and more visible. It has been said that by 1985 half the new members of the Dramatists Guild were women, who comprised 32 percent of the total membership. Two women won the Pulitzer Prize—Beth Henley for *Crimes of the Heart* in 1981 and Marsha Norman for *'night, Mother* in 1983. It had been more than twenty years since a woman last won the Pulitzer Prize for drama, and before that only five had been awarded to women in the almost forty years since the first prizes were given in 1918. In 1978 the substantial Susan Smith Blackburn Prize for an "outstanding English-language play" written by a woman was established and by 1987 had honored, along with writers in England, Barbara Schneider, Marsha Norman, Wendy Kesselman, and Mary Gallagher and Ellen McLaughlin, who shared the prize in that year. For the first time significant anthologies of plays by women began to appear—some for forgotten writers of the past in Rachel France's *A Century of Plays by American Women* and Judith Barlow's *Plays by American Women: The Early Years*, some for the new voices in Honor Moore's *The New Women's Theatre* and Julia Miles' several volumes from The Women's Project of the American Place Theatre. Other anthologies such as Margaret B. Wilkerson's *9 Plays by Black Women* included both old and new. Newspapers and magazines began occasionally to headline the "new strength" of women playwrights, several of whom won Guggenheim fellowships. In 1983 the Sunday Magazine section of *The New York Times* featured an article by critic Mel Gussow on "Women Playwrights: New Voices in the Theatre." In his piece mainly about Marsha Norman and other women in the mainstream Broadway, off Broadway and regional theatre, Gussow did briefly survey what he called the "wave of adventurous young women playwrights," and identified their emergence as one of "the most encouraging and auspicious aspects of the current American theatre."[1]

A number of the better-known of these "adventurous" theatre artists have spoken out in *Interviews with Contemporary Women Playwrights*, edited by Kathleen Betsko and Rachel Koenig in 1986, the first collection of its kind.[2] Previous anthologies about playwrights almost totally ignored women. From these rich interviews and some others, we can isolate a few of the issues of common concern to a wide variety of playwrights. Their individual, theatrical, and ideological differences are very important; other sections of our book detail some of the varied theatre impulses from which women dramatists come. Here we want only to suggest something of what the crucial decade and a half of the women's movement has meant to a diverse group, to suggest how they now look at a few aspects of themselves, their work, and their theatre.

To start with, the very designation "woman playwright" still stirs controversy. As early as 1941 Lillian Hellman had turned on an interviewer who called her "a woman playwright," saying "I am a *playwright*. You wouldn't refer to Eugene O'Neill as one of America's foremost *male* playwrights," and throughout her career she found the appellation "irritating."[3] Even for some whose feminist consciousness came through the women's movement of the 1970's, the term remains "dicey," as Eve Merriam, the doyen of current women writers, put it. "I guess there's still something pejorative about it. I *don't* want to be a 'woman playwright,' because I don't want to have my things done in a woman's theatre exclusively. It smacks of a certain kind of ghettoization, even if one chooses it."[4] Corinne Jacker suggests that the modifier " 'woman' makes the 'evaluation' drop a couple of notches," and one is not taken "seriously" as a writer. Yet she says she writes from her "female experience" and doesn't "want to deny what feminism has given me."[5] Although Adrienne Kennedy is no longer bothered by the label, she is bothered by the reality behind it, which is that "as a black woman, or as a woman writer, or as a black writer, I don't stand in line for the income and the rewards."[6] In discussing the "whole issue of whether women playwrights are a separate category," Wendy Wasserstein insisted: "We are all playwrights. I think that is very important. But for now, any minority group must be labeled. Our idea of a playwright is a white male—all the others are separated into subsets: black playwrights, gay playwrights, women playwrights, and so on. The point is, we are all in it together. I listen to my plays, and as I hear them, I distance myself, and I still think: 'A woman wrote this.'"[7] Janet Neipris accepts the designation because, as she puts it, "that's who I am."[8]

Certainly most of the women playwrights who have been interviewed by Kathleen Betsko and Rachel Koenig and others believe that the critics respond to them as "women playwrights." To the critics who proclaim their "male-dominated values" as "*the* universal values," a women "writing from her own point of view," says Gretchen Cryer, is "a revolutionary . . . from outside the system—unless she has absorbed a male sensibility."[9] Beth Henley finds that some critics writing about her plays, for example, identify their female subject matter, but don't "look for any of the deeper meanings or the spiritual levels in the play."[10] Studying thirty years of reviews for their collection of interviews led Kathleen Betsko to the conclusion that "the concerns, the irony, the innovations, and intentions of women playwrights are, for the most part, woefully lost on the majority of our critics. Gender bias is rampant in the language. With notable exceptions, commentary runs from paternal tolerance to aggressive misogyny."[11]

The power of the critics, as many see it, not only closes shows but closes off creativity. Corinne Jacker explains that she "stopped writing for ten years" when a critic of her first show, an adaptation of Katherine Anne Porter's *Pale Horse, Pale Rider*, said that she and Porter "wrote in eyeshadow."[12] It took Adrienne Kennedy two years "to recover" from the response to *Funnyhouse of a Negro*. Emily Mann was "devastated, depressed, enraged" by the direct "attack" she felt was made on her by critics of *Still Life*.[13] Eve Merriam felt that male critics attacked *The Club* because she had done the "unpardonable," which is to "hold the male power structure up to ridicule." The show was saved, she believes, by the New York women critics, Edith Oliver, Marilyn Stasio and Erika Munk. Some writers, however, complain that women critics often accept the male approach and provide little support.[14]

Although some women playwrights speak about open discrimination in the hierarchical professional theatre, Janet Neipris, who is chair of the dramatic writing program at New York University, suggests that "we have gone way beyond all that." Rather she finds the obstacles to be differences in taste and "incompatible production aesthetics"—which may, of course, amount to the same thing.[15] Marsha Norman believes that "more attention is given" to women playwrights now. Susan Yankowitz finds that what happens now, especially in regional theatres, is that "you get your play up through the woman who is in second command, and when the script ascends finally to the top, the person who really has the power is a man, and the man says no."[16]

Although exact statistics are hard to come by, there is little question that most of those at the top must still be saying "no" to women's work. A study done a decade ago by the group calling itself Action for Women in Theatre calculated that only 7 percent of all plays produced in fifty not-for-profit theatres were written by women. Their findings, as we report in our Sourcebook, precipitated action by individuals, theatres, and professional associations, including the creation of The Women's Project of the American Place Theatre by Julia Miles in 1978. That first year 700 scripts were submitted, a sharp answer to the accusation that there were not enough plays by women available.[17] From that date through 1986, when The Women's Project had 197 playwright and director members, the group staged 35 productions and 218 rehearsed readings.[18]

In the traditional venues, however, not that much has changed for women playwrights despite some conspicuous and highly touted improvements. Even when Mel Gussow of *The New York Times* heralded the arrival of the new women playwrights in 1983, there was only one play by a woman playing on Broadway and little more off Broadway, a fact noted in a collection of critical responses to his article published in *Performing Arts Journal* in November of that year. An informal survey of some two hundred theatres in TCG's biennial guide to regional theatres, *Theatre Profiles 7*, indicates that in the 1984–85 season, except for theatres dedicated to women's work, a quarter of the theatres had produced no plays by women; roughly 40 percent had one play by a woman out of anything from five to ten or twelve productions. Only the Eureka Theatre in California had an equal number of plays by men and women—three by each.[19] On Broadway in 1986 as this book was being prepared, only one play by a woman was produced, Emily Mann's *Execution of Justice*, which she also directed, but it closed quickly. France Burke, a playwright who has chaired the Committee for Women of the Dramatists Guild, has pointed out that "it is ironic that women have arrived in playwriting and directorial positions just as the fabulous invalid is going through a particularly spectacular series of seizures. It is hard for anyone to raise money for productions now, especially of new work, by a new team, that does not have a track record."[20] Who will listen to the new voices of women playwrights is something that troubles Wendy Wasserstein. "I worry about the theatre itself more than the women writers. I think, who is coming these days? Couples who come once a year for their anniversary? Is it really part of our culture anymore? Do people still talk about plays at the dinner table?"[21]

Even many of the women playwrights working in the mainstream rather than in feminist, political or avant-garde venues thus see that the central question of how "womanhood affects women's work" must include economic, institutional, and cultural questions. Corinne Jacker among others has suggested that women need to go beyond simply complaining that "critics and producers don't take us seriously enough." What is needed is to undertake "the formidable task of developing an aesthetic" that will reveal what is distinctive about women's plays and women's lives out of which their authentic creative vision must come.[22] Many more plays by women in both the mainstream and the alternative theatres will have to be produced and published, something that usually only follows staging, before we'll be able to answer fully the question "Plays by Women: What's the Difference?"—the topic of a Dramatists Guild Committee for Women panel in 1985. With some of the new resources now available to us about women playwrights, however, we have begun to make a rough start on the "formidable task." The previous section of our book surveyed the feminist theatres; subsequent sections briefly explore avant-garde, ethnic, community, and political dramatists. Here let's see what a few of the parameters of a woman's life in the theatre are—as reported by playwrights from some of the different and sometimes overlapping venues in which they work.

Getting started as a playwright is always a very difficult first step, especially for women. Here's how it happened for some who were to succeed. Lillian Hellman, always the benchmark for women playwrights, told Bill Moyers in 1974 that she "didn't know anything else." She had been around the theatre as a play reader for Anne Nichols of *Abie's Irish Rose* fame and for MGM during her marriage to Arthur Kober and was part of the Hollywood scene as the girlfriend of Dashiell Hammett, who suggested to her the plot of her first play, *The Children's Hour*. "My play *The Bridge at Belharbour* is what initially got me going," says Janet Neipris. "I did not know a bloody thing about playwriting. I was in grad school when I wrote that. It was a straight shoot from the heart. . . ."[23] Adrienne Kennedy was always "taking writing courses" when she came to New York with her husband and child in the 1950's, but it was her close relationship with her mother, "a terrific storyteller," and a year in Africa, where she discovered "a strength in being a black person and a connection to West Africa," that were the powerful influences that led to *Funnyhouse of a Negro*, which was produced by Edward Albee's workshop.[24] "What the hell am I doing?" is the question Donna de Matteo, associated with the HB Studio, says she asked herself one morning. "I had a terrific husband, two great kids, but something was missing, and I discovered that what was missing was *me*."[25] Such new consciousness led not only to individual expression but also to the group creations of the feminist theatres.

Many women have come to writing from acting, an obvious route. Alice Childress, the award-winning playwright and novelist, was an actress on Broadway and even did movies and television. "But racial prejudice was such that I was considered 'too light' to play my real self and they would not cast light-skinned blacks in white roles. . . . I decided I'd rather create from the start, create good roles I'd like to play by writing them."[26] She has not, however, played the fine women's roles she has written. Mary Gallagher, the winner of the Susan Blackburn Prize for *How to Say Goodbye*, followed her talent as an actress first, but playwriting brought her the kind of approval she sought. The enthusiastic audience response to her first play gave her extraordinary feelings. "I had released some force, some tremendous energy, inside me! . . . I had a sense of power like I'd never had before."[27] "Before I knew that I wanted to write, I wanted to act," Beth Henley recalls, but she found the acting world "tough." "It was so much more difficult than writing."[28] Attracted to the magic of theatre through her mother's acting in community theatre, she wrote her first play, *Am I Blue*, under the pseudonym Amy Peach during her college years.

Not many women recall important female role models. "The only woman playwright I knew," said Janet Neipris, "was Lillian Hellman and I couldn't figure out where my Dashiell Hammett was. My life didn't seem to be anything like hers."[29] For Marsha Norman, too, "Lillian Hellman was it. . . . She was my only indication that this kind of life was possible."[30] Emily Mann speaks of Caryl Churchill as someone to emulate; Karen Malpede, herself devoted to a poetic theatre, mentions Lady Augusta Gregory and Gertrude Stein; Ntozake Shange credits Alice Childress, who came from the "same part of South Carolina as my family," as an important influence. Rochelle Owens recalls the impact when she was twelve of reading an "allegorical morality" play by poet Mary Caroline Davies, who was associated with the Provincetown Players. Megan Terry claims that she was fortunate to have worked as a youngster in Seattle with Florence James, an inspirational director and teacher of acting who had studied in Moscow with Stanislavsky. She also credits the pioneer women in her family for her own feminist strength, manifested from the experimental sixties to her present work with the Omaha Magic Theatre. Some other writers also credit female family members, especially mothers, as either inspirational models or as spurs to achievement because of their opposition to or neglect of their daughters' aspirations.

Having children or the decision not to has been very important to many women writers. Karen Malpede believes that although it involves difficult considerations, pregnancy "can be a tremendously creative time in the life of a woman."[31] Beth Henley, however, discussing the "recurrence of barren women in her work," says that she herself doesn't want children. "I have a fear of being tied down. My mother was. I know my fear is based on her being trapped in with all that talent that she had, by kids and husband and the world."[32] Gretchen Cryer, who organized the Committee for Women of the Dramatists Guild, has said that women must balance having "to spend their creative energy on the children and home," against the positive aspects of having "your experience . . . definitely deepened from having children."[33] Even Merriam has commented on the "profound" effect of motherhood on her art. "I didn't have children until I was in my mid-thirties because I thought I could not reconcile my writing career and motherhood. And then when I *wanted* to have children, there was nothing rational about it, it just came on me. . . . Some of my best work has been about reconciling motherhood and a career, of dealing with that continuing dilemma."[34] Tina Howe made childbirth and raising children the subject of her ritualistic play *Birth and After Birth*, which has never been produced. "It's so incendiary I'm afraid critics would stone me to death," Howe once said.[35] JoAnne Akalaitis fought for day care in the Mabou Mines group; younger playwrights traveling to regional theatres to work on their shows are asking producers to provide housing for baby and babysitter in addition to themselves.

Earning a living confronts most women playwrights. Adrienne Kennedy's conclusion echoes that of many of them. After about twenty years at her craft, she realized "that although I had many first-class productions, apart from grants my plays did not seem to generate an income. . . . I had been living on grants, and hadn't quite realized that."[36] Teaching, acting, directing and film work as well as family support have helped to make it possible for many to keep on with their writing. As we have seen, few women playwrights have had productions on Broadway, and even these were not "money shows." Some have careers outside of New York, but the economics of playwriting make earning a living from one's art a hard task.

The creative process itself is highly individual. The late Jane Chambers, who made lesbians visible on the stage, called it "mystical" in a note about "The Birth of a Play" in the program for *My Blue Heaven*. "I'd like it to stay that way. I write in a kind of alpha state and am not fully aware of what has happened in the play until the first draft is complete and I reread it." In the early stage the playwright is at the typewriter, "taking dictation" from the characters who "materialize in the room and play the play." Later "the conscious work" begins as "craft is applied. . . . I have ceased to be secretary to my creation. I now decide its fate."[37]

Rehearsal behavior suggests some of the problems confronted and solved by women working outside of the collectivist theatres. Beth Henley has said that she loves the rehearsal process, "especially watching the actors work." She may do "some rewriting during rehearsals," but since she works from "excessive notes, charts, outlines" even before writing dialogue, she doesn't usually have to do "major rewrites."[38] Corinne Jacker would prefer "being considered a dead writer, one who can't rewrite from the grave. If it has to be done, I want to do it, but I want to be sure it has to be done." Like most of the others, she "behaves well" during the rehearsal process and she claims to be "cowardly" in urging her views on directors.[39] A director told Donna de Matteo when she objected that he had not discussed her play with her, "Look, this isn't Off-Off Broadway. You're in the commercial theatre now. . . ." She interpreted his comment as "If you want this production, you'll do it my way," and talking herself into " believing that what he wanted was correct," she was "passive," indeed "comatose," during rehearsals.[40] Susan Yankowitz finds that the "inevitable power struggle between playwright and director is always exacerbated by the male-female situation."[41]

Maria Irene Fornes, winner of an Obie for "Sustained Achievement" that includes innovative writing and directing, says that the playwright, whether a woman or a man, is the "female" in the production group, being taken care of by the "male" director. She, therefore, feels it "essential" to direct her own plays. "I didn't know I had to direct my own work right away, but I did find out immediately that the position of the playwright is unbearable. I went to the very first rehearsal of a work of mine. . . . I had never been to a rehearsal of anything in my life. . . . To me it was a world of madness. I learned as a playwright you 'behave.'" Even though women directors have great difficulty gaining opportunities to work, Fornes believes the woman playwright-director can be successful if she masters the essential crafts so that she can work with "people who believe" in her work. "Then I have a power that is almost hypnotic."[42]

Mary Gallagher claims that the combined power of a woman's being both playwright and director is discouraged by producers and wonders: "Was I afraid of that power in myself?"[43] She has high praise for several women directors of her plays, calling Mary Robinson the "best director" she has ever worked with. Tina Howe also has high praise for the director of her biggest successes, *Painting Churches* and *Coastal Disturbances*, Carole Rothman of The Second Stage. Howe is not certain whether their good relationship is the result of Rothman's being a woman or of her talent. "I think it's a combination of the two. . . . To have a woman who's not only sensitive to my point of view but who is also completely workmanlike is astonishing."[44]

On the question of a "female aesthetic" these women writers have expressed varied views. Maria Irene Fornes declares: "How could there possibly not be? Not only is there a women's aesthetic, each woman has her own aesthetic and so does each man. . . . How could we, as women, have nothing in common?"[45] Eve Merriam believes that there is a "female aesthetic," despite the fact that it is unfashionable to hold that view. "We women are more tuned in to our bodies, and I think our language sometimes reflects that. . . . The men may stay at the 'fuck you' verbal level, but frequently women have an *erotic* quality in their work. . . . The longing and the attachment for another human contact may be more accessible to women playwrights than to men . . . and acceptance and joyousness of the body, which is something the Women's Movement has brought about."[46] For Rosalyn Drexler "the female aesthetic is to be *un*aesthetic. When I think of *aesthetic*, I think of something too finely placed, too much in good taste. Women are trying to be a little sloppier, changing forms, getting stronger, letting ideas come in—and that is unaesthetic."[47]

Although Beth Henley finds talking about a "woman's aesthetic" "too much like school for me to be excited," her own attraction to "split images," to "the grotesque combined with the innocent" as a "metaphor for my view of life," suggests the recurrent interest, in women's plays, in duality and fragmentation.[48] Adrienne Kennedy recalls that it was "a huge breakthrough for me when my main characters began to have other personas—it was in fact my biggest breakthrough as a writer. . . . That's when I decided to use historical people as an extension of the main character."[49] At the same time she also began to incorporate symbolism that came from her dreams. Corinne Jacker talks about using "the male side of me" in her work. "Can we admit to ourselves that we *are able to imagine* what it's like to be a man? It's a kind of schizophrenia." She also opts for plays that don't "supply a resolution and an answer," but that ask the audience to "figure it out."[50]

Emily Mann wonders if her "theatre of testimony" may not be the result of "being female." "Women sit around and talk to each other about their memories of traumatic, devastating events in their lives. . . . I hear the stories, then I let *you*, the audience, have the same experience I had as a listener." In letting the audience hear the individual and the community, she takes advantage of the fact that in "the theatre you can hear many voices at once; it is a wonderful aspect of live theatre that can't actually be reproduced in film."[51]

The different sensibilities and dramatic strategies suggested by these observations have led some of these women writers to question the validity of "realism and naturalism" as styles appropriate for their vision. Many feel new forms are needed for the new content of women's plays. Eve Merriam puts the argument in these terms. Speaking of realism, "it doesn't give me any new insights. It doesn't teach me something that I didn't know before. . . . The realistic theatre confirms what goes on. . . . I find that larger-than-life, or smaller-than-life, if you have some strange miniatures, is what turns me on. Not the 'well-made play.'"[52] Anne Commire also rejects the "'male climax' in terms of a gun going off or a punch in the nose," for what she calls "minimalism."[53]

The personal story, which has been attacked as the main subject matter of many American writers—female and male—is, however, not seen as limiting by some of the women writers. Mary Gallagher tells of visiting theatre artists in Nicaragua, where they spoke always of "how the only valid theatre is collective theatre telling the collective story of a people." Although she felt as if she had "*naturalism* tattooed on my forehead," she realized that "working from the need to convey a political message . . . they still had to show personal detail, human nature, to express their feelings and beliefs and to communicate. Those of us who begin at the other end, with the need to express a feeling or belief, also wind up with plays that have a political and social message, any time we address a serious and complex issue. Good theatre incorporates the personal, the social, the political, seamlessly. That's what I learned."[54]

In her study of women writers in *Feminist Theatre*, Helene Keyssar also came to the conclusion that "the presence or absence of realism is not *the* central issue for feminist drama." Among the many distinctions she identified in the work of the American and English women dramatists studied, Keyssar considered the "strategy of transformation, the theatrical manifestation of metamorphosis of contexts, actions and, most crucially, of characters" to be the most important. In place of Aristotelian "self-recognition," she found in feminist plays "recognition of others and a concomitant transformation of the self and the world." This drama "asserts the possibility for change," which seems to be at the heart of the new women's theatre.[55]

Although women are often accused of writing about "trifles," many of the writers insist that they "handle a bigger subject than women are normally given credit for," as Rosalyn Drexler put it of one of her plays.[56] In Corinne Jacker's view, "the world-large, political actions actually revolve around what happens in domestic situations." She has pointed out that great male writers have themselves shown how for women the political is "inextricably connected to the personal" — witness Antigone or Cordelia.[57]

Karen Malpede has suggested that the feminist impulse which legitimated the connection between personal and political made an "extraordinary impact." "I suppose it's hard for people who didn't live through it to understand the absolutely cataclysmic force with which first the civil rights and peace movements and then feminism entered our lives. We actually felt, and it's a feeling that has never left me, that some great change for the good is possible, that our lives *are* a constant process of creation and that whatever we can understand about ourselves, about the nature of our victimization, our own oppression, our own fears and our own resistance can be transferred into social life."[58]

Just how feminist or how political women's drama is or ought to be has been variously interpreted. Beth Henley, for example, prefers to "write about people. The problems of just being here are more pressing and exciting to me than politics. Politics generally deal with the facades of our more desperate problems. I don't really feel like changing the world, I want to look at the world." She talks of the "existential madness that we—everyone—are born into. There's a sense of powerlessness in the world."[59] Tina Howe, whose own concerns are more "aesthetic than they are social or political," suggests that "in times of political chaos, many artists go inward because the outer landscape is so appalling," and out of this "move inwards . . . very exciting work is done as a result."[60] Susan Yankowitz is most attracted to works with a "political dimension," that try to "understand a relationship between the individual situation and a condition in the world."[61] Mary Gallagher takes a slightly different view, suggesting that "all good theatre is deeply political, revolutionary, when the society's values are as warped as our society's are now."[62] Ntozake Shange, whose *For Colored Girls . . .* was the first feminist play to reach Broadway, says, "I think the dangerous mistake that women make is to assume the personal is not political. When I make a personal statement, it is to me a political statement."[63]

Something most women playwrights seem to agree on is the importance of the female characters in their work. In Marsha Norman's view "the notion of an *active* central character is required for the theatre," but women could not write such female characters until they began to realize, as they have, that "they can be, and indeed are, the central characters in their own lives." She believes that women have "secrets to tell." They have a "new definition of survival" in which "Mother looms large." "As women, our historical role has been to clean up the mess. . . . We are not afraid to look under the bed, or to wash the sheets; and we know that life is messy. . . . This fearless 'looking under the bed' is what you see in so many plays by women, and it's exciting."[64]

It can also be dangerous, as Tina Howe pointed out some years ago. "If a woman really explored the areas that make her unique as a woman, was radical in her femininity, the commercial theatre would be terrified."[65] The pain of self-editing or self-censorship disturbs many women artists, especially now when some see it as the price for economic success. Ntozake Shange, for example, works in "alternative spaces" because working in the "commercial theatre" is "dangerous for somebody who is trying to explore because you can only explore so much when all that money is being invested in you. . . . It's important to have power over one's work."[66]

The need "to have power over one's work" brought some of these women playwrights together as early as 1968, when Maria Irene Fornes organized and ran New York Theatre Strategy, which advocated a "theatre without compromise and sexism." Emily Mann, for example, looks to women who were part of that group—Megan Terry, Rochelle Owens, Rosalyn Drexler—and to Ntozake Shange as the ones who "revolutionized the theatre in the seventies . . . who radicalized our perception and our consciousness about theatre."[67] Others have been part of Women's Interart Theatre or Ellen Stewart's Cafe La Mama or the Women's Project of the American Place Theatre. Some have come from feminist theatres; others from supportive regional venues.

Although women playwrights vigorously debate their differing views of aesthetics, politics, and feminism, most of them are using whatever hard-won power they have to "tell the stories that haven't been told" about their own experience and the world in which they live. Rachel Koenig offers a vivid personal distillation of the many plays she read or saw in preparing the book of interviews she and Kathleen Betsko edited. Her summary serves well not only to conclude this brief discussion but also to open up for future detailed study the achievement and the possibilities of women playwrights:

> I was both confronted with nonviolent dramatic conflict and positioned as a nonvoyeuristic spectator, asked not to passively observe a reenactment of a violent act, but to actively listen and evaluate valuable human testimony. Likewise I was witness to the lush landscape of female sexuality which bypassed the dynamic of sadomasochism so dependent on the hatred and denial of the 'other' . . . and embraced nature, desire and erotic knowledge

without fear. . . . I saw mature women, married and unmarried, mothers and grandmothers who (like their creators) were not fragile or impassive, used up, or too old, but vivid, erotic, rebellious, *alive.* I saw women across the spectrum of age, race, and class taking action, bearing witness, responding to and making an effect upon the world. I saw the expression of female will and saw the exertion of this will go unpunished. . . . I saw our ambivalence . . . reflected in the dramatic conflict between mother and daughter. I saw the split selves of a tortured psyche heal. A tradition of female action in the world was revealed to me. . . . I saw regimes interrogated. . . . I saw the notion of freedom considered and reconsidered. . . . I saw continuity, the generations, the cycles of birth and death and rebirth, fertility and decay. I saw the shape of time transgress the linear beginning, middle and ending of all things. I saw dramas which described a purely feminine quest, dramas in which compelling, powerful women created their own destiny. . . . I also saw women succumb to a patriarchal siren song . . . but . . . rather than passively accept their extinction, I was forced to mourn their fate, and therefore question and revise my own. . . . I was shown the dark side of human nature, but I was also given humor and hope, for in the enactment of these works I saw visions of the possible become actual. And I saw the agent of these visions, a dramatist, a woman, hold the power to shape the manifold of experience into new unities . . . broadening our sense of the range of human possibility.[68]

WOMEN BACKSTAGE AND OUT FRONT

HELEN KRICH CHINOY

Women who work backstage and out front—producers, managers, directors, designers, dramaturgs, technicians, agents, critics—still often face formidable obstacles to their full participation in theatre. The nature of their work can make them even more dependent on institutional structures than actors or playwrights. As women in professional theatre organizations many feel themselves to be the "new kids on the block," and despite their evident talent, top training, and outstanding track records, they have to pull down many barriers—the most difficult being the "Broadway barrier"—to make a place for themselves in the crafts and business of theatre institutions still largely run by a white, male hierarchy. Those specialists who work outside of the commercial arena operate in terms of the alternative values found in the feminist, experimental, community, ethnic, and political theatres. Here often "everyone does everything" to sustain their collective production, an approach that presents for them important advantages but also possible problems of "burnout" and stunted growth. As the 1980's opened, however, there seemed to be considerable mobility and opportunity for women to choose to work in the different kinds of theatres. By the second half of the decade the situation for these specialists, as for actors and playwrights, was a complicated, confusing one, which we have dubbed "The Turning Point" in our preface. What follows here is a mosaic of data, opinion, argument, and ideas to suggest what is happening for women in some of these crucial areas of theatre. Limited by constraints of space, time, and the availability of data, these few pages concentrate on a sampling of producers, directors, and designers mainly working on and Off Broadway and in the regional theatres, with some concluding references to the problems of critics and criticism.

In late 1986 when the Outer Circle Critics organized a panel at Sardi's on "Women on Broadway: Do They Make a Difference?" some of those working in the mainstream, even those who have "made it," said the situation for women was grim. Elizabeth McCann, the "Golden Lady" of many hit shows like *Amadeus*, spoke of producing: "Women in this industry are not plugged into the power network that can make the difference. They're not running the unions, and they're not running the real estate. There is not one theatre that can be booked in the ladies' room. We've got to get plugged into that network and stop letting men make all the deals."[1]

While the power structure of Broadway remains, as McCann puts it, the "last closed door," it is important to note that there is a fascinating "old girls' network" of women producers. One strand stretches back from Elizabeth McCann and her former associate Nelle Nugent through Cheryl Crawford, in whose office Nugent started out, to Theresa Helburn of the Theatre Guild. Cheryl Crawford, for example, survived in the business for over fifty-five years till her death in 1986. When she started out in the mid-1920's after attending Smith College, she wanted to get a job as a stage manager only to be told that there had been only "one woman stage manager in the professional theatre."[2] She quickly learned that "females are actresses or nothing." Yet shortly thereafter she did get her start with the Theatre Guild when Helburn, perhaps wanting "to give another woman a break," [3] took her on as "casting secretary" and "assistant stage manager."

In a long career on Broadway, Crawford had many notable successes including *Brigadoon* and four of Tennessee Williams' major plays. Unlike most people in the business, however, she also gave herself fully to several major alternative ideas of theatre, from the Theatre Guild itself, to the Group Theatre of which she was one of the founders with Harold Clurman and Lee Strasberg, to the American Repertory Theatre with Eva Le Gallienne and Margaret Webster, ANTA, and the Actors Studio. Looking back on her life in her autobiography Crawford expressed the tension between idealistic vision and individual success. "Ever since the Group days I had truly wanted to be involved in a theatre that had a core and continuity, theatre that enriched the theatre itself. When the ART and ANTA died aborning, I became again that naked individual I had tried to avoid."[4]

Crawford's many different activities as well as her desire to be more than just "one naked individual" serve to remind us that "producers in skirts,"[5] which is what newspapers in the 1930's dubbed women like her, go back not only to Crawford and Helburn but well into the nineteenth century. Most of them must have had that "ton of nerve" and some of the "philosophy of a gambler" that Crawford once said was essential to be a producer. But some in the past and a number today seem to think women have something special to contribute, a vision of theatre that enriches the idea of theatre itself. Elizabeth McCann, like Crawford very successful on Broadway, has suggested that women are not concerned with power the same way men are; they are more interested in ideas than buildings. With these values women are more likely to find the way to revive theatre.

Lyn Austin, producing director of the Music-Theatre Group/Lenox Arts Center, like Elizabeth McCann knows the Broadway theatre well; she had been for many years a leading producer associated with Roger Stevens. In the last ten years, however, she has nurtured an "idea" that grew out of dissatisfaction with Broadway, which nevertheless gave her the experience to carry out her current work effectively. But she grew tired, she says, of "seeing writers fall apart in the Ritz in Boston" during out-of-town tryouts. She wanted to find a "formula for artists to do what they wanted to do" in a supportive structure that would provide them "enough money and time" to be truly creative.[6]

Her "idea" as a producer was to "commit to an artist" rather than just produce shows. Since a number of theatre artists she knew wanted to use music, she helped them process the intricate mixing of the arts. The result has been the unique avant-garde accomplishments of such artists as Anne Bogart and Martha Clarke. Austin, who got her start in theatre at Vassar College, is "proud" that the work of women has been featured, but says she chose the artists not because they were women but because "they were the best in the field." She prizes "excellence" above all else, believing that theatre seeks out gifted people. It has been Lyn Austin's dream to do just that in a unique, modest, but highly skilled professional producing venture.

Among the "alternative" producers in New York, Ellen Stewart is surely La Mama of them all. Working in her intensely personal, idiosyncratic way completely outside show business, she has survived for twenty-five years as a unique magician of the theatre, an accomplishment acknowledged by the MacArthur "Genius" Award in 1987. Her uncritical openness, governed only by her intuition, has literally taken in the whole world. "The diversity of the La Mama population has grown to staggering proportions, reflecting Ellen's nurturing self," writes the composer Elizabeth Swados, one of those "raised" by her, in a glowing tribute.[7]

Ellen Stewart's accomplishments, which are far too numerous to describe here except to say that almost every modern theatrical innovation seems to have found a place with her, are not the result of any precise aesthetic or ideological intention. She insists that she "reads people" rather than texts, and supports those who "go beyond the norm," who "stretch the boundaries of theatre" to make a communication that can be played to anybody in the world.[8] Her major contribution to women has been as a "role model" who urges them, as she has urged her La Mama artists, to go out and do what they want. In response to complaints about "inability to get ahead in the field," she urges women to get their own "pushcart"—that is, "to start their own theatres"—as she was urged to do at the beginning of her career. "Look into yourself to note where you were shortchanged artistically along the way and begin to make a balance of payments, but don't just talk about it; show me and make it artistic." She questions women about what kind of contribution they want to make to their "fellow human beings." She urges them to be concerned with "communication and the universe." "If you aspire to the performing arts," she says, "aspire to give what is inspirational to audiences." By precept, example, and making opportunities for others, she herself has become a source of inspiration to women in theatre.

There are a number of other women in New York and across the country who have become producers because of their dedication to an "idea" rather than to buildings, box office, or self-advancement. Miriam Colon, who has acted on Broadway and on television and was the first Puerto Rican taken into the Actors Studio, of which she has been a member for twenty-five years, founded the Puerto Rican Traveling Theatre in 1967 because of her "desire to share with thousands and thousands of people in the inner communities the message of what we are and how we think, our defeats, our dreams, our rage, our humor."[9] She had never "studied business administration or anything about directing a group." "I have to confess that it was done without all the planning and structuring that supposedly should be done." It was the dream of a "traveling theatre for the masses" that thrust her into the job of producer. "Needless to say, I had no idea of the horror that fundraising is. But I started and thank God I did not know that it was going to be so hard. Had I known and had I become very technical and very scientific, I never would have started. Thank God for my naivete."

After years of nomadic existence in the borough of New York, the Puerto Rican Traveling Theatre saw their "dream fulfilled" when they found a home in a West 47th Street firehouse leased to them by the city of New York. Here they play their important bilingual repertoire and conduct their training program for young people from the community they serve. "When they gave me the building, I was ecstatic," Miriam Colon has said, but in 1986 she explained that "we have not solved the riddle of survival. Even though to all appearances we are eminently successful, we still are struggling with the great dilemma of economics. . . . We are still learning our values, but as we look back we are very, very proud that we have served as the showcase of plays, not only from Puerto Rico . . . [but also] the best in Latin American dramatic literature, always with an eye to the Hispanic playwright who concentrates on the Hispanic experience."

Combining the tasks of producing with directing, a number of women have become artistic directors of their own theatres. Most of these women found that they had to start or be in charge of their own theatres if they were to have opportunities to direct, for directing, it would seem, has been even more closed to women—especially on Broadway—than producing. Both Carole Rothman of Second Stage and Lynne Meadow of the Manhattan Theatre Club, like Zelda Fichandler before them, exemplify women who got into producing for this reason.

"It was just too hard to get opportunities to direct before that," Carole Rothman has said of her reasons for starting her theatre with Robyn Goodman. "I would direct things, but for some reason I wasn't making that jump from a workshop production to the main stage, even though my work was praised by the critics and all that."[10] She has indicated that she "felt a lot of frustration over the lack of opportunities for female directors. Robyn and I had both come to the realization that we were at a plateau in our careers, and we wanted to take charge of our own lives and create jobs for ourselves. I'm a feminist, and I thought it would be a good idea not only to direct myself, but to give other women directors the chance to direct. Doing plays by women was also a goal."[11]

They started the Second Stage in 1979 in rented spaces; by 1984 they moved into their own theatre at Broadway and 76th Street. Here they were best able to realize the special "idea" of their theatre—to resurrect American plays that had been done once. "When we started, there were a lot of Off Broadway and Off-Off Broadway theatres, mostly doing new plays," Rothman has said. "It seemed like there was a fast-food mentality—everybody had to have new, new, new. We felt there were plays that were slipping through the cracks." In addition to the revivals to which they have been dedicated, several new plays have been produced. *Painting Churches* and *Coastal Disturbances*, for example, were the result of a fruitful association between Carole Rothman and Tina Howe, who calls Rothman "an inspired director," and the work at the Second Stage "the most innovative and exciting" in New York.

Lynne Meadow, who celebrated fifteen years at Manhattan Theatre Club in 1986, also felt that she had to head her own theatre in order to have opportunities to direct. From Bryn Mawr College, she went to Yale Drama School, where she was the only woman director in her class; "there were no women directors in the class ahead of me and no women in the class behind me."[12] Without role models, she nevertheless absorbed the tough professional training at Yale and made her way to New York. As a "brainy fledgling director,"[13] she was brought in to run the Manhattan Theatre Club, where she has produced and/or directed new plays and significant revivals—among them David Rudkin's *Ashes* and *Ain't Misbehavin'* (their big money-maker), as well as the challenging plays of Athol Fugard. Looking back, she has said that her "dream was to have a major institution in New York City, one about which people would say, 'I know their work and it's good.'"[14]

Although Lynne Meadow has not done as much directing as she had hoped to at Manhattan Theatre Club, she has enjoyed the challenges of producing, even overcoming the "math anxiety" of her college days, an inhibition that often deters women. Although she considers herself a feminist and recognizes that her progress has been made "through the changing landscape of feminism," [15] women's work has not been a special issue in her theatre. Yet MTC has done plays by Joanna Glass, Sybille Pearson, and Pam Gems, as well as Beth Henley's *Crimes of the Heart*, which went on to win the Pulitzer Prize, and such women as Julianne Boyd, Geraldine Fitzgerald, Nancy Meckler, and Sharon Ott have directed there.

Because she thinks creative work is highly individual, Lynne Meadow does not like to generalize about a specifically female approach or sensibility, insisting that women should direct any plays they are attracted to. She is enthusiastic about the fact that women are not just writing "about mothers and daughters," but about large issues as well. "The basis of my artistic vision is a kind of eclecticism and love of diversity, though we do have certain strong inclinations. We have a history of doing a certain number of plays that speak out on social or political issues." [16] As a recent mother, she is "impressed with how women have managed to do it all," with few cultural or social supports. Recognizing that the current state of theatre is grim, she is still optimistic, believing that theatre ups and downs are cyclical. She believes that for women "the situation is changing. These days there are more women directors and more women who are deciding to become directors because there are more models that have been provided and more opportunities." [17]

Among the women directors providing models are a number of leading actors—Zoe Caldwell, Colleen Dewhurst, Geraldine Fitzgerald, Lee Grant, Estelle Parsons, Joanne Woodward—who have turned to directing. With recognizable names and solid accomplishments behind them, they, like the artistic directors, are able to achieve the authority other aspiring directors have difficulty winning. Even these stars, however, have to convince producers they can handle the "big bucks" involved on Broadway.

For unattached, free-lance directors, a large, talented cohort that includes Sue Lawless, Emily Mann, Timothy Near, Elinor Renfield, Nancy Rhodes, Mary Robinson and Amy Saltz, the opportunities are still hardly plentiful. A 1983 study by the League of Professional Theatre Women documents the five seasons from 1977 to 1982, showing that of the 261 plays produced on Broadway, only 9—roughly 3 percent—were directed by women. [18] Studies of the regional not-for-profit theatres done in 1976 and 1980 ("Action for Women in Theatre" and "Women Directing in Theatre") came up with similarly bleak figures. Of some 50 theatres studied, only 6 percent of productions were directed by women. However, surveys in the next few years of theatres that are members of Theatre Communications Group show considerable improvement, some of it accounted for by a few women artistic directors doing numerous productions in their own theatres. Julianne Boyd, coordinator of the League of Professional Theatre Women study with Kay Carney, summarized the major points: "We found that in general, women could get just so far as directors, and then they'd run up against what we called the broken-ladder syndrome. Women can direct in regional theatres, Off Broadway or Off-Off Broadway, but when it comes to large commercial Broadway productions, producers are not willing to put their millions of dollars, as well as their faith and belief, in a woman director." Their study discovered that women who wanted to direct were discouraged from doing so in both liberal arts colleges and professional training programs, where they were usually advised to study acting instead. Once in the profession, they find that progress is slower for women than for men and that women "have to be better than the men around them." They report "an unarticulated negative attitude toward women directors," who feel excluded from the powerful networks or cliques through which the top jobs are allocated. Tokenism, especially in high-paying regional theatres, was apparent in remarks like "we've hired a woman this season." Also a woman's failure on Broadway is viewed as a failure for all women.

How women directors perceive themselves and how other women in theatre respond to them were especially interesting findings in the study. Respondents pondered "How does a woman 'sell' herself and what will a man 'buy'?" Women felt caught in a double-bind in seeking jobs: "If we come on strong and confident and have the answers, some men . . . are scared and threatened. If we come in low-key, quiet but confident, then they might think we are not competent or skilled." Once at work, however, they listed as advantages in being a woman their emotional openness, sensitivity to others, patience, compassion, nurturing capacity. The most painful form of discrimination experienced was by women in positions of power. Although many report getting a start in the profession through other women, several told of being rejected by women producers and playwrights who wanted to protect the success of their "property" by having a man direct women's work.

Julianne Boyd's own experience as a free-lance director captures the triumphs and frustrations of working on and Off Broadway. With no models or mentors, she says it took her years to feel confident enough to say "I am a director," especially since she was always being used as an actress or a teacher. (She earned a Ph.D. along the way.)[19] After a variety of modest Off Broadway ventures, sandwiched between husband, children, and academic study, she came up with a project that propelled her to Broadway, where she was the only woman directing in 1978. Guiding *Eubie*, her musical which ran with great success for a year, through the whole Broadway production process gave her a unique education. She recalls that people involved in the show were suspicious of her because she was a young, female newcomer. She was advised to cut her hair to look older; she was questioned about her ability to take overall charge and to deal with stagehands, who turned out to be wonderful in working with her.

Even with the good luck of "starting at the top," Julianne Boyd has found that the things "that appeal" to her most often don't appeal to male producers;

that women producers and playwrights sometimes use a woman director to develop a play that then is turned over to a male director for final staging; that while male directors are hired to direct shows by and about women, women directors are told they cannot direct shows by and about men. Developing her own projects remained the best way to take charge of her career. For example, her next success, A . . . My Name Is Alice, conceived and directed with Joan Micklin Silver, grew initially out of a benefit for the National Abortion Rights Action League, for which over a hundred people were invited to contribute pieces. In a lengthy workshop process at the Women's Project of the American Place Theatre, they then sifted, cut, and replaced items. "Who else but Julia Miles and the Project would have let us do this, develop the show without commercial pressures?" "I wanted the material to reflect where we and our friends and our daughters feel we are today. . . . We seem more relaxed, more confident, less defensive than in the past. We didn't want to do a diatribe." They felt that women want to "see things that deal with themselves and their experiences." The success of the show, which eventually had an extended run at the Top of the Gate in Greenwich Village, confirmed their assumption and rewarded their accomplishments. The show also stirred up critical controversy about what a musical about women should be and do.[20] Since that production, she has turned down a number of scripts that repeat the Alice format, not wanting to repeat herself or become "a woman's director." Although she acknowledges that "right now is a bad time for everyone in the theatre; lots of friends—male and female directors—are unemployed," Julianne Boyd with her lively optimism says she'll continue to look for new projects.

The "Broadway barrier" that has excluded most women directors has worked even more effectively against women scenic designers, according to the 1983 League of Professional Theatre Women study discussed above.[21] Their investigation of women in design disclosed that women costume and lighting designers felt few inequities since they often shared the field with men, indeed sometimes outnumbering them. One thinks of costumers Theoni V. Aldredge, Lucinda Ballard, Judy Dearing, Franne Lee, Willa Kim, Florence Klotz, and Patricia Zipprodt, and of lighting designers Pat Collins, Arden Fingerhut, Peggy Clark Kelley, Tharon Musser, Jean Rosenthal, and Jennifer Tipton. Costume design involves sewing and fashion skills and interpersonal experience available to many women, while lighting design, being a new and underpaid field, found most takers among women. Scenic design differs sharply in part because it is identified with male skills—carpentry, physical prowess and technical know-how—and male power—money, position and old-boy networks.

The women scenic artists questioned were a well-trained and experienced group with graduate degrees, membership in the United Scenic Artists and experience everywhere except Broadway, where only one had worked in the previous year, 1982. They reported many different types of discrimination. Some said they had been less seriously treated than male design students, and most felt excluded from several of the powerful networks through which jobs seemed to be distributed. While it was difficult to document precisely discrimination in hiring or on the job, most agreed that "women must work constantly to overcome inherent mistrust of their abilities." Some blamed themselves and their upbringing for "not being taught about business and finance," or "how to compete aggressively in the marketplace." Family versus career pressures and the problems of "sacrifice and quality of life" were also cited. Women scenic artists were not satisfied with where they were in their careers, and despite criticism of aspects of New York theatre, they were eager to work in the commercial arena and had confidence in their "skills, talent or vision," "their working knowledge of construction methods and materials," and their proven success with and acceptance by scenic shops and stagehands. They identified the "combination that works against the women scenic designer" as "fear of risk, money, anxious producers (mostly male), nervous directors (mostly male)." There was hope that "changing times will increase opportunities for women in scenic design," and that soon "there will not be male designers or female designers, but simply people who happen to love designing scenery."[21]

The experience of Marjorie Bradley Kellogg, who became the spokesperson for the design study, suggests strikingly some of the problems of the concerned, talented woman artist in the second half of the 1980's. A graduate of Vassar College, she became the apprentice of Ming Cho Lee, and also worked with Robin Wagner and Boris Aronson. Before long she moved into the field to become a designer of growing reputation across the country, averaging about ten productions a year, the number usually done by a hard-working professional. On Broadway her sets were seen in *American Buffalo, Steaming, Da, The Best Little Whorehouse in Texas, Arsenic and Old Lace.* All her work is widely admired by directors, actors and critics.

That Marjorie Kellogg has been able to develop an important career and earn such high esteem makes her a "groundbreaker" among women in American scenic design. Not since Aline Bernstein in the twenties has a woman been able to work on Broadway as she has. She attributes this in part to the "change in producing habits." Producers today use shows that have "proven values in the regionals or Off Broadway and often, those shows come with designers. Like me— *Whorehouse, Da,* and *Solomon's Child* were all transferred. *Steaming* is about the only Broadway show I've done that I didn't start somewhere else. The Broadway scene has changed and women are being given a chance to prove themselves because they're coming with these projects."[22]

Marjorie Kellogg has dedicated time and energy to improvement for women designers. In 1984 in *American Theatre* magazine she wrote: "These days the first (and sometimes the only) question I get asked is if it's harder being a woman scenic designer. . . . But the question persists, and in their persistence is their answer. By setting women apart to press that question, they prove that the answer must inevitably be yes."[23] A few more women designers like Heidi Landesman have broken the Broadway barrier, but in the grim 1987 season Kellogg acknowledged that opportunities for women, despite initial expectations, had not much improved.

What had changed was her own relationship to the issue, and perhaps "the choice of methods for enlarging opportunities."[24] She had become so "totally identified" with women's problems that she felt her "work was not being dealt with," something which made her back off from being a spokesperson. Despite feeling guilty about "not being on the barricades," she needed to "just do her work" and to be "able to grow," for the work is what she went into theatre for. Without denying the help the women's movement gave her and others, she, like a number of other women in theatre, felt uncomfortable with the constraints of political activism. "I didn't like being called the woman designer. I'm perfectly willing to talk about whether there are differences between how women and men design. I love working with women. But I get impatient with the labels."

Of her own designing which may reflect her female sensibility, she observed: "I think I have a more environmental consciousness, a more empathetic consciousness that translates in scenery that is very responsive to the actor, but maybe recessive to the audience. It doesn't make a big splash, but actors never complain." She sees herself as "a maker of places" where "the actor and language" create meaning. Her mentor, Ming Cho Lee, praises her scenery for being "grounded in the lives and ideas of the characters in a play, and draw[ing] its strength from their behavior." [25] She has enjoyed very successful collaboration with several women associates, costume and lighting designers, directors, and playwrights, noting among them "the instant acceptance of certain values which we don't have to work at."[26] Without more productions by women designers, she is unsure what could be attributed to the individual and what to gender patterns in the work. What is sure is that as a designer and as a "gadfly" she has made us aware of women in scenic art.

Many of the issues Marjorie Kellogg and the others raise concerning feminist activism, gender, and the relationship of women's art to the important variables of economics, family life, institutional structures, class, and race also touch women managers, agents, and technicians. Although opportunities for them seem to have greatly increased since the women's movement and, it has been suggested, since the departure of many skilled men to higher-paying television, they too face these complex challenges. "Matrix," the final section of this book, explores some of the ways of thinking through the dynamics of women's life and work today. A few brief concluding questions concerning criticism by and about women here serve as a kind of preface to the conceptualizations about women and theatre that follow.

Since women as professional critics, especially in major newspapers and magazines, remain fairly rare, it is heartening to note the continued vitality of Sylvie Drake, Edith Oliver, and Marilyn Stasio, and the recognition of new voices through the George Jean Nathan Award for Dramatic Criticism, which was given to Carolyn Clay and Sylviane Gold jointly in 1982 and to Bonnie Marranca in 1985. *The Village Voice* under the theatre editorship of Erika Munk continues to offer diversity of opinion including that of several women critics such as Alisa Solomon and Eileen Blumenthal. Important critical articles by and about women in theatre have appeared in various theatre magazines, including *Women & Performance*, a new journal of feminist criticism, and in recent books on feminist theatre and women in theatre.

All who are concerned agree that woman's perception is needed in critical discourse as it is in artistic expression. What is open to discussion and to often vigorous and even acrimonious debate is what woman's criticism does or should involve beyond the sensibility and bias of the individual critic. The most intense quest in the critical arena comes today from women theatre artists, especially those in feminist theatre, who strongly feel the need for critical feedback for their own artistic growth. Because so much of their work is still under siege from outside economic and political forces that undermine its existence, must the criticism be positive only, limited to the kind of mutual back-slapping that women needed in the early stages when they first ventured out creatively? Should there now be one kind of in-house critical response during the production process and another that is a public performance evaluation? Is women's criticism for women's work only? Is it for just women's issues in any plays examined? Is it written from some implied women's aesthetic? Is it a political basis that tends to ignore the so-called traditional questions of dramatic criticism? What is the significance of gender in criticism? Must women's criticism be feminist? What does feminism mean when analyzing theatre? What responsibility does the critic have to the performance, the performers, to women's theatres, to audiences, to the larger state of theatre itself? Frank confrontation of these questions is central to the emerging new perspective on women in theatre.

DOUBLY MARGINALIZED:
WOMEN IN THE AVANT-GARDE

ALISA SOLOMON

Women in the avant-garde are doubly marginalized: just as women are written out of history, the avant-garde rarely makes it into official accounts of theatre. Those women theatre artists who finally do achieve wide recognition, even if their subjects are radically female, generally work in dramatic styles

Alisa Solomon is a teacher, dramaturg, and critic in New York; she writes regularly for *The Village Voice*. All quotations are taken from interviews conducted by the author in New York in November and December, 1986.

that play by conventional rules. But the six artists featured here challenge traditional theatrical forms, and often remain unnoticed by all but a faithful following; when the avant-garde finds broader acceptance, it is usually its men who get touted first.

Yet lumping these artists together can be doubly ghettoizing. If a volume on women in theatre even inadvertently suggests that women automatically create art that is somehow itself female, describing six experimental artists in a short piece within such a book might imply that they are all conducting the same experiment. With that warning in mind, though, they can be distinguished from traditional artists by some common characteristics.

The three preeminent artists considered here—JoAnne Akalaitis, Elizabeth LeCompte, and Meredith Monk—have all been making theatre for some twenty years. They grew up artistically in the alternative theatre movement of the '60's, itself spawned by the antiwar and civil rights movements. If we lack such a coherent, sweeping social movement now, these artists have retained the radical spirit behind the theatre techniques developed two decades ago (many of which have been superficially absorbed by such mainstream forms as the Broadway musical). Easily accepted today, environmental staging, self-conscious attention to breaking dramatic illusion, and the blurring of the separation between actor and character began as defiant breaks with tradition. Contemporary experiments retain that original impulse, and still connect such techniques to an attempt to see the world with new vision. Their work does not necessarily rely on linear development, narrative, or even language, but is often imagistic and associative, emphasizing the visual over the verbal, easily incorporating dance, film, video and other media. Just as important, such work tends to be created in a manner that deliberately replaces the traditional hierarchical structure of theatre-making with a collective, or at least an ensemble, in which actors contribute creatively to the work's development.

Out of these methods, a sort of performance-auteur emerged, a theatre-maker who wasn't exactly a playwright, nor precisely a director, but a deviser of theatre pieces who might create texts, music, visual design and choreography. This auteur might also perform with as well as direct a collaborating company. I have chosen to concentrate here on six women who more or less take such eclectic roles. As major accomplished figures, LeCompte, Monk, and Akalaitis offer a varied if incomplete introduction to women in the avant-garde. Following sketches of their work, I've more briefly outlined work by the younger generation they've influenced. My choices here—puppeteer Theodora Skipitares, director Anne Bogart, and performance artist Jerri Allyn—represent divergent but intersecting areas of contemporary experimental theatre.

Elizabeth LeCompte was a visual artist in the '60's, "alienated," she says, "by the very male-oriented painting world." Hooking up with actor Spalding Gray, she moved to New York City in the late '60's and "gravitated toward the theatre which was so active at the time. Richard Schechner [with whom Gray was already working] needed an assistant and offered me a job: I got into theatre for the money." When Schechner decided to leave his Performance Group for a while, LeCompte inherited *Commune*, a piece he was developing from company improvisation. "I didn't know what acting or staging were supposed to be, so I made things up," LeCompte recalls. "I could tell people trusted me." Indeed, in the ensuing years, making things up in an atmosphere of trust has characterized LeCompte's work with the seven core actors of the Wooster Group.

What LeCompte calls "a little constellation next to the Performance Group" emerged as an independent company in 1975 (taking its name from the street where its theatre is located) with its first production, *Sakonnet Point*. This playful pastorale built of improvisations based on Gray's childhood bears little tonal resemblance to the feverish, even brutal intensity of more recent works. But the relative unimportance of language, the absence of any representational meaning, and the basic mechanism whereby the audience must project its own associations onto the nonlinear juxtaposition of seemingly unrelated events and objects have all remained traits of the Group's subsequent work.

LeCompte has never tried to integrate the various elements that make these juxtapositions, but "just puts them next to each other." "The choice of elements can be arbitrary," she explains. "Material can be anything. Not just written text. Something comes in the mail, or a record I hear at a party, or a performer does something that gives me pleasure."

In *Rumstick Road* (1977), LeCompte mixed autobiographical material (the suicide of Gray's mother), documentary material (slides of Gray's family snapshots, letters, recorded conversations with Gray's mother's psychiatrist), and imaginative, nondiscursive material (a silly sequence, for instance, in which a man demonstrated a method of massaging a woman's midriff with his mouth while she writhed and giggled hysterically). *Nayatt School* (1978) added an element that would become part of the Wooster Group aesthetic— the referential, irreverent use of an established dramatic text. (Here, a group of children, parodying adult behavior, performed parts of Eliot's *The Cocktail Party*.)

While the Wooster Group made differing sensibilities collide onstage, it has had to fight offstage battles, too. Some people objected to what they deemed an invasion of privacy in the use of the secretly recorded phone conversations in *Rumstick Road*. More volatile, though, have been the issues surrounding *Route 1 & 9* (1981) and *L.S.D.* (1984). In *Route 1 & 9* videotaped scenes from Thornton Wilder's *Our Town* played in soap opera close-up rub against five white actors in blackface who make party preparations below the video monitors, and then play out Pigmeat Markham vaudeville routines. Sudden spurts of loud music well up for frenzied dances, then subside. Finally the overhead screens show a hitchhiking couple getting picked up by a truck, while an onstage TV monitor projects the Group's homemade porn movie.

The Wilder estate made some noises about the Group's scrambled use of the *Our Town* text, and some feminists objected to the pornography, but the larger debate centered on the use of blackface. Some critics condemned the production as racist, while others defended it, saying it criticized racial stereotypes. LeCompte found such judgments absurd, arguing that the use of blackface was a choice involving the quotation of theatrical material, not one made out of a political point of view.

The brouhaha around *L.S.D.* was less open to subjective interpretation; here Arthur Miller denounced the Group's cutting and pasting of *The Crucible* text, which LeCompte juxtaposed against diaries and debates of Timothy Leary and G. Gordon Liddy (with some quasi-flamenco dance routines interspersed), offering a vision of history as hallucination. Miller refused rights, and then threatened court action, so the *Crucible* excerpts were finally replaced by a text by Michael Kirby.

Such controversy surprises LeCompte. "I wanted to interpret *The Crucible* like a director does," she says, "but I can't stick to the play even when I want to; I can't settle on one meaning." Instead, she sees language as one unprivileged element among many. Some critics have suggested that such postmodern dramaturgy is inherently feminist, but LeCompte isn't so sure: "I couldn't really say whether deconstruction is feminist, but there is something from a feminine side, a denial of certain kinds of playwriting and form. Somewhere, I just don't relate to a lot of plays."

If LeCompte is reluctant to ascribe her style to some vague notion of a female aesthetic, she does consider the Group's organization feminist: "The reason a company like this survived and made such enduring work is that a woman runs it. If I were a man, I'd have more recognition, but then the company wouldn't be able to work the way it does. And working with the company is the supreme pleasure. Remembering that is how I survive."

When Meredith Monk received the prestigious Obie Award for Sustained Achievement in 1985, her citation said she "has pared down forms from various traditions of music, dance, and theatre, and has expanded into new ones of her own invention. Her works are sonatas of distilled aural and visual images—all harnessed to transmit deeply emotive, highly personal testimony." Indeed, over the past twenty-five years, Monk has alchemically fashioned a lovely, resonant theatrical style that is most difficult to characterize— as her own classifications for her work suggest: she called *Juice* (1969) a theatre cantata, *Needlebrain Lloyd and the Systems Kid* (1970) a live movie, *Vessel* (1971) an opera epic, and *Education of a Girlchild* (1972–73) and *Quarry* (1976) operas. Such subtitles, Monk says, "are working titles for me to clarify the forms I was trying to work in. I'm always interested in making a crossover form. That's been difficult for people though. Grants organizations pass my applications around and around from one department to another. And audience members watching my pieces spend three-quarters of the time worrying about trying to figure out what it is. I've spent most of my life trying to break that down."

In the mid-'60's Monk was known primarily as a choreographer in the postmodern Judson tradition. But while Cage-inspired Judsonites pursued a pure formalism built of chance compositions, repetition and fragmentation, games, and tasks for performers, Monk applied similar techniques to much more personal, deliberate, affective ends. A lot of formalist work, Monk says, has to do with distance, "but my work comes from an emotional base; it's about engaging. The function of the avant-garde used to be to shock the bourgeoisie out of the status quo. Now we live in such a multiplicitous culture, I'm not sure that kind of tactic is effective. I'm more interested in trying to see life in a fresh way. With *Recent Ruins, Specimen Days,* and *Turtle Dreams* I felt it was important to do warning pieces, to state what's wrong. Now it's more important to offer an alternative—not in the sense of '60's alternative life-styles, but in terms of ways of seeing things."

Quarry represents a culmination of Monk's early experiments with seeing the world's urgency in new ways. Revived in 1985, this timeless work subtly examines the way memory works in a person, a people, in history. A child in her pajamas (played by Monk) begins the piece, chanting her complaints of illness. She lies down under a quilt center stage while action of daily life carries on in the four corners surrounding her. Later, these same actors play dictators; they are followed by a chorus of thirty who erase their traces. Later still, returning to their original roles, they become victims. Quietly *Quarry* gathers a sinister momentum, evoking the Holocaust with a depth that makes it feel like preconscious knowledge, and calling forth the palpable danger of revising history with selective memory.

As in all her works, music plays an integral role here, starting off sweetly, harmoniously, and then gradually acquiring an ominous edge. Typically Monk's music is based on the capabilities of her versatile voice. Trained to sing opera and lieder, Monk also warbles, yodels, shrieks, whoops, belts, and ululates, often recalling archetypal, primitive musical forms.

"Music doesn't have to deal with meaning in the same way as theatre," explains Monk. "Even when you're working primarily with images in theatre, text is implied." For several years in the early '80's, says Monk, she could only do music. "The directness of musical communication creates a heart-to-heart relationship," she believes. "But in theatre, things have to be thought of carefully in terms of the objective. These are the questions you go through your whole life: theatre as a vital form—what does it mean? What are we doing in terms of our culture and is it useful? At times I've wondered why I don't go out and start working for the homeless instead of making art."

More than LeCompte or Monk, JoAnne Akalaitis has begun to be accepted by mainstream theatre. Though she's devised nonnarrative collage performances with Mabou Mines, the experimental collective of which she's a founding member, she's emerged in recent years as an independent director as well, and has begun to work in regional theatres and other venues. (By contrast, LeCompte says "taking a job as a director of a play would be like taking a job as a waitress.") Perhaps Akalaitis's broader acceptance is possible now because the idea of director's theatre has solidly taken hold. Still, Akalaitis says, "Coming from the avant-garde scares people. They want to know if you can handle a budget, if you know how to block a play."

Akalaitis began as a performer in Mabou Mines in 1969, and gradually started directing her own pieces; she acquired a fine reputation for visual elegance, creating such stunning productions as *Dressed like an Egg* (1977), a plotless evocation of Colette; a 1976 adaptation of Beckett's *Cascando*; *Southern Exposure* (1979), a minimalist portrait of polar explorers; and *Dead End Kids* (1980), a history of nuclear power that combines stand-up comedy, alchemical treatises, civil defense documents, and excerpts from Madame Curie's diaries into a magically ironic romp. (She directed a film version in 1986.) Recently, Akalaitis has taken on more traditional dramatic texts, approaching them, she says, as any director would. Still, her Americanized, feminist version of Kroetz's *Request Concert* (1981), her stark, hyperreal take on his *Through the Leaves* (1984), her lavish production of Genet's *The Balcony* (1985) and her controversially specific setting for Beckett's *Endgame* (1984) all reflect the milieu she was trained in. Though her productions don't cut up, rearrange, or radically alter dramatic texts as LeCompte's do, they do emphasize the visual, physical, and musical as much as the text. It's not surprising, for instance, that in her *Balcony*, Madame and Carmen danced a tango while conversing.

Not at all interested in psychological naturalism or its methods, Akalaitis uses rehearsal techniques associated with alternative theatre even when she's working in mainstream venues. "I always start rehearsal with dancing to music whose mood I pick for its appropriateness to the play," she explains. "For *Endgame* we danced to the Doors; for *Balcony* [which she set in Latin America], it was salsa." When she encounters resistance from actors, she thinks it comes both from a mistrust of experimental techniques and from her being a woman. "People who aren't used to doing those things question my directions. At the American Rep, which has a closely knit male atmosphere, I was full of fear and apprehension about not allowing smoking or coffee in rehearsal. Guys complained and I was scared of them. If a man were directing, they'd complain behind his back, but they felt empowered to complain to my face."

On the other hand, though, coming from a collective approach to theatre, Akalaitis believes she's "probably more collaborative than most directors. And being a woman, it's less of a power play, less of a manipulation. It wouldn't occur to me to pull a tantrum or humiliate an actor."

Trying to negotiate all her projects while raising two children has politicized her, Akalaitis says. "Every regional theatre should have a line in its budget for quality child care. Because unlike other jobs where there's a regularity to the schedule, theatre is crazy. Once you're in tech rehearsal, forget it. Forget everything. Forget life. *You* can do that, but children still need stuff like dinner. Women in theatre must work to truly revolutionize society or being a woman in theatre will remain suicidal."

For younger women just beginning to make a mark on the experimental theatre scene, Akalaitis, Monk, and LeCompte have served as role models, if not more. "Monk's *Education of a Girlchild* downright inspired me," says puppeteer Theodora Skipitares. At the same time, if artists now in their thirties were born too late to catch the tide of '60's political activism that carried the alternative theatre movement, they rode the crest of feminism. "I felt encouraged to try things in performance," continues Skipitares, who began as a sculptor, "absolutely as a result of the women's movement."

Skipitares's *The Age of Invention* (1985) ironically examines the ingenuity of Ben Franklin, Thomas Edison, and a twentieth-century quack doctor, all played by life-sized puppets. Between-scene interludes feature songs by smaller puppet-dioramas of women pioneers or Rosie-the-Riveters, implying an alternative view of history. "I'm interested in that tension," Skipitares explains. "I'm usually dredging up material that was part of a sexist culture, so certain people are forgotten or facts are hidden; I bring them back to remind people that history is not just exceptional men in exceptional moments. In *Age* the women act as the common thread of humanity, the ordinary or everyday in life."

Cooking with the Elements (1986), which starred a life-sized Madame Curie and Charles Darwin, continued to explore what Skipitares calls "the irony of what science says it's doing and what it is really doing." Her first performances, however, were autobiographical, like those of so many artists who started out in the gallery scene of the '70's. Early works used large murals and body coverings to describe the personal conflict of being between two cultures (Greek and American). "But there came a point around 1980 when autobiography seemed dried up for me," she says. "There was always a social-consciousness thread through my work that I wanted to turn outward, so I turned to puppets." These figures provide an emblem of the feminist principle of making the personal political: "At first I was making self-portraits. Even when I built Franklin, Edison, and the Doctor, I used my face, my mask, but stretched. It's not overtly me, but I'm still using myself that way."

Director Anne Bogart has followed more on the path forged by Akalaitis. Since 1980 she's collaborated on creating dance-theatre works as well as directing classics like *The Lower Depths*, *Danton's Death*, *Spring Awakening*, and *South Pacific*. She's also fashioned theatre-movement collages based on William Inge, Bertolt Brecht, Gertrude Stein's *Making of Americans*, and on testimony from the House Un-American Activities Committee of the '50's.

Bogart's work is most distinguished by her choreographic sense of stage movement and by her frequent use of cross-casting. These techniques are based in a physical approach to performance, guided by her ongoing practice of Tai Chi and Aikido. Martial arts' philosophy of movement, she explains, is applicable on stage. "The philosophy of not meeting force with force, and of continuing a line of movement, viscerally opens up the experience for the audience. Like in a painting, when the eyes follow a line without really knowing it, a line of movement can guide the audience to the stage's energy."

Bogart says of cross-casting (a woman, for instance, played Stanley Kowalski in her 1982 Massachusetts production of *Streetcar*) that "it's Gertrude Stein's idea of the same only different. Different actors playing the same character, even if they have the same words, movements, and gestures, evoke completely different universes. Rather than the audience merely identifying with the characters, they think about how the character and the gender categories are creations."

Jerri Allyn turned to performance from the visual arts precisely because it was a way to integrate feminism with art. Having studied at Los Angeles' influential Women's Building, she's emerged from a community of socially engaged performance artists that includes such remarkable women as Rachel Rosenthal, Suzanne Lacey, and Deena Metzger. Allyn says that the Women's Building, founded in the mid-'70's, "offered a crash course in women's history and consciousness raising" and radically altered her work. "I was always a political person," she explains, "and then I went to art school and was surprised. It was all about form and structure; we were never asked to think about what we wanted to say or who our audiences were. The Women's Building introduced me to performance art and also allowed feminism to bring my art and politics together."

Allyn's early work included guerrilla performances by a group called The Waitresses: "We thought the waitress's position was analogous to or emblematic of women's position in society." They presented vignettes in cooperating restaurants, and followed them with evening panel discussions. The Sisters of Survival, a five-woman group dressed in multicolored habits staging antinuclear spectacles, was founded, she says, "as a response to a call for help from the European peace movement."

Since moving to New York in 1981, Allyn has concentrated more on solo performances. In pieces like *Machine Scream* (1986), she tells stories about herself, but enlarges them into a broad, ironic perspective. The stories are recorded on tapes which are built into kitchen gadgets from the '50's. By operating these hand-cranked ice crushers, blow-dryers, and manual orange-juice squeezers, she activates the tape recorders to orchestrate a verbal fugue. The juxtapositions and repetitions of the backtracking tapes sharpen the movement between the personal and political so that her ruminations on Chernobyl, for instance, end up commenting on her silly story about the FBI; her comically awed description of the Michigan Womyn's Music Festival similarly connects to a later story called "S&M Dyke Bar." Currently, Allyn is at work on a more ambitious project, slated to tour the country's diners. *American Dining: Labor in the '80s*, says Allyn, represents the culmination of her work thus far. Recorded stories about waitresses' work will be installed in the little jukeboxes at booths in diners, and a series of placemats about women and labor will challenge diner patrons to "Name That Dame."

While Allyn, Bogart, and Skipitares carry on legacies of women who have come before them, each moves theatre forward in her own unique direction.

At the same time, Akalaitis, Monk, and LeCompte themselves keep working, keep exploring, challenging their own preconceptions of theatrical purpose and possibility as they challenge ours. "Our culture," Monk complains, "makes the woman artist and the avant-garde artist a crazy person. That's the tone of it. The man is a visionary; the female, an eccentric crazy person. We all have to deal with that. But the most important thing is that the work itself, what you see on the stage, transcends all categories."

MATRIX: NEW INTERSECTIONS OF GENDER, IDENTITY AND POLITICS

LINDA WALSH JENKINS

Feminists in all fields have long observed that "woman" and "man" (and their correlatives "feminine" and "masculine") are to a large extent social and political constructions taught and enforced on the basis of primary sex characteristics. However, elaborate social, political, and economic systems have been constructed that separate, stereotype, and privilege or oppress not only according to sex, but also according to skin color, occupation, money and property ownership, beliefs, dialects, and other such factors. These systems, based on difference and privilege, are manifest in the material culture; all who participate in theatre (whether creators, audience, or teachers) must examine how theatre aids, challenges or "revisions" them.

American theatre in the late 1980's is being vigorously stimulated by both the analysis of gender and the important intersections of gender and other crucial variables. This introduction explores briefly some of the varied interpretations of gender and then suggests the relationship of gender to race, class, and other important differences among women. What then follows is a sampling of theatre practices guided by the new theories and a concluding vision of the future of theatre by Judith Malina of the Living Theatre, who brings together feminism, politics, and aesthetic experiment.

The concept of gender in relation to theatre is marked by so much argument and variation that discussion could easily fill several books. Gender studies in theatre encompass a huge realm; as Sue-Ellen Case says, "The representation of women on the stage, the experiences of women in real life, and the discursive knowledge about women exist in a contiguous relationship with one another."[1] And since men too are affected by the way society engenders us all, the topic becomes vast.

Here is a simplified gender analysis: Women have the tasks of giving birth to and breastfeeding infants on the basis of primary biological sex characteristics; infant care becomes thought of as women's work; the behavior that is required in infant care—gentleness, patience, quiet speaking, keeping the body soft like a nest, selflessness—because it is associated with a female task becomes "feminine" behavior. The converse happens for the male who, on the basis of secondary sex characteristics of musculature, may be assigned the task of lifting heavy loads. Further roles are assigned and behavior presumed that are entirely gender-related, masculine/feminine defined, and have no real connection with biological sex. Further complications occur as males dominate a society and the naming of roles, and as women's authority is confined within private domestic spheres. Masculine and feminine "streams" are imprinted in the social and psychological construction of a people.

Numerous feminist theorists have addressed the implications of engendered society for theatre and vice versa. Their collective observations survey many of the major ideas current in the mid-'80's. Jill Dolan, one of the founders of the journal *Women & Performance*, observes:

> Sexual difference and its concomitant gender identification are embedded in both Western civilization and the stage that has reflected it. . . . Gender polarization has been a historical fact based on male economic and political necessity. It manifests a particular ideology that in turn reflects a particular hegemonic structure. Gender, it seems to me, isn't the perspective, but the evidence. Once this evidence is clear, it demands a certain kind of critique. I would suggests that feminism is the critique. Feminism exposes and deconstructs these underlying gender assumptions. The theatre, in its peculiar position as the mirrored stage, reflective of "real life" while not being real life, is an appropriate place for feminists to continue this ideological investigation. . . .
>
> We can safely say that both men and women, lesbians and gay men, are implicated in the polarized gender structure theatre reflects. Men, however, are implicated and involved as the subject of theatrical representation. Women, absent from the system and constituted only as Other, are in the outsider's critical position. In terms of deconstructing gender opposition, then, the feminist perspective edges out the others. Those who look at gender as a crucial issue are those who have the most at stake if the gendered status quo is maintained: women, as historical subjects, who no longer want to be the "woman" constructed as a biological, mythological imperative; and lesbians, who are caught in the netherworld between the polarized genders—as Monique Wittig writes, "not man, not woman." . . .
>
> A feminist perspective on gender has to foreground theatre's representational apparatus. We must make it clear that the hands holding the mirror up to nature have not been our own. Lesbians, in particular, have to debunk the myth that woman even exists, to reveal instead that she has been created to serve a particular ideological order. . . . We might have to question the mirror as an apt analogy for theatre.
>
> Adjusting this analogy would mean adjusting a wealth of expectations. It would no longer be possible to attend theatre hoping for a truthful reflection of oneself. Theatre might become more of a workplace than a

showplace. Our socially constructed gender roles are inscribed in our language and in our bodies. The stage, then, is a proper place to explore gender ambiguity, not to cathartically expunge it from society, but to play with, confound and deconstruct gender categories. If we stop considering the stage as a mirror of reality, we can use it as a laboratory in which to reconstruct new, nongenderized identities. And in the process, we can change the nature of theatre itself.[2]

Dolan's comments cover most of the topics related to gender that theatre theorists and experimentalists are exploring, especially "Man" as the Subject of narratives and actions, and "Woman" as the male-constructed heterosexual Other who is the object of male desire, the male gaze, and/or male action. She is the virgin, the whore, the mother, the betrayer, the sister, the sidekick; but she is always peripheral to the male action and isolated from relationships with other women that are not male-centered.

Monique Wittig and Sande Zeig have both written and experimented with the question of the lesbian "location" in heterosexual gender hierarchy. Wittig argues that there is only one gender, the feminine, because "the masculine is not the masculine but the general."[3] Wittig and Zeig advocate female appropriation of the general or "universal" gestures, language and roles that have been claimed by males. For some theorists, this means that lesbians choose to be masculine or feminine or consciously androgynous (does androgyny collapse the gender polarity or heighten awareness of it?), but that lesbians don't erase the binary pattern.

Alternatively, to follow this theoretical path further, if males have ownership of action and "the general," when a heterosexual female assumes an active role she splits, becoming "masculine" by virtue of taking action yet remaining "feminine" by virtue of her gender assignment. In assuming the masculine, she may be accused by other women of betraying the culture. This pressure on a female not to assume the masculine is especially evident in minority cultures that enforce heterosexual hierarchy in order to survive as a people in the face of oppression by the dominant culture. If a heterosexual female accepts the marginalized passive role and complies with the notion of male experience as universal, she undermines the authority of her own existence, participating in the devaluation and diminution of female experience. Lesbians who appropriate the gesture and behavior of "the general" argue they are not split because they have not accepted the assignment to "woman" or "feminine." These ideas are hotly argued. As most of the leading theorists in the mid-'80's are lesbian, the heterosexual female position has not been given much attention or articulation.

The female whose self is split frequently experiences some ambivalence as she uses the gestural, verbal, and cultural languages of both female and male experience. Sue-Ellen Case points out, quoting Sartre: "She resembles the thief Genet, . . . 'obliged, by error, to use a language which is not his own, which belongs only to legitimate children. By virtue of his mere existence he disturbs the natural order and the social order.'"[4] Marsha Norman's Arlie/ Arlene in *Getting Out* is a familiar American split subject. Case notes that those feminists forming a collective subject (like Split Britches) have dispersed and displaced the traditional gender assignments, and that this collective or displaced subject may be a solution to the dilemma.

One feminist theatre response to gendered difference and the marginalized Woman/Other has been to create a new woman-consciousness. Rosemary Curb has offered a description of this response:

[Woman-conscious drama is] all drama by and about women characterized by multiple interior reflections of women's lives and perceptions. This is comparable to "the private eye" to which Mary Ann Caws refers in her theory of perception of visual art: "I see the visual object not as an exterior element, but rather inside the subject in what I think of as an inner seen." Such theatre of "the private eye" necessarily represents many layers of women's experiences which have been hidden, silenced, ridiculed, trivialized, erased. Popular American realism cannot represent this diversity, because it presents only a single and often superficial layer of human perception, focusing on the masculinist status quo. Communicating the hidden layers of women's perceptions in the dramatic text and theatrical performance demands the creation of a new and more complex common woman's language, what Linda Jenkins has called "the mother tongue."

The drama and theatre that I am seeing as woman-conscious may be called feminist or lesbian or lesbian/feminist or postmodern, or it may eschew labels. It may be called "theatre of the oppressed" (Augusto Boal's term) or "disloyal to civilization" (Adrienne Rich's term) or "obscene." Woman-conscious theatre presents a multidimensional unravelling of women's collective imagination in a psychic replay of myth and history. All time is present to it. It emphasizes sociopolitical realities rather than the dilemmas of individual characters. Transformations of characters and fragmented personalities illustrate women's multiple reflections. It is polymorphous and antihierarchical, if not downright anarchistic and iconoclastic.[5]

Woman-conscious drama recognizes the bind of gender polarity, but honors women and brings to the stage the language of female experience, from the three sisters giggling around their mother's kitchen table in Beth Henley's *Crimes of the Heart* to the complicated passions of Maria Irene Fornes's *Sarita*. What men have condescended to as mundane or trivial has been given new value by women in theatre—from Susan Glaspell's *Trifles* to the feminist theatre movement's playful display of objects, phrases, and dialogues from women's "inner seens."

Intriguing theatrical experimentation in response to these gender puzzles may lead us into new territory that theory alone cannot. Males have played women characters, and occasionally females have played men, all through the history of Western and non-Western theatre, but deliberate "gender bending" in order to expose and revision gender is a contemporary phenomenon. Many feminist and alternative theatres have manipulated gender, but this technique has taken more sophisticated turns in the '80's, as is documented in the following essay on Role Over Productions.

Sande Zeig and Monique Wittig co-taught a workshop course at NYU in 1984 called the "Dynamics of Language and the Semiotics of Gesture," in which they experimented with techniques "directed toward finding one's 'impersonator'; that is, the person one would be if one were of the opposite sex."[6] This experiment involved detailed movement analysis and neutral exercises that permit one to "deconstruct one's own sex class gender system." Richard Schechner directed *Don Juan* at Florida State University in 1987; he cast across gender, interrupted the text, and repeated the same scene with multiple variations to display the role of gender in the construct of "the lover."

Performers at Cafe WOW in New York, the home of the Split Britches company, parody gender coding in every performance: "Women performing there dress in male and female drag while maintaining lesbian identities, so that the performances become not about men, and not about women, but about lesbians. WOW is socially and theatrically subversive because it represents women to women within the performance/spectator/stage apparatus— something the feminist theorists said couldn't be done."[7]

There is by no means agreement among women in American theatre over these ideas about gender, but the debates have begun in the '80's in a fashion not imagined twenty years ago. There are women theatre artists who feel that artists have so much in common that gender difference may not play such a strong role in theatre as it does in the culture at large. Some argue that it is inappropriate to speak of gender tendencies when speaking of artists, because artists are by nature individuals who break social rules, who are not governed by group tendencies. And little consideration has been given to the ways in which the physical presence of a female actor can subvert the male dramatist's construction of a "woman" character. Yet although the arguments continue over the notion of gender difference, most people nod with recognition at comedian Jay Leno's observation that the "difference between men and women is that men crack up over the Three Stooges and women think they're idiots. Moe hits Larry in the face with a shovel; men laugh, women say turn it off."[8]

The gender debates have opened up new discussions and discoveries, however; and surely that is the goal of speculation, experimentation, and theory. For example, Gertrude Stein's radical poetics have become more accessible, her "landscapes" liberating, and her refusal to assign character to text now comprehensible and political in a way not understood well before. Perhaps critic Annette Kolodny sums up best the aims of gender theory which are in fact being realized in the field of theatre and in the society at large: "Our task is to initiate nothing less than a playful pluralism, responsive to the possibilities of multiple critical schools and methods."[9]

In keeping with this notion of playful pluralism, it is essential to recognize that gender is by necessity an incomplete concept. Females in our society are socialized as "women" (and males as "men") through constructs of race, class, region, religion and other social factors—a qualification feminist research and writing has not often taken sufficiently into account. For example, the various geographical regions of our country acculturate people through traditions, dialects, rituals and values. In the South, which has itself been marginalized and stereotyped by the more urban and industrial northern states that have dominated U.S. culture, some women are working *through*, not separately *from*, regional aspects of their identity, as Cindy Lutenbacher has documented.

A black female doesn't choose whether she is black or female, but her social and political circumstances and conditioning lead her to be in some ways a different "woman" than a white female is led to be. Bernice Johnson Reagon has described the black woman's experience with racism in white feminism: "So here you are, and you grew up and you speak English and you know about this word 'woman' and you know you one, and you walk into this 'woman only' space and you ain't there. Because 'woman' in that space does not mean 'woman' from your world."[10] So too the Chicana must negotiate the intersection of gender with the history, language, and other realities of her culture. As Yvonne Yarbro-Bejarano points out, an Aztec woman, Malintzín Tenepal, was Cortes' mistress; she is "La Malinche," the Mexican/Chicano Eve who betrayed her people and represents La Vendida (the woman who sells out to the white race). La Virgen is constructed from the Catholic Madonna, the Mother who is pure and asexual.[11] The Chicana must find her way through the maze of these and other culture-specific roles.

The following essays demonstrate some of the approaches women are taking in theory and practice to revision the ways in which theatre participates in social constructions of identity and beliefs. As the entire nation faces the issue of dismantling structures of privilege, females may well provide the matrix for deconstruction and change. Some women in theatre are theorizing about gender, class, race, and culture as variables in the construction of identity and political behavior; some are exploring these issues and providing new directions through creative efforts; some are doing both. Some are focusing on collective political issues such as nuclear arms, with feminism informing their critiques. Some women work through people's theatre and indigenous culture to achieve change.

These essays can only hint at the rich diversity and extraordinary creativity and courage women today are bringing to the task of revolutionizing the consciousness of a nation that two hundred years ago did not even think to include women in its political constitution.

ROLE OVER PRODUCTIONS

SUSAN OGDEN MALOUF

Pamela Carter Joern and I created Role Over Productions in 1986 to examine contemporary gender/cultural roles through open casting. Our work, which we produce in a theatre we lease in Minneapolis, focuses on familial and community patterns of relationship. *Common Place*, by Joern, explores violence as a community/cultural problem, as two adolescent girls are caught up in a web of interconnecting violent relationships with family, friends, and the community. Simone de Beauvoir's *Who Shall Die?* deals with a thirteenth-century village under siege whose inhabitants decide to sacrifice the women, children, and elderly to preserve diminishing provisions for the fighting men.

Cross-gender characterization is approached externally in rehearsal, using techniques derived from the work of Bertolt Brecht, Joseph Chaikin and Augusto Boal among others. In a recent showcase performance, a blind male actor portrayed Juliet in the balcony scene. Not only did the cross-gender casting (Romeo was played by a female actor) underline the gender stratification which is present in this (and virtually any other) love scene; in addition, the actor's handicap became an asset, serving as a powerful metaphor of Juliet's condition and clearly differentiating her experience from Romeo's.

In the Role Over rehearsal process actors must physically and psychologically enter into the experience of the opposite sex. Women learning to play male roles are encouraged to use larger, more direct gestures, to take up a lot of space, to use direct eye contact, and to display the chest and pelvic areas. Men learning to play female characters are coached in the opposite direction. Scanty tight dresses, bras, and high heels help them experience the confinement and exposure often associated with feminine clothing.

We really do not know very much about one another's life experiences. Female actors, with little experience of direct power, have difficulty understanding and thus playing the subtle jockeying for position that characterizes much of male-to-male interaction; similarly, white male actors, having little experience of true powerlessness, have difficulty giving up center stage and learning to influence a scene from a peripheral position. In rehearsal we teach one another, sharing from our experience and breaking down the cultural taboos that have kept us ignorant of one another.

For the audience member, the alienation caused by the distance between the character's and the actor's physical attributes opens perception, allowing for a more objective examination of display behavior. In addition, the experience of identifying with a character of the same sex as portrayed without trivialization

Susan Ogden Malouf earned a Ph.D. in Theatre at Northwestern and was Director of Theatre at Bryn Mawr before beginning Role Over Productions.

by an actor of the opposite sex invites audience members to question the subject/object dualism upon which sexism is based.

Traditionally, the focus of the theatre has been individual (male) experience and achievement. In keeping with this, action and conflict are often cited as the essence of the dramatic form. For instance, Hamlet's tragic flaw is perceived to be his inability to act; more specifically, he cannot face the necessary conflict with his mother and stepfather, and therefore his life and the action of the drama (being one and the same) are stagnated. For me, however, Hamlet's tragedy lies in the fact that he is locked into relationships that give him such meager options: to deny his own experience (his conviction that his father was murdered), to validate his experience by killing those who would deny it, or to suffer extreme isolation, ending ultimately in death. I find it very much to his credit that it takes him four long acts to decide which of these suicidal paths to follow. For me the tragic flaw lies not in the individual, but in the vicious patterns of relationship these individuals have created and sustained as a group.

Our lives too are encumbered by patterns that entangle us, often causing great pain and human waste. And yet, since it is we who have designed these patterns, and we who recreate them on a day-to-day basis, it is we who can change them, making them richer, fuller, and more humane.

FEMALE BODY AS TEXT IN WOMEN'S PERFORMANCE ART

JEANIE FORTE

Simultaneously with the rise of feminist theory, women have virtually taken over the postmodernist genre of performance art. Choosing this problematic mode which blurs the boundaries between art and life, defying conventional definition and critical analysis, women performance artists use its unlimited strategies to pursue inherently feminist questions concerning the cultural construction of gender. When Rachel Rosenthal shaves her head or Laurie Anderson dresses in a man's tuxedo, "woman," and by extension, gender itself, is revealed as a fictional construct produced and enforced by a patriarchal culture. In Meredith Monk's *Education of a Girlchild* (New York, 1972), for example, an old woman regresses in memory to a young girl, demonstrating the process of gender conditioning in reverse.

Jeanie K. Forte is a director, dramaturg, and Assistant Professor of Modern Drama in the English Department at the University of Tennessee (Knoxville). She has published in *Theater, Women & Performance* and *High Performance*. This essay is excerpted from a paper delivered at the Modern Language Association convention in Chicago, 1985, which in turn derives from a soon-to-be-published longer work, "Women in Performance Art: Feminism and Postmodernism."

Women's performance art has particular disruptive potential because it poses a woman as subject, throwing this "speaking subject" into process, into doubt, opposing the traditional conception of the single, unified (male) subject. The very placement of the female body in the context of performance art positions a woman and her sexuality as speaking subject, an action which cuts across numerous sign-systems. Such a strategy combines physical presence, real time, and real women in dissonance with their representations, creating semiotic havoc and threatening the patriarchal structure with the revolutionary text of their actual female bodies. Carolee Schneemann's piece *Interior Scroll* (New York, 1975) is one example; she stood nude, extracting a long, minutely folded paper rope from her vagina, reading from it of the discrimination against her as a woman filmmaker. In this striking piece it seems as though her vagina itself is reporting the sexism. Linda Montano's pieces as "Chickenwoman" (San Francisco, 1972) were strangely redolent of a celebratory female energy and sexuality, and often involved exposing odd parts of her body in a sensual way. Martha Rosler had every inch of her body measured with exacting detail by two male "researchers" in *Vital Statistics* (San Diego, 1973), after which she and other women recited a litany of crimes against women and ceremoniously "cleansed" their bodies. Laurie Anderson fit parts of a drum machine into her suit, so that hitting various spots on her body produced eerie resonances (1984). In stunning "body" performances, Pat Oleszko used her breasts to create a face in a kind of postmodern puppet show, and made films of her vagina as a speaking mouth with a beard (1984). Countless others perform in the nude, not as actresses providing anonymous titillation for an audience, but actual women simultaneously revealing their vulnerability and their sexuality. They literally expose the female body as a sign while also reclaiming it as their own, in defiance of the oppressive system of representation and patriarchal encoding.

The female body in performance art articulates women's sexuality in ways never before possible. Women's performance art subverts the canon of codified sexuality imbedded in centuries of theatre and cultural works. It reveals binary sexuality as another construction complicit in the oppression of women and female sexuality. Bonnie Greer's *Vigil* (New York, 1982) highlighted the erasure of a black woman's sexuality in her bondage to white culture. In *Leave Her in Naxos* (Los Angeles, 1981), Rachel Rosenthal showed slides of her various lovers, male and female, and discussed intimate aspects of her relationship with each, speaking herself in different sexualities. A group of lesbian performance artists performed *An Oral Herstory of Lesbianism* (Los Angeles, 1979), in which each spoke of her particular oppression as a lesbian while also frankly revealing sexual intimacies.

Women's performance art explores the female body as female subject, returning subjectivity to women through the assertion of sexuality, rejecting the body's patriarchal "text," and providing new, multiple "texts" arising from the undeniable voice of authentic difference. By recognizing the female body as the textual basis for a repressive system of representation, deconstructing this text and reclaiming their own bodies and sexuality, women performance artists engage in a radical disruption of patriarchal culture.

"SO MUCH MORE THAN JUST MYSELF": WOMEN THEATRE ARTISTS IN THE SOUTH

CINDY LUTENBACHER

Most contemporary southern women theatre artists I have interviewed are affiliated with ensemble companies that also have at heart the commitment to community. All wear several theatrical hats at once (writer, performer, director, etc.). Their primary work grows from the indigenous culture of each individually defined constituency; their art not only makes the audience a vital participant in the performance, it also heightens the audience's awareness of itself as a community. For example the last "act" of Pearl Cleage's and Zeke Burnett's performance is an onstage dance with the audience lasting until some unordained hour of the morning, and Road Company's *Echoes and Postcards* concludes with a community's honoring of its dead.

Jo Carson, a writer and performer living in Johnson City, Tennessee, writes in almost every genre—plays, stories, essays, and a blend of anecdote, tale, commentary, memory and local voices that she has named "People Pieces." She has performed her People Pieces over 200 times all across the United States, as well as in Nicaragua and on National Public Radio's *All Things Considered*. Carson performs many of her works as a solo artist, as well as in collaboration with theatre groups, especially Road Company, also of Johnson City. Road Company's 1986 work, *Echoes and Postcards*, revolving around the images and ideas of Tennessee life, is a collaborative collage of scenes, memories, songs, and anecdotes. For example, Carson performs a piece about youthful attempts to sing like Patsy Cline while atop her grandmother's coal bin and in the family car. "Jo, honey, *please*," says her mother. Late in the show, when Carson finally does sing, with unabashed fervor, Hank Williams' "Your Cheatin' Heart," the entire audience cheers, as they share in the experience of childhood-wish fulfillment. Carson's work is deeply rooted in the language, images, thoughts and feelings of the mountain region. She believes in knowing the place from and in which you write because otherwise, as she says, "I suspect about the best you'll be able to do is gossip."

Pearl Cleage has lived in Atlanta for eighteen years and has spent four of

---

Cindy Lutenbacher is completing her Ph.D. in Theatre and Drama at Northwestern University. This essay is excerpted from a paper presented at the 1987 Themes in Drama conference, Riverside, California.

them as playwright-in-residence with Just Us Theatre Company. Cleage writes in several genres, but always with the idea of performance: "I don't think so much about the form, I just talk to people." Her plays include *Puppetplay, Good News, Essentials*, and *Hospice*, which won five AUDELCO awards in 1983. Cleage primarily writes for a black audience; her voice and concerns are those of a black woman. In her piece about buying her first 45 record—The Temptations—Cleage writes of the desires, fears, and treasures of a black girlhood: "I was looking for the music that made you know something good was coming to you in the next couple of years."

Linda Parris-Bailey is artistic director of Carpetbag Theatre in Knoxville, Tennessee, one of the oldest continuously operating black companies in the country. Carpetbag tours the region, playing in the usual theatre spaces as well as in many nontraditional places such as churches and prisons—"wherever the people are." The company develops original works that speak from the heart and history of the community, in order to "give something back to the community—its own positive image reflected." Carpetbag's repertory includes *Red Summer*, based on the Knoxville race riot of 1919, *Cric?Crac!*, a collage of African, Haitian and American southern black folktales, and *Dark Cowgirls and Prairie Queens*, originally created in part as a response to requests by teacher and principals in Knoxville for a performance for Black History Month. Written by Parris-Bailey in collaboration with the rest of the ensemble, *Cowgirls* is based upon the stories of black women who were part of the move west.

Angelyn DeBord is one of the mainstays of Roadside Theater, a touring, teaching, tale-telling company out of Whitesburg, Kentucky. Roadside, now entering its sixteenth year, performs stories and tales from Appalachia, as well as original, ensemble-created plays based upon characters and stories from the mountains. Roadside's repertory includes *Pretty Polly*, a play based upon the real life of Polly Branham, a mountain woman tale-teller who took her stories into the mountain schools and communities in the 1930's. "*Pretty Polly*," explains Debord, "begins with an introduction of how we are each the *history* that school history books know nothing about. The piece is a series of stories creating the saga of a woman's experiences; dark and light sides of life are shown from her youth until her ancient years when she reaches a state of acceptance and of grace. The show ends with a hymn which the audience joins in singing: "Bright mornin' stars are risin'/Where are our dear mothers?/ They have gone to heaven a-shoutin'/Day is a-breakin' in our souls." Debord acts Polly; she was also one of the collaborators in the creation of the script. In addition to her position as performer-director-writer, shared with the three men and two women of the company, DeBord is an artist-in-residence in the public schools in eastern Kentucky's hollers and way-backs. She teaches storytelling and performance, always drawing students to their own heritage of stories and mountain living.

And there's so much more: Lee Heuermann recreating political cabaret in

Atlanta, Jan Villarrubia's plays and "characters" from New Orleans, Rebecca Ranson's works in Atlanta, Cynthia Levee writing in "the Cajun-Jewish tradition," Marsha Jackson and Jomandi, Sallie Bingham in Louisville, Maya Levy in Louisiana, Rebecca Wackler with Southern Theater Conspiracy, and Linda Gregoric of Contemporary Arts in New Orleans. Then there's *Cabbagetown: 3 Women . . . An Oral History Play with Music*, which depicts life in a mill village now part of Atlanta; and *Louisville 200*, the celebration based on 250 oral history interviews created by TriCenter Theatre Company for Louisville, Georgia's 200th celebration; and. . . .

One has the sense that wherever a noncommercial theatre has arisen in the South, its goals and commitments have been based in the needs, issues, and inheritance of a community. Women are invariably either leading or participating in these theatres.

FEMINISM AND POLITICAL THEATRE

LINDA WALSH JENKINS

While it can be argued that all feminist theatre is political, some women in American theatre combine feminist consciousness with theatre that is specially and consistently concerned with political change. For Maxine Klein, producing director of the Massachusetts-based Little Flags Theatre, political theatre "deals with large collective economic, social and political issues that working people face—such as automation, nuclear proliferation and joblessness." Political theatre has a legacy of at least fifty years in the U.S., with the strongest surge occurring in the workers' theatre movement of the 1930's. Among the companies exemplifying feminist political theatre strategies in the 1980's are the San Francisco Mime Troupe, the Little Flags Theatre, and the Berkeley-based Ladies Against Women.

The San Francisco Mime Troupe, begun by R. G. Davis in 1959, evolved into the country's major political theatre first through participation in Vietnam street protests and then most decisively with two plays: *A Minstrel Show, or Civil Rights in a Cracker Barrel*, by Davis and Saul Landau, and their "commedia dell'arte" adaptation of Goldoni's *L'Amante Militaire*, writer/adaptor Joan Holden's first work with the group in 1967. The play won an Obie during its New York residency. When the theatre reconstituted as a collective and Davis departed in 1970, Holden became the company's primary scriptwriter. Although she has sometimes performed and now usually travels with the group,

---

Written from materials provided by the theatres, reviews of their work, personal knowledge of the theatres and individuals, newspaper articles, Ruby Cohn's "Joan Holden and the San Francisco Mime Troupe" (*The Drama Review*, vol. 24, no. 2, June 1980, 41–49), and William Kleb's "The San Francisco Mime Troupe a Quarter of a Century Later" (*Theater*, vol. 16, no. 2, Spring 1985, 58–61).

her forte has been political scripting from collective concerns. She described in an interview with Bernard Weiner the evolution of the troupe's work:

> In those times ['60's], we were seeking moments of confrontation, seeking outrage. We thought we were guerrillas—Che was our model—and that spontaneous outbreaks would occur wherever we performed. We truly expected to see a revolution in America within two or three years. We had no long view of the struggle. It never entered my head in 1967 that I'd still be here in [the 1980's].
>
> We used to end our plays with explosions. One time we shouted out phony credit card phone numbers to use. This was symbolic of our image of revolutionary action. Now, our shows tend to end on people struggling to keep in the struggle—people faced with the dilemma of giving up or making an immense effort and continuing the fight. Our message— whether the show is about nuclear disarmament or poverty or U.S. militarism or whatever—always is that people can change, that individuals do make history.

Over the years the Mime Troupe (once pronounced "meem" but now usually pronounced conventionally) has built a reputation for broad physical humor and musical satire designed for outdoor settings, always intended to provoke an audience to take action to make changes in their own lives. In the summer they always perform free theatre in parks, supplementing this through the year with indoor and outdoor shows across the U.S. and Europe. Their 1967–68 Obie citation salutes them "for uniting theatre and revolution and grooving in the park." In 1987 they won the Tony for "outstanding regional theatre."

The troupe has become multiracial and multiethnic, with strong guidance from women. Actress/director Sharon Lockwood has performed with them since 1969; Wilma Bonet plays Latina (*Last Tango in Huahuatenango, Steeltown*) and non-Latina roles (robot in *Factwino Meets the Moral Majority*); Audrey Smith plays a variety of black roles. All three often play men. María Acosta Colón was administrative manager from 1979–86.

NEA granted them $90,000 for the 1986 season, allowing them to provide health benefits and increase salaries of the approximately ten-member company to $230 a week. Families and other jobs are juggled with the demands of the collective, which owns its own building in the Mission District. Holden, for example, who has three daughters, teaches playwriting on and off at the University of California at Davis and the People's School of Dramatic Arts, and received a Rockefeller playwriting grant in 1986.

The very titles of the theatre's productions signal the political issues they've taken on: *The Independent Female, or A Man Has His Pride* (Holden's first feminist work and the first work of the new collective in 1970), *Soledad* (1971), *Frozen Wages* (1972), *Americans, or Last Tango in Huahuatenango* (1981), *Factwino Meets the Moral Majority* (1981), and *Factwino vs. Armageddonman* (1982). *Seize the*

Time (1970) was a documentary presentation of Black Panther Bobby Seale's Chicago 8 trial; *The Dragon Lady's Revenge* (1971, revived in 1987) attacked CIA involvement in Vietnam drug traffic using a combination of comic-strip style and spy-movies parody; and *Steeltown* (1984) approached steel mill closings and the history of the American labor movement with a more serious format designed solely for indoor playing in a conventionally darkened audience house.

Joan Holden explained her and the Mime Troupe's feelings about politics and theatre in the '80's in an interview with William Kleb:

> The politics of the '60's and ours in the '70's were very programmatic. We knew what the issues were, we were Marxists, the message was clear, the foreign models were clear. We're still Marxists, but the models aren't clear anymore. The American Revolution is going to be homemade, and nobody knows what it's going to be like. Theory isn't going to convince people that it needs to happen, they have to be convinced out of their own experience. So we're dealing with people's experience at a more particular level, trying to join the personal with the political.
>
> I don't feel either in myself or in other people in the company any fundamental change in attitude. Yes, we have to get subsidy. No, we can't live at the welfare level for the rest of our lives. . . . I don't feel that I'm coming from a different place than I ever was coming from since I started doing this. I still know who the enemy is, who is poisoning us and starving Africa, who is getting ready to blow up the world if we don't stop them! I know who I want to kill in my plays and who I want to exalt. Who I think deserves to die and who produces the wealth and should have the power. Those things that come from inside you aren't changing.

Little Flags, a company of men and women committed to "people's theatre," originated in Boston in 1974 but moved to Belchertown in 1986. Founder and producing director Maxine Klein had written and directed experimental and political theatre for years as a faculty member at the University of Minnesota and then Boston University. Her direction of Megan Terry's *Approaching Simone* won an Obie in 1970. She resigned from BU to produce with Little Flags plays dealing with and for "segments of society usually not treated by establishment drama." Her husband, James Oesterich, is the company's composer, and she is director, writer, acting teacher, and frequently performer.

Members of the group (which takes its name from a poem by Ho Chi Minh) do not have to espouse one political ideology, but, Klein says, they are bonded by a "belief in the 'struggle,' the right to be heard, and workers' control." Productions have included *Tania* (their first show, based on one of Che Guevara's comrades), *Fanshen*, *The Furies of Mother Jones* (about the famous mine-workers organizer), *Winds of the People* (celebrating the labor and liberation movements), *Marx on Her Mind* (about a fast-food waitress who is a union organizer and writes jazz), *The New Rise of the Master Race*, *Emma* (a portrait of

Emma Goldman), *Split Shift, Windfall, Ah, Woman!, To the People, Mysterious Death of C. T. List*, and *Boston Remembers* (a composite of histories of Boston's working class). Although the stories and character conflicts are political, the work itself is musical and humorous, with an emphasis on giving an audience a very good time. Songs and scripts are published by and available through South End Press and the company.

An itinerant group based in Klein's and Oesterich's home, Little Flags owns its own bus, which it uses to go into neighborhoods, workplaces, prisons, union halls, and factories where the audience often participates in a play. They have toured the U.S. and in 1983 performed at an International Peace Festival in Baku, Azerbaidzhan, and in Moscow. When creating a performance in a factory, Klein helps the workers create their own material. She explains, "It takes awhile. You sit around and tell stories about all of your lives. This is one way I do it. I tell stories about my life, they tell stories about theirs, and then we start improvising on common themes and create plays out of their lives."

Klein's notion of people's theatre is expressed by the title of her book, *Theatre for the 98%*. In an interview she amplified this concept:

> Theatre until now in this country has been extraordinarily elitist, not only in terms of its subject matter but in terms of whom it includes. We're living in a large society; we can't do art for the one or the two or we exclude most of the people, which is what art in this country has done. So I'm part of the movement that is concerned about finding art in all of us and bringing art to all of us.
>
> We've been taught to despise ourselves. That's what celebrity theatre does. You look at all those celebrities on stage and think, "Oh, dear, I could never be like that. There's something wrong with me; either I smell or my hair isn't combed right." That's what I call a theatre of protest—against the individual human form and need and spirit. Quite the contrary, people's theatre is a theatre that gets people involved, that celebrates human values. I mean the values of the majority. Now, it may at the same time take issue with something that's oppressing them. That's perfectly legitimate. But it is not only about what oppresses them; it is also about what exults them.

Ladies Against Women is a subgroup of the larger satirical collective the Plutonium Players, which formed in San Francisco in 1977 as the Theatre Collective of People Against Nuclear Power. The women, and sometimes men, of L.A.W. perform stage shows and theatrical events (which they call street adventures) dressed as antifeminists (1950's dresses, pillbox hats, white gloves). For Women's Week at Northwestern University in 1986, they held a *Bake Sale for the Pentagon* and handed out flyers that read:

> We are Ladies Against Women, an organization dedicated to the notion that women of quality don't need equality! We know that what all college-aged women really want is that wonderful man to fill your life with his career and

an array of avocado green kitchen appliances! Quit wasting your father's hard-earned $15,000 a year and get yourself a man—that's what we say. In the past we have held campaigns to establish a national dress code and to make virginity a high school graduation requirement. We have struggled for the rights of the unconceived ("Sperm are people, too!") and have been proud sponsors of the "Myth Northwestern" pageant.

Our current project shows that even real ladies can be concerned with doing God's will while never having to leave our kitchens! At our Bake Sale, we are offering our sugar cookies, made only with the finest white sugar and white flour at $3 billion dollars apiece, or $15 billion for a half-dozen. The all-American Twinkie is $9 billion, and Ho-Ho's will be only $6 billion. And just look at what your money will buy! One Twinkie will buy *nine* nuclear submarines, and a single sugar cookie will purchase torture instruments for 15,000 Nicaraguan freedom fighters. (May God bless them! We're not talking about some place like Vietnam this time—these boys are fighting communism that we can drive to!!)

As real patriotic Americans, we know that you will want to help us in this endeavor. Remember, nuclear families support nuclear arms.

Our efforts are encouraged by: The Bedtime for Bonzo Anti-Evolutionary League, Mutants for A Nuclear Society, American Society for the Advancement of Rich, White, Straight Men, Students for an Apathetic Society, No Pinkos in Academia, Inc.

Ladies Against Women encourages chapters to form for street-action projects such as local demonstrations and picket lines; anyone interested should write them to register the chapter and obtain some of their scenarios and suggestions. But only the original Berkeley-based group has the copyright to appear at political rallies and fundraisers around the country.

ABOUT THE FUTURE

JUDITH MALINA TALKS TO JOANIE FRITZ

What I really want to talk about is the future. Julian and I have always had a commitment to using all our art, all our work, all our time, all our effort, and all our communication to answering the question: How can our work make it better? And what is this "it"? The suffering. That's a very big category. And very generalized. But then when we put on a play, it's no longer so gener-

---

Judith Malina—actor, director, writer, founder in 1947 with the late Julian Beck of the provocative and challenging Living Theatre—was interviewed in 1986 by Joanie Fritz as part of her study of women in alternative performance. The wide-ranging discussion ended with this look to the future. Joanie Fritz, an actor and activist who lives and works in the Lower East Side of New York City, co-founded Protean Forms Theater Collective.

alized. In the Living Theatre we try to combine each of our lives, every aspect of our lives—our sexual life, our domestic life, our economic life, our personal life, our artistic life, our political life—into as holistic a community as possible.

When I think in terms of the next step in theatre, it seems to me that what I see now is not so much a shattered scene, but an immobilized scene. Everything seems to be in stasis. It's as if everyone were paralyzed, because we have seen this vision, and we have no idea how to move toward it. And we're just hanging in there, just being good till the next movement occurs. That has to happen. It will happen eventually. This social malaise has got to be temporary. It could last a long time; we could go into the Dark Ages. But I don't think so.

When I speak to young people, under all the cynicism and all the little layers of easy answers that come over the television, over MTV, I see a real desire for something to break through, a real hope in the younger kids that it's going to change.

It seems to me this is a very new moment. I'm interested in what this moment can show us. I'm working on the creation of a theatre in New York that's going to be valid to our situation politically, culturally, humanly, artistically; a theatre that speaks for people in our time. I have a thousand thoughts describing the directions in which that lies.

In the theatre a new form should be shown first as a theatrical form and not as a theory. Then you say, "Now you see, the theory was . . . ," and in retrospect describe it dramaturgically. On the other hand, in order to get some funding, we will write a proposal of what work we plan to do. But right now, it's in a better stage than that. Right now, it's brewing. And that's a good stage. We are again answering the question: What's really necessary? What's the next step we really need to take?

I think this is where my main energy now is. At a time when the Living Theatre has lost the strong, energetic force of Julian Beck, we have to find ways to take the next step. The puzzle in New York City at this time is very interesting and very difficult; it's good to work at something very hard. The social scene, overwhelmed by real estate, from condominiums to gentrification to the plight of the homeless, is all one problem—how to use the land on this island and in the surrounding boroughs in some sort of a humane way. We haven't really figured it out.

I don't know how one can really function in this world without adhering to some principles. The anarchists like to say that we have to build the new structure in the shell of the old. That is, we're living in the old structure, and we have to create a new structure. If we're pacifists, we don't want to create by killing off a lot of people and bursting the shell forcibly. We have to create both clarity of theory and as many examples of substructures as we possibly can within this society without our getting too discouraged by the fact that it's very hard to do that, and that they often fail. Yet when they fail, they're valuable, because they're examples and lessons that keep the thread going. They inspire people and get them thinking in the right direction.

Paul Goodman said a very interesting thing in his book *Drawing the Line*: "Everyone draws their line and cowers behind it." That is, each of us takes a moral stance. You make certain conditions. You make an agreement with life that you'll tolerate that much and no more. Beyond that, you'll break or you'll crack or you'll freak or you'll change or you'll do something else. But that line becomes a position that we take. And we sometimes draw that line close to ourselves, protectively, fitfully. This is certainly a time when nobody can afford to risk too much. Because we understand that we're in a precarious situation. We don't know how to make a change. Yet we have to go all the way. But all the way isn't with money. It isn't with a coercive state structure, a punitive legal system. Reforms of all those structures are part-way measures.

To think of replacing those things is so frightening that people are paralyzed. We know too much, and we're not good enough. We can be good to each other or bad to each other. I don't think anybody's bad. But a lot of good people behave very badly. I really think there's a possibility for changing who we think we are to each other. And that's what I'm interested in. Because that's political, and that's very much the subject and object of art. Who is this person looking at this painting? Who is the audience whom I address? Who are we to each other? And that leads to a study of something which is perhaps the most taboo thing in our entire structure, or the most taboo word in our language.

The taboo words are not fuck, suck, shit, cock, prick, cunt. Those are not the real taboos. Nobody raises an eyebrow if you say any of those things. But if you say the word goodness—that's right, everyone says, "Oh come on, goodness? What do you mean, goodness? Sunday School has goodness, we don't." Kindness? Tenderness? Gentleness? That's taboo, that's sentimentality.

When the Living Theatre was going to move to Paris, some of our enemies wrote a little article in *Le Monde*, saying, "We don't want the Living Theatre to come back here unless it is willing to abandon its idealistic, utopian infantilism." But think what that means! Think what's taboo! What's taboo about us? Not that we took our clothes off. Not that anybody said "fuck." But again to quote Paul Goodman, "Utopia means they don't want you to do it."

SOURCEBOOK

AWARDS

Following are some of the honors American women have received for their contributions to the theatre. Only Tony and Obie awards which are not women's categories are listed.

1. Awards of the American Theatre Association (ATA ended existence in 1986.)

ATA Awards of Merit
1961 Rosamond Gilder
1971 Winifred Ward
1982 Geraldine B. Siks
    Dina Rees Evans Shaw

ATA Citation for Distinguished Service to the Theatre
1969 Helen Hayes
1972 Eva Le Gallienne
1974 Peggy Wood
1981 Cheryl Crawford

ATA-ITI World Theatre Award
1975 Ellen Stewart
1977 Rosamond Gilder

ATA Special Citation
1971 Irene Ryan

Jennie Heiden Award (children's theatre)
1968 Nellie McCaslin
1975 Ann S. Hill
1976 Sara Spencer
1977 Marjorie Sigley

2. Susan Smith Blackburn Prize (for best play written by a woman in English)

1979 Mary O'Malley, *Once a Catholic*
1980 Barbara Schneider, *Details without a Map*
1981 Wendy Kesselman, *My Sister in This House*
1982 Nell Dunn, *Steaming*
1983 Marsha Norman, *'night, Mother*
1984 Caryl Churchill, *Fen*
1985 Shirley Gee, *Never in My Lifetime*
1986 Anne Devlin, *Ourselves Alone*
1987 Mary Gallagher, *How to Say Goodbye*
    Ellen McLaughlin, *A Narrow Bed*

3. Brandeis University Creative Arts Award

1957–58 Hallie F. Davis, medal
1960–61 Lillian Hellman, medal
    Julian Beck and Judith Malina, citation
1963–64 Cheryl Crawford, medal
1965–66 Eva Le Gallienne, medal
1966–67 Ellen Stewart, citation
1971–72 Alfred Lunt and Lynn Fontanne, medal
1973–74 Helen Hayes, medal
1982 Jennifer Tipton

4. Jane Chambers Playwriting Award (Women's Program and American College Theatre Festival)

1984 Karen Boetcher-Tate, *Evensong*
1985 Charlotte Anker and Irene Rosenberg, *The Third Child*
1986 Patricia Montley, *Rosvitha's Review*
1987 Micki Goldthorpe, *Conversation*

5. Common Wealth Award (American Theatre Wing) Service to Dramatic Arts

1981 Agnes de Mille
1985 Zelda Fichandler

6. Drama Desk Awards (Association of New York drama reporters, critics, editors)

1980 Costumes—Franne Lee, *Sweeney Todd*
    Patricia Zipprodt, *King of Hearts*
1983 Lighting—Tharon Musser, *Dreamgirls*
    Marcia Madeira, *Nine*
1984–85 Scenic design—Heidi Landesman, *Big River*
    One Person Show—Whoopi Goldberg
    Special award to Claudette Colbert

7. Drama League Awards

1936 Helen Hayes
1979 Frances Sternhagen
1985 Katherine Rao, *The Women of Cedar Creek*
1986 Bernadette Peters
1986 Lavonne Mueller, *Five in the Killing Zone*

8. Dramatists Guild Awards

Committee for Women Annual Award
1982 Alice Childress
1983 Megan Terry

1984 Gretchen Cryer
1985 Margot Lewitin and Julia Miles
1986 Emily Mann and Elsa Rael

Elizabeth Hull-Kate Warriner Award

1982–83 Marsha Norman

9. John Gassner Memorial Playwriting Award—New England Theatre Conference

1984 Tina Howe, *Painting Churches*
1985 Jane Waterhouse, *Private Apartments*
1986 Ruth Angell Purkey, *The Lady and the Lass*

10. Hall of Fame (American Theatre Critics Association)

1981 Betty Comden, Carol Channing, Colleen Dewhurst, Uta Hagen, Molly Picon, Maureen Stapleton, Margaret Sullivan, Gwen Verdon
1983 Angela Lansbury
1984 Mrs. John Drew, Mildred Dunnock
1985 Geraldine Fitzgerald, Rosemary Harris

11. George Jean Nathan Award for Dramatic Criticism

1967 Elizabeth Hardwick
1982 Carolyn Clay and Sylviane Gold
1985 Bonnie Marranca

12. National Institute of Arts and Letters, American Academy of Arts and Letters

1964 Lillian Hellman—Gold Medal
1985 Maria Irene Fornes—Special Literature Award
1986 Marsha Norman—Distinction in Playwriting

13. National Theatre Conference— Person of the Year Award

1967 Hallie Flanagan Davis
1968 Rosamond Gilder
1971 Zelda Fichandler
1973 Ruth Mayleas
1981 Ellen Stewart
1986 Martha Coigney

14. New York Drama Critics Circle Awards, Best American Play

1941 Lillian Hellman, *Watch on the Rhine*
1950 Carson McCullers, *The Member of the Wedding*
1956 Frances Goodrich and Albert Hackett, *Diary of Anne Frank*
1958 Ketti Frings, *Look Homeward, Angel*
1959 Lorraine Hansberry, *A Raisin in the Sun*
1960 Lillian Hellman, *Toys in the Attic*
1981 Beth Henley, *Crimes of the Heart*
1985 Lily Tomlin, Jane Wagner, *Search for Signs of Intelligent Life in the Universe*—special citation

15. Obies, Off Broadway Awards established by *The Village Voice*, 1956. Categories have changed over the years and in 1969 awards were made for distinguished achievement rather than citations for specific categories.

Best Musical
1959 *A Party with Betty Comden and Adolph Green*
1968 *In Circles* (Gertrude Stein and Al Carmines)
1970 *The Last Sweet Days of Isaac* (Gretchen Cryer and Nancy Ford)

Distinguished Play
1964 *Home Movies* (Rosalyn Drexler)
Funnyhouse of a Negro (Adrienne Kennedy)
1965 *Promenade* and *The Successful Life of 3* (Maria Irene Fornes)
1967 *Futz* (Rochelle Owens)

Distinguished Production
1977 *The Club* (Eve Merriam)
For Colored Girls Who Have Considered Suicide/When the Rainbow Is Enuf (Ntozake Shange)
Dressed like an Egg (JoAnne Akalaitis)

Best Play/Best New American Play
1970 *Approaching Simone* (Megan Terry)
1981 *Still Life* (Emily Mann)
1983 *The Danube, Mud,* and *Sarita* (Maria Irene Fornes)
1983 *The Art of Dining* (Tina Howe)
1985 *The Conduct of Life* (Maria Irene Fornes)
1985 *Transients Welcome* (Rosalyn Drexler)

Best Director
1964 Judith Malina, *The Brig*

Distinguished Direction
1970 Maxine Klein, *Approaching Simone*
1976 JoAnne Akalaitis, *Cascando*

1978 Elizabeth Swados, *Runaways*
1983 JoAnne Akalaitis, *Through the Leaves*
1984 Barbara Vann, *Bound to Rise*

Sustained excellence in direction
1987 Carole Rothman

Music
1972 Micki Grant, Liz Swados
1969 *Awards*
The Living Theatre, *Frankenstein*
Julie Bovasso, *Gloria and Esperanza*
Judith Malina and Julian Beck, *Antigone*
Arlene Rothlein, *The Poor Little Match Girl*

Sets, Lights, Costumes
1958 Nikola Cernovich
1965 Willa Kim—Costumes
1974 Theoni Aldredge—Costumes
1983 Anne Militello—Lighting
1984 Judy Dearing—Costume design
1984 Loren Sherman—Set design

Sustained achievement
1982 Maria Irene Fornes
1985 Meredith Monk

Sustained excellence in performance
1984 Pamela Reed
1985 Frances Foster
1987 Black-Eyed Susan

16. The Pulitzer Prize

1921 Zona Gale, *Miss Lulu Bett*
1931 Susan Glaspell, *Alison's House*
1935 Zoe Akins, *The Old Maid*
1945 Mary Chase, *Harvey*
1958 Ketti Frings, *Look Homeward, Angel*
1981 Beth Henley, *Crimes of the Heart*
1983 Marsha Norman, *'night, Mother*

17. Charles H. Sergel Drama Prize (est. 1935, for full-length play, not previously published or produced)

1938 Rosalie Moore
1948 Julie Ragir
1951 Mildred Kuner
1972 Doris H. Schwerin

18. Stanley Drama Award (est. 1957, for full-length play, not previously produced or commercially published)

1963 Adrienne Kennedy, *Funnyhouse of a Negro, The Owl Answers*
1964 Megan Terry, *Hothouse*
1976 Carol Mack, *A Safe Place*

19. The Tony Award. Created in 1947 in honor of actress-director Antoinette Perry by the American Theatre Wing, a service organization of theatre professionals. The award is given in numerous categories under

the direction of the League of New York Theatres and Producers, Inc. The awards are for "distinguished achievement in the theatre" (essentially Broadway). Sometimes there is more than one winner, sometimes there are none. No award for lighting was given until 1970. From 1947 to 1955 only winners were announced, but since that time nominees have been announced. The Tony Award nominees are listed since 1955 and in those lists one can see women honored by the nomination, such as in 1960 when Lillian Hellman's *Toys in the Attic* and Lorraine Hansberry's *Raisin in the Sun* both lost to William Gibson's *The Miracle Worker.*

Choreography
1947 Agnes de Mille, *Brigadoon*
1950 Helen Tamiris, *Touch and Go*
1962 Agnes de Mille, *Kwamina*

Costumes
1947 Lucinda Ballard, *Happy Birthday; Another Part of the Forest; Street Scene; John Loves Mary; The Chocolate Soldier*
1948 Mary Percy Schenck, *The Heiress*
1950 Aline Bernstein, *Regina*
1952 Irene Sharaff, *The King and I*
1958 Motley, *The First Gentleman*
1962 Lucinda Ballard, *The Gay Life*
1965 Patricia Zipprodt, *Fiddler on the Roof*
1966 Gunilla Palstierna-Weiss, *Marat/Sade*
1967 Patricia Zipprodt, *Cabaret*
1972 Florence Klotz, *Follies*
1973 Florence Klotz, *A Little Night Music*
1974 Franne Lee, *Candide*
1976 Florence Klotz, *Pacific Overtures*
1977 Theoni V. Aldredge, *Annie*
1979 Franne Lee, *Sweeney Todd*
1980 Theoni V. Aldredge, *Barnum*
1981 Willa Kim, *Sophisticated Ladies*
1984 Theoni V. Aldredge, *La Cage Aux Folles*
1985 Florence Klotz, *Grind*
1986 Patricia Zipprodt, *Sweet Charity*

Costume Design (Dramatic)
1961 Motley, *Becket*

Best Play
1956 Frances Goodrich and Albert Hackett, *Diary of Anne Frank*

Producer, Dramatic
1951 Cheryl Crawford, *The Rose Tattoo*
1958 Lawrence Langner, Theresa Helburn, Armina Marshall and Dore Schary, *Sunrise at Campobello*
1965 Claire Nichtern, *Luv*
1971 Helen Bonfils, Morton Gottlieb and Michael White, *Sleuth*

1987 Carole Shorenstein Hays, *Fences*

Scenic Design
1974 Franne and Eugene Lee, *Candide*
1985 Heidi Landesman, *Big River*

Lighting
1977 Jennifer Tipton, *The Cherry Orchard*

1982 Tharon Musser, *Dreamgirls*
1985 Pat Collins, *I'm Not Rappaport*

Musical
1949 *Kiss Me Kate,* book by Bella and Samuel Spewack
1953 *Wonderful Town,* lyrics by Betty Comden and Adolph Green
1959 *Redhead,* by Herbert and Dorothy Fields, Sidney Sheldon and David Shaw, lyrics by Dorothy Fields
1968 *Hallelujah, Baby!,* lyrics by Betty Comden and Adolph Green
1970 *Applause,* book by Betty Comden and Adolph Green

Authors (Musical)
1949 Bella and Samuel Spewack, *Kiss Me Kate*

1959 Herbert and Dorothy Fields et al., *Redhead*

Producer (Musical)
1968 Albert Selden, Hal James, Jane C. Nusbaum and Harry Rigby, *Hallelujah, Baby!*

The Lawrence Langer Award for Lifetime Achievement
1977 Cheryl Crawford
1980 Helen Hayes

ORGANIZATIONS, STUDIES, CONFERENCES, FESTIVALS

The following listing suggests a few of the ways in which women have worked together in recent years.

ORGANIZATIONS AND STUDIES

The Women's Program of the American Theatre Association, organized in 1976, has held an annual two-day Women's Program Pre-Convention since 1980. They have sponsored the Jane Chambers Playwriting Award for a "new play that addresses women's experiences in which the central character is a woman and which has a majority of principal roles for women. Application by women playwrights is especially encouraged."

The Women and Theatre Program, which replaced the above-mentioned program at the demise of the American Theatre Association in 1986, is continuing its general work, the annual conference structure, and the Jane Chambers Playwriting Award. Rhonda Blair, Theatre Department, Hampshire College, Amherst, MA 01002, President.

Action for Women in Theatre was a ground-breaking survey done in 1976 by a number of playwrights and directors—Nancy Rhodes, Gloria Albee, Jane Chambers, Jan P. Eliasberg, Dolores Ferraro, and Carole Rothman. Figures on the employment of women in fifty nonprofit theatres that received more than $50,000 a year in grants from both public and private foundations revealed that only 7 percent of the plays produced were written by women and only 6 percent were directed by women. To correct these discriminatory practices, changes in the granting and training procedures were recommended and a long list of available experienced, professional women directors and playwrights was issued.

Updates of these 1976 statistics were done in several quarters by Susan Clement, Geraldine Court, and especially by Susan Lehman in her 1980 study Women Directing in Theatre for the Women's Project of the American Place Theatre. They show that by 1978–79 17 percent of plays in theatres covered by the Theatre Communications Group reports were directed by women, but much of this increase was attributed to a single woman director who dominates her theatre's work. The list of theatres using no women directors or less than the 17 percent average remained long. On Off-Off Broadway in the same season, 42 percent of the plays were directed by women, but on Broadway the percentage of women directors was only 4 percent.

The Directors and Designers Report on Sex Discrimination in Theatre done by members of the League of Professional Theatre Women/New York in 1983 showed that of the 262 plays produced on Broadway from 1977 to 1982, only 9 shows (3 percent) were directed by women and even fewer were designed by women. A detailed analysis of a questionnaire sent to women directors was prepared by Julianne Boyd and Kay Carney. The report on women scenic designers was prepared by Marjorie Kellogg.

The Women's Project of the American Place Theatre was organized by Julia Miles in 1978 with a grant from the Ford Foundation to provide a variety of production opportunities for women playwrights and directors. Inspired in part by the Action for Women in Theatre survey noted above, the project offered women "a supportive, professional theatre environment" in which, between 1978 and 1986, 35 productions and 218 readings were developed. In 1986, when their membership included 197 playwrights and directors, they were awarded a $1 million grant by Kentucky playwright Sallie Bingham. Julia Miles, Women's Project of the American Place Theatre, 111 West 46th St., New York, NY 10036.

The Committee for Women of the Dramatists Guild, organized in 1979, holds monthly meetings and an annual event at which an award is given for significant contributions to women in theatre. Katherine Griffith, Chair, Dramatists Guild, 234 West 44th St., New York, NY 10036.

The League of Professional Theatre Women/New York, organized in 1982, was in part inspired by the Women's

Program of ATA to serve the needs of all professional women in theatre. Co-presidents Lynda Sturner and Berenice Weiler, Suite 2001, 1501 Broadway, New York, NY 10036.

Women in Theatre (WIT) Network, Inc. is a "network of people from all areas of the theatrical community united to focus, reinforce, and advocate woman's vital contribution to theatre." WIT Network, Box F, 29 West 15th St., New York, NY 10011.

CONFERENCES AND FESTIVALS

Women's One World Festival, produced in 1980 and 1981 in New York City, the genesis for the East Village's Cafe WOW.

Women in Theatre, Feb. 24–March 31, 1982, a lecture/performance/discussion series jointly sponsored by Albertus Magnus College and the New Haven Theatre of Light and Shadow, New Haven.

Critical Stages: Women in American Theatre: March 18–20, 1983, sponsored by Women's Studies Program and others, State University of New York/Albany.

First National Festival of Women's Theatre, May 16–22, 1983, Santa Cruz, CA.

A Conference on Women Playwrights, April 27–29, 1984, sponsored by the Center for Research on Women, the Drama Department, and the Humanities Center, Stanford University, CA.

Boston Women's Theatre Festivals '85, '86, '87, national and international showcase for new work by women playwrights and performers. Sophie Parker, Director, 64 Wyman St., Jamaica Plains, MA 02130.

1985: The Next Stage: Women Transforming Theatre, May 25–26, Theatre Festival of the Americas, Montreal, Canada.

1987: Women in Theatre, Feb. 13–15, The Annual Themes in Drama Conference, College of Humanities and Social Sciences, University of California, Riverside, CA 92521. Selected papers will appear in the annual *Themes in Drama*, edited by James M. Redmond and published by Cambridge University Press.

FEMINIST THEATRES INDEX

Geographical location and years of operation are shown where known. An asterisk indicates theatres known to be in operation at press time. Contact persons are shown, if known, for these theatres. Readers with additional information are urged to contact Linda Jenkins via the publisher.

Actor's Sorority (1976–82) Kansas City MO
Ain't I a Woman Theater (1978–?) Denver
Alive and Trucking Theatre Minneapolis
*Astarte Mettle (1985–) Evanston IL, Northwestern Women's Center
**At the Foot of the Mountain* (1974–) Minneapolis, Phyllis Rose
B & O Women's Theatre Champaign IL
Big Mama Poetry Theatre Cleveland
Black Orchid Third World Theatre Company Cambridge MA
Black Star Theatre (1978–?) Cambridge MA
Boulder Feminist Theatre Collective (1975–78) Durango CO
**Braided Circle Theater* (1983–) Boulder CO, Marie Cartier
Bread and Roses Theatre (1974–?) Los Angeles
*Cafe WOW, New York, Lois Weaver
Calliope Feminist Theatre Hartford CT
The Cambridge Ensemble Cambridge MA
Caravan Theatre (1965–78) Boston
Caught in the Act (1977–78) San Francisco
Chicago Women's Theatre Group (1977–?)
**Chrysalis Theatre Eclectic* (1978–) Northampton MA, Andrea Hairston
Circle of the Witch (1973–78) Minneapolis
Commonplace Pageant (1972–77) Cambridge MA
Common Threads San Francisco
The Co Respondents (1972–?) Olympia WA
Crazy Alice Ltd (1982–?) New York
The Cutting Edge (1975–?) New York
**Double Edge Theatre* (1982–) Boston, Andrea Dishy
Earth Onion Woman's Theatre Washington DC
**Eccentric Circles Theatre* (1980–) Montclair NJ, Paula Kay Pierce
Emmatroupe (1975–?) New York

Encompass Theatre New York
Era Productions Chicago
First Street Playhouse (1981–) (aka Mother's Theater, Inc.) Ithaca NY, Carolyn Fellman
Flamboyant Ladies Theatre Company, New York
Garage 59, Jamaica Plain MA
Gertrude Stein Opera Company San Francisco
The Great Grand Daughters of the American Revolution Denver
Greenville Feminist Theatre (1973–77) Greenville SC
Harrison and Tyler New York
Horizons Theatre (1983–) (formerly *Pro Femina,* members formerly with WAFT) Washington DC, Carole Myers
Hot Flashes San Diego
Indiana State University Listener's Theatre (1975–77) Terre Haute IN
Invisible Theatre Tucson AZ
It's All Right to Be Woman Theatre (1970–76) New York
It's Just a Stage (1975–?) San Francisco
Janice Perry (aka "GAL") Ferrisburg VT
Kate Kasten Comedy Theatre (1982–?) Adel IA, Kate Kasten
The Kathy and Mo Show (1982?–), Kathy Najimy
Kuku Ryku Theatre New York
Ladies Against Women (1984?–) San Francisco, Plutonium Players
Las Cucarachas San Francisco
Lavender Cellar Theatre (1973–75) Minneapolis
Lesbian Feminist Theatre Collective Pittsburgh
Lilith (1974–86) San Francisco
Lion Walk Center Pittsburgh
Little Flags Theatre Collective (1974–) Belchertown MA (formerly Boston), Maxine Klein
Los Angeles Feminist Theatre (1969–?)
Maidenhair Truth and Comedy Theatre Oakland CA
Mamalution Santa Cruz CA
Mass Transit Street Theatre Bronx NY
Medusa's Revenge (1977–) New York
Mermaid Theater (1977–?) Cambridge MA
The Migrant Theatre Taos NM
Mischief Mime (1974–) Ithaca NY
Mixed Company Ashland OR
More Fire! Productions New York
Mothertongue San Francisco
Motion: The Women's Performing Collective San Anselmo CA
Mouth of the Wolf Productions (1986–) (members formerly with *Lilith*) San Francisco, Joan Mankin
Narratives Performing Company New York
Necessary Luxury (1976–78) New York
New Africa Company Boston, Lynda Patton
Newbury Street Theatre Boston
New Cycle Theater (1977–?) Brooklyn
New Feminist Repertory Theatre Los Angeles
New World Theatre/Other Side of Today Shop Schenectady NY
New York Feminist Theatre Troupe (1969–mid 70's) Brooklyn
New York Tea Party New York
Nickel and Dime Productions Missoula MT
Northwest Touring Theatre (1980–) Eugene OR, Jane Van Boskirk
Omaha Magic Theatre (1969–) Jo Ann Schmidman/Megan Terry
Only One Monkey (1975–) (formerly *Performing Dance Collective*) Albion CA, Karen Rakofsky
Onyx Women's Theatre (1973–?) South Ozone Park NY
The Open Stage New York
Orange County Feminist/Repertory Theatre (1971–) Anaheim CA, Rosalie M. Gresser Abrams
Other Girls Productions
Other Voices Atlanta
Pagoda Playhouse (1978–) St. Augustine FL
The People's Playhouse (1975–?) Elmhurst NY

Pocket Theatre (1975–?) Durham NC
Poor Sid Theatre Madison WI
*POW (Professional Older Women's) Theatre (1985–) New York, Elsa Rael
Pro Femina Theatre (see *Horizons*) (1977–83) Washington DC
Puppets and Politics San Francisco
Rainbow Company Van Nuys CA
Rattling the Chains Theatre St. Louis MO
Reality Theatre (1976–?) Boston
The Red Dyke Theatre (1974–?) Atlanta
Rhode Island Feminist Theatre (1973–86?) Providence
Rites of Women Lesbian Feminist Theatre Philadelphia
River Queen Women's Center Guernewood Park CA
*Role Over Productions (1986–) Minneapolis, Susan Ogden Malouf
Rule of Thumb Chicago
*Samantha Rastles the Woman Question (1982–) Minneapolis, Jane Curry
Sisters of Light Denver
Sisters on Stage (1976–81) San Diego, Carol O. Perkins
*Snapdragon: Ozark Feminist Theater (1980–) Fayetteville AR, Judy Jones
Speak Its Name Chicago
*Spiderwoman Theatre Workshop (1975–) Brooklyn, Muriel Miguel
*Split Britches (1980–) New York, Lois Weaver
Streetfeet Women's Touring Company (1980–?) Roxbury MA
The Sunshine Company (aka *Ventura Feminist Theatre*) (1975–?) Ventura CA
Synthaxis Theatre Company North Hollywood CA
Thank You Theatre Los Angeles
*Theater Three Minneapolis
*Theater, Too Amherst MA
Theaterworks Boston
Theatre Company of Ann Arbor
Theatre of Light and Shadow (1978–?) Fair Haven CT
Theatre of Process Santa Barbara CA
Three Clowns (1976–79) Boston
Three for the Show Chevy Chase MD
*Thunder Thigh Review Baltimore
Uncommon Lady from Bloomsbury El Segundo CA
*Underground Railway Theater (1976–) Cambridge MA, Rosemarie Straijer
Union Sister Productions Washington DC, Jehane Dyllan
Valentina Productions San Jose
Vermont Women's Theatre Richmond VT
Violet Ray Theater Arts, Inc. Northampton MA
The Waitresses (1970's) LA
Walking the Tightrope: Herstory Ypsilanti MI
Washington Area Feminist Theatre (1973–78) DC
*Watermelon Studio (1978–) Jamaica Plain MA, Tita Wernimont
Westbeth Playwrights Feminist Collective (1970–mid 70's) New York
Westchester County Women's Theatre
Who's a Lady Company Newton Hill MD
Wilma Project Philadelphia
Woman Chief Productions Boulder CO
Womanrite Theatre Ensemble (1972–77) New York
Woman's Collage Theatre (1976–?) New York
Woman's Ensemble Palo Alto CA
Woman's Ensemble Los Angeles
Womanshine Productions (1977–?) Indianapolis
Womansong Theatre (1974–?) Atlanta
Womanspace Theatre New York
*Womenlight Players (1982–) (formerly *Tri City Players*) Tempe AZ, Jana Ruth
Women of the Burning City (aka *Painted Women Theatre*) (1970)
Women's Coffee Coven Seattle

Women's Community Theatre Northampton MA
Women's Ensemble Theatre (1984–) New York, June Guralnick
Women's Experimental Theatre (1977–) New York, Roberta Sklar
Women's Interart Center, Inc. (1969–) New York, Margot Lewitin
Women's Patrol Minneapolis
Women's Poetry Workshop Columbus OH
The Women's Project/The American Place Theatre (1978–) New York, Julia Miles
Women's Street Theatre San Francisco
Women's Theatre Council New York
Women's Theatre of Cincinnati
Women's Theatre Project of Minnesota Minneapolis
The Womyn's Theatre (1976–?) Seattle
Word of Mouth Productions (1978–) Boston, Susan Eisenberg
The World Women's Culture Caravan Stamford CT

SELECTED REFERENCE WORKS ON WOMEN AND THEATRE

The following lists are not intended to be inclusive, but to suggest the wide range of existing resources on women in theatre. Women performers from other countries who toured extensively in the U.S., thereby contributing to the shape of American theatre, are listed in the "American" section; play reviews are not included (see the *Women Studies Abstracts*, the *Left Index*, and the *Alternative Press Index*); and the section "Additional Works on Women in Theatre" addresses itself to sources other than biographies.

Women & Performance: A Journal of Feminist Theory (published biannually since 1983, NYU/TSOA, 721 Broadway, 6th Floor, New York, NY 10003) contains interviews, reviews, scripts, and essays.

More complete bibliographies of feminist dramatic criticism are also available; write to the editors of this book in care of the publisher. Also, see my brief overview of the literature with a comprehensive bibliography in *Women & Performance*, 1987.

Both the Omaha Magic Theatre and At the Foot of the Mountain have published newsletters, and Linda Walsh Jenkins edited *Women in Performing Arts Newsletter*, 1974–81. See archival collections for these.

Where no place of publication is indicated below, New York may be assumed.

WOMEN IN AMERICAN THEATRE: SELECTED BIBLIOGRAPHY

I: BOOKS

Abramson, Doris E. *Negro Playwrights in the American Theatre.* Columbia UP, 1969.

Anderson, Mary. *A Few Memories.* Harper and Brothers, 1896.

Ashley, Elizabeth, with Ross Firestone. *Actress: Postcards from the Road.* M. Evans and Co., 1978.

Auster, Albert. *Actresses and Suffragists: Women in the American Theatre.* Praeger Publishers, 1984.

Bacall, Lauren. *By Myself.* Knopf, 1979.

Bankhead, Tallulah. *Tallulah: My Autobiography.* Harper & Row, 1975.

Barnes, Eric Woolencrott. *The Lady of Fashion: The Life and Times of Anna Cora Mowatt.* Charles Scribner's Sons, 1954.

Barrymore, Ethel. *Memories: An Autobiography.* Harper and Row, 1955.

Betsko, Kathleen, and Rachel Koenig. *Interviews with Contem-*

porary Women Playwrights. Beech Tree Books/Morrow, 1987.

Binns, Archie. *Mrs. Fiske and the American Theatre.* Crown, 1955.

Bix, Cynthia, and Ann Dillon. *Contributions of Women: Theatre.* Minneapolis: Dillon Press, 1978.

Brown, Janet. *Feminist Drama: Definition and Critical Analysis.* Metuchen, NJ: Scarecrow Press, 1979.

Chinoy, Helen Krich. *Reunion: A Self-Portrait of the Group Theatre.* Drama Book Specialists, 1976.

Coleman, Marion. *Fair Rosalind: The American Career of Helena Modjeska.* Cheshire, CT: Cherry Hill Books, 1969.

Comtois, M. E., and Lynn F. Miller, eds. *Contemporary American Theater Critics: A Dictionary and Anthology of Their Works.* Metuchen, NJ: Scarecrow Press, 1977.

Corio, Ann, with Joe DiMona. *This Was Burlesque.* Madison Square Press, 1968.

Cornell, Katharine, as told to Ruth

Woodbury Sedgwick. *I Wanted to Be an Actress.* Random House, 1938.

Courtney, Marguerite. *Laurette.* Rinehart, 1955.

Coven, Brenda. *American Women Dramatists of the Twentieth Century: A Bibliography.* Metuchen, NJ: Scarecrow Press, 1982.

Crawford, Cheryl. *One Naked Individual: My Fifty Years in the Theatre.* Indianapolis: Bobbs-Merrill, 1977.

Creahan, John. *The Life of Laura Keene.* Philadelphia: Rodgers Publishing Co., 1897.

Davis, R. G. *The San Francisco Mime Troupe: The First Ten Years.* Palo Alto, CA: Ramparts Press, 1975.

Dempsey, David, with Raymond P. Baldwin. *The Triumphs and Trials of Lotta Crabtree.* William Morrow, 1968.

Doty, Gresdna A. *Career of Mrs. Anne Brunton Merry in the American Theatre.* Baton Rouge: Louisiana State UP, 1971.

Draper, Ruth. *The Art of Ruth*

Draper: Her Dramas and Characters: With a Memoir by Morton Dauwen Zabel. Doubleday, 1960.

Epstein, Helen. *The Companies She Keeps: Tina Packer Builds a Theater.* Cambridge, MA: Plunkett Lake Press, 1985.

Flanagan, Hallie. *Arena.* Duell, Sloan & Pearce, 1940.

Gordon, Ruth. *My Side: The Autobiography of Ruth Gordon.* Harper & Row, 1976.

Gottlieb, Lois C. *Rachel Crothers.* Boston: Twayne Publishers, 1979.

Hagen, Uta. *Sources.* Performing Arts, 1983.

Hayes, Helen, with Lewis Funke. *A Gift of Joy.* M. Evans & Co., 1956.

Hellman, Lillian. *Three: An Unfinished Woman, Pentimento, Scoundrel Time.* Boston: Little, Brown, 1979.

Heys, Sandra. *Contemporary Stage Roles for Women: A Descriptive Catalogue.* Westport, CT: Greenwood, 1985.

Higham, Charles. *Kate: The Life of Katharine Hepburn.* W. W. Norton, 1975.

Hotchkiss, Marlow. *Firehouse Theatre.* Minneapolis: Firehouse Theatre, 1969.

Janis, Elsie. *So Far, So Good! An Autobiography.* E. P. Dutton, 1932.

Johnson, Claudia. *American Actress: Perspective on the Nineteenth Century.* Chicago: Nelson-Hall, 1984.

Jones, Margo. *Theatre in the Round.* Rinehart, 1951.

Keyssar, Helene. *Feminist Theatre: An Introduction to Plays of Contemporary British and American Women.* Grove Press, 1985.

Klein, Maxine. *Theatre for the 98%.* Boston: South End Press, 1978.

Le Gallienne, Eva. *At 33.* Longmans, Green, 1939.

———. *With a Quiet Heart.* 1953. Westport, CT: Greenwood Press, 1974.

Leach, Joseph. *Bright Particular Star: The Life and Times of Charlotte Cushman.* New Haven, CT: Yale UP, 1970.

Leavitt, Dinah Luise. *Feminist Theatre Groups.* Jefferson, NC: McFarland and Co., 1980.

Lee, Gypsy Rose. *Gypsy: A Memoir.* Harper & Bros., 1957.

Lesser, Allen. *Enchanting Rebel: The Secret of Adah Isaacs Menken.* Beechhurst, 1947.

Logan, Olive. *Apropos of Women and the Theatre.* Carleton: Carleton Publishers, 1869.

Lucia, Ellis. *Klondike Kate: The Life and Legend of Kitty Rockwell, the*

Queen of the Yukon. Hastings House, 1962.

McKay, Frederick E., and Charles E. L. Wingate. *Famous American Actors of To-Day.* 2 vols. Thomas Y. Crowell, 1896.

Malina, Judith. *The Diaries of Judith Malina: 1947–1957.* Grove Press, 1984.

Malpede, Karen, ed. *Women in Theatre: Compassion and Hope.* Drama Book Specialists, 1981.

Mapp, Edward. *Directory of Blacks in the Performing Arts.* Metuchen, NJ: Scarecrow Press, 1978.

Marranca, Bonnie. *Theatrewritings.* Performing Arts Publications, 1984.

Martin, Mary. *My Heart Belongs.* Morrow & Co., 1976.

Mills, Earl. *Dorothy Dandridge: A Portrait in Black.* Los Angeles: Holloway House, 1970.

Mitchell, Loften. *Voices of the Black Theatre.* Clifton, NJ: James T. White, 1975.

Morris, Clara. *Life of a Star.* McClure, 1906.

Morrow, Lee Alan, and Frank Pike. *Creating Theater: The Professionals' Approach to New Plays.* Random House, 1986.

Mosel, Ted, and Gertrude Macy. *Leading Lady: The World and Theatre of Katharine Cornell.* Boston: Little, Brown, 1978.

Mullin, Donald, ed. *Victorian Actors and Actresses in Review: A Dictionary of Contemporary Views of Representative British and American Actors and Actresses, 1837–1901.* Westport, CT: Greenwood Press, 1983.

Natalle, Elizabeth J. *Feminist Theatre: A Study in Persuasion.* Metuchen, NJ: Scarecrow Press, 1985.

Nemiroff, Robert. *To Be Young, Gifted and Black: Lorraine Hansberry in Her Own Words.* Englewood Cliffs, NJ: Prentice-Hall, 1969.

Olauson, Judith. *The American Woman Playwright: A View of Criticism and Characterization.* Troy, NY: Whitson, 1981.

Pearce, T. M. *Mary Hunter Austin.* Twayne, 1965.

Philips, Julien. *Stars of the Ziegfeld Follies.* Minneapolis: Lerner Publications, 1972.

Picon, Molly, with Jean Bergantini Grillo. *Molly! An Autobiography.* Simon & Schuster, 1980.

Robinson, Alice M., Vera Mowry Roberts and Milly S. Barranger, eds. *Notable Women in the American Theatre.* Washington, DC: University Publications of America, Inc. Forthcoming.

Rosenthal, Jean, and Lael Werten-

baker. *The Magic of Light: The Craft and Career of Jean Rosenthal, Pioneer in Lighting for the Modern Stage.* Boston: Little, Brown, in association with Theatre Arts Books, 1972.

Roth, Moira, ed. *The Amazing Decade: Women and Performance Art in America 1970–1980.* Los Angeles: Astro Artz, 1983.

Rourke, Constance. *Troupers of the Gold Coast: Or, The Rise of Lotta Crabtree.* Harcourt, Brace, 1928.

Sainer, Arthur. *Radical Theatre Notebook.* Avon, 1975.

Seldes, Marian. *The Bright Lights: A Theatre Life.* Boston: Houghton Mifflin Company, 1978.

Seller, Maxine S., ed. *Ethnic Theatre in the United States.* Westport, CT: Greenwood Press, 1983.

Skinner, Cornelia Otis. *Family Circle.* Boston: Houghton, 1948.

Sothern, E. H. *Julia Marlowe's Story.* Rinehart & Co., 1954.

Staples, Shirley. *Male-Female Comedy Teams in American Vaudeville, 1865–1932.* Ann Arbor, MI: UMI Research Press, 1984.

Starhawk. *The Spiral Dance.* San Francisco: Harper, 1979.

Stevenson, Isabelle, ed. *The Tony Award: A Complete Listing of Winners and Nominees with a History of the American Theatre Wing.* Crown, 1985.

Taylor, Karen Malpede. *People's Theatre in Amerika.* Drama Book Specialists, 1972.

Webster, Margaret. *Don't Put Your Daughter on the Stage.* Knopf, 1972.

Wilson, Garff B. *A History of American Acting.* Bloomington: Indiana UP, 1966.

Wister, Fanny Kemble, ed. *Fanny, the American Kemble.* South Pass Press, 1972.

Wood, Peggy. *Actors—and People.* Appleton, 1930.

Woollcott, Alexander. *Mrs. Fiske: Her Views on the Stage, Recorded by Alexander Woollcott.* Benjamin Blom, 1917.

Wortley, Richard. *A Pictorial History of Striptease: 100 Years of Undressing to Music.* Secaucus, NJ: Chartwell Books, 1976.

Young, William C. *Famous Actors and Actresses on the American Stage.* 2 vols. Bowker, 1975.

II. ESSAYS AND ARTICLES

Note: *Women and Performance: A Journal of Feminist Theory* is abbreviated below as *W & P*.

Baker, Rob. "The Visionary Art of Meredith Monk." *American The-*

atre Oct. 1984: 4+.

Bank, Rosemarie K. "Theatre and Narrative Fiction in the Work of the Nineteenth-Century American Playwright, Louisa Medina." *Theatre History Studies* 3 (1983): 55–67.

Barker, Barbara. "Maria Bonfanti and *The Black Crook*, New Orleans, 1872." *Theatre Journal* 31 (1979): 88–97.

Bell, Gay. "From a Resistance to Lesbian Theatre to a Lesbian Theatre of Resistance." *Resources for Feminist Research* 12 (March 1983): 30–34.

Billman, Carol. "Women and the Family in American Drama." *The Arizona Quarterly* 36 (Spring 1980): 35–48.

Brown, Janet, and Pamela Loy. "Cinderella and Slippery Jack: Sex Roles and Social Mobility Themes in Early Musical Comedy." *International Journal of Women's Studies* 4 (1981): 507–16.

Butruille, Susan G. "Acting Out! Curtain Going Up on Women's History." *Ms.* March 1984: 95–98.

Coss, Clare, Sondra Segal, and Roberta Sklar. "Why Do We Need a Feminist Theatre?" *W & P* 1.1 (1983): 15–18.

Cryer, Gretchen, and others. "Where Are the Women Playwrights?" *New York Times* 20 May 1973, sec. 2: 1+.

Curb, Rosemary K., "Fragmented Selves in Adrienne Kennedy's *Funnyhouse of a Negro* and *The Owl Answers*." *Theatre Journal* 32 (1980): 180–95.

Dell'Olio, Anselma. "The Founding of the New Feminist Theatre." *Notes from the Second Year: Major Writings of Radical Feminists*. Radical Feminism Press, 1970.

Dolan, Jill. "Gender Impersonation Onstage: Destroying or Maintaining the Mirror of Gender Roles." *W & P* 2.2 (1985): 5–11.

———. "Women's Theatre Program ATA: Creating a Feminist Forum." *W & P* 1.2 (1984): 5–13.

Dullea, Georgia. "Dreams Are What a Feminist Group's Plays Are Made Of." *New York Times* 21 Dec. 1972: 42.

———. "Whose Role Is It Anyway? Mary Tyler Moore and Other Actresses Are Playing Roles Written for Men." *Ms.* August 1980: 81–82.

Fornes, Maria Irene. "I Write These Messages That Come." *Drama Review* 21.4 (1977): 25–40.

———, and Tina Howe. "Women's Work: Tina Howe and Maria Irene Fornes Explore the Wom-

an's Voice in Drama." *American Theatre* Sept. 1985: 10–15.

Forte, Jeanie. "Rachel Rosenthal: Feminism and Performance Art." *W & P* 2.2 (1985): 27–37.

Friedman, Sharon. "Feminism as Theme in Twentieth-Century American Women's Drama." *American Studies* 25 (Spring 1984): 69–89.

Gipson, R. "Martha Morton: America's First Professional Woman Playwright." *Theatre Survey* 23 (Nov. 1982): 213–22.

Goldberg, Marianne. "Transformative Aspects of Meredith Monk's *Education of the Girlchild*." *W & P* 1.1 (1983): 19–28.

Gottlieb, Lois C. "The Perils of Freedom: The New Woman in Three American Plays of the 1900's." *Canadian Review of American Studies* (1975): 4–98.

Goulianos, Joan. "Women and the Avant-Garde Theatre." In *Women: An Issue*. Ed. Lee Edwards, Mary Heath, and Lisa Baskin. Boston: Little, Brown, 1972. 257–67.

Gussow, Mel. "Women Playwrights: New Voices in the Theater." *New York Times Magazine* 1 May 1983: 22–40.

Harbin, Billy J. "The Role of Mrs. Hallam in the Hodgkinson-Hallam Controversy: 1794–1797." *Theatre Journal* 32 (1980): 213–22.

Hewitt, Barnard. "Mrs. John Wood and the Lost Art of Burlesque Acting." *Educational Theatre Journal* 13.2 (1961): 82–85.

Jay, Karla. "Carol Grosberg on Lesbian Theatre." *Win* 26 June 1975: 15–17.

Jenkins, Linda Walsh. "Locating the Language of Gender Experience." *W & P* 2.1 (1984): 5–20.

Kaplan, E. Ann. "Theories of Melodrama: A Feminist Perspective." *W & P* 1.1 (1983): 40–48.

Kennedy, Adrienne. "A Growth of Images." *Drama Review* 21.4 (1977): 41–48.

Kolb, Deborah S. "The Rise and Fall of the New Woman in American Drama." *Educational Theatre Journal* 27 (1975): 149–60.

———. "The Story of Anna O: Performing a Case History." *W & P* 2.1 (1984): 75–80.

Lamb, Margaret. "Feminist Criticism." *Drama Review* 18.3 (1974): 46–50.

Landau, Penny. "Jane Chambers: In Memoriam." *W & P* 1.2 (1984): 55–57.

Londré, Felicia Hardison. "The Two Edith Ellises." *Theatre Journal* 32 (1980): 518–19.

Lowell, Sandra. "Art Comes to the Elevator: Women's Guerrilla Theatre." *Women: A Journal of Liberation* 2.1 (1970): 50.

———. "New Feminist Theatre." *Ms.* August 1972: 17–23.

Loy, Pamela and Janet Brown. "Red Hot Mamas, Sex Kittens and Sweet Young Things: Role Engulfment in the Lives of Musical Comedy Performers." *International Journal of Women's Studies* 2 (Sept.–Oct. 1982): 338–47.

McKay, B. "Whatever Happened to the Ingenue?" *Saturday Review World* 27 July 1974: 42–43.

———. "Women on the Rocks." *Saturday Review World* 6 April 1974: 48–49.

Mael, Phyllis. "Beyond Hellman and Hansberry: The Impact of Feminism on a Decade of Drama." *Kansas Quarterly* 12.4 (1980): 141–44.

Malnig, Julie, Judy C. Rosenthal and Anne B. Wyma. "Orgasmo Adulto Escapes from the Zoo: An Interview with Estelle Parsons." *W & P* 2.1 (1984): 49–62.

Malpede, Karen. "Tending the Avant Garden: Can Feminism Save Avant Garde Theater?" *Soho News* Oct. 13, 1981: 17–18.

———. "What Freud Didn't Tell Us About Oedipus." *Soho News* May 27, 1981: 24.

Melville, Margarita B. "Female and Male in Chicano Theatre." In *Hispanic Theatre in the United States*. Ed. Nicolas Kanellos. Houston: Arte Publico, 1984. 71–79.

Moody, Richard. "Uncle Tom, the Theatre, and Mrs. Stowe." *American Heritage* 6 (Oct. 1955): 28+.

Moore, Gaylen. "Ellen Stewart—the Mama of LaMama." *Ms.* April 1982: 48–56.

Moore, Honor. "Theatre Will Never Be the Same." *Ms.* Dec. 1977: 36+.

Morton, Carlos. "Sugarcoated Socialism." *Drama Review* 19.2 (1975): 61–68.

Murray, Timothy. "Patriarchal Panopticism, or The Seduction of a Bad Joke: *Getting Out* in Theory." *Theatre Journal* 35 (1983): 376–88.

Nathan, George Jean. "The Status of the Female Playwrights." *The Entertainment of a Nation*. Knopf, 1941. 34–41.

Norman, Marsha. "Articles of Faith: A Conversation with Lillian Hellman." *American Theatre* May 1984: 10–15.

O'Brien, S. "The Image of Women in Tony-Award Winning Plays." *Journal of American Culture* 6

(Fall 1983): 45–49.

Oliveros, Pauline. "Crow Two, a Ceremonial Opera." *alcheringa/ethnopoetics* 1.2 (1975): 89–92.

Patraka, Vivian M. "*Apple Pie* and *Signs of Life*: Contrasting Forms in Feminist Drama." *W & P* 1.2 (1984): 58–72.

Perinciolo, Lillian. "Feminist Theatre: They're Playing in Peoria." *Ms.* Oct. 1975: 101–4.

Rea, Charlotte. "The New York Feminist Theatre Troupe." *Drama Review* 18.3 (1974): 132–33.

———. "Women for Women." *Drama Review* 18.4 (1974): 77–78.

———. "Women's Theatre Groups." *Drama Review* 16.2 (1972): 79–89.

Richards, S. L. "Conflicting Images in the Plays of Ntozake Shange." *Black American Literature Forum* 17 (Summer 1983): 73–78.

———. "Negative Forces and Positive Non-Entities: Images of Women in the Dramas of Amiri Baraka." *Theatre Journal* 34 (1982): 233–40.

Robinson, Harlow. "Dreams of a Prophetic Past: Novelist Toni Morrison Tries Her Hand at Playwriting." *American Theatre* Jan. 1986: 17–19.

Roth, Martha. "Notes toward a Feminist Performance Aesthetic." *W & P* 1.1 (1983): 5–14.

Schwartz, Barbara, and Mara Shelby. "A Survey of Women's Feminist/Lesbian Theatre Groups in New York." *Christopher Street* (Gay Theatre Issue) 2.12 (June 1978): 28–32.

Segal, Sondra, and Roberta Sklar. "The Women's Experimental Theatre." *Drama Review* 27.4 (1983): 74–75.

Shafer, Yvonne. "The Liberated Woman in American Plays of the Past." *Players* 49.3–4 (1974): 95–100.

Shange, Ntozake. "Unrecovered Losses." *The Black Scholar* 10.10 (1979): 7–8.

Simmons, Christina. "Companionate Marriage and the Lesbian Threat." *Frontiers* 4.3 (Fall 1979): 54–59.

Sklar, Roberta. "'Sisters' or Never Trust Anyone outside the Family." *W & P* 1.1 (1983): 58–63.

Skurnik, Jennifer. "San Francisco Mime Troupe Criticized." *Off Our Backs* Jan. 1983: 14.

Smith, Beverly A. "Women's Work—Trifles? The Skill of Playwright Susan Glaspell." *International Journal of Women's Studies* 5 (March-April 1982): 172–84.

Sommer, S. R. "JoAnne Akalaitis of Mabou Mines." *Drama Review* 20.3 (1976): 3–16.

———. "Loie Fuller." *Drama Review* 19.1 (1975): 53–67.

Stasio, Marilyn. "The Night the Critics Lost Their Cool." *Ms.* Sep. 1975: 37–41.

Stephens, J. L. "Why Marry? The New Woman of 1918." *Theatre Journal* 34 (1982): 183–96.

———. "Sister/Sister—Working It Out on Stage." *Ms.* Nov. 1978: 40–45.

Suntree, Susan. "Women's Theatre: Creating the Dream Now." *Women's Culture: The Women's Renaissance of the Seventies.* Ed. Gayle Kimball. Metuchen, NJ: Scarecrow Press, 1981. 106–16.

Sutherland, Cynthia. "American Women Playwrights as Mediators of the 'Woman Problem.'" *Modern Drama* 21 (1978): 319–36.

Tener, Robert L. "Theatre of Identity: Adrienne Kennedy's Portrait of the Black Woman." *Studies in Black Literature* 6.2

(1975): 1–5.

Terry, Megan. "Two Pages a Day." *Drama Review* 21.4 (1977): 59–64.

———, and others. "Women as Dramatists: Five Playwrights Talk about Theatre without Compromise and Sexism." *Mademoiselle* Aug. 1972: 288–91.

Van Kleef, Deborah. "Pillbox Hats, White Gloves and Ladies Against Women." *Theater* 13.3 (1982): 74–75.

Wegner, William H. "Alvina Krause Revisited." *Educational Theatre Journal* 31 (1977): 221–30.

Wetzsteon, Ross. "The Mad, Mad World of Tina Howe." *New York* 28 Nov. 1983: 58–71.

Wilkerson, Margaret B. "*A Raisin in the Sun*: Anniversary of an American Classic." *Theatre Journal* 38 (1986): 441–52.

Wilshire, Donna. "Feminist Theater Melds Politics with Art." *New Directions for Women* March–April 1981: 6.

Winer, Lucy. "Staging for Consciousness-Raising." *Emergency Librarian* 2.4–5 (1975): 18–23.

Wolverton, Terry. "An Oral Herstory of Lesbianism." *Frontiers* 4.3 (1979): 52–53.

"The 'Woman' Playwright Issue." *Performing Arts Journal* 7.3 (1983): 87–102.

Yarbro-Bejarano, Yvonne. "Chicanas' Experience in Collective Theatre: Ideology and Form." *W & P* 2.2 (1985): 45–58.

———. "The Female Subject in Chicano Theatre: Sexuality, 'Race,' and Class." *Theatre Journal* 38 (1986): 389–407.

Zucker, Barbara. "Women in the Theatre." *Centerpoint* 2.3–4 (1980): 31–37.

ADDITIONAL SELECTED READINGS IN WOMEN AND THEATRE

I: BOOKS

Bamber, Linda. *Comic Women, Tragic Men: A Study of Gender and Genre in Shakespeare.* Stanford UP, 1982.

Case, Sue-Ellen. *Feminism and Theatre.* Methuen, 1987.

Cotton, Nancy. *Women Playwrights in England, 1363–1750.* Bucknell UP, 1980.

Dash, Irene G. *Wooing, Wedding and Power: Women in Shakespeare's Plays.* Columbia UP, 1981.

Dusinberre, Juliet. *Shakespeare and the Nature of Women.* Barnes and Noble, 1979.

Fraser, Antonia. *The Weaker Vessel.* Alfred A. Knopf, 1984.

French, Marilyn. *Shakespeare's Division of Experience.* Summit Books, 1981.

Gilder, Rosamond. *Enter the Actress: The First Women in the Theatre.* Houghton Mifflin, 1931.

Goreau, Angeline. *Reconstructing Aphra: A Social Biography of Aphra Behn.* Dial Press, 1980.

Holledge, Julie. *Innocent Flowers: Women in the Edwardian Theater.*

Salem, NH: Merrimack Pubs. Circle, 1983.

Jardine, Lisa. *Still Harping on Daughters: Women and Drama in the Age of Shakespeare.* Sussex, England: The Harvester Press, 1983.

Lenz, Carolyn R. Swift, Gayle Green, and Carol Thomas Neely. *The Woman's Part: Feminist Criticism of Shakespeare.* University of Illinois Press, 1980.

McDonald, Margaret L. *The Independent Woman in the Restoration Comedy of Manners.* Salzburg Studies in English Literature:

Poetic Drama and Poetic Theory,
No. 32. Atlantic Highlands, NJ:
Humanities Press International,
1976.

McKendrick, Malveena. *Women and
Society in the Spanish Drama of
the Golden Age.* Cambridge UP,
1974.

Novy, Marianne. *Love's Argument:
Gender Relations in Shakespeare.*
University of North Carolina
Press, 1984.

Pitt, Angela. *Shakespeare's Women.*
Barnes and Noble, 1981.

Shepherd, Simon. *Amazons and Warrior Women: Varieties of Feminism
in Seventeenth-Century Drama.*
St. Martins, 1981.

Todd, Susan, ed. *Women and Theatre:
Calling the Shots.* Faber and Faber, 1984.

Vanovitch, Katherine. *Female Roles in
East German Drama 1949–1977:
A Selective History of Drama in
the GDR.* Lang, 1981.

Wandor, Michelene. *Understudies:
Theatre and Sexual Politics.* Methuen, 1981.

———. *Carry On, Understudies.*
Rev. ed. Routledge & Kegan
Paul, Inc., 1986.

II: ESSAYS AND ARTICLES

Bardsley, Barney. "The Young Blood
of Theatre: Women's Theatre
Groups." *Drama* 152 (1984): 25–
29.

Blair, Rhonda. "Shakespeare and the
Feminist Actor." *W & P* 2.2
(1985): 18–26.

Case, Sue-Ellen. "Gender as Play:
Simone Benmussa's *The Singular
Life of Albert Nobbs*." *W & P* 1.2
(1984): 21–24.

———, and Ellen Donkin. "FIT:
Germany's First Conference for
Women in Theatre." *W & P* 2.2
(1985): 65–73.

———, and Jeanie K. Forte. "From
Formalism to Feminism." *Theater* 16.2 (1985): 62–65.

Feral, Josette. "Writing and Dis-
placement: Women in the Theatre." *Modern Drama* 27 (1984):
549–63.

Lister, Rota H. "Bibliography of Canadian Plays about Older Wom-
en." *Resources for Feminist
Research*, 11.2 (1982): 238–40.

Parrish, Sue. "The Flavour of '84?"
Plays and Players 368 (May
1984): 34.

Savonna, Jeannette Laillou. "French
Feminism and Theatre: An Introduction." *Modern Drama* 27
(1984): 540–45.

Solomon, Alisa. "Witches, Ranters
and The Middle Class: The

Plays of Caryl Churchill." *Theater* 12.2 (1981): 49–55.

Wandor, Micheline. "The Personal Is
Political: Feminism and Theatre." *Dreams and Deconstruc-
tions: Alternative Theatre in
Britain.* Ed. Sandy Craig. Der-
byshire, England: Amber Lane
Press, 1980. 49–58.

Woddis, Carole. "Twenty Writers:
Ten Women." *Plays and Players*
368 (May 1984): 14–17.

JOURNALS:
SPECIAL ISSUES

*Feminist Criticism of Shakespeare.
Women's Studies* 9.1 (1981).

*Feminist Criticism of Shakespeare, II.
Women's Studies* 9.2 (1982).

*Lorraine Hansberry: Art of Thunder,
Vision of Light. Freedomways* 19.4
(1979).

Staging Gender. Theatre Journal 37.3
(1985). Includes: Sue-Ellen Case,
"Classic Drag: The Greek Crea-
tion of Female Parts"; Rosemary
K. Curb, "Re/cognition, Re/pre-
sentation, Re/creation in
Woman-Conscious Drama: The
Seer, The Seen, The Scene, The
Obscene"; Elin Diamond, "Re-
fusing the Romanticism of Iden-
tity: Narrative Interventions in
Churchill, Benmussa, Duras";
Kathleen A. McLennan, "Wom-
an's Place: *Marriage* in America's
Gilded Age"; Phyllis Rackin,
"Anti-Historians: Women's Roles
in Shakespeare's Histories";
Sharon Willis, "Hélène Cixous's
Portrait de Dora: The Unseen
and the Un-scene."

Theater 17.1 (Winter 1985). Includes:
Serena Anderlini, "Franca
Rame: Her Life and Works";
Ruby Cohn, "Ariane
Mnouchkine: Twenty-one Years
of Théâtre de Soleil"; Jane Ann
Crum, "Three Generations of
Lighting Design: An Interview
with Peggy Clark Kelley, Jen-
nifer Tipton, and Danianne
Mizzy"; Scott Cummings,
"Seeing with Clarity: The Vi-
sions of Maria Irene Fornes";
Nadine Honigberg, "The Wom-
en's Project: An Interview with
Julia Miles"; Linda Walsh
Jenkins and Susan Ogden-Mal-
ouf, "The (Female) Actor Pre-
pares"; Rosette C. Lamont,
"Rosalyn Drexler's Semiotics of
Instability"; Susan Mason, "An
Interview with Kristin
Linklater."

*Women and Performance Issue. The
Drama Review* 24.2 (1980). In-

cludes: Jessica Abbe, "Anne
Bogart's Journeys"; Cornelia
Brunner, "Roberta Sklar: Toward
Creating a Women's Theatre";
Ruby Cohn, "Joan Holden and
the San Francisco Mime
Troupe"; Mel Gordon, "Laurie
Anderson: Performance Artist";
Jim O'Quinn, "Linda Muss-
man's Time and Space Limited
Theatre."

*Women in Canadian Theatre. Canadian
Drama* 5.2 (1979).

Women in Theatre. Drama 152 (1984).
Articles on women in contemporary British theatre.

*Women in Theatre. Room of One's
Own.* 8.2 (July 31, 1983). Arti-
cles on women in contemporary
Canadian theatre.

Women in Theatre. The Theatre Annual
40 (1985). Includes: Beverley
Byers-Pevitts, "Imaging Women
in Theatre: Departures from
Dramatic Tradition"; Winona L.
Fletcher, "From Genteel Poet to
Revolutionary Playwright:
Georgia Douglas Johnson";
Eileen Kerney, "Teresa Deevy:
Ireland's Forgotten Second Lady
of the Abbey Theatre"; Felicia
Londré, "Ermolova's Revolution-
ary Realism before and after the
Revolution"; Madonne Miner,
"'What's These Bars Doin'
Here?'—The Impossibility of
Getting Out"; Vivian Patraka,
"Foodtalk in the Plays of Caryl
Churchill and Joan Schenkar";
Yvonne Shafer, "The Liberated
Woman in Ibsen's *The Lady from
the Sea*"; Judith L. Stephens,
"The Compatibility of Tradi-
tional Dramatic Forms and Fem-
inist Expressions"; Margaret
Wilkerson, "Diverse Angles of
Vision: Two Black Women
Playwrights."

Women's Theatre. Theatre News 10
(Nov. 1977).

*Susan M. Flierl Steadman is a freelance
teacher, director, and playwright in
Dallas.*

DISSERTATIONS ON WOMEN IN AMERICAN THEATRE

ARRANGED ALPHABETICALLY BY THEATRE PERSONALITIES

Maude Adams
Eileen Karen Kuehnl. *Maude Adams, An American Idol: True Womanhood Triumphant in the Late-Nineteenth and Early-Twentieth Century Theatre*. University of Wisconsin-Madison, 1984.

Stella Adler
Joanna-Helen Rotte. *The Principles of Acting According to Stella Adler*. City University of New York, 1983.

Viola Allen
Rita Plotnicki. *The Evolution of a Star: The Career of Viola Allen, 1882–1918*. City University of New York, 1979.

Mary Anderson
Raymond Sawyer. *The Shakespearean Acting of Mary Anderson: 1884–1889*. University of Illinois, 1975.

Margaret Anglin
Gordon Johnson. *The Greek Productions of Margaret Anglin*. Case Western Reserve University, 1971.

Sarah Bernhardt
Richard G. Smith. *Sarah Bernhardt in America: The Factors in Her Success*. University of Illinois, 1971.

Aline Bernstein
Mike Alan Barton. *Aline Bernstein: A History and Evaluation*. Indiana University, 1971.

Donald Stowell. *The New Costuming in America: The Ideas and Practices of Robert Edmond Jones, Norman Bel Geddes, Lee Simonson, and Aline Bernstein*. University of Texas, 1972.

Laura Justine Bonstelle-Stuart
William Luther Deam. *A Biographical Study of Miss Laura Justine Bonstelle-Stuart Together with an Evaluation of Her Own Contributions to the Modern Theatre World*. University of Michigan, 1954.

Fanny Brice
Barbara Grossman. *Fanny Brice*. Tufts University, 1985.

Alice Brady
William Lang. *The Career of Alice Brady, Stage and Screen Actress*. University of Illinois, 1971.

Mrs. Leslie Carter
Charles H. Harper. *Mrs. Leslie Carter: Her Life and Acting Career 1864–1937*. University of Nebraska, 1978.

Katharine Cornell
Lynda Moss. *An Historical Study of Katharine Cornell as an Actress-Producer: 1931–1960*. University of Southern California, 1972.

Ida Van Cortland
Doris Jane Katheleen Fraser. *Theatrical Touring in Late Nineteenth-Century Canada: Ida Van Cortland and the Tavernier Company, 1877–1896*. University of Western Ontario, 1985.

Lotta Crabtree
Irene Comer. *"Little Nell and the Marchioness": Milestone in the Development of American Musical Comedy*. Tufts University, 1979.

Rachel Crothers
Irving Abrahamson. *The Career of Rachel Crothers in the American Drama*. University of Chicago, 1956.

Sharon Friedman. *Feminist Concerns in the Works of Four Twentieth-Century American Women Dramatists: Susan Glaspell, Rachel Crothers, Lillian Hellman, and Lorraine Hansberry*. New York University, 1977.

Zoe Kaplan. *Woman in Focus in Major Plays and Productions of Rachel Crothers*. City University of New York, 1979.

Merrell Williams. *The Changing Role of the Woman as Represented in Selected Plays by Rachel Crothers: 1899–1937*. University of Denver, 1971.

Charlotte Cushman
Lisa Merrill. *Charlotte Cushman: American Actress on the Vanguard of New Roles for Women*. New York University, 1985.

Treva Rose Tumbleson. *Three Female Hamlets: Charlotte Cushman, Sarah Bernhardt, and Eva Le Gallienne*. University of Oregon, 1981.

James Willis Yeater. *Charlotte Cushman, American Actress*. University of Illinois, 1954.

Fanny Davenport
R. C. Whitlatch. *Fanny Davenport: Actress and Manager*. University of Illinois, 1962.

Mrs. Alexander Drake
James W. Swain. *Mrs. Alexander Drake: A Biographical Study*. Tulane University, 1970.

Marie Dressler
Roberta Raider. *A Descriptive Study of the Acting of Marie Dressler*. University of Michigan, 1970.

Louisa Lane Drew
Noreen Barnes. *Actress of All Work: A Survey of the Performance Career of Louisa Lane Drew*. Tufts University, 1986.

Dorothy Stolp. *Mrs. John Drew, American Actress-Manager, 1820–1897*. Louisiana State University, 1953.

Isadora Duncan
B. P. Beiswanger. *The Ideational Sources of the Modern Dance in America as Expressed in the Works of Two Leading Exponents, Isadora Duncan and Ruth St. Denis*. New York University, 1944.

Geraldine Farrar
Elizabeth Nash. *Geraldine Farrar: Singing Actress*. Indiana University, 1975.

Zelda Fichandler
B. A. Coyne. *A History of Arena Stage, Washington, D.C.* Tulane University, 1965.

Minnie Maddern Fiske
Ellen Donkin. *Mrs. Fiske's 1897 "Tess of the D'Urbervilles": A Structural Analysis of the 1887–98 Production*. University of Washington, 1982.

Ciesla Mary A.A. Messano. *Minnie Maddern Fiske: Her Battle with the Theatrical Syndicate*. New York University, 1982.

Elizabeth Neill. *The Art of Minnie Maddern Fiske: A Study of Her Realistic Acting*. Tufts University, 1970.

J. Edgar Webb. *Harrison Grey Fiske's Management of the Manhattan Theatre, 1901–1906*. Indiana University, 1971.

Hallie Flanagan
Barbara Mendoza. *Hallie Flanagan: Her Role in American Theatre, 1924–1935*. New York University, 1976.

Patricia Ridge. *The Contributions of Hallie Flanagan to the American Theatre*. University of Colorado, 1971.

Cheryl Dianne Swiss. *Hallie Flanagan and the Federal Theatre Project: An Experiment in Form*. University of Wisconsin, 1982.

Loie Fuller
Sally Sommer. *Loie Fuller: From the Theater of Popular Entertainment to the Parisian Avant-Garde*. New York University, 1979.

Mrs. G. H. Gilbert
Richard Andrew. *Augustin Daly's Big Four: John Drew, Ada Rehan,*

James Lewis and Mrs. G. H. Gilbert. University of Illinois, 1971.

Rosamond Gilder
Caroline Dodge. *Rosamond Gilder and the Theatre.* University of Illinois, 1974.

Susan Glaspell
Sharon Friedman. See Rachel Crothers.

Marcia Noe. *A Critical Biography of Susan Glaspell.* University of Iowa, 1976.

Arthur E. Waterman. *A Critical Study of Susan Glaspell's Works and Her Contributions to Modern American Drama.* University of Wisconsin, 1956.

Martha Graham
Ned Hitchcock. *An Approach to the Criticism of the Modern Dance.* Case Western Reserve University, 1973.

Herbert Propper. *Space/Symbol: The Spatial Concepts in Selected Dances of Martha Graham* (volumes I and II). University of Michigan, 1977.

Lorraine Hansberry
Sharon Friedman. See Rachel Crothers.

Deborah-Jean Wood. *The Plays of Lorraine Hansberry: Studies in Dramatic Form.* University of Wisconsin-Madison, 1985.

Uta Hagen
Susan Jane Spector. *Uta Hagen: The Early Years: 1919–1951.* New York University, 1982.

Julia Dean Hayne
Ralph E. Margetts. *A Study of the Theatrical Career of Julia Dean Hayne.* University of Utah, 1959.

Edith Head
Virginia Hirsch. *Edith Head, Film Costume Designer.* University of Kansas, 1973.

Lillian Head
Meredith Ackley. *The Plays of Lillian Hellman,* University of Pennsylvania, 1969.

Carrol Angermeier. *Moral and Social Protest in the Plays of Lillian Hellman.* University of Texas, 1971.

Debrah Ann Beck-Horn. *Types of Love in Selected Plays of Lillian Hellman.* North Texas State University, 1983.

Sister Carol Blitgen. *The Overlooked Hellman.* University of California, 1972.

John O. Brockington. *A Critical Analysis of the Plays of Lillian Hellman.* Yale University, 1962.

Eugene T. Carlson. *Lillian Hellman's Plays as a Reflection of the Southern Mind.* University of Southern California, 1975.

Sharon Friedman. See Rachel Crothers.

Charles Haller. *The Concepts of Moral Failure in the Eight Original Plays of Lillian Hellman.* Tulane University, 1967.

Annette Johnson. *A Study of Recurrent Character Types in the Plays of Lillian Hellman.* University of Massachusetts, 1971.

A. J. Keller. *Form and Content in the Plays of Lillian Hellman: A Structural Analysis.* Stanford University, 1965.

Cynthia Larimer. *A Study of Female Characters in the Eight Plays of Lillian Hellman.* Purdue University, 1970.

Michael L. McPherson. *Lillian Hellman and Her Critics.* University of Denver, 1976.

Vivian Patraka. *Lillian Hellman, Dramatist of the Second Sex.* University of Michigan, 1977.

Sara Hurdis Shaver. *Feminist Criticism as Role Analysis for the Interpreter: Women in Lillian Hellman's Major Plays.* University of Arizona, 1984.

Glenn Whitesides. *Lillian Hellman: A Biographical and Critical Study.* Florida State University, 1968.

Matilda Heron
Alberta L. Humble. *Matilda Heron, American Actress.* University of Illinois, 1959.

Karen Horney
William Jaeger. *The Application of the Psycho-Analytic Theories of Karen Horney to the Stanislavski System of Acting.* New York University, 1965.

Edith Isaacs
Nafe Edmund Katter. "Theatre Arts" under the Editorship of Edith J. R. Isaacs. University of Michigan, 1964.

Catherine-Ann Tabor. *Edith Juliet Rich Isaacs: An Examination of Her Theories and Influence on the American Theatre.* University of Wisconsin-Madison, 1984.

Margo Jones
June Larson. *A Biographical Study of Margo Jones.* City University of New York, 1980.

Amanda Rudisill. *The Contributions of Eva Le Gallienne, Margaret Webster, Margo Jones, and Joan Littlewood to the Establishment of Repertory Theatre in the United States and Great Britain.* Northwestern University, 1972.

Don Wilmeth. *A History of the Margo Jones Theatre.* University of Illinois, 1965.

Edith King and Dorothy Coit
Ellen Rene Rodman. *Edith King and Dorothy Coit and the King-Coit School and Children's Theatre.* New York University, 1980.

Alvina Krause
David Press. *The Acting Career of Alvina Krause: Theory and Practice.* Carnegie-Mellon University, 1971.

Clare Kummer
V. L. Finizio. *Clare Kummer: An Analysis of Her Plays and Musicals.* University of Iowa, 1965.

Eva Le Gallienne
Paul Cooper. *Eva Le Gallienne's Civic Repertory Theatre.* University of Illinois, 1968.

Amanda Rudisill. See Margo Jones.

Robert A. Schanke. *Eva Le Gallienne: First Lady of Repertory.* University of Nebraska, 1975.

Susanne K. Langer
Samuel David Abel. *Susanne Langer and the Rhythm of Dramatic Action.* Indiana University, 1984.

David K. Rod. *Kenneth Burke and Susanne K. Langer: Dramatic Theorists.* University of Kansas, 1985.

Charlotte Ramsey Lennox
Elizabeth G. Hayes. *Charlotte Ramsey Lennox: The Female Quixote; or, The Adventures of Arabella.* Edited with an Introduction and Notes. Stanford University, 1964.

Miriam Small. *The Life and Literary Relations of Charlotte Lennox.* Yale University, 1925.

Rosetta LeNoire
Linda Kerr Norflett. *The Theatre Career of Rosetta LeNoire.* New York University, 1983.

Mary Todd Lincoln
Alfred Dumais. *An Analysis of the Dramaturgical Use of History in the Writing of Two Full Length Plays About Mary Todd Lincoln.* New York University, 1978.

Olive Logan
Robert J. Wills. *The Riddle of Olive Logan.* Case Western Reserve University, 1971.

Kitty Madison
Joel Harvey. *American Burlesque as Reflected through the Career of Kitty Madison.* Florida State University, 1980.

Clare Tree Major
Michael W. Gamble. *Clare Tree Major: Children's Theatre, 1923–1954.* New York University, 1976.

Julia Marlowe

Sallie Mitchell. *The Early Career of Julia Marlowe: The Making of a Star*. University of Illinois, 1976.

A. Sogliuzzo. *Edward Sothern and Julia Marlowe*. Indiana University, 1967.

Anne Brunton Merry
Gresdna A. Doty. *The Career of Mrs. Anne Brunton Merry in the American Theatre*. Indiana University, 1968.

Edna St. Vincent Millay
John Patton. *Edna St. Vincent Millay as a Verse Dramatist*. University of Colorado, 1963.

Tanya Moiseiwitsch
Patricia Vandenberg Blom. *Tanya Moiseiwitsch, Costume Designer: The Creative Process*. University of Michigan, 1982.

Dennis Lorman Behl. *Tanya Moiseiwitsch: Her Contribution to Theatre Arts from 1935–1980*. Kent State University, 1981.

Anna Morgan
Joyce L. Sozen. *Anna Morgan: Reader, Teacher, and Director*. University of Illinois, 1961.

Clara Morris
Mildred L. Howard. *The Acting of Clara Morris*. University of Illinois, 1957.

Motley
Barbara Jean Costa. *Motley: An Analysis of the Costume Designs of Elizabeth Montgomery, Margaret Harris and Sophie Devine*. Florida State University, 1980.

Anna Cora Mowatt
Marius Blesi. *The Life and Letters of Anna Cora Mowatt*. University of Virginia, 1938.

Alla Nazimova
Margaret McKerron. *A Descriptive Study of the Acting of Alla Nazimova*. San Diego State University, 1974.

Olga Nethersole
Joy Harriman Reilly. *From Wicked Woman of the Stage to New Woman: The Career of Olga Nethersole*. Ohio State University, 1984.

Ada Rehan
Richard Andrew. See Mrs. G. H. Gilbert.

Elizabeth Robins
Mary Gay Gibson. *Elizabeth Robins: Ibsen Actress/Manageress*.

Cornell University, 1978.

Jane Conner Marcus. *Elizabeth Robins*. Northwestern University, 1973.

Ruth St. Denis
Barbara P. Beiswanger. See Isadora Duncan.

Christena L. Schlundt. *The Role of Ruth St. Denis in the History of American Dance 1906–1922*. Claremont Graduate School, 1959.

Caroline Schaffner
Martha Frances Stover Langford. *The Tent Repertoire Theatre of Neil and Caroline Schaffner: A Case in Tent Repertoire Theatre as Communication*. University of Colorado, 1978.

Zelda Sears
Denny Bettisworth. *The Life and Career of Zelda Sears*. University of Georgia, 1974.

Mary Shaw
John Irving. *Mary Shaw, Actress, Suffragist, Activist*. Columbia University, 1978.

Cornelia Otis Skinner
Bruce Loganbill. *Cornelia Otis Skinner and her Art Form of Monologue-Drama*. Michigan State University, 1961.

Viola Spolin
Bruce Levitt. *The Historical and Practical Evolution of Viola Spolin's Theatre Games*. University of Michigan, 1976.

Maureen Stapleton
Esther M. Ropsen. *Maureen Stapleton, American Actress*. University of Arizona, 1983.

Gertrude Stein
Elizabeth Armatage. *The Mother of Us All: The Woman in the Writings of Gertrude Stein*. University of Toronto, 1974.

Mary Irwin Bainum. *Gertrude Stein's Theatre*. University of Wisconsin, Madison, 1981.

Wilford Leach. *Gertrude Stein and the Modern Theatre*. University of Illinois, 1956.

Betsy Alayne Ryan. *Gertrude Stein's Theatre of the Absolute*. University of Illinois at Urbana, 1980.

Megan Terry
Elizabeth Anne Barron. *A Struc-

tural Analysis of Representative Plays of Megan Terry*. University of Louisville, 1983.

Phyllis Wagner. *Megan Terry: Practical Playwright*. University of Denver, 1972.

Lydia Thompson
Marilyn Moses. *Lydia Thompson and the "British Blondes" in the United States*. University of Oregon, 1978.

Sophie Treadwell
Louise Heck-Rabi. *Sophie Treadwell: Subjects and Structures in 20th Century American Drama*. Wayne State University, 1976.

Nancy Edith Wynn. *Sophie Treadwell: The Career of a Twentieth-Century American Feminist Playwright*. City University of New York, 1982.

Madame Vestris
Lillian S. Casey. *Madame Vestris in America*. University of Michigan, 1976.

Mercy Otis Warren
Maud M. Hutcheson. *Mercy Otis Warren: A Study of Her Life and Works*. American University, 1951.

Margaret Webster
Janet Carroll. *A Promptbook Study of Margaret Webster's Production of Othello*. Louisiana State University, 1977.

Amanda Rudisill. See Margo Jones.

Ely Silverman. *Margaret Webster's Theory and Practice of Shakespearean Production in the United States (1937–1953)*. New York University, 1969.

Oak Song. *A Promptbook Study of Margaret Webster's Production of "Macbeth."* University of Oregon, 1982.

Ronald Worsley. *Margaret Webster: A Study of Her Contributions to the American Theatre*. Wayne State University, 1972.

Peggy Wood
Barbara Ann Simon. *Twentieth Century American Performing Arts as Viewed through the Career of Peggy Wood*. New York University, 1981.

ADDITIONAL DISSERTATION TITLES ARRANGED ALPHABETICALLY BY TITLE

Ralph Klein. *The American Military Heroes and the Heroines of the Revolutionary War, the War of 1812, and the Civil War: An Analysis of Character Based on Representative American Plays Written Between the Years of 1774 and 1907*. Uni-

versity of Denver, 1967.

Linda Sue Long. *The Art of Beatrice Herford, Cissie Loftus, and Dorothy Sands within the Tradition of Solo Performance*. University of Texas at Austin, 1982.

Shirley Louise Staples. *From

"Barney's Courtship" to Burns and Allen: Male-Female Teams in American Vaudeville, 1865–1932*. Tufts University, 1981.

Piankhi Maisha L. A. Hazzard. *Black Love on Stage: A Profile of Courtship and Marriage Relation-

ships in Selected Broadway Shows by Black Dramatists, 1959–1979, and an Original Play. Bowling Green State University, 1983.

Judith Stephens. *The Central Female Characters in the Pulitzer Prize Plays, 1918–1949*. Kent State University, 1977.

Doyne Mraz. *The Changing Image of Female Characters in the Works of Tennessee Williams*. University of Southern California, 1967.

Jo Loudin. *The Changing Role of the Comic Heroine in American Drama from 1900 to 1940*. University of Washington, 1974.

George D. Haskell. *Complicated Charms. The Literary Activities of 18th Century Actresses*. Fordham University, 1960.

Mary H. Newell. *The Contributions of Selected Women Directors in 20th Century American Theatre*. Wayne State University, 1975.

Judith Marie Babnich. *A Consciousness Raising Theatre in America: The History of the Omaha Magic Theatre from 1969 to 1980*. University of California, Los Angeles, 1981.

Elaine S. Klein. *The Development of the Leading Feminine Character in Selected Librettos of American Musicals from 1900 to 1960*. Columbia University, 1962.

William Morgan. *An Experimental Study and Comparison of the Responses of Men and the Responses of Women in Theatre Audiences*. University of Iowa, 1951.

Teri S. Kwal. *An Experimental Study of Sex as a Factor Influencing Audience Evaluation of Performer Effectiveness and Audience Comprehension of Performance for Selected Dramatic Monologues*. New York University, 1976.

Dorothy S. Pam. *Exploitation, Independence, and Solidarity: The Changing Role of American Working Women as Reflected in the Working-Girl Melodrama, 1870–1910*. New York University, 1980.

Meredith Flynn. *The Feeling Circle, Company Collaboration, and Ritual Drama: Three Conventions Developed by the Women's Theater, At the Foot of the Mountain*. Bowling Green State University, 1984.

William M. Dawson. *The Female Characters of August Strindberg, Eugene O'Neill, and Tennessee Williams*. University of Wisconsin, 1964.

Janet P. Brown. *Feminist Drama: Definition and Critical Analysis*. University of Missouri, 1978.

Dinah L. Leavitt. *Feminist Theatre Groups in America: Four Case Studies*. University of Colorado, 1978.

Beverley Byers Pevitts. *Feminist Thematic Trends in Plays Written by Women for the American Theatre: 1970–1979*. Southern Illinois University at Carbondale, 1980.

Louise Cheryl Mason. *The Fight to Be an American Woman and a Playwright: A Critical History from 1772 to the Present*. University of California, Berkeley, 1983.

Lyn Stiefel Hill. *Heroes, Heroines and Villains in English and American Melodrama: 1850–1900*. City University of New York, 1982.

Georgiana Von Tornow. *The Heroine in American Drama and Theatre Down to the Civil War, and Her Relation to Life and the Novels of the Times*. Cornell University, 1945.

Christine Ruth Birdwell. *Heroines of American Midwestern Repertoire Theatre Comedy-Dramas (Melodrama, Tent Shows, Popular Culture)*. Michigan State University, 1984.

William P. Zahler. *The Husband and Wife Relationship in American Drama from 1919 to 1939*. Kent State University, 1973.

S. H. Regina Turner. *Images of Black Women in the Plays of Black Female Playwrights*. Bowling Green University, 1982.

Ruth B. Manser. *The Influence of the American Actress on the Development of the American Theatre from 1835–1935*. New York University, 1938.

Gary L. Smith. *The International Ladies Garment Workers Union's Labor Stage, A Propagandistic Venture*. Kent State University, 1975.

Terryl Wright Hallquist. *The Makings of a Classical Actress in the Modern Twentieth-Century Western Theatre: A Comparative Study (Frances Hyland, Martha Henry, Rosemary Harris, Zoe Caldwell, Irene Worth)*. University of Michigan, 1985.

Marilyn Baxter. *Modern Woman as Heroine in Representative Plays by S. N. Behrman*. University of Wisconsin, 1973.

Ruth McKenzie. *Organization, Production and Management at the Chestnut Street Theatre, Philadelphia, from 1791–1820*. Stanford University, 1952.

Marjorie Thomas. *An Overview of Miss Anne: White Women as Seen by Black Playwrights*. Florida State University, 1973.

Kathryn Elizabeth Carter. *A Phe-nomenology of Feminist Theatre and Criticism*. Southern Illinois University at Carbondale, 1985.

Charlotte Winburn Macarthur. *Portraitists in Performance—Four Women Originals (Sacchetto, Germany; Guilbert, France; Draper, Enters; United States)*. University of Pittsburgh, 1983.

Pauline W. Schaffer. *The Position of Women in Society as Reflected in Serious American Drama from 1890–1928*. Stanford University, 1966.

James Taliaferro. *The Propagandistic Role of Women in Selected American Plays from 1763 to 1860*. New York University, 1976.

Marilyn Louise Mckay, *The Relationship Between the Female Performer and the Female Character in the American Musical: 1920–1974*. University of Georgia, 1983.

Judith Louise Baxter Olauson. *Representative American Women Playwrights, 1930–1970, and a Study of Their Characters*. University of Utah, 1976.

Jeannine Wilkins. *Robert Anderson's Women: Their Ritual Role*. Ohio State University, 1976.

Gary Sheldon Luter. *Sexual Reform on the American Stage in the Progressive Era, 1900–1915*. University of Florida, 1981.

Helen Russell. *Social Comment as Depicted in the Plays of American Women Dramatists*. University of Denver, 1959.

Debra Gonsher. *Stereotypes of Women in Contemporary American Drama 1958–1978*. City University of New York, 1980.

Sylvia Zastrow. *The Structure of Selected Plays by American Women Playwrights: 1920–1970*. Northwestern University, 1975.

Charles Wiley. *A Study of the American Woman as She Is Presented in the American Drama of the 1920s*. University of New Mexico, 1957.

Joseph Epolito. *A Study of Characters in Selected Plays of William Inge*. Ohio State University, 1974.

Donald Koster. *The Theme of Divorce in American Drama, 1871–1939*. University of Pennsylvania, 1941.

Robert Edward Ericson. *Touring Entertainment in Nevada During the Peak Years of the Mining Boom*. University of Oregon, 1970.

Charlene Edwards. *The Tradition for Breeches in the Three Centuries That Professional Actresses Have Played Male Roles on the English-Speaking Stage*. University of Denver, 1957.

Shirlee Hennigan. *The Woman Direc-*

tor in the Contemporary, Professional Theatre. Washington State University, 1983.
Martin Sidney Tackel. *Women and American Pageantry: 1908 to 1918.* City University of New

York, 1982.
Phyllis Ferguson. *Women Dramatists in the American Theatre 1901–1940.* University of Pittsburgh, 1957.
Nancy Vunovich. *The Women in the*

Plays of Eugene O'Neill. University of Kansas, 1966.

Originally compiled by Caroline J. Dodge Latta; updated by HKC.

SELECTED FILM, VIDEO AND AUDIO RESOURCES

The New York Public Library's Lincoln Center Collection has video recordings of many live New York productions, as well as copies of televised theatre. Advance notice is required for viewing.

1986 *Index Directory of Women's Media,* Martha Leslie Allen, ed. Women's Institute for Freedom of the Press, Washington, DC. Published annually since 1975.
Alternate Currents, c/o Marilyn Rivchin, 107 East Spencer St., Ithaca, NY 14850. Interviews with feminist writers and artists.
Caedmon Records, 1995 Broadway, New York, NY 10023. Titles include: *Lorraine Hansberry Speaks Out, A Raisin in the Sun, To Be Young, Gifted and Black.*
Icarus Films, 200 Park Ave. S., Suite 1319, New York, NY 10003. *Troupers,* documentary of San Francisco Mime Troupe.
Junkie! A film by Martha Boesing and Kathleen Laughlin. At the Foot of the Mountain, Attn: Dorothy Crabb, 2000 South 5th St., Minneapolis, MN 55454.
Lorraine Hansberry in Her Own Words. Seven-hour radio tribute by 61 theatre artists performing

her work. 1967. Pacifica Tape Library, Los Angeles, BB4497.01 and BB5348.02.
Lorraine Hansberry: The Black Experience in the Creation of Drama. 16mm color film. *Films for the Humanities,* P.O. Box 2053, Princeton, NJ 08540.
Paz Press Productions, P.O. Box 3146, Fayetteville, AR 72702. Dramatic reading plus interviews by Juana Maria Paz, with local women.
Phoenix Films, 470 Park Ave. S., New York, NY 10016. Films include *The Girl with the Incredible Feeling* (about Elizabeth Swados), *Helen Hayes, What Are You Woman?* (collage of dramatic scenes about women).
Point of View Productions, 2477 Folsom St., San Francisco, CA 94110. Documentaries, dramatic programs, talk shows. Karil Daniels.
To Be Young, Gifted and Black. 90-minute film produced by

WNET, 1972. Indiana University, Audio-Visual Center, Bloomington, IN 47405.
Video Women, 1150 Greenfield Ave., Pittsburgh, PA 15217. Interviews with feminist writers and artists. Katholeen Kampfe.
The Women's Access Coalition, 6 Bowdoin Park, Dorchester, MA 02122. Catherine Russo.
Women in the Director's Chair, P.O. Box 4044, Chicago, IL 60654. Films and videos of the work of women theatre artists. Nalani McClendon.
Women Make Movies, Inc., 19 West 21st St., 2nd Floor, Box A, New York, NY 10010. Videos include: *Electra Tries to Speak, Lies, Window, Three Story Suite.* M.H. Berg.
Women's Video Collective, P.O. Box 1609, Cambridge, MA 02238.

Deborah Peifer is a theatre doctoral student at Northwestern University.

PLAYLIST

Our compilation of American women playwrights and their plays is a selected guide to hundreds of women and thousands of plays since the beginning of the United States. Included are: published writers (we include all plays by that writer, published or not); writers who've won major prizes or recognition, like the Susan Smith Blackburn Prize or development at the O'Neill conference; writers who've been produced by feminist theatres and/or major not-for-profit Equity companies; and children's plays if significant new work in that literature. We apologize for any mistaken exclusions.

Publication information is either given in full or keyed to the list immediately following this introduction; so, for example, Ruth Wolff's *The Abdication* is followed by (Moore), which means that the reader should refer to Moore in the key to see that the reference is to Honor Moore's anthology.

The playlist is organized alphabetically by author. The plays are listed alphabetically because chronology is too difficult to determine. We provide the following information, when known, on writers and plays: city where writer lives; dates of birth/death; feminist theatre(s) that have produced the writer's work; collaborators; one publication source; date of writing or first production of play if significantly different from date of publication; date of writing of unpublished play; major awards play has won; and other publication sources for the writer's work, as appropriate.

Many plays are published through major catalogue sources. Because of the enormous number of plays by women published in these sources, we do not key the catalogues in this revised playlist. Usually, if we do not show a publication or production source for a writer she is listed in one or more of these catalogues:

Applause Theatre Books, 211 West 71 St., NY, NY 10023.

Baker's Plays, 100 Chauncy St., Boston, MA 02111.

Broadway Play Publishing, 357 West 20th St., NY, NY 10011.

Dramatic Publishing Co., 311 Washington St., Woodstock, IL 60098.

Dramatists Play Service, 440 Park Ave. S., NY, NY 10016.

Performance Publishing Co., 978 North McLean Blvd., Elgin, IL 60120.

Pioneer Drama Service, 2172 South Colorado Blvd., Box 22555, Denver, CO 80222.

Samuel French Publishing Company, 45 West 25 St., NY, NY 10010.

For guidance in finding unpublished plays by black women, please consult James V. Hatch, *Black Image on the American Stage: A Bibliography of Plays and Musicals, 1770–1970*, Drama Book Specialists Publications, 1970; James V. Hatch and OMANii Abdullah, eds., *Black Playwrights, 1823–1977: An Annotated Bibliography of Plays*, Bowker, 1977; Karamu Theatre ms. collection, Cleveland, Ohio; Negro Ensemble Company ms. collection, St. Mark's Place and 2nd Ave., NY; Schomburg Collection of Negro Literature and History, 103 West 135 St., NY; and the Yale Univ. Library, James Weldon Johnson Memorial Collection.

Other useful ms. collections include American Place Theatre, NY; Federal Theatre Project Collection, George Mason Univ.; Harris Collection, Brown Univ.; Library of Congress; Northwestern Univ. Library/Special Collections; Performing Arts Library, Lincoln Center, NY; and the Sophia Smith Collection, Smith College.

KEY

(published in New York City unless otherwise noted)

BAP	*Best American Plays*, series. John Gassner, ed., Crown
BOAP	*Best One Act Plays of 19–*. Margaret Mayorga, ed., Dodd, Mead
BP	*Best Plays of 19–: The Burns Mantle Yearbook*, Dodd, Mead
BSP	*Best Short Plays of 19–*. Stanley Richards, ed., Chilton
NP	*New Plays USA* series, Theatre Communications Group
OOB	*The Off Off Broadway Book*, Albert Poland and Bruce Mailmen, eds., Bobbs Merrill, 1972
POY	John C. Trewin, ed., *Plays of the Year*, several editions, Ungar
PIP	*Plays in Process*, Theatre Communications Group
PT	*Playwrights for Tomorrow*, series. Arthur Ballet, ed., U. of Minn. Press
RAD	*Representative American Dramas, National and Local*, Montrose Jonas Moses, ed., Little, Brown, sev. eds.
RAP	*Representative American Plays*, Arthur Hobson Quinn, ed., Century (Appleton/Century/Crofts), sev. eds.
ROAP	*Representative One-Act Plays by American Authors*, Margaret Mayorga, ed., Little, Brown, 1937
RPAD	*Representative Plays by American Dramatists, from 1765 to the Present Day*, 3 vols., Montrose Jonas Moses, ed., Dutton, 1925; Arno, 1964
The Scene	Series. Stanley Nelson, ed., The Smith, Horizon Press and Drama Book Specialists
VPT	*From Valley Playwrights Theatre*, vol. 1, Susan Vick, ed., Playwrights Press, Amherst, MA
WCP	*West Coast Plays*, P.O. Box 7206, Berkeley, CA 94707
WH	*Women Heroes: Six Short Plays from the Women's Project*, Julia Miles, ed., Applause, 1986
Wordplays	Series, PAJ Publications
WP 1/2	*The Women's Project Anthology*, Julia Miles, ed., vols. 1 (1980)/2 (1984), PAJ Publications
Barlow	Judith Barlow, ed., *Plays by American Women 1900–1930*, Applause, 1985
Benedikt	Michael Benedikt, ed., *Theatre Experiment, 17 Plays*, Doubleday, 1967
Bullins	Ed Bullins, ed., *New Plays from the Black Theatre, 11 Plays*, Bantam, 1969
Childress	Alice Childress, ed., *Black Scenes*, Doubleday, 1971
Clements	Colin Campbell Clements, ed., *Sea Plays*, London, Robert Holden, 1926
Cohen	Helen Louise Cohen, ed., *One-Act Plays by Modern Authors*, Harcourt, 1934
Cordell	Kathrun C. Cordell and William H. Cordell, eds., *The Pulitzer Prize Plays, 1918–1934*, Random House, 1940
Delgado	Ramon Delgado, ed., *Best Short Plays of 1986*, Applause, 1986
France	Rachel France, ed., *A Century of Plays by American Women*, Richards Rosen Press, 1979
Galbraith	Esther E. Galbraith, ed., *Plays without Footlights*, Harcourt, 1945
Hatch	James V. Hatch and Ted Shine, eds., *Black Theatre USA: 45 Plays by Black Americans 1847–1974*, The Free Press, 1974
Hoffman	William Hoffman, ed., *Gay Plays*, Avon, 1979
King	Woodie King and Ron Milner, eds., *Black Drama Anthology*, New American Library, 1971
Koch	Frederick Henry Koch, ed., *Carolina Folk Plays*, Holt, 1941
Kozelka	Paul Kozelka, ed., *Fifteen American One-Act Plays*, Pocket Books, 1961
LaTempa	Susan LaTempa, ed., *New Plays by Women*, Berkeley, Shameless Hussy Press, 1979
Lifton	Betty Jean Lifton, ed., *Contemporary Children's Theatre*, Avon, 1974
Locke	Alain Locke and Montgomery Gregory, eds., *Plays of Negro Life*, Harper, 1927
McDermott	Kate McDermott, ed., *Places, Please*, Aunt Lute Press, 1985

Moore   Honor Moore, ed., *The New Women's Theatre: Ten Plays by Contemporary American Women*, Vintage, 1977

Osborn   M. Elizabeth Osborn, ed., *On New Ground: Contemporary Hispanic-American Plays*, Theatre Communications Group, 1987

Owens   Rochelle Owens, ed., *Spontaneous Combustion: Eight New American Plays*, Winter House, 1972

Parone   Edward Parone, ed., *Collision Course*, Random, 1968

Patterson   Lindsay Patterson, ed., *Black Theatre*, Dodd, 1971

Richardson 1   Willis Richardson and May Miller, eds., *Plays and Pageants from the Life of the Negro*, Washington, Associated Publishers, 1930

Richardson 2   Willis Richardson and May Miller, eds., *Negro History in 13 Plays*, Washington, Associated Publishers, 1935

Sanchez   Sonia Sanchez, ed., *Three Hundred Sixty Degrees of Blackness Comin' at You*, 5X Pub. Co., 1971

Shay 1   Frank Shay and Pierre Loving, eds., *Fifty Contemporary One-Act Plays*, Cincinnati, Stewart Kidd, 1920

Shay 2   Frank Shay, ed., *Fifty More Contemporary One-Act Plays*, Appleton, 1928

Shay 3   Frank Shay, ed., *Twenty Contemporary One-Act Plays (American)*, Cincinnati, Stewart Kidd, 1922

Shay 4   Frank Shay, ed., *A Treasury of Plays for Women*, Little, Brown, 1922

Smith   Betty Smith, ed., *Twenty-Five Non-Royalty One-Act Plays for All Girl Casts*, Greenberg, 1942

Sullivan   Victoria Sullivan and James Hatch, eds., *Plays by and about Women*, Vintage, 1973

Swortzell   Lowell Swortzell, ed., *All the World's a Stage: Modern Plays for Young People*, Delacorte, 1972

Wilkerson   Margaret Wilkerson, ed., *Nine Plays by Black Women*, New American Library, 1986

Joyce Aaron. *Acrobatics* (w Luna Tarlo; WP 1)

Dolores Abramson. *The Light* (Sanchez)

Kathy Acker. *The Birth of the Poet* (Wordplays 5)

Sheila K. Adams. *Melancholy Baby*

Jo Adamson. (The Womyn's Theatre) *Bound in Shallows; Wax Candle*

Dorothy Ahmad. *Papa's Daughter* (*Drama Review* 12(4): Summer 1968)

Gertine Ahrens. *Ah, Togetherness!*

Joan Aiken. *The Mooncusser's Daughter* (Viking, 1974); *Winterthing* (Holt, 1972)

JoAnne Akalaitis, NY. *Dead End Kids: A History of Nuclear Power* (*Theater*, 13, 3, 1982); *Dressed like an Egg* (Wordplays 4)

Zoe Akins (1886–1958). *Another Darling* (1950); *Cake upon the Waters* (The Century Co., 1919); *Daddy's Gone A-Hunting* (Boni and Liveright, 1924); *Declassé* (1919; Boni and Liveright, 1924); *Foot-Loose* (1920); *The Furies* (1928); *Greatness* (Boni and Liveright, 1924); *The Greeks Had a Word for It* (1929); *The Happy Days* (from Claude-Andre Puget; 1941); *The Human Element* (from Maugham; American Play Co., 1948?); *The Little Miracle* (Harper, 1936); *The Magical City* (Forum, 1916); *The Morning Glory;* Mrs. January and Mr. Ex- (1942, as *Plans for Tomorrow*, 1948); *The Old Maid* (from Edith Wharton; Appleton-Century Co., 1935; Pulitzer, 1935); *Papa, An Amorality in Three Acts* (M. Kennedy, NY, 1913); *Portrait of Turo* (1929); *A Royal Fandango* (1924); *Such a Charming Young Man* (1924); *The Swallow's Nest* (1951); *The Texas Nightingale* (see

Greatness; 1922); *Thou Desperate Pilot* (1927); *The Varying Shore* (1921)

Gloria Albee. *Medea* (*Female Studies X*: 1975)

Rose Albert. *Release* (*Four Full-Length Plays*, Hatcher Hughes et al., ed., Appleton, 1928)

Maude M. Aldrich. *Filmy-Cooperation* (Signal Press, 1940's)

Lynne Alvarez. *Graciela; The Guitarron* (Osborn); *Hidden Parts; Latinos; Mundo; Thin Air*

Dorothy Allensworth. *Interurban* (w Carl Allensworth)

Lola E. Amis. (*Three Plays*, NY, Exposition, 1965); *The Deal; The New Nigger or Who's Afraid of William Faulkner* (1975) (Both: *Exploring the Black Experience in America*. Franklin Square, NY, F. Peters, 1976); *Helen; The Other Side of the Wall; Places of Wrath*

Trudy Anderson. (Pagoda Playhouse, 1979) *An Afternoon of S and M; Maraccas; The Weighting Room*

Charlotte Anker. (w Irene Rosenberg) *The Third Child*

Joyce Antler. *Year One of the Empire* (w Elinor Fuchs; Houghton Mifflin, 1973)

Margaret Applegarth. *Were You There?* (*Four Playettes*, NY, Friendship Press, 1956)

Marjorie (M. H.) Appleman, NY. *The Bedroom* (1977); *The Best Is Yet to Be* (1975); *The Commuter* (Confrontation, Long Island Univ., 1985); *Fox Trot on Longboat Bay* (1984); *Intermission* (1985); *Nice Place You Have Here* (1971); *Penelope's Odyssey* (1978); *Seduction Duet* (1982; *Off Off Broadway Festival Plays*, Sixth Series); *Seduction Quartet* (1982); *Space*

(1983); *Thirty-Nine Seconds and Counting* (1983)

Trisha Arlin. (The Womyn's Theatre) *Stifled*

Kay Arthur. *When Altars Burn*

Sandra Fenichel Asher. *Afterthoughts in Eden* (LA Feminist Theatre Publishing, 1974)

Ruth Ashton. *The Sunny Side of the Atom* (BOAP, 1948)

Mary Austin. *The Arrowmaker* (Houghton Mifflin, 1915)

Bobbi Ausubel, Lexington, MA. (Caravan) *Focus on Me!; Fossils, Relics and Other Treasures of Family Life; Tell Me a Riddle* (from Tillie Olsen)

Rietta Winn Bailey. *Mourners to Glory; Washed in the Glory* (1937; Samuel Selden, ed. *International Folk Plays*, U. of No. Carolina Press, 1949)

Doris Baizley, Venice, CA. *Beowulf and the Tapes* (1980); *Bugs* (1976); *Catholic Girls* (1979; WCP 11/12); *A Christmas Carol* (1977); *Concrete Dreams* (1978); *Daniel in Babylon* (1982; WCP 19/20); *Darkest Africa: A Ladies Guide to the Nile* (1972); *Dolls: An Evening with the Women of Jacqueline Susann* (1985); *Guns* (1975); *Lines* (1977); *Mary Dyer Hanged in Boston* (1971); *Mrs. California* (1986); *Nevada 62* (1981); *Orange Trees* (1976)

Andrea Balis. (The Cutting Edge) *Croon* (1978)

Frances Banks. *The Last Leaf*

Kay Bannerman. *All for Mary; Don't Tell Father; Let Sleeping Wives Lie*

Anna Marie Barlow, NY. *Ambassador; The Artists; The Bicycle Riders; Cold Christmas; Cruising Speed 500 MPH; Dance to the El; Ferryboat; The Frizzly Hen; Glory!*

Hallelujah!; Half Past Wednesday; Limb of Snow; The Meeting; Mr. Biggs (Robert Corrigan, ed., *New American Plays*, vol. 1, Hill and Wang, 1965); *On Cobweb Time; Other Voices Other Rooms; Out of Track; Spit in the Ocean; Taffy; Where the Music Is*

Charlotte M. S. Barnes (1818–63). *(Plays, Prose, and Poetry,* 1848, Scholarly Reprint, 1976); *Octavia Bragaldi, or The Confession; The Forest Princess, or, Two Centuries* (1844)

Djuna Barnes. *An Irish Triangle; Kurzy of the Sea; Three from the Earth* (France)

Margaret Ayer Barnes. *Dishonored Lady* (w Edward Sheldon, 1932); *Jenny* (w ES, 1929); *Years of Grace* (Houghton Mifflin, 1931)

Gina Barnett. *Blood Bond* (Delgado)

Madalene Demarest Barnum. *Our Aunt from California*

Betty Barr. *The Good and Obedient Young Man* (1932)

Ramona Bass. (Rites and Reason Theatre, Brown University) *Run the Rail; The I-Run House; To Be a Bethune*

Lucy Bate. *The Great Silkie of Sule Skerry* (Scripts 1(8): June 1972)

Sidney Frances Bateman (1823–81). *Evangeline* (1860); *Geraldine, or Love's Victory* (1859); *Self* (1856; RPAD); *The Golden Calf, or, Marriage a la Mode* (1857; Scholarly Reprints, 1976)

Susan Batson. *Hoodoo Talkin* (1971; Sanchez)

Terry Baum. (Lilith) (Both: McDermott) *Dos Lesbos* (w Carolyn Myers); *Immediate Family;* see Michele Linfante

Marie Baumer. *It's an Ill Wind* (1929)

Eleanor Bayer. *Third Best Sport* (w Leo Bayer)

Mary Hayley Bell. *Duet for Two Hands*

Barbara Benedetti. (The Womyn's Theatre) *De Ja Vu*

Dorothy Bennett. *Fly Away Home* (w Irving White); (all following w Link Hannah) *Lovely Duckling; Sixteen in August; Woman's a Fool to Be Clever* (1938)

Sally Benson. *Memphis-Bound* (w Albert Barker, BP, 1944–45); *Seventeen* (BP, 1951–52); *The Young and the Beautiful*

Shelley Berc. *Burn Out; Dual Heads; Guildford Digs; Lulu* (adaptation); *Shooting Shiva*

Gertrude Berg (1900–66). *Me and Molly* (BP, 1947)

Candice Bergen. *The Freezer* (BSP, 1968)

Julie Berns. *Uncle Willie* (w Irving Ellman)

Mary Fournier Bill. *An Infinite Deal*

of Nothing; The Welcoming

Sallie Bingham, Prospect, KY. (Women's Project) *Couvade* (1983); *In the Presence* (1986); *Milk of Paradise* (1980); *Paducah* (1984); *The Wall Between* (1983)

Jean Ferguson Black. *Penny Wise*

Elizabeth Blake. *The Man Nobody Saw* (Plays for Living Series, Family Service Association of America, 1969)

Lisabeth Blake. *Brewsie and Willie* (w Ellen Violett, from Gertrude Stein)

Margaret Bland. *Land and Larnin'; Lighted Candles* (Koch)

Dorothy Blankfort. *Monique* (w Michael Blankfort)

Rita McDonald Bleiman, Northampton, MA. *Broken Roses; Poker Faces; Walking on Eggshells; What Are Friends For?* (VPT)

Anita Rowe Block. *Love and Kisses* (1964)

Martha Boesing, Minneapolis (At the Foot of the Mountain; some written in group collaboration) *Accent of Fools; Antigone Too: Rites of Love and Defiance* (1983); *Ashes, Ashes We All Fall Down* (1982); *Dora Du Fran's Wild West Extravaganza or The Real Low Down on Calamity Jane* (1979); *Earth Song* (1970); *The Gelding* (1974); *Journey to Canaan* (1974); *Junkie!; Labia Wings* (1979); *The Last Fire: An Illumination* (1981); *Love Song for An Amazon* (1976); *Mad Emma* (1976); *The Moontree* (1976); *The Mothers of Ludlow* (1983); *Pimp* (1973); *Prehistoric Visions for Revolting Hags* (1979); *Raped: A Woman's Look at Brecht's The Exception and The Rule* (1976/87); *River Journal* (1975); *Song for Johanna* (1981); *The Story of a Mother* (1977/87); *Trespasso* (1977); *The Wanderer* (1969); *The Web* (1981; PIP)

Karen Boetcher-Tate. *Evensong*

Bridget Boland. *Cockpit* (POY, 1948–49); *Gordon* (POY, 1951–52); *The Prisoner* (POY, 1953–54); *The Return* (POY, 1953); *The Zodiac in the Establishment* (Evans, 1963)

Ludmilla Bollow, Milwaukee. *The Beach Club; Between the Dark and the Daylight; Children of the Universe; Choke Cherry Corners—Tavern & Dance Hall* (1985); *Dr. Zastro's Sanatorium for the Ailments of Women—Mental, Physical & Sexual; The Golden Gate Bridge; Harper's Bizarre!; In the Rest Room at Rosenbloom's; King of the Beach; Late/Late—Computer Date!; Martha's Boy; Paper Houses; Royal Americans; St. Francis; The Silvery Spangly Summer; The Smile on the Kewpie Doll; Where*

Have All the Flowers Gone?; Where It Stops, Nobody Knows

Marita O. Bonner. *Exit an Illusion* (Crisis 36 (10): Oct. 1929); *The Pot-Maker* (Opportunity 5 (2): Feb. 1927); *The Purple Flower* (Crisis 35 (1): Jan. 1928)

Sue Booker. *The Flags* (Cry at Birth, M. D. Booker, ed., McGraw-Hill, 1971)

Julie Bovasso, NY. *Down by the River Where the Waterlilies Are Disfigured Every Day* (1972); *El Rancho del Rey; The Final Experiment; Gloria and Esperanza* (1968; OOB; Obie); *Monday On the Way to Mercury Island* (1971); *The Moon Dreamers* (1967); *The Nothing Kid* (1974); *Schubert's Last Serenade* (1971; Owens); *Standard Safety* (1976; BSP); *Super Lover, Schubert's Serenade, and the Final Analysis* (1975)

Jane Bowles (1917–73). *At the Jumping Bean* (1955; *Feminine Wiles*, Black Sparrow, 1976); *In the Summer House* (Collected Works, Farrar Straus, 1966)

Frances Bowyer. *Shadow of a Cross*

Neith Boyce. *Two Sons* (1910's); *Winter's Night* (France)

Julianne Boyd. *A . . . My Name Is Alice* (w Joan Micklin Silver)

Susan Boyd. *St. Mael and the Maldunkian Penguins* (LaTempa)

Mary Boylan. *Curley McDimple*

Joan Brampton. *Dilemma*

Dorothy Brandon. *The Outsider*

Esther M. Broner. *Summer Is a Foreign Land* (Wayne State Univ. Press, 1966)

Eleanor Brooke. see Jean Kerr

Charlotte Brooks. *Firm Foundations* (Negro History Bulletin, 1954)

Brigid Brophy. *The Burglar* (Holt, 1967); *The Waste-Disposal Unit* (Best Short Plays of World Theatre, 1968–73, Crown, 1973)

Alice Brown. *Children of Earth: A Play of New England* (Macmillan, 1915); *Sugar House* (1916)

Annie K. Brown. *Voice on Wire* (Counselor Print, 1919)

Sonia Brown. *Strange Rain* (BOAP, 1945)

Alice Browne and W. Gault. *Mr. Butte from Montana* (Clyde, Ohio, Ames Publishing Co., 1903)

Felicity Browne. *Family Dance*

Nancy Buell. see Deborah Fortson

Katherine S. Burgess. *Duetto* (1927)

France Burke, NY. (POW; Women's Project) *Minehill* (1977); *The New World Monkey* (1978); *The Invisible Fire* (1979); *Haze* (1980); *Virginia & Vanessa* (1980); *Tough Turkey* (1981); *Christmas Cover* (1982); *The Totem Meal* (1983); *Will O' the Wisp* (1984); *The*

Housesitters (1985); *Ruby's Place* (1986)

Barbara Burnham. *Girls in Uniforms*

Inez Burke. *Two Races* (Richardson 1)

Frances Hodgson Burnett. *Little Lord Fauntleroy* (1889)

Sophy Burnham. *The Art Crowd* (McKay, 1973)

Anne Burr. *Huui Huui* (1968); *Mert and Phil* (1974); *Solid State*

Mary Burrill. *Aftermath* (France); *They That Sit in Darkness* (1919)

Ida M. Buxton. *Tit for Tat* (Clyde, Ohio, A. D. Ames, 1884)

Ann Caldwell. *The Magnolia Lady* (BP, 1924–25)

Mary C. Canfield. *The Duchess Says Her Prayers* (Shay 2)

Alice Cannon. *Great Day in the Morning* (1962)

Vinnette Carroll. see Micki Grant

Beatrix Carter. *All Set for Murder*

Stephanie Caruana. *The Rip-Off* (West Coast Women Publishing Co., 1972)

Rosemary Casey. *Late Love, Velvet Glove*

Vera Caspary. *Laura* (w George Sklar, 1945)

Mary Lou Cassidy. *A Penny Friend* (w Ed Graczyk)

Marisha Chamberlain, St. Paul, MN. (Theater Three; Women's Project) *Aviation* (1982); *Desert in Flower* (1981); *Little Women* (1986); *The Nightingale* (1984); *Miracle Gardening* (1985); *Scheherazade* (1984, BP); *Slumming* (1985); *Snow in the Virgin Islands* (1982); *Stargazer* (1980); *Those Who Favor Fire* (1980); *Willa* (1983); *Winter Camera* (1982)

Jane Chambers. (Women's Interart) *Deadly Nightshade; Eye of the Gull; Kudzu; Last Summer at Bluefish Cove*; *A Late Snow* (William Hoffman, ed., *Gay Plays: The First Collection*, Avon, 1979); *My Blue Heaven*

Martie Charles. *Black Cycle* (King); *Job Security* (1970)

Monica Jane Charles. *Yanowis* (*The Indian Historian* 4(3):44–51, Fall 1971)

Mary Coyle Chase (1907–81). *Bernardine* (BP; 1952); *Cocktails with Mimi* (1973); *The Dog Sitters* (children's play, 1963); *Harvey* (BP; Pulitzer, 1945); *Loretta Mason Potts* (1958); *Mickey* (with puppets, 1968); *Midgie Purvis* (1961); *Mrs. McThing* (BP; 1951); *Now You've Done It* (1937); *The Prize Play* (1961); *Too Much Business* (1938); *The Wicked Pigeon Ladies in the Garden* (1968)

Alice Childress. *The African Garden* (Childress); *Florence* (1950); *Gold Through the Trees* (1952); *Let's*

Hear It for the Queen (children's play, Coward, 1976); *Martin Luther King at Montgomery, Alabama; Mojo* (*Best Short Plays of the World Theatre, 1968–73*, Chilton, 1974); *String* (1969); *Trouble in Mind* (1955; Lindsay Patterson, ed., *Black Theatre*, Dodd, 1971); *Wedding Band* (1966; Wilkerson); *When the Rattlesnake Sounds* (Coward, 1975); *Wine in the Wilderness* (Sullivan); *The World on a Hill* (*Plays to Remember*, Macmillan, 1968)

Elinor Chipp. *The Honor and the Glory* (1949)

Charlotte Chorpenning. (Children's Theatre Press—C) *Abe Lincoln—New Salem Days* (Coach House Press, Chicago, 1954); *Adventures of Tom Sawyer* (1946); *Alice in Wonderland* (1946); *Cinderella* (C, 1940); *The Emperor's New Clothes* (1932); *Flibberty Gibbet* (C, 1952); *Hans Brinker and the Silver Skates* (C, 1938); *The Indian Captive* (C, 1937); *Jack and the Beanstalk* (C, 1935); *James Thurber's Many Moons* (1946); *Lincoln's Secret Messenger* (Coach House Press, 1955); *Little Black Sambo and the Tigers* (w Shirley Graham Du Bois, 1938); *Little Red Riding Hood* (C, 1946); *The Prince and the Pauper* (1938); *Radio Rescue* (1938); *Rama and the Tigers* (Coach House Press, 1954); *The Return of Rip Van Winkle* (1938); *Rhodopes, the First Cinderella* (1936); *Robinson Crusoe* (C, 1952); *Rumplestiltskin* (C, 1944); *The Secret Weapon* (N.E.A., Washington, D.C., 1944); *Sleeping Beauty* (C,, 1947); *The Three Bears* (C, 1949); *Tom Sawyer's Treasure Hunt* (1937)

Dorothy Christie. *His Excellency* (POY, 1951); *Touch of Fear* (w Campbell Christie)

Paula Cizmar, Hollywood, CA. (Women's Project; Women's Theatre Project of Minnesota) *Al's Lunchette*Stationers*Drink Coca Cola* (1985); *Apocryphal Stories, Exceptional Friends* (1984); *Cafe Odessa* (1985); *Candy & Shelley Go to the Desert* (1984; WP 2); *Cupcakes* (1981); *The Death of a Miner* (1982); *The Girl Room* (Poet's Theatre, Ailanthus Press, 1981); *The Legend of the Ice Birds* (1985); *Madonna of the Powder Room* (1983); *You Can't Always Get What You Want* (1986)

Patricia Clapp. *A Candle on the Table*

China Clark. *The Chinese Screen; In Sorrow's Room* (Era, Box 1829, G.P.O., New York, NY 10011); *Neffie* (Era); *Profection in Black* (*Scripts* 1(7), 1972)

Sylvia Clarke. *Rosie at the Train* (*On the Air: 15 Plays for Broadcast and for Classroom Use*, ed. Garrett Leverton, French, 1944)

Pearl Cleage. *Essentials; Good News; Hospice; Puppetplay*

Susan Clement. *Foodfright* (w Barbara Harrington)

Dorothy Clifford. *December Seventh* (Smith)

Margaret Ellen Clifford (1908–71). *The Secret of the Worn-Out Shoes; Sleeping Beauty; see Hallie Flanagan*

Darrah Cloud, NY. *The House Across the Street; The Mud Angel; The Stick Wife*

Lenore Coffee. *Family Portrait* (W. J. Cowen, 1938–39)

Gertrude Coffin. *Plays* (Koch)

Kathleen Collins, Upper Nyack, NY. (Women's Project) *Begin the Beguine* (1984); *The Brothers* (1982, Wilkerson); *The Reading* (1984); *In the Midnight Hour* (1978; WP 1); *Only the Sky Is Free* (1985); *While Older Men Speak* (1986)

Betty Comden. (w Adolph Green) *Applause* (Random House, 1971; Tony); *Bells Are Ringing* (Random House, 1957); *Billion Dollar Baby* (1945); *Bonanza Bound* (Crawford Music, 1947); *Hallelujah Baby!* (1968; Tony); *On the Town; On the Twentieth Century; A Party with Betty Comden and Adolph Green* (1959; Obie); *Peter Pan; Singin' in the Rain* (Loew's, 1952); *Wonderful Town* (1953; Tony); (see *Comden and Green on Broadway*, Drama Book Specialists, 1980)

Anne Commire, Waterford, CT. *Melody Sisters* (1983); *Put Them All Together* (1978); *Shay* (1973)

Constance Congdon, Longmeadow, MA. *Boarders: Three Short Plays with an Epilogue by the Landlady; The Bride; A Conversation with Georgia O'Keeffe; Fourteen Brilliant Colors; The Gilded Age* (after Mark Twain); *Gilgamesh; Native American; No Mercy* (PIP); *Phantomnation* (w Bennett Cohen and Mac Wellman); *Raggedy Ann and Andy; Tales of the Lost Formicans*

Louise Conkling. *Let 'em Eat Steak*

Alice Carter Cook. *Komateekay* (Bruce Humphries, Inc., Boston, 1936)

Cynthia L. Cooper, NY. (Women's Project; Women's Theatre Project of Minnesota) *Dirty Laundry* (1982); *Fox and Hounds* (1983); *How to Be a Bum* (1983); *How She Played the Game* (1986; WH); *The Light Before Christmas* (1983); *New Friends* (1986); *Reachin'* (1986); *Peripheral Vision* (1986); *Sisters of Sisters* (1984)

Susan Cooper. *Foxfire* (w Hume Cronyn)

Clare Coss, NY. (Women's Experimental Theatre) *Daughters* (w Sondra Segal and Roberta Sklar); (*Massachusetts Review* 24, 1, 1983); *Lillian Wald: At Home on Henry Street*

Sada Cowan (d. 1943). *Auf Wiedersehen* (1930's; France); *In the Morgue* (1920; Shay 1); *Sintram of Skagerrak* (1917; ROAP)

Constance Cox. *Miss Letitia*

Myrtle Crawford. *Negro Builds a Pyramid* (*Social Studies* 32, Jan. 1941)

Rachel Crothers (1878–1958). (*Six One-Act Plays by Rachel Crothers*, Walter N. Baker, Boston, 1925— S; *Three Plays*, Brentano's, 1923—T3; *Three Plays*, Brentano's, 1924—T4) *As Husbands Go* (BP, 1930); *The Coming of Mrs. Patrick*; *Criss-Cross* (1930's, France); *Expressing Willie* (T4); *He and She* (1911, RAP); *The Heart of Paddy Whack*; *The Importance of Being Clothed* (S); *The Importance of Being Married* (S); *The Importance of Being Nice* (S); *The Importance of Being a Woman* (S); *Katy Did*; *A Lady's Virtue*; *Let Us Be Gay*; *A Little Journey* (T3); *A Man's World* (Barlow); *Mary the Third* (T3); *Myself-Bettina*; *Nice People* (T4); *Old Lady 31* (T3); *Once Upon a Time*; *Ourselves*; *Peggy* (S); *Pollyanna*; *The Rector* (1902); *Susan and God* (1937); *The Three of Us* (1906); *Venue* (1927); *What They Think* (S); *When Ladies Meet* (1932); *Young Wisdom*; *39 East* (T4)

Julie Beckett Crutcher. *Approaching Lavendar*

Gretchen Cryer. (all w Nancy Ford) *Hanging On to the Good Times* (1987); *I'm Getting My Act Together and Taking It on the Road*; *The Last Sweet Days of Isaac* (Obie, 1970); *Now Is the Time for All Good Men*; *Shelter*

Maud Cuney-Hare, *Antar of Araby* (1929, Richardson 1)

Jane Curtin. *Pretzels* (w Fred Gandy and Judy Kahan)

Catherine Chisholm Cushing. *Pollyanna* (from Porter)

Barbara Damashek. see Molly Newman

Clemence Dane. *Adam's Opera*; *Bill of Divorcement* (1921); *For Katharine Cornell*; *Granite* (Samuel Marion Tucker, ed., *Modern American and British Plays*, Harper, 1931); *Mariners*; *Naboth's Vineyard* (1926); *The Way Things Happen*; *Wild December* (1932); *Will Shakespeare*

Barbara Daniel. *Bathrains*

Gwen Davenport. *The Bachelor's Baby*; *Belvedere*

Mary Carolyn Davies. *The Slave with Two Faces* (1918; Shay 1)

Katherine Dayton. *First Lady* (w George S. Kaufman, Random House, 1935); *Loose Leaves* (Doubleday, 1923); *Save Me a Waltz* (1937)

Sandra De Helen (formerly McCorkle). see Kate Kasten

Vina Delmar. *Midsummer*; *Rich Full Life*; *Warm Wednesday*

Donna de Matteo, NY. *Almost on a Runway*; *Animal Lovers*; *The Barbecue Pit* (1969); *The Flip Side*; *The Paradise Kid*; *Rocky Road*; *The Silver Fox*

Alexis De Veaux, NY. *Circles* (1973); *No* (w Glenda Dickerson, 1981); *A Season to Unravel* (1979); *The Tapestry* (1976; Wilkerson)

Elaine Denholtz. *The Highchairs*

Priscilla B. Dewey, Millis, MA. *Dearo Family* (w David Downing and Tom Megan, 1979); *King Arthur's Knights and Days* (w Tony Hutchins, 1972); *The Mouse in the White House* (1970); *Pied Piper* (w TH, 1975); *Prime Time* (1971); *Rip's New Wrinkle* (1972); *To Find a Rose* (w TH, 1978); *Two if by Sea* (w TH, 1970); *The Unsinkable Helen of Troy* (1970); *Young Country* (w TH, 1975)

Glenda Dickerson, NY. (Women's Interart) *Every Step I Take*; *The Golden Stool*; *Jesus Christ, Lawd Today*; *Jump at the Sun* (from Zora Neale Hurston); *Magic and Lions* (from Ernestine Jackson); *No* (from Alexis DeVeaux, 1981); *Owen's Song* (w Mike Malone); *Praise Singer*; *Tale of Madame Zora*; *Tar Baby*; *The Unfinished Song*; *Winti Train*

Elizabeth Diggs, NY. *Close Ties* (Fireside Book Club, 1981); *Dumping Ground* (1981); *Goodbye Freddy* (1983)

Dorothy Dinroe. *Ododo* (with Joseph Walker, 1968)

Beulah Marie Dix. *The Road to Yesterday*

Helen Dortch. *Companion Mate Maggie* (*Carolina Folk Comedies*, French, 1931)

Felicity Douglas. *According to the Evidence*; *Alibi for a Judge*; *It's Never Too Late*

Jeannette Dowling. *The Young Elizabeth* (POY, 1951–52)

Laura Downing. *Defending the Flag*; *or the Message Boy* (A. D. Ames Publishing Co., Clyde, Ohio, 1894)

Olive Tilford Dragan. *The Woods of Ada* (*Century* 74, Aug. 1907)

Jane Dransfield (1875–1955). *Blood of*

Kings (*The American Scene*, Clark & Nicholson, ed., D. Appleton & Co., 1930); *The Lost Pleiad* (1910; Shay 4)

Ida Drapkin. *Lucy* (Smith)

Mary Drayton. *The Playroom* (Random House, 1966)

Sarah Dreher, Amherst, MA. *Alumnae News, The Doris Day Years* (1986); *Backward, Turn Backward* (1984); *Base Camp* (1983); *Hollandia '45* (1983); *Ruby Christmas* (1981; McDermott); *8x10 Glossy* (1985; McDermott)

Rosalyn Drexler, NY. (Omaha Magic Theatre) *The Bed Was Full*; *Delicate Feelings* (1984); *Graven Image* (1980); *Home Movies* (1964, Obie); *Hot Buttered Roll* (1966); *The Ice Queen* (1965); *The Investigation* (1966); *The Line of Least Existence* (1964); *The Mandrake* (1983); *A Matter of Life and Death* (1986); *Room 17C* (1984); *She Who Was He* (1974); *Skywriting* (Parone); *Softly* (1964); *Consider the Nearness* (1964); *Starburn and the Story of Jenni Love* (1983); *Transients Welcome* (1985; Obie); *Travesty Parade* (1974); *Vulgar Lives* (1979); *The Writer's Opera* (1979; Obie); (see *The Line of Least Existence and Other Plays*, Random House, 1967)

Shirley Graham Du Bois (also Shirley Graham). *Coal Dust* (1930); *Dust to Earth* (c 1940); *Elijah's Ravens* (c 1930); *I Gotta Home* (1939); *It's Morning* (c 1940); *The Swing Mikado* (1938); *Tom-Tom* (1932); *Track Thirteen* (Expression Co., Boston, 1940); see Charlotte Chorpenning

Maureen Duffy. *Capital* (Braziller, 1976); *Rites* (Sullivan)

Louisa Duls. *Lighted Candles* (Koch)

Daphne Du Maurier. *Rebecca*; *September Tide* (V. Gollancz, 1949)

Alice Dunbar-Nelson. *The Author's Evening at Home* (*The Smart Set*, Sept. 1900); *Mine Eyes Have Seen* (1918)

Thelma Myrtle Duncan. *The Scarlet Shawl*; *Black Magic* (*The Yearbook of Short Plays*, 1st series, Wise and Snook, ed., Row Peterson, 1931); *The Death Dance* (Locke); *Sacrifice* (Richardson 1)

Andrea Dworkin. (Encompass Theatre) *A Girl Starts Out . . . with George Eliot*

Susan Dworkin. *The Farm Bill*; *Galilee*; *Mama's God of Love*; *The Miami Dog*; *Picking Up Pieces*; *The Public Good*; *Roses*

Fay Ehlert. *The Undercurrent* (1929)

Ida L. Ehrlich. *Changing Places*; *Winners All* (Shay 2)

Deborah Eisenberg. *Pastorale*

Susan Eisenberg, Jamaica Plain,

MA. (Word of Mouth) *Calamity Jane! Tales of a Preacher's Daughter Who Ran Away from Home First Chance She Got* (1978); *Me!* (1984); *Mother Country* (1986); *We're All Gonna Die Someday Anyway* (1982); *Why Don't You Find a Rich Guy and Marry Him?* (1980)

Edith Ellis. *Adventure; Because I Love You; Ben of Broken Bow* (1925); *Betty's Last Bet* (T. S. Denison, Chicago, 1921); *Bravo Claudia; Captives; Cleopatra; Contrary Mary* (1912); *The Devil's Garden* (1913); *Fields of Flax; If You Think It's So, It's So* (w Oliver Erlan); *The Illustrious Tartaria* (Rosenfield, 1922); *The Judsons Entertain* (1922); *The Lady of La Paz; The Last Chapter; The Last of the Crusoes* (w Robert Sneddon); *Love in Danger* (1910's); *The Love Wager; Madame Is Amused* (1933); *Make Your Fortune; Making Dick Over; The Man Higher Up; Mary and John; Mary Jane's Pa* (M. Kennerly, 1914); *The Moon and Sixpence* (from Maugham; see also her play *Strickland*, 1923); *The Mothers* (1910; France); *Mrs. B. O'Shaughnessy; Mrs. Jimmie Thompson* (w Norman Rose); *My Man; Never Too Late; New Wine; Open the Door* (Knopf, 1935); *The Pixy* (1910's); *The Point of View; Seven Sisters* (from Herzog, 1938); *Sonya; Storms on the Equator; The Subjection of Kezia* (1910; Shay 2); *We Knew These Men* (Knopf, 1942); *White Collars* (1926); *The White Villa; Whose Little Bride Are You?* (Denison, 1919); *Women; The Wrong Man*

Lizzie May Elwyn. *Millie the Quadroon; or Out of Bondage* (A. D. Ames, Clyde, Ohio, 1888)

Eve Ensler. (Women's Interart) *The Depot*

Angna Enters. *Love Possessed Juana* (Queen of Castile) (Twice a Year Press, New York, 1939)

Phoebe Ephron. (w Henry Ephron) *Howie; My Daughter, Your Son; Take Her, She's Mine; Three's a Family*

Raima Evan, NY. *Goodnight Firefly Ravine* (*Dramatics Magazine*, Sept. 1986)

Dorothy Evans. *June Dawn* (w John Ware)

Margaret Evans. *Faith* (*Poet Lore* 33, Spring 1922)

Victoria Nancy Fales. see Nancy Fales Garrett

Laura Farabough, Sausalito, CA. *Femme Fatale: The Invention of Personality; Liquid Distance/Timed Approach* (1984); *Obedience*

School; Surface Tension* (WCP 11/12); *Under Construction*

Margaretta Bleecker Faugeres. *Belisarius: A Tragedy* (T & J Swords, 1795)

Mary Feldhaus-Weber. *Annie's Dead; Frog Frog; Prodigal* (*Minnesota Review 7*); *The Royal Flesh; The Virgin, The Lizard, and The Lamb* (James Laughlin, ed., *New Directions in Prose and Poetry*, New Directions, 1968); *The World Tipped Over and Laying on Its Side* (1967; PT, vol. 4)

Edna Ferber (1885–1968). *Bravo; Dinner at Eight* (w George S. Kaufman; Doubleday, 1932); *The Eldest* (1919; France); *The Land Is Bright; Minick* (w GSK; 1925); *The Royal Family* (w GSK; Doubleday, 1928); *Stage Door*

Ada Reed Ferguson. *Yesterday, Today and Tomorrow* (1930's; Signal Press, no date)

Peggy Fernway. *The Glamour Girl*

Barbara Field, Minneapolis. *Camille* (from Dumas fils, 1980); *A Christmas Carol* (from Dickens, 1975); *Coming of Age* (1980); *El Capitan* (G. Shirmer); *Great Expectations* (from Dickens, 1983); *The Late Show; Marriage* (from Gogol, 1978); *Materia Medica* (1971); *Matrix* (1974); *Monsieur de Moliere* (from Bulgakov, 1979); *Neutral Countries* (1983); *Pantagleize* (from Gheldorode, 1977); *Pen* (1979); *Playground; Quality Time* (1986); *The Renaissance of Barnabe Barnes* (1973); *The Renaissance Man* (1984); *She Sells Sea Shells; Townfolk* (from Gorki, 1982); *Trip* (1975); *Rosina* (1980); *Visiting Angels* (1973); *Winds of Change* (1976)

Rachel Lyman Field (1894–1942). *The Bad Penny* (1931); *Cinderella Married; Columbine in Business; The Fifteenth Candle* (1921); *The Londonderry Air; The Patchwork Quilt; Theories and Thumbs; Three Pills in a Bottle; Wisdom Teeth* (see *Three Plays*, Scribner's, 1924)

Dorothy Fields (lyricist and librettist). *Annie Get Your Gun* (w Herbert Fields, 1946); *Arms and the Girl* (w HF and Rouben Mamoulien, 1950); *Blackbirds of 1928* (w Lew Leslie); *By the Beautiful Sea* (w HF, 1954); *Hello, Daddy* (1928); *The International Revue* (1930); *Let's Face It* (w HF, 1941); *Mexican Hayride* (w HF, 1944); *Redhead* (w HF and Sidney Sheldon, 1959; Tony); *Rhapsody in Blue* (1931); *Seesaw* (1973); *Shoot the Works* (1931); *Singin' the Blues* (1931); *Something for the Boys* (w HF, 1943);

Stars in Your Eyes (w HF, 1939); *Sugar Babies; Sweet Charity* (w Neil Simon, 1966); *A Tree Grows in Brooklyn* (1951); *Up in Central Park* (w HF, 1945); *The Vanderbuilt Revue* (1930)

Louisa May Fields. *Twelve Years a Slave* (1897)

Maxine Wood Finsterwald. *May Moon; On Whitman Avenue* (1946)

Ann Flagg, *Great Gettin' Up Mornin'* (1964)

Hallie Flanagan (Davis) (1890–1969). *Can You Hear Their Voices* (w Margaret Ellen Clifford, 1931; *The Curtain*; $E = mc^2$

Hildegard Flanner. *Mansions* (Shay 1)

Lucille Fletcher. *The Hitch-Hiker* (1943); *Night Watch* (1922); *Sorry, Wrong Number* (1948)

Anne Crawford Flexner. *Aged 26; All Souls Eve; The Blue Pearl; A Lucky Star; The Marriage Game* (B. W. Huebsch, 1916); *Miranda of the Balcony* (G. W. Kauser, NY, 1901); *Mrs. Wiggs of the Cabbage Patch* (1924)

Harriet French Ford (1869–1949). *Are Men Superior?* (1932); *Audrey* (1903); *The Bride* (1924); *Christopher Rand* (w Mrs. August Belmont, 1929); *The Dummy* (1925); *The Durni Afflatus* (1931); *The Fourth Estate* (w Joseph M. Patterson, 1919); *A Gentleman of France* (1902); *The Greatest Thing in the World* (w Beatrice de Mille, 1900); *The Happy Hoboes* (1928); *Heroic Treatment* (1933); *In the Next Room* (w Elenor Robson, 1925); *The Land of the Free* (w Fannie Hurst, 1919); *A Little Brother of the Rich* (w JMP, 1919); *Youth Must Be Served* (1926); (following w Harvey O'Higgins) *The Argyle Case* (1927); *The Dickey Bird* (1925); *Main Street; Mr. Lazarus* (1926); *Old P. Q.* (1928); *On the Hiring Line* (1923); *Orphan Aggie* (1927); *Polygamy* (1921); *When a Feller Needs a Friend* (1921)

Ruth Ford. *Requiem for a Nun* (1959, w William Faulkner, Random House, 1959)

Joanne Forman, Taos. (The Migrant Theater) *Daisies; Polly Baker*

Maria Irene Fornes, NY. *Abingdon Square* (1987); *The Annunciation* (1967); *Aurora* (1974); *Baboon!!!* (1972); *Cap-a-Pie* (1975); *Cold Air* (from Virgilio Piñera; NP3); *The Conduct of Life* (1985; Obie); *The Curse of the Langston House; The Danube* (1983; Obie); *Dr. Kheal* (1968; France); *Drowning* (Orchards, Knopf, 1986); *Evelyn Brown* (A Diary); *Fefu and Her*

Friends (Wordplays 1); *Eyes of the Harem* (1979); *Lovers and Keepers* (1986; PIP); *Molly's Dream* (1968; OOB); *The Mothers* (1987); *Mud* (1984; Obie); *The Office* (1964); *Oscar and Berta* (1987; Osborn); *Promenade* (1965; Obie); *The Red Burning Light, or Mission XQ3* (1968); *Sarita* (1982; Obie); *The Successful Life of 3* (1965; PT 2; Obie); *Tango Palace* (1963; PT 2); *A Visit* (1981); *A Vietnamese Wedding* (1967); *The Widow* (published as *La Viuda*, in *Cuatro Autores Cubanos*, Havana, Casa del las Americas, 1961); (see *Maria Irene Fornes, Promenade & Other Plays*, Winter House, 1971/PAJ Publications, 1987; and *Marie Irene Fornes: Plays*, PAJ Publications, 1986)

Deborah Fortson, Brookline, MA. (Commonplace Pageant; Mermaid Theater) *Baby Steps* (1985); *Baggage* (1976); *Mermaids* (1978); *Vagabond Skin* (1987)

Sister Mary Francis. *La Madre; The Smallest of All*

Caroline Francke, *Exceeding Small; Father of the Bride* (from Edward Streeter); *The Fighting Littles* (from Booth Tarkington); *The 49th Cousin* (w Florence Lowe)

Florence K. Frank. *The Home for the Friendly* (Shay 2)

Doris Frankel. *Journey for an Unknown Soldier* (1940's; France); *Love Me Long* (1949)

Rose D. Franken. *Another Language* (1931; BP); *Claudia* (Farrar and Rinehart, 1941); *Doctors Disagree; The Hallams* (1947); *Outrageous Fortune* (1943; BP); *Soldier's Wife* (1944; BP)

J. e Franklin. *Black Girl* (1969); *Cut Out the Lights and Call the Law; First Step to Freedom* (1964); *Four Women; The In-Crowd* (1965); *Mau-Mau Room* (1972); *The Prodigal Sister* (1974, w Micki Grant); *Two Flowers*

Carol Freeman. *The Suicide* (LeRoi Jones and Larry Neal, eds., *Black Fire*, Morrow, 1968).

Ketti Frings. *Look Homeward Angel* (BAP; Pulitzer, 1958); *The Long Dream* (1960; BP); *Mr. Sycamore; Walking Happy* (w Roger Hirshon)

Elinor Fuchs. see Joyce Antler

Martha Ayers Fuentes. *Go Stare at the Moon; Mama Don't Make Me Go to College, My Head Hurts; Two Characters in Search of an Agreement* (Contemporary Drama Service)

Enid Futterman (lyricist and librettist). *An Open Window; Portrait of Jennie* (from Robert Nathan, w Dennis Rosa, 1982; Richard Rodgers Award); *Yours, Anne* (from Anne Frank, 1985)

Sophie Gage. *These Golden Days*

Esther E. Galbraith. *The Brink of Silence* (1917; Clements)

Zona Gale (1874–1938). *Faint Perfume* (1923); *Miss Lulu Bett* (Barlow; Pulitzer, 1921); *Mr. Pitt* (1924); *The Neighbors* (1914; Kozelka)

Mary Gallagher. *Buddies; Chocolate Cake; Dog Eat Dog; Father Dreams; Fly Away Home; How to Say Goodbye* (Blackburn Prize); *Little Bird;* see Ara Watson

Terry Galloway, Austin, TX. *Heart of a Dog* (WP 2)

Becky Gardiner. *Damn Your Honor* (1929, w Bayard Veiller; BP)

Dorothy Gardner. *Eastward in Eden* (1947–48; BP)

Nancy Fales Garrett (aka Victoria Nancy Fales), Delhi, NY. (Women's Project) *Ark* (1975); *The Baby Sitter; Casserole: An Illusion* (1974); *The City and the Self; Damaging Evidence; A Harvard Man; How They Made It* (1969); *Indianhead* (1979); *Nicole Willing* (1978); *The Orchard; Passion and Garbage; Playing in Local Bands* (1982); *Predicates: A Dance* (1971); *Refracted Light; The Secret Life of Women* (1984); *Some Sweet Day* (1985); *Surviving Death in Three Acts* (1973); *Travel: Long Distance* (1983); *Zone of Middle Dimensions* (1977)

Barbara Garson, NY. *The Co-op* (1971); *The Department* (1983); *The Dinosaur Door* (1976; Obie); *F.T.A.* (w Fred Gardner, Herb Gardner, Jules Feiffer, et al., 1971); *MacBird* (1966, Grove Press); *Take Care, Take Care* (w Lou Coles, Ossie Davis, Micki Grant, 1981); *You Gotta Be Kidding*

Ellen Gruber Garvey. *Soup* (McDermott)

(Mary) Eleanor Gates. *Apronstrings* (1918); *Darling of the World* (1922); *Fire* (1927); *Fish-Bait* (1928); *Memories* (1933, w Laughton George); *Out of the West* (1924); *The Poor Little Rich Girl* (The Arrow Publishing Co., 1916); *The Twinkling of an Eye* (1934); *We Are Seven* (1913)

Alice Gerstenberg. *Ever Young* (1920; Shay 3); *A Patroness* (1917; Shay 3); *Tuning In* (1931; ROAP); (all following in *Ten One-Act Plays*, Brentano's, 1921); *Attuned; Beyond; Fourteen; He Said and She Said; Heart; The Illuminati in Drama Libre; Overtones* (1913; Sullivan); *The Pot Boiler* (1916); *Time for Romance; The Unseen* (see *Comedies All, Short Plays by Alice Gerstenberg*, Longmans

Green, 1930)

Elizabeth Gibson. (w C. B. Gilford) *The Blackboard Jungle; Widow's Mite*

Martha Norwood Gibson. *Will the Ladies Please Come to Order*

P. J. Gibson, NY. *Brown Silk and Magenta Sunsets* (1985; Wilkerson); *Long Time Since Yesterday*

Ilsa Gilbert, NY. (Eccentric Circles) *The Black Carousel* (1979); *Berlin Blues* (1982); *The Bundle Man* (1967); *Circus* (1972); *The Dead Dentist* (1968); *A Dialogue between Didey Warbucks and Mama Vaseline* (1970); *The First Word* (1983); *Little Onion Annie* (1973); *The Many Faces of Eve* (1981); *Pardon the Prisoner* (1971; *The Scene* 3); *The Soul of a Stripper* (1971); *Travellers* (1981)

Penelope Gilliatt, NY. (Women's Project) *But When All's Said and Done* (1981); *Nobody's Business; Property* (WP 1)

Charlotte Perkins Gilman. (Both: *The Forerunner*) *Something to Vote For* (2 (6): 143–153); *Three Women* (11 (5): 115–123)

Natalia Ginzburg. *The Advertisement* (1968; Sullivan); *I Married You for Fun* (1965); *The Secretary* (1968)

Marisa Gioffre. *Trouble; Bread and Roses*

Ruth Giorloff. *Lavender and Red Pepper* (*New Plays for Women and Girls*, French, 1932); *The Way Out* (1932)

Susan Glaspell (1876–1948). (*Plays*, Small, Maynard, 1920—P; *Three Plays*, E. Benn Ltd., London, 1924—T) *Alison's House* (1930; Cordell; Pulitzer); *Bernice* (1919; P; T); *Close the Book* (P); *The Inheritors* (1921; T); *The Outside* (1917; P); *The People* (P); *Suppressed Desires* (w George Cram Cook, 1917; P); *Tickless Time* (w GCC; P); *Trifles* (1916; Barlow; *The Verge* (1921; T); *A Woman's Honor* (1918; P)

Joanna McClelland Glass, NY. *Artichoke* (1975); *Canadian Gothic/American Modern* (1972); *The Last Chalice* (1977); *Play Memory* (1983); *Santacqua* (1969); *To Grandmother's House We Go* (1980); *Towering Babble* (1985)

Ruth Goetz (w Augustus Goetz). *The Heiress* (from Henry James's *Washington Square*, 1948); *The Hidden River* (from Storm Jameson); *The Immoralist* (from Gide, 1954)

Frances Goforth. *Ark of Safety* (w Howard Richardson, from *Tall Tales from Old Smokey* by C. Hodge Mathes); *Evening Star* (w HR)

Rose Leiman Goldemberg, NY. (Women's Project) *Absolutely Everything; Apples in Eden* (1985); *The Crossroad; Gandhiji* (BP, 1982–3); *Letters Home* (1980; WP 1); *A Little Traveling Music; Love One Another* (1974); *Marching as to War; The Merry War* (1973); *The Rabinowitz Gambit* (1973); *Rites of Passage* (1972); *Sophie* (1987)

Gloria Goldsmith. *Womanspeak* (Pioneer Drama Service)

Micki Goldthorpe. *Conversation*

Gloria Gonzales. *Black Thoughts on a Bright Monday; Cuba; The Economy Class; Curtains* (1975; BSP); *A Day in the Port Authority* (The Scene 3); *A Former Gotham Girl; The Glad Man* (Knopf, 1975); *Lights; Moving On!* (1971); *The New America* (1971); *The Puppet Trip; Revolutionaries Don't Sit in the Orchestra*

Ellen Goodfellow. *If Women Worked as Men Do*

Frances Goodrich. *The Diary of Anne Frank* (w Albert Hackett, 1956; NY Drama Critics Circle Award)

Ruth Gordon (1896–1986). *The Leading Lady* (1949); *Over Twenty-One* (Random House, 1944); *A Very Rich Woman; Years Ago* (Viking, 1947)

Mona Graham. *Spring Journey* (w John Ware)

Shirley Graham. see Shirley Graham Du Bois

Suzanne Granfield. *From This Time Forward; Tide of Voices; Whispers in the Grass*

Micki Grant, NY. *The Boogie-Woogie Rumble of a Dream Deferred* (w Vinnette Carroll, 1982; aka *Step Lively, Boy*); *Croesus & the Witch* (w VC, 1973); *Don't Bother Me, I Can't Cope* (1972; see J. e Franklin); *Hansel & Gretel in the 1980's* (w Marie Thomas, 1981); *Hazel* (w Ted Key); *It's So Nice to Be Civilized* (1980); *Phillis* (w Leslie Lee); *The Ups and Downs of Theophilus Maitland* (w VC, 1985); *Working* (w Studs Terkel, Stephen Schwartz, et al., 1980); *Your Arms Too Short to Box with God* (w VC and Alex Bradford, 1976)

Elizabeth A. Gray, LA. *The Instant Dream Game; Lunch or Something* (1980); *The Powder Room; Tidepool*

Tamu Gray. (Womanrite Theatre Ensemble) *Voice of a Black Woman* (w Tracy Schultz)

Virginia H. Gray. *Willie's Lie Detector*

Carolyn Green. *Janus*

Erma Green. *Fixin's* (Koch)

Suzin Green. (Violet Ray Theater Arts) *A Woman's Journey through Space and Time* (1977); see Irene Yesner-Ringawa

Elizabeth Gregory. *Hope Springs Eternal*

Joyce Grenfill. *George, Don't Do That!*

Roma Greth, Reading, PA. (WAFT; Westchester County Women's Theatre; Women's Project) *The American War Women* (1972); *But What Will We Do about Betty?* (1977); *Curtain Call; Four Lanes to Jersey* (1984); *A Ful Good Woman* (1979); *Ghost of Cemetery Ridge; The Greatest Day of the Century* (1978); *Half Way; Happy Birthday, America, from Your Daughters; The Happy Hunting Ground; The Heaven Mother; Interview* (The Scene 3); *Nightmare* (as LeRoma Greth); *North Light* (1985); *November People; On Summer Days* (1978); *The Pottstown Carnival; President's Daughter, President's Wife* (1976); *A Second Summer; Watchnight* (1984); *Windfall Apples* (1977); *Worms* (1970; The Scene 1)

Susan Griffin. *Cat and the Cock; Dear Sky; The Everlasting Reich; The Little Deaths; Voices* (1975; Feminist Press)

Angelina Weld Grimke (1880–1958). *Rachel* (1916; Hatch)

Suzanne Grossmann, NY. (adaptations and translations) *Alpha and Omega* (Sten Kaaloe); *Amphitryon* (1981; von Kleist); *Chemin de Fer* (The Chemmy Circle) (w Paxton Whitehead; Feydeau); *The Dance of Death* (Strindberg; PIP); *A Flea in Her Ear* (w PW; Feydeau); *The Grand Hunt* (1980; Gyula Hernady; PIP); *The Lady of the Camellias* (1979; Dumas fils); *La Guerre, Yes Sir* (Roch Carrier); *La Vie Parisienne* (Offenbach, Meilhac, Halevy); *Number Our Days* (1982, Myerhoff); *Summer Days* (Romain Weingarten); *There's One in Every Marriage* (w PW; Feydeau); *A Very Selfish Person* (w PW; Françoise Dorin)

Dorothy Guinn. *Out of the Dark* (1924; Richardson 1)

Gwendolyn Gunn. (Westbeth) *Across the Street* (1971); *The Confessions of Clara* (1970's; Fly You (1973)

Frances Gunner. *The Light of Women* (1930; Richardson 1)

Elizabeth Guptill. *The Little Heroine of the Revolution* (March Brothers, Lebanon, Ohio, 1906)

Andrea Hairston, Northampton, MA. (Chrysalis) *Einstein, An Imaginary Realization* (1973); *The Enemy's Not on Safari Coming to Round Us Up in the Jungle No More* (1980); *Hungry* (1974); *In the Middle Ground the Focus Blurs*

(1977); *On Display Do Not Touch* (Hellcoal Press, 1977); *Virginia, Sylvia & Anne* (1976); *Withdrawal Is Deadly* (1977).

Eleanor Hakim. (Medusa's Revenge) *Eliphant and Flamingo Vaudeville* (Scripts 1 (10): 1972); *A Lesbian Play for Lucy* (1978)

Ruth Hale. (w Nathan Hale) *Lilacs in the Rain; Love Comes in Full Array; Melody Jones; Runaway Heart*

Doris F. Halman. *Johnny Pickup; The Playroom* (1920); *The Voice of the Snake; Will o' the Wisp* (1916; Clements)

Cicely Hamilton (1872–1952). *The Beggar Prince* (1929); *Diana of Dobson's* (1908); *How the Vote Was Won* (w Christopher St. John, 1909; France); *Just to Get Married* (1910); *The Pot and the Kettle* (w CSJ, 1909)

Denise Hamilton, NY. (Women's Project) *Parallax* (1986; WH)

Nancy Hamilton. *One for the Money*

Lorraine Hansberry (1930–65). *The Drinking Gourd* (1960; Random House, 1972); *Les Blancs* (Random House, 1972); *A Raisin in the Sun* (1959; New American Library, 1987); *The Sign in Sidney Brustein's Window* (1964; BAP); *To Be Young, Gifted, and Black* (compiled by Robert Nemiroff); *Toussaint: Excerpt from Act I of a Work in Progress* (1961; Wilkerson); *What Use Are Flowers?* (Random House, 1972)

Barbara Harrington. see Susan Clement

Laura Harrington. (Women's Project) *Angel Face; Cheat; Countdown; Free Fall; Lucy's Lapses; Night Luster; 'Round Midnight; Women and Shoes; The Wrong Man*

Bernice Harris. *Judgement Come to Dan'l* (1933; *Folk Plays of Eastern Carolina*, B. Harris, ed., Chapel Hill, University Press, 1940)

Helen Webb Harris. *Genefrede* (Richardson 2)

Margaret Harton. (*Blackfriars Series of Original Plays*, Lester Raines, ed., Alabama Univ.); *Blessed Be the Bride* (no. 43); *Night Life of a Teacher* (w Leslie Davis, 1940; no. 6)

Charlotte Hastings. *High Ground; Soft September Air; Uncertain Joy* (POY, 1955)

Fanny Hatton. *Lombardi, Ltd.* (w Frederick Hatton)

June Havoc. *I, Said the Fly* (1969); *The Love Regatta; The Great Elinor Glyn Emancipation Proclamation Gun Powder Plot* (1974); *Marathon 33* (1963)

Esther M. Hawley. *On the Way Home* (1940's; France)

Ruth Hawthorne. see Mary Kennedy

Marijane Hayes. (w Joseph Hayes) *And Came Spring; Change of Heart; Come Over to Our House; Head in the Clouds; Life of the Party; June Wedding; Mister Peepers; Once in Every Family; Penny; Too Many Dates; Turn Back the Clock; Too Young, Too Old*

Eleanor & Elizabeth Hazard. *An Old Plantation Night* (Dick & Fitzgerald, NY, 1890)

Alvira Hazzard. (*Saturday Evening Quill*); *Little Heads* (1929); *Mother Liked It* (1928)

Frances Healey. *Creeds* (Shay 2)

Theresa Helburn. *Enter the Hero* (1918; Shay 1)

Lillian Hellman (1905–84). *Another Part of the Forest* (1946); *The Autumn Garden* (1950); *Candide* (from Voltaire; Random House, 1957); *The Children's Hour* (1934); *Days to Come* (1936; Modern Library); *The Lark* (from Anouilh); *The Little Foxes* (1939); *Montserrat* (from Emmanuel Robles; 1950); *My Mother, My Father, and Me* (from Burt Blechman; 1963); *Regina* (1949); *The Searching Wind* (1944); *Toys in the Attic* (1960; NY Drama Critics Circle Award); *Watch on the Rhine* (1941) (see *Six Plays by Lillian Hellman*, Vintage, 1979; *The Collected Plays of Lillian Hellman*, Little, Brown, 1972)

Nancy Wallace Henderson, Chapel Hill, NC. (Eccentric Circles) *Celebrate America* (1978; Julian Messner); *Feel Free* (w Charlotte Kraft, 1970); *Hot Pink Blues* (1969); *Lo, the Angel* (1951); *Medusa of Forty-Seventh Street; Monochrome* (1968); *96 A* (1980); *Penelope* (1986); *Speed, Bonnie Boat* (1954; Row, Peterson); *Walk Together: Five Plays on Human Rights* (1972; Julian Messner)

Beth Henley, LA. *Am I Blue?* (BSP, 1983); *Crimes of the Heart* (1979; Pulitzer; NY Drama Critics Circle Award); *The Debutante Ball* (1985); *The Lucky Spot; The Miss Firecracker Contest* (1984; PIP); *The Wake of Jamey Foster*

Dorothy Heyward. *Little Girl Blue* (w DeJagers); *Love in a Cupboard* (1920's); *Mamba's Daughters* (w Dubose Heyward; Farrar and Rinehart, 1939); *Nancy Ann* (1920's); *New Georgia* (1944); *Porgy* (w DH; George H. Doran, 1925); *Set My People Free* (1948); *South Pacific* (w Howard Rigsby, 1943)

Kay Hill. *Three to Get Married* (*Beyond the Footlights*, H. D.

McKellar, ed., Edward Arnold, London, 1964)

Eleanor Holmes Hinkley. *A Flitch of Bacon* (*Plays of the 47 Workshop*, George Pierce Baker, ed., Brentano's, 1920)

Charlotte Teller Hirsh. *Hagar and Ishmael* (*Crisis*, May 1913)

Jane S. Hitchcock. (Women's Project) *Bhutan, a Comedy of Bad Manners* (1983); *Grace* (1981); *The Custom of the Country* (from Edith Wharton, 1984); *Kohoutek: A Family Play* (1984); *New Listings* (1971); *Spirits* (1985)

Joan Holden, SF. (most are collaborations w San Francisco Mime Troupe) *Accidental Death of an Anarchist* (from Dario Fo, 1984); *L'Amant Militaire* (from Goldoni; Al Lavalley, ed., *The New Consciousness*, Rutgers, 1968); *Americans, or Last Tango in Huahuatenango* (1981); *The Dragon Lady's Revenge* (1971); *Electrobucks* (1978); *Factperson* (1980); *Factwino Meets the Moral Majority* (1981); *Factwino vs. Armageddonman* (1982); *False Promises/Nos Enganaron* (1976); *Frijoles* (1975); *Frozen Wages* (1972); *The Great Air Robbery* (1974); *The Hotel Universe* (1977); *The Independent Female, or A Man Has His Pride* (1970; France); *The Loon's Rage* (w Dell'Arte Players); *Power Play* (1975); *Ruzzante, or The Veteran* (from Beolco; 1978); *San Fran Scandals* (1973); *Seize the Time* (1970); *Soledad* (1971); *Steeltown* (1984) (see anthology *By Popular Demand*, San Francisco Mime Troupe, 1980)

Marjorie Holmes. *Two from Galilee*

Rochelle Holt. (Omaha Magic Theatre) *Walking Into Dawn—A Celebration* (*Valhalla-4*, 1977)

Pauline Elizabeth Hopkins. *One Scene from the Drama of Early Days* (*Phylon* 33 (1): Spring 1972); *Slaves' Escape or the Underground Railroad* (later entitled *Peculiar Sam; c* 1880)

Pauline Hopkins. *That Brewster Boy*

Patricia Horan. (Westbeth) *Egos* (1973); *God Bless God; Hand and Foot* (1973); *She Needs It*

Katharine Houghton. *Antigone* (from Anouilh; 1979); *Buddha* (1984); *Merlin* (1983); *On the Shady Side* (1985); *The Right Number* (1986); *Sailing to Byzantium* (1985); *The Thought Castle* (1986); *To Heaven in a Swing* (1982); *Two Beastly Tales* (w J. B. Grant, 1975; Lamplighters Roadway Press, Freestone, CA); *The Wizard's Daughter* (1984)

Alice H. Houstle. *The Kentucky Marriage Proposal* (from Chekhov)

Eleanor Harris Howard. *Mating Dance* (w Helen McAvity)

Julia Ward Howe (1819–1910). *Hippolytus* (1857; Clark); *Lenora, or, The World's Own* (1857; RAP)

Tina Howe. *Appearances* (1981); *The Art of Dining* (1979); *Birth and After Birth* (1974; Moore); *Coastal Disturbances* (1986); *Columbine String Quartet Tonight!* (1981); *Museum* (1976); *The Nest* (1970); *Painting Churches* (1982) (see *Three Plays by Tina Howe*, Avon, 1984)

Camm Hubert. *Rites of Passage* (*Room of One's Own* 3 (2))

Babette Hughes. *Angelica* (1934); *Greek to You* (1938); *If the Shoe Pinches* (1937); *The Liar and the Unicorn* (Shay 2); *Mrs. Harper's Bazaar; Murder! Murder!; One Egg; Sisters Under the Skin* (1949); *Three Players, a Fopp and a Duchess* (1928)

Elwil Hughes. (Washington Area Feminist Theatre) *Floury Tails* (1973)

Ruby Hult. *The Saga of George W. Bush* (*Negro Digest*, Sept. 1962)

Elizabeth Maddox Huntley. *What Ye Sow* (Comet Press Books, 1955)

Kathy Hurley, NY. *The Alchemist's Book; At the Bus Stop; The Black Princess* (children's play); *Byron; For an Eggshell*

Zora Neale Hurston. *Color Struck* (1920's); *Fast & Furious* (w Forbes Randall et al., 1931; BP); *The First One* (1927; Books for Libraries, Freeport, NY, 1971); *From Sun to Sun; Great Day* (1927); *Mule Bone* (w Langston Hughes, 1930); *Polk County, A Comedy of Negro Life on a Sawmill Camp* (w Dorothy Waring, 1944)

Maude Phelps Hutchins. *Aunt Julia's Caesar* (Spearhead: Ten Years' Experimental Writing in America, New Directions, 1947); *The Case of Astrolabe* (Laughlin, 1944); *A Play About Joseph M. Smith, Jr.* (Laughlin, 1944); *The Wandering Jew* (Laughlin, 1951)

Momoko Iko. *The Gold Watch; Second City Flat*

Corinne Jacker, NY. *After the Season* (1980); *Bits and Pieces* (1974; Moore; Obie); *Breakfast, Lunch and Dinner* (1974); *Chinese Restaurant Syndrome* (BSP, 1977); *Dancing in the Dark* (1986); *Domestic Issues* (1981); *Harry Outside* (1975; Obie); *In Place* (BSP, 1984); *Later* (1975); *Making It; My Life* (1976); *Night Thoughts* (1976); *The Other People's Tables* (1975); *Terminal* (1976); *Travellers*

Elaine Jackson. *Paper Dolls* (1983; Wilkerson); *Toe Jam* (King)

Josephine Jackson. *The Believers* (w

Joseph A. Walker, subtitled *The Black Experience in Song*; BP, 1967–68)

Leslie Jacobson. (Washington Area Feminist Theatre) *The Amateur: Reflections of Zelda* (1974); *In Good Company* (1975); *Women's Voices* (1975)

Laurie James, Dix Hills, NY. *The Roots of Rebellion; Still Beat Noble Hearts; The Yellow Wallpaper* (from Charlotte Perkins Gilman)

Jennifer Jarrett. *Storm Town* (1985); *Winter Chicken*

Pamela Johanson. *Orange Blossom* (BOAP, 1942–43)

Bertha Johnson. *Pax, America* (w Albert Johnson)

Carleene Johnson. *The Odyssey of Jeremy Jack* (w Mark Medoff)

Christine Johnson. *Zwadi Ya Afrika Kwe Dunwa (Africa's Gift to the World*, children's play; Free Black Press, Chicago, c 1970)

Elizabeth Johnson. *A Bad Play for an Old Lady* (PT, vol. 1)

Georgia Douglas Johnson (1886–1966). *A Bill to Be Passed; Blue Blood* (1920's; Shay 2); *Blue Eyed Black Boy; Frederick Douglass* (Richardson 2); *Plumes* (Barlow); *Safe; The Starting Point; A Sunday Morning in the South: With Negro Church Background* (1925); *A Sunday Morning in the South: With White Church Background; William and Ellen Craft* (Richardson 2)

Karen Johnson. *I'll Die if I Can't Live Forever*

Kitty Johnson, LA. *Final Arrangements; Houston, Houston* (w Joseph Scott Kierland and Doug Katsaras); *Mirror, Mirror; Strawberry Envy* (1983); *Triplet* (1982) (see Kierland, ed., *Best One-Act Plays*, Panjandrum Books, LA, 1985)

Elinor Jones. *Box Office; What Would Jeanne Moreau?*

Gayl Jones. *Beyond Yourself (The Midnight Confessions) for Brother Ahh* (*Blacks on Paper*, Brown Univ., 1975); *Chile Woman* (Shubert Playbook Series, John Emigh, ed., 2 (5): 1974); *Mama Easter*

Gwenyth Jones. *The Ass and the Philosopher* (BOAP, 1956–57)

Pamela Jones. *The Schoolhouse Is Burning* (*Yale/Theatre* 2 (2): 1969)

Elizabeth Garver Jordan. *The Lady of Oklahoma: A Comedy* (Harper, 1911)

Patricia Joudry. *The Song of Louise in the Morning; Teach Me How to Cry; Three Rings for Michelle*

Sherry Kafka. *The Man Who Loved God* (BSP, 1968)

Diane Kagan, NY. (Women's Project) *The Corridor; High Time; Luminosity—A Self Portrait; Marvelous Gray* (1982); *On the Rocks; Phoebus; Stolen Goods*

Judy Kahan. see Jane Curtin

Lucille Kallen. *Maybe Tuesday*

Judith Kandel. *Play, Genius, Play!* (BP, 1935–36)

Susan J. Kander, NY. (Women's Project) *A Good Year for the Roses* (1984); *Just Last August* (1982); *Milly* (1986; WH); *Murphy's Law* (1980); *Stop-Time Rag* (1982)

Fay Kanin. *Goodbye, My Fancy* (1948); *The High Life;* (w Michael Kanin) *His and Hers; Rashomon*

Sharleen Kap. *The Interview* (1986; VPT)

Ella Gerber Kasakoff. (w Howard Richardson) *A Thread of Scarlet*

Kate Kasten, Adel, IA. (At the Foot of the Mountain) *Transcendental Trepidation*; (all following w Sandra de Helen) *Body Talk; The Clue in the Old Birdbath; Death after Death; The Notorious McCorkle Sisters; On the Elevator; The Rex Family: Jocasta and Oedipus*

Judith Katz. (Chrysalis; Omaha Magic Theatre; Washington Area Feminist Theatre) *Breakfast: A Kitchen Comedy* (Valhalla-4); *The Franny Chicago Play* (1974); *Temporary Insanity* (1975); *100,001 Horror Stories of the Plains* (w Megan Terry and James Larson, 1977); *Tribes: A Play of Dreams* (1979)

Esther Kaufman. *Worm in the Horseradish*

Florence Aquino Kaufman. *The Winner!*

Lynne Kaufman, SF. *The Couch* (1985); *Roshi* (1987)

Katherine Kavanaugh. *The Million Dollar Butler* (1933); *The Wrong Professor* (1946)

Molly Kazan. *The Egghead* (1957)

Eloise Keeler. *Grandma Steps Out*

Sallie Kemper. *An Old Chester Street Secret* (*Boston Theatre Guild Plays*, Frank W. C. Hershey, ed., W. H. Baker, Boston, 1924)

Adrienne Kennedy (1931–). *A Beast's Story* (1966); *Boats* (1969); *Diary of Lights* (1954); *Funnyhouse of a Negro* (1962; BSP; Obie); *The Lennon Play* (from John Lennon, 1967); *A Lesson in a Dead Language* (1964; Parone); *A Movie Star Has to Star in Black and White* (Wordplays 3); *The Owl Answers* (1963; Hatch); *The Pale Blue Flower; A Rat's Mass* (1965; OOB); *Sun: A Poem for Malcolm X Inspired by His Murder* (1969; Owens); (see also Paul Carter Harrison, ed., *Kuntu Drama*, Grove Press, 1974)

Mary Kennedy. *Mrs. Partridge Presents* (BP, 1924–25)

Jean Kerr. *Finishing Touches* (BP, 1972); *Goldilocks* (1958); *Jenny Kissed Me* (1949); *King of Hearts* (w Eleanor Brooke, Doubleday, 1954); *Lunch Hour* (1980); *Mary, Mary* (1960, BAP); *Please Don't Eat the Daisies* (Doubleday, 1957); *Poor Richard* (1964)

Sophie Kerr. *Big Hearted Herbert; They're None of Them Perfect*

Wendy Kesselman. *The Juniper Tree* (1982); *My Sister in This House* (Blackburn Prize)

Kathleen Kimball. *The Meat Rack* (Scripts 7, 1972)

Ramona King. *Steal Away*

Maxine Klein, Belchertown, MA. (Little Flags) *Ah, Women!; Boston Remembers; Marx on Her Mind; Mysterious Death of C. T. List; Tania; To the People; Winds of the People;* all following in *Playbook*, South End Press, 1986: *The Furies of .Mother Jones* (1977); *New Rise of the Master Race* (1979); *Split Shift* (aka *Brainchild;* 1986); *Windfall* (1978)

Florence Clay Knox, *For Distinguished Service* (1918; Shay 4)

Joanne Koch, Evanston, IL. *Haymarket: Footnote to a Bombing; Grant 5742* (1983); *Nesting Dolls* (1986); *Teeth* (1979); *XX-XY* (1981)

Sarah Monson Koebnick. *Fair Beckoning One* (1968; PT, vol. 4)

Mary Koisch. (Washington Area Feminist Theatre) *When Wombs Were Tombs and Mothers, Glass* (1975)

Felicia Komai. *Cry, the Beloved Country* (w Josephine Douglas from Alan Paton, Friendship Press, NY, 1955)

Joanna Halpert Kraus, Rochester, NY. *Circus Home* (1978); *The Ice Wolf* (1965; Moore); *Kimchi Kid; The Last Baron of Arizona* (1984); *Mean to Be Free* (1967); *The Shaggy Dog Murder Trial; Why Am I Invisible—Especially at Lunch?* (1983) (see New Plays for Children)

Ruth Krauss. *A Beautiful Day* (1963; OOB); *The Cantilever Rainbow* (Pantheon, 1965); *If Only* (Toad Press, 1969); *The Little King, The Little Queen, The Little Monster* (children's play, Toad Press); *Poem-Plays* (1961; Benedikt); *There's a Little Ambiguity Over There Among the Blue Bells* (Something Else Press, 1968); *This Beast Gothic* (Bookstore Press, 1973); *Under Twenty* (Toad Press, 1970)

Margaret Kressman. *Apple Pie*

Helen Kromer. *Take Any Street* (Friendship Press); *Under One*

Roof (*We, Too, Belong*, Dell); *For Heaven's Sake! Hannah, A Parable in Music; Like It Is; Sure as You're Born; Verdict of One*

Clare Kummer. *Be Calm, Camilla* (1922); *Good Gracious, Annabelle* (1910's); *Her Master's Voice; Open Storage; Papera; The Robbery; Rollo's Wild Oat* (1922)

Myrna Lamb. (New Feminist Repertory; Women's Interart) *Apple Pie* (1975); *Ballad of Brooklyn; Because I Said So; But What Have You Done for Me Lately; The Butcher Shop* (Aphra 1, 2, Winter 1970); *Crab Quadrille; The Comeback Act; I Lost a Pair of Gloves Yesterday* (1972; Moore); *In the Shadow of the Crematorium; Jillila; The Mod Donna; Mother Ann; Olympic Park; The Sacrifice; Scyklon Z; The Serving Girl and the Lady; The Two Party System* (see *The Mod Donna and Scyklon Z: Plays of Women's Liberation*, Pathfinder Press, 1971)

Beth Lambert. *The Riddle Machine* (1966; Lifton)

Diane Charlotte Lampert (lyricist). *Nell Gwyn* (1984); *Shout Up a Morning* (1986)

Eula A. Lamphere. *Crosses on the Hill*

V. R. Lang (1924–56). (*Poems and Plays*, Random House, 1973) *Fire Exit* (1952); *I Too Have Lived in Arcadia* (1954)

Armina Marshall Langer. (w Lawrence Langer) *The Pursuit of Happiness*

Susan LaTempa, Culver City, CA. *A Play of One's Own . . . The Story of Virginia Woolf* (1976); *At Home on Location* (1980); *The Folk Singer's Guide to Love Songs* (1986); *Gentle Arts* (1981); *Hardboiled* (1983); *The Life of the Party* (LaTempa); *Prologue to a Dance by Rudy Perez* (1984); *Queen of the Angels* (1981); *Scenes from University Life* (1982); *Sunset Beach* (*Plays from Padua Hills*, Pomona College, 1982); *Untitled, 1957* (1983); *Vampire Guts* (1984)

Jean Lee Latham. *The Ghost of Rhodes Manor*

Shirley Lauro, NY. (Women's Project) *The Coal Diamond* (BSP, 1982); *The Contest* (1976); *I Don't Know Where You're Coming From at All; In the Garden of Eden; Margaret and Kit; Nothing Immediate; Open Admissions* (1983); *Pearls on the Moon; Set Up; Sunday Go to Meeting*

Elizabeth A. Lay. *Trista* (1941); *When Witches Rise* (Koch)

Ellen Lay. *In Dixon's Kitchen* (Koch)

Barbara Lebow, Atlanta. *The Adventures of Homer McGundy; Aqua-*

marine and Tangerine: A Fantasy; The Boy and the Spirits; Cinderella and the Green-Eyed Monster; Circus!; Cyparis; Dream Windows; The Fourth Ring; I Can't Help It; I Love You, Bobby; Little Joe Monaghan; Moyngin; Night Witch (w Frank Wittow); *People of the Brick; Playground; Rally 'Round; Red Ridinghood Rides Again; Rosita and the Bandit; Sandburg, Yes!; A Shayna Maidel* (PIP); *Sola; The Square Egg of Gratchitt; The Trashcan Kid; Windows; Yesterday's Children*

Maryat Lee. *Dope* (1952; France); *Four Men and a Monster; Fuse* (1971)

Eva Le Gallienne. *Alice in Wonderland* (from Carroll); *The Strong Are Lonely*

Pamela Lengyl. *The Super Reality of Duane Danson* (The Scene, no. 3)

Lois Lenski. *The Bean-Pickers* (National Council of Churches, New York, 1952)

Eugenie Leontovich. See Elena Miramova

Jennette Letton. *The Young Elizabeth* (w Francis Letton)

Maya Levy. *Daughters*

Kate Lewis. (*Alabama Folk Plays*, Kate Lewis, ed., Univ. Press, Chapel Hill, 1940) *The Scarlet Petticoat; Three Links O'Chaine; Watermelon Time*

Betty Jean Lifton. *Kap the Kappa* (Lifton)

Abbey Lincoln. *A Streak O'Lean* (1967; Childress)

Michele Linfante, SF. (At the Foot of the Mountain; Lilith; Snapdragon; Theatre Three) *Androcles and the Lion; Beguine* (1974); *Cafe Iowa* (w ensemble at Iowa State U.); *Crossing Borders* (w Steve Most and SF Mime Troupe); *Exit the Maids* (w Margo Gomez and Lilith, 1981); *Family Album* (1983); *Field Nurse* (1981); *Flight Nurse* (aka *Private Parts*, 1982); *Malpractice or Love's the Best Doctor* (from Molière, w Jael Weisman, Michael Fields, and Donald Forrest; 1983); *Manifesto* (from Dacia Maraini, 1979); *Moonlighting* (w Terry Baum and Carolyn Myers, 1976); *Pizza* (WCP 6); *The Road Not Taken* (w Dell' Arte Players, 1985); *Sacrifices* (w TB and CM, 1978)

Jessica Litwak, NY. *Emma Goldman* (WH)

Myrtle S. Livingston. *For Unborn Children* (Crisis 32 (3): July 1926)

Ruby Livingston. *In Review* (1920's; Signal Press)

Fran Lohman. *The Telegram* (1971;

The Scene 1)

Katharine Long. *Ariel Bright* (Delgado); *Two Part Harmony*

Anita Loos (1893–1981). *Gentlemen Prefer Blondes* (w John Emerson, Century Play Co., NY, 1926); *Gigi* (from Colette; Random House, 1952); *Happy Birthday* (1946); *The Whole Town's Talking* (Longmans Green, 1925)

Mimi Loring. (Omaha Magic Theatre) *Astral White: A Musical Comedy about the Holy Order of Divine Illumination*

Shellen Lubin, NY. (POW) *Jewish Daughters; Ladies!; Leah* (1986); *Molly's Daughters; Womansong*

Clare Boothe (Luce) (1903–). *Abide with Me* (1935); *Child of the Morning; Europe in the Spring* (1940); *Kiss the Boys Goodbye* (1938; BP); *Margin for Error* (1939; BP); *Slam the Door Softly* (1970, from *A Doll's House*; France); *Stuffed Shirts* (1931); *The Women* (Random House, 1937)

Ada McAllister. (Rhode Island Feminist Theatre) *Internal Injury* (1978)

Pauline Macauley. *The Astrakhan Coat* (1968); *The Creeper* (POY, 1965); *Monica* (1966)

Helen McAvity. *Everybody Has to Be Somebody*; see Eleanor Harris Howard

Audrey McBain. *Cast Off Five*

Gertrude Parthenia McBrown. (see *Negro History Bulletin*) *Birthday Surprise* (Feb. 1953); *Bought with Cookies* (April 1949)

Sara S. McCarty. *Three's a Crowd* (w Clayton McCarty; Zachar)

Clarice Vallette McCauley. *The Conflict* (1920; Shay 4); *The Queen's Hour* (Drama 10: June 1920); *The Threshold* (Shay 2)

Marcie McCreary. *Three Needles in a Haystack* (w Bill McCreary)

Carson McCullers (1917–67). *The Member of the Wedding* (New Directions); *The Square Root of Wonderful* (1957)

Heather McDonald. *Available Light; Faulkner's Bicycle*

Elizabeth McFadden. *Double Door*

Leueen MacGrath. *Amicable Parting* (w George S. Kaufman); *Fancy Meeting You Again* (w GSK; 1951); *The Small Hours* (w GSK; 1951)

Anne McGravie, Chicago. *Chicago in the Morning* (1985); *Christmas at Seven; The Deaths of Anna May Wong* (1987); *Oona and the Oyster Girl* (aka *Orphans*, 1982); *Rose Cat and Cat Bush* (Scott, Foresman); *Sweet Dreams* (Scott, Foresman); *Wonderella* (Scott Foresman); *Wrens* (1985)

Helen MacInnes. *Home Is the Hunter*

(Harcourt Brace, 1964)

Carol K. Mack, NY. (Women's Project) *A.K.A. Marleen; American Dreamer* (1985); *Esther* (1976); *Gazebo* (1982); *Half Time at Halcyon Days* (BSP, 1985); *Hi Tech; The Magenta Shift* (1986); *Postcards* (1983); *Revisions on Eden Rock; A Safe Place; Survival Games* (1980); *Territorial Rites* (1983; WP 2); *Unprogrammed*

Grace McKeaney, LA. *Brothers, Keepers* (1973); *The Coming of Mr. Pine* (1976); *Deadfall* (1987); *Fits and Starts* (1976); *Jubilee* (1975); *On-the-Fritzz* (1976); *Run Deep* (1979-80); *Who They Are and How It Is with Them* (1979)

Patricia McLain. *Love Is Contagious*

Ellen McLaughlin. *Days and Nights Within* (PIP); *A Narrow Bed* (Blackburn Prize)

Mary MacMillan. *The Shadowed Star* (1913; Shay 1)

Patricia Malango. *The Boy Who Changed the World*

Karen Malpede (Taylor), Brooklyn, NY. (New Cycle) *The End of War* (1977); *A Lament for Three Women* (France); *Making Peace* (1979); *A Monster Has Stolen the Sun; Rebeccah* (1977); *Sappho and Aphrodite* (see *A Monster Has Stolen the Sun and Other Plays*, Marlboro Press, 1987)

Dorothy Manley. *The Stigma* (w Donald Duff and Doralyne Spence, 1929)

Emily Mann. (Women's Project) *Annulla, An Autobiography* (1976; PIP, 1985); *Betsey Brown* (w Ntozake Shange); *Execution of Justice* (NP 3); *Nights and Days* (from Pierre Laville, 1985); *Still Life* (1979; Obie; James Reston, Jr., ed., *Coming to Terms, American Plays & the Vietnam War,* Theatre Communications Group, 1985)

Mary Mann. (Synthaxis) *The Senator's Daughter* (1978)

Hilda Manning. *On the Air* (1944); *A Young Man's Fancy* (1944)

Jeannette Marks (1875–1964). *The Merry Merry Cuckoo* (1911; ROAP); *Welsh Honeymoon* (1916; Cohen)

Anne Coulter Martens. *Blue Beads*

Joyce F. Martins. *Rosemary for Remembrance*

Tanyss Rhea Martula. *The Three Boys* (1986; VPT); *Two Women from Waldo, Arkansas*

Judi Ann Mason. *$Living Fat$; A Star Ain't Nothin' but a Hole in Heaven* (1976)

Lillian Masters. (w Robert Masters) *Off a Pewter Platter; Our Night Out*

Elaine May. *Adaptation* (1968; BP);

Not Enough Rope (1962)

Edith Meiser. *The Strangler Fig* (BP, 1939–40)

Mary Melwood. *Five Minutes to Morning* (Lifton); *The Tingalary Bird* (Swortzell)

Mary Mercier. *Johnny No-Trump* (1966; Marilyn Stasio, ed., *Broadway's Beautiful Losers,* Delacorte, 1972)

Elizabeth (Avery) Meriwether. *Ku Klux Klan; or, the Carpet Bagger in New Orleans* (South Baptist Publ. Co., Memphis, 1877)

Eve Merriam, NY. *And I Ain't Finished Yet* (1982); *At Her Age* (1979); *The Classic Question* (1986); *The Club* (1976); *Dialogue for Lovers* (1981); *The Good Life: Lady MacBeth of Westport* (1979); *Out of Our Fathers' House* (w Paula Wagner and Jack Hofsiss, 1975; Moore); *Plagues for Our Time* (1983); *Street Dreams, The Inner City Musical* (aka *Inner City,* 1981); *Viva Reviva* (1977); *Wedlocked* (1984); *Woman Alive: Conversation against Death* (1977)

Felicia Metcalfe. *Shooting High* (w Wall Spence)

Henriette Metcalfe. *Come Easy*

Annie Nathan Meyer. *Black Souls* (Reynolds Press, Bedford, Mass., 1932)

Edna St. Vincent Millay (1892–1950) *Aria da Capo* (1919; Kozelka); *The King's Henchman* (1927; Harper); *The Lamp and the Bell* (1921; Harper); *The Murder of Lidice* (1942); *The Princess Marries the Page* (1917; Harper); *Two Slatterns and a King* (1921; Harper)

Alice Miller. *Charm School*; see Florence Ryerson

Helen Miller. see Eve Merriam

May Miller. *The Bog Guide* (1925); *Christophe's Daughters* (Richardson 2); *The Cuss'd Thing* (1926); *Freedom's Children on the March* (c 1943); *Graven Images; Harriet Tubman* (Richardson 1); *Nails and Thorns* (c 1933); *Riding the Goat* (Richardson 71); *Samory* (Richardson 2); *Scratches* (*Carolina Magazine* 59 (7): Apr. 1929); *Sojourner Truth* (Richardson 2); *Stragglers in the Dust* (c 1930); *Within the Shadow* (c 1920)

Susan Miller, LA. (Women's Interart) *Arts and Leisure* (1985); *Confessions of a Female Disorder* (Hoffman); *Cross Country* (1976; WCP 1); *Daddy/A Commotion of Zebras; Denim Lecture; Flux* (1975); *Nasty Rumors and Final Remarks* (1979; Obie); *No One Is Exactly 23* (*Pyramid Magazine* 1, 1968); *Silverstein and Co.*

Wendy Miller. *Death Rite* (w Loren Partridge; *Womanspirit* 5 (8): 1978)

Jane Milmore. (w William Van Zandt) *Having a Wonderful Time, Wish You Were Her!; Lie, Cheat, and Genuflect; A Little Quickie; Love, Sex, and the IRS; Playing Doctor; Suitehearts*

Nerissa Long Milton. *The Challenge—A Fantasy* (*Negro History Bulletin,* Oct. 1953)

Elena Miramova. *Dark Eyes* (w Eugenie Leontovich, 1943)

Anita Velez Mitchell, NY. *The Salsamerican Connection* (1984); *Vainlove* (1981); *Venezuelan Scrub*

Norma Mitchell. *Cradle Snatchers* (w Russell G. Medcroft); *Post Road* (w Wilbur Daniel Steele)

Yvonne Mitchell. *The Same Sky* (POY, 1951)

Barbara Molette, Houston, TX. (w Carlton Molette) *Booji; Dr. B. S. Black; Noah's Ark; Rosalee Pritchett* (1972)

Ursule Molinare, NY. *The Abstract Wife* (William Hoffman, ed., *New American Plays,* vol. 2, Hill and Wang, 1971); *After the Wash* (1963); *Antiques* (1963); *Breakfast Past Noon* (1964; Moore); *The Contest* (Quixote, 1959); *The Engagement* (*San Francisco Review,* 1962?); *The Great Emancipation* (1965); *The Happy Hexagon* (1970); *Innocent; The Mine* (1964); *The Sundial* (1962); *The Thirteenth Christmas* (1960); *The Tourniquet* (1961); *Tyrant* (1984); (several plays published in *Chelsea,* 1960–63)

Dorothy Monet. *Cyprienne*

Debra Monk (et al.). *Pump Boys and Dinettes*

Harriet Monroe. *The Passing Show* (5 *Modern Plays in Verse,* Houghton Mifflin, c 1903)

Patricia Montley. *Bible Herstory; Not So Grim Fairy Tales; Rosvitha's Review*

Elvie A. Moore. *Angela Is Happening* (Abe C. Ravitz, ed., *The Disinherited,* Encino, CA, Dickenson, 1974)

Honor Moore, NY. *Mourning Pictures* (Moore); *The Terry Project; Years*

Cherrie Moraga. *Giving Up the Ghost* (West End Press, LA, 1986)

Alice Morgan (d. 1970). *The Grand Street Follies*

Robin Morgan. *Art and Feminism* (*Going Too Far,* Random, 1977)

Judith Morley, Roslyn Harbor, NY. (Eccentric Circles, Women's Interart) *Agave* (1984); *Bloodfeud, The Life and Death of Clytemnestra* (1981); *The Fledgling; The Haircult; Ham and Borscht; Jo Ella; Miss Laughinghouse and the Lis-*

tener (1981); *Mother's Day* (1977); *A Nice Boy for Joanie* (NYS Community Theatre Journal 4, 1); *No Vacancy; The Oresteia* (1983); *Short Hop to Ohio; Travel Lightly; The True Story of Adam and Eve* (1985)

Katherine Morrill. *A Distant Bell*

Angela Morris. *Dorinda Dares* (Boston Theatre Guild Plays, 1924)

Aldyth Morris, Honolulu, HI. *The Clone; The Damien Plays* (I, II, III, *Damien Letter); The Dog That Was; The Dragon of the Six Resemblances* (Fingernail of My Beloved); *Fourth Son* (The Carefree Tree); *Secret Concubine; Sword and Samurai; Tusitala: Robert Louis Stevenson in the Pacific; The Wall*

Anne Morrison. *Jonesy; Pigs; Their First Anniversary* (1934); *Wild Wescotts*

Lillian Mortimer. *No Mother to Guide Her* (1905; *America's Lost Plays*, Indiana Univ. Press)

Martha Morton. *A Bachelor's Romance*

Jean Mountaingrove. *Our Circle Our Cauldron* (Womanspirit 4 (14): Winter 1977)

Anna Cora Mowatt (Ritchie) (1819–70). *Armand, or the Peer and the Peasant* (1847); *Fashion, or, Life in New York* (1845; RAP); *Gulzara, the Persian Slave* (1840)

Lavonne Mueller, NY. (Women's Project) *Breaking the Prairie Wolf Code* (1985); *Colette in Love* (1986; WH); *Crimes and Dreams* (1980); *Isolates* (1970); *Killings on the Last Line* (1980); *Little Victories* (1983; WP 2); *The Only Woman General* (1984); *Oyster Crackers, Undershirts, and Mauve Lemonade* (1975); *Warriors from a Long Childhood* (1979)

Grace Murphy. *Kamiano, the Story of Damien* (Theatre for Tomorrow, Longmans, London, 1940)

Carolyn Myers. see Terry Baum, Michele Linfante

Leah Napolin. *Yentl* (w Isaac Bashevis Singer, 1977)

Elyse Nass. *Avenue of Dreams* (1983); *Admit One* (1983); *Backwards; Detours; Floaters* (1986); *Love from the Madhouse* (Dekalb Literary Arts Journal, 1972); *Mango; The Marriage Museum; Memory Shop; Reunion '68; The Real Wife Beater* (1984); *Second Chance* (BSP, 1980); *Washington Squares*

Marcia Naufrecht. *Welfare*

Janet Neipris, NY. (Women's Project) *The Agreement* (Delgado); *Almost in Vegas* (1985); *The Bridge at Belharbour; The Desert; Exhibition; Flying Horses; Jeremy and the Thinking Machine; Out of Order; Separations; Statues*

Alice D. Nelson. *Mine Eyes Have Seen* (Crisis, April 1918)

Claris Nelson. *Passing Fancy*

Mariah Burton Nelson. *Out of Bounds* (McDermott)

Natalie Nelson. (New Dimensions, 1970) *Things That Happen to Us; More Things That Happen to Us*

Sally Nemeth, Chicago. (Women's Project) *Aviator Season* (1985); *Flight* (1981); *Holding the Bag* (1985); *Holy Days* (1984); *Modern Lit* (1982); *Swansong for a Unicorn* (1981)

Molly Newman, Denver. *Quilters* (w Barbara Damashek); *Shooting Stars*

Anne Nichols (1891–1966). *Abie's Irish Rose* (Grosset and Dunlap, 1927); *Down Limerick Way* (1920); *The Happy Cavalier* (1918); *Heart's Desire* (w Adelaide Matthews, 1916); *Just Married* (w AM, 1921); *Linger Longer Letty* (1919); *A Little Bit Old-Fashioned* (1918); *The Man from Wicklow* (1917); *Marry in Haste* (1921); *Pre-Honeymoon* (w Alfred Van Ronkel; BP, 1935–36); *Springtime in Mayo* (1919)

Josefina Niggli (1910–83). *The Cry of Dolores; The Fair-God* (Malinche) (1936); *Miracle at Blaise; The Ring of General Macia* (1943; John Sweet and Kenneth Lunn, eds., *Designs for Reading: Plays*, Houghton Mifflin, 1969); *This Bull Ate Nutmeg* (1937; Galbraith); *This Is Villa* (1938); (all the following: *Mexican Folk Plays*, Univ. of North Carolina Press, 1938) *Azteca; The Red Velvet Goat* (1935); *Soldadera* (Soldier-Women) (1937); *Sunday Costs Five Pesos* (1937); *Tooth or Shave*

Nora F. Nixon. *Cunjer Joe* (1935)

Marsha Norman, NY. *Circus Valentine* (1979); *Getting Out* (1977; Avon); *The Holdup* (1980); *'night, Mother* (1981; Hill and Wang; Pulitzer; Blackburn Prize); *Third and Oak* (1978); *Traveler in the Dark* (1983)

Nina Nsabe. *Moma Don't Know What Love Is* (Sanchez)

Joyce Carol Oates. *In the Region of Ice* (Black Sparrow Press, 1974); *The Hungry Ghosts: Seven Allusive Comedies; Miracle Play*

Edna O'Brien. *A Cheap Bunch of Nice Flowers* (POY, 1962–63); *A Pagan Place* (Faber, 1972); *A Wedding Dress* (Mademoiselle 58, 1963)

Mary O'Hara. *The Catch Colt*

Esther Olson. *Let's Make Up; Mister Co-Ed; A Question of Figures; Swing Fever*

Sally Ordway, NY. (Westbeth; Women's Interart; Women's Project) *Allison* (1970); *Australia Play* (1971); *Binoculars* (1982); *The*

Chinese Caper (1973); *Crabs* (Scripts, Fall 1971); *A Desolate Place Near a Deep Hole* (1965); *Family, Family* (The Scene, 1974); *Free! Free! Free!* (1965); *Film Festival* (1979); *The Hostess* (1975); *Memorial Day* (1974); *Ike and Mamie, A Nuclear Romance* (1985); *Movie, Movie on the Wall* (Scripts, Fall 1971); *No More Chattanooga Choo Choo* (1981); *Once upon a Woman* (1978); *A Passage through Bohemia* (1966); *Playthings* (1973); *A Pretty Passion* (1982); *Promise Her Anything* (1980); *San Fernando Valley* (Scripts, Fall 1971); *Sex Warfare* (1974); *S.W.A.K.* (Sealed with a Kiss) (1977); *There's a Wall Between Us, Darling* (Yale/Theatre, 1968); *Translators* (1984); *War Party* (1974); *We Agree* (1970)

Jeannine Bails O'Reilly. *Bread Basket; I Got on Point Late in Life; L'Etat* (1974; The Scene 3); *Strains; A Tribute to Mother Jade; The Umbilical Cord of Howard Lostfogil; Timberlines*

Mary Orr. *Grass Widows* (1976); *Women Must Weep* (1963); *Women Must Work* (1963); (all following w Reginald Denham) *Be Your Age; Dark Hammock; Minor Murder; Wallflower; The Wisdom of Eve*

Peggy Adams Osborne. *The Meeting* (Afro-American Pub. Co., Chicago, 1968)

Rochelle Owens, Norman, OK. (Women's Interart) *Beclich; Chucky's Hunch* (Obie; Wordplays 2); *Coconut Folksinger* (1972); *Emma Instigated Me* (Performing Arts Journal 1, 1, 1976); *Farmer's Almanac* (1968); *Futz and What Came After* (1965; OOB; Obie); *A Game of Billiards; He Wants Shih!* (1968); *Homo* (1966); *Istanboul; The Karl Marx Play* (1973); *Kontraption* (1970; Scripts 2); *Mountain Rites; O. K. Certaldo* (1973); *The Queen of Greece; The String Game; The Widow and the Colonel* (BSP, 1977); *Who Do You Want, Peire Vidal?; (see collected plays in Futz and What Came After, Random House, 1968; The Karl Marx Play and Others, Dutton, 1974)*

Anita Page. *Noodle-Doodle Box* (w Alex Page)

Dorothy Parker (1893–1967). *Here We Are* (1931; Bennett Cerf and Van Cartmell, eds. *Twenty-four Favorite One-Act Plays*, Doubleday, 1958); *Ladies of the Corridor* (w Arnaud d'Usseau, 1953)

Linda Parris-Bailey. *Circus Maxim* (w David Fuller); *Dark Cowgirls and Prairie Queens*

Loren Partridge. see Wendy Miller

Josephine Preston Peabody (1874–1922). *The Chameleon* (1917); *Fortune and Men's Eyes* (1900; *Helen Louise Cohen*, ed., *One-Act Plays by Modern Authors*, Harcourt, 1934); *Marlowe* (1901); *The Piper* (1910; RAD); *Portrait of Mrs. W.* (1922); *The Wings* (1905); *The Wolf of Gubbio* (1913)

Marjean Perry. *A Trap Is a Small Place* (1953; France)

Pauline Phelps. *Shavings* (w Marion Short)

Peggy Phillips. *Brass Ring; The Brink of Glory; A Golden Sorrow; It Never Was You; Listen Professor; Paper Moon; The Summer Soldier; To Charlie, with Love*

Eden Philpotts. *Farmer's Wife*

Alice Pierratt. *Days' End* (1920's; France)

June Pierson. *Vital Statistics*

Sylvia Plath (1932–63). *Three Women* (1962; see *Winter Trees*, Harper, 1972)

Agnes Porter. *The Man with the Book* (*Four Full-Length Plays*, Hatcher Hughes et al., eds., Appleton, 1928)

Estela Portillo. *Black Light; The Day of the Swallows* (Robert Garza, ed. *Contemporary Chicano Theatre*, U. of Notre Dame, 1976); *Morality Play; Sor Juana* (*Sor Juana and Other Plays*, Bilingual Press, 1983)

Toni Press. *Mash Note to an Old Codger* (LaTempa)

Doris Price. *The Bright Medallion; The Eyes of the Old* (Both: *Univ. of Michigan Plays*, Kenneth Rowe, ed., Univ. of Mich. Press, 1932); *Two Gods: A Minaret* (*Opportunity*, Dec. 1932)

Deborah Pryor, Virginia Beach, VA. *Burrhead* (PIP, 1984); *The Love Talker; Wetter than Water* (PIP)

Madeline Puccioni. *Laundromat* (LaTempa)

Ruth Angell Purkey. *The Lady and the Lass*

Phyllis Purscell, Newtown, PA. (Women's Project) *Duets* (1981); *A Killing Frost* (1984); *RomCom: A Romantic Comedy* (1986); *Separate Ceremonies* (WP 1); *Square One* (1981)

Linda Putnam. (Reality Theatre) *Evergreen Solitude* (1976–77)

Mary Putnam. *Tragedy of Errors* (Ticknor & Fields, Boston, 1862)

Mary Thurman Pyle. *Little Strangers* (Smith, 1942)

Elsa Rael, NY. (Encompass; POW) *The Baal Shen Tov; A Day at Summer's End; The Girl on the Via Flaminia; The Illusionless Man; Mama Bett* (1985); *Mateo and the Genie; My Bride Is Freedom; Sally Hemings; Snow White* (1985)

Aishah Rahman. *Unfinished Women Cry in No Man's Land While a Bird Dies in a Gilded Cage* (Wilkerson)

Glenda Raikes. (Synthaxis) *Lily Pad Launch*

Ayn Rand. *Night of January 16th* (Longmans Green, 1936)

Katherine Jones Rao, NY. *Calamity Jane* (1984); *Difficult Friends* (1980); *A Fairytale for Adults* (1967); *The Myth of Annie Beckman* (1983); *On the Edge* (*American Literature Quarterly*, 1983); *Somewhere In Between; Two in One* (1982); *The Women of Cedar Creek* (1985)

Celeste Raspanti. *I Never Saw Another Butterfly* (1971)

Helen Ratcliffe. (Washington Area Feminist Theatre) *Lorraine, Gloria and Bootsie; The Railroad Women* (LaTempa)

Ellen Ratner, NY. *Personality* (w Gina Wendkos; WH)

Joyce Rayburn. *Cat in the Bag; Don't Start without Me; The Man Most Likely; Out on a Limb*

Bernice Reagon. *Upon This Rock*

Jean Reavey. *Adora; American Kaleidoscope; The Blandergets; Cracks in the Grand Old Manse; Eldorado Dream Train; The Incredible Julia; Mercy Me; Telephone Pole; Ten Ton Toys; Who Stole the American Crown Jewels?; Window*

M. Kilburg Reedy, NY. *Second Lady* (1983)

Mary Katherine Reely (1881–1959). *Flittermouse* (1927; Galbraith)

Edwena Reed. *A Man Always Keeps His Word* (*Negro History Bulletin* 26 (4): Jan. 1963)

Sylvia Regan. *The Fifth Season; The Golem; Great to Be Alive; Morning Star* (1940); *The Twelfth Hour; The Wind Up Toys; Zelda*

Muriel Resnik. *Any Wednesday* (1964)

Anna Helen Reuter. see Jane Trahey

Beah Richards, LA. *A Black Woman Speaks* (1950; Wilkerson); *One Is a Crowd* (1971)

Gillian Richards, NY. *Americas; In His 80th Year*

Anne Ridler. *The Departure* (*Some Time After and Other Poems*, Faber, 1972); *How Bitter the Bread* (Faber, 1963); *The Jesse Tree* (Lyrebird, 1972); *Who Is My Neighbor?* (*Some Time After*)

Alice C. D. Riley. *The Weathervane Elopes*

Mary Roberts Rinehart. (w A. Hopgood) *The Bat* (1932); *Seven Days* (1931)

Susan Rivers. *Maud Gonne Says No to the Poet* (WCP 3)

Barbara Robinson. *The Best Christmas Pageant Ever!*

Betsy Julia Robinson. *The Shanglers* (LaTempa)

Audrey Roos. *Speaking of Murder* (w Bill Roos)

Irene Rosenberg. see Charlotte Anker

Judith Ross. *An Almost Perfect Person; Via Galactica*

Beatrice Roth. *Seventeen: A Theatre Piece* (*Massachusetts Review* 24, 1, 1983); included in *A Trilogy* with *At That Time I Was Studying Carole Lombard* and *The Father*

Susanna H. Rowson (1762–1824). *Americans in England* (1797); *Slaves in Algiers* (1794; Scholarly Facsimiles, 1976)

Enid Rudd, West Orange, NJ. *Broadway; The Ashes of Mrs. Reasoner; Does Anybody Here Do the Peabody?; Father of the Bride; Locked In; The Other Side of Newark; Peterpat* (aka *The Marriage Gambol*, 1965); *Reign; A Step Out of Line; What a Lot of Blarney!*

Joanna Russ. *Communique from the Front* (*South* 4 (1), 1971); *Window Dressing* (1969; Moore)

Miriam Ryan. *All About Love*

Florence Ryerson. *The Third Angle* (Shay 2); (next three w Alice D. G. Miller) *Follow the Dream; Little Scandal; Sky High*; (all following w Colin Clements) *Angels Don't Marry; The Divine Flora; Ever Since Eve; Harriet* (1942); *Hot Lemonade* (1929); *June Mad; Ladies Alone; Oh! Susanna; Spring Green; Strange Bedfellows; The Tenth Word; The Willow Plate*

Christopher St. John. *The Good Hope* (1903); *Paphnutius* (from Hrosvitha, the Medieval Library Series); *The Rising Sun* (1929); see Cicely Hamilton

Salimu. *Growin' into Blackness* (Bullins)

Gertrude Samuels. *The Assignment; The Corrupters* (BSP); *Judah the Maccabee and Me* (*Dekalb College Literary Arts Journal*); *Kibbutz; Reckonings*

Milcha Sanchez-Scott. *The Cuban Swimmer* (PIP); *Dog Lady* (Delgado); *Latina; Roosters* (Osborn)

Sonia Sanchez. *The Bronx Is Next* (*Drama Review*, 1968); *Dirty Hearts* (1971; Scripts 1); *Malcolm Man Don't Live Here No More* (*Black Theatre*, no. 6); *Sister Son/Ji* (Bullins); *Uh, Uh, But How Do It Free Us?* (Ed Bullins, ed., *The New Lafayette Theatre Presents, 6 Plays*, Doubleday, 1974)

Nahma Sandrow. *Kuni Leml*

Susan Sandler. *Crossing Delancey*

Amelia Sanford. *The Ghost of an Idea* (The Penn. Publ. Co., Philadelphia, 1898)

Carol de Santa. *Thom & Jerri*

Caroline Schaffner. (w Neil Schaffner) *Natalie Needs a Nightie; Right Bed, Wrong Husband*

Edna Schappert, NY. *Abstract of a Present Day; At a Cocktail Party; The Big Shot* (1979); *Celebrate Me!* (1971); *The Crow Flyeth!; Enzymes at Work; Granny Grass; Hairy Tales of Evolution* (1979); *Holiday in Space; How to Survive in Spite of It All; The Ice Cubes* (1977; The Scene); *Lonely Friends* (1983); *Mechanical Bugs* (1972); *The Money Committee; Oh! What Fools We Morsels Be . . . ; The Onion and the Strawberry Seed* (1983); *The Pandas* (1974); *Regret Me Not* (Hunter Press, 1979); *Teddy* (1971); *The Trouble Maker* (1971); *Water Strike!* (1971); *Will O' The W.A.S.P.* (1978); (see collection published by Edgemore Publishing Company, 1971)

Joan Schenkar. (Women's Project) *Between the Acts; Bucks and Does; Cabin Fever* (1977); *Family Pride in the 50's* (1986); *Fulfilling Koch's Postulate* (1985); *Joan of Arc: The First Course* (1986); *The Last of Hitler* (1981); *Last Words* (1979); *The Lodger* (1979); *Mr. Monster* (1980); *The Next Thing; Nothing Is Funnier Than Death; Signs of Life* (WP 1); *Things Could Happen; The Tree*

Jo Ann Schmidman, Omaha. (Omaha Magic Theatre) *Aliens Under Glass; Astro*Bride* (New Plays from the Best of America's Regional Theatres*, Broadway Play Publishing, 1987); *Change Yer Image* (1981); *100,001 Horror Stories of the Plains* (1976); *The Initiation; Mutation Show* (w Open Theatre); *Nightwalk* (w Open Theatre; Obie); *Running Gag* (1980); *Sea of Forms* (w Megan Terry) (Valhalla 4, Ragnarok Press, 1974); *Velveeta Meltdown; Watch Where We Walk; X-Rayed-iate: E-Motion in Action* (w MT, 1984); (see *High Energy Musicals from the Omaha Magic Theatre*, Broadway Play Publishing, 1983; Omaha Magic Theatre Press)

Carolee Schneemann. *Meat Joy* (1964; Benedikt); *More than Meat Joy* (Documentext, New Paltz, NY, 1978)

Barbara Schneider. *Details without a Map* (Blackburn Prize)

Barbara Schottenfeld. *I Can't Keep Running in Place*

Pat Schneider. *After the Applebox; Counterpoint in Straw* (Laurel Review); *Crossroad to Bethlehem;*

Crosswalk; Peter; A Question of Place (VPT); *Three Flights Down* (Westminster Press); *The Undertaking* (Abingdon Press); *The Wake*

Mary Schulz. see Tamu Gray

Natalie V. Scott. *Zombi* (Plays of American Life and Fantasy, Edith Isaacs, ed., Coward-McCann, New York, 1929)

Ellen Sebastian. *Your Place Is No Longer with Us* (WCP 13/14)

Marilyn Seven, St. Paul, MN. (At the Foot of the Mountain) *The Barber-Surgeon Had a Wife* (1986); *Controlling the Rent* (1987); *Double Dutch* (1982); *The Ladies Who Lunch* (1985); *Life upon the Wicked Stage* (1976); *Mother's Little Helper* (1986)

Ann Seymour. *Lawd, Does You Undahstan'?* (ROAP)

Laura Shamas, Denver. *Amelia; Amelia Lives; Babylon Revisited* (1984); *Fitness Lady Like; The Last Slumber Party; Living Doll; Mr. and Mrs. Abbey's Difficulties* (1984); *Nancy Drew and the Swami's Ring* (1982); *The Other Shakespeare* (1980); *Picnic at Hanging Rock* (1987); *Runestone Hill; Telling Time; Unicorn Song*

Ntozake Shange. *Betsey Brown* (adapt. from her novel, w Emily Mann); *Black & White Two-Dimensional Planes* (1979); *Bocas: A Daughter's Geography & Three for a Full Moon* (1982); *Boogie-Woogie Landscapes* (1979); *Educating Rita* (adaptation); *For Colored Girls Who Have Considered Suicide/ When the Rainbow Is Enuf* (1976; Obie; Outer Critics Circle Award; Bantam); *From Okra to Greens* (1978); *Mother Courage and Her Children* (from Brecht, 1980; Obie); *A Photograph, A Study of Cruelty* (1977); *Shapes, Sadness and the Witch; Spell #7* (1979); *Where the Mississippi Meets the Amazon* (w J. Hagedorn and T. Davis, 1977)

Adele Edling Shank, SF. (Women's Project) *Dry Smoke* (1981); *Fox & Co.* (from Ben Jonson, 1977); *The Grass House* (1983; PIP); *Innocence Abroad* (1981); *Sand Castles* (1981; WCP 15/16); *Stuck* (1980; PIP); *Sunset/Sunrise: A Hyperreal Comedy* (1979; WCP 4); *Tumbleweed; War Horses* (1984); *Winterplay* (NP 1)

Marsha Sheiness. *Clair and the Chair; Dealer's Choice; Monkey Monkey Bottle of Beer, How Many Monkeys Have We Here?; Pancho Pancho; Professor George; Reception; The Spelling Bee; Stop the Parade*

Elsa Shelley. *Foxhole in the Parlor; Pick-Up Girl* (BP, 1943–44)

Nina Shengold. *Homesteaders*

Marcia Ann Shenk. *Diary*

Lisa Shipley. (The Womyn's Theatre) *The Bathtub* (WCP 5); *Dear Child*

Rima Shore. *Life in America* (Conditions: Three 1 (3): 1978)

Marion Short. see Pauline Phelps

Joan Micklin Silver. see Julianne Boyd

Susie Smith Sinclair. *Graveyard Day* (Smith)

Rosemary Sisson. *A Ghost on Tiptoe* (w Robert Morley); *The Splendid Outcasts* (POY, 1959)

Cornelia Otis Skinner. *One Woman Show* (1974); *The Pleasure of His Company* (w Samuel Taylor)

Susan Slade. *Ready When You Are, C.B.*

Betty Smith (1904–72). *Fun After Supper* (1940); *Heroes Just Happen* (w Robert Finch); *A Tree Grows in Brooklyn* (w George Abbott; Harper, 1951); *Youth Takes Over*

Beverly Smith. *Family Portrait* (WCP 17/18)

Dodie Smith. *Call It a Day* (BP, 1935–36); *Dear Octopus; I Capture the Castle*

Jean Smith. *O. C.'s Heart* (Negro Digest, April 1970)

Pauline W. Snapp. *Accidentally Yours*

Edith Sommer. *A Roomful of Roses* (1955)

Carol Sorgenfrei. *Medea: A Noh Cycle Based on the Greek Myth*

Katherine Githa Sowerby. *Rutherford and Son* (Dickinson, 1912)

Muriel Spark. *Doctors of Philosophy* (Knopf, 1966)

Doralyne Spence. see Dorothy Manley

Eulalie Spence. *Foreign Mail* (1927); *Fool's Errand* (1927); *Help Wanted* (Saturday Evening Quill, Boston, April 1929); *Her* (1927); *The Hunch* (1927); *The Starter* (Locke); *Undertow* (Hatch)

Bella Spewack. *Boy Meets Girl* (w Samuel Spewack, 1953); *Clear All Wires* (1932); *The Festival* (w SS, 1955); *Kiss Me Kate* (1948; Harms, 1951); *Leave It to Me* (Hart, 1938); *Miss Swann Expects* (Trousers to Match) (w SS, 1939); *My Three Angels* (w SS, 1952); *Poppa; The Solitaire Man* (1934); *Spring Song* (w SS; Random, 1936); *Woman Bites Dog* (w SS)

Lezley Steele (aka Lezley Havard), Philadelphia. *The Actors* (1981); *Arrangements* (1984); *The Courting* (1985); *Dear John* (1983); *Hide and Seek* (aka *Jill*; 1977); *In the Bag* (1982); *In the Name of the Father* (1980); *Session* (1986); *Termination Point; Victims* (1978); *A Woman's Place* (1983); *What Ever Happened to Charity?*

Gertrude Stein (1874–1946). (Geogra-

ingale (1922); *Plumes in the Dust* (1936)

Francine L. Trevens. *Applejuice* (The Scene 2); *Best Life; Best of Strangers; Little Boy Lost; Marriage of Inconvenience; No One; Shortages; This'll Kill Ya*

Margaret Turnbull. *At the Mitre*

Catherine Turney. *My Dear Children* (w Jerry Horwin)

Willie Tyson. (Washington Area Feminist Theatre) *Bless These Women* (1975)

Ethel Van der Veer. *Babuuscka* (1929); *The Feast of Barking Women; Romance of the Willow Pattern* (1942); *St. Cyprian and the Devil* (1928)

Joan Vatsek. *Mark's Place*

Susan Vick. *Generations* (aka *Investments*); *If You Only Loved Birds the Way I Do; Only Just a Minute; Ord-Way Ames-Gay; Quandry; When I Was Your Age* (VPT)

Ellen Violett. see Lisabeth Blake

Paula Vogel. *Meg* (1977)

Lula Vollmer (1898–1955). *The Dunce Boy* (1925); *The Hill Between* (Longmans Green, 1939); *Moonshine and Honeysuckle* (1934); *Sentinels* (1931; BP); *The Shame Woman* (1923); *Sun-Up* (RAP); *Trigger* (1927)

Rebecca Wackler. *Tent Meeting* (w Larry Larson and Levi Lee; PIP)

Jane Wagner. *The Search for Signs of Intelligent Life in the Universe* (Harper & Row, 1986; NY Drama Critics Circle Special Citation)

Dolores Walker. (Westbeth) *Abide in Darkness* (1971); *Recess* (1968, w Andrew Piotrowski)

Nancy Walter. *Blessings* (1970); *Rags* (1969; PT); *Stab and Dance* (1972); *Still Falling* (1971; Arthur Sainer, ed., *The Radical Theatre Notebook*, Avon, 1975); *The Window* (1972); *Traveling Light* (1972); *Trinity* (1968)

Alice H. Ware. *Like a Flame; Together* (Both: *Theatre Workshop Magazine* 11, 1938; *Mighty Wind A'Blowin'* (1938); *The Open Door* (1923)

Dorothy Waring. see Zora Neale Hurston

Rose Warner. *Lavender and Old Lace*

Mercy Otis Warren (1728–1814). *The Adulateur* (Boston, 1773); *The Blockheads, or, The Affrighted Officers* (attributed to her, 1776); *The Defeat* (1773); *The Group* (1775; RPAD); *The Motley Assembly* (attributed to her, 1779); (see Norman Philbrick, ed., *Trumpets Sounding: Propaganda Plays of the American Revolution*, Blom, 1972)

Wendy Wasserstein. *Isn't It Romantic; Miami* (w Jack Feldman and Bruce Sussman); *Sunset at Camp*

O'Henry; Tender Offers; Uncommon Women and Others (Avon, 1978)

Jane Waterhouse. *Fannies* (1985); *House of Cards* (1981); *Neon Hearts* (1984); *Private Apartments* (1983); *Public Domain* (1985); *Specialties of the House* (1984)

Maurine Watkins. *Chicago* (1926); *Revelry* (1927); *Marshland*

Ara Watson. *Bite the Hand* (1984); *Blue Light Dancing* (1986); *A Different Moon* (1982); *The Duck Pond* (1979); *Family Things* (w Mary Gallagher, 1983); *Final Placement* (1980); *HPB* (1984); *In Between Time* (1985); *Just a Little Hiccup on the Road* (1984); *Little Miss Fresno* (w MG, 1983); *Reunion* (1979); *Scarecrows* (1978)

Billie Lou Watt. *Phillis* (Friendship Press, NY, 1969)

Anne Weatherby. *Undertow*

Abiola Roselle Weaver. *The Matriarchs* (c 1976)

Margaret H. Weber. *George Washington Fourth* (Row, Peterson & Co., 1942)

Jean Webster. *Daddy Long Legs; Love from Judy*

Elizabeth Wehner. *Little Immortal* (Smith)

Rita Weiman. *The Acquittal* (*Footlights*, 1919)

Rae Welch. *Let's Get Out of Here* (BOAP, 1957–58)

Rita Wellman. *For All Time* (1918; Shay 1); *Funiculi, Funicula* (1910's)

Ruth Welty. *A Hint of Lilacs* (Smith)

Gina Wendkos, NY. (Women's Project) *Personality* (WH)

Mae West. *The Constant Sinner* (Macauley, 1931); *Diamond Lil* (Macauley, 1932); *The Drag* (1927); *Pleasure Man* (BP, 1928–29); *Sex* (1926); *Sextet* (1961)

Lucy White. *Bird Child* (1922; Locke)

Natalie E. White. *Seven Nuns at Las Vegas; Seven Nuns South of the Border*

May Hoyt Wiborg. *Taboo* (BP, 1921–22)

Sally Dixon Wiener, NY. *The Blue Magi* (1972); *Flyin' Turtles* (1976); *Jude's People* (1985); *Marjorie Daw* (1970); *Mlle. Olympe Zabriski* (1983); *The Pimienta Pancakes* (1976); *Second Battle of Baltimore* (1981); *Show Me a Hero* (1979); *Stag Party* (1985); *Telemachus, Friend* (1972)

Kate Douglas Wiggin (1856–1923). *The Old Peabody Pew*

Allene Tupper Wilkes. *Creaking Chair*

Doris Willens. *Piano Bar*

June Vanleer Williams, Cleveland. *A Bit of Almsgiving; The Eyes of the Lofty* (1984); *The Face of Job*

(1980); *The Meek Won't Inherit S—!; Two Wandering Sons of Ham; Will the Real You Please Stand Up?* (Dorrance and Co.)

Margaret Williams. (w Hugh Williams) *Flip Side; Grass Is Greener; The Irregular Verb to Love* (1963); *Past Imperfect*

Marjorie Williams. *Out of the Night* (w Harold Hutchinson)

Jane Willis. *Slam!* (Delgado)

Julia Willis. *Going Up* (McDermott)

Alice T. Wilson. *How a Poet Made Money & Forget-Me-Nots* (Pageant Press, NY, 1968)

Elizabeth Wilson. *The Lord and Hacksaw Sadie* (BOAP, 1946–47)

Marian Winters. *All Is Bright; All Saint's Day* (*A Is For All*, 1968); *Animal Keepers; Assembly Line; Breadwinner; Getting There Soon; The Tour*

Kathleen Witherspoon. *Jule* (Three Southwest Plays, Play Anthology Reprint Series, Books for Libraries Press, Freeport, NY, 1942/1970)

Ruth Wolff, NY. *The Abdication* (Moore); *Arabic Two; Eden Again; Eleanor of Aquitaine* (1965); *Empress of China* (1974); *The Fall of Athens; Folly Cove; George and Frederic; The Golem* (from H. Leivick, 1959); *The Perfect Marriage* (1983); *Sarah in America* (1981); *Still Life with Apples*

Margaret Wood. *Home Is the Sailor* (BP, 1956–57)

Maxine Wood. *On Whitman Avenue*

Elizabeth Wray, SF. (both in Mac Wellman, ed., *Theater of Wonders*, Sun & Moon Press, 1985); *Border* (1981); *Forecast* (1982)

Olwen Wymark. (*The Gymnasium & Other Plays*, Calder, 1971—G; *Three Plays*, Calder, 1967—T) *Coda* (T); *Find Me* (c 1979); *The Gymnasium* (1967; G); *The Inhabitants* (T); *Jack the Giant Killer* (G); *Lunchtime Concert* (1966; T); *Neither Here nor There* (1971; G); *Stay Where You Are* (1969; G); *The Technicians* (1969; G)

Wakako Yamauchi. *And the Soul Shall Dance* (WCP 11/12)

Susan Yankowitz, NY. (Omaha Magic Theatre; Westbeth; Women's Interart) *Acts of Love* (1973); *America Piece* (1974); *Baby* (1982); *Basics* (1972); *Boxes* (1972; PT); *The Cage* (1965); *The Ha-Ha Play* (Scripts 10); *A Knife in the Heart* (1982); *The Lamb* (1970); *Monk's Revenge* (1983); *Monologues for the Wicked Women Revue* (1973); *Nightmare* (1967); *Positions* (1972); *Qui Est Anna Mark?; Rats' Alley* (1969); *Sideshow; Slaughterhouse Play* (*Yale/Theater* 2, 2, 1969); *Still Life*

(1977); *Terminal* (w Open The-
atre, 1973; *Scripts* 1); *That Old
Rock-A-Bye*; *Transplant* (1971);
True Romances (1978); *Who Done
It?* (1982); *Wooden Nickels* (1973)
Elizabeth H. Yates. *The Slave* (*Small
Plays for Small Casts*, Penn.
Publ. Co., Philadelphia, 1926)
Lorees Yerby. *Save Me a Place at For-
est Lawn*
Irene Yesner-Ringawa. (Violet Ray
Theater Arts) *Double Visions*,

Tales and Dreams (w Suzin
Green); *My Name Is Alice* (1977);
Tender Alchemy (1978); *We Are
Your Sisters* (w SG, 1976);
Wrinkly Old Lady Dancer
(1977–78)
Charlotte Zaltsberg. *Raisin* (w
Robert Nemiroff; from
Hansberry)
Suzan L. Zeder, Dallas. *Because You
Never Asked Me* (1984); *The
Death and Life of Sherlock Holmes*

(from Doyle, 1987); *Doors*
(1981); *In a Room Somewhere*
(1986); *The Miser* (from Molière,
1986); *Mother Hicks* (1983); *Ozma
of Oz: A Tale of Time* (1978); *The
Play Called Noah's Flood* (1972);
Something with Jamie in the Title
(1975); *Spa!* (1982); *Step on a
Crack* (1974); *Wiley and the Hairy
Man* (1972); (see Anchorage
Press)

Text Notes

Sex Roles and Shamans

1. Knud Rasmussen. *Across Arctic
America.* G. P. Putnam's Sons,
1927, pp. 71–72.
2. Joseph Epes Brown, ed. *The Sacred
Pipe.* Penguin reprint, 1972.
3. See for further discussion Peggy
V. Beck and A. L. Walters, *The
Sacred: Ways of Knowledge, Sources
of Life.* Navajo Community College, Tsaile, Arizona, Navajo Nation, 1977.
4. John G. Neihardt. *Black Elk Speaks.*
Simon & Schuster, Pocket Books,
and University of Nebraska
Press, copyright John G.
Neihardt 1959, 1961.
5. Charlotte Johnson Frisbie. *Kinaal-
dá.* Wesleyan University Press,
1967.
6. Franz Boas. *Kwakiutl Ethnography.*
Helen Codere, ed. University of
Chicago Press, 1966. Reprinted
by permission of the University
of Chicago Press.
7. Ruth Murray Underhill. *Singing for
Power.* University of California
Press, 1938.
8. Mircea Eliade. *Shamanism.* Willard
R. Trask, trans. Princeton University Press, 1964.
9. Beck and Walters. See for more
discussion of Native American
shamans.
10. R. G. Wasson et al. *María Sabina
and Her Mazatec Mushroom Vela-
da.* Harcourt Brace Jovanovich,
1974. Contemporary poet Anne
Waldman's poem/chant "Fast
Speaking Woman" is based on
María Sabina's chant. *Fast Speaking Woman & Other Chants.* City
Lights, 1975.
11. Wasson et al. as quoted by Joan
Halifax, ed. in *Shamanic Voices.*
E. P. Dutton, 1979, pp. 212–13.
12. See playwright Mary Austin's *The*

Arrow-Maker, Houghton Mifflin,
1915. She builds the dramatic
conflict around the desire of her
heroine, the Chisera, to be both
a shaman and a married woman
with children.

Trampling Out the Vintage

1. W. C. Steel. *The Woman's Temperance Movement, A Concise History
of the War on Alcohol.* Introduction by Dio Lewis. New York:
National Temperance Society &
Publication House, 1874, pp. 36–
37.
2. Eliza Jane Trimble Thompson, Her
Two Daughters, and Frances
Willard. *Hillsboro Crusade Sketches
and Family Records.* Cincinnati:
Cranston & Curts, 1896, pp. 57–
149.
3. Mrs. Annie Wittenmyer. *History of
the Woman's Temperance Crusade.*
Philadelphia: Office of the
Christian Woman, 1878, p. 659.
4. Steel, p. 12.
5. Jane E. Stebbins. *Fifty Years' History of the Temperance Cause, With
a Full Description of the New Plan
of Labor by the Women Up to the
Present Time.* Hartford: Published
by L. Stebbins, 1874, p. 323.
6. Wittenmyer, p. 352.
7. Reverend W. H. Daniels, ed. *The
Temperance Reform and Its Great
Reformers.* New York: Nelson &
Phillips, 1878, p. 294.
8. Mother Stewart. *Memories of the
Crusade, A Thrilling Account of the
Great Uprising of the Women of
Ohio in 1873, Against the Liquor
Crime.* Chicago: H. J. Smith &
Co., 1890, p. 194.
9. Mrs. Matilda Gilruth Carpenter.
*The Crusade: Its Origin and De-
velopment at Washington Court
House and Its Results.* Columbus:

W. G. Hubbard & Co., Pub-
lishers, 1893, p. 71.
10. J. H. Beadle. *The Women's War on
Whiskey: Its History, Theory, and
Prospects.* Cincinnati: Wilstach,
Baldwin & Co., 1874, pp. 47–48.
11. Steel, p. 46.
12. Wittenmyer source for this section, pp. 264, 208, 224, 176, 210–
11, 450, 81, 184, 156, 685, 199.
13. Stewart, p. 188.
14. Stebbins, pp. 324–25.
15. Wittenmyer source for this section, pp. 333, 193, 265, 448, 54.
16. *Cincinnati Commercial*, March 7,
1874.
17. *Springfield Republic*, January 7,
1874.
18. Stewart, p. 336; see also *New-York
Daily Tribune*, March 7, 1874.
19. Steel, p. 27.
20. Carpenter, p. 104.
21. Steel, pp. 30–31.
22. Wittenmyer, p. 50.
23. Stewart, p. 220.
24. *Minutes of the First Convention of
the National Woman's Christian
Temperance Union.* Chicago:
Woman's Temperance Publication Association, 1889, pp. 3–40.
25. *Union Signal*, December 20, 1883.
26. Wittenmyer, p. 16.

Friendship and Ritual in the WTUL

1. *Signs*, vol. I, pp. 1–29, 1975. See
also Keith E. Melder. *Beginnings
of Sisterhood: The American
Woman's Rights Movement, 1800–
1850.* Schocken Books, 1977, pp.
30–48. Nancy F. Cott. *The Bonds
of Womanhood: "Woman's Sphere"
in New England, 1780–1835.* Yale,
1977, pp. 160–96.
2. Rosalyn Baxandall, Linda Gordon,
and Susan Reverby, eds. *America's Working Women: A*

Documentary History—1600 to the Present. Vintage, 1976, p. xviii.
3. Quoted in Mary E. Dreier to Margaret Dreier Robins and Raymond Robins, January 29, 1941. Margaret Dreier Robins Papers, University of Florida, Gainesville, Florida.
4. Rose Schneiderman to Margaret Dreier Robins, June 4, 1936, Robins Papers; Ricki Myers Cohen. *Fannie Cohn and the International Ladies' Garment Workers Union.* Ph.D. thesis, University of Southern California, 1976, p. 200.
5. Anna Rudnitzky. "Time Is Passing." *Life and Labor,* vol. 2 (April 1912), p. 99.
6. Barry Schwartz. "The Social Psychology of the Gift." *The American Journal of Sociology,* vol. 73 (July 1967), p. 3.
7. In quieter factories, women workers often found diversion on the job. "To drown the monotony of work," glove-worker Agnes Nestor recalled, "we used to sing." Agnes Nestor. *Woman's Labor Leader: An Autobiography of Agnes Nestor.* Rockford, Illinois: Bellevue Books Publishing Co., 1954, p. 28.
8. Margaret Dreier Robins quoted in "Educational Side of Women's Trade Unionism," *New York Tribune,* October 12, 1919; *Some of the Happy Features of the Women's Trade Union League of Chicago,* WTUL of Chicago, Leaflet No. 3, June 1909. See also William L. O'Neill, *Everyone Was Brave, A History of Feminism in America.* Quadrangle Books, 1969, pp. 104–16.
9. S. M. Franklin. "The Fifth Biennial." *Life and Labor,* vol. 5 (July 1915), p. 116.
10. For the use of birthday parties as a bonding mechanism among an age-based group see Elizabeth Colson, "The Least Common Denominator," in *Secular Ritual,* Moore and Myerhoff, pp. 189–98.
11. Agnes Nestor to Margaret Dreier Robins, April 29, 1924, Robins Papers.
12. Margaret Dreier Robins, "The Human Side of the Industrial South." Address presented at Southern Session, Eleventh Convention of the National Women's Trade Union League, May 9, 1929, Robins Papers.
13. Schwartz, pp. 2–3.
14. *Life and Labor,* vol. 6 (April 1916), p. 59.
15. See, for example, William H. Chafe, *The American Woman, Her Changing Social, Economic and Political Roles, 1920–1970.* Oxford

University Press, 1972, pp. 73–74.
16. Leonora O'Reilly, Diary 16, March 17, 1909. Papers of Leonora O'Reilly, Schlesinger Library, Radcliffe College, Cambridge, Massachusetts.

Rites and Rights

1. Lavinia Egan. "The Seneca Falls Conference." *Equal Rights,* vol. 1, no. 25 (August 4, 1923), p. 198.
2. Hazel Mackaye. "Campaigning with Pageantry." *Equal Rights,* vol. 1, no. 39 (November 10, 1923), p. 389.
3. The Woman's Party's journal, *Equal Rights,* contains a rich variety and an abundant quantity of articles on the party's pageants and its attitudes regarding their role as a vanguard of idealists. For a representative selection of citations in which both themes appear, see especially vol. 1 (1923), pp. 18, 22–24, 29–31, 35.

"Lesson I Bleed"

1. Edward Parone, ed. *Collision Course.* Random House, 1968, p. 35.
2. Janice Delaney, Mary Jane Lupton, and Emily Toth. *The Curse: A Cultural History of Menstruation.* New American Library, 1976. I am indebted to Anne Harmon for calling my attention to certain culturally conditioned rites of passage, such as the practice of African genital mutilation performed on girls as young as five years of age in parts of Africa today. See also Mary Daly, *Gyn/Ecology: The Metaethics of Radical Feminism.* Beacon Press, 1978, especially Chapter Five, pp. 153–177.
3. Kennedy's grotesque imagery comes from her own nightmares which she has recorded in dream journals as described in an interview with Lisa Lehman: "*A Rat's Mass* was based on a dream I once had when I was on a train . . . going from Paris to Rome, . . . I had this dream in which I was being pursued by red, bloodied rats. It was a very powerful dream, and when I woke up the train had stopped in the Alps. It was at night. I had never felt that way. It was a crucial night in my life. So, I was just haunted by that image for years, about being pursued by these big, red rats." "A Growth of Images." *The Drama Review,*

vol. 21, no. 4 (1977), p. 44.
4. Adrienne Kennedy. *A Rat's Mass,* in *New Black Playwrights,* edited by William Couch. Avon Books, 1970, p. 87.
5. Robert L. Tener. "Theatre of Identity: Adrienne Kennedy's Portrait of Black Woman." *Studies in Black Literature,* vol. 6, no. 5 (1975), p. 3. To illuminate the imagery in this play, see also Merlin Stone, *When God Was a Woman.* Harcourt Brace Jovanovich, 1976, pp. 214–16.

Anne Brunton Merry

1. Anne Brunton married Robert Merry in 1791. She subsequently married Thomas Wignell in 1803, and William Warren in 1806. Although most often remembered by historians as Mrs. Merry, she always performed under the name of the man to whom she was married.
2. Philadelphia, *Gazette of the United States and Philadelphia Daily Advertiser,* December 7, 1796, hereinafter cited as *Gazette of the United States.*
3. William Dunlap. *History of the American Theatre.* London, 1833, vol. I, pp. 336–37.
4. James L. Clifford. "Robert Merry—a pre-Byronic Hero," *Bulletin of the John Rylands Library,* vol. XXVII (1942), pp. 74–92.
5. Charlotte Barrett, ed. *Diary and Letters of Madam D'Arblay,* July 1791–April 1802. London, 1904–1905, pp. 39–40.
6. Dunlap, *History of the American Theatre,* vol. II, pp. 148–49.
7. William I. Warren. Journals. Channing Pollock Theatre Collection, Howard University, Washington, D.C., June 14, 1801. Hereinafter cited as Warren, Journals.
8. Charles Durang. "The Philadelphia Stage from the Year 1749 to the year 1885," *Philadelphia Sunday Dispatch,* Chapter XXXIV, December 24, 1854.
9. James Fennell. *An Apology for the Life of James Fennell.* Philadelphia, 1814, p. 366. See also Thomas Condie, "Biographical Anecdotes of Mrs. Merry of the Theatre, Philadelphia." *Philadelphia Monthly Magazine,* or *Universal Repository of Knowledge and Entertainment,* vol. I (April 1798), p. 187.
10. Durang, "The Philadelphia Stage," Chapter XXXI, December 3, 1854.
11. Durang, "The Philadelphia Stage," Chapter XXXII, December 10, 1854.
12. Durang, "The Philadelphia Stage."
13. *New York Evening Post,* June 25,

1805, June 27, 1805.

14. Durang, "The Philadelphia Stage," Chapter XXXIX, January 28, 1855.

15. William Dunlap. *Diary of William Dunlap*. 3 vols., vol. II. New York, 1930, p. 419.

16. *New York Evening Post*, March 3, 1807.

Enter the Harlot

1. Winthrop S. Huson, *American Protestantism*. University of Chicago Press, pp. 96–110.

2. James Monroe Buckley. *Christians and the Theatre*. Nelson and Philips, 1875, pp. 10–18, 116. David Grimsted. *Melodrama Unveiled*. University of Chicago Press, 1968, p. 25.

3. Robert Hatfield. *The Theatre*. Methodist Book Depository, 1866, pp. 27, 28.

4. Thomas DeWitt Talmadge. *Sports That Kill*. Harper and Brothers, 1875, p. 17.

5. John Hodgkinson. *Narrative of His Connection with the Old America Company*. Oram, 1797, p. 22.

6. Frances Trollope. *Domestic Manners of the Americans*. Alfred A. Knopf, rpt 1949, p. 564.

7. Albert A. Palmer. "American Theatres," *One Hundred Years of American Commerce*. Haynes Publishing Company, 1895, p. 157.

8. Daniel Frohman. *Daniel Frohman Presents*. C. Kendall and W. Sharp, 1935, p. 44.

9. Anna Cora Mowatt. *The Autobiography of an Actress*. Ticknor, Reed and Fields, 1854, pp. 214, 445.

10. Clara Morris. *Stage Confidences*. Lothrop Publishing Company, 1902, pp. 13–32.

11. William Wood. *Personal Recollections of the Stage*. H. C. Baird, 1855, p. 208.

12. Noah Ludlow. *Dramatic Life as I Found It*. G. I. Jones, 1880, p. 347. Sol Smith. *Theatrical Management in the West and South for Thirty Years*. Harper and Brothers, 1868, p. 60. Mrs. Maud Skinner. *One Man in His Time: The Adventures of H. Watkins, Strolling Player*, 1845, 1863, pp. 38, 47.

13. Hatfield, p. 24.

14. Joseph N. Ireland. *Mrs. Duff*. James R. Osgood, 1822, pp. 134–41.

15. Margaret Armstrong. *Fanny Kemble: Passionate Victorian*. Macmillan, 1938, pp. 151, 153, 184. Fanny Kemble Wister, ed. *Fanny, the American Kemble*. South Pass Press, 1972, pp. 37, 92.

16. Olive Logan. *Apropos of Women and the Theatre*. Carleton Publishers, 1869, p. 8.

17. Buckley, pp. 64, 65.

18. David Hayes Agnew. *Theatrical Amusements*. W. S. Young, 1857, pp. 6, 7.

19. Buckley, p. 65.

20. Talmadge, p. 18.

21. Robert Turnbull. *The Theatre*. Caufield and Robins, 1837, p. 92

22. Trollope, p. 74.

23. Buckley, pp. 50–65.

24. Samuel G. Winchester. *The Theatre*. W. S. Martien, 1840, p. 196.

25. "A Letter to Respectable Ladies Who Frequent the Theatre." *The Christian Spectator*, vol. I, no. 8 (August 1827), pp. 415, 416.

26. Winchester, p. 199.

27. Tyrone Power. *Impressions of America During the Years 1832, 1834, 1835*. Richard Bentley, 1836, vol. I, pp. 62, 172, 211, 352; vol. II, pp. 172, 191.

28. Charles Dickens. *American Notes*. Chapman and Hall, 1842, vol. I, p. 141.

29. Meade Minnigerode. *The Fabulous Forties*. G. P. Putnam's Sons, 1924, pp. 150–56.

30. W. W. Clapp. *Record of the Boston Stage*. B. Blom, 1868, p. 298.

31. William Davidge. *The Drama Defended*. Samuel French, 1859, pp. 13, 14.

32. Mowatt, pp. 214–313.

33. Elizabeth Dexter. *Career Women of America: 1876–1940*. Marshall Jones Company, 1950, p. 87. In *American Actress: Perspectives on the Nineteenth Century* (Chicago, Nelson-Hall, 1984) Claudia Johnson points to the many advantages of a theatre career where a woman could gain "financial reward, professional status, and even a surprising equality with men." In a time when a teacher could earn $600 a year plus room and board, an ordinary actress could earn from $5,000 to $20,000 a year for what would seem to be easier and more rewarding work.

Women in Male Roles

1. All quotations in this section from George C. Odell, *Annals of the New York Stage*. Columbia University Press, 1927, vol. II, p. 560, vol. III, pp. 138, 249, 306.

2. Joseph Leach. *Bright Particular Star*. Yale University Press, 1970, p. 205.

3. Odell, vol. III, p. 575.

4. Unidentified clippings, Charlotte Cushman Scrapbook, Folger Shakespeare Library, Washington, D.C., n.d.,n.p.

5. Leach, p. 241.

6. Leach, p. 65.

7. Emma Stebbins, ed. *Charlotte Cushman: Her Letters and Memories of Her Life*. Houghton, Osgood, 1972, p. 60.

8. Leach, p. 175.

9. Undated letter, Players Club Library, New York City.

10. Eleanor Ruggles. *Prince of Players*. W. W. Norton, 1953, p. 133.

11. Lawrence Barrett. *Charlotte Cushman*. Dunlap Society, 1889, p. 21.

12. Stebbins, p. 59.

13. W. T. Price. *A Life of Charlotte Cushman*, Brentano's, 1894, p.138.

14. William Winter. *Other Days*, Moffat, Yard, 1908, p. 154.

15. Ruggles, p. 116.

16. Leach, p. 305.

17. Leach, p. 180.

18. Leach, p. 310.

19. Leach, p. 277.

20. Ruggles, p. 61.

21. Leach, p. 209.

22. Leach, p. 310.

23. Ruggles, p. 130.

24. Leach, p. 179.

Adah Isaacs Menken

1. Paul Lewis. *Queen of the Plaza*. New York, 1964, p. 124. Confusion abounds concerning the dates of Menken's *Mazeppa* and many of the other "facts" of her life.

2. One of the first friends with whom she used the name was Augustin Daly in 1861. *Bell's Life*, London, lists this as her real name. She gave notes for a biography to Daly—he never wrote it, but published the notes in the *New York Times*, September 6, 1868.

3. James Murdoch. *The Stage*. Philadelphia, 1880, p. 243.

4. Quote from clipping in *The Menken Portfolio*, Players Collection. Lincoln Center Library for the Performing Arts.

5. The *Albany Express* review was quoted by the *Sunday Mercury*, June 9, 1861.

6. Robert Henry Newell (alias D. C. Kerr). *My Life with Adah Isaacs Menken*. New York. No copies are extant in libraries. Lewis uses this as a source for numerous stories, though where he obtained a copy remains a mystery; perhaps from his general source, Mr. Ewing Hibbard, collector of Menken

memorabilia.
7. Bernard Falk. *The Naked Lady*. London, 1934, p. 65. Quoted from a letter found in the Harvard Theatre Collection.
8. This is quoted by Charles Warren Stoddard, "La Belle Menken." *National Magazine* (February 1905), p. 479. Falk and Lewis quote it as a *New York Tribune* comment, which it is not.
9. Allan Lesser, in *Enchanting Rebel*, New York, 1947, makes this estimate; source not known.
10. Ed James. *The Life and Times of Adah Isaacs Menken*. New York, 1881. Although this book, as well as the Newell biography, is not extant, there is proof that it actually existed. It is mentioned in a clipping from *Music and Drama*, June 24, 1882, in the *Players Collection*. As for Adah's "diary," referred to by Lewis, Harvard Library disclaims all knowledge of it.
11. Lewis, pp. 6, 16, 17 for quotations in this section.
12. Falk, p. 155.
13. Lewis, pp. 139, 140.
14. *Menken Portfolio, Players Collection*, clipping.
15. *Menken Portfolio, Players Collection*, clipping.
16. Lewis, p. 124. Lewis uses this quote and the following ones from undated newspapers and seems simply to attribute them to his time slot for the first New York performance in 1861, even though such reviews for that date do not exist.
17. The *New York Clipper*, May 7, 1886.
18. Lewis, p. 20.
19. Falk, p. 164.
20. Lewis, p. 17.

Lydia Thompson and the "British Blondes"

1. Bernard Sobel. *A Pictorial History of Burlesque*. G. P. Putnam's Sons, 1956. Irving Zeidman. *The American Burlesque Show*. Hawthorn Books, Inc., 1967. Ann Coria and Joseph Di Mona. *This Was Burlesque*. Grosset and Dunlap, 1968.
2. Olive Logan. *Before the Footlights and Behind the Scenes*, 1870, p. 585.
3. June 5, 1869. Clipping from the Theatre Collection, New York Public Library.
4. Brander Matthews. *These Many Years: Recollections of a New Yorker*. Charles Scribner's Sons, 1917, p. 153.
5. "The Return of Miss Lydia Thompson," *The Sketch*. October 30, 1895. Clipping from the Vic-

toria and Albert Museum Theatre Collection.
6. February 17, 1895, p. 4. Clipping from the Harvard Theatre Collection.
7. *The New York Herald*, February 17, 1895, p. 4. Clipping from the Harvard Theatre Collection.

Henrietta Vinton Davis

1. *Washington Bee*, July 21, 1883.
2. *New York Globe*, August 4, 1883.
3. Quoted in *New York Age*, April 28, 1888.
4. Quoted in *New York Age*, May 9, 1891.
5. *New York Freeman*, March 26, 1887.
6. Reprinted in *New York Age*, April 4, 1885.

Mary Shaw

1. Unmarked newspaper clipping. Theatre Collection, New York Public Library.
2. *New York Sun*, October 17, 1912.
3. Souvenir Book of Woman's Exhibition, 1902, p. 53. Theatre Collection, New York Public Library.
4. *New York Morning Telegraph*. n.d.
5. Unmarked newspaper clipping. Theatre Collection. New York Public Library.
6. Quoted in Einar Haugen, "Ibsen in America." *Norwegian-American Studies and Records*, 1959, vol. 20, p. 5.
7. Interview with Mary Shaw, February 14, 1903, Theatre Collection, New York Public Library.
8. Arthur W. Row. "Great Moments in Great Acting." *Poet Lore*, vol. 29 (1918), pp. 359–60.
9. *London Times*, July 1, 1899.
10. "Mary Shaw—A Woman of Thought and Action." *The Theatre*, vol. 2 (August 1902), p. 21.
11. William Winter. *Wallet of Time*. Moffat, Yard, and Company, 1913, vol. 2, p. 570.
12. *New York Dramatic News*, December 25, 1902.
13. Joseph P. Dannenburg. "Playing Ibsen in the Badlands." *The Theatre*, vol. 6 (August 6, 1906), pp. 219–21.
14. Untitled newspaper clipping, February 28, 1904. Theatre Collection, New York Public Library.
15. *Chicago Evening Post*, March 3, 1904.
16. *New York Magazine Program*, n.d. Theatre Collection, New York Public Library.
17. "My Plays Advocate Moral Reform!" *The Theatre*, vol. 5 (December 1905), p. 298. Mary

Shaw. "My Immoral Play." *McClure's*, vol. 38 (April 1912), p. 690.
18. See for details: *New York Commercial Advertiser*, October 25, 1905; *New York Times*, October 9, 1905; *New York Tribune, New York American, New York Herald* of October 31, 1905.
19. Quoted in Archibald Henderson, *George Bernard Shaw: Man of the Century*. Appleton-Century-Crofts, 1956, p. 511.
20. Rose Young. "Suffrage as Seen by Mary Shaw." *Harper's Weekly*, vol. 60 (May 8, 1915), p. 456.
21. Unmarked newspaper clipping, Theatre Collection, New York Public Library.
22. Ada Patterson. "Actresses' Clubs in America." *The Theatre*, vol. 20 (October 1914), p. 187.
23. Gamut Club pamphlet. Theatre Collection, New York Public Library.
24. Unmarked newspaper clipping. Theatre Collection, New York Public Library.
25. *Cleveland Leader*, February 2, 1913.
26. *New York Herald*, January 6, 1912.
27. For details in this section see Gamut Club pamphlet and the following: *New York Sun*, October 17, 1912; *New York Morning Telegraph*, August 8, 1914; September 8, 1914; *New York Mail*, August 27, 1914.
28. Unmarked newspaper clipping, Theatre Collection, New York Public Library.
29. *Equity* magazine, May 1930, p. 23.

The Art of Ruth Draper

1. An interview with Ruth Draper. "Talk of the Town." *New Yorker*, March 6, 1954.
2. R. D. Skinner. "Ruth Draper, Dramatist." *Commonweal*, vol. 11 (January 8, 1930), pp. 283–84.
3. R. D. Skinner, p. 284.
4. Other useful sources: Iris Origo. "Ruth Draper and Her Company of Characters." *Cornhill Magazine*, vol. 169 (Winter 1957), pp. 383–93. Iris Origo. "Ruth Draper." *Atlantic Monthly*, vol. 202 (October 1958), pp. 56–60. M. D. Zabel. *The Art of Ruth Draper, Her Dramas and Characters, with a Memoir*. Doubleday, 1960.

Women Mimes in America

R. J. Broadbent. *A History of Pantomime*. Citadel Press, 1965 (first published 1901).
Dance Index, vol. I, no. 3 (March 1942).
Angna Enters. *Silly Girl*. Houghton

Mifflin Co., 1944.

Angna Enters. *Artist's Life.* Coward-McCann, 1958.

Ric Estrada. "To Be a Clown." *Dance* (August 1968).

Trudi Schoop. *Won't You Join the Dance?* National Press Books, 1974.

Marian Hannah Winter. *The Theatre of Marvels.* Benjamin Blom, Inc., 1964.

Critical reviews of Enters, Schoop, and Goslar in various periodicals.

Mercy Warren

Plays

(Warren, Mercy Otis). *The Adulateur* Boston, 1773.

(Warren, Mercy Otis). *The Adulateur* (excerpts) in *The Massachusetts Spy,* March 26 and April 23, 1772.

(Warren, Mercy Otis). *The Defeat* (excerpts) in the *Boston Gazette,* May 24 and July 19, 1773.

(Warren, Mercy Otis). *The Group.* Edes and Gill, 1775.

(Warren, Mercy Otis). *The Group* (excerpts) in the *Boston Gazette,* January 23, 1775.

Books

Anthony, Katharine. *First Lady of the Revolution: The Life of Mercy Otis Warren.* Doubleday and Company, Inc., 1958.

Brown, Alice. *Mercy Warren. (Women of Colonial and Revolutionary Times).* Charles Scribner's Sons, 1896.

Hosmer, James K. *The Life of Thomas Hutchinson.* Houghton Mifflin and Company, 1896.

Quinn, Arthur Hobson. *A History of the American Drama from the Beginnings to the Civil War,* vol. I, 2nd ed. F. S. Crofts and Co., 1946.

Warren, Mercy Otis. *History of the Rise, Progress and Termination of the American Revolution Interspersed with Biographical, Political and Moral Observations.* 3 vols. E. Larkin, 1805.

Warren-Adams Letters, Being chiefly a correspondence among John Adams, Samuel Adams, and James Warren, vol. I. The Massachusetts Historical Society, 1917.

Articles and Unpublished Material

Ford, Worthington Chauncey. "Mrs. Warren's *The Group.*" *Massachusetts Historical Society Proceedings,* vol. LXII (1928–1929), pp. 15–22.

Hutcheson, Maud Macdonald. "Mercy Warren, 1728–1814," *The William and Mary Quarterly,* 3rd series, vol. X, no. 3 (July 1953), pp. 378–402.

Robinson, Alice McDonnell. "The Developing Ideas of Individual Freedom and National Unity as Reflected in American Plays and the Theatre, 1772–1819." Unpublished Ph.D. dissertation, Stanford University, Stanford, California, 1965.

Looking to Women

Unless otherwise indicated, texts used are individually published editions of Crothers's plays. Manuscripts are found in the Burnside-Frohman Collection, Theatre Collection, New York Public Library, and Rare Books, University of Pennsylvania Library.

1. Djuna Barnes. "The Tireless Rachel Crothers," *Theatre Guild,* vol. 8 (May 1931), p. 18.

2. Dates in parentheses refer to first production, usually in New York.

3. Undated clipping from an unknown Boston newspaper in Crothers Scrapbook, Special Collections, Illinois State University Library. Crothers's reference to her production of *He and She* suggests 1911 as the date of her remarks.

4. In this argument Crothers reflects the view of a woman she greatly admired, Katherine Bement Davis. Appointed New York City Commissioner of Corrections in 1914, Davis was the former supervisor of the Woman's Reformatory at Bedford, after which Crothers modeled the reform home in Act I of *Ourselves.*

5. Amy Bulley, English feminist, cited in Elaine Showalter, *A Literature of Their Own: British Women Novelists from Brontë to Lessing.* Princeton, 1977, p. 186. I am indebted to Showalter, especially in Chapter 7, "Feminist Novelists," for her clear distinction between the moderate and radical positions of feminists on the subject of woman's evolution, which she demonstrates was a central concept of feminist ideology.

6. Crothers quoted in an interview with Marguerite Mooers Marshall, "What Do Women Think of Other Women?" *New York World,* 1915. Crothers Scrapbook, Special Collections, Illinois State University Library.

7. Interview with Marguerite Mooers Marshall.

8. Rachel Crothers. "Troubles of a Playwright." *Harper's Bazaar,* vol. 45 (January 1911), p. 14.

9. *New York Sun,* January 4, 1914, in Crothers Scrapbook, vol. I, compiled by Irving Abrahamson, available on microfilm from University of Chicago Library.

10. In *Representative American Dramas National and Local,* ed. Montrose J. Moses. Boston, 1925.

11. In *Mary the Third, Old Lady 31,* and *A Little Journey,* New York, 1923, p. 147. Subsequent references to this edition are in the text.

12. In *Representative Modern Plays,* ed. Richard Cordell. New York, 1930.

13. *Six One-Act Plays.* Boston, 1925.

14. No known manuscripts of the play exist. A review by Brooks Atkinson, in the *New York Times,* December 26, 1927, summarizes its plot and comments on characters. In Irving Abrahamson, "The Career of Rachel Crothers in the American Theater," an unpublished Ph.D. dissertation, University of Chicago, 1956, p. 378.

15. Deborah S. Kolb. "The Rise and Fall of the New Woman in American Drama." *Educational Theatre Journal,* vol. 27 (May 1975), pp. 158–60.

16. Rachel Crothers. "The Construction of a Play," in *The Art of Playwriting.* Foreword by Arthur H. Quinn, 1928, rpt. New York, 1967, p. 117.

17. Eleanor Flexner. *American Playwrights: 1918–1938.* rpt. Freeport, N.Y., 1969.

Apropos of Women and the Folk Play

1. Frederick H. Koch. *American Folk Plays.* D. Appleton-Century Company, 1939, p. xiv.

2. Quoted in Montrose J. Moses, *The American Dramatist,* 1925, reprint, Benjamin Blom, 1964, p. 8.

3. Ruth Suckow. "The Folk Idea in American Life." *Scribner's Magazine,* September 8, 1930, p. 247.

4. Zona Gale. *The Neighbors,* in *Wisconsin Plays,* Thomas H. Dickinson, ed. B. W. Huebsch, 1914.

5. Alice Brown. *Children of the Earth.* Macmillan Company, 1915.

6. Margaret G. Mayorga. *A Short History of the American Drama: Commentaries on Plays Prior to 1920.* Dodd, Mead and Company, 1944, p. 31.

7. Neith Boyce. *Winter's Night,* in *Fifty More Contemporary One-Act Plays,* Frank Shay, ed. D. Appleton, 1934.

8. Arthur E. Waterman. *Susan Glaspell.* Twayne Publishers, 1966, p. 69.
9. Susan Glaspell. *Trifles,* in *Literary Heritage: Drama I,* Marjorie Westcott Barrows, ed. Macmillan Company, 1962.
10. Arthur Hobson Quinn, ed. *Representative American Plays: From 1767 to the Present Day.* Appleton-Century-Crofts, Inc., 1953, p. 983.
11. Burns Mantle. *American Playwrights of Today.* Dodd, Mead and Company, 1929, p. 193.
12. Lula Vollmer, *Sun-Up,* in Quinn, *Representative American Plays.*

Anne Nichols

1. "Anne Nichols Is Dead at 75; Author of *Abie's Irish Rose.*" *New York Times,* September 16, 1966, p. 37.
2. Arthur Gelb. "Author of *Abie's Irish Rose* Reviews 40 Years." *New York Times,* May 21, 1962, p. 40.
3. *Encyclopedia Americana.* International Edition, 1975.
4. George Jean Nathan. *The Entertainment of a Nation or Three-Sheets in the Wind.* Alfred A. Knopf, 1942, p. 34.
5. Mary Braggiotti. "Abie's Rose Grows an Olive Leaf." *New York Post,* June 26, 1943, n. pag., col. 3, Theatre Collection, Lincoln Center for the Performing Arts, New York.
6. Jean Meegan. "Old Man Abie, He Just Goes Rolling." *Milwaukee Journal,* October 3, 1943, n. pag., cols. 3–4, Theatre Collection, Lincoln Center for the Performing Arts, New York.
7. Braggiotti, col. 3.
8. Gelb, p. 40.
9. Anne Nichols. "The Million Dollar Hit." *Theatre Arts* (July 1924), p. 19.
10. Braggiotti, col. 2.
11. "Anne Nichols Is Dead at 75," p. 37.
12. William B. Chase. "*Abie's Irish Rose* Funny." *New York Times,* May 24, 1922, p. 22.
13. Nichols, p. 19. See also Braggiotti, cols. 2–3.
14. "Anne Nichols Is Dead at 75," p. 37.
15. George Jean Nathan. *Materia Critica.* Alfred A. Knopf, 1924, p. 229.
16. Montrose J. Moses and John Mason Brown, eds. *The American Theatre as Seen by Its Critics, 1752–1934.* W. W. Norton and Co., 1934, pp. 260–62.
17. Nathan. *Materia Critica,* pp. 229–33.
18. Robert Littell. *Read America First.* Harcourt, Brace and World, 1926, pp. 244–45.
19. Nichols, p. 19.
20. "Anne Nichols Is Dead at 75," p. 37.
21. Gelb, p. 40.
22. Nichols, p. 19.
23. Gelb, p. 40.
24. Chase, p. 22.
25. "Anne Nichols Is Dead at 75," p. 37. See also Abe Laufe. *Anatomy of a Hit.* Hawthorn Books, Inc., 1966, p. 66.
26. Gelb, p. 40.

The Comic Muse of Mary Chase

1. Lynette Carpenter. "The Stuff that Dreams are Made of": *American Culture and Its Literature and Film, 1940–1953,* diss. Indiana University, 1979, pp. 83–92.
2. Not everyone has approved of Mrs. Chase's satire, as evidenced in Lillian Herlands Hornstein, "'Though This Be Madness': Insanity in the Theater." *College English,* vol. 7 (1945), pp. 7–9. More positive views are voiced in a rejoinder to the Hornstein article: Florence R. Scott. "*Harvey:* Or Sanity in the Theater." *College English,* vol. 8. (1946), pp. 37–38. An excellent appreciation of *Harvey* may be found in Jordan Y. Miller, *American Dramatic Literature.* McGraw-Hill, 1961, pp. 467–69.
3. Mary Chase. *Harvey.* Oxford University Press, 1953. (Parentheses following quotations indicate page numbers in this edition.)
4. It is ironic that in John L. Toohey, *A History of the Pulitzer Prize Plays,* Citadel Press, 1967, p. 201, Mr. Toohey says he would have awarded the Pulitzer Prize *Harvey* received to Tennessee Williams's *The Glass Menagerie,* for Williams's drama is very much a serious rendering of the themes Mary Chase handles with comic vitality.
5. Mary Chase. *Mrs. McThing.* Oxford University Press, 1952.
6. Mary Chase. *Bernardine.* Oxford University Press, 1953. (Parentheses following quotations indicate page numbers in this edition.)

Lorraine Hansberry

1. Interview with Lorraine Hansberry conducted by Eleanor Fisher for Columbia Broadcasting Company, June 7, 1961.
2. Lorraine Hansberry, *To Be Young,*
Gifted and Black, Englewood Cliffs, NJ, Prentice-Hall, 1969, pp. 11–12.
3. Interview, *op. cit.*
4. *A Raisin in the Sun/The Sign in Sidney Brustein's Window,* New York, New American Library, 1958, p. 286.
5. *Ibid.,* p. 317.

Woman Alone, Women Together

Unless otherwise indicated, plays discussed have been published in *The New Woman's Theatre,* edited by Honor Moore. Vintage, 1977.
1. Gail Kriegel Mallin. *Holy Places.* Workshop production at the Women's Project, the American Place Theatre, 1979.
2. Francine Stone. *Dead Sure.* Workshop production at the Circle Repertory Theatre, 1977. Quotes are from the manuscript.
3. Myrna Lamb. *Apple Pie.* An opera. Libretto by Lamb, music by Nicholas Meyers. Workshop production at the Public Theatre, 1976, full production 1977. Quotes are from notes on production.
4. Marsha Norman. *Getting Out.* Produced at the Actors Theatre, Louisville, 1977, Mark Taper Forum, 1978, Phoenix Theatre, New York City, 1978, Theatre de Lys, 1979. Published by Dramatists Play Service, 1980. Quotes from notes on Theatre de Lys production.
5. Ntozake Shange. *For Colored Girls Who Have Considered Suicide/ When The Rainbow Is Enuf, A Choreopoem.* Produced by Papp at the New York Shakespeare Festival Public Theatre, 1976. Booth Theatre (Broadway), 1976. Macmillan, 1977. Shange's second choreopoem, *Spell #7,* had a long run at the Public Theatre in 1979. In this piece the chorus included men as well as women.
6. Susan Griffin. *Voices.* Produced on California Public Television, 1974. Published by the Feminist Press, 1977. (Out of Print.) Quotes from published version.
7. Wendy Wasserstein. *Uncommon Women and Others.* Produced at the O'Neill Theatre Center, National Playwrights' Conference 1977; Phoenix Theatre, New York City, 1977. Published by Avon Books, 1979 and by the Dramatists Play Service, 1977.
8. Leigh Curran. *The Lunch Girls,* 1977. Produced at the Long Wharf Theatre, New Haven, 1977.
9. Aishah Rahman. *Unfinished Women*

Cry in No Man's Land While a Bird
Dies in a Gilded Cage. Produced
by New York Shakespeare Fes-
tival Mobile Unit, 1977, and at
the New York Shakespeare Fes-
tival Public Theatre, 1978.
10. Feminist concerns and aspirations
have been dealt with in the work
of women's theatre groups like
Women's Experimental Theatre
(New York City), the Caravan
Theatre (Cambridge, Mass.), and
At the Foot of the Mountain
(Minneapolis).
11. Tina Howe. *The Art of Dining.*
Produced by Joseph Papp and
the Kennedy Center at the New
York Shakespeare Festival Public
Theatre and the Eisenhower
Theatre, Kennedy Center, 1979.
Quotes from the manuscript.

Women Open Augusta's First Theatre

1. Mary Julia Curtis. *The Early
Charleston Stage: 1703–1798.*
Ph.D. dissertation, Indiana University, 1968, pp. 122–37, 145,
167–72.
2. Thomas Cooper and David J.
McCord, eds. *Statutes at Large of
South Carolina.* 10 vols. A. S.
Johnston, 1836–1841, vol. v, act.
no. 1376, pp. 41–44.
3. David Ritchey. "The Maryland
Company of Comedians." *Educational Theatre Journal*, vol. 24
(1972), pp. 355–62.
4. *Georgia State Gazette* (Augusta),
August 9, August 23, September
13, September 27, 1788.
5. *Chronicle*, September 4, September
18, October 2, 6, 27, November
13, 20, 1790.
6. *Chronicle*, May 7, 1791.
7. *Chronicle*, April 16, 1791.
8. *Chronicle*, May 21, 1791.
9. Virginia E. deTreville. "The First
President Visits Augusta." *Richmond County History*, vol. 4
(1972), pp. 38–53.
10. Minutes of the Trustees, April 7,
1794.
11. *City Gazette and Daily Advertiser*
(Charleston), March 30, 1799.
12. City Council Minutes (Richmond
County Court House, Augusta),
Receipts and Expenditures from
April 1805 to April 1806.
13. Monique Davis Boyce. *The First
Forty Years of the Augusta, Georgia, Theatre.* M.A. Thesis, University of Georgia, 1957, p. 45.

Art Theatre in Hull-House

1. Jane Addams. "The Subjective Ne-

cessity for Social Settlements," in
*Philanthropy and Social Progress:
Seven Essays*, by Jane Addams,
Robert A. Woods, and others.
1893; rpt. McGrath Publishing
Company, 1969, pp. 10, 22.
2. Jane Addams. *Twenty Years at
Hull-House.* Macmillan Pub-
lishing Company, 1938, pp. 112,
385.
3. Robert A. Woods and Albert J.
Kennedy. *The Settlement Horizon.*
Russell Sage Foundation, 1922,
p. 156.
4. Addams, *Twenty Years*, pp. 383–85.
5. Woods and Kennedy, p. 157.
6. Addams, *Twenty Years*, p. 388.
7. *Hull-House Bulletin*, vol. 1, no. 2
(February 1896), p. 7. Hull-
House Association Papers, Jane
Addams Memorial Collection,
University of Illinois–Chicago
Circle.
8. Walter Pietsch, Letter to Jane
Addams, March 7, 1928, Jane
Addams Papers, Swarthmore
College Peace Collection,
Swarthmore College, Pennsylvania.
9. *Hull-House Bulletin*, vol. 3, no. 6
(October 1898), p. 5.
10. Addams, *Twenty Years*, p. 388.
11. *Hull-House Bulletin*, vol. 3, no. 12
(November and December 1899),
p. 2.
12. Woods and Kennedy, p. 158.
13. Addams, *Twenty Years*, pp. 387–91.
14. William Dean Howells, Letter to
Jane Addams, October 26, 1899,
Jane Addams Papers.
15. Laura Pelham herself dated her
directorship from 1901; however,
programs of plays, etc., among
the collections at the Jane
Addams Hull-House at the University of Illinois at Chicago Circle indicate that the 1900 date is
correct.
16. In published works, Jane
Addams makes no mention of
Walter Pietsch as the original
director of drama at Hull-House.
She credits Pelham as the original founder of the theatre.
Pietsch's 1928 letter to Addams
states that he resigned because
he was about to be married.
17. *Hull-House Bulletin*, vol. 4, no. 3
(Autumn 1900), p. 6.
18. Laura Dainty Pelham. "The Story
of the Hull-House Players." *The
Drama*, May 22, 1916, pp. 250–
51.
19. Pelham, pp. 251–61.
20. Constance D'Arcy MacKaye. *The
Little Theatre in the United States.*
Henry Holt, 1917, p. 115.
21. Maurice Browne. *Too Late To Lament.* Indiana University Press,
1956, p. 128.

Women Directors—The Early Years

1. Burns Mantle, ed., *The Best Plays
of 1925–26 and the Year Book of
Drama in America* (New York:
Dodd, Mead and Company,
1926), pp. 627–31.
2. These names are drawn from the
listing in the Burns Mantle *Best
Plays* series.
3. Information about Agnes Morgan
can be found in Walter Rigdon,
ed., *Biographical Encyclopedia and
Who's Who of American Theatre*
(New York: James H.
Heinemann, Inc., 1965) and *Notable Names in American Theatre.*
4. Much of this information is
drawn from *Souvenir Program:
Grand Street Follies*, 1929
Edition.
5. "Women Rush into Rivalry in Producing," *American* (New York),
30 October 1927 (page numbers
cut off in clipping).
6. "Society Women Fail in Efforts to
Save 'Maya,'" *New York Telegraph*, 28 February 1928 (page
numbers cut off in clipping).
7. *Newport Casino Theatre Program*, 6
August 1935, p. 9.
8. Telephone interview with Wade
Miller, General Manager of the
Paper Mill Playhouse, Millburn,
NJ, 25 September 1982.

Hallie Flanagan

1. Francis Fergusson, "The Search
for New Standards in the Theatre." Address given at Barnard
College, April, 1955, reprint in
Theatre Collection, Lincoln Center, New York Public Library.
2. Quotations from Hallie Flanagan
talks and articles: "A Theatre for
the People"; "Federal Theatre,"
speech at Civitas Club, New
York; "Farewell Address to
members of the Federal Theatre
Summer Theatre," July, 1937.
3. "What Are We Doing with Our
Chance?" *Federal Theatre*, 1936.
4. " A Theatre for the People."
5. "Federal Theatre Tomorrow," May,
1936.
6. "Art and Geography," *The Magazine of Art*, Washington, DC,
August, 1938.
7. *Ibid.* Also, "The Tractor Invades
the Theatre," *Theatre Guild Magazine*, December, 1930.

8. "Federal Theatre," BBC Radio Talk, March 24, 1939.
9. *The Idea of a Theatre*, Princeton University Press, 1949, p. 14.
10. Letter to the author, April 26, 1983, from London.

Matriarchs of the Regional Theatre

1. Margo Jones. *Theatre-in-the-Round*. Rinehart, 1951, p. 92.
2. Joseph W. Zeigler. *Regional Theatre: The Revolutionary Stage*. University of Minnesota Press, 1973, p. 17.
3. Jones, pp. 40–63, 92, for her story.
4. Zeigler, p. 30.
5. Zeigler, p. 31.
6. Zeigler, p. 188.
7. Zeigler, p. 25.
8. Address, American Educational Theatre Association Convention. New York, August 1967.
9. Stuart W. Little. *Off-Broadway: The Prophetic Theatre*. Coward, McCann and Geoghegan, 1972, p. 168.
10. Zeigler, p. 194.

The Lady Is a Critic

Unless otherwise stated, quotations are from personal interviews.
1. M. F. Comtois and Lynn F. Miller, compilers. *Contemporary American Theater Critics: A Directory and Anthology of Their Works*. Scarecrow Press, 1977, pp. 951–56.
2. Mary Pat Daly. *Journalistic Criticism of Theater in Eighteenth Century America*. Ph.D. dissertation, Case Western Reserve University, 1975, pp. 4, 14, 30, for historical references.
3. James Townsend. "Mildred Aldrich." *American Women Writers: A Critical Guide from Colonial Times to the Present*, ed. Lina Mainiero. Frederick Ungar Publishing Company, 1979, vol. I, p. 37.
4. James D. Arnquist. "Amy Leslie." *Notable American Women: A Biographical Dictionary*, ed. Edward James. The Belknap Press of Harvard University, 1971, vol. II, p. 389.
5. Ishbel Ross. *Ladies of the Press*. Harper and Brothers, 1936, p. 409.
6. Brooks Atkinson. *Broadway*. Macmillan Co., 1970, pp. 258–65.
7. Eleanor Flexner. *American Playwrights 1918–38*. Simon and Schuster, Inc., 1938, p. 25.
8. Jane W. Sledman. "Claudia." *Opera News*. October 31, 1970, p. 23.

9. Lehman Engel. *The Critics*. Macmillan Co., 1976, p. 217.
10. Rosamond Gilder. "A One-Foot Shelf." *Theatre Arts* (July 1925), p. 449.
11. Caroline J. Dodge. *Rosamond Gilder and the Theatre*. Dissertation, University of Illinois, 1974, pp. 50–53.
12. Edith Oliver. *The New Yorker*, May 15, 1978, p. 116.
13. *Time*, September 3, 1965, p. 74.
14. Claudia Cassidy in Engel, p. 229.
15. *Contemporary American Theater Critics*, pp. 335–58. The editors asked each critic to submit two examples of his/her writing. That Ms. Holmes selected this piece is, in my opinion, indicative of her overwhelming concern in this area.
16. Clurman in Engel, p. 225.
17. Engel, p. 231.
18. Rosamond Gilder's views are drawn from the following issues of *Theatre Arts*: April 1945; February 1942; March 1944; June 1942; October 1943.
19. Engel, p. 222.
20. Basic Books, Inc., 1965, p. 56.
21. Claudia Cassidy. *Europe on-the-Aisle*. Random House, 1954, p. 224.
22. "What offsets off-off Broadway's revels in amateurishness . . . is the fun of it." *Cue*, November 30, 1968, p. 10.

The Second Face of the Idol

1. The favorable climate toward melodrama has been summarized recently by Joseph Donohue in his review of Cross's *Next Week—East Lynne*, *Theatre Survey*, vol. xx, no. 1 (May 1979), pp. 134–45.
2. David Grimsted. *Melodrama Unveiled: American Theatre and Culture, 1800–1850*. University of Chicago Press, 1968. My purpose here is only to present Professor Grimsted's conclusions as I understand them. Subsequent research may well establish that women characters in melodrama have always been more assertive than is commonly thought, even in the 1800 to 1850 period Grimsted examines. I suspect this to be, but I am only discussing the latter part of the nineteenth century here.
3. The sample plays are as follows:
1863—L. Wallack, *Rosedale*
1867—A. Daly, *Under the Gaslight*
1870—J. McCloskey and O. D. Byron, *Across the Continent*
1871—A. Daly, *Horizon*
1874—F. Murdock, *Davy Crockett*

1879—B. Campbell, *My Partner*
1881—J. Miller, *Forty-Nine*
1882—B. Campbell, *The White Slave*
1883—J. O'Neill, *The Count of Monte Cristo*
1886—H. C. deMille and C. Barnard, *Main Line*
1893—D. Belasco and F. Fyles, *The Girl I Left behind Me*
1895—P. M. Potter, *Trilby*
1895—E. M. Alfriend and A. C. Wheeler, *The Diamond Robbery*
c.1898—C. Bennett, *The Royal Slave*
1900—A. Thomas, *Arizona*
1904—O. Wister and K. LaShelle, *The Virginian*
1905—D. Belasco, *Girl of the Golden West*
1905—L. Mortimer, *No Mother to Guide Her*
1906—W. Woods, *Billy the Kid*
1906—W. V. Moody, *The Great Divide*
1907—W. C. deMille, *The Warrens of Virginia*
4. *My Partner, The White Slave, The Diamond Robbery*.
5. *Main Line, Trilby, The Virginian*.
6. *Girl of the Golden West, The Great Divide*.
7. Tom Taylor, *The Ticket-of-Leave Man*, in *Nineteenth Century Plays*, ed. by George Rowell. Oxford University Press, 1972.
8. Augustin Daly, *Under the Gaslight*, in *Hiss the Villian*, ed. by Michael R. Booth. London: Eyre and Spottiswoode, 1964.
9. Bartley Campbell, *My Partner*, in *America's Lost Plays*, vol. 19, ed. by Napier Wilt. Indiana University Press, 1965.
10. Nellie to the "fallen" Jennie in Walter Woods' *Billy the Kid*, in *America's Lost Plays*, vol. 8, ed. by Garrett H. Leverton. Indiana University Press, 1963. Reprint of 1940 edition.
11. Rosemarie K. Bank, "Melodrama as a Social Document: Social Factors in the American Frontier Play." *Theatre Studies*, vol. 22 (1975–76), pp. 42–49.
12. Grimsted appears to see the tug-of-war as typical of melodrama during the first half of the century.
13. Grimsted sees the heroine as buffer as a frequent feature of the melodrama he studied.

Women in Pulitzer Prize Plays, 1918–1949

1. Montrose J. Moses. *The American Dramatist*, 1925, reprint, Benjamin Blom, 1964, p. 420. John Gassner. *Dramatic Soundings: Evaluations and Retractions Culled from Thirty Years of Dramatic Criticism*. Crown, 1968, p. 374. Wil-

liam Lyon Phelps, Introduction, *A New Edition of the Pulitzer Prize Plays*, ed. by Kathryn Coe and William Cordell. Random House, 1940. Gerald Weales. *American Drama Since World War II*. Harcourt Brace and World, 1962, p. 154. Jane Bonin. *Prize Winning American Drama: A Bibliographical and Descriptive Guide*. Scarecrow Press, 1973, p. xi. John Toohey. *A History of the Pulitzer Prize Plays*. Citadel Press, 1967, p. 8. John Hohenberg. *The Pulitzer Prizes: A History of the Awards in Books, Drama, Music, and Journalism, Based on the Private Files Over Six Decades*. Columbia University Press, 1974, p. 354.

2. Edmond M. Gagey. *Revolution in American Drama*. Columbia University Press, 1947, pp. 1–19. Joseph Wood Krutch. *The American Drama Since 1918: An Informal History*. George Braziller (revised edition 1967), p. 11.

3. John Gassner, "Preface," *American Playwrights 1918–1938*, by Eleanor Flexner. Simon and Schuster, 1938, p. vii.

4. Hohenberg, p. 176.

5. Joanna Russ. "What Can a Heroine Do?" in *Images of Women in Fiction: Feminist Perspectives*, ed. by Susan Koppelman Cornillon. Bowling Green University Press, 1973, p. 9.

6. Simone de Beauvoir. *The Second Sex*, trans. and ed. by H. M. Parshley. Bantam Books, 1952, p. 236.

7. June B. West. *Attitudes Towards American Women as Reflected in American Literature Between the Two World Wars*. Ph.D. dissertation, University of Denver, 1954, p. 202.

8. Katherine M. Rogers. *The Troublesome Helpmate: A History of Misogyny in Literature*. University of Washington Press, 1966, p. 232.

9. Leslie Fiedler. *Love and Death in the American Novel*. Stein and Day (revised edition 1966), p. 296.

10. Judith H. Montgomery. "The American Galatea," *College English*, vol. 32 (May 1971), p. 899.

11. Mary Anne Ferguson, compiler. *Images of Women in Literature*. Houghton Mifflin, 1972, pp. 31–88.

12. Carolyn Heilbrun. "The Woman as Hero." *Texas Quarterly*, vol. 4 (Winter 1965), p. 133.

13. Hubert C. Heffner. "The Nature of Drama," in *An Introduction to Literature*, ed. by Gordon N. Ray. Houghton Mifflin, 1959, pp. 346–49. Francis Hodge. *Play Directing: Analysis, Communication and Style*. Prentice Hall, 1971, p. 41. Brander Matthews. *Dramatic Characterization, A Study of the Drama*, Houghton Mifflin, 1910, p. 152.

The Women's World of Glaspell's Trifles

1. Susan Glaspell. *Plays*. Small, Maynard, 1920.

2. Elaine Hedges. "Quilts and Women's Culture." *The Radical Teacher*, vol. 8 (March 4, 1977). For an art critic's assessment of the esthetics of women's quilts, see Patricia Mainardi, "Quilts: The Great American Art." *Radical America*, vol. 7, no. 1 (1973), pp. 36–68.

3. Caroll Smith-Rosenberg. "The Female World of Love and Ritual: Relations Between Women in Nineteenth Century America." *Signs: Journal of Women in Culture and Society*, vol. 1, no. 1 (Autumn 1975), pp. 1–29.

Black Women in Plays by Black Playwrights

1. *The Journal of Negro Education*, vol. 2 (April 1933), pp. 179–203.

2. *The Escape; or, A Leap for Freedom*. Boston: R. F. Wallcut, 1858.

3. *Rachel*. Boston: The Cornhill Company, 1920.

4. "A Woman Playwright Speaks Her Mind," *Anthology of the American Negro in the Theatre: A Critical Approach*, ed. Lindsay Patterson. Publishers Company, Inc., 1969, pp. 75–79.

5. *Masses and Mainstream*, vol. 3 (October 1950), pp. 34–47.

6. *Black Theater*, ed. Lindsay Patterson. Dodd, Mead, 1971, pp. 135–74.

7. *Wine in the Wilderness*. Dramatists Play Service, 1969.

8. *Wedding Band*. Samuel French, 1972.

9. *Black Theater*, ed. Lindsay Patterson, pp. 221–76.

10. *Les Blancs: The Collected Last Plays of Lorraine Hansberry*. Vintage Books, 1973, pp. 217–313.

11. *Contemporary Black Drama*, ed. Clinton F. Oliver and Stephanie Sills, Charles Scribner's Sons, 1971, pp. 187–205.

12. *Cities in Bezique*, Samuel French, 1969, pp. 3–29.

Who Put the "Tragic" in the Tragic Mulatto?

1. Webster Smalley, ed. *Five Plays by Langston Hughes*. Indiana University Press, 1963, pp. x–xi. Copyright 1926 by Alfred A. Knopf, Inc., and renewed 1954 by Langston Hughes. Reprinted from *The Selected Poems of Langston Hughes* by Langston Hughes, by permission of Alfred A. Knopf, Inc.

2. Arthur Calhoun. *A Social History of the American Family from Colonial Times to the Present*. Arno Press and the New York Times, 1973, vol. I, p. 210. Edward Reuter. *The Mulatto in the United States*. Negro Universities Press, 1969, p. 111. George W. Williams. *History of the Negro Race in America*. Arno Press, 1968. Bernard C. Steiner. *A History of Slavery in Connecticut*. Johns Hopkins Press, 1893. John H. Russell. *The Free Negro in Virginia*. Johns Hopkins Press, 1913. See other state histories for specific state laws. Sidney G. Fisher. *Men, Women and Manners in Colonial Times*. Lippincott and Co., 1898, vol. II, p. 118. Edward R. Turner. *The Negro in Pennsylvania: Slavery-Servitude-Freedom, 1639–1861*. American Historical Association, 1911, p. 31. Two plays of the '30's on this theme are: DeBose Heyward's *Brass Ankle* (1931), and Samuel Raphaelson's *White Man* (1936). The 1979 weekly television appearance of the Norman Lear characters Tom and Helen on "The Jeffersons" is a reminder of the continuing popularity of this theme.

3. James V. Hatch and Ted Shine, eds. *Black Theatre, U.S.A.: Forty-Five Plays by Black Americans*. The Free Press, 1974, p. 184.

4. Grandma Carlson clearly reflects the attitude of the "New Negro" writers of the Harlem Renaissance. See Claude McKay's *Home to Harlem*, Harper and Brothers, 1928, and Countee Cullen's *One Way to Heaven*, Harper and Brothers, 1932, as examples of nondramatic treatment of the subject.

5. The Reverend Charles Elliott's strong admonition to the South reveals attitudes toward this illegal amalgamation. See Charles Elliott, *Sinfulness of American Slavery*. L. Swormstedt & J. H. Power, 1850, vol. I, p. 154.

6. In Hollywood, Peola, the tragic mulatto of *Imitation of Life* (1934 film of the Fannie Hurst novel), was flashing a similar brand of militancy on the screen; her whiteness, not her blackness, prompted her rebellion. By the

1949 revival *(Pinky)* not even a real-life mulatto could qualify for the role, and Jeanne Crain, white actress, appeared in the title role.

7. Adrienne Kennedy discusses her real-life mulatto aunt (the model for Clara) who "didn't belong anywhere" and herself as a writer in "A Growth of Images," *Drama Review*, vol. 21, no. 4 (December 1977), pp. 41–48.

8. There are many variations on this theme; the following ditty expresses one of the most common:

If you're white, you're right,
If you're light, you can fight,
If you're brown, stick around,
But if you're black, get back!

Creative Drama

1. Four studies with particularly strong evidence of sources related to sex are: E. C. Irwin, *The Effect of a Program of Creative Dramatics Upon Personality as Measured by the California Test of Personality, Sociograms, Teacher Ratings and Grades*, Ph.D. dissertation, University of Pittsburgh, 1963; Elissa Goforth, "Fostering Creativity in Kindergarten Children Through the Use of Creative Drama," M.A. thesis, Arizona State University, 1974; Lin Sommers Wright, *The Effects of Creative Drama on Person Perception*, Ph.D. dissertation, University of Minnesota, 1972; Mary E. Lunz, "Creative Dramatics and Communication Effectiveness," *Children's Theatre Review*, vol.13, no.3 (1974), pp. 2–3.

2. Irwin, pp. 41–44.
3. Goforth, pp. 35–36.
4. Wright, pp. 63–65A.
5. Lunz, pp. 3–5.
6. Irwin, p. 42.
7. Lunz, p. 5.
8. Alice Dalgliesh. *The Courage of Sarah Noble*. Scribner's, 1964. Madeleine L'Engle. *A Wrinkle in Time*. Ariel Books, 1962. Astrid Lindgren, *Pippi Longstocking, Pippi Goes on Board, Pippi in the South Seas, Pippi on the Run*. Viking Press. Jean Merrill. *Pushcart War*. Scott, 1964. E. B. White. *Charlotte's Web*. Harper, 1952.
9. David Saar is the Drama Specialist for grades K-6 in the Mesa Public Schools in Mesa, Arizona.

Feminist Theatre: A Rhetorical Phenomenon

1. Both the New Feminist Theatre (New York City) and the Los Angeles Feminist Theatre claim to be the oldest. Probably the NFT predates LAFT by only a few months. For information about the national phenomenon, I am indebted to Betty Moseley Davis, "Feminist Theatre: An Identity Crisis," paper delivered at Southeastern Theatre Conference, Norfolk, Virginia, March 1977. See also, Lillian Perinciolo, "Feminist Theater: They're Playing in Peoria," *Ms.* (October 1975), pp. 101–4; *Ms.* (December 1977), see especially pp. 35–39, 70–75, 89–90; Charlotte Rea, "Women's Theatre Groups," *Drama Review*, vol. 18, no. 4 (1974), pp. 77-87; *Theatre News*, vol. 10, no. 2 (1977).

2. *Quarry*, "an opera . . . pageant . . . play . . . multi-media spectacle," revived by Women's Interart in 1976, won an Obie, as did Joyce Aaron for her work with *Acrobatics*, which she directed, coauthored, and in which she performed (produced by Interart, April 1976). Sy Syna, mimeographed transcript of a program performed on WNYC-TV, December 21, 1976; Sy Syna, "Review," *Wisdom's Child* (New York), Apr. 17, 1976, p. 13.

3. In 1851 the Bloomer rage hit London. Perhaps as many as a dozen Bloomer plays were on the boards during that year at the Strand, the Adelphi, and the Olympic theatres. I am indebted to Richard Moody of Indiana University for alerting me to these works.

4. Many books and articles treat the political and experimental theatres of the 1960's. Among those which I found useful were Oscar G. Brockett and Robert R. Findlay. *Century of Innovation: A History of European and American Theatre and Drama Since 1870.* Prentice-Hall, 1973; Oscar G. Brockett. *Perspectives on Contemporary Theatre*. Louisiana State University Press, 1971; Margaret Croyden. *Lunatics, Lovers and Poets: The Contemporary Experimental Theatre*. New York: McGraw-Hill, 1974; James Schevill. *Break Out! In Search of New Theatrical Environments*. Chicago: Swallow Press, 1973.

5. For this information I am indebted to Betty Moseley Davis, "Women of the Open Theatre," paper presented at the annual convention of the Southern Speech Communication Asso-

ciation, Knoxville, Tennessee, April 1977. Davis cites as her source Joseph Chaikin, telephone interview, July 19, 1976.

6. Davis, "Feminist Theatre." See, for example, Bobbie Spalter-Roth. "WAFT Comes Out: The Franny Chicago Play," *Off Our Backs* (October 1974), p. 22; John C. Meyers. "I Want to Wake Up and Be Free," Providence (R.I.) *Sunday Journal Magazine*, February 29, 1976, pp. 14–17.

7. I relied most heavily on three studies: Karlyn Kohrs Campbell. "The Rhetoric of Women's Liberation: An Oxymoron." *Quarterly Journal of Speech*, vol. 58 (1972), pp. 264–71. Eva M. McMahan. "Pragmatic Paradox: The Rhetorical Challenge to Advocates of Women's Equality," paper presented at the annual convention of the Southern Speech Communication Association, Knoxville, Tennessee, April 1977. Brenda Robinson Hancock. "Affirmation by Negation in the Women's Liberation Movement." *Quarterly Journal of Speech*, vol. 58 (1972), pp. 264–71.

8. Campbell, pp. 75, 84, 78–81, 83–84. Italics are Campbell's.

9. Many books and articles deal with promoting radical change, such as Saul D. Alinsky, *Rules for Radicals: A Practical Primer for Realistic Radicals*. New York: Random House, 1971.

10. See Delmer H. Hilyard, "Research Models and Designs for the Study of Conflict," in Fred E. Jandt, ed., *Conflict Resolution Through Communication* (Harper & Row, 1973), pp. 448–50. Campbell, p. 86. For a discussion of theatre as symbol, see Northrop Frye, *Anatomy of Criticism: Four Essays*. Princeton University Press, 1957, pp. 83–84.

11. Campbell, pp. 83–84.

12. For information about both Women's Interart Theatre and It's All Right to Be Woman Theatre I am indebted to the research efforts of Cheryl Black.

13. Survey by Action for Women in Theatre, cited by the National Commission on the Observance of International Women's Year, *The Creative Woman: A Report of the Committee on the Arts and Humanities*. Washington, D.C.: Department of State, 1976, p. 6.

14. Gretchen Cryer, "Where Are the Women Playwrights?" *New York Times*, May 20, 1973, sec. 2, p. 1.

15. National Commission on the Observance of International Women's Year, p. 6.

16. An overview of the situation against which such women's groups revolted is provided by the National Commission on the Observance of International Women's Year, pp. 6–10.

17. Margo Lewitin of Interart Theatre stresses that the theatre is "not an outpost for women's lib," but asserts that the group is "certainly political if you define politics as the need for getting women together." Margo Lewitin, telephone interview with Cheryl Black, April 8, 1977. See also Bill Marvel, "Woman's Place Is in the Center." *National Observer*, August 16, 1975, p. 26; and the Foundation Grant Application, New York State Council on the Arts, 1976.

18. Foundation Grant Application, New York State Council on the Arts, 1970–71. Also cited by Karen Malpede Taylor, *People's Theatre in Amerika*. New York: Drama Book Specialists, 1973, p. 325.

19. Ronnog Seaberg. "Womansong Theatre: Militant and Tender." *Great Speckled Bird*, April 29, 1974, p. 17.

20. "Women of Burning City." *Rat*, November 17–December 6, [1970?], p. 21. "The Cutting Edge." Jedediah Wheeler, tour manager, to Patti Gillespie, November 18, 1976 (mimeographed enclosure).

21. Georgia Dullea. "Dreams Are What a Feminist Group's Plays Are Made Of." *New York Times*, December 21, 1972, p. 42.

22. Performed by the New Feminist Theatre first as a benefit for the Redstockings Abortion Hearings in March 1969.

23. Sondra Lowell. "Art Comes to the Elevator: Women's Guerrilla Theater." *Women*, vol. 2, no. 1 (1970), pp. 50–51.

24. Rosalyn Regelson. "Is Motherhood Holy? Not Any More." *New York Times*, May 18, 1969, sec. 2, p. 5.

25. Application for a Foundation Grant, cited by Taylor, p. 326.

26. "The Cutting Edge" as reported by Mel Gussow, "Theater: Women's Work: Cutting Edges 'Croon' at Performing Garage." *New York Times*, March 30, 1976, p. 39.

27. It's All Right to Be Woman Theatre, according to Rea, "Women for Women," p. 79.

28. "Women of Burning City," p. 21.

29. I have here adopted the summary of "antirhetorical" style put forth by Campbell, p. 78.

30. Mel Gussow, "Stage: Feminist Musical: *What Time of Night Strongly Provocative.*" *New York Times*, June 19, 1973, p. 30, says: "The show works both as a course in consciousness raising and as a call to arms." An unidentified woman upon seeing a performance of "Women of the Burning City" (see note 43) remarked, "It's like three years of consciousness raising packed into one hour." See also remarks by Roberta Sklar reported by Rea, "Women for Women," p. 81.

31. See Hancock, pp. 265–67.

32. The technique is discussed in Pamela Kearon, "Power as a Function of the Group," in *Notes from the Second Year*, ed. Shulamith Firestone. New York: Shulamith Firestone, 1970, pp. 108–10. Sandra L. Bem and Daryl J. Bem. "Training the Woman to Know Her Place: The Power of a Nonconscious Ideology," in *Roles Women Play: Readings Toward Women's Liberation*, ed. Michele Hoffnung Garskof. Belmont, Ca.: Brooks/Cole, 1971, pp. 84–96.

33. Campbell, p. 86.

A Rainbow of Voices

1. Carl G. Jung. *Two Essays on Analytical Psychology*. Meridian, 1956, p. 182.

2. Jolande Jacobi. *The Psychology of C. G. Jung*. Yale University Press, 1973, pp. 132–33.

3. Harriet Perl and Gay Abarbanell. *Guidelines to Feminist Consciousness Raising*. National Task Force on Consciousness Raising for the National Organization for Women, 1976, p. 2.

4. Honor Moore, ed. Introduction, in *The New Women's Theatre*. Vintage, 1977, p. xxxv.

5. Adrienne Rich. Introduction, in Susan Griffin, *Voices*. Old Westbury: The Feminist Press, 1975, p. 10.

6. Rich, p. 12.

7. Moore, p. xxxvi.

8. Eve Merriam, ed. *Growing Up Female in America: Ten Lives*. Dell, 1971, p. 18.

9. Moore, p. xxxv.

10. Ntozake Shange. *For Colored Girls Who Have Considered Suicide/When the Rainbow Is Enuf.* Macmillan, 1977, p. xv.

11. Phyllis Funke. "Beneath the Sur-

face of Shange." *Los Angeles Times*, "Calendar," August 7, 1977, p. 54.

12. Funke, p. 54.

13. Toni Cade Bambara. "For Colored Girls—and White Girls Too." *Ms.*, vol. 5 (September 1976), p. 38.

The Female Actor

Quotations are listed in sequence from sources.

1. Cornelia Brunner, "Roberta Sklar: Toward Creating a Women's Theatre," *The Drama Review*, Vol. 24, #2, June, 1980, pp. 30, 35, 38, 39, 40.

2. Sondra Segal and Roberta Sklar interviewed by Helen Krich Chinoy and Linda Walsh Jenkins, October 19, 1986.

3. Viola Spolin, *Improvisation for the Theatre*, Northwestern University Press, 1963, pp. 3–17 *passim*.

4. Biographies distributed by Columbia Pictures and Universal Studios, 1984.

5. Universal Studios Biography, 1984; Frank Van Riper, "Linda Hunt Measures Up," Leisure Section, *New York Daily News*, April 29, 1984; Christopher Sharp, "A Small Sensation Named Linda Hunt," Arts and People Section, *Women's Wear Daily*, January 25, 1983; Leslie Bennetts, "Breakthrough Season Arrives for Linda Hunt," *New York Times*, February 12, 1983.

6. Robbie McCauley interviewed by Joanie Fritz, January 15, 1986.

7. Louise Sweeney, "Colleen Dewhurst; America's 'Mother Courage' Now Leaves Them Laughing," *Christian Science Monitor*, May 12, 1983; Bruce Chadwick, "Colleen Takes Her Act onto the Stage," *New York Daily News*, September 26, 1982.

8. Helen Stuart Barthelmess, "A Slice of Life According to Colleen Dewhurst," *Westport News*, July 24, 1986.

9. Chadwick, *Daily News*; Kay Gardella, "Colleen Dewhurst," Sunday's People, *New York Daily News*, March 9, 1986.

10. Judy Stone, "An Interview with Actress Colleen Dewhurst," *Playgirl*, April, 1975, pp. 48, 89, 118, 119; Ann Pinkerton, "TV—or not TV," Eye View, *Women's Wear Daily*, August 27, 1976.

11. Pinkerton, *Women's Wear Daily*; "Colleen Dewhurst," *Quest*, May, 1978; Sweeney, *Christian Science Monitor*.

12. Kathy Larkin, "A Grand Old-

style Party," Manhattan Section, *New York Daily News*, April 7, 1983.

13. Colette Dowling, "Joanne Woodward: With *Candida* she has again expanded the role of Woman," *Playbill*, October, 1981.

14. Florence Graves and Nina Easton, "Joanne Woodward: On Women and War," *Common Cause Magazine*, November–December, 1983; Dowling, *Playbill*.

15. Rex Reed, "The Three Dimensions of Joanne," Leisure Section, *New York Daily News*, October 11, 1981.

16. Mark Goodman, "The Dominant Member of the Paul Newman Menage Is a Green-eyed Feminist," *People*, July 21, 1975; "National Conference to Prevent Nuclear War," *Los Angeles Times*, May 13, 1985.

17. Graves and Easton, *Common Cause; People*.

18. Graves and Easton, *Common Cause*.

19. Ron Cohen, "Estelle Parsons' One-Woman Marathon," Arts and People, *Women's Wear Daily*, July 21, 1983; "Guests of the Nation," Great Performances Press Release, January 29, 1982.

20. Stephen Saban, "Estelle Parsons: Oscar in the Closet," *Soho Weekly News*, January 20, 1977; AP News Features, February 14 (undated clipping).

21. Terri Jentz, "Estelle Parsons: A Great Actress Stars in a Major Feminist Play," *West Side TV Shopper*, August 27–September 2, 1983; Cohen, *Women's Wear Daily*; Jentz, *West Side TV Shopper*.

22. Carol Lawson, "Broadway," *New York Times*, August 26, 1983; Jentz, *West Side TV Shopper*.

23. Robin Brantley, "Estelle Parsons's New Role: Director," *New York Times*, May 26, 1978.

24. William Harris, "Off and On," *Soho Weekly News*, April 19, 1979.

25. Martin Burden, "Parsons Keynote Is to Open the B'way Door to Women," *New York Times*, January 4, 1983.

26. Helen Hayes, "Helen Hayes Relives Her Roles," *New York Times Magazine*, December 7, 1958, pp. 40–48 *passim*.

27. "Hayes 80th Birthday at Actors' Fund Home in Englewood, N.J." *New York Times*, October 13, 1980.

28. "All of My Stages," as told to Nanette Kutner, *Good Housekeeping*, February, 1959.

Here Are the Women Playwrights

1. May 1, 1983.
2. Kathleen Betsko and Rachel Koenig, *Interviews with Contemporary Women Playwrights*. New York: Beech Tree Books, William Morrow, 1987. Quotations from this invaluable source are identified as B/K with page reference. They are used by the generous permission of the editors and the publisher.
3. William Wright, *Lillian Hellman: The Image, The Woman*. New York, Simon and Schuster, 1986, p. 98.
4. B/K, p. 302.
5. B/K, p. 240.
6. B/K, p. 258.
7. B/K, p. 430.
8. B/K, p. 323.
9. B/K, p. 96.
10. B/K, p. 219.
11. B/K, p. 457.
12. B/K, p. 241–42.
13. B/K, p. 281.
14. B/K, p. 320.
15. B/K, p. 322, 312.
16. B/K, p. 434.
17. *Backstage*, February 12, 1982.
18. Letter from Julia Miles to editors, Sept. 10, 1986.
19. *Theatre Profiles*, Special 25th Anniversary Edition, 1986.
20. Typescript, "The Woman Playwright," 1985, used by permission of France Burke.
21. *America's Arena*, Arena Stage, clipping, 1985.
22. B/K, p. 240.
23. B/K, p. 313.
24. B/K, p. 249.
25. B/K, p. 109.
26. B/K, p. 67–68.
27. B/K, p. 171–72.
28. B/K, p. 211.
29. B/K, p. 316.
30. B/K, p. 341.
31. B/K, p. 267.
32. B/K, p. 220.
33. B/K, p. 99.
34. B/K, p. 302–3.
35. B/K, p. 224.
36. B/K, p. 254–55.
37. June 1981 production of *My Blue Heaven*.
38. B/K, p. 212.
39. B/K, p. 243–44.
40. B/K, p. 113.
41. B/K, p. 445.
42. B/K, p. 158–60 *passim*.
43. B/K, p. 172.
44. B/K, p. 228.
45. B/K, p. 163.
46. B/K, p. 299.
47. B/K, p. 138.
48. B/K, p. 215–16.
49. B/K, p. 251.
50. B/K, p. 238–39.
51. B/K, p. 281.
52. B/K, p. 293.
53. B/K, p. 90.
54. B/K, p. 180–81.
55. Helen Keyssar, *Feminist Theatre*, p. xiii.
56. B/K, p. 131.
57. B/K, p. 240.
58. B/K, p. 261–62.
59. B/K, p. 221.
60. B/K, p. 234.
61. B/K, p. 442.
62. B/K, p. 176.
63. B/K, p. 370.
64. B/K, p. 338.
65. B/K, p. 235.
66. B/K, p. 369.
67. B/K, p. 282.
68. B/K, p. 13–14.

Women Backstage and Out Front

1. Leslie Bennetts, "Is the Road to a Theatre Career Rockier for Women? *New York Times*, November 2, 1986.
2. Cheryl Crawford. *One Naked Individual: My Fifty Years in the Theatre*. Indianapolis: Bobbs-Merrill Company, 1977, p. 31.
3. *Ibid.*, p. 33.
4. *Ibid*.
5. *Ibid.*, p. 104.
6. Interview with Lyn Austin by Helen Krich Chinoy, Oct. 15, 1986, New York City.
7. Elizabeth Swados, "Stretching Boundaries: The Merlin of La Mama," Arts and Leisure, *New York Times*, October 26, 1986.
8. Quotations from two addresses by Ellen Stewart, at Women's Program of American Theatre Association, 1980, and Women in Theatre, Theatre of Light and Shadow and Albertus Magnus College, New Haven, Connecticut, March 24, 1982.
9. Miriam Colon address, Luncheon, American Society for Theatre Research and Theatre Library Association, November, 1986. See also Richard F. Shepard, "For Street Troupe at 20, Life's Both Buena y Good," *New York Times*, April 18, 1987, p. 9.
10. Leslie Bennetts, "Women Directing More Plays but Broadway Is Still Elusive," *New York Times*, January 16, 1984.
11. Leslie Bennetts, "For the Second Stage, Its First New Theatre," *New York Times*, March 10, 1984, contains this and the following quotations about Carole Rothman.
12. Leslie Bennetts, "Women Directing . . . ," *op. cit.*

13. Jeremy Gerard, "How a 'Chamber Theater' Grew to Fill the Orchestra," Arts and Leisure, *New York Times*, November 9, 1986.
14. *Ibid*.
15. Eleanor Munro, "Lynne Meadow, Impresario," People column, *Ms.*, February, 1980, p. 82.
16. Interview with Lynne Meadow by Helen Krich Chinoy, October 14, 1986, New York City.
17. Leslie Bennetts, "Women Directing . . . ," *op. cit.*
18. "Directors and Designers Report on Sex Discrimination in the Theatre," League of Professional Theatre Women, March 8, 1983. Summary in Leslie Bennetts, "Women Directing . . . ," *op. cit.*
19. Interview with Julianne Boyd by Helen Krich Chinoy, October 17, 1986, New York City.
20. Frank Rich noted with approval that the "show's feminism is worn lightly" (*New York Times*, February 27, 1984), while Erika Munk felt that "women's situation in 1984 deserves a bit of bite, a snarl of satire" (*Village Voice*, March 6, 1984).
21. From League of Professional Women in Theatre Study, *op. cit.* See also Marjorie Bradley Kellogg, "Women's Caucus Puzzles Over Lack of Set Designers," *Variety*, January 12, 1983.
22. Bruce Bossard, "Set Designers Marjorie Kellogg and Ming Cho Lee," *Back Stage*, November 25, 1983.
23. Marjorie Kellogg, *American Theatre*, May, 1984.
24. Interview with Marjorie Bradley Kellogg by Helen Krich Chinoy, November 18, 1986, New York City.
25. Alexis Greene, "I never dream about scenery," *Vassar Quarterly*, Fall, 1980 (Vol. LXXVII, No. 1), 16.
26. Arnold Aronson, "Marjorie Bradley Kellogg," *American Set Design*, New York, Theatre Communications Group, 1985, p. 67.

Matrix

1. Sue Ellen Case, "From Split Subject to Split Britches," unpublished ms., 1986, 1.
2. Jill Dolan, "Gender Impersonation Onstage: Destroying or Maintaining the Mirror of Gender Roles?," *Women & Performance* 2, 2 (1985), 5–11. Dolan refers to Monique Wittig's writings in *Feminist Issues*, particularly "The Straight Mind" (Summer 1980), "One Is Not Born a Woman" (Winter 1981), and "The Category of Sex" (Fall 1982).
3. Sande Zeig, "The Actor as Activator: Deconstructing Gender through Gesture," *Women & Performance* 2, 2 (1985), 15.
4. Case, 12.
5. Rosemary K. Curb, "Re/cognition, Re/presentation, Re/creation in Woman-Conscious Drama: The Seer, The Seen, The Scene, The Obscene," *Theatre Journal* 37, 3 (1985) 302–3. She cites Mary Ann Caws, *The Eye in the Text: Essays on Perception, Mannerist to Modern* (Princeton University Press, 1981), 3; and Linda Walsh Jenkins, "Locating the Language of Gender Experience," *Women & Performance* 2, 1 (1984), 5–20.
6. Zeig, 14.
7. Jill Dolan, "The Politics of Feminist Performance," *Theatre Times* 5, 6 (July/August, 1986), 12.
8. Jay Leno, interview on *Good Morning America*, ABC-TV, June 13, 1986.
9. Annette Kolodny, "Dancing Through the Minefield," ed. Elaine Showalter, *The New Feminist Criticism: Essays on Women, Literature, and Theory* (Pantheon, 1985), 161. See also Deborah Cameron, *Feminism and Linguistic Theory* (St. Martin's Press, 1985), for an excellent survey and critique of feminist theory in humanities and social sciences.
10. Bernice Johnson Reagon, "Coalition Politics: Turning the Century," *Home Girls: A Black Feminist Anthology*, ed. Barbara Smith (New York: Kitchen Table: Women of Color Press), 360. See also Barbara Hilkert Andolsen, *Daughters of Jefferson, Daughters of Bootblacks: Racism and American Feminism* (Mercer University Press, 1986); and Gloria I. Joseph and Jill Lewis, *Common Differences: Conflicts in Black and White Feminist Perspectives* (Anchor/Doubleday, 1981).
11. Yvonne Yarbro-Bejarano, "The Female Subject in Chicano Theatre: Sexuality, 'Race,' and Class," *Theatre Journal* 38, 4 (December 1986), 389–407.

INDEX

435

ACKNOWLEDGMENTS

Although the editors are responsible for the contents and the organization, the work on the two editions of this book has been done over a period of time by many people whose contributions go well beyond that usually noted in acknowledgments. To them all our deepest gratitude for their participation in the adventure of finding women in American theatre:

Members of the American Theatre Association under whose auspices this project was started: the late Professor Barnard Hewitt, Professors Oscar Brockett, Esther Jackson, Vera Mowry Roberts, and the late Professor George Bogush.

Librarians and archivists who facilitated our task: Mary Henderson and Wendy Warnken, Museum of the City of New York; Dorothy Swerdlove, Theatre Collection, Lincoln Center Library for the Performing Arts; Rosemary L. Cullen, Special Collection, Brown University Library; Jeanne Newlin, Theatre Collection, Harvard University; Mary Trott, Susan Griggs, Susan Boone, Eleanor Lewis, Dorothy Greene, Archives and Sophia Smith Collection, Smith College; Sarah Sherman, Women's Collection, Northwestern University Library.

Officials and members of professional theatre organizations: Julia Miles, Susan Lehman, Amy Ober, Women's Project, American Place Theatre; Beverly B. Pevitts, Association for Theatre in Higher Education; Sophie Parker, Boston Women in Theatre Festival; Gretchen Cryer, France Burke, Peggy Gold, Katharine Griffith, Maggie Grove, Alison Jones, Paula Pierce, Committee for Women, Dramatists Guild; Nancy Rhodes, Encompass Theatre; David J. Skal, Theatre Communications Group; Nick Wilkerson, Phoenix Theatre; Marjorie Gunner and Joan Nourse, Outer Critics Circle; Betsy Shevy; Mildred Traube, Society of Stage Directors and Choreographers; Rhonda Blair, Women's Program; Lynne Meadow, Manhattan Theatre Club; Lyn Austin, Anne Bogart, Music-Theater Group/Lenox Arts Center; Julianne Boyd, Marjorie Bradley Kellogg, League of Professional Women in Theatre/New York; Joanie Fritz, Protean Forms Collective.

Academic colleagues, students, friends, relatives who contributed in various important ways to the manuscript: Roy Wood and Leslie Hinderyckx, Northwestern University; Len Berkman, Erica Bianci-Jones, Sally Donohue, Kendall, Claire Joley, Jacqueline Van Voris, Smith College; Judith Barlow, Kathleen Betsko, Rachel Koenig, Lynda Moss, Gail Cohen, Susan Clement, Mary Poole, Nancy Weiss, Debra Woodard, Jan Zimmerman, Terry McCabe, Rosemary Curb, Caroline Dodge Latta, Winona Fletcher, Patti Gillespie, Dinah Leavitt, Phyllis Mael, Yvonne Shafer, Bari Watkins, Marijane Datson, Sue-Ellen Case, Joanne Bentley, Aron Krich, Michael and Claire Nicole Chinoy.

Those who participated in the symposium on Women in Theatre in honor of the retirement of Helen Krich Chinoy at Smith College, April 19, 1986: Karen Malpede and Susan Spector, moderators; Kay Carney, Andrea Hairston, Linda Walsh Jenkins, Beverley May, Tina Packer, Mary Robinson, Kiki Smith, Roberta Sklar.

All whose names are listed in the table of contents and within individual pieces; publishers credited in the text for permission to reprint material; the many interested persons, too numerous to name, who corresponded with us about aspects of our work.

Our editors and others who were most helpful in preparing this revised and enlarged edition at Theatre Communications Group: Terence Nemeth, M. Elizabeth Osborn, Laura Ross, John Istel; and our original editor, Virginia Wentworth, Crown Publishers.

Finally, we want to acknowledge our unusual collaboration. Separated by a thousand miles, but very close in spirit and interest, we have worked together in the greatest harmony, sharing tasks in accordance with our talents and facilities, learning from each other and growing together in the rewarding experience of bringing both the first and the second edition of this volume to completion.

ABOUT THE AUTHORS

Helen Krich Chinoy, professor emeritus in the theatre department of Smith College, edited *Actors on Acting* and *Directors on Directing* with Toby Cole, basic texts that have remained continuously in print for over thirty years. She has published many articles in journals and books and is now completing a study of the Group Theatre of the 1930's that grows out of her earlier volume *Reunion: A Self-Portrait of the Group Theatre*, and is consultant to an upcoming WNET/PBS special on The Group.

Linda Walsh Jenkins, associate professor in the theatre department, Northwestern University, has edited two volumes of plays from the Children's Theatre Company of the Minneapolis Institute of Arts, where she was an actor and literary editor. She has produced newsletters on women in the performing arts and Native American theatre, topics on which she has written articles published in *The Drama Review*, *Yale/Theatre*, and *Theatre News*. She has performed in films, written plays, and is currently dramaturg for Wisdom Bridge Theatre in Chicago.